MULTIVARIATE STATISTICS IN THE SOCIAL SCIENCES:

A RESEARCHER'S GUIDE

TO TOM AND TO BARBARA

MULTIVARIATE STATISTICS IN THE SOCIAL SCIENCES:

A RESEARCHER'S GUIDE

LEONARD A. MARASCUILO
University of California, Berkeley

JOEL R. LEVIN
University of Wisconsin, Madison

BROOKS/COLE PUBLISHING COMPANY
Monterey, California

Consulting Editor: Roger E. Kirk, Baylor University

Brooks/Cole Publishing Company
A Division of Wadsworth, Inc.

Printed in the United States of America

10 9 8 7 6 5 4 3 2

Library of Congress Cataloging in Publication Data

Marascuilo, Leonard A.
Multivariate statistics in the social sciences.

Bibliography: p.
Includes index.
1. Multivariate analysis. 2. Social sciences—Statistical methods. I. Levin, Joel R. II. Title.
HA31.3.M37 1983 300'.519535 82-20618
ISBN 0-534-01147-0

Subject Editor: C. Deborah Laughton
Manuscript Editor: Margaret E. Hill
Production: Unicorn Production Services, Inc.
Interior Design: Katherine Minerva
Cover Design: Debbie Wunsch
Typesetting: The Alden Press Ltd.
Printing and Binding: Halliday Lithograph

PREFACE

A FEW WORDS ABOUT THIS BOOK

In recent years, the number of books devoted to the presentation of advanced statistical methods for use by researchers seems to have increased in a regular geometric progression. This book adds to that progression, but we hope in a different way. After many years of experience as teachers, consultants, and researchers—roles in which we have had to apply multivariate methods—we have acquired a number of insights into multivariate data and their interpretation. As far as we can tell, many of these insights have not been documented in the books on multivariate analysis that are commonly used in the social sciences. Thus, feeling that there was a gap in the practice of the art, we decided to make our small contribution to help close that gap.

Although we may have been able to make our ideas known through articles written for various professional journals, it seemed that a book format was more appropriate. With it, we could develop our ideas more extensively. In addition, because our primary goal was one of *pedagogy,* a textbook would indeed appear to be the correct mode of communication. We have attempted to make our book a pedagogically sound vehicle for you, the consumer, and we hope that you will agree that we have succeeded.

When we first started writing, we generated a traditional type of preface. Because it proved to be exceptionally lengthy, however, we chose to incorporate it into Chapter 1. There we present our views on univariate and multivariate methods. We also provide a chapter-by-chapter preview of the topics that appear in the remainder of the book. This material is described in Sections 1-1 through 1-6. In addition, a compact representation of the book's contents appears on the inside front cover.

A question of obvious concern to potential consumers of this book is how its contents can be mastered most effectively within the context of a college-level course on multivariate analysis. We will address this question by describing the way we have used the written manuscript in its various forms, as it evolved into what you see here.

With some modifications in chapter coverage, we have covered the various topics within the duration of either a 10-week quarter (LAM) or a 16-week semester (JRL). Most of our students come from graduate programs within a School of Education, although many also come from psychology, sociology, speech and communication, and other departments within the social sciences. A prerequisite to enrollment in our courses is completion of a full year of exposure to (two or three courses in) statistical methods in the social sciences. From this training we assume knowledge about hypothesis testing, confidence intervals, and the analysis of variance, including knowledge about the Scheffé, Tukey, and Dunn-Bonferroni models of multiple comparisons. We further assume that students are familiar with concepts from simple correlation and regression, and that they possess the skills required to use commonly available computer packages such as SPSS, BMD, and SAS. These topics form the core on which our presentations in this book are based.

Although many of the correlation-and-regression concepts in Chapters 1 through 3 are familiar to our students, many of the specific procedures and the associated discussion are new. Moreover, and as we point out in Section 1-4, we devote considerable space and time to these topics for two reasons. First, we have been surprised to discover that students have a tendency to forget (suppress?) topics in correlation and regression more rapidly than those in other areas. This is undoubtedly somewhat a result of differences in emphasis given in our own introductory courses, but a result as well of the preferential treatment given to analysis-of-variance-designed studies that appear in most of the empirical research journals in the social sciences.

Following this extension of simple correlation procedures to those based on multiple correlation, we cover matrix algebra and canonical correlation in Chapters 4 and 5. Our goal in Chapter 4 is not to teach the theory of matrix algebra or linear forms, but instead to enable students to recognize the relationship between scalar arithmetic concepts and those presented in matrix notation. In Chapter 5, we give careful consideration to the most "versatile" of all measures of relationship, canonical correlation, building on the material presented in Chapters 1 through 4.

A chapter on principal component analysis (Chapter 6) follows, but those who wish to spend more time on other material (ourselves included) can readily omit this chapter with no loss in continuity. The same comments apply to the chapter on the analysis of qualitative data (Chapter 10). The main reason that these two specialized chapters were included in the first place was to provide the social science researcher with a brief exposure to the "ballparks" encompassed by the respective topics.

Chapters 7, 8, and 9 on linear discriminant analysis and multivariate analysis-of-variance procedures constitute a major part of our teaching effort. Much of our own statistical training and philosophy dictate this emphasis, and the particular techniques discussed are closely related to those covered in earlier chapters and courses. In this portion of the course especially, many student-run computer exercises are included. Assignments consist of conducting multivariate analyses of both real and simulated data, reporting the results of such analyses in the context of a Results section of a journal article, and critiquing existing data analyses that appear in the literature of the student's own discipline.

We hope that most readers of this book will find credible and creditable our approach to multivariate data analysis in the social sciences. Our examples are worked out in sufficient detail that a researcher should be able to adapt his or her particular questions to the models discussed. Finally, a personal plea: We plan to revise this book at a later date. We know that other researchers have their own unique insights into multivariate analysis that are not presently included in existing textbooks. Because of this, we invite our readers to write us and let us know how we can make improvements that will benefit students and researchers. Any suggestions that we are able to incorporate into subsequent revisions of this book will be both appreciated and gratefully acknowledged.

ACKNOWLEDGMENTS

Like a fine wine, this book has been well aged before it was set out for consumption. Indeed, start to finish of this project occupied the better part of a decade. We would be aging still were it not for the assistance of many dedicated individuals. The Brooks/Cole Publishing Company has been extremely patient with us. Thanks to you all and, in particular, to Debbie Laughton and Todd Lueders. Thanks also to Michael Michaud of Unicorn Production Services, Inc., for helping us get the manuscript into print. We further wish to thank Rob Slaughter for computer analyzing some of the examples, and our Berkeley and Wisconsin students for providing us with much needed field-testing feedback. For reviews of initial manuscript versions, we are grateful to Pat Busk, Elliott Cramer, Harvey Goldstein, Al Hexter, Henry Kaiser, Dennis Leitner, David Stern, Neil Timm, Becky Zwick, and our series editor, Roger Kirk. The invaluable substantive contributions of our friend and colleague, Ron Serlin, were especially appreciated. Finally, and above all, thanks to Tom Little for his unerring translation into type all those miles and miles of single-spaced, handwritten, illegible text that came across his desk.

LAM and JRL
December 23, 1982

CONTENTS

Chapter 3. Multiple Correlation and Regression Theory 75

Chapter 4. Matrix Algebra and Multiple Regression Theory 141

CHAPTER ONE

PREVIEW AND REVIEW

1-1. A functional history of multivariate statistics

Perhaps a book whose primary objective is to introduce social science researchers to multivariate statistics should begin with a brief history of multivariate methods, followed by an argument convincing the researchers why multivariate methods are for them. Because other authors have done this before, and they have done it well (see Cattell, 1966; and Whitla, 1968), there is no need for us to repeat their writings. Anyone who is particularly interested in the history of multivariate procedures and the important role they play in social science research should consult the various multivariate textbooks cited throughout this book.

Presenting a history of multivariate methods contributes little to the objectives of this book. However, note that the *functional* history of multivariate analysis did not begin until the appearance of the high-speed electronic computer and not until accompanying computer programs were written with the researcher in mind. Among the first truly useful computer programs to be written and to gain worldwide acceptance were those included in the Biomedical Series or BMD programs that were prepared by Dixon and his associates at UCLA. This set of programs first appeared in 1961. This, more than any other event, made multivariate methods available to researchers who had access to an electronic computer. The BMD package has been revised several times, and with each revision it has become increasingly more versatile and more responsive to users' needs. Its success encouraged the development of other computer packages, of which the most frequently used are the *Statistical Package for the Social Sciences* (SPSS) by Nie and others, which is available from the McGraw-Hill Publishing Company of New York. Also available are Statistical Analysis System (SAS), from SAS Institute, Inc., Cary, North Carolina, and *Multivariance* by Finn, from National Education Resources Inc., Ann Arbor, Michigan. Most of the numerical examples appearing in this book were analyzed using one or more of these four programs.

1-2. Multivariate versus univariate analysis

Loosely defined, *univariate analyses* concentrate on only one variable at a time, whereas *multivariate analyses* concentrate on two or more simultaneously. We would be the last ones to argue that multivariate analyses are invariably preferable to univariate analyses. Indeed, we can enumerate a number of situations in which univariate analyses are definitely preferable, and we do so throughout the book. On the other hand, in some situations multivariate methods constitute the only rational approach to a research problem, and to use a univariate approach would be in error. We provide examples of these later. Thus, whether or not a potential multivariate problem is analyzed 'multivariately' is a function of the researcher's perceptions of the problem and corresponding desired substantive interpretations of the data. In this statistical domain, as in others, a variety of data-analysis options is available for answering a given research question.

Here we provide researchers with a number of data-analysis strategies to consider when tackling *potential* multivariate problems. A preliminary sketch of these strategies can be obtained by examining the table of contents, as well as the chapter-by-chapter overview presented in this chapter. Throughout the book, guidelines are provided for many specific problems that are unique to research on data collected on human subjects. We hope that our book is of significant utility to researchers in the social sciences.

1-3. The authors' pedagogical philosophy

A textbook on multivariate analysis can be written at many different levels of sophistication. After reviewing the currently available texts on this subject, we concluded that many writers chose to adopt a mathematically complex level of presentation, often with little or no emphasis on practical applications and interpretations of multivariate techniques in the social sciences. We purposely adopted the opposite view in this text. Our primary emphasis here is on applications and interpretations of multivariate techniques. As a result, we pay less attention to the complex mathematical and theoretical underpinnings of the techniques discussed.

This kind of practical focus is consistent with the teaching philosophy shared by the authors. As applied especially to the learning of relatively complex material, our philosophy boils down to one of *clarification* and *simplification*. Throughout the text, we attempt to translate otherwise esoteric statistical methods into a form that can be easily understood by potential consumers of these methods in the social sciences. To this end, we offer numerous verbal and pictorial examples, analogies, and simplifications. By presenting the material in a comparatively simple, and often intuitive, form we hope to introduce applied multivariate techniques to students and researchers who otherwise might have consciously avoided them.

The approach we have adopted is not without its drawbacks. For one, our coverage of the material is not always technically complete from a theoretical purist's point of view. Given a modest amount of "poetic license," we do strive to be technically accurate throughout the book, and specifically acknowledge any departures from exactitude. A unique feature of this book is the "simplified statistics" section found at the end of most chapters. Here we present easy-to-use univariate analogs of the multivariate technique(s) being discussed in the particular chapter. We introduce the simplified statistical procedures as *approximations* to the exact multivariate techniques, in keeping with our philosophy of simplicity in the name of improved understanding. Of course, we recognize that simplified statistical techniques, by definition, represent less-than-perfect, one-to-one correspondences with the companion multivariate techniques, but nonetheless we offer these for two reasons. First, as has already been mentioned, often our simplified procedures will greatly help the reader understand aspects of the particular multivariate technique being discussed. Second, in applied situations, a researcher frequently requires only an approximate, rather than an exact, statistical solution. In such cases, our simplified procedures will lead to far quicker and more manageable computations which, as such, would be recommended in the interest of economy.

1-4. Extent of coverage

Before we summarize the chapter contents, a few comments about topic coverage are in order. A glance at the chapter headings will reveal that the material in this and the next chapter does not deal with *multivariate* statistics at all, but rather with *bivariate* (two-variable) statistical concepts and procedures. We have included this material because we acknowledge the almost certain heterogeneous backgrounds of our readers and want to introduce our readers to the terminology, symbolic notation, and conceptual approach used throughout the book. Some readers may also be familiar with the multiple regression material in Chapters 3 and 4. We included multiple regression in this book not just because we consider it to fall legitimately within the "multivariate" domain, but primarily because it represents such an important building block for almost all of the material discussed in later chapters. In sum, even though the first part of the book's contents may appear to overlap with what the reader already knows, we personally view this overlap as healthy for two reasons. First, we continually relate early developments to the later multivariate techniques as a comprehension-enhancing device. Second, we believe that our coverage will serve to complement and extend the statistical backgrounds possessed by our readers. On both accounts, we view the inclusion of Chapters 1–4 as extremely important from a pedagogical standpoint.

Naturally, a book of this scope cannot encompass all topics related to multivariate analysis. Among the particular chapters we have chosen to exclude are different regression models and structural equations, time-series analysis, factor analysis, and multidimensional scaling. It is not that we think that such techniques are without their value. Rather, we focus here on the more-or-less "traditional" multivariate methods that are frequently used by social science researchers. The topics omitted often occupy books of their own; accordingly, we could not easily expand the present coverage to include them here.

1-5. How to use this book

We do not provide computational algorithms for the models presented because we assume that all multivariate investigations will be done using a computer. This is not to say that desk or hand calculators will not be necessary. It is our experience that computer programs perform all of the heavy computations but that extra analyses based on means, standard deviations, and correlation coefficients must still be done by hand. Many of the analyses presented in this book were conducted in such a manner. Thus we suggest that complicated analyses be done via canned computer programs and that secondary analyses be done with a desk or hand calculator.

One of the best ways to learn how to use multivariate procedures is to practice. With this in mind, we have provided exercises at the end of each chapter. We recommend that they be used to master the methods presented in this book.

1-6. Chapter contents

In Chapter 1 we begin by providing a detailed review of simple regression and correlation problems; that is, problems with one predictor variable and one criterion variable. Here the correlation coefficient is defined, as are the slope and intercept values of regression problems. Two different uses of regression equations are indicated, followed by a presentation of least squares estimation theory and its associated properties. In anticipation of the matrix algebra presentation in Chapter

4, Cramer's Rule for solving sets of linear equations is illustrated. Finally, we begin our discussion of simplified statistics, a topic that is developed more fully in later chapters. As stated previously, we believe that simple procedures are often just as appropriate for analyzing data as the more complex multivariate methods that we present in each chapter, and sometimes they are even more appropriate.

Chapter 2 begins with the important distinction between correlation and regression models. The notion of "variance accounted for" is presented, and then selected hypothesis-testing and confidence-interval procedures are illustrated. Pooling correlation coefficients is considered and the within-sample estimator of a correlation coefficient is presented. This latter measure of association plays an important role in the theory of linear discriminant analysis and the multivariate analysis of variance. Regression theory is examined in some detail. Hypotheses related to two or more regression lines in terms of tests of equal slopes, equal intercepts (analysis of covariance), and of identity are illustrated. Planned and post hoc comparisons for these hypotheses are presented. The chapter closes with guidelines on how to handle missing data, the nemesis of multivariate methodology.

Chapter 3 begins our development of multivariate methods with an in-depth presentation of multiple regression theory. Partial correlations are presented for one dependent variable and two independent variables, along with the corresponding significance test. Beta weights, methods for interpreting them, and corresponding statistical inference procedures are discussed. The relationship of the beta weight to measures of residual variance is examined, and the multiple correlation coefficient is introduced. Tests of significance for the multiple correlation coefficient are also provided. Next, part correlation is presented and a discussion of the percent of variance explained by individual predictors is made. Stepwise regression theory is introduced, and the method of forward selection is presented. How to perform an analysis of variance (ANOVA) in terms of dummy coding is illustrated, and the analysis of covariance hypothesis is reexamined in terms of dummy coding. The rudiments of the explanatory system, path analysis, are then described. Finally, simplified statistical procedures for multiple regression close the chapter.

In Chapter 4, in preparation for the methods to follow in later chapters, we repeat the presentation of Chapter 3, but in terms of vectors and matrices and for $P > 2$ predictor variables. Vectors and matrices are defined and illustrated. Rules for adding, subtracting, multiplying, and dividing matrices are presented, and examples are provided. Inverse matrices are introduced and the method of least squares is reexamined in matrix terms. Linear combinations of variables, and the associated statistical comparisons, are examined in terms of matrix notation. The multiple correlation coefficient is also examined under this system for representing multivariate data. Finally, testing for the equality of K independent variance-covariance matrices is considered in light of the new matrix representation.

Chapter 5 provides a thorough description of canonical correlation theory. Characteristic equations, eigen values, and eigen vectors are presented. Statistical tests for the significance of canonical variates are provided in the context of a simple example. Correlations between canonical variates and the original variables are presented, and a discussion of the differences between pattern and structure matrices is begun. Using the canonical variates in an ANOVA investigation is illustrated, and the assumptions underlying canonical correlation analysis are discussed. Then it is shown how most of the methods discussed in this text are in reality special cases of canonical correlation theory. The chapter closes with a simplified statistical procedure for approximating the first pair of canonical variates.

In Chapter 6 we deviate from the mainstream of measuring correlations and comparing group means to a discussion that rightfully belongs to a treatise on factor analysis. We provide an in-depth presentation of principal components, rotation of principal components, the determination of principal component scores, and their use in ANOVA designs. We complete the discussion of structure and pattern matrices, describe the rudiments of factor analysis, and close the chapter with simplified procedures for principal component analysis.

Chapter 7 provides a return to the mainstream of multivariate analysis. Linear discriminant analysis is presented as a special case of multiple regression in which the dependent variable is dichotomous. Next the model is examined according to the model first proposed by R. A. Fisher and is then represented as a problem in matrix algebra. Hotelling's T^2 is presented and planned and post hoc procedures for comparing two groups on P variables are examined. Mahalanobis's D^2 is presented and its connection to Hotelling's T^2 and Fisher's discriminant functions are discussed. Finally, simplified procedures are presented.

Chapter 8 continues the discussion started in Chapter 7, but for three or more groups of observations. Wilks's and Roy's criteria are presented. Multivariate analysis of variance is discussed in terms of these two statistics. Bartlett's test is presented and Rao's test is illustrated. Rules are given as to when Roy's criterion is likely to be preferred to the methods based on Wilks's criterion. Classification for the K-group problem is represented, and simplified statistics for the one-way multivariate analysis of variance close the chapter.

In Chapter 9 we extend multivariate analysis of variance notions to encompass more complex designs. First, univariate factorial ANOVA designs are reviewed and then extended to the multivariate case. Two types of factorial models, interaction and simple effects, are distinguished between, and the problem of unequal cell frequencies is considered. Multiple comparison procedures, appropriate for the models discussed, are presented. Brief mention is made of the multivariate analysis of covariance model. We then discuss in detail the multivariate analysis of within-subject designs, either accompanied or not by between-subject factors. Procedures for examining trends are included in this discussion. The chapter ends with a consideration of simplified statistics for factorial multivariate analysis of variance (MANOVA) designs.

Chapter 10, the final chapter of the book, focuses on the kind of qualitative data that typically appears in contingency tables. Various alternatives to the traditional Pearson Chi-square test are introduced. The first procedure is a test for trend in a single $I \times 2$ contingency table, which is then extended to more than one $I \times 2$ table. Log-linear analysis, an analog to analysis of variance for qualitative dependent variables, is then described. Omnibus tests, multiple comparison procedures, and measures of association are presented for both the interaction and simple effects models. Finally, contingency table analysis is related to the problem of canonical correlation, as discussed in Chapter 5.

1-7. An example

A large part of multivariate statistical theory and methodology is based upon simple two-variable correlation and regression models. Because so much of multivariate theory is actually a generalization of the familiar two-variable theory, it becomes useful to examine the simple models in great detail so as to aid the understanding of the seemingly more complex models presented in the following chapters. To achieve this goal, we will examine the simple models in terms of the data of Table 1-1, which are based on a random sampling of 40 students from the listing of complete data for 216 students enrolled in a beginning sociology class at a midwestern university. The complete data for all 216 students are reported in Table A-1 of the appendix.

TABLE 1-1. Random sample of 40 subjects selected from the population of Table A-1

						Variable						
	1	2	3	4	5	6	7	8	9	10	11	12
Student Number	*SC*	*Sex*	*GPA*	*CB*	*HSS*	*M*	*PT*	*M1*	*M2*	*F*	*E*	*C*
003	2	1	3.55	410	0	1	17	43	61	129	3	2
004	2	1	2.70	390	0	2	20	50	47	60	1	1
010	2	1	3.50	510	0	4	22	47	79	119	1	1
014	3	1	2.91	430	0	1	13	24	40	—	1	2
018	2	1	3.10	600	0	—	16	47	60	79	—	1
020	3	1	3.49	610	0	2	28	57	59	99	1	1
032	1	0	3.17	610	0	4	14	42	61	92	3	1
040	2	1	3.57	560	0	4	10	42	79	107	2	2
050	3	1	3.76	700	1	1	28	69	83	156	1	1
052	2	0	3.81	460	1	1	30	48	67	110	1	2
055	2	0	3.60	590	1	3	28	59	74	116	1	1
070	3	—	3.10	500	1	1	15	21	40	49	1	1
072	1	1	—	410	0	4	24	52	71	107	5	2
076	2	—	3.50	470	1	5	15	35	40	125	1	1
080	2	1	3.43	210	1	5	26	35	57	64	5	2
083	2	0	3.39	610	0	1	16	59	58	100	1	1
089	2	0	3.76	510	1	1	25	68	66	138	2	1
091	3	0	3.71	600	0	1	3	38	58	63	1	1
103	2	1	3.00	470	1	—	5	45	24	82	3	1
104	2	0	—	460	0	5	16	37	48	73	3	1
106	2	1	3.69	800	1	2	28	54	100	132	2	1
108	1	1	3.24	610	0	3	13	45	83	87	2	1
117	2	1	3.46	490	0	2	9	31	70	89	2	2
118	2	0	3.39	470	0	2	13	39	48	99	1	2
128	2	0	3.90	610	1	3	30	67	85	119	—	1
143	1	—	2.76	580	0	3	10	30	14	—	1	2
150	2	1	2.70	410	0	2	13	19	—	—	2	2
166	1	1	3.77	630	1	—	8	71	100	166	3	1
171	2	1	4.00	790	1	4	29	80	94	111	2	1
174	3	1	3.40	490	0	4	17	47	45	110	1	2
179	2	0	3.09	400	0	—	—	46	58	93	1	1
183	2	1	3.80	610	1	1	16	59	90	141	2	1
188	1	1	3.28	610	1	1	13	48	84	99	2	2
193	1	1	3.70	500	1	2	30	68	81	114	5	1
195	2	1	3.42	430	1	1	17	43	49	96	1	1
196	3	1	3.09	540	0	1	17	31	54	39	1	2
199	1	1	3.70	610	0	3	25	64	87	149	4	2
207	2	1	2.69	400	0	3	10	19	36	53	3	2
208	3	1	3.40	390	0	4	23	43	51	39	1	2
211	1	0	2.95	490	0	2	18	20	—	—	1	2

The variables investigated are as follows:

1. Social class:

   1. High 2. Middle 3. Low

2. Sex:

   0. Male 1. Female

3. High school grade point average.
4. College Board test score.
5. Response to the question: "Did you take high school classes where topics in sociology were presented?":

   0. No 1. Yes

6. College major:

   1. Natural Sciences 2. Social Sciences
   3. Humanities 4. Other 5. Unknown

7. Score on a 30-point pretest designed to measure knowledge in sociology.
8. Score on the first 100-point midterm.
9. Score on the second 100-point midterm.
10. Score on the 200-point final.
11. Response, at the end of the semester, to the question: "What is your overall evaluation of this course?":

    1. Very Positive 2. Positive 3. Neutral
    4. Negative 5. Very Negative

12. A followup of every student to determine whether or not they selected a sociology-related career:

    1. Yes 2. No

Note that the values of some of the variables are *coded*. For example, sex is coded in terms of 0 and 1, with 0 representing Male and 1 representing Female. Codes are also used for variables 1, 5, 6, 11, and 12. We will have more to say about coding in Section 3-16.

The 216 students of this study represent a sample of students who, over time, could enroll for a beginning course in sociology. Statistical analysis would normally involve the data for all 216 students. However, for expository purposes, we will assume that the 216 students constitute a population of students and that the study will be based on a simple random sample of 40 students selected from the population of 216.

As will soon be apparent, only a few of these variables are considered in this chapter. Complete data are reported in Table 1-1 for subsequent reference, as each of the variables will appear at one point or another in later chapters. In many of the analyses that follow, certain of the variables will be called *predictor* variables, in that they will serve to predict students' scores on some or all of the remaining variables, called *criterion* variables. In other analyses, no distinction will be made between predictor and criterion variables. Variables that are used as predictors are also referred to as *independent* variables, whereas the variables being predicted are called *dependent* variables. Even though independent variables are often associated with the *experimental* variables deliberately manipulated by a researcher, this restrictive definition is not adhered to in statistical analysis. Independent variables in statistics are much broader in nature and conform more closely to the mathematical definition of an independent variable. For example, college major, sex, social class, and so on can be considered as independent variables even though they are not randomly assigned by researchers, but are rather assigned by nature or society. Some researchers refer to these variables as *demographic*, *organismic*, or *status* variables. Following the mathematical tradition, we denote independent variables by $X_1, X_2, \ldots, X_P$ and dependent variables by $Y_1, Y_2, \ldots, Y_Q$. In this sense, an independent variable will be viewed as any variable that can be used to predict the values of a dependent variable.

1-8. Summarizing the data for a two-variable investigation

Suppose we were interested in the relationship between students' performance on the pretest (variable 7 in Table 1-1) and their performance on the first midterm (variable 8). The data for these two variables are reported in Table 1-2. With the pretest represented by X and the first midterm as Y, they are displayed in the scatter diagram of Figure 1-1. Because a pretest score is missing for one student, we will use the information for only 39 students. Later, in Section 2-10, we will consider the problem of missing data. Note that there appears to be a positive relationship between these two variables in that midterm scores tend to increase with increases in pretest scores.

Notation and formulas useful for summarizing data such as those in Table 1-2 are given in Table 1-3. Here we find that:

$$\bar{X} = \frac{710}{39} = 18.2051 \qquad \bar{Y} = \frac{1796}{39} = 46.0513$$

$$S_X^2 = \frac{39(15066) - (710)^2}{39(38)} = 56.3252 \qquad S_Y^2 = \frac{39(91952) - (1796)^2}{39(38)} = 243.2604$$

$$S_X = \sqrt{56.3252} = 7.5050 \qquad S_Y = \sqrt{243.2604} = 15.5968$$

$$S_{XY} = \frac{39(35162) - 710(1796)}{39(38)} = 64.8839$$

$$r_{XY} = \frac{3(35162) - 710(1796)}{\sqrt{[39(15066) - (710)^2]\,[39(91952) - (1796)^2]}} = .5543$$

TABLE 1-2. Scores on the pretest, *X*, and first midterm, *Y*, for the 39 students with complete data

Student number	*PT*	*M1*	*Student number*	*PT*	*M1*
003	17	43	106	28	54
004	20	50	108	13	45
010	22	47	117	9	31
014	13	24	118	13	39
018	16	47	128	30	67
020	28	57	143	10	30
032	14	42	150	13	19
040	10	42	166	8	71
050	28	69	171	29	80
052	30	48	174	17	47
055	28	59	183	16	59
070	15	21	188	13	48
072	24	52	193	30	68
076	15	35	195	17	43
080	26	35	196	17	31
083	16	59	199	25	64
089	25	68	207	10	19
091	3	38	208	23	43
103	5	45	211	18	20
104	16	37			

TABLE 1-3. Basic notation and formulas for summarizing bivariate data

1. Sample means ($\bar{X}$ and $\bar{Y}$)

$$\bar{X} = \frac{\sum_{i=1}^{N} X_i}{N} \qquad \bar{Y} = \frac{\sum_{i=1}^{N} Y_i}{N}$$

2. Sample variances (S_X^2 and S_Y^2)

   a. Definitional formulas

$$S_X^2 = \frac{\sum_{i=1}^{N} (X_i - \bar{X})^2}{N - 1} \qquad S_Y^2 = \frac{\sum_{i=1}^{N} (Y_i - \bar{Y})^2}{N - 1}$$

   b. Computational formulas

$$S_X^2 = \frac{N \sum_{i=1}^{N} X_i^2 - \left(\sum_{i=1}^{N} X_i\right)^2}{N(N-1)} \qquad S_Y^2 = \frac{N \sum_{i=1}^{N} Y_i^2 - \left(\sum_{i=1}^{N} Y_i\right)^2}{N(N-1)}$$

3. Sample standard deviations (S_X and S_Y)

$$S_X = \sqrt{S_X^2} \qquad S_Y = \sqrt{S_Y^2}$$

4. Standard scores (Z_X and Z_Y)

$$Z_X = \frac{X - \bar{X}}{S_X} \qquad Z_Y = \frac{Y - \bar{Y}}{S_Y}$$

5. Sample covariance (S_{XY})
   a. Definitional formula

$$S_{XY} = \frac{\sum_{i=1}^{N} (X_i - \bar{X})(Y_i - \bar{Y})}{N - 1}$$

   b. Computational formula

$$S_{XY} = \frac{N \sum_{i=1}^{N} X_i Y_i - \left(\sum_{i=1}^{N} X_i\right)\left(\sum_{i=1}^{N} Y_i\right)}{N(N - 1)}$$

6. Sample correlation coefficient (r_{XY})
   a. Definitional formula

$$r_{XY} = \frac{S_{XY}}{S_X S_Y}$$

   b. Computational formula (raw scores)

$$r_{XY} = \frac{N \sum_{i=1}^{N} X_i Y_i - \left(\sum_{i=1}^{N} X_i\right)\left(\sum_{i=1}^{N} Y_i\right)}{\sqrt{\left[N \sum_{i=1}^{N} X_i^2 - \left(\sum_{i=1}^{N} X_i\right)^2\right]\left[N \sum_{i=1}^{N} Y_i^2 - \left(\sum_{i=1}^{N} Y_i\right)^2\right]}}$$

   c. Computational formula (standard scores)

$$r_{XY} = \frac{\sum_{i=1}^{N} Z_{X_i} Z_{Y_i}}{N - 1}$$

7. Slope of the sample regression line to predict Y from X (B_1 or b_1)
   a. Applied to raw scores

$$B_1 = r_{XY} \frac{S_Y}{S_X}$$

$$= \frac{S_{XY}}{S_X^2}$$

   b. Applied to standard scores

$$b_1 = B_1 \frac{S_X}{S_Y}$$

$$= r_{XY}$$

8. Intercept of the sample regression line to predict Y from X (B_0 or b_0)
   a. Applied to raw scores

$$B_0 = \bar{Y} - B_1 \bar{X}$$

   b. Applied to standard scores

$$b_0 = 0$$

9. Equation of the best-fitting straight line to predict Y from X ($\hat{Y}$ or $\hat{Z}_Y$)
   a. Applied to raw scores

$$\hat{Y} = B_0 + B_1 X$$

   b. Applied to standard scores

$$\hat{Z}_Y = r_{XY} Z_X$$

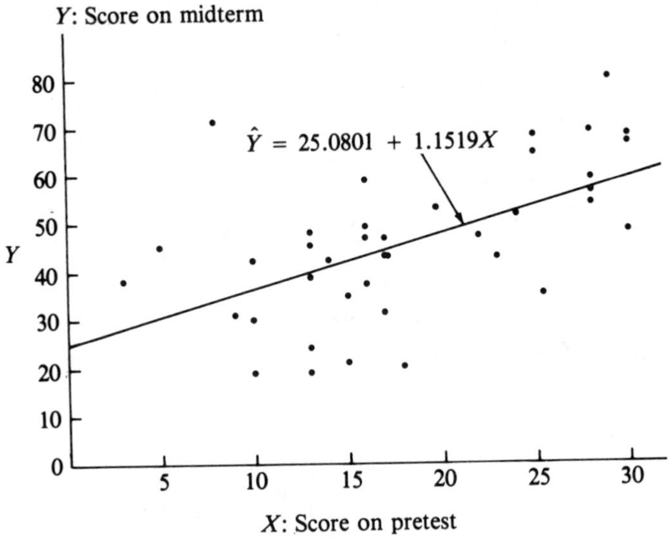

Figure 1-1. Scatter diagram and regression line for scores on the sociology pretest and the first midterm for the 39 students who took both tests.

Thus, for these data a moderate positive correlation of $r_{XY} = .55$ exists between pretest and midterm scores.

Let us now determine the best-fitting straight line for predicting first midterm scores (Y) from the pretest (X), where "best-fitting" will be defined in Section 1-9. Of course, in terms of standard scores:

$$\hat{Z}_Y = .5543 Z_X$$

which means that, say, an individual whose Z score on the pretest was 1 standard deviation above the mean would be expected to have a first midterm score that is .5543 standard deviations above the mean. In terms of raw scores, we see that:

$$B_1 = .5543\left(\frac{15.5968}{7.5050}\right) = 1.1519$$

and

$$B_0 = 46.0513 - 1.1519(18.2051) = 25.0801$$

which yields:

$$\hat{Y} = 25.0801 + 1.1519X$$

and which is displayed in Figure 1-1. Thus, for example, consider again an individual who scored one standard deviation above the mean of the pretest. With $\bar{X} = 18.2051$ and $S_X = 7.5050$, this represents a score of $X = 25.7101$. According to the equation, this individual's predicted score on the first midterm is given by:

$$\hat{Y} = 25.0801 + 1.1519(25.7101)$$
$$= 54.6956$$

With $\bar{Y} = 46.0513$ and $S_Y = 15.5968$, we see that a score of 54.6956 may be represented as:

$$\hat{Z}_Y = \frac{54.6956 - 46.0513}{15.5968}$$
$$= .5542$$

which, within rounding errors, is the same distance above the Y mean as was indicated directly by the standard score version of the regression equation ($r_{XY} = .5543$). Note also that the relatively closer-to-the-mean performance on Y than X, which was predicted for this individual, is captured by the term *regression toward the mean*.

1-9. The method of least squares

Many multivariate methods are based on the method of least squares. The nature of the method can be illustrated by referring to the hypothetical data and regression line in Figure 1-2. Each vertical deviation between an observed value and its corresponding value on the regression line is shown there and defined by:

$$D_i = Y_i - \hat{Y}_i = Y_i - (B_0 + B_1X_i)$$

Thus:

$$D_1 = Y_1 - (B_0 + B_1X_1)$$
$$D_2 = Y_2 - (B_0 + B_1X_2)$$
$$\vdots \qquad \vdots$$
$$D_N = Y_N - (B_0 + B_1X_N)$$

Consider the sum of the squared deviations:

$$\sum_{i=1}^{N} D_i^2 = \sum_{i=1}^{N} [Y_i - (B_0 + B_1X_i)]^2$$

Note from the preceding formula that the sum of the D_i^2 may be made as large as we please by merely changing the values of B_0 and B_1. The method of least squares states that we should select B_0 and B_1 so as to give the best fit to the points that are scattered about the line. The values of B_0 and B_1 that achieve the best fit, in the sense of least squares, are the two numbers that minimize the value of $\sum_{i=1}^{N} D_i^2$. These two

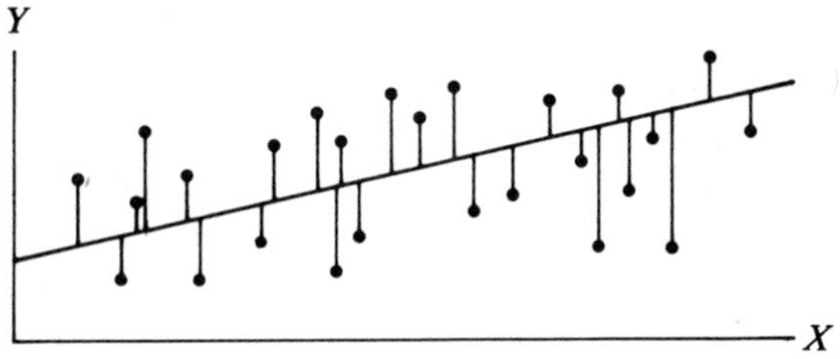

Figure 1-2. Deviations about the best-fitting straight line.

values are easy to determine. The determination involves the simple calculus problem of minimizing the value of $\sum_{i=1}^{N} D_i^2$.

To obtain the minimum, we need only differentiate $\sum_{i=1}^{N} D_i^2$ with respect to B_0 and B_1, and then solve the resulting equations. If we follow this process, we are eventually led to two equations which are commonly referred to as the *normal equations*. The solution to these equations gives rise to formulas for determining the values of B_0 and B_1.

The normal equations for $\hat{Y} = B_0 + B_1X$.
Let N, $\sum_{i=1}^{N} X_i$, $\sum_{i=1}^{N} Y_i$, $\sum_{i=1}^{N} X_i^2$, and $\sum_{i=1}^{N} X_iY_i = \sum_{i=1}^{N} Y_iX_i$ be determined for a set of data. The normal equations for determining B_0 and B_1 are given by:

$$\sum_{i=1}^{N} Y_i = (N)B_0 + \left(\sum_{i=1}^{N} X_i\right)B_1$$

$$\sum_{i=1}^{N} Y_iX_i = \left(\sum_{i=1}^{N} X_i\right)B_0 + \left(\sum_{i=1}^{N} X_i^2\right)B_1$$

The solutions to these equations are called the least squares estimates of the corresponding population values, β_0 and β_1, which are introduced in Chapter 2.

For the pretest and midterm scores of Table 1-2, the two normal equations are given by:

$$1796 = 39B_0 + 710B_1$$

$$35162 = 710B_0 + 15066B_1$$

We will illustrate the solution of these equations by means of *determinants* and *Cramer's rule*.

A determinant with two rows and two columns is a configuration of four real numbers which reduces to a single real number, according to the following rule.

Definition of a 2 × 2 determinant.
Consider the four real numbers a_1, a_2, a_3, and a_4, as arranged between the two vertical lines. Such an array is called a determinant whose numerical value may be determined as:

$$\Delta = \begin{vmatrix} a_1 & a_2 \\ a_3 & a_4 \end{vmatrix} = a_1a_4 - a_2a_3$$

According to the preceding definition:

$$\Delta = \begin{vmatrix} N & \sum_{i=1}^{N} X_i \\ \sum_{i=1}^{N} X_i & \sum_{i=1}^{N} X_i^2 \end{vmatrix} = \begin{vmatrix} 39 & 710 \\ 710 & 15066 \end{vmatrix}$$

$$= 39(15066) - 710(710) = 83474$$

This determinant serves as the building block for Cramer's rule which is used to determine B_0 and B_1.

Cramer's rule for determining the values of B_0 and B_1.

Step 1. Determine the value of:

$$\Delta = \begin{vmatrix} N & \sum\limits_{i=1}^{N} X_i \\ \sum\limits_{i=1}^{N} X_i & \sum\limits_{i=1}^{N} X_i^2 \end{vmatrix}$$

Step 2. Replace column 1 of Δ by the left-hand column of the normal equations. Compute this determinant, designated by Δ_{B_0}.

Step 3. The value of B_0 is given by $B_0 = \Delta_{B_0}/\Delta$.

Step 4. Replace column 2 of Δ by the left-hand column of the normal equations. Compute this determinant, designated by Δ_{B_1}.

Step 5. The value of B_1 is given by $B_1 = \Delta_{B_1}/\Delta$.

For the example under consideration:

$$\Delta_{B_0} = \begin{vmatrix} 1796 & 710 \\ 35162 & 15066 \end{vmatrix} = 1796(15066) - 710(35162) = 2093516$$

so that:

$$B_0 = \frac{\Delta_{B_0}}{\Delta} = \frac{2093516}{83474} = 25.0799 \simeq 25.08$$

In like manner:

$$\Delta_{B_1} = \begin{vmatrix} 39 & 1796 \\ 710 & 35162 \end{vmatrix} = 39(35162) - 1796(710) = 96158$$

so that:

$$B_1 = \frac{\Delta_{B_1}}{\Delta} = \frac{96158}{83474} = 1.1520 \simeq 1.15$$

Thus the equation of the least squares regression line to four decimal points is given by:

$$\hat{Y} = 25.0799 + 1.1520X$$

and to two decimal points is given by:

$$\hat{Y} = 25.08 + 1.15X$$

This equation differs only slightly from the results obtained in Section 1-8, where it was shown that:

$$\hat{Y} = 25.0801 + 1.1519X$$

The difference is merely a result of rounding errors. In general, the method of this section is preferred to the method of Section 1-8 for determining the values of B_0 and

B_1 because it minimizes rounding errors, just as the previously given computational formulas do for the sample variance and correlation coefficient. However, as can be seen in this case, both methods produce the same results when rounded to the nearest hundredths.

1-10. Predicted values and goodness of fit based on least squares

The regression equation resulting from the normal equations of the method of least squares has two major uses: the prediction of unknown values and the evaluation of the resulting regression line as to how well it fits the data.

As an example of the predictive or *forecasting* use, consider a student with a pretest score of 20 who was not included in the sample from which the regression line was determined. On the basis of the regression equation, we would predict this student's final score to be a number close to:

$$\hat{Y} = 25.08 + 1.15(20) = 48.08 \simeq 48$$

Naturally we could not expect to predict the score exactly. However, we do know that among students who had a pretest score of 20, the average value on the first midterm will be a number close to 48.08. In fact, if we examine the data of Table A-1, we would see that seven students had pretest scores of 20. Their first midterm scores were equal to 18, 50, 50, 50, 50, 57, and 77. The average value of these seven scores is 50.29, a number fairly close to 48.08.

Four properties of predicted values for the observations that produce the least squares estimates of B_0 and B_1 are as follows.

1. *The mean of predicted scores*. The mean of the predicted scores, $\bar{\hat{Y}}$, is equal to the mean of the observed scores, $\bar{Y}$. By definition:

$$\bar{\hat{Y}} = \frac{1}{N}\sum_{i=1}^{N} \hat{Y}_i = \frac{1}{N}\sum_{i=1}^{N} [\bar{Y} + B_1(X_i - \bar{X})]$$

Thus:

$$\bar{\hat{Y}} = \frac{1}{N}\sum_{i=1}^{N} \bar{Y} + \frac{B_1}{N}\sum_{i=1}^{N} (X_i - \bar{X}) = \frac{1}{N} N\bar{Y} + \frac{B_1}{N}(0) = \bar{Y}$$

2. *The variance of predicted scores*. The variance of the predicted scores, $S_{\hat{Y}}^2$, can never be larger than the variance of the observed scores, S_Y^2. For the special case where $r_{XY} = 1.00$ or $r_{XY} = -1.00$, then $S_{\hat{Y}}^2 = S_Y^2$. These statements can be appreciated through the application of some simple algebra, which in turn leads to a very important connection between variance and the value of the correlation coefficient. The connection will simply be derived here without additional comment. An extensive discussion of it and its function as an important building block for multivariate analysis will be reserved for Chapter 2. By definition and Property 1:

$$S_{\hat{Y}}^2 = \frac{1}{N-1}\sum_{i=1}^{N} (\hat{Y}_i - \bar{\hat{Y}})^2 = \frac{1}{N-1}\sum_{i=1}^{N} [\bar{Y} + B_1(X_i - \bar{X}) - \bar{Y}]^2$$

$$= \frac{1}{N-1}\sum_{i=1}^{N} [B_1(X_i - \bar{X})]^2 = B_1^2\left(\frac{1}{N-1}\sum_{i=1}^{N} (X_i - \bar{X})^2\right)$$

$$= B_1^2 S_X^2 = \left(r_{XY}^2 \frac{S_Y^2}{S_X^2}\right) S_X^2 = r_{XY}^2 S_Y^2$$

3. *The correlation between predicted and actual scores.* A rather surprising property of the regression line is that the correlation between predicted and observed scores, $r_{\hat{Y}Y}$, is identical to r_{XY}. This important property will arise in multiple regression theory which will be discussed in Chapter 3. By definition:

$$r_{\hat{Y}Y} = \frac{1}{N-1} \sum_{i=1}^{N} \left(\frac{\hat{Y}_i - \bar{\hat{Y}}}{S_{\hat{Y}}}\right)\left(\frac{Y_i - \bar{Y}}{S_Y}\right)$$

Using Properties 1 and 2, it follows that:

$$\frac{\hat{Y}_i - \bar{\hat{Y}}}{S_{\hat{Y}}} = \frac{[\bar{Y} + B_1(X_i - \bar{X})] - \bar{Y}}{B_1 S_X} = \frac{X_i - \bar{X}}{S_X}$$

Thus:

$$r_{\hat{Y}Y} = \frac{1}{N-1} \sum_{i=1}^{N} \left(\frac{X_i - \bar{X}}{S_X}\right)\left(\frac{Y_i - \bar{Y}}{S_Y}\right) = r_{XY}$$

The second or *evaluative* use of regression equations is one of determining how well the equation fits the data at hand. That is, with respect to the data available, one can ask how good the fit was between what was actually observed for each individual, Y_i, and what had been predicted for that same individual according to the regression equation, $\hat{Y}_i$.

4. *Least squares property.* As noted previously, B_0 and B_1 are determined so that $\sum_{i=1}^{N} (Y_i - \hat{Y}_i)^2$ will be minimized. Thus, one property of the regression line is that it is the best-fitting straight line in the sense of minimizing the sum of squared vertical deviations about it, as in Figure 1-2. Any other values of B_0 and B_1, that is, any other straight line, must produce a larger sum of squared vertical deviations. Thus, if the sum of squared deviations is small, the fit between data and the regression line is deemed a good fit. Otherwise it is said to represent a poor fit. We will have more to say on this subject in later chapters.

1-11. Simplified statistics for simple linear regression

Borrowing from the properties of regression equations, as outlined in Section 1-10, we present the basis for our first simplified statistic that will be developed more fully in later chapters.

Within the context of the evaluative use of regression equations, two kinds of best fit may be desired. The first is complete, or *absolute,* best fit, where the least squares property of the regression line (Property 4) applies. In such cases, to achieve the best fit one must base the prediction on the least squares regression equation, $\hat{Y} = B_0 + B_1 X$, or on its standard score analogue, $\hat{Z}_Y = r_{XY} Z_X$.

In contrast, sometimes we are not concerned with determining how well an individual's actual score on Y is predicted, but rather how well his or her relative standing on Y is predicted. If a simple *relative* prediction rule will suffice, instead of employing the standardized regression equation, $\hat{Z}_Y = r_{XY} Z_X$, we can adopt only the simpler intuitive standardized equation: $\hat{Z}_Y = Z_X$ for positive values of r_{XY}; and $\hat{Z}_Y = -Z_X$ for negative values of r_{XY}. That is, whenever only relative prediction is desired, regression toward the mean, as reflected by the inclusion of r_{XY}, may be ignored. It will now be shown that the "goodness" of a relative prediction rule will be exactly the same for the preceding intuitive rule as when r_{XY} is included in the equation.

Consider the five pairs of scores reported in Table 1-4, for which $r_{XY} = .80$. The Z scores associated with the X variable are shown in Table 1-4, along with the predicted Z scores on Y. According to this procedure, each $\hat{Z}_Y$ is exactly .8 times the value of its original Z_X, and in terms of individuals' relative standings on $\hat{Z}_Y$, nothing has changed. In particular, not only have the individuals' rank orderings been preserved, but so have the relative score distances. Thus the difference between the first and third individual's scores is twice as large as the difference between the first and second individual's scores, and so on, just as it was on Z_X. So, to predict Z_X rather than $\hat{Z}_Y$ would yield identical relative prediction accuracy. Note also that $r_{\hat{Z}_Y Y} = r_{Z_X Y} = r_{XY}$.

What has been demonstrated by this example is that r_{XY} has the property of *invariance* with respect to linear transformations of one or both variables. For further discussion of this topic see Glass and Stanley (1970, pp. 119–120). In terms of goodness of fit in a relative sense, we need not include r_{XY} in the prediction rule. Although the exclusion of r_{XY} may seem trivial, remember that we are dealing with only two variables here. Formal regression equations become more complex as the number of predictor variables increases, and it is in just such situations that the present approach will prove most helpful. For now, we summarize an intuitive standardized relative prediction rule as follows.

Simplified prediction models.

Step 1. If X and Y are positively correlated, use $\hat{Z}_Y = Z_X$ to predict an individual's relative standing on Y. This rule will result in as good a fit to the relative data as the formal standardized regression equation, $\hat{Z}_Y = r_{XY}Z_X$.

Step 2. If X and Y are negatively correlated, use $\hat{Z}_Y = -Z_X$, with similar results.

Step 3. If X and Y are uncorrelated, that is, if $r_{XY} = 0$, the best standardized relative prediction rule is $\hat{Z}_Y = 0$.

Note that when $r_{XY} = 0$, a predicted standardized score of zero on Y is the same as predicting the standardized mean of Y, which is our best guess about any individual's score in the absence of additional information. To state that X and Y are uncorrelated is to acknowledge that, in a linear sense, nothing about Y is learned from knowledge of X.

TABLE 1-4. Data to illustrate relative and absolute prediction

X	Y	Z_X	$\hat{Z}_Y = r_{XY}Z_X$
1	2	−1.265	−1.012
2	1	−.632	−.506
3	3	.000	.000
4	5	.632	.506
5	4	1.265	1.012

1-12. Summary

In this chapter, the basic models for two-variable regression and correlation studies were presented. As will be seen, these models lead directly into the multivariate procedures described in later chapters. One of the major objectives of social science research is the identification of cause-and-effect relationships. Unfortunately the disentanglement of cause from effect is not easy. In any case, the first step in establishing causation is to show that an association exists between the variables that are believed to be joined in a causative relationship. The most commonly used measure of the strength of the association between an independent variable, X, and a dependent variable, Y, is the Pearson product moment correlation coefficient. This measure can be viewed as an average of the product of the paired standard scores of X and Y measured on a sample of N unique elements. In particular, if $(X_1, Y_1), (X_2, Y_2), \ldots, (X_N, Y_N)$ represent a sample of N paired observations made on N distinct units drawn from a population of interest, then:

$$r_{XY} = \frac{1}{N-1} \sum_{i=1}^{N} \left(\frac{X_i - \bar{X}}{S_X}\right)\left(\frac{Y_i - \bar{Y}}{S_Y}\right) = \frac{1}{N-1} \sum_{i=1}^{N} Z_{X_i} Z_{Y_i}$$

where $\bar{X}$ and $\bar{Y}$ are the mean values of X and Y, respectively, and where S_X and S_Y are the corresponding standard deviations of the two to-be-correlated variables. This measure ranges from a low value of -1 to a high value of $+1$. These extreme values are encountered whenever X and Y are mathematically related in terms of a linear functional relationship defined by:

$$Y = B_0 + B_1 X$$

The sample regression equation $\hat{Y} = B_0 + B_1 X$ is used to predict the value of Y for specified values of X. If we were to determine the predicted value of Y for each sample element and if the standard scores associated with each X and $\hat{Y}$ were to be computed, we would find that the relationship between $\hat{Z}_Y$ and Z_X would be given by:

$$\hat{Z}_Y = r_{XY} Z_X$$

This mathematical relationship shows that a predicted Z score on Y is $(100)\, r_{XY}\%$ of the observed Z score on X. If r_{XY} does not equal -1 or $+1$, $\hat{Z}_{Y_i}$ is closer to a mean value of zero than is Z_{X_i}. The predicted score is said to be regressed toward the mean of the dependent variable. For this reason, the equation used to predict Y from X is called a regression equation. If this equation were used to predict each Y score and if they were paired as $(Y_1, \hat{Y}_1), (Y_2, \hat{Y}_2), \ldots, (Y_N, \hat{Y}_N)$, it can be shown that:

1. The mean of the $\hat{Y}$ values is identical to $\bar{Y}$, that is, $\bar{\hat{Y}} = \bar{Y}$.
2. The variance of the $\hat{Y}$ values is $(100)\, r_{XY}^2\%$ of the variance of Y, that is, $S_{\hat{Y}}^2 = r_{XY}^2 S_Y^2$.
3. The correlation between Y and $\hat{Y}$ is identical to r_{XY}, that is, $r_{Y\hat{Y}} = r_{XY}$.

These three properties are encountered repeatedly in the multivariate methods described in the later chapters. In fact, the multiple correlation coefficient will be defined as $r_{Y\hat{Y}}$.

In the population from which a sample of N pairs of X and Y observations are drawn, the population correspondences to B_0 and B_1 are unknown and must be estimated. The method of *least squares* (Property 4 of the regression equation) is used to provide useful estimators. For the method of least squares, compute for each data pair, (X_i, Y_i), $D_i = Y_i - B_0 - B_1X_i$ and then determine the sum of squared deviations:

$$\sum_{i=1}^{N} D_i^2 = \sum_{i=1}^{N} (Y_i - B_0 - B_1X_i)^2$$

With judicious choices for B_0 and B_1, this sum can be made exceedingly large or limitedly small. The specific values of B_0 and B_1 that minimize the sum of the squared deviations are the least square estimators. They can be computed from the sample data as:

$$B_1 = r_{XY}\frac{S_Y}{S_X} \quad \text{and} \quad B_0 = \bar{Y} - B_1\bar{X}$$

If we substituted these estimators into the equation $\hat{Y} = B_0 + B_1X$ and computed each D_i, we would find that:

$$\sum_{i=1}^{N} D_i^2 = \sum_{i=1}^{N} (Y_i - \hat{Y}_i)^2$$

is as small as it could be, given the original data.

Finally, this chapter closed with a discussion of relative and absolute prediction. Two points were made: rank order of predicted Y values (based on Z scores) is the same for both types of prediction and the main difference is that, with absolute prediction, predicted values are regressed to the mean. It was suggested that if only rank order were of interest, this simplified procedure was recommended. In addition, it will prove useful for understanding many of the multivariate concepts discussed in this book.

1-13. Exercises

Starred exercises are most easily performed using a computer and canned program.

1-1. Select a random sample of 40 students from the roster of Table A-1. Transfer the information to data entry cards using the following code scheme. Make a second copy of your data deck for safekeeping and as a protection against card loss and damage. Extensive use will be made of this sample in other exercises following each chapter.

Column(s)	*Variable*	*Column(s)*	*Variable*	*Column(s)*	*Variable*
1, 2, 3	Student number	16	Blank	28, 29, 30	Midterm
4	Blank	17	High school sociology unit	31	Blank
5	Social class	18	Blank	32, 33, 34	Final score
6	Blank	19	College major	35	Blank
7	Sex of subject	20	Blank	36	Evaluation of course
8	Blank	21, 22	Pretest score	37	Blank
9, 10, 11	Grade point average	23	Blank	38	Career choice
12	Blank	24, 25, 26	Midterm 1		
13, 14, 15	College Board score	27	Blank		

***1-2.** For your sample of 40 subjects, make a scatter diagram and use the pretest score as the independent variable (X) and first midterm score as the dependent variable (Y). Compare your scatter diagram to the one shown in Figure 1-1. What do the two graphs show about the relationship between the two variables being studied?

***1-3.** Determine $\bar{X}$, S_X, $\bar{Y}$, S_Y, and r_{XY} for the variables of Exercise 1-2 and compare them to the figures reported in the text for the data of Table 1-2.

***1-4.** Determine the values of B_0 and B_1 for the data of Exercise 1-2. Compare your values to those reported in the text for Table 1-2.

1-5. Draw in the regression line for the data of Exercise 1-2. Comment on the following factors that have a profound effect on the magnitude and interpretation of a correlation coefficient:

a. *Nonlinear relationship.* Is there some systematic relationship apparent between X and Y other than a straight-line relationship?

b. *Variance heteroscedasticity.* Does the variation about the regression line appear to differ at different values of X?

c. *Distribution truncation.* Does either variable appear to be restricted in terms of the practical score extremes obtainable? Large numbers of scores at the top or bottom of either variable ("ceiling" and "floor" effects, respectively) would indicate this.

d. *The appearance of outliers.* Are there one or a few scores considerably higher or lower than the others on either variable?

If the answer to any of these questions is yes, an assumption related to proper interpretation of correlation coefficients and regression equations may be questioned.

1-6. Use your prediction equation to predict the value of Y for $X = \bar{X} + S_X$. Compute the Z score for your predicted Y value. What relationship has the predicted $\hat{Y}$ value to $Y = \bar{Y} + S_Y$? Explain what has happened.

1-7. Can the equation $\hat{Y} = B_0 + B_1X$ be solved for X and then used as a way to predict X? Why?

1-8. Solve your equation for X and compare it to the regression equation for $\hat{X}$ in which the intercept is given by $\bar{X} - [r_{XY}(S_X/S_Y)]\bar{Y}$ and the slope is given by $r_{XY}(S_X/S_Y)$. Compare this to the equation derived in Exercise 1-7. Explain what is happening.

1-9. Estimate the value of Y from your equation for $X = 20$. Compare it to the conditional mean value of Table A-1 for which $\bar{Y}$ is equal to 50.3, given that $X = 20$.

1-10. Explain what is meant by the method of least squares.

1-11. Use the normal equations and Cramer's rule to verify the values of B_0 and B_1 obtained in Exercise 1-4.

***1-12.** Determine $\hat{Y}$ for each of the 40 X values in your sample. Compute the variance of these predicted scores, $S_{\hat{Y}}^2$, and verify that $S_{\hat{Y}}^2 = r_{XY}^2 S_Y^2$.

1-13. Explain why $r_{\hat{Y}Y} = r_{XY}$.

1-14. Evaluate:

$$\Delta_1 = \begin{vmatrix} 3 & 9 \\ 7 & 2 \end{vmatrix} \quad \text{and} \quad \Delta_2 = \begin{vmatrix} -2 & 6 \\ 0 & 5 \end{vmatrix}$$

1-15. A determinant with three rows and three columns can be evaluated in terms of the elements of the first row by alternating algebraic signs and repeated application of the rule for 2 by 2 determinants. For example:

$$\Delta = \begin{vmatrix} 3 & 9 & 2 \\ 7 & 6 & 1 \\ 4 & 3 & -2 \end{vmatrix}$$

$$= 3\begin{vmatrix} 6 & 1 \\ 3 & -2 \end{vmatrix} - 9\begin{vmatrix} 7 & 1 \\ 4 & -2 \end{vmatrix} + 2\begin{vmatrix} 7 & 6 \\ 4 & 3 \end{vmatrix}$$

Find the value of Δ.

1-16. A determinant with four rows and four columns can be evaluated in terms of the elements of the first row by alternating algebraic signs and repeated application of the rule for 3 by 3 determinants. For example:

$$\Delta = \begin{vmatrix} 3 & 9 & 2 & 2 \\ 7 & 6 & 1 & 0 \\ 4 & 3 & -2 & 3 \\ 0 & 1 & 0 & -7 \end{vmatrix}$$

$$= 3\begin{vmatrix} 6 & 1 & 0 \\ 3 & -2 & 3 \\ 1 & 0 & -7 \end{vmatrix} - 9\begin{vmatrix} 7 & 1 & 0 \\ 4 & -2 & 3 \\ 0 & 0 & -7 \end{vmatrix}$$

$$+ 2\begin{vmatrix} 7 & 6 & 0 \\ 4 & 3 & 3 \\ 0 & 1 & -7 \end{vmatrix} - 2\begin{vmatrix} 7 & 6 & 1 \\ 4 & 3 & -2 \\ 0 & 1 & 0 \end{vmatrix}$$

Find the value of Δ.

CHAPTER TWO

STATISTICAL INFERENCE PROCEDURES FOR TWO-VARIABLE CORRELATION AND REGRESSION PROBLEMS

2-1. Correlation theory versus regression theory

In Chapter 1, we presented the underlying rationale and procedures for either describing the association between two variables or for predicting outcomes on one variable from knowledge of another. These two techniques are referred to as simple correlation and simple linear regression, respectively. In this chapter, we provide a more formal distinction between correlation and regression models. In addition, the important, but often neglected, distinction between samples and populations is made. From this discussion we will leave the more familiar methods of *descriptive* statistics and turn to the realm of *inferential* statistics. In applying statistical inference procedures, we recognize that any given relationship observed in a sample is one based on statistics determined from a finite number of cases. Thus we may wish to determine whether or not what is observed in the sample also holds for the sampled population. This generalization depends on the application of sampling and probability theory to evaluate how well sample statistics serve as estimators of fixed, unknown population parameters. As will be shown in this chapter, the principles of statistical inference will serve as the basis for testing hypotheses about, and estimating the values of, correlation and regression coefficients.

The major distinction between correlation theory and regression theory is in the nature of the X variable; that is, the independent variable. In the regression model, there is a true independent and a true dependent variable. This means that for each element in the sample, X is assumed to be fixed and measured without error. As a consequence, the distribution of Y is conditioned on the particular X values included in the sample (see Cramer & Appelbaum, 1978). It is assumed that these conditional distributions are normal in form and are characterized by three parameters, β_0, β_1, and $\sigma^2_{Y \cdot X}$ [or $\text{Var}(Y \cdot X)$, to be defined shortly], which are estimated in the sample by B_0, B_1 and $S^2_{Y \cdot X}$, respectively. On the other hand, the correlation model does not differentiate between the independent and dependent variables. Both X and Y are treated as being mutually dependent, with a joint probability distribution. The mathematical model that represents their joint probability distribution is the simple extension of the univariate normal distribution. In particular, it is assumed that X and Y have a joint distribution that is *bivariate normal* and is defined by five parameters, μ_X, μ_Y, σ^2_X, σ^2_Y, and ρ_{XY}. The sample analogs to these parameters are given, respectively, by $\bar{X}$, $\bar{Y}$, S^2_X, S^2_Y, and r_{XY}, as defined in Chapter 1. Knowledge of these five parameters completely specifies the nature of the joint distribution of X and Y.

Expected values of the two models. The graphic representation of the correlation model involves three dimensions with a reference system defined by a right angle grid on a horizontal plane and the probability, or more appropriately, the *likelihood*, graphed vertically to the plane. When the graph is viewed from an outside position, an elongated "bell" may be seen, as illustrated in Figure 2-1. If $\rho_{XY} = 0$, the bell is not distorted even though the contours made on the bell, horizontal to the reference plane, will be elliptical. If, in addition, $\sigma_Y = \sigma_X$, the contours reduce to circles. Any plane passing through the bell, perpendicular to the horizontal reference plane but parallel to either of the right angle grids, generates a normal curve whose expected value lies on one of two straight lines. The straight lines trace out the *conditional expected values* for the distributions and are given by:

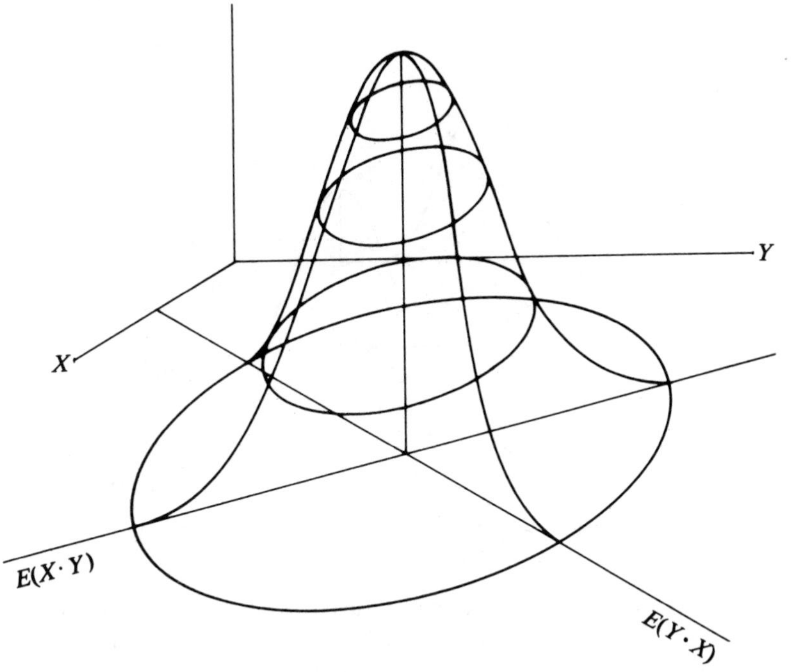

Figure 2-1. Geometric model of the bivariate normal distribution.

$$E(Y \cdot X) = \mu_Y + \rho_{XY}\frac{\sigma_Y}{\sigma_X}(X - \mu_X)$$

and

$$E(X \cdot Y) = \mu_X + \rho_{XY}\frac{\sigma_X}{\sigma_Y}(Y - \mu_Y)$$

The $E(Y \cdot X)$ corresponds to the population values of the sample best-fitting straight line described in Chapter 1. In fact, $E(Y \cdot X)$ is the population equation for predicting Y from knowledge of X, and $E(X \cdot Y)$ is the population equation for predicting X from Y.

In the regression model, there is one and only one regression line given by:

$$E(Y \cdot X) = \beta_0 + \beta_1 X$$

and estimated by B_0 and B_1 as defined in Section 1-8. When this model is represented graphically, it takes on the appearance of a "loaf of bread," similar to what is shown in Figure 2-2. Note that each "slice" traces out a normal distribution with $E(Y \cdot X)$ as just defined.

From this brief discussion, we can begin to see the distinction between correlation and regression theory. With the former, two best-fitting straight lines may be drawn, whereas with the latter, there is only one. Note that the two prediction equations of correlation theory become identical if $\rho_{XY} = 1.00$. Otherwise, they cross at the point

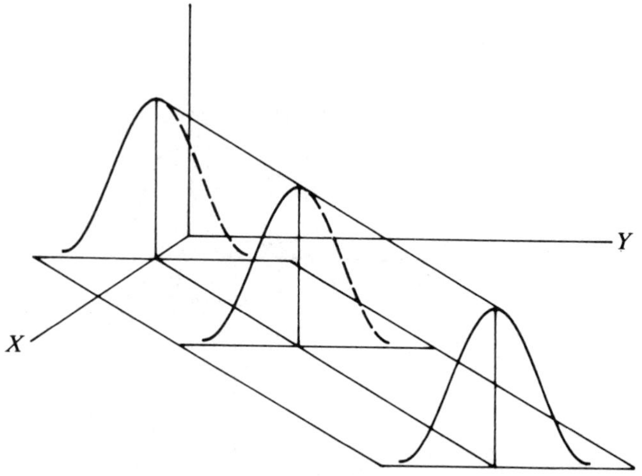

Figure 2-2. Geometric model of the univariate regression model with conditional normal distribution.

(μ_X, μ_Y), which is called the *centroid* of the joint distribution. It can be shown that the sample equations of Chapter 1 serve as unbiased estimators of the corresponding population equations. Even though we have emphasized the procedures for estimating $E(Y \cdot X)$ in Chapter 1, it is easy to see that in estimating $E(X \cdot Y)$, we simply interchange the X and Y values in all of the previously described equations and formulas.

Variances of the two models. In the correlation model, there are two conditional variances. The variance of Y for fixed values of X is defined as:

$$\text{Var}(Y \cdot X) = \sigma_Y^2(1 - \rho_{XY}^2)$$

and the variance of X for fixed values of Y is defined as:

$$\text{Var}(X \cdot Y) = \sigma_X^2(1 - \rho_{XY}^2)$$

In the regression model, there is only one conditional variance. It is identical to $\text{Var}(Y \cdot X)$ of the preceding correlation model.

To help understand the distinction between correlation and regression theory, consider the student of Table 1-2 with code number 143, for whom $X = 10$ and $Y = 30$. According to the theoretical regression model, it is assumed that $X = 10$ and $Y = \beta_0 + 10\beta_1 + \varepsilon_Y = 30$, where ε_Y is an error component coming from a univariate normal distribution with $E(\varepsilon_Y) = 0$ and $\text{Var}(\varepsilon_Y) = \text{Var}(Y \cdot X) = \sigma_Y^2(1 - \rho_{XY}^2)$. Here ρ_{XY} represents the correlation between X and Y or, equivalently, between X and ε_Y. In contrast, under the theoretical correlation model, it is assumed that

$$Y = \mu_Y + \rho_{XY}(\sigma_Y/\sigma_X)(10 - \mu_X) + \varepsilon_Y = 30, \text{ and}$$

$$X = \mu_X + \rho_{XY}(\sigma_X/\sigma_Y)(30 - \mu_Y) + \varepsilon_X = 10.$$

Here ε_X and ε_Y have a joint bivariate normal distribution with $E(\varepsilon_Y) = 0$, $E(\varepsilon_X) = 0$, $\text{Var}(\varepsilon_Y) = \sigma_Y^2(1 - \rho_{XY}^2)$, $\text{Var}(\varepsilon_X) = \sigma_X^2(1 - \rho_{XY}^2)$, and $\rho_{\varepsilon_X \varepsilon_Y} = \rho_{XY}$.

2-2. Variation about the regression line and its interpretation

As was stated in Exercise 1-5, the interpretation of a sample correlation coefficient depends on homoscedastic variation (that is, equal Y variation at each level of X). If the condition is satisfied, we can estimate the variation of the Y scores about the regression line to evaluate the goodness of fit of the line to the data. If the variation about the line is small, relative to the total variance in the sample, the fit is good; otherwise, it is poor. The variation about a straight line is measured as follows. Let $Y_1, Y_2, \ldots, Y_i, \ldots, Y_N$ be the observed values of the dependent variable. Let $\hat{Y}_1, \hat{Y}_2, \ldots, \hat{Y}_i, \ldots, \hat{Y}_N$ be the values of the dependent variable determined from the best-fitting prediction equation $\hat{Y} = B_0 + B_1X$. Variation about the line will be denoted SS_U and is computed as follows:

$$SS_U = \sum_{i=1}^{N} (Y_i - \hat{Y}_i)^2$$

An appreciation of the geometry associated with this definition may be gained from Figure 2-3. As indicated, the variation is found by computing the deviation between each value of Y_i and its value predicted from the best-fitting line, $\hat{Y}_i$. These deviations are squared and then added. Using analysis of variance terminology, we call this sum of squared deviations a *sum of squares*. In addition, a *mean square* is simply a sum of squares divided by its associated degrees of freedom. In the present situation, we will note that the degrees of freedom associated with SS_U are given by

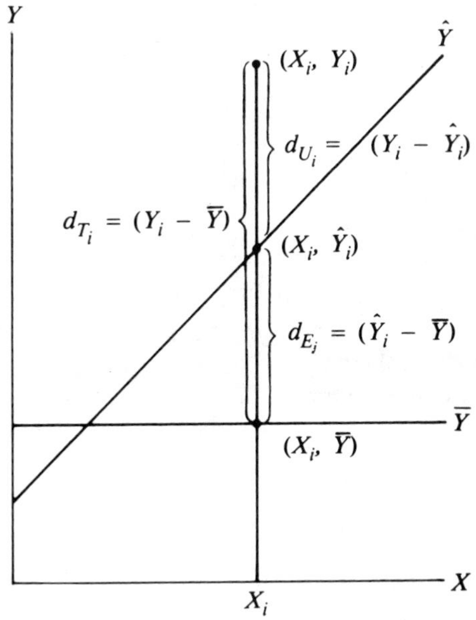

Figure 2-3. The geometry of explained, unexplained, and total deviations about a regression line.

$\nu = N - 2$ and that the corresponding mean square is actually a sample variance based on these $N - 2$ degrees of freedom.

Consider the geometry illustrated in Figure 2-3. For the discussion, let (X_i, Y_i) be the values of X and Y observed in the ith sample element. Let $\bar{Y}$ be the sample mean of the N values of the dependent variable, Y, and let $\hat{Y}_i = B_0 + B_1X_i$ be the estimate of Y_i determined from the best-fitting straight line. Here we see that:

$Y_i - \bar{Y}$ = the total deviation of the ith observation from the sample mean on the dependent variable Y.

$Y_i - \hat{Y}_i$ = the deviation between the ith observation and its value, predicted from the equation $\hat{Y}_i = B_0 + B_1X_i$.

$\hat{Y}_i - \bar{Y}$ = the deviation between the predicted value for the ith observation and the mean of the sample on the dependent variable Y.

Further, note that:

$$(Y_i - \bar{Y}) = (Y_i - \hat{Y}_i) + (\hat{Y}_i - \bar{Y})$$

Recall from Chapter 1 that if B_1 were found to equal zero, the best-fitting equation would be given simply as $\hat{Y} = \bar{Y}$, and the value of $\hat{Y}_i - \bar{Y}$ would equal zero for every observation. In all other cases, $\hat{Y}_i - \bar{Y}$ would be different from zero. This means that $\hat{Y}_i - \bar{Y}$ provides another means for describing the extent of the relationship between X and Y. This deviation is called the *explained component* of the total deviation of Y_i from $\bar{Y}$ and will be denoted d_{E_i}. On the other hand, $Y_i - \hat{Y}_i$ measures the deviation between the observed value Y_i and its predicted value $\hat{Y}_i$. This deviation is called the *unexplained component* and will be denoted d_{U_i}. Finally, the deviation $Y_i - \bar{Y}$ will be referred to as the *total deviation* and will be denoted d_{T_i}. Thus:

Total deviation = Unexplained deviation + Explained deviation

or:

$$d_{T_i} = d_{U_i} + d_{E_i}$$

If the regression line has a slope of zero, then $d_{E_i} = 0$ for each observation since $\hat{Y}_i$ and $\bar{Y}$ would coincide. As a result, $d_{T_i} = d_{U_i}$, so that each total deviation is unexplainable. On the other hand, if all observations were to lie on the regression line, then $d_{U_i} = 0$ for each observation. As a result, $d_{T_i} = d_{E_i}$, so that each total deviation is completely explainable by the perfect correlation that exists between X and Y. We illustrate the determination of these values for the first pair of observations in Table 1-2. For $Y_1 = 43$, the predicted value is given by:

$$\hat{Y}_1 = 25.08 + 1.15(17) = 44.66$$

For the entire sample of 39 students, $\bar{Y} = 46.05$. Thus:

$$d_{T_1} = Y_1 - \bar{Y} = 43 - 46.05 = -3.05$$

$$d_{U_1} = Y_1 - \hat{Y}_1 = 43 - 44.66 = -1.66$$

$$d_{E_1} = \hat{Y}_1 - \bar{Y} = 44.66 - 46.05 = -1.39$$

As can be seen:

$d_{T_1} = d_{U_1} + d_{E_1} = -1.66 + (-1.39) = -3.05$

The remaining values of d_{T_i}, d_{U_i}, and d_{E_i} are summarized in Table 2-1. Note that, except for rounding errors:

$$\sum_{i=1}^{N} d_{T_i} = \sum_{i=1}^{N} d_{U_i} = \sum_{i=1}^{N} d_{E_i} = 0$$

TABLE 2-1. Total deviations, unexplained deviations, and explained deviations for each of the $N = 39$ observations of Table 1-2 for which $\hat{Y} = 25.0801 + 1.1519X_i$ and $\bar{Y} = 46.0513$

Student number	X_i	Y_i	$\hat{Y}_i$	$d_{T_i} = Y_i - \bar{Y}$	$d_{U_i} = Y_i - \hat{Y}_i$	$d_{E_i} = \hat{Y}_i - \bar{Y}$
003	17	43	44.66	− 3.05	− 1.66	− 1.39
004	20	50	48.12	3.95	1.88	2.07
010	22	47	50.42	− .95	− 3.42	4.37
014	13	24	40.05	− 22.05	− 16.05	− 6.00
018	16	47	43.51	.95	3.49	− 2.54
020	28	57	57.33	10.95	− .33	11.28
032	14	42	41.21	− 4.05	.79	− 4.84
040	10	42	36.60	− 4.05	5.40	− 9.45
050	28	69	57.33	22.95	11.67	11.28
052	30	48	59.64	1.95	− 11.64	13.59
055	28	59	57.33	12.95	1.67	11.28
070	15	21	42.36	− 25.05	− 21.36	− 3.69
072	24	52	52.73	5.95	− .73	6.68
076	15	35	42.36	− 11.05	− 7.36	− 3.69
080	26	35	55.03	− 11.05	− 20.03	8.98
083	16	59	43.51	12.95	15.49	− 2.54
089	25	68	53.88	21.95	14.12	7.83
091	3	38	28.53	− 8.05	9.47	− 17.52
103	5	45	30.84	− 1.05	14.16	− 15.21
104	16	37	43.51	− 9.05	− 6.51	− 2.54
106	28	54	57.33	7.95	− 3.33	11.28
108	13	45	40.05	− 1.05	4.95	− 6.00
117	9	31	35.45	− 15.05	− 4.45	− 10.60
118	13	39	40.05	− 7.05	− 1.05	− 6.00
128	30	67	59.64	20.95	7.36	13.59
143	10	30	36.60	− 16.05	− 6.60	− 9.45
150	13	19	40.05	− 27.05	− 21.05	− 6.00
166	8	71	34.30	24.95	36.70	− 11.75
171	29	80	58.49	33.95	21.51	12.44
174	17	47	44.66	.95	2.34	− 1.39
183	16	59	43.51	12.95	15.49	− 2.54
188	13	48	40.05	1.95	7.95	− 6.00
193	30	68	59.64	21.95	8.36	13.59
195	17	43	44.66	− 3.05	− 1.66	− 1.39
196	17	31	44.66	− 15.05	− 13.66	− 1.39
199	25	64	53.88	17.95	10.12	7.83
207	10	19	36.60	− 27.05	− 17.60	− 9.45
208	23	43	51.57	− 3.05	− 8.57	5.52
211	18	20	45.81	− 26.05	− 25.81	− .24
Total	710	1796	1795.95	.05	.05	.00

Because all these sums are equal to zero, we consider the squares of each deviation, as we did for defining SS_U. Using the present notation and data, we see that:

1. Sum of squares of the unexplained deviations equals:

$$SS_U = \sum_{i=1}^{N} (Y_i - \hat{Y}_i)^2$$
$$= (-1.66)^2 + (1.88)^2 + \cdots + (-25.81)^2$$
$$= 6403.6576 \simeq 6404$$

2. Sum of squares of the explained deviations equals:

$$SS_E = \sum_{i=1}^{N} (\hat{Y}_i - \bar{Y})^2$$
$$= (-1.39)^2 + (2.07)^2 + \cdots + (-.24)^2$$
$$= 2840.2398 \simeq 2840$$

3. Sum of squares of the total deviations equals:

$$SS_T = \sum_{i=1}^{N} (Y_i - \bar{Y})^2$$
$$= (-3.05)^2 + (3.95)^2 + \cdots + (-26.05)^2$$
$$= 9243.8974 \simeq 9244$$

From this we see that:

$$SS_T = SS_U + SS_E$$

From the preceding, it may be noted that the total variation, as reflected by the total sum of squared deviations, is given by $SS_T = 9244$. As a percentage of this total variation, we see that the explained variation accounts for:

$$\frac{SS_E}{SS_T}(100) = \frac{2840}{9244}(100) = 30.7\%$$

This suggests that almost one-third of the variation in the midterm scores can be explained by the variation in the pretest scores. This is not too surprising since we have already seen in Chapter 1 that the correlation coefficient between the two sets of scores is given by $r_{XY} = .5543$. However, what is remarkable is that r_{XY} is related in a direct numerical fashion to the ratio of SS_E to SS_T. In fact, $r^2_{XY} = SS_E/SS_T$. For this example, $r^2_{XY} = .5543^2 = .307$. This means that r^2_{XY} has a simple interpretation. In particular, it represents the proportion of the variation in the dependent variable, as defined by the sum of squared deviations about the mean, that is explainable in terms of the linear relationship between X and Y. In this case, it would be said that about 31% of the variation in the first midterm scores can be explained by the variation of the scores on the pretest given to the students at the beginning of the sociology class. Low scores on the first midterm tend to be made by students who had low pretest scores, whereas high scores tend to be earned by students who scored high on the pretest.

Although r_{XY} is difficult to interpret, r^2_{XY} is not. The importance of this statement cannot be overemphasized. Research is performed to determine the percent of variation in a dependent variable that is explainable by its correlation with an independent variable. The determination of the percent of explained variation is given simply as r^2_{XY}. This means that we need not perform the lengthy calculations shown in Table 2-1 to determine this value. We only need to compute the value of r_{XY} and then square it.

It is worth mentioning at this point the distinction between testing for the statistical significance of a correlation coefficient such as H_0: $\rho_{XY} = 0$, as discussed in Section 2-3, and assessing its practical significance as reflected by the strength of the relationship between X and Y, that is, r^2_{XY} as discussed here. Even though we reject the hypothesis that $\rho_{XY} = 0$, we must still base our interpretation of the strength of the relationship by referring to r^2_{XY}. The statistical test is dependent on sample size, and very small rejection probabilities (for example, rejecting H_0: $\rho_{XY} = 0$ at $p < .001$) may reflect a large sample size rather than a strong relationship. Thus, whenever the hypothesis H_0: $\rho_{XY} = 0$ is rejected, thereby indicating that the relationship is real, we should routinely gauge the magnitude of r^2_{XY} to ascertain whether or not the relationship is large, so that our enthusiasm and interpretations are framed appropriately.

2-3. Testing hypotheses about a regression coefficient

One may apply tests of statistical significance to either correlation coefficients or regression coefficients. In the case of the slope of the regression line B_1, one may assess whether H_0: $\beta_1 = 0$ in the population. If H_0 were not rejected, it would imply that the population regression line had no slope, that is, it was flat. Given the assumptions of normality, homoscedasticity, independence among observations, and linearity of regression, a statistical test of the hypothesis H_0: $\beta_1 = 0$ against the alternative H_1: $\beta_1 \neq 0$ may be conducted. This test can be performed either as a t test or as an F test. Since both methods arise in multivariate models, both will be considered here. In developing the procedures, we will continue to use the notation and terminology of the analysis of variance.

Often it will be convenient to compute the respective sums of squares directly from the sample statistics S^2_Y and r_{XY}. Because a sum of squares is merely the numerator of a mean square and since the total variance in the dependent variable S^2_Y is based on $v = (N - 1)$ degrees of freedom, we know that:

$$SS_T = (N - 1)S^2_Y = SS_Y$$

Similarly, because r^2_{XY} represents the proportion of SS_T accounted for by SS_E, we may compute:

$$SS_E = r^2_{XY}SS_T = (N - 1)r^2_{XY}S^2_Y = r^2_{XY}SS_Y$$

Furthermore, because $1 - r^2_{XY}$ represents the unexplained proportion of SS_T, it follows that:

$$SS_U = (1 - r^2_{XY})SS_T = (N - 1)(1 - r^2_{XY})S^2_Y = (1 - r^2_{XY})SS_Y$$

Note that SS_E represents that portion of SS_T which is associated with the regression line and thus can be alternatively referred to as SS_{Reg}. Similarly, SS_U represents the sum of squares not associated with the regression line. It is often referred to as the *residual sum of squares* and can be written as SS_{Res}. Table 2-2 provides a

TABLE 2-2. The analysis of variance table for a simple regression model

Source	*d/f*	*Sum of squares*	*Mean square*	*F ratio*
Regression	1	$r^2_{XY}SS_Y$	$MS_{\text{Reg}} = r^2_{XY}SS_Y$	$\dfrac{MS_{\text{Reg}}}{MS_{\text{Res}}} = \dfrac{(N-2)r^2_{XY}}{1-r^2_{XY}}$
Residual	$N-2$	$(1-r^2_{XY})SS_Y$	$MS_{\text{Res}} = \dfrac{(1-r^2_{XY})SS_Y}{N-2}$	
Total	$N-1$	SS_Y		

representation of these and other analysis of variance developments that follow.

As just noted, a mean square in the analysis of variance may be computed by dividing a sum of squares by its degrees of freedom v. Thus, the mean square total S^2_Y is simply $SS_T/(N-1)$, as the total variance of Y is based on $v = N - 1$. In analogous fashion, the mean square residual MS_{Res} is defined by $SS_{\text{Res}}/(N-2)$. Alternatively written as $S^2_{Y \cdot X}$, the mean square residual represents the variance in Y that still remains after having removed the variance due to the linear relationship between X and Y. The $v = N - 2$ for the residual arises from the fact that the deviations $Y_i - \hat{Y}_i$ comprising SS_{Res} are restricted by the values of B_0 and B_1 determined from the sample. This means that the number of independent deviations v is equal to $N - 2$ and not $N - 1$ as it is in the case of SS_T, whose deviations are restricted only by $\bar{Y}$. Finally, the degrees of freedom associated with the mean square regression, MS_{Reg}, must be 1 because, by subtraction:

$$\begin{aligned} v_{\text{Tot}} &= v_{\text{Reg}} + v_{\text{Res}} \\ N - 1 &= v_{\text{Reg}} + (N-2) \\ v_{\text{Reg}} &= 1 \end{aligned}$$

Because MS_{Res} serves as an unbiased estimator of the population residual variance and because MS_{Reg} provides a second independent estimator under the truth of H_0, an F statistic may be formed by taking the ratio $MS_{\text{Reg}}/MS_{\text{Res}}$. This ratio can be referred to the F distribution based on 1 and $N - 2$ degrees of freedom and can be used to test the hypothesis H_0: $\beta_1 = 0$ against H_1: $\beta_1 \neq 0$. An analysis of variance table, based on the data of Table 1-2 and the previously discussed formulas for computing the sums of squares, is presented as Table 2-3. In this table, the observed F ratio:

$$F = \frac{MS_{\text{Reg}}}{MS_{\text{Res}}} = \frac{\dfrac{2840.2398}{1}}{\dfrac{6403.6576}{37}} = \frac{2840.2398}{173.0718} = 16.41$$

is referred to the tabled F distribution in Table B-1, based on $v_1 = 1$ and $v_2 = N - 2 = 37$. For a type I error probability of $\alpha = .05$, the critical value of F needed for rejection is given by $F_{1,37:.95} = 4.11$. Since $F = 16.40 > 4.11$, the hypothesis H_0: $\beta_1 = 0$ is rejected. It is concluded that the regression line is not parallel to the X axis, but rather makes an angle with the horizontal reference axis.

Two interesting properties associated with the preceding test of hypothesis should be pointed out. First, since $F = MS_{\text{Reg}}/MS_{\text{Res}}$ has an F distribution with $v_1 = 1$ and

TABLE 2-3. The analysis of variance table for the data of Table 1-2

Source	*d/f*	*Sum of squares*	*Mean square*	*F ratio*
Regression	1	2840.2398	2840.2398	16.41
Residual	37	6403.6576	173.0718	
Total	38	9243.8974		

$F_{1,37:.95} = 4.11$

$\nu_2 = N - 2$, it is immediately known that $\sqrt{F}$ has a t distribution with $\nu = N - 2$. This follows from the known relationship between the t and F distributions, as shown in Marascuilo (1971), for example. Moreover:

$$\sqrt{F} = \sqrt{\frac{MS_{\text{Reg}}}{MS_{\text{Res}}}}$$

$$= \sqrt{\frac{\dfrac{(N-1)r_{XY}^2 S_Y^2}{1}}{\dfrac{(N-1)(1-r_{XY}^2)S_Y^2}{N-2}}} = \sqrt{\frac{r_{XY}^2(N-2)}{1-r_{XY}^2}} = \frac{r_{XY}\sqrt{N-2}}{\sqrt{1-r_{XY}^2}} = t$$

This latter result is the familiar t test of the hypothesis, H_0: $\rho_{XY} = 0$, which appears in most elementary statistics tests (see Marascuilo, 1971).

It is now apparent that the tests of the hypotheses $\beta_1 = 0$ and $\rho_{XY} = 0$ are identical, being based on the same statistic and the t distribution with $\nu = N - 2$. Thus, although simple correlation and regression models are conceptually different, the tests of hypothesis about no relationship are algebraically identical in the two models. Thus, if we conclude that $\rho_{XY} = 0$, we would also conclude that $\beta_1 = 0$, and vice versa. Similarly, if we conclude that $\rho_{XY} \neq 0$, we would conclude that $\beta_1 \neq 0$, and vice versa.

The test statistic for testing $\rho_{XY} = 0$ or $\beta_1 = 0$ represents a special case of a more general formula. Because this relationship will be seen in several different contexts throughout the remaining chapters of this book, we provide directions for the test.

Procedure for testing a correlation for significance.

Step 1. Let θ be any measure of association for which a test of the hypothesis:

$$H_0\text{:}\quad \theta = 0$$

against:

$$H_1\text{:}\quad \theta \neq 0$$

is to be made.

Step 2. Let $\hat{\theta}$ be the sample estimator of θ.

Step 3. Let ν_1 = number of degrees of freedom associated with $\hat{\theta}^2$ and $SS_{\text{Regression}}$.

Step 4. Let ν_2 = number of degrees of freedom associated with $(1 - \hat{\theta}^2)$ and SS_{Residual}.

Step 5. The general form of the F statistic is given as:

$$F = \frac{MS_{\text{Regression}}}{MS_{\text{Residual}}} = \frac{\nu_2}{\nu_1}\left(\frac{\hat{\theta}^2}{1-\hat{\theta}^2}\right)$$

In the present situation, $\nu_1 = 1$, $\nu_2 = N - 2$, and $\hat{\theta} = r_{XY}$, so that:

$$F = \frac{\nu_2}{\nu_1}\left(\frac{\hat{\theta}^2}{1 - \hat{\theta}^2}\right) = (N - 2)\frac{r_{XY}^2}{1 - r_{XY}^2}$$

Whenever $\nu_1 = 1$, the square root of the general F ratio will afford a t test of the same hypothesis based on ν_2 degrees of freedom.

The second point of interest that will prove useful later on is that we could similarly test the hypothesis H_0: $\beta_1 = 0$ against H_1: $\beta_1 \neq 0$, using the t distribution, by directly comparing the sample regression coefficient B_1 to its standard error SE_{B_1}. As will be shown in Section 4-5, the standard error of B_1 can be written as:

$$SE_{B_1} = \sqrt{\frac{MS_{\text{Res}}}{SS_X}} = \sqrt{\frac{MS_{\text{Res}}}{(N - 1)S_X^2}}$$

For the data of Table 1-2:

$$SE_{B_1} = \sqrt{\frac{173.0718}{(39 - 1)(56.3252)}} = \sqrt{.0809} = .2844$$

and with $B_1 = 1.1519$, we have:

$$t = \frac{B_1}{SE_{B_1}} = \frac{1.1519}{.2844} = 4.05$$

which, within rounding errors, is equal to $\sqrt{16.41}$, the square root of the F ratio reported in Table 2-3.

The two-tailed critical values of t are found through interpolation in Table B-2 as $t_{37:.025} = -2.03$ and $t_{37:.975} = 2.03$. Because $t = 4.05$ exceeds 2.03 in absolute value, the hypothesis that the slope is zero, or that there is no linear relationship between X and Y, is rejected. As in the case of testing the sample correlation coefficient, a one-tailed test would most certainly have been performed for this example, in which case the critical value would have been given by $t_{37:.95} = 1.69$. Finally, we should mention that the numerator of t is really a special case of $B_1 - \beta_{1_0}$. Thus the same statistic can be used to test the hypothesis that β_1 is equal to some specified value, β_{1_0}. For example, if it were posited that X and Y increase at equal rates with $\beta_{1_0} = 1.00$, the numerator of t would become $B_1 - 1.00$ and the statistical test would proceed accordingly. For completeness, we provide directions for testing H_0: $\beta_1 = 0$ or $\beta_1 = \beta_{1_0}$.

Procedure for testing H_0: $\beta_1 = 0$ or H_0: $\beta_1 = \beta_{1_0}$.

Step 1. For testing H_0: $\beta_1 = 0$, perform an analysis of variance as summarized in Table 2-2.

Step 2. Compute:

$$F = \frac{MS_{\text{Reg}}}{MS_{\text{Res}}}$$

and reject H_0 if:

$$F > F_{1, N-2:1-\alpha}$$

Step 3. For testing either H_0: $\beta_1 = \beta_{1_0}$ or H_0: $\beta_1 = 0$, compute:

$$t = \frac{B_1 - \beta_{1_0}}{SE_{B_1}}$$

where:

$$SE^2_{B_1} = \frac{MS_{\text{Res}}}{SS_X}$$

$$SS_X = (N - 1)S^2_X$$

Step 4. Reject H_0 if $t < t_{N-2:\alpha/2}$ or if $t > t_{N-2:1-\alpha/2}$.

Step 5. The two-sided $100(1 - \alpha)\%$ confidence interval for β_1 is given by:

$$B_1 - t_{N-2:1-\alpha/2}SE_{B_1} < \beta_1 < B_1 + t_{N-2:1-\alpha/2}SE_{B_1}$$

For the data of Table 1-2, the 95% confidence interval for β_1 is given by:

$$1.1519 - 2.03(.2844) < \beta_1 < 1.1519 + 2.03(.2844)$$

$$1.1519 - .5773 < \beta_1 < 1.1519 + .5773$$

$$.5746 < \beta_1 < 1.7292$$

The assumptions for this test are:

1. Each of the Y_i values is statistically independent of all other Y_i values.
2. Each X_i is fixed and measured without error.
3. The variance about the regression line is constant for all values of X_i.
4. The errors associated with the Y_i values are normally distributed.

The fourth assumption can be weakened, provided that the sample size is large, where large usually means an N greater than 25 or 30. It should also be mentioned that, because of this normality assumption, no transformation of B_1 is necessary when building confidence intervals, as is needed for r_{XY} (see Marascuilo, 1971). The only direct correspondence between the conclusions about β_1 and ρ_{XY} comes from the respective tests $\beta_1 = 0$ and $\rho_{XY} = 0$. This is not true for the tests of $\beta_1 = \beta_{1_0}$ and $\rho_{XY} = \rho_{XY(0)}$, or for interval estimates in these two cases.

Finally, in addition to testing hypotheses about the slope of the regression line β_1, we can test hypotheses related to the intercept β_0. For example, in the physical sciences it is often important to determine whether the regression line passes through the origin, such that $\beta_0 = 0$. It is also possible to construct confidence bands (in this case, hyperbolas) around the regression line itself. That is, we can determine the upper and lower limits of $\hat{Y} = \beta_0 + \beta_1 X$ for some, or for all, values of X. Moreover, we can build a confidence interval about an individual predicted score $\hat{Y}_i$. Though such procedures are not discussed here, examples are provided in Exercises 2-5, 2-6, and 2-7.

2-4. Testing hypotheses about two or more independent regression coefficients

As was noted in Section 2-3, a test of the hypothesis H_0: $\beta_1 = 0$ is algebraically identical to a test of the hypothesis H_0: $\rho_{XY} = 0$. Thus, when $r_{XY} = 0$, B_1 must also equal 0. Interestingly, the generalization of this statement to a comparison of two or more coefficients is not true. That is, testing the hypothesis that $\rho_{XY(1)} = \rho_{XY(2)}$ (see

Marascuilo, 1971) is not the same as testing the hypothesis to be discussed here that $\beta_{1(1)} = \beta_{1(2)}$. To state this simply, the test for equality of correlation coefficients examines whether the scale-free strength of relationship is comparable across populations. In contrast, the test for equality of regression coefficients examines whether the scale-dependent increases in Y as a function of X are comparable.

Thus it is possible for two correlation coefficients to be equal, even though the two corresponding regression coefficients are not. Because a regression coefficient is defined in terms of the ratio of two standard deviations, if the ratio differs across populations, the regression coefficients will also differ even though the correlation coefficients are identical. The left panel of Figure 2-4 shows two relationships of similar magnitude, as defined by the least squares criterion, yet with quite nonparallel slopes. This example points out a popular misconception held by many who believe that the slope of the regression line directly reflects the strength of the relationship. This is simply not correct, as steep slopes may arise from large standard deviation ratios rather than from large correlations. Thus steepness is a function of scale. What determines the strength of the relationship is the closeness of the points to the regression line or, in visually descriptive terms, the thinness of the football-like ellipses. The right panel of Figure 2-4 shows two populations with differing correlation coefficients but with comparable regression coefficients. These two examples should clearly reveal that no necessary relationship exists between testing hypotheses about the equality of two or more regression coefficients on the one hand, and two or more correlation coefficients on the other, except in the special case in which all correlations are equal to zero.

With this introduction, let us consider the problem of deciding whether the slopes of $K(\geq 2)$ independent regression lines are parallel. This is a common question in educational and psychological research, especially when, say, two populations represent different treatments (such as Method 1 and Method 2), the X variable represents some particular subject characteristic (such as age, ability, or aptitude), and the Y variable represents performance on some dependent measure. Note that this test of parallelism provides a more sensitive test of *aptitude-by-treatment interactions* (ATIs) than would be obtained by categorizing the X variable as high, medium, and low and seeking a statistical interaction with treatments via a factorial

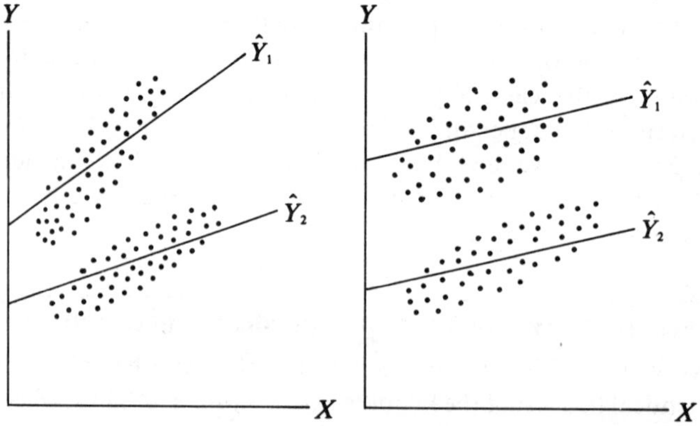

Figure 2-4. Comparing two correlation coefficients versus comparing two regression coefficients.

analysis of variance (Cronbach and Snow, 1977). In this context, the question of interest is whether the two treatments produce similar performance profiles, across the aptitude variable, as reflected by the slopes of the two regression lines.

Incorporating the assumptions of one-sample regression hypothesis testing for each sample, along with the assumptions that between-sample observations are independent and that the variation about the regression line is the same in each sample, we can test the hypothesis that the regression lines in K populations are parallel or, equivalently, that their slopes are the same. This test of parallelism can be performed if it is assumed that:

1. The distribution of the dependent variable for each of the K universes sampled is normal or that the sample sizes are large enough to justify the use of the Central Limit Theorem.
2. The measures of variation about each regression line are equal.
3. Observations between samples are independent.
4. Observations within samples are independent.
5. The regression lines are linear with homoscedastic variation about them.

If these five conditions are satisfied, a test of:

$$\text{H}_0: \quad \beta_{1(1)} = \beta_{1(2)} = \cdots = \beta_{1(k)} = \cdots = \beta_{1(K)}$$

against:

$$\text{H}_1: \quad \text{H}_0 \text{ is false}$$

can be performed using the following F statistic:

$$F = \frac{\dfrac{1}{K-1}\left(\sum_{k=1}^{K} W_k B_{1(k)}^2 - B_{1(W)}^2 \sum_{k=1}^{K} W_k\right)}{MS_{\text{Res}}} = \frac{MS_{\text{Par}}}{MS_{\text{Res}}}$$

where:

$$MS_{\text{Res}} = \frac{\sum_{k=1}^{K} (N_k - 2) MS_{\text{Res}(k)}}{\sum_{k=1}^{K} (N_k - 2)} = \frac{\sum_{k=1}^{K} SS_{\text{Res}(k)}}{N - 2K}$$

$$W_k = (N_k - 1)S_{X(k)}^2 = SS_{X(k)}$$

and $B_{1(W)}$ represents the *pooled within-sample regression coefficient*, which is defined as:

$$B_{1(W)} = \frac{\sum_{k=1}^{K} SS_{X(k)} B_{1(k)}}{\sum_{k=1}^{K} SS_{X(k)}} = \frac{\sum_{k=1}^{K} W_k B_{1(k)}}{\sum_{k=1}^{K} W_k}$$

The value MS_{Par} in the numerator represents deviations from parallelism of the K regression lines. The resulting F statistic is referred to the standard F distribution with $\nu_1 = K - 1$ and $\nu_2 = N - 2K$ degrees of freedom.

The division of the numerator of F by $K - 1$ is required because the quantity enclosed by the parentheses actually represents a sum of squares, and to convert to a mean square we must divide by the appropriate number of degrees of freedom. Because K regression slopes are compared, the degrees of freedom are given by

$\nu_1 = K - 1$. In the two-group case, this term was implicit in the formula, since $\nu_1 = 1$.

Procedure for testing the parallelism of *K* independent regression lines, in terms of sample statistics.

Step 1. Perform a regression analysis on each sample and compute $W_1, W_2, \ldots, W_K$, where $W_k = (N_k - 1)S^2_{X(k)} = SS_{X(k)}$.

Step 2. Determine $B_{1(1)}, B_{1(2)}, \ldots, B_{1(K)}$, and:

$$B_{1(W)} = \frac{\sum_{k=1}^{K} W_k B_{1(k)}}{\sum_{k=1}^{K} W_k}$$

Step 3. Compute:

$$MS_{\text{Par}} = \frac{1}{K-1}\left(\sum_{k=1}^{K} W_k B^2_{1(k)} - B^2_{1(W)} \sum_{k=1}^{K} W_k\right)$$

$$MS_{\text{Res}} = \frac{\sum_{k=1}^{K} (N_k - 2) MS_{\text{Res}(k)}}{N - 2K} = \frac{1}{N - 2K} \sum_{k=1}^{K} SS_{\text{Res}(k)}$$

$$= \frac{1}{N - 2K} \sum_{k=1}^{K} (N_k - 1)(1 - r^2_{XY(k)}) S^2_{Y(k)}$$

and

$$F = \frac{MS_{\text{Par}}}{MS_{\text{Res}}}$$

Step 4. Reject H_0 if F exceeds $F_{K-1, N-2K:1-\alpha}$.

Although the immediately preceding form of the test for parallelism may be useful in many situations, there are times when the sample regression coefficients $B_{1(k)}$ are not readily accessible. Fortunately, an alternative, algebraically equivalent, formula is available. For this alternative formula, we introduce the notion of a *sum of cross-products*, which is simply the numerator of the covariance between X and Y, S_{XY}, as defined in Section 1-8. The sum of cross-products, or sum of *products*, will be denoted by SP_{XY}.

Definition of a Sum of Cross-Products.
A sum of cross-products of a sample of size N is defined as the numerator of the sample covariance. Thus:

$$SP_{XY} = \sum_{i=1}^{N} (X_i - \bar{X})(Y_i - \bar{Y}) = (N - 1)S_{XY}$$

Note, as a result, that we can define the sample correlation coefficient in terms of sums of squares and cross-products as:

$$r_{XY} = \frac{S_{XY}}{S_X S_Y} = \frac{(N-1)S_{XY}}{\sqrt{[(N-1)S^2_X]\,[(N-1)S^2_Y]}} = \frac{SP_{XY}}{\sqrt{SS_X SS_Y}}$$

With this new notation:

$$SS_{\text{Par}} = \sum_{k=1}^{K} \frac{SP^2_{XY(k)}}{SS_{X(k)}} - \frac{\left(\sum_{k=1}^{K} SP_{XY(k)}\right)^2}{\sum_{k=1}^{K} SS_{X(k)}} = \sum_{k=1}^{K} \frac{SP^2_{XY(k)}}{SS_{X(k)}} - \frac{SP^2_{XY(W)}}{SS_{X(W)}} \quad \text{and}$$

$$SS_{\text{Res}} = \sum_{k=1}^{K} SS_{Y(k)} - \sum_{k=1}^{K} \frac{SP^2_{XY(k)}}{SS_{X(k)}} = SS_{Y(W)} - \sum_{k=1}^{K} \frac{SP^2_{XY(k)}}{SS_{X(k)}}$$

where $SP_{XY(W)}$, $SS_{X(W)}$, and $SS_{Y(W)}$ represent pooled within-sample values. We now give directions for performing a test of parallelism in terms of sums of squares and cross-products.

Procedure for testing the parallelism of *K* independent regression lines, in terms of sums of squares and cross-products.

Step 1. For each sample, determine $SS_{X(k)}$, $SP_{XY(k)}$, and $SS_{Y(k)}$.

Step 2. Compute:

$$SS_{\text{Par}} = \sum_{k=1}^{K} \frac{SP^2_{XY(k)}}{SS_{X(k)}} - \frac{\left(\sum_{k=1}^{K} SP_{XY(k)}\right)^2}{\sum_{k=1}^{K} SS_{X(k)}} \quad \text{and}$$

$$SS_{\text{Res}} = \sum_{k=1}^{K} SS_{Y(k)} - \sum_{k=1}^{K} \frac{SP^2_{XY(k)}}{SS_{X(k)}}$$

Step 3. Compute:

$$MS_{\text{Par}} = \frac{SS_{\text{Par}}}{K-1}$$

$$MS_{\text{Res}} = \frac{SS_{\text{Res}}}{N-2K} \quad \text{and}$$

$$F = \frac{MS_{\text{Par}}}{MS_{\text{Res}}}$$

Step 4. Reject H_0 if F exceeds $F_{K-1,N-2K:1-\alpha}$.

If desired, we can summarize these results, as in the analysis of variance format of Table 2-4.

As an example, consider the data of Table A-1 for *X*: Pretest and *Y*: Final for the following four groups:

Group 1. Males who selected sociology-related careers
Group 2. Males who selected nonsociology-related careers
Group 3. Females who selected sociology-related careers
Group 4. Females who selected nonsociology-related careers

We will treat these data as representing a random sample of $N = 216$ selected from a population of students who could enroll in the class. The summary statistics for these four groups are presented in Table 2-5. For these data:

$$B_{1(W)} = \frac{(4307.0733)(1.2618) + \cdots + (2184.9565)(1.7529)}{4307.0733 + \cdots + 2184.9565}$$

$$= \frac{16427.1556}{12605.7974} = 1.3031$$

$$MS_{\text{Par}} = \frac{1}{4-1}[(4307.0733)(1.2618)^2 + \cdots + (2184.9565)(1.7529)^2 - (12605.7974)(1.3031)^2]$$

$$= \frac{1}{3}(22492.5379 - 21405.5215) = 362.3388$$

and

$$MS_{\text{Res}} = \frac{1}{216-8}[67(687.7216) + \cdots + 37(464.2212)]$$

$$= \frac{139834.1032}{208} = 672.2793$$

so that:

$$F = \frac{MS_{\text{Par}}}{MS_{\text{Res}}} = \frac{362.3388}{672.2793} = .54$$

TABLE 2-4. Analysis of variance table for testing the hypothesis of equal slopes in K independent samples, using sum of squares and cross-product notation

Source	*d/f*	*Sum of squares*	*Mean square*	*F*
Parallelism	$K-1$	$\sum_{k=1}^{K} \frac{SP^2_{XY(k)}}{SS_{X(k)}} - \frac{SP^2_{XY(W)}}{SS_{X(W)}}$	$\frac{SS_{\text{Par}}}{K-1}$	$\frac{MS_{\text{Par}}}{MS_{\text{Res}}}$
Residual	$N-2K$	$SS_{Y(W)} - \sum_{k=1}^{K} \frac{SP^2_{XY(k)}}{SS_{X(k)}}$	$\frac{SS_{\text{Res}}}{N-2K}$	
Total	$N-K-1$	$SS_{Y(W)} - \frac{SP^2_{XY(W)}}{SS_{X(W)}}$		

TABLE 2-5. Summary statistics for four groups of students taken from Table A-1 for X (Pretest) and Y (Final)

	Group 1: males in sociology-related career	*Group 2: males in non-sociology-related career*	*Group 3: females in sociology-related career*	*Group 4: females in non-sociology-related career*
N_k	69	67	41	39
$SS_{X(k)}$	4307.0733	3745.7391	2368.0285	2184.9565
$SS_{Y(k)}$	52935.2950	54637.0267	30865.8025	23889.8553
$SP_{XY(k)}$	5434.3255	3510.6444	3652.2752	3829.8870
$r_{XY(k)}$	.3599	.2454	.4272	.5301
$B_{1(k)}$	1.2618	.9372	1.5422	1.7529
$B_{0(k)}$	82.1733	75.0042	76.5269	66.1044
$MS_{\text{Res}(k)}$	687.7216	789.9537	647.0149	464.2212
$\bar{X}_k$	16.8841	16.9403	19.0000	17.0256
$\bar{Y}_k$	103.4783	90.8806	105.8293	95.9487
$\bar{Y}_k^A$	104.0576	91.3867	103.6514	96.3437

With $v_1 = 3$ and $v_2 = 208$, the $\alpha = .05$ value of the F distribution is given by $F_{3,208:.95} = 2.65$. Thus we conclude that the four regression lines are parallel.

In terms of the sum of squares and cross-products, we have:

$$SS_{Y(W)} = \sum_{k=1}^{K} SS_{Y(k)} = 52935.2950 + \cdots + 23889.8553 = 162327.9795$$

$$SS_{X(W)} = \sum_{k=1}^{K} SS_{X(k)} = 4307.0733 + \cdots + 2184.9565 = 12605.7974 \quad \text{and}$$

$$SP_{XY(W)} = \sum_{k=1}^{K} SP_{XY(k)} = 5434.3255 + \cdots + 3829.8870 = 16427.1321$$

so that:

$$SS_{\text{Par}} = \left(\frac{5434.3255^2}{4307.0733} + \cdots + \frac{3829.8870^2}{2184.9565}\right) - \frac{(16427.1321)^2}{12605.7974}$$
$$= 22493.1054 - 21406.8702 = 1086.2352$$

$$SS_{\text{Res}} = 162327.9795 - 22493.1054 = 139834.8741$$

The results, within rounding errors, are summarized in Table 2-6.

To conclude this section, recall that the preceding test for equal slopes depends on the assumption that the K population variances about their respective regression lines, $MS_{\text{Res}(k)}$, are equal. Fortunately, however, an analog to the same test can be performed, even in the absence of homogeneous residual variances. This test is based on the statistic:

$$U_0 = W_1 B_{1(1)}^2 + W_2 B_{1(2)}^2 + \cdots + W_K B_{1(K)}^2 - W_0 B_{1(0)}^2$$

where:

$$W_k = \frac{SS_{X(k)}}{MS_{\text{Res}(k)}}$$

$$W_0 = \sum_{k=1}^{K} W_k \quad \text{and}$$

$$B_{1(0)} = \frac{\sum_{k=1}^{K} W_k B_{1(k)}}{\sum_{k=1}^{K} W_k}$$

U_0 has a distribution that is approximately Chi-square (χ^2) with $v = K - 1$ (see Table B-3).

At the same time, it must be noted that the validity of the preceding χ^2

TABLE 2-6. Analysis of variance table for testing that the slopes of Table 2-5 are equal

Source	*d/f*	*Sum of squares*	*Mean square*	*F*
Parallelism	3	1086.2352	362.0784	.54
Residual	208	139834.8741	672.2830	
Total	211	140921.1093		

$F_{3,208:.95} = 2.65$

approximation depends on large sample sizes (for example, all $N_k > 30$). In the absence of large samples, an analogous test based on an approximation to the F distribution is available, and is given by:

$$F^* = \frac{U_0}{(K-1)\left[1 + \frac{2(K-2)}{K^2-1}\Lambda\right]}$$

where:

$$\Lambda = \sum_{k=1}^{K} \frac{1}{N_k - 2}\left[1 - \frac{W_k}{W_0}\right]^2$$

F^* is referred to as an "F-like" statistic, and is based on $\nu_1 = K - 1$ and an approximate ν_2 given by:

$$\nu_2^* = \frac{K^2 - 1}{3\Lambda}$$

See Li (1964) for further details about F^* in the one-way ANOVA model. Also, a recent Monte Carlo investigation by Dretzke, Levin, and Serlin (1982) found that the F^* statistic is decidedly superior to the usual F test of parallelism—in terms of controlling type I errors—when the equal residual variance assumption is violated and the various sample sizes are not equal. Interestingly, an analogous conclusion has been reached for testing hypotheses about equal means when the homogeneity-of-variance assumption is violated (see Glass, Peckham, and Sanders, 1972).

2-5. Multiple comparisons for regression slopes

If the parallelism hypothesis had been rejected, post hoc simultaneous confidence intervals based on the $\beta_{1(k)}$ values could have been constructed according to Scheffé's (1953) method to determine reasons for the rejection. Using advanced methods, Scheffé demonstrated that a more precise hypothesis and alternative of the analysis-of-variance F test is given by:

H_0: All $\psi = 0$

versus:

H_1: At least one $\psi \neq 0$

where, in this case, ψ is a linear contrast in the $\beta_{1(k)}$ defined as:

$$\psi = \sum_{k=1}^{K} a_k \beta_{1(k)}$$

with $\sum_{k=1}^{K} a_k = 0$.

Thus rejection of the null hypothesis implies that at least one contrast exists that is statistically different from zero. It is then up to the researcher to determine whether or not one or more contrasts that carry substantive meaning are included in the set of contrasts that differ from zero. Scheffé's procedure enables a researcher to examine as many post hoc comparisons as desired, while guaranteeing an overall type I error probability of alpha for the entire set of comparisons. An infinite number of comparisons is subsumed by the Scheffé model, but nonetheless we are guaranteed with probability $1 - \alpha$ that no type I errors will be made in the entire set. Of course, this implies that the probability of making *at least one* type I error in the entire set of comparisons is alpha. We will refer to sets of comparisons as *families* of comparisons and will call the risk of making at least one type I error the *familywise* type I error rate (see Kirk, 1982).

We now provide directions for Scheffé's multiple comparison procedure, as applied to contrasts involving the $B_{1(k)}$.

Procedure for performing a post hoc analysis of a rejected test of parallelism using Scheffé's method of multiple comparisons.

Step 1. Define any *linear contrast* in the $\beta_{1(k)}$ that is of substantive interest. Let such a contrast be denoted by:

$$\psi = \sum_{k=1}^{K} a_k \beta_{1(k)}$$

where the a_k are contrast coefficients chosen so that:

$$a_1 + a_2 + \cdots + a_K = 0$$

Step 2. Estimate the contrast in the data by:

$$\hat{\psi} = \sum_{k=1}^{K} a_k B_{1(k)}$$

Step 3. Determine the standard error of this contrast as:

$$SE_{\hat{\psi}} = \sqrt{MS_{\text{Res}}\left(\frac{a_1^2}{W_1} + \frac{a_2^2}{W_2} + \cdots + \frac{a_K^2}{W_K}\right)}$$

where:

$$W_k = SS_{X(k)} = (N_k - 1)S^2_{X(k)}$$

Step 4. Compute:

$$t = \hat{\psi}/SE_{\hat{\psi}}$$

Step 5. With a *familywise type I error probability* of α, reject H_0: $\psi = 0$ in favor of H_1: $\psi \neq 0$ if $|t| > \mathbf{S}$, where $\mathbf{S} = \sqrt{\nu_1 F_{\nu_1,\nu_2:1-\alpha}}$, with $\nu_1 = K - 1$ and $\nu_2 = N - 2K$. In this case, the familywise error rate refers to the probability of making *at least one* type I error in the entire (infinite) set of Scheffé comparisons that theoretically could be investigated.

In the present example, H_0 was not rejected and, therefore, no post hoc Scheffé contrasts involving the $B_{1(k)}$ will be significant using a simultaneous type I error probability of $\alpha = .05$. Let us, nonetheless, perform a post hoc comparison for illustrative purposes only. In this comparison, suppose we had reason to believe that the slopes of the two male career groups were comparable, but different from those of the two female career groups, which are also comparable. For the males, the common slope of the regression line is given by:

$$B_{1(M)} = \frac{W_1 B_{1(1)} + W_2 B_{1(2)}}{W_1 + W_2}$$

In like manner, the common slope of the females' regression line is given by:

$$B_{1(F)} = \frac{W_3 B_{1(3)} + W_4 B_{1(4)}}{W_3 + W_4}$$

Thus, a contrast in these pooled slopes is defined by:

$$\begin{aligned}\hat{\psi} &= B_{1(M)} - B_{1(F)} \\ &= \frac{W_1 B_{1(1)} + W_2 B_{1(2)}}{W_1 + W_2} - \frac{W_3 B_{1(3)} + W_4 B_{1(4)}}{W_3 + W_4}\end{aligned}$$

This is a legitimate contrast in that:

$$a_1 = \frac{W_1}{W_1 + W_2} \qquad a_2 = \frac{W_2}{W_1 + W_2}$$

$$a_3 = \frac{-W_3}{W_3 + W_4} \qquad a_4 = \frac{-W_4}{W_3 + W_4}$$

and

$$\sum_{k=1}^{4} a_k = \frac{W_1 + W_2}{W_1 + W_2} - \frac{W_3 + W_4}{W_3 + W_4} = 1 - 1 = 0$$

With these coefficients:

$$\begin{aligned}\hat{\psi} &= \frac{4307.0733(1.2618) + 3745.7391(.9372)}{4307.0733 + 3745.7391} - \frac{2368.0285(1.5422) + 2184.9565(1.7529)}{2368.0285 + 2184.9565} \\ &= \frac{8945.1718}{8052.8124} - \frac{7481.9838}{4552.9850} = 1.1108 - 1.6433 = -.5325\end{aligned}$$

For this contrast:

$$\begin{aligned}SE^2_{\hat{\psi}} &= \frac{1}{(W_1 + W_2)^2}\left(W_1^2 \frac{MS_{\text{Res}}}{W_1} + W_2^2 \frac{MS_{\text{Res}}}{W_2}\right) + \frac{1}{(W_3 + W_4)^2}\left(W_3^2 \frac{MS_{\text{Res}}}{W_3} + W_4^2 \frac{MS_{\text{Res}}}{W_4}\right) \\ &= MS_{\text{Res}}\left(\frac{1}{W_1 + W_2} + \frac{1}{W_3 + W_4}\right) \\ &= 672.2830\left(\frac{1}{8052.8124} + \frac{1}{4552.9850}\right) = .2311\end{aligned}$$

so that:

$$SE_{\hat{\psi}} = \sqrt{.2311} = .4807$$

Accordingly:

$$t = \frac{-.5325}{.4807} = -1.11$$

which is compared to the Scheffé (familywise $\alpha = .05$) value given by:

$$\mathbf{S} = \sqrt{3F_{3,208:.95}} = \sqrt{3(2.65)} = \sqrt{7.95} = 2.82$$

Because $t = -1.11$ is less in absolute value than $\mathbf{S} = 2.82$, we conclude that the contrast is not significant. In other words, we assume that the common regression line of the males is parallel to that of the females.

Consider the hypothesis in a bit more detail. The actual hypothesis under test is that all $\psi = 0$, with the risk of a type I error distributed across an infinite set of contrasts that is subsumed by the F test. Consequently we may wonder about the cost entailed in distributing alpha across so many contrasts, most of which are not of substantive interest. It turns out that, in practice, the cost is generally high in comparison to other methods that can be employed. One very attractive alternative is for a researcher to generate a finite set of substantively interesting contrasts before the data are collected. When this is done, the family of contrasts produced is referred to as a set of *a priori* or *planned* comparisons. With this approach, we bypass the F test completely and compute t statistics only for those contrasts in the a priori set. Generally speaking, *efficiency*, in the form of smaller required t values and narrower intervals, is gained in adopting a planned, rather than a Scheffé post hoc, approach. Intuitively we can appreciate this by realizing that, with the planned approach, there are fewer comparisons across which the familywise α needs to be distributed. In particular, the familywise α is divided among just those contrasts in the a priori set. The smaller this set is, the more efficient a planned approach is, relative to Scheffé's post hoc approach. A formal treatment of type I error probabilities in a set of C planned comparisons is dealt with in what is known as the *Bonferroni inequality*, which we now define.

Definition of the Bonferroni inequality for multiple comparisons.
Consider C contrasts, $\psi_1, \psi_2, \ldots, \psi_C$, which are to be tested for significance in terms of H_{0_c}: $\psi_c = 0$ versus H_{1_c}: $\psi_c \neq 0$. Let the risk of a type I error for each hypothesis be denoted by $\alpha_1, \alpha_2, \ldots, \alpha_C$. The maximum familywise type I error probability in the set of C contrasts is given by:

$$\alpha \leq \alpha_1 + \alpha_2 + \cdots + \alpha_C$$

Tables for the Bonferroni model were originally prepared by Dunn (1961) for the case in which $\alpha_1 = \alpha_2 = \cdots = \alpha_C$. More useful tables have recently been prepared by Dayton and Schafer (1973), and these appear as Table B-4. The utility of these latter tables is twofold: they lend themselves to unequal allocations of α in situations where that is deemed desirable, and they can be referred to directly for either one-tailed (directional) or two-tailed (nondirectional) statistical tests, of which only the latter is directly handled by the Dunn tables. To illustrate the use of the Dayton and Schafer tables, suppose we decided to perform all $\binom{4}{2} = 6$ pairwise slope comparisons, $\hat{\psi}_1$ through $\hat{\psi}_6$, as well as the complex comparison involving the two combined male career groups and the two combined female career groups, $\hat{\psi}_7$. Thus

$C = 7$. For a nondirectional test of each hypothesis, with $\alpha_1 = \alpha_2 = \cdots = \alpha_7$ and $.05/7 = .0071$, we enter Table B-4 with

$$\frac{a_i}{\Sigma a_i} = \frac{\alpha_c}{2\alpha} = \frac{.05/7}{2(.05)} = \frac{1}{14}$$

For $v_2 = 100$, $t_{100:.9965} = 2.75$ and for $v_2 = 250$, $t_{250:.9965} = 2.71$. With interpolation, $t_{208:.9965} = 2.72$. Since 2.72 is smaller than the corresponding Scheffé value, or $\sqrt{3F_{3,208:.95}} = \sqrt{7.95} = 2.82$, the Dunn procedure would be recommended in this case. On the other hand, for directional tests of the same hypotheses, we would use:

$$\frac{a_i}{\Sigma a_i} = \frac{\alpha_c}{\alpha} = \frac{.05/7}{.05} = \frac{1}{7}$$

Finally, suppose we wished to partition $\alpha = .05$ in the following manner:

$\alpha_1 = .0025$ (two-tailed)

$\alpha_2 = .0025$ (one-tailed)

$\alpha_3 = .005$ (two-tailed)

$\alpha_4 = .005$ (one-tailed)

$\alpha_5 = .01$ (two-tailed)

$\alpha_6 = .01$ (one-tailed)

$\alpha_7 = .015$ (two-tailed)

The corresponding $a_i/\Sigma a_i$ and critical t values in Table B-4 would be determined as follows:

$$\frac{\alpha_1}{2\alpha} = \frac{.05/20}{2(.05)} = \frac{1}{40} \quad \text{with } t = \pm 3.07$$

[*Note:* This value had to be determined by interpolating in the regular t tables (e.g., Table B-2), based on $t_{208:.99875}$, because Table B-4 does not go as high as 1/40.]

$$\frac{\alpha_2}{\alpha} = \frac{.05/20}{.05} = \frac{1}{20} \quad \text{with } t = 2.84$$

$$\frac{\alpha_3}{2\alpha} = \frac{.05/10}{2(.05)} = \frac{1}{20} \quad \text{with } t = \pm 2.84$$

$$\frac{\alpha_4}{\alpha} = \frac{.05/10}{.05} = \frac{1}{10} \quad \text{with } t = 2.61$$

$$\frac{\alpha_5}{2\alpha} = \frac{.05/5}{2(.05)} = \frac{1}{10} \quad \text{with } t = \pm 2.61$$

$$\frac{\alpha_6}{\alpha} = \frac{.05/5}{.05} = \frac{1}{5} \quad \text{with } t = 2.35$$

$$\frac{\alpha_7}{2\alpha} = \frac{.05/3.33}{2(.05)} = \frac{1}{6.67} = \frac{3}{20} \quad \text{with } t = \pm 2.46$$

Procedure for performing an a priori analysis on the slopes of K regression equations (Bonferroni method).

Step 1. Follow the first four steps of the Scheffé method.

Step 2. Replace **S** by $t_{\nu_2:1-\alpha_c/2}$, which is determined from Table B-4 by letting $\nu_2 = N - 2K$ and C = the number of planned comparisons.

Step 3. To use the Dayton and Schafer tables, proceed as follows:
(a) Once α (familywise) has been determined, define C and $\alpha_1, \alpha_2, \ldots, \alpha_C$.
(b) For one-tailed tests, enter the tables for each contrast with:

$$\frac{a_i}{\Sigma a_i} = \frac{\alpha_c}{\alpha}$$

(c) For two-tailed tests, enter the tables for each contrast with:

$$\frac{a_i}{\Sigma a_i} = \frac{\alpha_c}{2\alpha}$$

Finally, we note that both planned and post hoc analyses can be performed on hypotheses rejected by U_0 and F^* as described in Section 2-4.

2-6. Test of the hypothesis H_0: $\beta_{1(W)} = 0$, assuming that the K independent regression lines are parallel

If a researcher knows or can assume that K independent regression lines are parallel, two other questions associated with the regression lines may arise. The first of these relates to testing the hypothesis that the two variables under investigation are uncorrelated within samples; that is, that the pooled within-sample regression coefficient is equal to zero. This hypothesis is examined in this section. Section 2-7 shows how we can test a second hypothesis that relates to the equality of the intercepts of the K regression lines. This second hypothesis is also referred to as the *analysis-of-covariance* hypothesis.

Under the assumption of parallel regression lines, both of these tests yield a revised estimate of the regression-adjusted residual variance. In particular, if the lines are parallel, the sum of squares due to nonparallelism represents a chance deviation from zero, and therefore it can be pooled with the previously defined residual sum of squares to obtain a more efficient estimator of the unknown variance about the assumed common slope. In particular:

$$MS^*_{\text{Res}} = \frac{SS_{\text{Par}} + SS_{\text{Res}}}{\nu_{\text{Par}} + \nu_{\text{Res}}} = \frac{SS^*_{\text{Res}}}{\nu^*_{\text{Res}}}$$

As we see:

$$\nu^*_{\text{Res}} = (K - 1) + (N - 2K) = N - K - 1$$

SS^*_{Res} is easily computed in terms of the sums of squares and cross-products as:

$$SS^*_{\text{Res}} = \sum_{k=1}^{K} SS_{Y(k)} - \frac{\left(\sum_{k=1}^{K} SP_{XY(k)}\right)^2}{\sum_{k=1}^{K} SS_{X(k)}} = SS_{Y(W)} - \frac{SP^2_{XY(W)}}{SS_{X(W)}}$$

Assuming parallelism, we can estimate the common within-sample slope as:

$$B_{1(W)} = \frac{\sum_{k=1}^{K} W_k B_{1(k)}}{\sum_{k=1}^{K} W_k} = \frac{\sum_{k=1}^{K} SP_{XY(k)}}{\sum_{k=1}^{K} SS_{X(k)}} = \frac{SP_{XY(W)}}{SS_{X(W)}}$$

The sum of squares associated with this common regression line may be computed as:

$$SS_{\text{Reg}(W)} = \frac{\left(\sum_{k=1}^{K} SP_{XY(k)}\right)^2}{\sum_{k=1}^{K} SS_{X(k)}} = \frac{SP^2_{XY(W)}}{SS_{X(W)}}$$

Since $v_{\text{Reg}(W)} = 1$, $MS_{\text{Reg}(W)} = SS_{\text{Reg}(W)}$. Finally, $F = MS_{\text{Reg}(W)}/MS^*_{\text{Res}}$ is referred to the F distribution with $v_1 = 1$ and $v_2 = N - K - 1$ degrees of freedom. Results can be summarized as in Table 2-7. Note that SS_{Tot} in this table is identical to the sum of squares within groups for a univariate analysis of the Y variable.

We demonstrate this procedure for the four groups of Table 2-5. Incorporating the present formulas and previous computations, we obtain:

$$SS_{\text{Reg}(W)} = MS_{\text{Reg}(W)} = \frac{(16427.1321)^2}{12605.7974} = 21406.8702$$

In addition, we see from Table 2-6 that:

$$SS^*_{\text{Res}} = 140921.1093$$

so that:

$$MS^*_{\text{Res}} = \frac{140921.1093}{211} = 667.8726$$

Finally:

$$F = \frac{21406.8702}{667.8726} = 32.05$$

with $v_1 = 1$ and $v_2 = 211$, $F_{1,211:.95} = 3.85$. Consequently H_0 is rejected with $\alpha = .05$. We therefore conclude that the common within-sample slope is not equal to zero. Rather, X and Y are assumed to be correlated within groups. The results are summarized in Table 2-8.

TABLE 2-7. Analysis of variance table for testing the hypothesis that $\beta_{1(W)}$ is equal to zero, assuming parallelism

Source	*d/f*	*Sum of squares*	*Mean square*	*F*
Regression	1	$\frac{SP^2_{XY(W)}}{SS_{X(W)}}$	$MS_{\text{Reg}(W)}$	$\frac{MS_{\text{Reg}(W)}}{MS^*_{\text{Res}}}$
Residual	$N - K - 1$	$SS_{Y(W)} - \frac{SP^2_{XY(W)}}{SS_{X(W)}}$	MS^*_{Res}	
Total	$N - K$	$SS_{Y(W)}$		

TABLE 2-8. Test that $\beta_{1(W)} = 0$ for the data of Table 2-5

Source	*d/f*	*Sum of squares*	*Mean square*	*F*
Regression	1	21406.8702	21406.8702	32.05
Residual	211	140921.1093	667.8726	
Total	212	162327.9795		

$F_{1,211:.95} = 3.85$

As in the one-sample case, it can be shown that the test H_0: $\beta_{1(W)} = 0$ is equivalent to the test H_0: $\rho_{XY(W)} = 0$, where $r_{XY(W)}$ estimates the common within-population correlation coefficient, based on pooling covariances and variances across the K samples. This pooled measure of association is defined as follows.

Definition of the within-sample correlation coefficient for K independent samples. Let:

$S^2_{X(1)}, S^2_{X(2)}, \ldots, S^2_{X(K)}$

$S^2_{Y(1)}, S^2_{Y(2)}, \ldots, S^2_{Y(K)}$ and

$S_{XY(1)}, S_{XY(2)}, \ldots S_{XY(K)}$

represent the variances and covariances of K independent samples based on $N_1, N_2, \ldots, N_K$ observations. The pooled estimate of their common correlation coefficient is defined as:

$$r_{XY(W)} = \frac{\sum_{k=1}^{K} \sum_{i=1}^{N_k} (X_{ik} - \bar{X}_k)(Y_{ik} - \bar{Y}_k)}{\sqrt{\sum_{k=1}^{K} \sum_{i=1}^{N_k} (X_{ik} - \bar{X}_k)^2} \sqrt{\sum_{k=1}^{K} \sum_{i=1}^{N_k} (Y_{ik} - \bar{Y}_k)^2}}$$

In terms of the variance-covariance notation of Section 2-3:

$$r_{XY(W)} = \frac{\sum_{k=1}^{K} (N_k - 1) S_{XY(k)}}{\sqrt{\sum_{k=1}^{K} (N_k - 1) S^2_{X(k)}} \sqrt{\sum_{k=1}^{K} (N_k - 1) S^2_{Y(k)}}}$$

which can now be written as:

$$r_{XY(W)} = \frac{\sum_{k=1}^{K} SP_{XY(k)}}{\sqrt{\sum_{k=1}^{K} SS_{X(k)}} \sqrt{\sum_{k=1}^{K} SS_{Y(k)}}}$$

Finally, in some cases it is more convenient to write the numerator in terms of the sample correlation coefficients, namely:

$$\sum_{k=1}^{K} SP_{XY(k)} = \sum_{k=1}^{K} (N_k - 1) r_{XY(k)} S_{X(k)} S_{Y(k)}$$

For the four groups represented in Table 2-5, we now compute $r_{XY(W)}$.

$$\sum_{k=1}^{4} SP_{XY(k)} = 5434.3255 + 3510.6444 + 3652.2752 + 3829.8870 = 16427.1321$$

In addition:

$$\sum_{k=1}^{4} SS_{X(k)} = 4307.0733 + 3745.7391 + 2368.0285 + 2184.9565$$
$$= 12605.7974$$

and

$$\sum_{k=1}^{4} SS_{Y(k)} = 52935.2950 + 54637.0267 + 30865.8025 + 23889.8553$$
$$= 162327.9795$$

so that:

$$r_{XY(W)} = \frac{16427.1321}{\sqrt{12605.7974}\sqrt{162327.9795}} = .3631$$

Recalling our previous comments in Section 2-3 about the generality of testing for the significance of a sample correlation coefficient, we can write:

$$t = \sqrt{\frac{v_2}{v_1}\left(\frac{r^2}{1 - r^2}\right)}$$

or equivalently:

$$F = \frac{v_2}{v_1}\left(\frac{r^2}{1 - r^2}\right)$$

With only one independent variable, $v_1 = 1$ and $v_2 = N - K - 1$. Therefore the appropriate test statistic for testing the significance of $r_{XY(W)}$ is given by:

$$F = \frac{(N - K - 1)r^2_{XY(W)}}{1 - r^2_{XY(W)}}$$

For the data of Table 2-5, $r_{XY(W)} = .3631$, so that:

$$F = \frac{(216 - 4 - 1)\,(.3631)^2}{1 - (.3631)^2} = \frac{211(.1318)}{.8682} = 32.04$$

which, within rounding errors, equals the previously computed F associated with the hypothesis, H_0: $\beta_{1(W)} = 0$.

If the hypothesis $\beta_{1(W)} = 0$ were not rejected, under the assumption of parallelism, it would follow that:

$$\beta_{1(1)} = \beta_{1(2)} = \cdots = \beta_{1(K)} = 0$$

In addition, it would be concluded that:

$$\rho_{XY(1)} = \rho_{XY(2)} = \cdots = \rho_{XY(K)} = 0$$

We now provide instructions for testing H_0: $\beta_{1(W)} = 0$ or H_0: $\rho_{XY(W)} = 0$.

Procedure for testing H_0: $\beta_{1(W)} = 0$ or H_0: $\rho_{XY(W)} = 0$.

Step 1. Obtain $SS_{X(k)}$, $SS_{Y(k)}$, and $SP_{XY(k)}$ for each sample.

Step 2. Compute:

$$SS_{\text{Reg}(W)} = \frac{\left(\sum_{k=1}^{K} SP_{XY(k)}\right)^2}{\sum_{k=1}^{K} SS_{X(k)}} \quad \text{and}$$

$$SS^*_{\text{Res}} = \sum_{k=1}^{K} SS_{Y(k)} - SS_{\text{Reg}(W)}$$

Step 3. Compute:

$$F = \frac{MS_{\text{Reg}(W)}}{MS^*_{\text{Res}}}$$

Step 4. Reject H_0 if $F > F_{\nu_1,\nu_2:1-\alpha}$

where:

$\nu_1 = 1$ and $\nu_2 = N - K - 1$

2-7. Testing K independent regression lines for equal intercepts, assuming parallelism (the analysis of covariance)

A second test of hypothesis that can be performed, once the assumption of equal slopes is tenable, is that the K intercepts are equal to a common unknown value. In particular, we can test the hypothesis:

H_0: $\beta_{0(1)} = \beta_{0(2)} = \cdots = \beta_{0(K)}$

against:

H_1: H_0 is false

provided the five assumptions of Section 2-4 are met.

Before we discuss this test, it is worth noting its mathematical identity to the analysis of covariance, which is frequently used to make regression-adjusted comparisons of means across groups. For simplicity of presentation we describe the model for only two groups, noting that it can be generalized in a direct manner to three or more groups.

Let the regression equations for the two groups, which are assumed parallel, be given in deviation form by:

$\hat{Y}_1 = \bar{Y}_1 + B_{1(W)}(X - \bar{X}_1)$ and

$\hat{Y}_2 = \bar{Y}_2 + B_{1(W)}(X - \bar{X}_2)$

We define the adjusted averages for these groups to be the values of $\hat{Y}_1$ and $\hat{Y}_2$ evaluated at the overall mean of $\bar{X}$. Thus:

$\bar{Y}_1^A = \bar{Y}_1 + B_{1(W)}(\bar{X} - \bar{X}_1) = (\bar{Y}_1 - B_{1(W)}\bar{X}_1) + B_{1(W)}\bar{X}$ and

$\bar{Y}_2^A = \bar{Y}_2 + B_{1(W)}(\bar{X} - \bar{X}_2) = (\bar{Y}_2 - B_{1(W)}\bar{X}_2) + B_{1(W)}\bar{X}$

If these adjusted averages were equal, it would follow that:

$$(\bar{Y}_1 - B_{1(W)}\bar{X}_1) = (\bar{Y}_2 - B_{1(W)}\bar{X}_2)$$

since $B_{1(W)}\bar{X}$ is a constant added to both adjusted averages. At this point, we see that:

$$B_{0(1)} = \bar{Y}_1 - B_{1(W)}\bar{X}_1$$

and that:

$$B_{0(2)} = \bar{Y}_2 - B_{1(W)}\bar{X}_2$$

so that $B_{0(1)} = B_{0(2)}$. Thus, obtaining equal adjusted means is synonymous to obtaining equal intercepts, provided that the regression lines are parallel. In this sense, testing for equal intercepts is like testing an analysis-of-covariance hypothesis.

On the basis of this discussion, we may wonder why the hypothesis of equal intercepts is related to the hypothesis of equal adjusted means. The reasons for the connection can be traced to simple geometric properties of parallelograms, as well as to the principles of modern-day statistical theory which state that, given two procedures for testing the same hypothesis with equal risks of a type I error, the test with the greater power or the smaller risk of a type II error should be selected.

Concerning the geometric argument, we recall that opposite sides of a parallelogram are of equal length and that the test of equal intercepts, to be described, is based on the assumption that the regression lines are parallel. Thus we know that differences in two intercepts measured in a sample by:

$$\Delta_{B0} = B_{0(1)} - B_{0(2)}$$

must equal the corresponding difference in the adjusted means measured by:

$$\Delta_{\bar{Y}^A} = \bar{Y}_1^A - \bar{Y}_2^A = (\bar{Y}_1 - \bar{Y}_2) - B_{1(W)}(\bar{X}_1 - \bar{X}_2)$$

since Δ_{B0} and $\Delta_{\bar{Y}^A}$ represent the distances on the opposite sides of a parallelogram defined by the parallel regression lines.

Concerning the statistical arguments, it can be shown that the standard error of $\Delta_{\bar{Y}^A}$ is smaller than the standard error of Δ_{B0}, so that the test about the adjusted means has greater power than the test about the intercepts. For these reasons, the hypothesis of equal intercepts can be evaluated whenever a test of equal adjusted means is conducted. Thus a test of equal adjusted means is synonymous with, but has greater statistical power than, a direct test of equal intercepts.

A test of the identity of K independent intercepts or, equivalently, of K adjusted means consequently can be generated as follows. First, fit a regression line to the total sample by completely ignoring the sample differences. Let the total regression line be denoted by:

$$\hat{Y}_T = \bar{Y} + B_{1(T)}(X - \bar{X})$$

With this fit, consider the geometry illustrated in Figure 2-5. In this figure, let $\hat{Y}_T$ represent the total regression line fitted to the total sample, and let:

$$\hat{Y}_k = \bar{Y}_k + B_{1(W)}(X - \bar{X}_k)$$

represent the regression line fitted to the kth sample under the assumption of

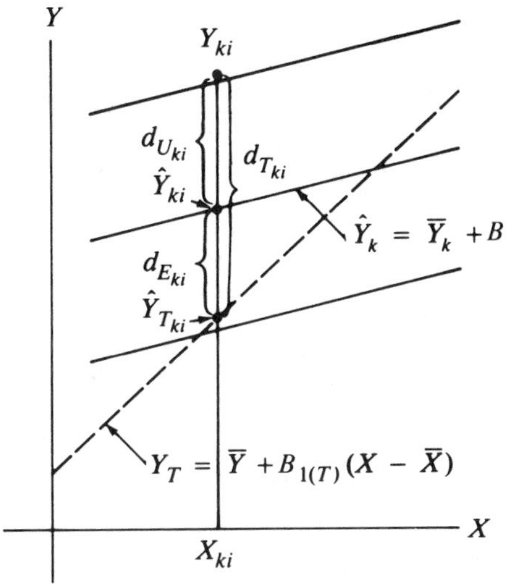

Figure 2-5. The geometry of testing for equal intercepts, assuming parallelism.

parallelism. Now consider a specific Y value in sample k, as illustrated in Figure 2-5. Let the deviation of Y_{ki} from its predicted value $\hat{Y}_{T_{ki}}$ be denoted by:

$$d_{T_{ki}} = (Y_{ki} - \hat{Y}_{T_{ki}}) = (Y_{ki} - \bar{Y}) - B_{1(T)}(X_{ki} - \bar{X})$$

As indicated in Figure 2-5, $d_{T_{ki}}$ can be decomposed into two elements. Let these elements be denoted by:

$$d_{U_{ki}} = (Y_{ki} - \hat{Y}_{ki}) = (Y_{ki} - \bar{Y}_k) - B_{1(W)}(X_{ki} - \bar{X}_k)$$

and

$$d_{E_{ki}} = d_{T_{ki}} - d_{U_{ki}} = (Y_{ki} - \hat{Y}_{T_{ki}}) - (Y_{ki} - \hat{Y}_{ki}) = (\hat{Y}_{ki} - \hat{Y}_{T_{ki}})$$

In terms of Figure 2-5, we see that $d_{E_{ki}}$ measures the deviation of the kth regression line from the total regression line. When each $d_{E_{ki}}$ equals 0, it follows that all K regression lines are identical to the total regression line, and therefore all K intercepts are equal. On the other hand, if the $d_{E_{ki}}$ are not all equal to 0, the K regression lines must deviate from the total regression line so that their intercepts are also different from that of the total line. This means that the information for identity of regression lines is contained in the set of $d_{E_{ki}}$ values. As a result, these values are used to generate a statistic that relates to the truth of H_0 or its alternative H_1. The derivation of this index requires a considerable amount of algebra which we wish to bypass. Thus we state the results without supplying a proof or demonstration.

Starting with the information available from Table 2-7, we have that:

$$SS_U = SS^*_{\text{Res}} = SS_{Y(W)} - \frac{SP^2_{XY(W)}}{SS_{X(W)}}$$

Similarly, if we now define sums of squares and cross-products across the total sample as:

$$SS_Y = \sum_{k=1}^{K} \sum_{i=1}^{N_k} (Y_{ki} - \bar{Y})^2$$

$$SP_{XY} = \sum_{k=1}^{K} \sum_{i=1}^{N_k} (X_{ki} - \bar{X})(Y_{ki} - \bar{Y})$$

and

$$SS_X = \sum_{k=1}^{K} \sum_{i=1}^{N_k} (X_{ki} - \bar{X})^2$$

Then:

$$SS^*_T = SS_Y - \frac{SP^2_{XY}}{SS_X}$$

Finally:

$$SS^*_E = SS_{\text{Intercepts}} = SS^*_T - SS^*_U$$

The degrees of freedom for SS^*_T are given by $\nu^*_T = N - 2$, since as with the one-sample model, the total deviations d_T are restricted by both the estimated total slope $\beta_{1(T)}$ and the estimated total intercept $\beta_{0(T)}$. The degrees of freedom for SS^*_U are given by $\nu^*_U = N - K - 1$, since K intercepts $\beta_{0(k)}$ and the common slope $\beta_{1(W)}$ must be estimated from the data. Finally, by subtraction, the degrees of freedom for SS^*_E are given by $\nu^*_E = (N - 2) - (N - K - 1) = K - 1$.

An analysis of variance table summarizing these developments is presented as Table 2-9. Directions for performing a test of equal intercepts are given as follows.

Procedure for testing *K* parallel regression lines for equal intercepts (or equal adjusted means).

Step 1. Perform a regression analysis on the entire sample and determine the values of:

$$SS^*_{\text{Tot}} = SS_Y - \frac{SP^2_{XY}}{SS_X}$$

Step 2. Determine:

$$SS^*_{\text{Res}} = SS_{Y(W)} - \frac{SP^2_{XY(W)}}{SS_{X(W)}} \quad \text{and}$$

$$SS_{\text{Int}} = SS^*_{\text{Tot}} - SS^*_{\text{Res}}$$

Step 3. Complete the ANOVA table summarized in Table 2-9.

Step 4. Reject H_0 if F exceeds the $100(1 - \alpha)$ percentile of the F distribution with $\nu_1 = K - 1$ and $\nu_2 = N - K - 1$.

We now test the hypothesis:

$$H_0: \quad \beta_{0(1)} = \beta_{0(2)} = \beta_{0(3)} = \beta_{0(4)}$$

for the data of Table 2-5. Since the values needed for SS^*_{Tot} are not provided in Table 2-5, we must first perform some intermediate arithmetic based on analysis-of-variance knowledge that:

TABLE 2-9. Analysis of variance table for testing hypotheses of equal intercepts (or equal adjusted means) in K independent samples, assuming parallelism

Source	*d/f*	*Sum of squares*	*Mean square*	*F*
Intercepts	$K - 1$	$\left(SS_Y - \frac{SP^2_{XY}}{SS_X}\right) - \left(SS_{Y(W)} - \frac{SP^2_{XY(W)}}{SS_{X(W)}}\right)$	MS_{Int}	$\frac{MS_{\text{Int}}}{MS^*_{\text{Res}}}$
Residual	$N - K - 1$	$SS_{Y(W)} - \frac{SP^2_{XY(W)}}{SS_{X(W)}}$	MS^*_{Res}	
Total	$N - 2$	$SS_Y - \frac{SP^2_{XY}}{SS_X}$		

$$SS_{\text{Total}} = SS_{\text{Between}} + SS_{\text{Within}}$$

As we have seen earlier, the SS_{Within} for the Y variable was given as:

$$SS_{Y(W)} = \sum_{k=1}^{K} SS_{Y(k)} = 162327.9795$$

In addition, SS_{Between} for the Y variable may be written as:

$$SS_{Y(B)} = \sum_{k=1}^{K} N_k(\bar{Y}_k - \bar{Y})^2$$

where:

$\bar{Y}$ = the grand mean of all Y observations

$$= \frac{\sum_{k=1}^{K} \sum_{i=1}^{N_k} Y_{ki}}{\sum_{k=1}^{K} N_k} = \frac{\sum_{k=1}^{K} N_k \bar{Y}_k}{\sum_{k=1}^{K} N_k}$$

For the data of Table 2-5:

$$\bar{Y} = \frac{69(103.4783) + \cdots + 39(95.9487)}{216} = 98.6574$$

$$SS_{Y(B)} = 69(103.4783 - 98.6574)^2 + \cdots + 39(95.9487 - 98.6574)^2$$
$$= 8050.7290$$

Thus, the SS_{Total} is given by:

$$SS_Y = 8050.7290 + 162327.9795 = 170378.7085$$

In similar fashion:

$$SS_{X(W)} = 12605.7974$$

$$\bar{X} = \frac{69(16.8841) + \cdots + 39(17.0256)}{216} = 17.3287$$

and

$$SS_{X(B)} = 69(16.8841 - 17.3287)^2 + \cdots + 39(17.0256 - 17.3287)^2$$
$$= 141.8523$$

TABLE 2-10. Analysis of variance table for testing equality of intercepts (or equal adjusted means) for the data of Table 2-5

Source	*d/f*	*Sum of squares*	*Mean square*	*F*
Intercepts	3	6773.2153	2257.7384	3.38
Residual	211	140921.1093	667.8726	
Total	214	147694.3246		

$F_{3,211:.95} = 2.65$

Thus:

$$SS_X = 141.8523 + 12605.7974 = 12747.6497$$

Finally:

$$SP_{XY(W)} = 16427.1321$$

$$\begin{aligned} SP_{XY(B)} &= 69(16.8841 - 17.3287)(103.4783 - 98.6574) + \cdots + \\ &\quad 39(17.0256 - 17.3287)(95.9487 - 98.6574) \\ &= 577.9430 \end{aligned}$$

and

$$SP_{XY} = 577.9430 + 16427.1321 = 17005.0751$$

Accordingly:

$$SS^*_{\text{Tot}} = 170378.7085 - \frac{(17005.0751)^2}{12747.6497} = 147694.3246$$

From previous calculations and as reported in Table 2-8:

$$SS^*_{\text{Res}} = 140921.1093$$

so that:

$$SS_{\text{Int}} = 147694.3246 - 140921.1093 = 6773.2153$$

Finally:

$$F = \frac{\dfrac{6773.2153}{3}}{\dfrac{140921.1093}{211}} = 3.38$$

and since this exceeds the critical value of $F_{3,211:.95} = 2.64$, the hypothesis H_0: $\beta_{0(1)} = \beta_{0(2)} = \beta_{0(3)} = \beta_{0(4)}$ is rejected. Results are summarized in Table 2-10.

The total degrees of freedom for the test of equal intercepts was given by $v = N - 2$ and not the familiar $N - 1$. However, this one-degree-of-freedom difference could be restored to perform a test of the linear relationship between the covariate X and the dependent variable Y. If this degree of freedom and corresponding sum of squares are returned to the analysis, the total degrees of freedom are given by $v = N - 1$ as in the analysis of variance. Using the residual displayed in Table 2-9, we can test the hypothesis that X and Y are related, based on $v_1 = 1$ and $v_2 = N - K - 1$.

A word of caution is in order for researchers who perform this test. In performing an analysis of covariance, we hope that the covariate selected is at least moderately related to the dependent variable. The greater the extent to which this is true, the greater the advantage in performing an analysis of covariance relative to a simple analysis of variance. The particular relationship of concern, however, is the within-sample relationship, as represented by $r_{XY(W)}$ or $B_{1(W)}$. Many computer programs provide a one-degree-of-freedom test, generally labeled "covariate" or "regression," which ostensibly assesses the significance of the relationship between X and Y. However, it must be recognized that the relationship assessed is not the within-sample relationship, but rather the relationship between X and Y across all individuals, as represented by $r_{XY(T)}$ or $B_{1(T)}$. In particular, it can be shown that such a test confounds the within-group regression with across-group mean differences and, as a result, it is uninformative with respect to interpreting the utility of an analysis of covariance.

Consider, for example, the pattern represented by Example One of Figure 3-2 in the next chapter. Here we see that the correlation within groups is much larger than the correlation across groups. In this case, the test of H_0: $\beta_{1(T)} = 0$ might not be rejected even though H_0: $\beta_{1(W)} = 0$ would be. Nonrejection of the former hypothesis would argue against performing an analysis of covariance, even though it might be quite advantageous to perform one. On the other hand, consider the pattern represented in Figure 3-1 of the next chapter. Here a test of H_0: $\beta_{1(T)} = 0$ might be rejected, and yet it is clearly suggested that $\beta_{1(W)} = 0$. In this case, an analysis of covariance should not be selected in preference to a simple analysis of variance as a result of cost considerations and loss of statistical power. See Feldt (1958) and Elashoff (1969) for these and other important conditions surrounding the proper use of the analysis of covariance. Because of the interpretive difficulties associated with the test of H_0: $\beta_{1(T)} = 0$ in this context, we recommend that researchers refrain from conducting or examining it. If one does wish to assess the unconfounded, within-sample, relationship between X and Y, the test of $\beta_{1(W)} = 0$ described in Section 2-6 is appropriate. We shed further light on the distinction between across- and within-group relationships, as represented by $B_{1(T)}$ and $B_{1(W)}$, respectively, in the context of partial correlation and stepwise multiple regression analysis in Chapter 3. For related discussion, see Robinson (1950).

If the hypothesis of equal intercepts is rejected, post hoc Scheffé comparisons may be performed, based on:

$$\psi = \hat{\psi} \pm \mathbf{S}\, SE_{\hat{\psi}}$$

where:

$$\hat{\psi} = \sum_{k=1}^{K} a_k \bar{Y}_k^A = \sum_{k=1}^{K} a_k[\bar{Y}_k - B_{1(W)}(\bar{X}_k - \bar{X})]$$

$$\mathbf{S} = \sqrt{(K-1)F_{K-1,N-K-1:1-\alpha}}$$

and

$$SE_{\hat{\psi}} = \sqrt{MS^*_{\text{Res}}\left(\sum_{k=1}^{K} \frac{a_k^2}{N_k} + \frac{\hat{\psi}_X^2}{SS_{X(W)}}\right)}$$

where $\hat{\psi}_X$ represents the same contrast applied to the X means, $\bar{X}_1, \bar{X}_2, \ldots, \bar{X}_K$, as to the adjusted Y means, $\bar{Y}_1^A, \bar{Y}_2^A, \ldots, \bar{Y}_K^A$. Obviously, the overall F test of equal intercepts may be bypassed in favor of a priori planned comparisons. In that case, the contrast and the standard error of the contrast are as just defined, and critical t values from Table B-4 would replace **S**. For completeness, we provide directions for assessing the significance of intercept differences in terms of post hoc contrasts. Note that contrasts are evaluated in terms of the $\bar{Y}_k^A$ values and not the $B_{0(k)}$ values associated with each regression line. If desired, we could recompute each interval and use $B_{0(k)} = \bar{Y}_k - B_{1(W)}\bar{X}_k$ in place of the $\bar{Y}_k^A$. However, nothing is gained in doing this as the value of the contrast will be the same under either substitution.

Procedure for performing post hoc comparisons among intercepts (or adjusted means).

Step 1. Compute:

$$\mathbf{S} = \sqrt{v_1 F_{v_1, v_2:1-\alpha}}$$

where $v_1 = K - 1$ and $v_2 = N - K - 1$.

Step 2. For each contrast of interest, compute:

$$\hat{\psi} = \sum_{k=1}^{K} a_k \bar{Y}_k^A = \sum_{k=1}^{K} a_k[\bar{Y}_k - B_{1(W)}(\bar{X}_k - \bar{X})]$$

Step 3. Determine the value of:

$$SE_{\hat{\psi}}^2 = MS_{\text{Res}}^* \left(\sum_{k=1}^{K} \frac{a_k^2}{N_k} + \frac{\hat{\psi}_X^2}{SS_{X(W)}} \right)$$

Step 4. Compute:

$$t = \frac{\hat{\psi}}{SE_{\hat{\psi}}}$$

and compare this to **S** in Step 1. Conclude that $\psi \neq 0$ if $|t| > \mathbf{S}$.

For the post hoc comparison of the intercepts of males in sociology- and nonsociology-related careers (Groups 1 and 2, respectively, from Table 2-5) we have:

$$\hat{\psi} = 104.0576 - 91.3867 = 12.6709$$

with:

$$SE_{\hat{\psi}}^2 = 667.8726\left[\frac{1}{69} + \frac{1}{67} + \frac{(16.8841 - 16.9403)^2}{12605.7974}\right] = 19.6477$$

$$\mathbf{S} = \sqrt{3F_{3,211:.95}} = \sqrt{3(2.65)} = \sqrt{7.95} = 2.82$$

Thus:

$$t = \frac{12.6709}{\sqrt{19.6477}} = 2.86$$

Since $t = 2.86 > \mathbf{S} = 2.82$, we would conclude that the intercepts of the two male career groups are different. In particular, males who entered sociology-related careers tended to do better on the final exam in comparison to males who did not end up in sociology-related careers, when the final was adjusted by pretest scores. On the average, the adjusted scores of sociology career males are about 12.67 points higher. Looking at the adjusted means in Table 2-5, we might also be inclined to compare the combined male–female sociology career groups, Groups 1 and 3, with the combined male–female nonsociology career groups, Groups 2 and 4. In this case, a post hoc comparison, weighted by sample size, would be given by:

$$\hat{\psi} = (a_1\bar{Y}_1^A + a_3\bar{Y}_3^A) - (a_2\bar{Y}_2^A + a_4\bar{Y}_4^A)$$

where $a_1 = 69/110$, $a_2 = 67/106$, $a_3 = 41/110$, and $a_4 = 39/106$.

Thus:

$$\hat{\psi} = \frac{69(104.0576) + 41(103.6514)}{110} - \frac{67(91.3867) + 39(96.3437)}{106}$$

$$= 103.9062 - 93.2105 = 10.6957$$

with:

$$SE_{\hat{\psi}}^2 = 667.8726\left(\frac{1}{110} + \frac{1}{106} + \frac{(17.6728 - 16.9717)^2}{12605.7974}\right) = 12.3983$$

As a result:

$$t = \frac{10.6957}{\sqrt{12.3983}} = 3.04$$

which also exceeds $\mathbf{S} = 2.82$. Thus students who ended up in sociology-related careers had higher adjusted final exam scores than students who ended up in nonsociology-related careers.

2-8. A single test for the identity of *K* independent regression lines

In preceding sections, we described separate tests that could be performed to ascertain whether K independent regression lines were parallel and, assuming they were, whether they had the same intercepts. As we see, nonrejection of both hypotheses would mean that the lines are identical. Dixon and Massey (1969) describe a single omnibus test that can be used to test the identity of two or more regression lines. In this test, the sums of squares and degrees of freedom associated with slope and intercept differences are pooled. The resulting mean square identity, MS_{Ident}, is then compared with the MS_{Res} based on $N - 2K$ degrees of freedom, as defined in Table 2-4. Nonrejection of the identity hypothesis enables us to conclude that the K regression lines are identical, which in turn implies that $\beta_{1(W)} = \beta_{1(T)}$. On the other hand, rejection of the hypothesis indicates that the regression lines differ with respect to slope and/or intercept. Although post hoc Scheffé contrasts could be examined to identify the specific loci of the differences according to this model, the resulting confidence intervals will invariably be more imprecise than the more direct confidence intervals that follow from the specialized tests for slopes and intercepts, discussed in Sections 2-5 and 2-7. For completeness, we present the omnibus test statistic associated with the identity hypothesis.

Procedure for testing the identity of K independent regression lines.

Step 1. To test the hypothesis

$$H_0: \beta_{0(1)} + \beta_{1(1)}X = \beta_{0(2)} + \beta_{1(2)}X = \cdots = \beta_{0(K)} + \beta_{1(K)}X$$

Compute:

$$MS_{\text{Ident}} = \frac{SS_{\text{Par}} + SS_{\text{Int}}}{\nu_{\text{Par}} + \nu_{\text{Int}}}$$

and

MS_{Res} = the mean square residual of the test for parallelism in Section 2-4

Step 2. Compute:

$$F = \frac{MS_{\text{Ident}}}{MS_{\text{Res}}}$$

and reject H_0 if

$$F > F_{2(K-1), N-2K:1-\alpha}$$

For the data of Table 2-5, we have that:

$$SS_{\text{Ident}} = 1086.2352 + 6773.2153 = 7859.4504$$

$$MS_{\text{Ident}} = \frac{7859.4504}{2(4-1)} = \frac{7859.4504}{6} = 1309.9084$$

Thus:

$$F = \frac{1309.9084}{672.2830} = 1.95$$

The results are summarized in Table 2-11.

Because $F = 1.95$ does not exceed the critical value of $F_{6,208:.95} = 2.12$, the four regression lines can be considered identical. It is worth mentioning in this regard that although differences in intercept were detected in Section 2-7, the test there was specifically designed for intercept differences, unlike the more diffuse test performed here. In that sense also, the test for intercepts in conjunction with the test for slopes would yield a combined maximum type I error probability of .10, and thus the single test performed here using $\alpha = .05$ is not strictly comparable. If the more liberal type I error probability is applied to the test just conducted, the critical F value is given by $F_{6,208:.90} = 1.80$, which would result in rejection of the hypothesis just as it did for the previous intercept test. This kind of consistency should not always be expected however.

The general ANOVA table associated with the test of identical regression lines is

TABLE 2-11. Analysis of variance table for testing the hypothesis of identical regression lines for the data of Table 2-5

Source	*d/f*	*Sum of Squares*	*Mean Square*	*F*
Identity	6	7859.4504	1309.9084	1.95
Residual	208	139834.8741	672.2830	
Total	214	147692.3245		

$F_{6,208:.95} = 2.12$

TABLE 2-12. Analysis of variance table for testing hypotheses of identical regression lines in K independent samples

Source	*d/f*	*Sum of squares*	*Mean square*	*F*
Identity	$2(K-1)$	$\left(SS_Y - \frac{SP^2_{XY}}{SS_X}\right) - \left(SS_{Y(W)} - \sum_{k=1}^{K} \frac{SP^2_{XY(k)}}{SS_{X(k)}}\right)$	MS_{Ident}	$\frac{MS_{\text{Ident}}}{MS_{\text{Res}}}$
Residual	$N-2K$	$SS_{Y(W)} - \sum_{k=1}^{K} \frac{SP^2_{XY(k)}}{SS_{X(k)}}$	MS_{Res}	
Total	$N-2$	$SS_Y - \frac{SP^2_{XY}}{SS_X}$		

presented as Table 2-12, and an overall schematic relating the various statistical tests and concepts discussed in Sections 2-4 through 2-8 is presented as Figure 2-6. The figure resulted from continued discussion with Professor Ronald Serlin of the University of Wisconsin, to whom we are most grateful.

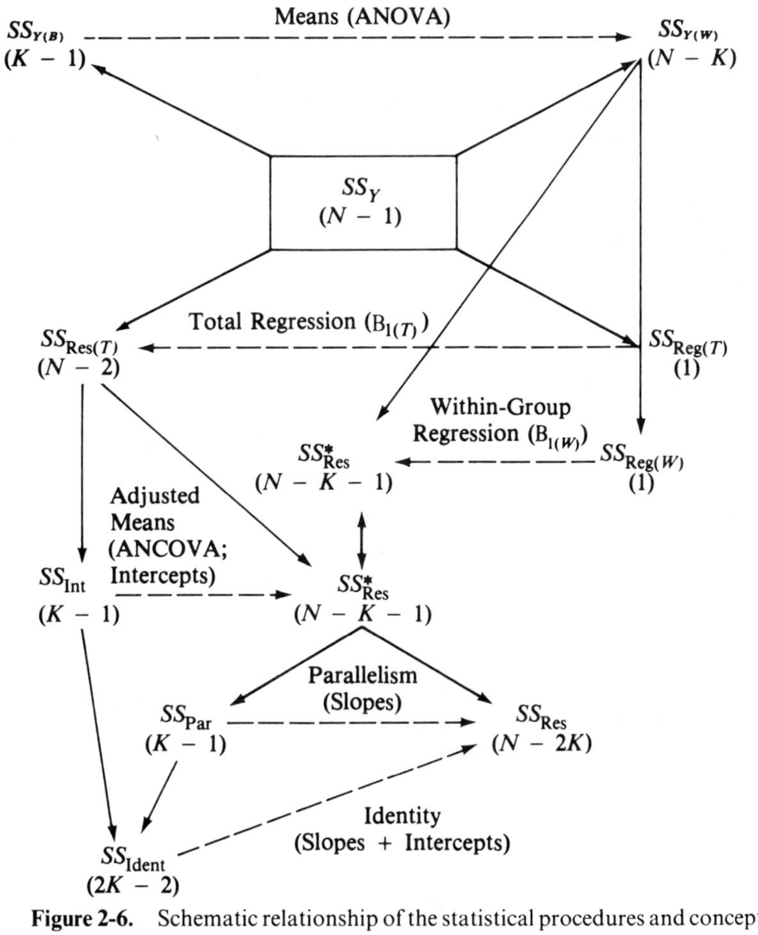

Figure 2-6. Schematic relationship of the statistical procedures and concepts discussed in this chapter.

Note: Solid arrows represent partitionings of sums of squares and degrees of freedom Broken arrows represent specific sources and associated residuals for hypothesis testing. Also shown is how SS^*_{Res} can be obtained in two different ways.

2-9. Comparison of two or more regression lines over a finite interval

Sometimes a researcher wishes to examine identity of regression lines only over a finite interval. This might happen, for example, in educational studies where standardized tests covering a finite range of values are employed for evaluation purposes, or when experimenter-selected lower and upper values of X are meaningful hypothesis-testing end points. Tsutakawa and Hewett (1978) have developed a test for just this situation. Their test can be used to test the hypothesis that, over a preselected range of values $X_L < X < X_U$, one regression line is uniformly greater than another regression line. In particular, their test is designed to test:

$$\text{H}_0\text{:} \quad \beta_{0(1)} + \beta_{1(1)}X = \beta_{0(2)} + \beta_{1(2)}X \qquad \text{for } X_L < X < X_U$$

against:

$$\text{H}_1\text{:} \quad \beta_{0(1)} + \beta_{1(1)}X > \beta_{0(2)} + \beta_{1(2)}X \qquad \text{for } X_L < X < X_U$$

where X_L and X_U refer, respectively, to the lower and upper values of X in the range of interest.

The assumptions for the test are exactly the same as those needed in Sections 2-3 and 2-4, that is, independence between and within samples, normality of errors, linearity of regressions, homoscedasticity, and equal residual variances. The test is easy to carry out and is performed as follows.

Procedure for testing the hypothesis that one regression line is uniformly above another over a preselected range of values.

Step 1. Choose the lower and upper limits on the independent variables that are of interest. Let these values be X_L and X_U.

Step 2. Obtain the least square estimates for the two regression lines. For each line determine for $k = 1$ and $k = 2$:

$$\hat{Y}_{L(k)} = B_{0(k)} + B_{1(k)}X_L$$

$$\hat{Y}_{U(k)} = B_{0(k)} + B_{1(k)}X_U$$

Step 3. Determine for each estimated value:

$$MS_{\text{Res}} = \frac{\sum_{k=1}^{2} (N_k - 1)(1 - r^2_{XY(k)})S^2_{Y(k)}}{N_1 + N_2 - 4}$$

$$= \frac{SS_{\text{Res}(1)} + SS_{\text{Res}(2)}}{N_1 + N_2 - 4}$$

$$SE^2_{\hat{Y}_{L(k)}} = MS_{\text{Res}}\left[\frac{1}{N_k} + \frac{(X_L - \bar{X}_k)^2}{SS_{X(k)}}\right]$$

$$SE^2_{\hat{Y}_{U(k)}} = MS_{\text{Res}}\left[\frac{1}{N_k} + \frac{(X_U - \bar{X}_k)^2}{SS_{X(k)}}\right]$$

Step 4. Compute:

$$t_L = \frac{\hat{Y}_{L(1)} - \hat{Y}_{L(2)}}{\sqrt{SE^2_{\hat{Y}_{L(1)}} + SE^2_{\hat{Y}_{L(2)}}}}$$

$$t_U = \frac{\hat{Y}_{U(1)} - \hat{Y}_{U(2)}}{\sqrt{SE^2_{\hat{Y}_{U(1)}} + SE^2_{\hat{Y}_{U(2)}}}}$$

and

$t = \text{minimum}\,(t_L, t_U)$

Step 5. With the risk of a type I error set at α, reject H_0, if:

$t > t_{v:1-\alpha}$

where $v = N_1 + N_2 - 4$

As an example of the use of this test, consider the data for Groups 1 and 2, summarized in Table 2-5. In particular, let us test the hypothesis that the regression line for the male students who select sociology-related careers is uniformly above the corresponding regression line for the male students who select nonsociology-related careers. Suppose further that one is interested in assessing this hypothesis between the values $X_L = 5$ and $X_U = 25$. In terms of these finite limits and the data of Table 2-5, we have:

$$MS_{\text{Res}} = \frac{67(687.7216) + 65(789.9537)}{67 + 65} = 738.0632$$

$$\hat{Y}_{L(1)} = 82.1733 + 5(1.2618) = 88.4823$$

$$\hat{Y}_{L(2)} = 75.0042 + 5(.9372) = 79.6902$$

$$\hat{Y}_{U(1)} = 82.1733 + 25(1.2618) = 113.7183$$

$$\hat{Y}_{U(2)} = 75.0042 + 25(.9372) = 98.4342$$

$$SE^2_{\hat{Y}_{L(1)}} = 738.0632\left[\frac{1}{69} + \frac{(5 - 16.8841)^2}{4307.0733}\right] = 34.8981$$

$$SE^2_{\hat{Y}_{L(2)}} = 738.0632\left[\frac{1}{67} + \frac{(5 - 16.9403)^2}{3745.7391}\right] = 39.1081$$

$$SE^2_{\hat{Y}_{U(1)}} = 738.0632\left[\frac{1}{69} + \frac{(25 - 16.8841)^2}{4307.0733}\right] = 21.9837$$

$$SE^2_{\hat{Y}_{U(2)}} = 738.0632\left[\frac{1}{67} + \frac{(25 - 16.9403)^2}{3745.7391}\right] = 23.8154$$

$$t_L = \frac{88.4823 - 79.6902}{\sqrt{34.8981 + 39.1081}} = \frac{8.7921}{8.6027} = 1.02$$

$$t_U = \frac{113.7183 - 98.4342}{\sqrt{21.9837 + 23.8154}} = \frac{15.2841}{6.7675} = 2.26$$

$$t = \text{minimum}\,(1.02, 2.26) = 1.02$$

H_0 is not rejected since $t = 1.02$ is less than $t_{132:.95} = 1.66$.

Note that even though two statistical tests are being performed, using α for each, the problem of type I error compounding is not the same here as it is in the multiple-comparison situation where the Bonferroni procedure is recommended.

This is because in the latter situation each contrast is examined separately and declared statistically significant if it exceeds some critical value. Of course, as more and more contrasts are examined, the probability that at least one will exceed the critical value *by chance* increases. On the other hand, for the two regression lines to differ according to the present procedure, *both* contrasts must be significant as specified by the minimum t criterion. Thus, because each contrast must be significant, the type I error probability is the same conceptually as that associated with conducting only a single statistical test.

It is easy to show how the power of the test is influenced by the values of X_L and X_U that are selected by a researcher. If $X_L = 0$ and $X_U = 30$ had been selected here, we could see that t = minimum (.64, 1.84) = .64, which is lower than the value of 1.02 that was obtained with the narrower interval bounded by $X_L = 5$ and $X_U = 25$. In contrast, for intervals even narrower than the one we selected, the minimum t value would increase. Actually this is not as undesirable as it seems, since our inference would be restricted to the range of values selected for the independent variable. This means that exact statements can be made about the regression lines only over a restricted set of X values. As always, decisions regarding the particular end points of interest should be made in advance of hypothesis testing.

Incidentally it is worth noting that the test provides some information about the parallelism of the regression lines. If t_L and t_U are close to one another in value, there is evidence that the lines may be parallel for most practical stituations. On the other hand, if t_L and t_U are far apart, the evidence favors the existence of an ordinal interaction, with the lines coming together as X increases if $t_L > t_U$ or separating if $t_L < t_U$. Of course, these decisions are not statistically based; they are conclusions that follow from logical, and not statistical, considerations. The test, as described, can also be used to test nondirectional alternatives, in which case the minimum t is compared with $t_{v:1-\alpha/2}$.

Finally, we note that the method can be extended to treat the case involving multiple regression lines. The simplest procedure would be to perform pairwise comparisons with a splitting of the risk of a type I error across the number of comparisons that are to be made. For $C = 6$ pairwise comparisons for the data of Table 2-5, use could be made of the Bonferroni values of Table B-4. Six different rules would have to be used since the degrees of freedom for each test are different. On the other hand, it might also be justified to use across-sample pooled estimates of MS_{Res} and v when conducting the comparisons.

2-10. The problem of missing data

A problem that a researcher must face when performing a multivariate analysis is that of missing data. Unfortunately this problem seems to be the rule and rarely the exception, especially in large-scale experiments or field studies. No one truly knows what to do about missing data. A number of suggestions have been proposed, some of which are quite sophisticated, such as that in Timm (1970). We will consider some of the simpler models and will illustrate them for the pretest data of Table 1-1. As we see, the student with code number 179 was eliminated from subsequent analyses since no pretest score was available. Thus one possibility for dealing with missing data is to *eliminate* from the sample any subject with one or more pieces of missing information, as was done here.

There are, however, a variety of procedures for *estimating* missing data in order that the original sample may remain intact. What follows are some proposed estimation procedures that we will apply through examples to subject number 179.

1. Replace the missing score by the mean value of the subjects similar to the subject with the missing data. Subject number 179 comes from the middle social class, is male, has not had a previous high school class in sociology, and has a College Board score of 400 and a GPA of 3.09. Subjects 083, 104, and 118 are also from the middle social class, are male, and have not had a previous high school course in sociology. For these students, $\tilde{X}_i = 1/3(16 + 16 + 13) = 15$ can be used as the estimated value. While this estimate is on the low side, it may not be low enough since the GPA and CB scores are lower than those of the three similar students. A disadvantage of this method is that enough "similar" subjects may not exist. In addition, the aura of subjectivity associated with locating good matches may dissuade potential users of this approach.

2. Substitute the sample mean or, for skewed distributions, the sample median. If we were to follow this procedure, the unknown pretest score would be replaced by $\tilde{X}_i = 18.20$, or 18 rounded to the nearest integer. This method has the disadvantage of reducing the variance of X. If there are many such estimated values, imprecision can ensue for many of the multivariate procedures to be described. Thus it should be considered only when a few missing values exist.

3. Replace the missing value by $\bar{X} + Z_i S_X$, where $\bar{X}$ is the sample mean for the complete data, S_X is the sample standard deviation for the complete data, and Z_i is a random normal deviate selected from Appendix B-5. From Appendix B-5, $Z_i = .79$ was selected at random. With this value, the estimated value is $\tilde{X}_i = 18.20 + .79(7.50) = 24.12$, or 24 to the nearest integer. This method has the advantage of not reducing the variance of X. It has the disadvantage that it does not take regression toward the mean into consideration since it ignores the correlation that exists with other variables.

4. Estimate the missing value from a regression equation in which X is predicted from Y. In this case:

$$\hat{X}_i = \bar{X} + r_{XY}\frac{S_X}{S_Y}(Y_i - \bar{Y})$$

$$= 18.2051 + .5543\frac{7.50}{15.60}(Y_i - 46.0513)$$

$$= 18.2051 + .2665(46 - 46.0513) = 18.19 \simeq 18$$

5. Use the estimate from the preceding regression equation, along with a random normal variate and $S_{X \cdot Y}$, the residual standard deviation. For these data:

$$S_{X \cdot Y} = \sqrt{\frac{N-1}{N-2} S_X^2 (1 - r_{XY}^2)} = \sqrt{\frac{38}{37}(7.50)^2(.6928)} = 6.33$$

With the random deviate $Z_i = -.94$, the estimated value is:

$$\tilde{X} = 18.19 - .94(6.33) = 12.24 \simeq 12$$

Other methods could be proposed, but these are probably the simplest. However, the five here do provide varying estimates of 15, 18, 24, 18, and 12.

Another procedure that is used for correlational analyses is known as the pairwise deletion method. According to this method, all subjects are retained, but they contribute only to those pairs of variables for which they have data. Thus a subject who has information on variables 1 and 2, but not 3, would be included when computing $r_{X_1X_2}$, but not $r_{X_1X_3}$ or $r_{X_2X_3}$. Cohen and Cohen (1975) describe some negative aspects of this method.

In univariate analysis, it is often recommended that one degree of freedom be subtracted for each estimated value. We do not adhere to this recommendation throughout the text because we will usually be working with large samples. In our reading of contemporary practice, it seems that most researchers ignore this problem and statisticians seem to offer no sound or consistent advice concerning the treatment of missing data. About all that we can say is that multivariate analysis is frequently based on incomplete data and, as such, we suggest that practitioners consult with methodologists on how best to handle their missing data problems.

In this regard, both the elimination and estimation procedures discussed in this section depend on randomness of missing observations. That is, it is assumed that data are unsystematically missing, which implies that the characteristics of subjects with missing data are, on the average, the same as the characteristics of subjects with complete data. This assumption is not warranted in a good many research contexts. For example, with questionnaire data or survey research, nonresponses to particular questions, especially sensitive ones, are likely to be missing for a reason. If subjects who answer such questions are demographically different from subjects who do not, randomness cannot be assumed. An interesting approach for dealing with this problem and subsequently using this information to analyze the results of complete-data subjects is presented by Cohen and Cohen (1975) in their Chapter 7. An actual research example using this approach is given by Stumpf (1978). This specific technique capitalizes on the concepts of partial correlation and multiple regression, which are discussed in Chapter 3.

2-11. Summary

This chapter began with a comparison of correlation theory with regression theory. We saw that the difference in the two models was one based on the way the X, or independent variable, was viewed. In the correlation model, X is treated as a random variable with structure defined as:

$$X_i = \mu_X + \rho_{XY}\frac{\sigma_X}{\sigma_Y}(Y_i - \mu_Y) + \varepsilon_{X_i}$$

with the ε_X having a joint distribution with the ε_Y defined from:

$$Y_i = \mu_Y + \rho_{XY}\frac{\sigma_Y}{\sigma_X}(X_i - \mu_X) + \varepsilon_{Y_i}$$

On the other hand, regression theory makes the simpler assumption that the X_i values in the sample are not random variables, but are constants that are measured without error.

Now, if we add the powerful assumption that (X, Y) has a joint bivariate normal distribution, we can test the hypothesis:

H_0: $\rho_{XY} = 0$

by relating the sample correlation coefficient, r_{XY}, to:

$$t = \frac{r_{XY}\sqrt{N-2}}{\sqrt{1 - r_{XY}^2}}$$

Correlational theory is very limiting, however, in that satisfactory models have not been worked out only because the mathematics are so difficult. Because of this, much bivariate research must fall back on the models provided by regression theory even though it is known that the models do not apply to the data at hand. Thus, if a researcher believed that a quantitative skill variable was measured without error and that $Y_i = \beta_0 + \beta_1 X_i + \varepsilon_{Y_i}$, a test can be made of $\beta_1 = 0$ or that $\beta_1 = \beta_{1_0}$. In either case, the test statistic is given by:

$$t = \frac{B_1 - \beta_{1_0}}{SE_{B_1}}$$

where:

$$SE_{B_1}^2 = \frac{S_{Y \cdot X}^2}{(N-1)S_X^2}$$

In either case, H_0 would be rejected if $t < t_{N-2:\alpha/2}$ or if $t > t_{N-2:1-\alpha/2}$. This is not like the correlational model since the test that $\rho = \rho_0$ must be approached via the normal distribution through the Fisher z transformation (see Marascuilo, 1971), whereas the test of $\beta = \beta_{1_0}$ is performed via the t distribution. This difference also extends to the two-sample case in which the normal distribution and Fisher's z are used for testing $\rho_{XY(1)} = \rho_{XY(2)}$, whereas the t distribution is used for testing $\beta_{1(1)} = \beta_{1(2)}$. While the test statistic for this two-sample test was not presented in an explicit way, it is easy to show that $t = \sqrt{F}$ and that:

$$t = \frac{B_{1(1)} - B_{1(2)}}{\sqrt{MS_{\text{Res}}\left(\frac{1}{W_1} + \frac{1}{W_2}\right)}}$$

where:

$$W_1 = (N_1 - 1)S_{X(1)}^2$$

$$W_2 = (N_2 - 1)S_{X(2)}^2 \quad \text{and}$$

$$MS_{\text{Res}} = \frac{SS_{\text{Res}(1)} + SS_{\text{Res}(2)}}{N_1 + N_2 - 4}$$

The assumptions for this test are:

1. Observations between and within samples are independent.
2. The X_{ki} are measured without error.
3. The Y_{ki} are univariate normal random variables.
4. Variance about each regression line is homoscedastic and equal in the two populations.

Starting in Section 2-2, we began a thorough description of regression analysis. Because it is a univariate and not a bivariate model, terminology from the analysis of variance was adopted. First, it was seen that the total sum of squares of the deviation from $\bar{Y}$ could be decomposed as follows:

$$\sum_{i=1}^{N} (Y_i - \bar{Y})^2 = \sum_{i=1}^{N} (\hat{Y}_i - \bar{Y})^2 + \sum_{i=1}^{N} (Y_i - \hat{Y}_i)^2$$

or as:

$$SS_{\text{Total}} = SS_{\text{Regression}} + SS_{\text{Residual}}$$

with degrees of freedom given by:

$$(N - 1) = 1 + (N - 2)$$

It was also seen that:

$$r^2_{XY} = \frac{\sum_{i=1}^{N} (\hat{Y}_i - \bar{Y})^2}{\sum_{i=1}^{N} (Y_i - \bar{Y})^2} = \frac{SS_{\text{Regression}}}{SS_{\text{Total}}}$$

and that $H_0\!: \ \rho = 0$ or $H_0\!: \ \beta_1 = 0$ could be tested as a special case of:

$$F = \frac{\nu_2}{\nu_1}\left(\frac{\hat{\theta}^2}{1 - \hat{\theta}^2}\right)$$

with $\nu_1 = 1$ and $\nu_2 = N - 2$, and $\hat{\theta}^2 = r^2_{XY}$, so that the test statistic is defined as:

$$F = (N - 2)\left(\frac{r^2_{XY}}{1 - r^2_{XY}}\right)$$

The test of parallelism of two or more regression lines was then discussed, with the hypothesis represented by:

$$H_0\!: \ \beta_{1(1)} = \beta_{1(2)} = \cdots = \beta_{1(K)}$$

The test statistic for this hypothesis was given as:

$$F = \frac{\frac{1}{K - 1}\left(\sum_{k=1}^{K} W_k B^2_{1(k)} - B^2_{1(W)} \sum_{k=1}^{K} W_k\right)}{MS_{\text{Res}}}$$

where:

$$W_k = (N_k - 1)S^2_{X(k)}$$

$$B_{1(k)} = r_{XY(k)} \frac{S_{Y(k)}}{S_{X(k)}}$$

$$B_{1(W)} = \frac{\sum_{k=1}^{K} W_k B_{1(k)}}{\sum_{k=1}^{K} W_k}$$

$$MS_{\text{Residual}} = \frac{\sum_{k=1}^{K} SS_{\text{Res}(k)}}{N - 2K}$$

H_0 is rejected if:

$$F > F_{\nu_1,\nu_2:1-\alpha}$$

where $\nu_1 = K - 1$ and $\nu_2 = N - 2K$.

Both planned and post hoc comparison procedures were described for testing:

$$H_0: \quad \psi = 0$$

with ψ estimated as:

$$\hat{\psi} = \sum_{k=1}^{K} a_k B_{1(k)}$$

with:

$$\sum_{k=1}^{K} a_k = 0$$

$$SE_{\hat{\psi}} = \sqrt{MS_{\text{Res}} \sum_{k=1}^{K} \frac{a_k^2}{W_k}}$$

For Scheffé post hoc comparisons, the critical value is given by:

$$\mathbf{S} = \sqrt{\nu_1 F_{\nu_1\nu_2:1-\alpha}}$$

whereas, for a planned analysis, we determine C, the number of contrasts of interest, and then enter Table B-4 with $\alpha/2C$.

The analysis of covariance was investigated and it was seen that the hypothesis of equal intercepts:

$$H_0: \quad \beta_{0(1)} = \beta_{0(2)} = \cdots = \beta_{0(K)}$$

is identical to the hypothesis of equal adjusted mean values. This intercepts hypothesis, of course, depends on the truth of the assumption that the regression lines are parallel. In this case, the corresponding F ratio is referred to the F distribution with $\nu_1 = K - 1$ and $\nu_2 = N - K - 1$, and planned and post hoc contrasts are estimated as:

$$\hat{\psi} = \sum_{i=1}^{K} a_k[\bar{Y}_k - B_{1(W)}(\bar{X}_k - \bar{X})]$$

with:

$$SE_{\hat{\psi}}^2 = MS^*_{\text{Res}}\left(\sum_{i=1}^{K} \frac{a_k^2}{N_k} + \frac{\hat{\psi}_X^2}{SS_{X(W)}}\right)$$

where:

$$MS^*_{\text{Res}} = \frac{SS_{\text{Par}} + SS_{\text{Res}}}{\nu_{\text{Par}} + \nu_{\text{Res}}}$$

from the test of parallelism.

In addition, tests were described for testing $\beta_{1(W)} = 0$ and $\beta_{1(T)} = 0$. Tests for the identity of K regression lines and parallelism of regression lines over a finite interval were described and procedures for estimating missing data were examined.

2-12. Exercises

2-1. Is there reason to believe, at $\alpha = .01$, that $\rho_{XY} = 0$ for X: Pretest and Y: First midterm, on the basis of your sample of 40 students?

*2-2. Now determine the regression coefficient for the students in sociology-related careers and for those in nonsociology-related careers. Is there reason to believe, at $\alpha = .05$, that $\beta_{1(1)} = \beta_{1(2)}$? That is, are the population regression lines parallel?

*2-3. For the data of Exercise 2-2, test the analysis-of-covariance hypothesis that $\beta_{0(1)} = \beta_{0(2)}$ or, equivalently, that $\mu^A_{Y_1} = \mu^A_{Y_2}$. Use $\alpha = .05$.

2-4. Determine MS_{Res} for your sample of 40 for X: Pretest and Y: First midterm, and:

a. Test H_0: $\beta_1 = 0$, using $\alpha = .01$.

b. Set up a 95% confidence interval for β_0.

2-5. Test the hypothesis that the intercept of your regression line is equal to 25; that is, H_0: $\beta_0 = 25$. To do this, compute B_0 and the standard error of B_0, which is given by:

$$SE_{B_0} = \sqrt{\frac{\sum\limits_{i=1}^{N} X_i^2}{N}} \; SE_{B_1}$$

(This formula is derived in Section 4-5.) Then compute a t statistic, based on $\nu = N - 2$, using:

$$t = \frac{B_0 - 25}{SE_{B_0}}$$

Let $\alpha = .05$. The two-sided $100\,(1 - \alpha)\%$ confidence interval for β_0 is given by:

$$B_0 - t_{N-2:1-\alpha/2}SE_{B_0} < \beta_0 < B_0 + t_{N-2:1-\alpha/2}SE_{B_0}$$

2-6. Determine the 95% confidence interval for your sample regression line for X: Pretest and Y: First midterm. The limits are defined for selected values of X_0:

$$\hat{Y}_{\text{Lower limit}} = (B_0 + B_1X_0) - t_{N-2:1-\alpha/2}SE_{\hat{Y}_{X_0}}$$

$$\hat{Y}_{\text{Upper limit}} = (B_0 + B_1X_0) + t_{N-2:1-\alpha/2}SE_{\hat{Y}_{X_0}}$$

with:

$$SE_{\hat{Y}_{X_0}} = \sqrt{MS_{\text{Residual}}\left[\frac{1}{N} + \frac{(X_0 - \bar{X})^2}{(N-1)S_X^2}\right]}$$

Compare the intervals at $X_0 = 0$ and $X_0 = \bar{X}$. Note that if we wished to construct *simultaneous intervals* (that is, for all possible values of X_0 with a familywise type I error of α), t in the preceding formulas should be replaced by:

$$S = \sqrt{2F_{2,N-2:1-\alpha}}$$

(For additional discussion, see Serlin & Levin, 1980.)

2-7. Determine the 95% confidence interval for Y for a hypothetical individual (not in your sample) with $X_i = 25$, using X: Pretest and Y: First midterm. In this case:

$$SE_{\hat{Y}_{X_i}} = \sqrt{MS_{\text{Residual}}\left[1 + \frac{1}{N} + \frac{(X_i - \bar{X})^2}{(N-1)S_X^2}\right]}$$

Note the slight difference between the standard error of scores coming from within the sample ($SE_{\hat{Y}_{X_0}}$) and the standard error of a hypothetical score from outside ($SE_{\hat{Y}_{X_i}}$). The inclusion of the quantity 1 in the latter sum produces a larger standard error (that is, greater uncertainty) arising from the measurement error associated with predicting a new individual's score.

2-8. Perform a test at $\alpha = .01$ to determine whether the slope of your regression line differs from the slope of the regression line presented in the text. For the data of Table 1-2, $N = 39$, $B_1 = 1.1519$, $MS_{\text{Res}} = 173.0718$, and $S_X^2 = 56.3252$. Build a 99% confidence interval that follows from the statistical test. Can you think of anything that could potentially invalidate the preceding procedures in this case?

2-9. Repeat the analysis of Exercise 2-8 over the finite range $5 \leq X \leq 30$.

2-10. In the summary, the test of $\beta_{1(1)} = \beta_{1(2)}$ is presented as a t test. Show that $t^2 = F$ for $K = 2$, where:

$$F = \frac{W_1 B_{1(1)}^2 + W_2 B_{1(2)}^2 - (W_1 + W_2)B_{1(W)}^2}{MS_{\text{Res}}}$$

and $\quad W_1 = SS_{X_1} \quad$ and $\quad W_2 = SS_{X_2}$

2-11. In a longitudinal study where 58 third-grade slow readers were tested on five different occasions, the following correlations were observed for the scores taken at different time periods:

Time period	One	Two	Three	Four	Five
One	1.00	0.73	0.62	0.51	0.38
Two		1.00	0.79	0.52	0.40
Three			1.00	0.63	0.61
Four				1.00	0.76
Five					1.00

a. Is there any reason to believe ($\alpha = .05$ per test) that:
1. $\rho_{12} = \rho_{15}$?
2. $\rho_{12} = \rho_{45}$?

The test statistics for these two hypotheses are:

$$Z_1 = \frac{\sqrt{N}(r_{12} - r_{15})}{\sqrt{(1 - r_{12}^2)^2 + (1 - r_{15}^2)^2 - 2r_{25}^3 - (2r_{25} - r_{12}r_{15})(1 - r_{12}^2 - r_{15}^2 - r_{25}^2)}}$$

$$Z_2 = \frac{\sqrt{N}(r_{12} - r_{45})}{\sqrt{\begin{array}{c}(1 - r_{12}^2)^2 + (1 - r_{45}^2)^2 - r_{12}r_{45}(r_{14}^2 + r_{15}^2 + r_{24}^2 + r_{25}^2) \\ - 2(r_{14}r_{25} + r_{15}r_{24}) + 2(r_{12}r_{14}r_{15} + r_{12}r_{24}r_{25} + r_{14}r_{24}r_{45} + r_{15}r_{25}r_{45})\end{array}}}$$

where Z_1 and Z_2 are referred to the standard normal distribution (Table B-11).

b. How would you go about testing H_{0_1}: $\rho_{12} = \rho_{13} = \rho_{14} = \rho_{15}$ or

H_{0_2}: $\rho_{13} = \rho_{24} = \rho_{35}$ given the preceding formulas and the desire to control the familywise α subsumed by each hypothesis at .05?

(Thanks to Professor Ingram Olkin of Stanford University and Geoffrey Billiu of the University of Wisconsin for verifying these formulas!)

2.12. In a learning experiment reported by Ghatala, Levin, and Subkoviak (1975), 120 children were randomly assigned in equal numbers to four conditions. In all conditions, three tasks were administered: Task 1 was a *frequency judgment* (FJ) task, where the children studied a list in which words were repeated varying numbers of times throughout the list. On the test trial, the child's task was to indicate how many times each word had been presented previously. The number of erroneous judgments made (out of 40 possible) was recorded. Task 2 was a *modality judgment* (MJ) task, in which the children were instructed to rehearse a designated random half of the items in a word list and not to rehearse the other half. On the test trial, a given word was presented, and the children simply had to indicate whether or not they had been instructed to rehearse it. The number of erroneous judgments made (out of 80 possible) was recorded. Task 3 was a *discrimination learning* (DL) task, where the children were presented a list of 24 word pairs, with one word designated "correct" in each pair. On the test trial, the children were required to point to the previously designated "correct" word for each pair. The number of erroneous choices (out of 24 possible) was recorded.

The four experimental conditions differed according to the instructions subjects were given for the MJ and DL tasks. (Instructions were identical in all conditions for the FJ task.) In the Vocalization-Control condition, the children were told to *pronounce* the designated words in the MJ task, and were not given any special strategy to employ in the DL task. In the Vocalization-Strategy condition, the children were told to *pronounce* the designated words in *both* the MJ and DL tasks. The Imagery-Control and Imagery-Strategy conditions paralleled those just described, with the exception that the children were instructed to *generate visual images* of the words' referents (all words were concrete nouns).

The data for the study are summarized in Table A-2. The major hypothesis of interest—based on theoretical analyses of the tasks' component processes—was that the FJ task would be predictive of DL performance in the two control conditions, whereas the MJ task would be predictive of DL performance in the two strategy conditions. Other hypotheses related to mean performance differences were also tested.

Test the hypothesis that $\rho_{13} = 0$ in each condition. (Use $\alpha = .05$, one-tailed, per test.) Then test the hypothesis that $\rho_{23} = 0$ in each condition. (Again, use $\alpha = .05$, one-tailed, per test.) Finally, use the appropriate formula of Exercise 2-11 to test the hypothesis that $\rho_{13} = \rho_{23}$ in each condition. (Use $\alpha = .05$, one-tailed according to the differential predictions, per test.)

2.13. Based on the data of Table A-2, let X = MJ and Y = DL.

a. Compute $B_{1(k)}$ and $MS_{\text{Res}(k)}$ for each of the four conditions. What do you notice?

b. Test the hypothesis that all $\beta_{1(k)}$ are equal, using the F, U_0, and F^* statistics presented in Section 2-4. Use $\alpha = .05$ for each test.

c. A simultaneous Scheffé-like comparison procedure can be applied if the hypothesis in part (b) is rejected. For the U_0 statistic, compare:

$$\hat{\psi} = \sum_{k=1}^{K} a_k B_{1(k)} \qquad \text{(as in Section 2-5)}$$

with:

$$\sqrt{\chi^2_{K-1:1-\alpha}}\, SE_{\hat{\psi}}$$

where:

$$SE^2_{\hat{\psi}} = \sum_{k=1}^{K} \frac{a_k^2 \, MS_{\text{Res}(k)}}{SS_{X(k)}}$$

Assuming that the U_0 test in part (b) was rejected, determine whether the two control groups' slopes differ from those of the two strategy groups (simultaneous $\alpha = .05$).

2.14. Ignoring the fact that the four regression lines of Exercise 2-13 may not be parallel (and that their residual variances may not be equal), perform the standard analysis-of-covariance F test ($\alpha = .05$) on the four groups. If the test is significant, use the Scheffé simultaneous contrast procedure to identify differences in the adjusted means.

2.15. Sixteen high school males (volunteers in a physical education class) were randomly assigned to four conditions in which they were permitted differing amounts of sleep on a particular night:
Condition 1: 0 hours of sleep
Condition 2: 3 hours of sleep
Condition 3: 6 hours of sleep
Condition 4: 9 hours of sleep
Conditions were supervised such that during the nonsleep periods, subjects were engaged in "stay-awake" recreational activities (for example, reading or watching a movie). The next morning, each subject was given a test containing 60 items: 20 from each of three subtests which measured vocabulary, reasoning, and arithmetic skills, respectively.

The data are reported in full in Table A-3 (in the order in which they were collected, that is, one subject per morning over 16 consecutive days).

Let IQ be the predictor variable (X) and vocabulary subtest score be the criterion variable (Y). Ignoring the fact that the sample sizes are too small ($N_1 = N_2 = N_3 = N_4 = 4$) to employ parametric analyses with confidence, complete the following.

a. Test for the significance ($\alpha = .05$) of the planned comparison,

$$\text{H}_0: \quad \beta_{1(1)} = 1/3(\beta_{1(2)} + \beta_{1(3)} + \beta_{1(4)})$$

or that the slope of the group with *no* sleep is equal to that of the groups with *some* sleep.

b. Assuming parallelism, now test for the significance ($\alpha = .05$) of the same contrast as applied to the intercepts or:

$$\text{H}_0: \quad \beta_{0(1)} = 1/3(\beta_{0(2)} + \beta_{0(3)} + \beta_{0(4)})$$

2-16. For the data of Table A-3:

a. Compute the pooled *within-groups* (sleep conditions) *correlation* between IQ and reasoning subtest performance. Does your obtained value differ significantly ($\alpha = .05$, one-tailed) from zero?

b. Now compute the *across-groups correlation* and assess its significance ($\alpha = .05$, one-tailed).

c. Compare the two correlation coefficients just computed. What do you notice?

CHAPTER THREE

MULTIPLE CORRELATION AND REGRESSION THEORY

3-1. Introduction

In Chapters 1 and 2, our discussion focused on the linear relationship between one independent or predictor variable and one dependent or criterion variable. Techniques appropriate for this model were described in terms of simple correlation theory and simple linear regression analysis. As soon as a researcher employs two or more predictor variables, $X_1, X_2, \ldots, X_P$, the models expand to what are generally referred to as multiple correlation and multiple regression theory. As will be seen, these extended procedures generate a new variable $\hat{Y}$, which is simply a linear combination or composite of the predictor variables and which is maximally correlated with the criterion Y. Once the composite predictor has been established, the model may be interpreted exactly the same as in the single predictor variable model. This means that we can continue to examine and evaluate best-fitting straight-line relationships, simple correlation coefficients, the percent of the total sum of squares associated with the predictors, and other related characteristics. These now refer to multiple predictors taken collectively, however, and not to a single independent variable.

The rationale behind the multiple predictor approach is an intuitively appealing one in that more detailed information about individuals or sampling units typically permits a researcher to make more precise predictions about performances than could be done with only one piece of information. For example, in determining the insurance premium to charge a particular automobile driver, decisions can be made about risk of accident in terms of a single predictor variable, such as the driver's age. Correlating age with the number, severity, or cost of accidents during a fiscal time period, premium prices could be established. Such a correlation is not likely to be as high as one obtained when additional predictors, such as average number of miles driven per week, geographic data relating to weather and road conditions, type of vehicle driven, number of previous accidents, and others, are included in the prediction model. It is assumed that these several predictors are correlated with the accident criterion in such a manner that more efficient prediction can be obtained by using all or some of the predictors as a set, rather than any one of them alone. Statistical criteria for evaluating the effectiveness of this assumption will be presented later in this chapter. As will also be seen, the degree to which we can improve the prediction using many predictors depends on the intercorrelations that exist among the predictors themselves, in addition to the correlation that exists between each predictor and the criterion of interest.

Perhaps the easiest way to introduce multiple correlation and regression theory is by means of an example. For the example, we will again consider the data of Table 1-1. In particular, we will see how final test scores are related to the two midterm test scores. We will let Y refer to scores on the final examination, X_1 to the scores on the first midterm, and X_2 to the scores on the second midterm. The scores are listed in Table 3-1.

The simplest model that we could use to predict Y from X_1 and X_2 is given as:

$$\hat{Y} = B_0 + B_1X_1 + B_2X_2$$

where B_0, B_1, and B_2 are sample estimators of the unknown parameters β_0, β_1, and

TABLE 3-1. Data matrix for scores on two midterms and a final examination for 40 subjects

Subject number	*First midterm score* (X_1)	*Second midterm score* (X_2)	*Final examination,* (Y)
003	43	61	129
004	50	47	60
010	47	79	119
014	24	40	*100**
018	47	60	79
020	57	59	99
032	42	61	92
040	42	79	107
050	69	83	156
052	48	67	110
055	59	74	116
070	21	40	49
072	52	71	107
076	35	40	125
080	35	57	64
083	59	58	100
089	68	66	138
091	38	58	63
103	45	24	82
104	37	48	73
106	54	100	132
108	45	83	87
117	31	70	89
118	39	48	99
128	67	85	119
143	30	14	*100*
150	19	*55*	*84*
166	71	100	166
171	80	94	111
174	47	45	110
179	46	58	93
183	59	90	141
188	48	84	99
193	68	81	114
195	43	49	96
196	31	54	39
199	64	87	149
207	19	36	53
208	43	51	39
211	20	*59*	*91*
Mean	46.0500	62.8750	99.4750
S.D.	15.3956	20.0872	30.3230

* Figures in italics are estimated values.

β_2. As indicated, this represents the simple extension of the one predictor model to two predictors. Moreover, this model assumes that the two variables X_1 and X_2 do not "interact" with respect to predicting Y. A simple model that would build in a possible interaction between X_1 and X_2 is given by:

$$\hat{Y} = B_0 + B_1X_1 + B_2X_2 + B_3X_1X_2$$

If we let $X_3 = X_1X_2$, this model reduces to:

$$\hat{Y} = B_0 + B_1X_1 + B_2X_2 + B_3X_3$$

which is similar to the first model except that three predictor variables are used to describe the relationship with Y.

In like manner, regression analysis involving nonlinear terms can also be subsumed under this model. For example, if a researcher believes that the relationship between a predictor and a criterion variable is best described by a polynomial of the form:

$$\hat{Y} = B_0 + B_1X + B_2X^2 + B_3X^3$$

then direct use of the methods described in this chapter can be achieved by letting:

$$X_1 = X, \qquad X_2 = X^2, \qquad \text{and } X_3 = X^3$$

so that the model reduces to:

$$\hat{Y} = B_0 + B_1X_1 + B_2X_2 + B_3X_3$$

As can be seen, this is now similar to the previous model.

Note that a linear or additive model, of which multiple linear regression is an example, means that the coefficients applied to the variable generate a linear function. Thus $Y = \beta_0\log_e(\beta_1 + \beta_2X^{\beta_3})$ does not satisfy the criterion of linearity in β_0, β_1, β_2, and β_3, nor is there any simple way to make it linear. From the present discussion, it should be clear that not all models need be linear. We will not discuss these higher order models here, but will develop the theory and models for predicting Y from two independent variables X_1 and X_2 that are linear in β_0, β_1, and β_2. Then we will generalize the theory and model to more than two predictors. This should cause no problem, especially if the material in Chapters 1 and 2 has been understood.

As will be seen, multiple correlation and regression theory are simple extensions of the models of Chapter 2. The major differences are that the notation is more complex and the arithmetic becomes excessive and involved. As a consequence, we arrive at an important juncture in the development. A dependency on high-speed electronic computers for arithmetic computations is necessary. To attempt a multivariate analysis without an electronic computer would be folly. For this reason, much of what appears in later pages is taken directly from computer printouts. This means that we will not illustrate computational procedures to the same extent as we did in Chapters 1 and 2. Instead we will emphasize the reading of computer printouts to help in the analysis and interpretation of multivariate data. It is worth mentioning that it is in these complex multivariate situations that our simplified statistics, as laid down in Section 1-11, will be especially useful.

Let us begin by examining the data of Table 3-1, which lists the final exam scores, the two midterm test scores, and the estimated scores for all pieces of missing data. The estimated missing scores are shown in italics in Table 3-1. As we have indicated, multivariate methods require complete data for each observed element of the sample. In this case, missing data were estimated subjectively, by using Method 1 of Section 2-10. Our use of this method is not an endorsement of its use. As was pointed out earlier, it is not without its problems. We are merely applying it as a device for generating scores in this fictitious example.

3-2. Partial correlation

One way to approach multiple correlation theory is through partial correlation theory. As an example, consider the final test scores of Table 3-1, and the corresponding first and second midterm scores. For these data, $r_{YX_1} = .64$, $r_{YX_2} = .58$, and $r_{X_1X_2} = .67$. The correlation, $r_{X_1X_2} = .67$, suggests that part of the correlation between Y and X_1 could be confounded by the correlation that Y has with X_2 or that X_1 has with X_2. If the correlation that Y and X_1 have with X_2 could be removed, we would have a purer, or more refined, measure of the association between Y and X_1 that is free of the correlations with X_2. Such a measure of association is called a *partial correlation coefficient*. It serves as a measure of association between two variables after the linear effects of one of the variables is removed. By "linear effects" we mean the correlation or linear relationship between a third variable and the two to-be-correlated variables. In subsequent discussion, the term "linear" will be dropped, even though implied. We will now proceed to develop the concept of partial correlation.

For this development, let three variables be denoted X_1, X_2, and X_3, and let us consider the correlation between X_1 and X_2 when the effects of X_3 are "removed," "controlled," or "partialed out." For this, consider the regression of X_1 on X_3 as:

$$\hat{X}_{1\cdot 3} = \bar{X}_1 + B_{1\cdot 3}(X_3 - \bar{X}_3)$$

and the regression of X_2 on X_3 as:

$$\hat{X}_{2\cdot 3} = \bar{X}_2 + B_{2\cdot 3}(X_3 - \bar{X}_3)$$

With this notation:

$$(X_1 - \bar{X}_1) = (X_1 - \hat{X}_{1\cdot 3}) + (\hat{X}_{1\cdot 3} - \bar{X}_1)$$

corresponds to:

$$d_{TX_1} = d_{UX_1} + d_{EX_1}$$

and:

$$(X_2 - \bar{X}_2) = (X_2 - \hat{X}_{2\cdot 3}) + (\hat{X}_{2\cdot 3} - \bar{X}_2)$$

corresponds to:

$$d_{TX_2} = d_{UX_2} + d_{EX_2}$$

As indicated, the explained portions of the deviations that are related to the correlation involving X_3 are d_{EX_1} and d_{EX_2}. This means that the d_{UX_1} and the d_{UX_2} are free of X_3. If we compute these paired deviations for each of the N subjects and then determine a correlation coefficient based on them, we will have estimated the correlation between X_1 and X_2 after the effects of X_3 have been removed. If we denote this correlation coefficient as $r_{X_1X_2\cdot X_3}$, then:

$$r_{X_1X_2\cdot X_3} = \frac{1}{N-1}\sum_{i=1}^{N}\left(\frac{d_{UX_1} - \bar{d}_{UX_1}}{S_{d_{UX_1}}}\right)\left(\frac{d_{UX_2} - \bar{d}_{UX_2}}{S_{d_{UX_2}}}\right)$$

If we now substitute sample statistics into this definition and perform the resulting algebra, we obtain the following computing formula for $r_{X_1X_2 \cdot X_3}$.

The computing formula for $r_{X_1X_2 \cdot X_3}$.
The computing formula for the sample partial correlation coefficient between variables X_1 and X_2 when the effects of X_3 are removed is given as:

$$r_{X_1X_2 \cdot X_3} = \frac{r_{X_1X_2} - r_{X_1X_3}r_{X_2X_3}}{\sqrt{1 - r^2_{X_1X_3}}\sqrt{1 - r^2_{X_2X_3}}}$$

We now return to our original notation in which Y represents a dependent variable and X_1 and X_2 represent independent variables. Although correlation coefficients are usually reported to two decimal places, the computations underlying them should be based on as many significant digits as possible. This will reduce the chances of error from rounding decimal values. Thus, for five-decimal-place accuracy, we have for the data of Table 3-1 that:

$$r_{YX_1 \cdot X_2} = \frac{r_{YX_1} - r_{YX_2}r_{X_1X_2}}{\sqrt{1 - r^2_{YX_2}}\sqrt{1 - r^2_{X_1X_2}}} = \frac{.64438 - (.58482)(.67120)}{\sqrt{1 - .58482^2}\sqrt{1 - .67120^2}}$$

$$= \frac{.25185}{\sqrt{(.65799)(.54949)}} = \frac{.25185}{.60130} = .41884 \simeq .42$$

and:

$$r_{YX_2 \cdot X_1} = \frac{r_{YX_2} - r_{YX_1}r_{X_2X_1}}{\sqrt{1 - r^2_{YX_1}}\sqrt{1 - r^2_{X_2X_1}}} = \frac{.58482 - (.64438)(.67120)}{\sqrt{1 - .64438^2}\sqrt{1 - .67120^2}}$$

$$= \frac{.15231}{\sqrt{(.58477)(.54949)}} = \frac{.15231}{.56685} = .26869 \simeq .27$$

As can be seen for this example, the partial correlation coefficients are somewhat smaller than the zero-order correlations of the dependent variable with the two independent variables. For the first midterm, $r_{YX_1} = .64$, whereas $r_{YX_1 \cdot X_2} = .42$; for the second midterm, $r_{YX_2} = .58$, whereas $r_{YX_2 \cdot X_1} = .27$.

This reduction in the partial correlation coefficients happens since, in this example, all three variables are positively correlated and thus some of the variance between any two variables is shared with the third variable. When this shared, or common, relationship is removed statistically, the unique relationship that remains is smaller. However, one should not infer on the basis of this example that all partial correlations will behave in the same fashion. In some cases, a partial correlation may be larger than its zero-order correlation and in still other cases it may even be different in sign.

For example, suppose that X_1 and Y are correlated, with $r_{YX_1} > 0$, but that X_2 and Y are uncorrelated, with $r_{YX_2} = 0$. In this case, $r_{YX_1 \cdot X_2}$ reduces to:

$$r_{YX_1 \cdot X_2} = \frac{r_{YX_1}}{\sqrt{1 - r^2_{X_1X_2}}}$$

Regardless of the value of $r_{X_1X_2}$, we immediately see that $r_{YX_1 \cdot X_2} > r_{YX_1}$. For example, if $r_{YX_1} = .50$ and $r_{X_1X_2} = .50$, then $r_{YX_1 \cdot X_2} = .58$. Thus, even though X_2 is not correlated with Y, it still has an impact on the correlation of X_1 and Y through its correlation with X_1. In this case, the impact is to elevate the correlation. In other situations, it may change the sign of the correlation. Consider, for the same example, the situation in which r_{YX_2} is not zero, but a value very close to zero and positive, for example, $r_{YX_2} = .10$. Now, computation shows:

$$
\begin{aligned}
r_{YX_2 \cdot X_1} &= \frac{r_{YX_2} - r_{YX_1} r_{X_1X_2}}{\sqrt{1 - r^2_{YX_1}}\sqrt{1 - r^2_{X_1X_2}}} \\
&= \frac{.10 - .50(.50)}{\sqrt{1 - (.50)^2}\sqrt{1 - (.50)^2}} \\
&= \frac{.10 - .25}{.75} = \frac{-.15}{.75} = -.20
\end{aligned}
$$

Variables that cause zero-order correlations to move further from zero or to change signs when partialed out are often referred to as *suppressor* variables. As can be inferred from the present illustrations, the effect of suppressor variables on a partial correlation can be devastating, as far as interpretation goes. In practice, a researcher should be aware of such potential problems, especially when many independent variables are "thrown into" a multiple regression analysis. For an extended discussion of suppressor variables, see Cohen and Cohen (1975, pp. 84–91).

For now, and as an intuitive demonstration of what partial correlation accomplishes, let us consider a simplified data set based on $N = 12$ cases, presented in Table 3-2 and in Figure 3-1. In this example, let us assume that a group of elementary school children in the second, third, and fourth grades took a common 25-point arithmetic test. Let X_1 equal the child's height in inches, Y equal the score on the arithmetic test, and X_2 equal grade level. From Figure 3-1, note that a strong relationship exists between X_1 and Y across levels of X_2, but not within levels of X_2. The across-grade relationship is reflected by the zero-order correlation coefficient, which may be computed to be $r_{YX_1} = .7895$. However, we can show that grade level is very highly correlated with both height and arithmetic performance, since

TABLE 3-2. Hypothetical data set to illustrate partial correlation

Student number	*Arithmetic (Y)*	*Height (X_1)*	*Grade (X_2)*
1	15	49	2
2	17	51	2
3	17	49	2
4	15	51	2
5	18	51	3
6	20	53	3
7	20	51	3
8	18	53	3
9	21	53	4
10	23	55	4
11	23	53	4
12	21	55	4

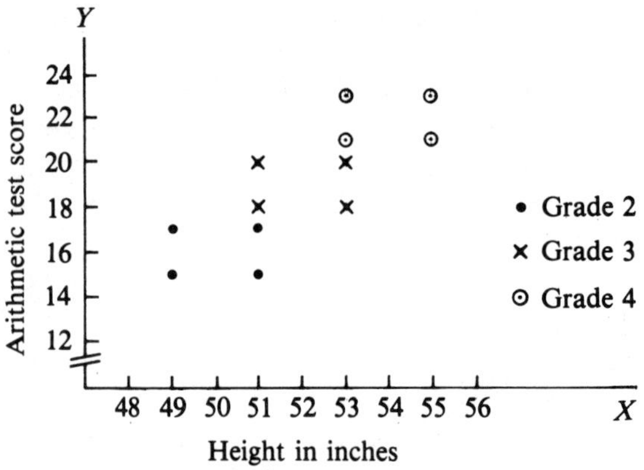

Figure 3-1. Scatterplot of the data of Table 3-2.

$r_{X_2X_1} = .8528$ and $r_{X_2Y} = .9258$. In fact, when these two correlations are considered in the numerator of $r_{YX_2 \cdot X_1}$, it is found that their product, .7895, is exactly equal to r_{YX_1}, thereby yielding a partial correlation $r_{YX_1 \cdot X_2} = 0$. Thus the partial correlation formula reproduces, statistically, what is visually apparent from Figure 3-1: no height-arithmetic relationship when grade level is controlled. The same conclusion would be reached by viewing the three grade levels as discrete groups and computing the pooled within-grade correlation as discussed in Section 2-6.

An example of a partial correlation exceeding its zero-order correlation is depicted in Figure 3-2, Example One, where the three ellipses represent levels of a third variable, X_2, such as age. Across X_2, the correlation is much smaller than it is within levels of X_2. Example Two of Figure 3-2 displays a positive relationship across levels of X_2, but a negative relationship within levels. Substantive illustrations to fit each of these examples may be found in the behavioral science and educational literature. In Example Two, for instance, X_1 and Y could represent the two variables typically used to measure the cognitive style construct known as reflectivity-impulsivity. Within any "homogeneous" population, the amount of time it takes to respond to a particular perceptual task (X_1) is found to be negatively correlated with the number of errors made on the task (Y). Consider the consequences, however, of including a large sample of students with visual-perceptual difficulties in the same study as their nonhandicapped age-mates. One might well expect the perceptually deficient students, $X_{2(2)}$, both to take the greatest amount of time to respond and to make the most errors, whereas nonhandicapped children, $X_{2(1)}$, would likely produce quicker response times and fewer errors. If so, the zero-order positive correlation between X_1 and Y would become a negative partial correlation between X_1 and Y, when X_2 is controlled. It is possible to construct a reasonable set of hypothetical data to fit each of these examples. The previously mentioned Cohen and Cohen (1975) discussion of suppressor effects is very relevant within the same context.

We provide here an intuitive explanation of how zero-order correlations and their associated partials can be opposite in sign. We do so by appealing to our prior discussion of across- and within-group relationships in Section 2-7. Recall that we assumed that K independent groups or levels of the X variable could be identified, as

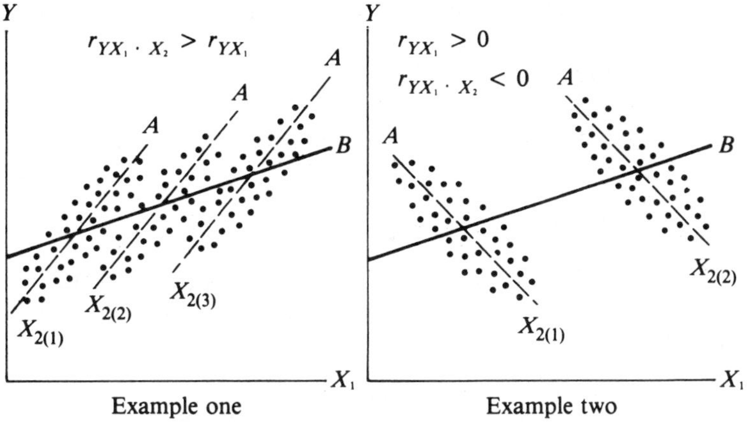

Figure 3-2. Examples of different across-variable and within-variable relationships.
Note: Line A represents the within-group relationship between X and Y; Line B represents the across-group relationship between X and Y.

required in the true regression problem. Given this assumption, the overall across-group relationship is reflected by $B_{1(T)}$ or $r_{XY(T)}$, and would have a numerator represented by the sum of cross-products:

$$SP_{XY(T)} = \sum_{k=1}^{K} \sum_{i=1}^{N_k} (X_{ki} - \bar{X})(Y_{ki} - \bar{Y})$$

However, by partitioning $SP_{XY(T)}$ in the manner of Section 2-7 so that

$$SP_{XY(T)} = SP_{XY(W)} + SP_{XY(B)},$$

we obtain:

$$SP_{XY(W)} = \sum_{k=1}^{K} \sum_{i=1}^{N_k} (X_{ki} - \bar{X}_k)(Y_{ki} - \bar{Y}_k)$$

$$\begin{aligned} SP_{XY(B)} &= SP_{XY(T)} - SP_{XY(W)} \\ &= \sum_{k=1}^{K} N_k(\bar{X}_k - \bar{X})(\bar{Y}_k - \bar{Y}) \end{aligned}$$

From this it is apparent that the across-group relationship $SP_{XY(T)}$ is derived from two additive components: the pooled within-group relationship, $SP_{XY(W)}$, and the relationship between X and Y produced by group centroid differences, $SP_{XY(B)}$. In analogous terms, the zero-order relationship, $SP_{XY(T)}$, is influenced not only by the first-order (partial) relationship, $SP_{XY(W)}$, but also by between-group effects, $SP_{XY(B)}$. When viewed from this perspective, we can appreciate how a positive zero-order correlation could be associated with a negative partial correlation, or vice versa. Specifically, suppose that $SP_{XY(W)}$ were negative. Now, $SP_{XY(T)}$ could be positive if the pattern of group centroid differences produced a positive relationship as, for instance, in Example Two of Figure 3-2. As long as the positive sum of cross-products associated with the group centroids $SP_{XY(B)}$ exceeded the negative sum of cross-products associated with the within-group relationship, $SP_{XY(W)}$, then $SP_{XY(T)}$ would be positive.

Partial correlations that involve the removal of two or more independent variables are encountered in great abundance in multivariate analysis. Since the arithmetic involved in determining higher order partial correlation coefficients is excessive, such correlations are usually found by means of electronic computers. The reason for this is easy to appreciate if we consider the partial correlation between two variables, X_1 and X_2, after having removed the effects of two other variables, X_3 and X_4. The appropriate formula is given by:

$$r_{X_1X_2 \cdot X_3X_4} = \frac{r_{X_1X_2 \cdot X_3} - r_{X_1X_4 \cdot X_3} r_{X_2X_4 \cdot X_3}}{\sqrt{1 - r^2_{X_1X_4 \cdot X_3}}\sqrt{1 - r^2_{X_2X_4 \cdot X_3}}}$$

and requires that $r_{X_1X_2 \cdot X_3}$, $r_{X_1X_4 \cdot X_3}$, and $r_{X_2X_4 \cdot X_3}$ be computed first. Alternatively the equivalent formula:

$$r_{X_1X_2 \cdot X_3X_4} = \frac{r_{X_1X_2 \cdot X_4} - r_{X_1X_3 \cdot X_4} r_{X_2X_3 \cdot X_4}}{\sqrt{1 - r^2_{X_1X_3 \cdot X_4}}\sqrt{1 - r^2_{X_2X_3 \cdot X_4}}}$$

requires that $r_{X_1X_2 \cdot X_4}$, $r_{X_1X_3 \cdot X_4}$, and $r_{X_2X_3 \cdot X_4}$ be computed first. In either case, it is apparent why a computer should be used to perform the necessary calculations. The results will have greater accuracy and less time will be wasted.

To help understand the nature of a partial correlation coefficient, we present a simple geometric demonstration of the properties of $r_{X_1X_2 \cdot X_3}$. For our geometric representation, consider the data of Table 3-3. Assume that each student is measured on three variables, X_1, X_2, and X_3. Now, suppose we wish to compute the correlation between X_1 and X_2 after the linear relationship between X_3 and each of these variables has been removed. Consider the regression of X_1 on X_3 and of X_2 on X_3, as depicted in Figure 3-3. Predicted values and unexplained deviations are reported in Table 3-4. As we recall, these unexplained deviations, or residuals, are

TABLE 3-3. Hypothetical set of three measures on five subjects

Subject number	X_1	*Variable* X_2	X_3
1	20	10	10
2	30	40	20
3	10	20	30
4	50	50	40
5	40	30	50

TABLE 3-4. Computations related to the data of Table 3-3, for which $\hat{X}_1 = 12.00 + .60X_3$ and $\hat{X}_2 = 15.00 + .50X_3$

Subject number	X_3	X_1	$\hat{X}_1$	du_{X_1}	X_2	$\hat{X}_2$	du_{X_2}
1	10	20	18	2	10	20	− 10
2	20	30	24	6	40	25	15
3	30	10	30	− 20	20	30	− 10
4	40	50	36	14	50	35	15
5	50	40	42	− 2	30	40	− 10

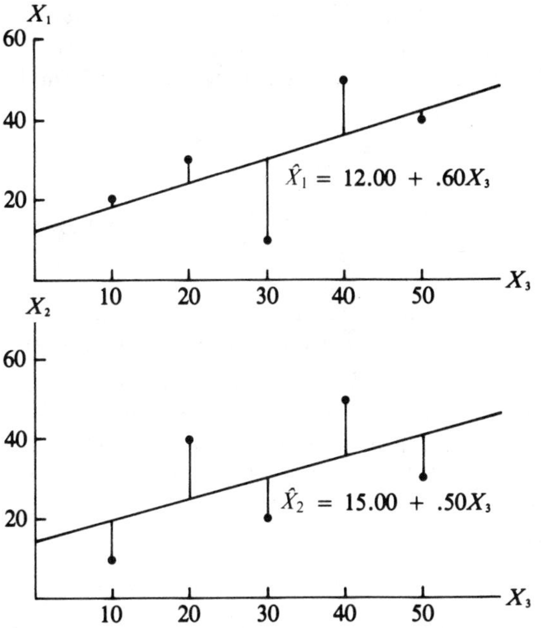

Figure 3-3. Regression of X_1 on X_3 and of X_2 on X_3 for the data of Table 3-3.

defined as the difference between a predicted and observed value. These are the vertical distances in Figure 3-3. Note when comparing the two sets of deviations of Table 3-4 or Figure 3-3 that the three students with the smallest residuals when predicting X_1 from X_3 (Students 1, 3, and 5) also have the smallest residuals when predicting X_2 from X_3. Similarly, the two students with the largest residuals when predicting X_2 from X_3 (Students 2 and 4) also have the largest residuals when X_1 is predicted from X_3. Thus the residuals appear to be correlated.

To see this from another point of view, examine Figure 3-4 where the paired

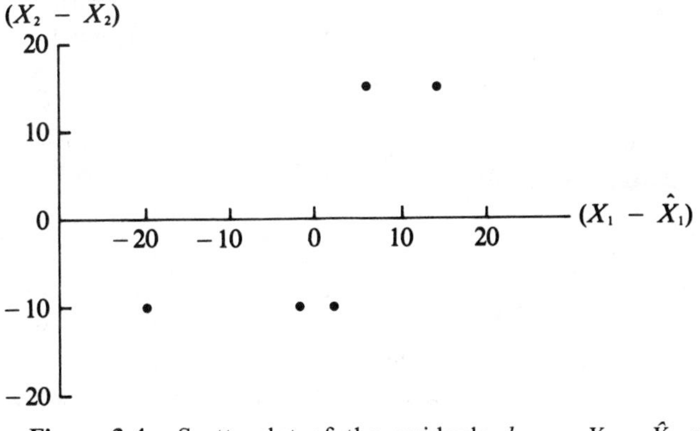

Figure 3-4. Scatterplot of the residuals $d_{U_{X_1}} = X_1 - \hat{X}_1$ and $d_{U_{X_2}} = X_2 - \hat{X}_2$ of Table 3-4.

residuals have been plotted. The correlation coefficient associated with these data is given by $r_{(X_1-\hat{X}_1)(X_2-\hat{X}_2)} = .722$. One can show that $r_{X_1X_3} = .60$, $r_{X_2X_3} = .50$, and $r_{X_1X_2} = .80$. Thus, according to the computational formula:

$$r_{X_1X_2 \cdot X_3} = \frac{.80 - .60(.50)}{\sqrt{(1 - .60^2)(1 - .50^2)}} = .72$$

the same value determined directly from the residuals.

3-3. Assessing the statistical significance of a partial correlation coefficient

The partial correlation coefficient $r_{X_1X_2 \cdot X_3}$ can be tested for statistical significance in similar fashion to that for a zero-order correlation coefficient $r_{X_1X_2}$, as discussed in Section 2-3. However, instead of the test being based on $N - 2$ degrees of freedom, it is based on $N - 3$ degrees of freedom. Thus the statistic:

$$t = \frac{r_{X_1X_2 \cdot X_3}\sqrt{N - 3}}{\sqrt{1 - r^2_{X_1X_2 \cdot X_3}}}$$

is referred to the t distribution with $\nu = N - 3$ degrees of freedom. In a similar way, $r_{X_1X_2 \cdot X_3X_4}$ can be tested with:

$$t = \frac{r_{X_1X_2 \cdot X_3X_4}\sqrt{N - 4}}{\sqrt{1 - r^2_{X_1X_2 \cdot X_3X_4}}}$$

and is referred to the t distribution with $\nu = N - 4$.

For the data of Table 3-1, we could test the hypothesis that there is no linear relationship between second midterm X_2 and final scores Y when the effect of first midterm scores X_1 has been removed. Thus let us test the statistical hypothesis:

$$H_0: \quad \rho_{YX_2 \cdot X_1} = 0$$

using $\alpha = .05$. With $N = 40$, $\nu = N - 3 = 37$, and the critical values are given by $t_{37:.025} = -2.03$ and $t_{37:.975} = 2.03$. If one could justify looking for a positive relationship only, the appropriate one-tailed critical value is given by $t_{37:.95} = 1.69$. For the observed data:

$$t = \frac{.26869\sqrt{40 - 3}}{\sqrt{1 - .26869^2}} = 1.70$$

which would be statistically significant according to the one-tailed decision rule, but not according to the two-tailed decision rule. Based on the one-tailed decision, we would conclude that second midterm and final scores were positively correlated, even when the first midterm scores were controlled. Based on the two-tailed decision, we would conclude that they were not correlated.

Procedure for testing a partial correlation coefficient for significance where the number of partialed out variables is equal to V.

Step 1. Compute the partial correlation coefficient of interest. Let r represent the partial correlation with V variables partialed out.

Step 2. To test H_0: $\rho = 0$, compute:

$$t = \frac{r\sqrt{(N-2) - V}}{\sqrt{1 - r^2}}$$

Step 3. Reject H_0 if:

$$t < t_{(N-2)-V:\alpha/2} \text{ or if } t > t_{(N-2)-V:1-\alpha/2}$$

It should be apparent from the preceding directions that these represent very general formulas that could be applied even in the case of zero-order correlations. There, no variables would be partialed out and thus $V = 0$.

Finally, as an extension of a comment made in Section 2-3, it is possible to test the hypothesis that a partial correlation is equal to some specified nonzero value, or that two or more partial correlations are equal to one another. To do so requires the use of the Fisher r-to-z transformation, however (see Marascuilo, 1971).

3-4. Estimation of the beta weights and residual variance

The computation of the *beta weights*, as they are referred to in both multiple correlation and regression theory, is an easy process once the partial correlation coefficients are known. For two independent variables, the formula for the beta weights is as follows.

The beta weights for two independent variables.
The beta weights for two independent variables are computed as:

$$B_1 = r_{YX_1 \cdot X_2}\left(\frac{S_Y\sqrt{1 - r^2_{YX_2}}}{S_{X_1}\sqrt{1 - r^2_{X_1X_2}}}\right)$$

$$B_2 = r_{YX_2 \cdot X_1}\left(\frac{S_Y\sqrt{1 - r^2_{YX_1}}}{S_{X_2}\sqrt{1 - r^2_{X_2X_1}}}\right) \quad \text{and}$$

$$B_0 = \bar{Y} - B_1\bar{X}_1 - B_2\bar{X}_2$$

As can be seen, these equations are simple extensions of the formulas given in Section 1-8 for estimating β_0 and β_1 for one independent variable. For more than two independent variables, these formulas generalize in an expected manner.

However, since they are always found by prewritten computer programs, we will not generalize the results.

Using the $S^2_{Y \cdot X}$ notation introduced in Chapter 2 to represent variance in one variable remaining after the variance due to its linear relationship with another variable is removed, we can make the formulas for B_1 and B_2 resemble the definition of a one-predictor variable beta weight given in Chapter 1. As we recall:

$$B_1 = r_{XY}\frac{S_Y}{S_X}$$

In like manner:

$$B_1 = r_{YX_1 \cdot X_2}\frac{S_{Y \cdot X_2}}{S_{X_1 \cdot X_2}}$$

where $r_{YX_1 \cdot X_2}$ is as defined in Section 3-2, and where $S^2_{Y \cdot X_2}$ is defined as:

$$S^2_{Y \cdot X_2} = \frac{(N-1)S^2_Y(1 - r^2_{YX_2})}{N-2} = \frac{SS_Y(1 - r^2_{YX_2})}{N-2} = MS_{\text{Res}(Y \cdot X_2)}$$

or the mean square residual when predicting Y from X_2. In similar fashion:

$$S^2_{X_1 \cdot X_2} = \frac{(N-1)S^2_{X_1}(1 - r^2_{X_1X_2})}{N-2} = \frac{SS_{X_1}(1 - r^2_{X_1X_2})}{N-2} = MS_{\text{Res}(X_1 \cdot X_2)}$$

represents the mean square residual when predicting X_1 from X_2. Thus the formula for B_1:

$$B_1 = r_{YX_1 \cdot X_2}\sqrt{\frac{MS_{\text{Res}(Y \cdot X_2)}}{MS_{\text{Res}(X_1 \cdot X_2)}}}$$

is identical to that given previously.

For the data of Table 3-1:

$$B_1 = (.41884)\frac{30.3230\sqrt{1 - .58482^2}}{15.3956\sqrt{1 - .67120^2}} = .9027$$

$$B_2 = (.26869)\frac{30.3230\sqrt{1 - .64438^2}}{20.0872\sqrt{1 - .67120^2}} = .4184 \quad \text{and}$$

$$\begin{aligned} B_0 &= 99.4750 - .9027(46.0500) - .4184(62.8750) \\ &= 31.5955 \end{aligned}$$

Thus the equation relating the final test scores to the two midterm scores is given by:

$$\hat{Y} = 31.5955 + .9027X_1 + .4184X_2$$

or, to two decimal points:

$$\hat{Y} = 31.60 + .90X_1 + .42X_2$$

To report the results in deviation form, we see that, to two decimal places:

$$\hat{Y} = \bar{Y} + B_1(X_1 - \bar{X}_1) + B_2(X_2 - \bar{X}_2)$$
$$= 99.48 + .90(X_1 - 46.05) + .42(X_2 - 62.88)$$

In terms of standard scores, the corresponding regression equation is given as:

$$\frac{\hat{Y} - \bar{Y}}{S_Y} = b_1\left(\frac{X_1 - \bar{X}_1}{S_{X_1}}\right) + b_2\left(\frac{X_2 - \bar{X}_2}{S_{X_2}}\right)$$

or

$$\hat{Z}_Y = b_1 Z_1 + b_2 Z_2$$

where:

$$b_1 = B_1 \frac{S_{X_1}}{S_Y} \quad \text{and} \quad b_2 = B_2 \frac{S_{X_2}}{S_Y}$$

In this form, the weights are called *standardized beta weights*. For the data of Table 3-1:

$$b_1 = .9027 \frac{15.3956}{30.3230} = .4583$$

$$b_2 = .4184 \frac{20.0872}{30.3230} = .2772$$

Thus, in terms of standard scores:

$$\hat{Z}_Y = .4583 Z_{X_1} + .2772 Z_{X_2}$$

This equation will be reexamined in Section 3-5, where its connection with measures of explained variance will be demonstrated.

For completeness, we define standardized beta weights and regression equations for P predictors.

Definition of standardized beta weights.
Let $B_1, B_2, \ldots, B_P$ be the estimates for:

$$\hat{Y} = B_0 + B_1 X_1 + B_2 X_2 + \cdots + B_P X_P$$

The standardized beta weights for the standard score regression equation:

$$\hat{Z}_Y = b_1 Z_{X_1} + b_2 Z_{X_2} + \cdots + b_P Z_{X_P}$$

are defined as:

$$b_1 = B_1 \frac{S_{X_1}}{S_Y}, b_2 = B_2 \frac{S_{X_2}}{S_Y}, \ldots, b_P = B_P \frac{S_{X_P}}{S_Y}$$

A little reflection shows that a standardized beta weight can be written as:

$$b_1 = r_{YX_1 \cdot X_2}\sqrt{\frac{1 - r^2_{YX_2}}{1 - r^2_{X_1X_2}}}$$

$$= \frac{r_{YX_1} - r_{YX_2}r_{X_1X_2}}{\sqrt{(1 - r^2_{YX_2})(1 - r^2_{X_1X_2})}}\sqrt{\frac{1 - r^2_{YX_2}}{1 - r^2_{X_1X_2}}}$$

$$= \frac{r_{YX_1} - r_{YX_2}r_{X_1X_2}}{1 - r^2_{X_1X_2}}$$

This form may be convenient for certain purposes. In all cases, b_1, and thus B_1, are closely tied to the corresponding partial correlation coefficient and will always bear the same sign, unlike the situation for partial and zero-order correlations as, for example, in Example Two of Figure 3-2. Some of these properties will prove useful in our later section on simplified statistics for multiple regression.

Three points should be made in relation to the standardized beta weights. First, they are directly comparable with one another since they are on the same scale, whereas unstandardized weights are not. This does not mean that they represent information concerning a particular variable's *importance* since they do not reveal the influence of suppressor variables (see Cohen and Cohen, 1975). Second, in the special case where there is only one predictor variable, it is obvious that $b_1 = r_{XY}$, since $B_1 = r_{XY}(S_Y/S_X)$ and $b_1 = B_1(S_X/S_Y)$. Finally, whenever the partialed out variable X_2 is equally correlated with its two constituents Y_1 and X_1, then $b_1 = r_{YX_1 \cdot X_2}$, so that the standardized beta weight is simply a partial correlation.

The interpretation of beta weights corresponds exactly to that given for the one-predictor problem. The value of B or b indicates the average increase in Y for every unit increase in X. For B these values are given in raw scale units, whereas for b they are given in standard deviation units. Thus, for the unstandardized equation:

$$\hat{Y} = 31.5995 + .9027X_1 + .4184X_2$$

we would conclude that an individual's final test score will be .9027 points higher for each additional first midterm point. Similarly, a one-point increase on the second midterm is worth .4184 points more on the final. The predicted final score (to two-decimal-point accuracy) for anyone whose score corresponded to the average on both midterms, $\bar{X}_1 = 46.05$ and $X_2 = 62.88$, is given by:

$$\hat{Y} = 31.60 + .90(46.05) + .42(62.88) = 99.45$$

or simply the mean on the final. For the standardized equation:

$$\hat{Z}_Y = .4583Z_{X_1} + .2772Z_{X_2}$$

we would conclude that an individual's final test score will be .4583 standard deviation units higher for each additional standard deviation unit increase on the first midterm and .2772 standard deviation units higher for each additional standard deviation unit increase on the second midterm. It is worth noting that, because $S_Y = 30.3230$ points, .4583 standard deviation units is equivalent to .4583(30.3230) = 13.8979 points. Also, since $S_{X_1} = 15.3956$ points, the ratio 13.8979/15.3956 indicates the amount of increase in Y relative to X. This will be found to equal .9027, or the unstandardized beta weight for X_1.

As an example of the use of $\hat{Y}$ as a prediction equation, we see that for Subject 003:

$$\hat{Y} = 31.5955 + .9027(43) + .4184(61) = 95.9371$$

Since the actual score on the test for Subject 003 is equal to $Y = 129$, the prediction is not too precise. The deviation between Y and $\hat{Y}$ for this subject is given by $Y - \hat{Y} = 33.0629$. The remaining estimated scores and residuals are reported in Table 3-5 with 2-place decimal accuracy.

The variance about the prediction plane can be computed directly from the residuals. Since the $\hat{Y}$ values are restricted by the three estimators B_0, B_1, and B_2, the

TABLE 3-5. Table of residuals for the 40 students of Table 3-1

Student number	Y_i	$\hat{Y}_i$	$Y_i - \hat{Y}_i$
003	129	95.94	33.06
004	60	96.40	− 36.40
010	119	107.08	11.92
014	100	70.00	30.00
018	79	99.13	− 20.13
020	99	107.74	− 8.74
032	92	95.03	− 3.03
040	107	102.57	4.43
050	156	128.61	27.39
052	110	102.96	7.04
055	116	115.82	0.18
070	49	67.29	− 18.29
072	107	108.25	− 1.25
076	125	79.93	45.07
080	64	87.04	− 23.04
083	100	109.13	− 9.13
089	138	120.60	17.40
091	63	90.17	− 27.17
103	82	82.26	− 0.26
104	73	85.08	− 12.08
106	132	122.19	9.81
108	87	106.95	− 19.95
117	89	88.87	0.13
118	99	86.89	12.11
128	119	127.64	− 8.64
143	100	64.54	35.46
150	84	71.76	12.24
166	166	137.53	28.47
171	111	143.15	− 32.15
174	110	92.85	17.15
179	93	97.39	− 4.39
183	141	122.52	18.48
188	99	110.07	− 11.07
193	114	126.87	− 12.87
195	96	90.92	5.08
196	39	82.18	− 43.18
199	149	125.77	23.23
207	53	63.81	− 10.81
208	39	91.75	− 52.75
211	91	74.34	16.66

residual variance is defined as:

$$MS_{\text{Res}(Y\cdot X_1X_2)} = S_U^2 = S_{Y\cdot X_1X_2}^2 = \sum_{i=1}^{N} \frac{(Y_i - \hat{Y}_i)^2}{N-3}$$

$$= \frac{1}{40-3}[(33.06)^2 + (-36.40)^2 + \cdots + (16.66)^2]$$

$$= \frac{1}{37}(19455.7420)$$

$$= 525.8309$$

with 4-place decimal accuracy.

Note that the sum of squares residual, unexplained, error, and so on is simply the numerator of $MS_{\text{Res}(Y\cdot X_1X_2)}$. In this case:

$$SS_{\text{Res}(Y\cdot X_1X_2)} = \sum_{i=1}^{N} (Y_i - \hat{Y}_i)^2 = 19455.7420$$

For P predictor variables, $MS_{\text{Res}(Y\cdot X_1X_2\ldots X_P)}$ is defined as follows.

Definition of the mean square residual for *P* predictors.
The estimate of the residual variance about the estimated regression equation for P predictor variables is given by:

$$MS_{\text{Res}(Y\cdot X_1X_2\ldots X_P)} = \frac{1}{N-P-1} \sum_{i=1}^{N} (Y_i - \hat{Y}_i)^2$$

For $P = 1$, the definition of $MS_{\text{Res}(Y\cdot X_1)}$ reduces to the form developed in Sections 2-2 and 2-3.

3-5. The multiple correlation coefficient

At this point, we introduce a statistic that will prove useful in understanding the rationale behind multiple regression. Recall that, for the Y variable in the two-variable model:

$$SS_{\text{Regression}} + SS_{\text{Residual}} = SS_{\text{Total}}$$

and that:

$$r_{XY}^2 = \frac{SS_{\text{Reg}}}{SS_{\text{Tot}}}$$

This partitioning of a sum of squares and determination of a measure of association can be extended to the case in which there is more than one predictor variable, so that we can similarly compute SS_{Reg}, SS_{Res}, and SS_{Tot} on the basis of all P predictor variables.

For our example with $P = 2$, we have seen that $SS_{\text{Res}} = 19456.11612$. In addition, we have seen that with two-decimal-point accuracy the total sum of squares for Y is given by

$$SS_{\text{Tot}} = (N-1)S_Y^2 = 39(30.3230)^2 = 35859.89.$$

In addition:

$SS_{\text{Reg}} = 35859.89 - 19456.12 = 16403.77$ and:

$SS_{\text{Reg}}/SS_{\text{Tot}} = 16403.77/35859.89 = .457.$

This ratio is analogous to r^2_{XY} and is called the squared *multiple correlation coefficient* and is denoted by $\hat{R}^2_{Y \cdot X_1 X_2}$. It is interpreted exactly like r^2_{XY} in the bivariate situation. For P predictor variables, we denote the squared multiple correlation coefficients as $\hat{R}^2_{Y \cdot X_1 X_2 \cdots Y_P}$. For completeness, we now provide a definition of the squared multiple correlation coefficient and its associated measure of unexplained variance.

Definition of the multiple correlation coefficient and unexplained variance. The square of the multiple correlation coefficient is defined as:

$$\hat{R}^2 = \frac{SS_{\text{Explained}}}{SS_{\text{Total}}} = \frac{\sum_{i=1}^{N} (\hat{Y}_i - \bar{Y})^2}{\sum_{i=1}^{N} (Y_i - \bar{Y})^2}$$

In terms of the squared multiple correlation coefficient:

$$S^2_{\text{Unexplained}} = S^2_U = MS_{\text{Res}(Y \cdot X_1 X_2 \ldots X_P)}$$

$$= \frac{N - 1}{N - P - 1} S^2_Y (1 - \hat{R}^2)$$

Another way to define $\hat{R}_{Y \cdot X_1 X_2 \ldots X_P}$ is to define it as the correlation coefficient between the observed Y values and their predicted values, $\hat{Y}$, determined from the prediction equation. Thus, $\hat{R}_{Y \cdot X_1 X_2 \ldots X_P} = \hat{R}_{Y\hat{Y}}$. Even though we have not provided a proof, it is of interest to mention that the B_P are derived so that $\hat{R}_{Y \cdot X_1 X_2 \ldots X_P}$ will be maximized, given the data. Thus, for the present example, there is no linear combination of X_1 and X_2 that will produce an $\hat{R}_{Y \cdot X_1 X_2}$ greater than $\sqrt{.457} = .676$, the value produced when the weights applied to X_1 and X_2 consist of $B_1 = .9027$ and $B_2 = .4184$.

Note that $\hat{R}_{Y \cdot X_1 X_2 \ldots X_P} = r_{\hat{Y}Y}$ represents a simple extension of the bivariate property, $r_{XY} = r_{\hat{Y}Y}$, as discussed in Section 1-10. At this point, another correspondence will be described. Recall that a squared correlation coefficient can be interpreted as the proportion of variance in Y accounted for by $\hat{Y}$. In Section 1-10, this was proved by showing that $S^2_{\hat{Y}} = r^2_{XY} S^2_Y$, so that $r^2_{XY} = S^2_{\hat{Y}}/S^2_Y$. Since $\hat{R}_{Y \cdot X_1 X_2 \ldots X_P}$ and r_{XY} have similar meanings, the same can be said for the squared multiple correlation $\hat{R}^2_{Y \cdot X_1 X_2 \ldots X_P}$. For this reason, it is possible to derive simple computing formulas for the multiple correlation coefficient. We now develop some of these formulas.

To do this, let us recall some basic concepts from elementary statistics. In particular, let V_1 and V_2 represent two random variables which are not necessarily independent. Suppose a new variable T is constructed from V_1 and V_2 and is defined as the linear combination, $T = a_1 V_1 + a_2 V_2$, where a_1 and a_2 represent chosen constants. If the variances of V_1 and V_2 are known, as well as the covariance between them, the variance of T is easily determined as:

$$\text{Var}(T) = a_1^2\text{Var}(V_1) + a_2^2\text{Var}(V_2) + 2a_1a_2\text{Cov}(V_1, V_2)$$

Let us now use this property, along with the fact that $\hat{R}^2_{Y \cdot X_1X_2 \ldots X_P} = S^2_{\hat{Y}}/S^2_Y$, to compute the multiple correlation coefficient for the case of $P = 2$.

As we saw in Section 3-4, the regression equation describing our present example can be written in standard form as:

$$\hat{Z}_Y = .4583Z_{X_1} + .2772Z_{X_2}$$

If we compute the variance of $\hat{Z}_Y$, we have:

$S^2_{\hat{Z}_Y} = (.4583)^2S^2_{Z_{X_1}} + (.2772)^2S^2_{Z_{X_2}} + 2(.4583)(.2772)S_{Z_{X_1}}S_{Z_{X_2}}r_{X_1X_2}$, where $S_{Z_{X_1}}S_{Z_{X_2}}r_{X_1X_2}$ is simply the covariance between Z_{X_1} and Z_{X_2}. Note that $r_{Z_{X_1}Z_{X_2}} = r_{X_1X_2}$ since, as shown in Section 1-10, the correlation between X and Y is not affected by standardization. For this example, $r_{X_1X_2} = .6712$. Recalling that $S^2_{Z_{X_1}} = S^2_{Z_{X_2}} = 1.00$, we find that:

$$\begin{aligned} S^2_{\hat{Z}_Y} &= .4583^2 + .2772^2 + 2(.4583)(.2772)(.6712) \\ &= .4574 = \hat{R}^2_{Y \cdot X_1X_2} \end{aligned}$$

Finally, since $S^2_{Z_Y} = 1.00$, we note that the ratio $\hat{R}^2_{Y \cdot X_1X_2} = S^2_{\hat{Z}_Y}/S^2_{Z_Y}$ reduces to $S^2_{\hat{Z}_Y}$. Thus, when the standardized regression equation is used, the variance of predicted scores is equal to the squared multiple correlation coefficient. In general, for $P = 2$:

$$\hat{R}_{Y \cdot X_1X_2} = \sqrt{b_1^2 + b_2^2 + 2b_1b_2r_{X_1X_2}}$$

which generalizes to $P > 2$ as:

$$\hat{R}_{Y \cdot X_1X_2 \ldots X_P} = \sqrt{\sum_{p=1}^{P} b_p^2 + 2\sum_{p=1}^{P}\sum_{p'=1}^{P} b_pb_{p'}r_{X_pX_{p'}}} \qquad p < p'$$

We now provide some alternative formulas for $\hat{R}_{Y \cdot X_1X_2 \ldots X_P}$ which may prove useful under different circumstances. These are developed by substituting equivalent terms. For standardized beta weights b_p written in terms of correlation coefficients only, it can be shown that for $P = 2$, a convenient computing formula is given by:

$$\hat{R}_{Y \cdot X_1X_2} = \sqrt{\frac{r^2_{YX_1} + r^2_{YX_2} - 2r_{YX_1}r_{YX_2}r_{X_1X_2}}{1 - r^2_{X_1X_2}}}$$

An algebraically equivalent version is given by:

$$\hat{R}_{Y \cdot X_1X_2} = \sqrt{r_{YX_1}b_1 + r_{YX_2}b_2}$$

which extends directly as:

$$\hat{R}_{Y \cdot X_1X_2 \ldots X_P} = \sqrt{\sum_{p=1}^{P} r_{YX_p}b_p}$$

For completeness, we give a general method for computing $\hat{R}^2_{Y \cdot X_1X_2 \ldots X_P}$.

Procedure for computing $\hat{R}^2_{Y \cdot X_1 X_2 \ldots X_P}$.

Step 1. Determine the correlation coefficients among the predictor or independent variables $X_1, X_2, \ldots, X_P$.

Step 2. Determine the correlation coefficients of each X_P with Y.

Step 3. Determine the P standardized beta weights, $b_1, b_2, \ldots, b_P$.

Step 4. Compute:

$$\hat{R}^2_{Y \cdot X_1 X_2 \ldots X_P} = \sum_{p=1}^{P} b_p^2 + 2 \sum_{p=1}^{P} \sum_{p'=1}^{P} b_p b_{p'} r_{X_p X_{p'}} \qquad p < p'$$

or, alternatively:

$$\hat{R}^2_{Y \cdot X_1 X_2 \ldots X_P} = \sum_{p=1}^{P} r_{YX_p} b_p$$

Before we leave this discussion, consider the computing formula for $\hat{R}^2_{Y \cdot X_1 X_2}$ in terms of r_{YX_1}, r_{YX_2}, and $r_{X_1 X_2}$. If $r_{X_1 X_2} = 0$, then $\hat{R}^2_{Y \cdot X_1 X_2}$ reduces to:

$$\hat{R}^2_{Y \cdot X_1 X_2} = r^2_{YX_1} + r^2_{YX_2}$$

From this it can be seen that a researcher will be wise to select predictor variables that are not highly correlated with one another. Consider, for example, the case where X_1 and X_2 are moderately correlated, such as $r_{X_1 X_2} = .50$. Here, $\hat{R}^2_{Y \cdot X_1 X_2}$ reduces to:

$$\hat{R}^2_{Y \cdot X_1 X_2} = \frac{r^2_{YX_1} + r^2_{YX_2} - r_{YX_1} r_{YX_2}}{.75}$$

If $r_{YX_1} = r_{YX_2} = .50$, then $\hat{R}^2_{Y \cdot X_1 X_2} = .33$, which is less than $r^2_{YX_1} + r^2_{YX_2} = .50$. Even if $r_{YX_1} = r_{YX_2} = .70$, with $r_{X_1 X_2} = .50$, $\hat{R}^2_{Y \cdot X_1 X_2} = .65$ is less than $r^2_{YX_1} + r^2_{YX_2} = .98$. This suggests that high correlations among the predictor variables require even higher correlations between the criterion variables and the predictors. Otherwise, the improvement in the prediction may be minimal. Intuitively, this comes about because highly correlated variables share a large amount of common variance and redundancy. As such, they do not contribute much independent information to the regression equation so as to improve the prediction and inflate $\hat{R}^2$.

3-6. Testing the multiple correlation coefficient for statistical significance

Recall that in the bivariate model, the hypothesis H_0: $\rho_{XY} = 0$ is equivalent to the hypothesis H_0: $\beta_1 = 0$, as shown in Section 2-3. For $P > 1$, this equivalence extends in a direct fashion. The hypothesis H_0: $R_{Y \cdot X_1 X_2 \ldots X_P} = 0$ is equivalent to the hypothesis H_0: All $\beta_p = 0$, since the only way that $R_{Y \cdot X_1 X_2 \ldots X_P}$ could equal zero would be if each constituent β_p were also equal to zero.

Also recall from Section 2-3 that a test of significance for r_{XY} was obtained through an F ratio defined as:

$$F = \frac{\nu_2}{\nu_1} \frac{\hat{\theta}^2}{1 - \hat{\theta}^2}$$

For the multiple regression analog, the relevant squared correlation coefficient is given by $\hat{\theta}^2 = \hat{R}^2_{Y \cdot X_1X_2\ldots X_P}$ with the respective degrees of freedom given by $\nu_1 = P$ and $\nu_2 = N - P - 1$. For $P = 1$, this reduces to r^2_{XY}, $\nu_1 = 1$, and $\nu_2 = N - 2$. Thus the multiple correlation coefficient may be tested for significance by referring:

$$F = \frac{N - P - 1}{P}\left(\frac{\hat{R}^2_{Y \cdot X_1X_2\ldots X_P}}{1 - \hat{R}^2_{Y \cdot X_1X_2\ldots X_P}}\right)$$

to an F distribution with P and $N - P - 1$ degrees of freedom. For the data of Table 3-1:

$$F = \frac{40 - 2 - 1}{2}\left(\frac{.4574}{1 - .4574}\right) = 15.60$$

Since $15.60 > F_{2,37:.95} = 3.26$, we can reject the hypothesis that $R^2_{Y \cdot X_1X_2} = 0$ with $\alpha = .05$.

With some very simple algebra beginning with:

$$1 = (1 - \hat{R}^2) + \hat{R}^2$$

we can derive F by multiplying both sides of this identity by S^2_Y to give:

$$S^2_Y = S^2_Y(1 - \hat{R}^2) + S^2_Y\hat{R}^2$$

Furthermore, if we now multiply both sides by $N - 1$, we have:

$$(N - 1)S^2_Y = (N - 1)S^2_Y(1 - \hat{R}^2) + (N - 1)S^2_Y\hat{R}^2$$

From this final equation, we see that:

$$SS_{\text{Total}} = (N - 1)S^2_Y \qquad \text{with } \nu_{\text{Tot}} = N - 1$$

$$SS_{\text{Regression}} = (N - 1)S^2_Y\hat{R}^2 \qquad \text{with } \nu_{\text{Reg}} = P$$

$$SS_{\text{Residual}} = (N - 1)S^2_Y(1 - \hat{R}^2) \qquad \text{with } \nu_{\text{Res}} = N - P - 1$$

so that:

$$F = \frac{MS_{\text{Reg}}}{MS_{\text{Res}}} = \frac{\dfrac{(N - 1)S^2_Y\hat{R}^2}{P}}{\dfrac{(N - 1)S^2_Y(1 - \hat{R}^2)}{N - P - 1}} = \frac{N - P - 1}{P}\left(\frac{\hat{R}^2}{1 - \hat{R}^2}\right)$$

For completeness, we have the test for H_0: $R^2 = 0$ against H_1: $R^2 \neq 0$ in the following form. Results of this test are usually summarized in an analysis of variance table similar to that of Table 3-6.

Procedure for testing H_0: $R^2_{Y \cdot X_1X_2\ldots X_P} = 0$.

Step 1. Compute:

$$\hat{R}^2_{Y \cdot X_1X_2\ldots X_P} \quad \text{and} \quad F = \frac{N - P - 1}{P}\left(\frac{\hat{R}^2}{1 - \hat{R}^2}\right)$$

Step 2. Reject H_0 if:

$$F > F_{P,N-P-1:1-\alpha}$$

TABLE 3-6. Analysis of variance table for multiple regression

Source	*d/f*	*Sum of squares*	*Mean square*	*F*
Regression	P	$(N-1)S_Y^2\hat{R}^2$	$\frac{N-1}{P}S_Y^2\hat{R}^2$	$\left(\frac{N-P-1}{P}\right)\frac{\hat{R}^2}{1-\hat{R}^2}$
Residual	$N-P-1$	$(N-1)S_Y^2(1-\hat{R}^2)$	$\frac{N-1}{N-P-1}S_Y^2(1-\hat{R}^2)$	
Total	$N-1$	$(N-1)S_Y^2$		

3-7. Comments about the sample $\hat{R}^2$

Although it is standard practice to test the hypothesis that R^2 in the population is equal to zero, a comment is in order when it comes to interpreting the magnitude of $\hat{R}^2$ in a sample. The more predictor variables P that are included in a particular multiple regression analysis involving N individuals or sampling units, the larger $\hat{R}^2$ can be expected to be.

This increase in $\hat{R}^2$ as a function of increases in P is a mathematical consequence of the method of least squares which we illustrated only for $P = 1$. As we also saw:

$$\hat{R}^2_{Y\cdot X_1X_2\ldots X_P} = r_{YX_1}b_1 + r_{YX_2}b_2 + \cdots + r_{YX_P}b_P$$

where $b_1, b_2, \ldots, b_P$ are solutions to the normal equations defined from the minimization of:

$$SS_{\text{Res}} = \sum_{i=1}^{N}(Y_i - \hat{Y}_i)^2$$

Because of this minimization process, a large correlation can be generated from small b_p and r_{YX_p} values. For example, suppose $P = 10, b_p = .08,$ and $r_{YX_p} = .25$ for each p. For this case, $\hat{R}^2 = 10(.08)(.25) = .20$, so that $\hat{R} = \sqrt{.20} = .45$. This means that small, but not statistically significant, correlations can influence the magnitude of $\hat{R}^2_{Y\cdot X_1X_2\ldots X_P}$. As these small effects accumulate, their contribution to $\hat{R}^2_{Y\cdot X_1X_2\ldots X_P}$ can become quite pronounced. Because of this, $\hat{R}^2_{Y\cdot X_1X_2\ldots X_P}$ is a biased estimator of the population squared multiple correlation coefficient. In general, $\hat{R}^2$ is larger than R^2.

Assuming that $R^2 = 0$, the expected value of $\hat{R}^2$ is given by:

$$E(\hat{R}^2_{Y\cdot X_1X_2\ldots X_P}) = \frac{P}{N-1}$$

Thus, whenever P is large relative to N, we can expect $\hat{R}^2$ to be large by chance alone. In the present example, with $P = 2$ and $N = 40$, $E(\hat{R}^2_{Y\cdot X_1X_2}) = 2/39 = .0513$, if H_0 is true. If $P = 10$ predictor variables were used instead, $E(\hat{R}^2_{Y\cdot X_1X_2\ldots X_{10}}) = 10/39 = .2564$. That is, we could expect to obtain a sample $\hat{R}^2$ of .2564 even though R^2 in the population were equal to zero. The ultimate consequence of this property arises when $P = N - 1$, in which case perfect prediction is achieved since $\hat{R}^2$ will always equal 1.00.

Fortunately the hypothesis testing procedure involving R^2 in the population is not compromised by the fact that $E(\hat{R}^2) \neq 0$, as shown by Serlin and Levin (1978). What is compromised, however, is our interpretation of the magnitude or importance of a given sample $\hat{R}^2$ when the statistical test of it has proven significant. Thus, in interpreting a particular $\hat{R}^2$, we should *correct* it with regard to its chance value, such as we might do when correcting a multiple-choice test score for guessing. This *shrunken* $\hat{R}^2$ may be computed according to the formula:

$$\hat{R}^2_C = 1 - (1 - \hat{R}^2)\left(\frac{N - 1}{N - P - 1}\right)$$

where $\hat{R}^2_C$ represents the corrected-for-chance squared multiple correlation coefficient. For our example:

$$\hat{R}^2_C = 1 - (1 - .457)(39/37) = 1 - .572 = .428$$

As a safe rule of thumb, we recommend that a researcher select a sample size so that $N > 10P$. Thus, for $N = 10P$:

$$\hat{R}^2_C = 1 - (1 - \hat{R}^2)\frac{10P - 1}{9P - 1} = 1 - (1 - \hat{R}^2)\left(1 + \frac{P}{9P - 1}\right)$$

so that the shrinkage will not exceed $P/(9P - 1)$, or about 11% on the average.

As is true for all sample statistics, $\hat{R}^2$ is also influenced by sampling variability. Although not shown here, $\hat{R}^2$ is actually derived from an optimal combination of the Xs, given N individuals. However, it is well known that the particular values of B or b that satisfy this condition are likely to change from one sample to the next as a function of sampling variability. Naturally, sample size and the resulting standard errors of the betas will determine how much change can be expected. Because of this, it is inevitable that the beta weights derived in one sample will not be optimal for the new sample. As a result, if the original betas are applied to the new sample members and the squared correlation with Y computed, this new $\hat{R}^2$ will be smaller than the original $\hat{R}^2$.

Cross-validation is a procedure used to determine how much a given $\hat{R}^2$ shrinks when the originally derived beta weights are applied to a new sample. Large shrinkage in $\hat{R}^2$ indicates that the original equation is not very useful for prediction, whereas small shrinkage indicates that it is quite useful. One recommendation often made by statisticians is for a researcher to collect data on more subjects than are used to derive the original regression equation, for example, twice as many, or $2N$. The second sample can thus serve as a cross-validation sample to which the originally derived regression weights are applied. It is possible to assess the resulting $\hat{R}^2$, both descriptively and statistically, to determine whether the prediction equation is still a useful one.

3-8. Testing the beta weights for statistical significance

It is possible to test for the statistical significance of each B_p, either separately or simultaneously (the latter via a Scheffé procedure), following the rejection of H_0: $R^2_{Y \cdot X_1 X_2 \ldots X_P} = 0$. The two approaches differ only with respect to the critical values selected to represent either per comparison or familywise type I error probabilities. In both cases, however, the test performed is a direct extension of the test described for $P = 1$ in Chapter 2 and is, as we will see, identical to the test that the partial correlation coefficient associated with a particular predictor is equal to zero.

Following standard statistical hypothesis-testing theory, we simply compare each B_p to its standard error. In the per comparison case, this ratio is referred to a t distribution with $N - P - 1$ degrees of freedom. In the familywise post hoc Scheffé model, the ratio is referred to $S = \sqrt{PF_{P,N-P-1:1-\alpha}}$. When $P = 1$, we recall that $v = N - 2$. This agrees with general result, $v = N - P - 1$. We note that the general result agrees with $v = N - 2 - V$, the degrees of freedom for testing the significance of a partial correlation. For example, with $P = 4$ predictor variables, the beta weight tests would be based on $N - 5$ degrees of freedom. In the same situation, testing for the significance of a correlation with all other predictor variables partialed out would yield $V = 3$, and thus the degrees of freedom would also equal $N - 5$.

With a little effort, it can be shown that the standard error of an unstandardized beta weight, such as B_1, is given by the following definition.

The standard error of an unstandardized beta coefficient.
The standard error of B_1 is given by:

$$SE_{B_1} = \sqrt{\frac{MS_{\text{Res}(Y \cdot X_1 X_2 \ldots X_P)}}{SS_{\text{Res}(X_1 \cdot X_2 X_3 \ldots X_P)}}}$$

where:

$$MS_{\text{Res}(Y \cdot X_1 X_2 \ldots X_P)} = \frac{SS_Y(1 - \hat{R}^2_{Y \cdot X_1 X_2 \ldots X_P})}{N - P - 1} = \frac{(N-1)S^2_Y(1 - \hat{R}^2_{Y \cdot X_1 X_2 \ldots X_P})}{N - P - 1}$$

$$SS_{\text{Res}(X_1 \cdot X_2 X_3 \ldots X_P)} = SS_{X_1}(1 - \hat{R}^2_{X_1 \cdot X_2 X_3 \ldots X_P}) = (N-1)S^2_{X_1}(1 - \hat{R}^2_{X_1 \cdot X_2 X_3 \ldots X_P})$$

The standard errors of $B_2, B_3, \ldots, B_P$ are defined in a similar fashion.

As indicated, the SE_{B_p} represent straightforward generalizations of the univariate SE_{B_1}.

The statistical tests of H_0: $\beta_p = 0$ proceed according to familiar test theory. The tests are as follows.

Procedure for testing H_0: $\beta_p = 0$ against H_1: $\beta_p \neq 0$.

Step 1. Compute:

$$t = \frac{B_p - 0}{SE_{B_p}}$$

Step 2. The hypothesis is rejected with a risk of a type I error set at α according to the following decision rule:

D.R. Reject H_0 if $t < t_{v:\alpha/2}$ or if $t > t_{v:1-\alpha/2}$ where $v = N - P - 1$.

We now apply these procedures to the data of Table 3-1, for which $B_1 = .90273$. To determine whether this value differs significantly from zero, we must first compute the SE_{B_1}. Using previously computed statistics, we find that:

$$MS_{\text{Res}(Y \cdot X_1 X_2)} = \frac{39(30.3230)^2(1 - .4574)}{37} = 525.8410$$

and, since $\hat{R}^2_{X_1 \cdot X_2} = r^2_{X_1 X_2}$:

$$SS_{\text{Res}(X_1 \cdot X_2)} = 39(15.3956)^2(1 - .6712^2) = 5079.4664$$

As a result:

$$SE_{B_1} = \sqrt{\frac{525.8410}{5079.4664}} = .3218 \quad \text{and}$$

$$t = \frac{.9027}{.3218} = 2.80$$

If a single test were performed using $\alpha = .05$, the critical values would be $t = \pm 2.02$, with $\nu = 37$. If each of the two beta weights were tested using $\alpha_1' = \alpha_2' = .025$, thereby yielding a familywise $\alpha \leq .05$ according to the Dunn-Bonferroni procedure, the critical values would be given by $t = \pm 2.33$. Finally, if a familywise Scheffé test were performed using $\alpha = .05$, the critical values are then defined by:

$$\mathbf{S} = \pm\sqrt{2F_{2,37:.95}} = \pm\sqrt{2(3.26)} = \pm 2.55$$

Thus, according to each of the preceding comparison procedures, we would conclude that B_1 differs significantly from zero. That is, first midterm performance is statistically related to performance on the final, even when the contribution of the second midterm is considered. On the other hand, it would be found that $H_0\colon \ \beta_2 = 0$ is not rejected under any of the models, since the statistical test of B_2 gives a t value of:

$$t = \frac{.4184}{.2466} = 1.70$$

It is worth mentioning that the two t values correspond exactly to those that would have been obtained for testing $H_0\colon \ \rho_{YX_1 \cdot X_2} = 0$ and $H_0\colon \ \rho_{YX_2 \cdot X_1} = 0$. The second of these was demonstrated in Section 3-3. This is exactly analogous to the simple regression model where the test of $\rho_{XY} = 0$ was seen to be identical to the test of $\beta_1 = 0$. This result should be expected since, generalizing from Section 3-4:

$$B_p = r_{YX_p \cdot X_1 X_2 \ldots X_{p-1} X_{p+1} \ldots X_P} \sqrt{\frac{MS_{\text{Res}(Y \cdot X_1 X_2 \ldots X_{p-1} X_{p+1} \ldots X_P)}}{MS_{\text{Res}(X_p \cdot X_1 X_2 \ldots X_{p-1} X_{p+1} \ldots X_P)}}}$$

Except for degenerate cases in which the correlations equal one or the standard deviations equal zero, the only way B_p could equal zero would be if the partial correlation coefficient were to equal zero.

Confidence intervals for the beta weights are determined according to familiar interval estimation procedures. For per comparison control of a type I error, we have the following model.

Confidence intervals for the beta weights.
The $100(1 - \alpha)\%$ confidence interval for β_p is given by:

$$B_p - t_{\nu:1-\alpha/2} SE_{B_p} < \beta_p < B_p + t_{\nu:1-\alpha/2} SE_{B_p}$$

where $\nu = N - P - 1$.

Confidence intervals based on a per comparison type I error probability of $\alpha = .05$, a planned analysis with two contrasts under the Dunn-Bonferroni model with $\alpha_1 = \alpha_2 = .025$, and a post hoc analysis under Scheffé's model with $\alpha = .05$ yield the respective confidence intervals for β_1:

$\beta_1 = .9027 \pm 2.02(.3218) = .90 \pm .65$

or:

$$.25 < \beta_1 < 1.55 \qquad \text{(Per comparison)}$$

$\beta_1 = .9027 \pm 2.33(.3218) = .90 \pm .75$

or:

$$.15 < \beta_1 < 1.65 \qquad \text{(Dunn-Bonferroni)}$$

$\beta_1 = .9027 \pm 2.55(.3218) = .90 \pm .82$

or:

$$.08 < \beta_1 < 1.72 \qquad \text{(Scheffé)}$$

Since zero is not included in any of the intervals, each indicates that $\beta_1 \neq 0$. These results are, of course, consistent with the tests of hypothesis that were previously performed.

Comparing corresponding beta weights in two different samples involves a direct extension of the methods of Section 2-4. Thus, to test H_0: $\beta_p^{(1)} = \beta_p^{(2)}$, we use:

$$t = \frac{B_p^{(1)} - B_p^{(2)}}{\sqrt{SE^2_{B_p^{(1)}} + SE^2_{B_p^{(2)}}}}$$

with $\nu = (N_1 - P - 1) + (N_2 - P - 1) = \nu_1 + \nu_2$ and with each standard error based on a pooled estimate of the common unknown variance. In this case:

$$MS_{\text{Res}} = \frac{\nu_1 MS_{\text{Res}(1)} + \nu_2 MS_{\text{Res}(2)}}{\nu_1 + \nu_2}$$

This model extends directly to cover the K-sample problem, as in Section 2-4. The assumptions required are:

1. Samples are independent.
2. Observations within samples are independent.
3. Variances and covariances within populations are equal.
4. Y has a normal distribution or that N_k are large enough to justify the use of the Central Limit Theorem. In the latter case we use $N_k = 20$ as a practical rule of thumb.

3-9. Attempts to assess each predictor variable's contribution to the regression equation

In Section 2-2 we saw that r^2_{XY} could be used as an estimate of the proportion of the variance in Y that could be explained by the linear relationship between X and Y. In Section 3-5 we saw that $\hat{R}^2_{Y \cdot X_1 X_2 \ldots X_P}$ could be used similarly as an estimate of the proportion of variance in Y that could be explained by the linear relationship of Y, with $X_1, X_2, \ldots, X_P$ taken collectively. It certainly makes sense to ask how much of the variance is explained by X_1 alone, by X_2 alone, and so on. Unfortunately, as soon as $P > 1$, there is no simple method recommended by statisticians to do this. In this case, there is a mathematical complication in that the components of variance associated uniquely with X_1, with X_2, and so on are not well-defined.

Consider, for example, the two methods for computing $\hat{R}_{Y \cdot X_1 X_2 \ldots X_P}$ as described in Section 3-5. As we recall, for $P = 2$, $\hat{R}^2$ reduces to:

$$\hat{R}^2 = b_1^2 + 2b_1 b_2 r_{X_1 X_2} + b_2^2$$

and for the example of Table 4-1, it follows that:

$$.4574 = .2100 + .1705 + .0768$$

We see that X_1 appears to account for 21.0% of the explained variance, that X_2 appears to account for 7.7% of the explained variance, and that together X_1 and X_2 appear to share 17.1% of the explained variance.

This explained covariance term makes it impossible to determine how much X_1 explains alone or how much X_2 explains alone. Although it is tempting to say that X_1 explains $100[.2100 + 1/2(.1705)] = 29.5\%$ of the variance and that X_2 explains $100[.0768 + 1/2(.1705)] = 16.2\%$ of the variance, the temptation should be avoided since it is most likely to be in error. The error becomes obvious if b_1, b_2, or $r_{X_1 X_2}$ is negative because under these conditions the middle term would have a negative algebraic value and, as we know, variances are always positive.

According to the second formula for computing $\hat{R}^2$, when $P = 2$:

$$\begin{aligned}\hat{R}^2 &= r_{YX_1} b_1 + r_{YX_2} b_2 \\ &= (.64438)(.4583) + (.58482)(.2772) \\ &= .2953 + .1621 \\ &= .4574\end{aligned}$$

so that the same percentage breakdowns are observed. However, we are advised against saying that X_1 explains 29.5% of the total variance, since r_{YX_1} does not have X_2 partialed out. In like manner, 16.2% is not the percent of explained variance associated with X_2, since r_{YX_2} does not have X_1 partialed out.

As these two methods for computing $\hat{R}^2$ illustrate, it is easy to fall into the trap of thinking that we can determine the percentage of variance explained individually by $X_1, X_2, \ldots, X_P$. However, it must be emphasized that this cannot be done. In addition, there is the substantive problem that the magnitude of any standardized beta weight and the apparent contribution of its associated variable to the regression equation are intimately related to the nature and number of other predictor variables included by the researcher in the analysis. The amount of variance explained by a variable, whether it is large or small, is strictly a function of how many other predictor variables accompany it in the equation, as well as the correlations among all variables. These problems have been articulated previously, but a particularly convincing presentation is made by Gordon (1968). Through several examples, he shows that two important considerations are the *redundancy* and *repetitiveness* associated with a set of predictor variables. With redundancy defined as the degree to which the variables in a set or subset are intercorrelated and repetitiveness referring to the number of such variables included in the set or subset, the beta weight of a particular variable is shown to be smaller under high levels of each in comparison to low levels of each. Although some of this information overlaps with standard presentations of the concept of *multicollinearity*, or high relatedness in a set of predictor variables, there is sufficiently unique information in Gordon's (1968) examples to illustrate some clear warnings inherent in interpreting multiple regression equations.

Attempts to specify the unique contribution of a particular variable are not without ambiguity and, even worse, can be potentially misleading. Gordon (1968), for example, shows how a predictor variable with the smallest zero-order correlation with the criterion variable may emerge with the largest standardized beta weight in the regression equation, simply as a function of the configuration of other predictor variables included. Nonetheless, procedures abound for determining optimal prediction equations and, a fortiori, the specific contributions of individual variables. Some of the more popular methods will now be described, though the reader is advised to see Draper and Smith (1981) for a more complete presentation.

3-10. The method of all possible regressions

One way that researchers have used to estimate the percent of explained variance associated with a particular variable is to examine the multiple correlation coefficients that are generated by all possible regression lines. As will be seen, the method is not very useful as it was originally designed to solve a different problem. The different problem is the determination of the minimum number of variables required to give a satisfactory prediction equation. The method is best illustrated by an example.

Consider predicting Y from the set of variables X_1, X_2, and X_3. If the cost of measurement were high, such as it often is in economic or industrial investigations, we may wish to use the fewest number of variables that give an adequate prediction for practical purposes. In this case, there are seven different possible regressions that could be used. Suppose the multiple correlations for these seven different regressions are as reported in Table 3-7. As we see, the use of X_1, X_2, and X_3 provides the best prediction, with $\hat{R}^2_{Y \cdot X_1X_2X_3} = .52$. The next best prediction is offered with X_2 and X_3 for which $\hat{R}^2_{Y \cdot X_2X_3} = .50$. If we now note that since $\hat{R}^2_{Y \cdot X_1X_2X_3} - \hat{R}^2_{Y \cdot X_2X_3} = .52 - .50 = .02$, one might conclude that X_1 accounts for 2% of the variance. Unfortunately this is in error, since .02 cannot be attributed to X_1 alone. Note that,

TABLE 3-7. An example of the method of all possible regressions

Variables used as predictors	*Value of* $\hat{R}^2$
X_1	.23
X_2	.29
X_1, X_2	.38
X_3	.45
X_1, X_3	.48
X_2, X_3	.50
X_1, X_2, X_3	.52

in an analogous fashion:

$$\hat{R}^2_{Y\cdot X_1X_3} - \hat{R}^2_{Y\cdot X_3} = .48 - .45 = .03$$

$$\hat{R}^2_{Y\cdot X_1X_2} - \hat{R}^2_{Y\cdot X_2} = .38 - .29 = .09$$

Thus we have three different values for the percentage of explained variance, 2%, 3%, and 9%, respectively, to attribute to X_1. None is a correct measure. $\hat{R}^2_{Y\cdot X_1X_2X_3} = .52$ measures the proportion of variance explained *jointly* by X_1, X_2, and X_3; $\hat{R}^2_{Y\cdot X_1X_3} = .48$ measures the proportion of variance explained *jointly* by X_1 and X_3; and $\hat{R}^2_{Y\cdot X_1X_2} = .38$ measures the proportion of variance explained *jointly* by X_1 and X_2. To reiterate the message of Section 3-9, the proportion of variance explained by X_1 *alone* is not determinable.

In any case, let us return to the real objective of the *method of all possible regressions*. The model is actually used to determine an economically sound prediction equation. Since $\hat{R}^2_{Y\cdot X_2X_3} = .50$ is almost equal to $\hat{R}^2_{Y\cdot X_1X_2X_3} = .52$, we might be advised to use X_2 and X_3 alone, since the expense involved in measuring X_1 increases the proportion of explained variance only minimally. In this example, even X_3 alone might be sufficient since $r^2_{YX_3} = .45$. This is only .05 less than the best two-variable solution and .07 less than the complete three-variable solution. In the final analysis, the economics of the situation will determine the best strategy.

Often a simple graphical method can be used to determine which and/or how many variables to retain. As the number of variables admitted to the regression equation increases, the value of $\hat{R}^2$ increases until it reaches $\hat{R}^2_{Y\cdot X_1X_2\ldots X_P}$. However, the increase is not necessarily linear with increases in P. In most practical applications, it tends to plateau, or asymptote, close to $\hat{R}^2_{Y\cdot X_1X_2\ldots X_P}$ even for small values of P. As an example, consider a graphical plot of $\hat{R}^2$ for a hypothetical $P = 4$ variable problem, as shown in Figure 3-5. As can be seen, the value of $\hat{R}^2$ begins to level off when X_2 and X_4 are used as predictors. If the cost of measuring X_1 and X_3 were high and only prediction were of interest, X_2 and X_4 might be sufficient. As mentioned previously, the primary use of this method is one of determining the most economical prediction equation, from a cost-benefit standpoint.

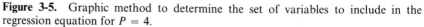

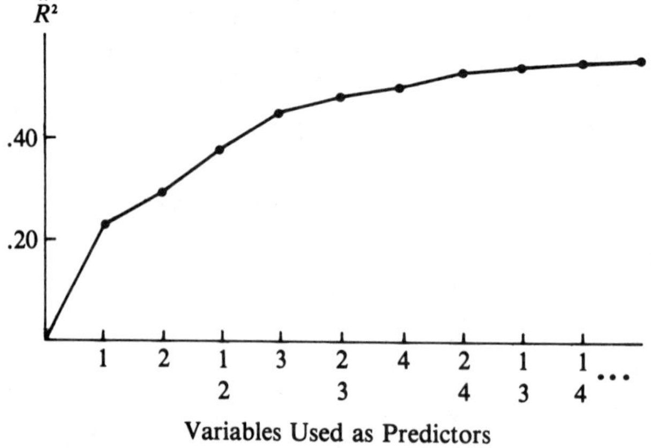

Figure 3-5. Graphic method to determine the set of variables to include in the regression equation for $P = 4$.

3-11. The method of backward elimination or backward selection

An alternative procedure has been proposed which alleviates the problem of examining all possible regressions. In many cases, this model is definitely preferable since the number of possible regression equations for P variables is given by:

$$T = 2^P - 1$$

Thus, for $P = 3$, $T = 7$; for $P = 4$, $T = 15$; for $P = 5$, $T = 31$; and for $P = 6$, $T = 63$. As we see, the number of possible regression equations for even moderate values of P is quite large. This method is called *backward elimination* or *backward selection*. We describe the method as follows.

Backward elimination begins with the full regression equation involving $X_1, X_2, \ldots, X_P$. For the full set of predictors, we compute $\hat{R}^2_{Y \cdot X_1 X_2 \ldots X_P}$. Next, we compute the P regression equations that result from the removal of one predictor variable. Then the various P values of $\hat{R}^2$ are computed and each is compared to $\hat{R}^2_{Y \cdot X_1 X_2 \ldots X_P}$. The equation that produces an $\hat{R}^2$ closest to the full squared correlation is retained. With this equation as a new starting point, we repeat the process by computing $P - 1$ regression equations and associated $\hat{R}^2$ values, by removing one variable from the remaining $P - 1$ variables. These $P - 1$ squared correlations are compared to the largest $\hat{R}^2$ in the previous step, and the largest one is retained. The process continues in this fashion. At any step along the way, however, whenever a noticeable decrease in $\hat{R}^2$ is observed, relative to $\hat{R}^2$ in the preceding step, the process is terminated.

For this model, the maximum number of regression equations to examine is given by:

$$t = P + (P - 1) + (P - 2) + \cdots + 2 + 1 = \frac{P(P + 1)}{2}$$

For $P = 2$, $(t = 3) = (T = 3)$; for $P = 3$, $(t = 6) < (T = 7)$; for $P = 4$, $(t = 10) < (T = 15)$; for $P = 5$, $(t = 15) < (T = 31)$; and for $P = 6$, $(t = 21) < (T = 63)$. As we see, the model has significant economic advantages for large values of P.

3-12. Part correlation

The most popular method in present-day use for selecting the fewest number of predictor variables necessary to guarantee a good fit or adequate prediction is based on a model referred to as *forward selection*, which is actually the reverse process of backward elimination. Before describing this model, we must first introduce a correlational index that serves an integral part of the procedure.

The index is known as a *part* or *semipartial* correlation coefficient, and is similar to a partial correlation coefficient. Whereas a partial correlation coefficient measures the correlation between, for instance, Y and X_1 from which the respective linear relationships with X_2 have been removed, a part correlation refers to the correlation between Y and X_1 but where only the linear relationship of X_2 with X_1 has been removed. More generally, a part correlation refers to the association that a dependent variable Y has with that part of X_1 that is free from the relationship that X_1 has with one or more other variables.

For the special case in which $P = 2$, we have seen that the partial correlation between Y and X_1, after the effects of X_2 have been removed from both variables, is given simply as the correlation between the residuals $Y - \hat{Y}$ and $X_1 - \hat{X}_1$ and is computed as:

$$r_{YX_1 \cdot X_2} = \frac{r_{YX_1} - r_{YX_2} r_{X_1X_2}}{\sqrt{1 - r^2_{YX_2}}\sqrt{1 - r^2_{X_1X_2}}}$$

In like manner, the part correlation between Y and X_1, after the effects of X_2 have been removed from X_1 alone, is given simply as the correlation between Y and the residual $X_1 - \hat{X}_1$ and is computed as:

$$r_{Y(X_1 \cdot X_2)} = \frac{r_{YX_1} - r_{YX_2} r_{X_1X_2}}{\sqrt{1 - r^2_{X_1X_2}}} = r_{YX_1 \cdot X_2}\sqrt{1 - r^2_{YX_2}}$$

The latter form is useful for computation purposes and because of its immediate generalization to multiple independent variables.

For completeness, we provide the following definition.

Definition of a part or semipartial correlation.
Consider the dependent variable Y and the set of independent variables $X_1, X_2, \ldots, X_P$. The part correlation of Y with X_1, where $X_2, X_3, \ldots, X_P$ have been removed from X_1, is given by:

$$r_{Y(X_1 \cdot X_2X_3 \ldots X_P)} = r_{YX_1 \cdot X_2 \ldots X_P}\sqrt{1 - \hat{R}^2_{Y \cdot X_2 \ldots X_P}}$$

Because $r_{YX_1 \cdot X_2}$ and $r_{Y(X_1 \cdot X_2)}$ differ only by the factor $\sqrt{1 - r^2_{YX_2}}$, which is less than or equal to one, we see that:

$$r_{Y(X_1 \cdot X_2)} \leq r_{YX_1 \cdot X_2}$$

Also, we see that $r_{Y(X_1 \cdot X_2)}$ can equal zero only if $r_{YX_1 \cdot X_2} = 0$. As a result of the connection between $r_{Y(X_1 \cdot X_2)}$ and $r_{YX_1 \cdot X_2}$, it can be shown that the test H_0: $\rho_{Y(X_1 \cdot X_2)} = 0$ is identical to the test H_0: $\rho_{YX_1 \cdot X_2} = 0$, except in the degenerate case where $r_{YX_2} = 1.00$.

For our present three-variable example, we recall that $r_{YX_1} = .64438$, $r_{YX_2} = .58482$, and $r_{X_1X_2} = .67120$, yielding $r_{YX_1 \cdot X_2} = .41884$ and $r_{YX_2 \cdot X_1} = .26869$. In terms of the computational formula:

$$r_{Y(X_1 \cdot X_2)} = .41884\sqrt{1 - .58482^2} = .33975$$

$$r_{Y(X_2 \cdot X_1)} = .26869\sqrt{1 - .64438^2} = .20547$$

Note that, as indicated, both of these part correlations are less than their respective partials.

The interpretive difference between $r_{YX_1 \cdot X_2X_3 \ldots X_P}$ and $r_{Y(X_1 \cdot X_2X_3 \ldots X_P)}$ is quite subtle and thus should be understood and appreciated. To aid this understanding, consider $r^2_{Y \cdot X_1X_2}$ and $r^2_{Y(X_1 \cdot X_2)}$. The squared part correlation coefficient $r^2_{Y(X_1 \cdot X_2)}$ may be interpreted as the proportion of Y variance explained by the portion of X_1 that is free of X_2. In contrast, the squared partial correlation coefficient $r^2_{YX_1 \cdot X_2}$ may be interpreted as the proportion of the portion of Y free of X_2 that is explained by the portion of X_1 that is also free of X_2. In this sense, a squared part correlation reflects the proportion of the total Y variance that is explained by a portion of X_1, whereas a squared partial correlation reflects a proportion of the conditional Y variance that is explained by the same portion of X_1. Here conditional refers to reduced variance in Y resulting from the relationship of Y with one or more other variables. We will illustrate this latter point more clearly in the next section. Following Cohen and Cohen (1975), a useful Venn diagram representation of the interrelationships among squared zero-order, multiple, partial, and part correlations is provided in Figure 3-6.

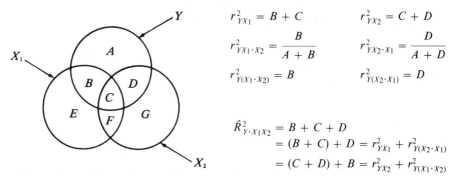

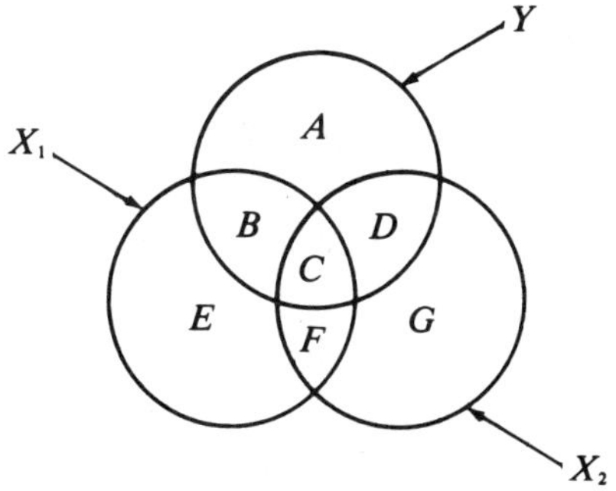

$$r^2_{YX_1} = B + C \qquad r^2_{YX_2} = C + D$$

$$r^2_{YX_1 \cdot X_2} = \frac{B}{A + B} \qquad r^2_{YX_2 \cdot X_1} = \frac{D}{A + D}$$

$$r^2_{Y(X_1 \cdot X_2)} = B \qquad r^2_{Y(X_2 \cdot X_1)} = D$$

$$\begin{aligned} \hat{R}^2_{Y \cdot X_1 X_2} &= B + C + D \\ &= (B + C) + D = r^2_{YX_1} + r^2_{Y(X_2 \cdot X_1)} \\ &= (C + D) + B = r^2_{YX_2} + r^2_{Y(X_1 \cdot X_2)} \end{aligned}$$

Figure 3-6. A Venn diagram illustration of squared zero-order, multiple, partial, and part correlations.

Note: The four areas identified within each circle represent variance proportions, with each four-area sum equalling 1.00.

3-13. The method of forward selection

We now examine the forward selection procedure. According to this method, the X variable exhibiting the highest zero-order correlation, in absolute value, with Y enters into the regression equation first. Let the first variable selected be X_1, the second X_2, and so on. Thus, with X_1 in the model, $\hat{R}^2$ is given simply by $r^2_{YX_1}$. In the second step, the next variable selected is the one that produces the greatest increment in $\hat{R}^2$. The X variable that satisfies this condition is the one with the largest squared partial correlation, $r^2_{YX_2 \cdot X_1}$, or equivalently the one with the largest squared part correlation, $r^2_{Y(X_2 \cdot X_1)}$. We prefer to talk in terms of part correlations because of their more direct interpretation in terms of explained variance.

At Step 2, it is possible to partition the proportion of explained variance in Y into two nonoverlapping components: that accounted for by X_1 and that accounted for by the part of X_2 that is free of X_1. In terms of squared correlation coefficients, we can see from Figure 3-6, that:

$$\hat{R}^2_{Y \cdot X_1 X_2} = r^2_{YX_1} + r^2_{Y(X_2 \cdot X_1)}$$

Thus, we can maximize $\hat{R}^2_{Y \cdot X_1 X_2}$ at Step 2 by selecting as X_2 the variable with the largest squared part correlation, $r^2_{Y(X_2 \cdot X_1)}$. Obviously the procedure extends in a straightforward fashion. To maximize $\hat{R}^2$ at Step 3, we should select as X_3 the variable with the largest squared part correlation, $r^2_{Y(X_3 \cdot X_1X_2)}$. With this selection:

$$\hat{R}^2_{Y \cdot X_1X_2X_3} = r^2_{YX_1} + r^2_{Y(X_2 \cdot X_1)} + r^2_{Y(X_3 \cdot X_1X_2)}$$

Proceeding in this fashion, we have, after P successive steps:

$$\hat{R}^2_{Y \cdot X_1X_2 \ldots X_P} = r^2_{YX_1} + r^2_{Y(X_2 \cdot X_1)} + r^2_{Y(X_3 \cdot X_1X_2)} + \ldots + r^2_{Y(X_P \cdot X_1X_2 \ldots X_{P-1})}$$

A useful complementary formula can easily be derived from that just given, by making use of the relationship between part and partial correlations originally defined in Section 3-12. In particular, it can be shown that:

$$1 - \hat{R}^2_{Y \cdot X_1X_2 \ldots X_P} = (1 - r^2_{YX_1})(1 - r^2_{YX_2 \cdot X_1})(1 - r^2_{YX_3 \cdot X_1X_2}) \ldots (1 - r^2_{YX_P \cdot X_1X_2 \ldots X_{P-1}})$$

which may be computationally convenient in certain circumstances. (We are grateful to Gary Price of the University of Wisconsin for pointing out this equivalence.)

As indicated, each step of the process terminates in a selection of an X variable with the highest squared part or partial correlation with Y. Corresponding to the other selection methods, a rough signal for stopping the selection would be a point at which little or no increase in the value of $\hat{R}^2$ is encountered.

For the present example:

$$\begin{aligned}\hat{R}^2_{Y \cdot X_1X_2} &= r^2_{YX_1} + r^2_{Y(X_2 \cdot X_1)} \\ &= .64438^2 + .20547^2 \\ &= .4574\end{aligned}$$

For completeness, we provide directions for this forward selection model and we note that, in the applied literature, the model is often called *stepwise regression.*

Procedure for performing a stepwise regression.

Step 1. Select the independent variable with the largest correlation with Y. Let it be X_1. The proportion of variance in Y explained by this variable is $r^2_{YX_1}$. Let $r^2_{YX_1} = \hat{R}^2_{YX_1}$.

Step 2. Compute, for the remaining $P - 1$ predictor variables, the squared part correlations with Y.

Step 3. Select the variable with the largest squared part correlation with Y and enter it into a multiple regression along with X_1. Let X_2 be the variable selected.

Step 4. Compute $\hat{R}^2_{Y \cdot X_1X_2}$. The difference, $\hat{R}^2_{Y \cdot X_1X_2} - \hat{R}^2_{YX_1}$, is the additional proportion of explained variance contributed by X_2 when taken with X_1 as the predicting set.

Step 5. Compute, for the remaining $(P - 2)$ predictor variables, the squared part correlations with Y.

Step 6. Select the variable with the largest squared part correlation with Y and enter it into a multiple regression along with X_1 and X_2. Let X_3 be the variable selected.

Step 7. Compute $\hat{R}^2_{Y \cdot X_1X_2X_3}$. The difference $\hat{R}^2_{Y \cdot X_1X_2X_3} - \hat{R}^2_{Y \cdot X_1X_2}$ is the additional proportion of explained variance contributed by X_3 when taken with X_1 and X_2 as the predicting set.

Step 8. Repeat the process until all P predictor variables have been included.

As can be seen, this process can be used to select the least number of X variables that give adequate prediction or fit. Since the $\hat{R}^2$ values must increase, a point is reached at which the addition of more and more predictors has less and less impact on the value of $\hat{R}^2$. As with the previous multiple-regression procedures, if the point at which the increase in $\hat{R}^2$ becomes negligible can be determined, then we can stop the stepwise regression process and use a smaller set of predictors.

3-14. Statistical bases for deciding which variables to include in a regression equation

As demonstrated in Section 3-8, it is possible to assess the statistical significance of each of the beta weights in the full P-variable multiple regression equation. This procedure has its dangers and is not recommended if its major objective is to serve as a screening device for determining which variables to retain and which to eliminate for prediction purposes. As was noted previously, a particular variable in a P-variable set may possess a small beta weight only because of the nature and number of other predictor variables accompanying it. As a result, that variable might be dropped from a regression equation on inappropriate grounds. A more desirable sequential approach, based on the forward selection method, will now be described. For completeness, we note that a similar development can be made, based on the backward elimination method, but it is not described here.

The basic statistical procedure accompanying the forward selection method is as follows. At each step we test for the statistical significance of the to-be-added predictor variable. It will be recalled that this variable is the one with the highest squared part correlation, given the variables already included in the model at previous steps. Thus, if at any step, the squared part correlation under consideration is statistically different from zero, its associated variable is added to the equation. If it does not differ from zero, the corresponding predictor variable is not added to the equation. The process is terminated in the latter case, and the regression equation is defined simply in terms of the variables previously included.

In order to employ this procedure, a statistical test of the part correlation coefficient must be conducted. As noted earlier, this test is identical to testing a partial correlation for significance, but where the testing involves only those variables that have already been included in the equation. A convenient version of this test is described here. To determine whether or not $r^2_{Y(X_2 \cdot X_1)}$ adds a statistically significant proportion of explained variance to the relationship already existing between Y and X_1, determine $r^2_{Y(X_2 \cdot X_1)}$ and $\hat{R}^2_{Y \cdot X_1 X_2}$. Consider the following identity:

$$1 = (1 - \hat{R}^2_{Y \cdot X_1 X_2}) + \hat{R}^2_{Y \cdot X_1 X_2}$$

In terms of part correlation, we know that:

$$\hat{R}^2_{Y \cdot X_1 X_2} = r^2_{YX_1} + r^2_{Y(X_2 \cdot X_1)}$$

If we substitute this latter result into the identity we have:

$$1 = (1 - \hat{R}^2_{Y \cdot X_1 X_2}) + r^2_{YX_1} + r^2_{Y(X_2 \cdot X_1)}$$

If we now multiply this equation by $(N - 1)S^2_Y = SS_{\text{Tot}}$, we have that:

$$SS_{\text{Tot}} = (1 - \hat{R}^2_{Y \cdot X_1 X_2})SS_{\text{Tot}} + r^2_{YX_1}SS_{\text{Tot}} + r^2_{Y(X_2 \cdot X_1)}SS_{\text{Tot}}$$

with associated degrees of freedom given by:

$$(N - 1) = (N - 3) + 1 + 1$$

In this notation, we see that:

$$SS_{\text{Tot}} = (N-1)S_Y^2$$
$$SS_{\text{Res}} = (N-1)(1-\hat{R}^2_{Y\cdot X_1X_2})S_Y^2$$
$$SS_{X_1} = (N-1)r^2_{YX_1}S_Y^2$$
$$SS_{X_2\cdot X_1} = (N-1)r^2_{Y(X_2\cdot X_1)}S_Y^2$$

so that:

$$MS_{\text{Added}} = \frac{(N-1)S_Y^2 r^2_{Y(X_2\cdot X_1)}}{1}$$

$$MS_{\text{Res}} = \frac{(N-1)S_Y^2(1-\hat{R}^2_{Y\cdot X_1X_2})}{N-3}$$

Thus we can construct an F ratio to test:

$$H_0: \quad \rho^2_{Y(X_2\cdot X_1)} = 0$$

by computing:

$$F = \frac{MS_{\text{Added}}}{MS_{\text{Res}}} = \frac{(N-1)S_Y^2 r^2_{Y(X_2\cdot X_1)}}{\dfrac{(N-1)S_Y^2(1-\hat{R}^2_{Y\cdot X_1X_2})}{N-3}}$$
$$= \frac{(N-3)r^2_{Y(X_2\cdot X_1)}}{1-\hat{R}^2_{Y\cdot X_1X_2}}$$

Note that this ratio differs somewhat from the general formula presented in Section 2-3:

$$F = \frac{\nu_2}{\nu_1}\left(\frac{\hat{\theta}^2}{1-\hat{\theta}^2}\right)$$

where, in this case, $\nu_1 = 1$ and $\nu_2 = N - P - 1 = N - 2 - 1 = N - 3$. The $1 - \hat{\theta}^2$ here is based on the total set of $P = 2$ predictor variables, and not just the one being tested. The resulting F ratio is often referred to as a partial F test. The hypothesis is rejected if $F > F_{\nu_1,\nu_2:1-\alpha}$ where $\nu_1 = 1$ and $\nu_2 = N - 3$. If $\rho^2_{Y(X_2\cdot X_1)} = 0$ is rejected, we test $\rho^2_{Y(X_3\cdot X_1X_2)}$ for significance. The general model is as follows.

Procedure for performing a partial F test.

Step 1. Suppose $X_1, X_2, \ldots, X_p$ have entered a regression equation. Let the sum of squares explained by $X_1, X_2, \ldots, X_p$ be denoted by $SS_{X_1,X_2,\ldots,X_p}$. For this sum of squares, $\nu_p = p$.

Step 2. Add X_{p+1} to the regression and let the sum of squares with this larger set of variables be denoted by $SS_{X_1,X_2,\ldots,X_{p+1}}$. For this sum of squares, $\nu_{p+1} = p + 1$.

Step 3. The addition to the sum of squares by X_{p+1} is given by:

$$SS_{X_1,X_2,\ldots,X_{p+1}} - SS_{X_1,X_2,\ldots,X_p} = SS_{\text{Added}}$$

and its degrees of freedom are given by $\nu_{\text{Added}} = \nu_{p+1} - \nu_p = (p+1) - p = 1$.

Step 4. With the first $p + 1$ variables in the equation, compute the sum of squares residual as:

$$SS_{\text{Res}} = [N - (p + 1) - 1]\, S_Y^2(1 - \hat{R}^2_{Y \cdot X \ldots X_{p+1}})$$

and the MS_{Res} as:

$$MS_{\text{Res}} = \frac{SS_{\text{Res}}}{N - (p + 1) - 1}$$

Step 5. Test the hypothesis:

$$\text{H}_0\text{:} \quad \rho^2_{Y(X_{p+1} \cdot X_1 X_2 \ldots X_p)} = 0$$

with:

$$F = \frac{MS_{\text{Added}}}{MS_{\text{Res}}}$$

and reject H_0 if $F > F_{1, N-(p+1)-1:1-\alpha}$. In terms of the squared part correlation coefficient:

$$F = \frac{[N - (p+1) - 1] r^2_{Y(X_{p+1} \cdot X_1 X_2 \ldots X_p)}}{1 - \hat{R}^2_{Y \cdot X_1 X_2 \ldots X_{p+1}}}$$

As a simple example of the forward selection procedure and its statistical basis, let us return to our example in which the two midterm scores were used to predict performance on the final. In this example, X_1: Midterm 1 would be selected first as a candidate for the regression equation, since $r_{YX_1} = .64438$ is greater than $r_{YX_2} = .58482$. Since r_{YX_1} is statistically different from zero, it would be entered into the equation in Step 1. In Step 2, we would evaluate the part correlation, $r_{Y(X_2 \cdot X_1)} = .20547$. With $\hat{R}^2_{Y \cdot X_1 X_2}$ given previously as .4574, we have, for the test of $\text{H}_0\text{:} \quad \rho_{Y(X_2 \cdot X_1)} = 0$, that:

$$F = \frac{40 - 2 - 1}{1}\left(\frac{.20547^2}{1 - .4574}\right) = 2.88$$

which, with $v_1 = 1$ and $v_2 = 37$, is not significant using $\alpha = .05$. If we wished to control the type I error rate at .05 for the set of $P = 2$ predictor variables here, we could have used the Dunn-Bonferroni procedure and conducted the tests in each step at $\alpha' = \alpha/2 = .05/2 = .025$. According to either procedure, first midterm scores would be included in the prediction equation, whereas second midterm scores would not. Note that $\sqrt{F} = \sqrt{2.88} = 1.70$, the value reported in Section 3-3 for testing $\text{H}_0\text{:} \quad \rho_{YX_2 \cdot X_1} = 0$.

For completeness, three final variations of this approach will be mentioned. First, the forward selection method has been modified to permit the removal of previously included variables that cease to be effective predictors at any step of the process. According to this procedure, at each step the partial correlation of each previously included predictor and the dependent variable is reexamined to determine whether it is still significantly different from zero, as it was when it was originally entered. If at any step the partial correlation is no longer statistically significant, that particular variable is removed from the equation. The process continues until no new variables are added and no old variables are removed. For more information on this topic, see Draper and Smith (1981).

The second variation consists of the situation in which researcher-defined sets of variables are to be added in groups, rather than individually, at each step of the forward selection process. In this case, the SS_{Added} represents the additional explained variance provided by the set of, for instance, Q' predictors beyond that explained by the previously entered P' predictors. The only change would come in the appropriate degrees of freedom for the F test, which would now be given by $\nu_1 = Q'$ and $\nu_2 = N - (P' + Q') - 1$. For further information, see Cohen and Cohen (1975).

Finally, a number of existing computer programs are not written to perform stepwise regression in the manner that we have been discussing. For these programs, the order of entry is not determined on the basis of the largest part correlation criterion that characterizes the forward selection method described in Section 3-13. Rather than adhering to what might be called a data-determined order of entry, based on decreasing part correlation values, these programs enter variables into the equation sequentially on the basis of a researcher- or user-determined order. Thus the researcher specifies the order of introduction of each predictor variable into the equation. The $\hat{R}^2$s and squared part correlations are given at each step of the process, which is terminated only after all variables have been entered. An appropriate usage of this user-determined approach is when the researcher has a priori theoretical or practical reasons for entering variables in a particular order. Under this model, the respective importance of each variable can be argued on substantive or theoretical grounds. The statistical tests are then performed in that order rather than by the order dictated by the magnitudes of the part correlations. Obviously, questions of appropriate type I error partitioning are relevant here as well.

3-15. An example

Consider the summary data graciously provided by Walter Loban of the University of California at Berkeley, which are presented in Table 3-8. In the Loban study, an attempt was made to predict verbal fluency of 97 third-grade boys on the basis of verbal measures taken in the first and second grades. The potential set of predictors consists of:

X_1: Fluency at Grade 1
X_2: Fluency at Grade 2
X_3: Freedom from mazes at Grade 1
X_4: Freedom from mazes at Grade 2
X_5: Use of dependent clauses at Grade 1
X_6: Use of dependent clauses at Grade 2

More complete definitions of these terms appear in Section 8-1. In addition, a psychometric measure of intelligence, Lorge-Thorndike IQ, was taken in Grade 3 and included as a predictor, X_7.

Examination of the correlation coefficients in Table 3-8 shows that verbal fluency in Grade 3 was most highly correlated with fluency in Grade 2 with $r_{YX_2} = .80149$. According to the data-determined forward selection procedure presented in Table 3-9, X_2 enters the regression equation first. The F test for this variable is indicated by $F = 170.64$, which is significant at $\alpha = .05$. At this first step it is seen that:

TABLE 3-8. Correlation matrix associated with the Loban data of Section 3-15

	X_1	X_2	X_3	X_4	X_5	X_6	X_7	Y
X_1	1.00000	0.73891	0.18323	− 0.02429	0.64103	0.42370	0.40786	0.70512
X_2		1.00000	0.13572	0.12423	0.42523	0.45152	0.38990	0.80149
X_3			1.00000	0.57431	0.10675	− 0.03824	− 0.17241	0.17844
X_4				1.00000	− 0.10708	− 0.09096	− 0.30531	0.10306
X_5					1.00000	0.55392	0.28937	0.47429
X_6						1.00000	0.37103	0.36657
X_7							1.00000	0.27953
Y								1.00000

TABLE 3-9. Stepwise regression analysis for selecting the prediction equation with the smallest set of predictors

Step One: Part 1

Source	*d/f*	*Sum of squares*	*Mean square*	*F*
Regression	1	113.02212	113.02212	170.64
Residual	95	62.92098	.66233	
Total	96	175.94310		

Step One: Part 2. Variables not in the equation

Variable	*Part correlations*
Fluency 1	.17
Mazes 1	.07
Mazes 2	.00
Dependent Clauses 1	.14
Dependent Clauses 2	.01
IQ score	− .04

Step Two: Part 1

Source	*d/f*	*Sum of squares*	*Mean square*	*Partial F*
Regression	2	117.96107		
Fluency 2	1	113.02212		
Fluency 1	1	4.93895	4.93895	8.01
Residual	94	57.98202	.61683	
Total	96	175.94310		

Step Two: Part 2. Variables not in the equation

Variable	*Part correlations*
Mazes 1	.05
Mazes 2	.03
Dependent Clauses 1	.07
Dependent Clauses 2	− .02
IQ Score	− .07+

Step Three: Part 1

Source	*d/f*	*Sum of squares*	*Mean square*	*Partial F*
Regression	3	118.80964		
Fluency 2	1	113.02212		
Fluency 1	1	4.93895		
IQ Score	1	.84857	.84857	1.38
Residual	93	57.13345	.61434	
Total	96	175.94310		

$$r^2_{YX_2} = \hat{R}^2_{Y \cdot X_2} = \frac{SS_{\text{Reg}}}{SS_{\text{Tot}}} = \frac{113.02212}{175.94310} = .64238 = .80149^2$$

The part correlations based on X_2 already included in the regression equation are reported in Part 2 of Step One in Table 3-9. Of these, variable X_1 or fluency in Grade 1, emerges with the largest value, $r_{Y(X_1 \cdot X_2)} = .17$. As a result, X_1 is selected for inclusion at Step Two. We therefore add this variable to the equation and determine:

$$\begin{aligned} SS_{\text{Added}} &= SS_{\text{Reg (Step Two)}} - SS_{\text{Reg (Step One)}} \\ &= 117.96107 - 113.02212 = 4.93895 \end{aligned}$$

With $MS_{\text{Res}} = .61683$, the partial F test for Fluency 1 is given by:

$$F = 4.93895/.61683 = 8.01$$

If $\alpha = .05$, the addition would be declared significant since F exceeds $F_{1,94:.95} = 3.96$. We also note that:

$$r^2_{Y(X_1 \cdot X_2)} = \frac{SS_{\text{Added}}}{SS_{\text{Tot}}} = \frac{4.93895}{175.94310} = .028 = .17^2$$

is not very large. Even so, X_1 represents a statistically significant addition to $\hat{R}^2$, which is now given by:

$$\hat{R}^2_{Y \cdot X_2 X_1} = \frac{SS_{\text{Reg (Step Two)}}}{SS_{\text{Tot}}} = \frac{117.96107}{175.94310} = .670$$

Alternatively:

$$\hat{R}^2_{Y \cdot X_2 X_1} = r^2_{YX_2} + r^2_{Y(X_1 \cdot X_2)} = .80^2 + .17^2 = .67$$

This is to be compared with the $\hat{R}^2_{Y \cdot X_2}$ figure of .640 that was obtained using Fluency 2 as a single predictor.

The remaining variables and their associated part correlations are given in Part 2 of Step Two of Table 3-9. Since IQ has the highest of the remaining part correlations, $r_{Y(X_7 \cdot X_1 X_2)} = -.07$, it enters the equation next. The partial F ratio associated with IQ is given in Part 1 of Step Three by $F = 1.38$, which is not statistically significant at $\alpha = .05$. Therefore IQ would not be included in the final equation and the process stops. Using formulas presented in Section 3-4, we can determine a $P = 2$ variable regression equation for predicting third-grade fluency by:

$$\hat{Y} = 1.3867 + .2400X_1 + .6191X_2$$

3-16. Dummy coding of qualitative variables

By now it should be somewhat obvious that regression analysis and the analysis of variance are somehow associated with one another, since we have been using the analysis of variance concepts of degrees of freedom, sums of squares, F ratios, and explained and unexplained variance in our discussion of regression. Though the connection is apparent, its nature may not be. In this section, we will attempt to show that the analysis of variance and its derivative, analysis of covariance, can be couched in a multiple regression framework and therefore can be subsumed under this more general model. We demonstrate the truth of this proposition by examples and not by any theoretical development even though this could be done. For the reader who requires such a formal development, we recommend the texts by Cohen and Cohen (1975), Timm (1975), and Kerlinger and Pedhazur (1973).

We can introduce a qualitative variable into a regression equation provided we quantify it properly. To achieve this quantification, we first count the number of levels and degrees of freedom associated with the qualitative variable to be quantified. If the number of levels is equal to K, the number of degrees of freedom associated with this variable is $K - 1$. This latter number tells us that we can incorporate into the regression model $K - 1$ linearly independent or noncollinear variables. We can introduce them by defining *dummy variables* as follows:

$$X_1 = \begin{cases} 1, \text{ if the individual is a member of Level 1} \\ 0, \text{ otherwise} \end{cases}$$

$$X_2 = \begin{cases} 1, \text{ if the individual is a member of Level 2} \\ 0, \text{ otherwise} \end{cases}$$

$$X_{K-1} = \begin{cases} 1, \text{ if the individual is a member of Level } K - 1 \\ 0, \text{ otherwise} \end{cases}$$

According to this model, dummy coding proceeds as follows.

Procedure for dummy coding a qualitative variable for analysis of variance.

Step 1. Determine the number of levels of the qualitative variable of interest. Let the number be denoted by K.

Step 2. Define $v = K - 1$ dummy variables, $X_1, X_2, \ldots, X_{K-1}$, which are given as follows:

Level	X_1	X_2	$\ldots$	X_{K-1}
1	1	0	$\ldots$	0
2	0	1	$\ldots$	0
$\vdots$	$\vdots$	$\vdots$	$\ddots$	$\vdots$
K	0	0	$\ldots$	0

As an example, consider the data of Table 3-10, which represent the first pretest scores of the 39 students of Table 1-2 classified by College Major: Natural Science, Social Science, Humanities, with Others and Unknowns treated as a fourth group. The analysis of variance table for these data is presented in Table 3-11, with mean values given by $\bar{Y}_1 = 17.500$, $\bar{Y}_2 = 19.875$, $\bar{Y}_3 = 19.333$, and $\bar{Y}_4 = 17.308$.

We now code all students with variables as follows:

	X_1	X_2	X_3
Natural Science	1	0	0
Social Science	0	1	0
Humanities	0	0	1
Others and Unknowns	0	0	0

Table 3-10. Quantification of qualitative data to convert an ANOVA into a regression model where Y: Score on pretest and where College Major: Natural Science, Social Science, and Humanities are coded as X_1, X_2, and X_3

Y	X_1	X_2	X_3
28	1	0	0
17	1	0	0
25	1	0	0
13	1	0	0
30	1	0	0
16	1	0	0
13	1	0	0
3	1	0	0
16	1	0	0
17	1	0	0
15	1	0	0
17	1	0	0
13	0	1	0
18	0	1	0
13	0	1	0
20	0	1	0
28	0	1	0
28	0	1	0
9	0	1	0
30	0	1	0
10	0	0	1
28	0	0	1
25	0	0	1
10	0	0	1
13	0	0	1
30	0	0	1
24	0	0	0
23	0	0	0
16	0	0	0
26	0	0	0
29	0	0	0
5	0	0	0
8	0	0	0
10	0	0	0
22	0	0	0
17	0	0	0
14	0	0	0
15	0	0	0
16	0	0	0

TABLE 3-11. Analysis of variance table for the data of Table 3-10

Source	*d/f*	*Sum of squares*	*Mean square*	*F*	$\hat{\eta}^2 = \frac{SS_{Bet}}{SS_{Tot}}$
Between groups	3	46.38	15.46	.26	.0217
Within groups	35	2093.98	59.83		
Total	38	2140.36	56.32		

Note that even though only three dummy variables were coded, students from all four college major levels can be uniquely identified according to a three-digit binary code: 100, 010, 001, and 000.

With these dummy-coded variables, the following sums are obtained: $\Sigma Y = 710$, $\Sigma X_1 = 12$, $\Sigma X_2 = 8$, $\Sigma X_3 = 6$; $\Sigma Y^2 = 15066$, $\Sigma X_1^2 = 12$, $\Sigma X_2^2 = 8$, $\Sigma X_3^2 = 6$; and $\Sigma X_1 Y = 210$, $\Sigma X_2 Y = 159$, $\Sigma X_3 Y = 116$, $\Sigma X_1 X_2 = 0$, $\Sigma X_1 X_3 = 0$, and $\Sigma X_2 X_3 = 0$. From these figures, the set of normal equations can be derived:

$$710 = 39B_0 + 12B_1 + 8B_2 + 6B_3$$

$$210 = 12B_0 + 12B_1 + 0B_2 + 0B_3$$

$$159 = 8B_0 + 0B_1 + 8B_2 + 0B_3$$

and

$$116 = 6B_0 + 0B_1 + 0B_2 + 6B_3$$

with solution given by:

$$\hat{Y} = 17.308 + .192X_1 + 2.567X_2 + 2.025X_3$$

From this equation, we see that:

$$\bar{\bar{Y}}_{\text{Natural Science}} = 17.308 + .192(1) + 2.567(0) + 2.025(0) = 17.500 = \bar{Y}_1$$

$$\bar{\bar{Y}}_{\text{Social Science}} = 17.308 + .192(0) + 2.567(1) + 2.025(0) = 19.875 = \bar{Y}_2$$

$$\bar{\bar{Y}}_{\text{Humanities}} = 17.308 + .192(0) + 2.567(0) + 2.025(1) = 19.333 = \bar{Y}_3$$

and

$$\bar{\bar{Y}}_{\text{Others}} = 17.308 + .192(0) + 2.567(0) + 2.025(0) = 17.308 = \bar{Y}_4$$

As indicated:

$$B_0 = \bar{Y}_4 = 17.308$$

$$B_1 = \bar{Y}_1 - \bar{Y}_4 = 17.500 - 17.308 = .192$$

$$B_2 = \bar{Y}_2 - \bar{Y}_4 = 19.875 - 17.308 = 2.567$$

and

$$B_3 = \bar{Y}_3 - \bar{Y}_4 = 19.333 - 17.308 = 2.025$$

The pattern for K groups of subjects is obvious. $\bar{Y}_K$ will always be associated with the group scored by $K - 1$ zero values. For this group $B_0 = \bar{Y}_K$. For the remaining groups, we have $B_k = \bar{Y}_k - \bar{Y}_K$.

To complete the analysis, we need the variances and covariances associated with the $K - 1$ dummy variable. From the previously reported sums:

$$S^2_{X_1} = \frac{39(12) - 12^2}{39(38)} = .2186$$

$$S_{X_1X_2} = \frac{39(0) - (12)(8)}{39(38)} = -.0648$$

The remaining values are reported in Table 3-12. Moreover the value of S^2_Y is given by:

$$S^2_Y = \frac{39(15066) - 710^2}{39(38)} = 56.3252$$

which is simply the MS_{Tot} of Table 3-11.

As we saw in Chapter 1, $r^2 = S^2_{\hat{Y}}/S^2_Y$ where, according to Section 3-5, $S^2_{\hat{Y}}$ can be written as:

$$S^2_{\hat{Y}} = B_1^2S^2_{X_1} + B_2^2S^2_{X_2} + B_3^2S^2_{X_3} + 2B_1B_2S_{X_1X_2} + 2B_1B_3S_{X_1X_3} + 2B_2B_3S_{X_2X_3}$$

TABLE 3-12. Variances and covariances for the dummy variables of Table 3-10

	X_1	X_2	X_3
X_1	.2186	− .0648	− .0486
X_2	− .0648	.1673	− .0324
X_3	− .0486	− .0324	.1336

Substituting the previously given values of B_k and the values of Table 3-12 into this equation, we find that:

$$S_{\hat{Y}}^2 = 1.2203$$

Finally:

$$\hat{R}^2 = \frac{S_{\hat{Y}}^2}{S_Y^2} = \frac{1.2203}{56.3250} = .0217$$

which corresponds with the value labeled $\hat{\eta}^2$ in Table 3-10. This statistic is called the *correlation ratio* and is defined as $\hat{\eta}^2 = SS_{\text{Bet}}/SS_{\text{Tot}}$. Thus we see that, except for rounding errors:

$$\begin{aligned} SS_{\text{Between groups}} &= (N-1)S_Y^2\hat{R}^2 = 38(56.3250)(.0217) \\ &= 46.37 = SS_{\text{Reg}} \\ SS_{\text{Within groups}} &= (N-1)S_Y^2(1-\hat{R}^2) = 38(56.3250)(.9783) \\ &= 2093.90 = SS_{\text{Res}} \end{aligned}$$

which are the same values reported in Table 3-10. Moreover, since $SS_{\text{Between}} = SS_{\text{Reg}}$ and $SS_{\text{Within}} = SS_{\text{Res}}$, it is not surprising that $\hat{\eta}^2$ of the analysis of variance model corresponds exactly to $\hat{R}^2$ of the multiple regression model.

Before concluding this discussion, we note that if statistical interactions were of interest, they too could be subsumed by the multiple regression model. For our example, if the researcher wished to include both sex and career in the regression equation, they could be entered by defining the main effect of sex X_S, the main effect of career X_C, and the interaction of sex by career $X_{S\times C}$ as:

$$X_S = \begin{cases} 1, \text{ if male} \\ 0, \text{ if female} \end{cases}$$

$$X_C = \begin{cases} 1, \text{ if sociology-related career} \\ 0, \text{ if nonsociology-related career} \end{cases}$$

$$X_{S\times C} = \begin{cases} 1 \times 1 = 1, \text{ if male and sociology-related career} \\ 1 \times 0 = 0, \text{ if male and nonsociology-related career} \\ 0 \times 1 = 0, \text{ if female and sociology-related career} \\ 0 \times 0 = 0, \text{ if female and nonsociology-related career} \end{cases}$$

Since each of these three sources of variance may be shown to have only one degree of freedom, each person would appear with the following three coded values:

	X_S	X_C	$X_{S\times C}$
Males in sociology-related careers	1	1	1
Males in nonsociology-related careers	1	0	0
Females in sociology-related careers	0	1	0
Females in nonsociology-related careers	0	0	0

We do not go into the details of the analysis here, but note that caution must be exercised in interpreting the results derived from multifactor, dummy-coded designs (or, more generally, from any *nonorthogonal* designs). The reason is that more than one solution is possible, depending on the order in which the various dummy variables (or factors) are entered into the regression equation. For multiple regression solutions to this problem, see Cohen and Cohen (1975) or Kerlinger and Pedhazur (1973). For discussion of the more general topic of nonorthogonal analysis of variance designs, see Overall and Spiegel (1969) and Carlson and Timm (1974). Suffice it to say that such designs present complex interpretive problems, which would get us into issues far beyond the scope of this book.

We now extend the dummy-coded multiple regression model to incorporate analysis of covariance designs. However, before proceeding we wish to emphasize that the various correspondences that can be demonstrated within an analysis of covariance framework are intended as mathematical identities and nothing more. That is, the analysis of covariance is one of the most restrictive statistical models with respect to its proper use and associated assumptions, as stated by Elashoff (1969). In the context of the present example, one or more of these assumptions are likely to be violated. For instance, because the experimental groups to be considered were self-selected rather than randomly formed, we would expect the distributions of the covariates not to be comparable from one group to the next. Because of the interpretive difficulties arising from violation of analysis of covariance assumptions such as this, we therefore present the following example without attaching substantive significance to the results. We certainly are not advocating its application in situations where we wish to "equate" for initial group differences. Rather, we view the primary function of the technique as *variance reducing* which will occur when X and Y are related within groups, rather than *bias removing* which will occur when groups differ considerably with respect to the covariate(s).

Consider a one-way analysis of variance design involving four independent groups in which three covariates are of theoretical or applied interest. If we perform a stepwise regression on the three covariates, we will reach a point where the effects of X_1, X_2, and X_3 have been removed from Y. If we now add the independent variable of interest to the model in terms of dummy variables, we would see that the sum of squares added to the explained source of variance is identical to the sum of squares associated with the adjusted scores of an analysis of covariance.

For the example, consider the 216 subjects of Table A-1 who are classified according to major and for which all missing data have been estimated. Let the groups be denoted:

G_1: Natural Science
G_2: Social Science
G_3: Humanities
G_4: Others and Unknowns

Let the covariates be:

X_1: High school grade point average (HSGPA)
X_2: Midterm 1 (M1)
X_3: Midterm 2 (M2)

and let the dependent variable be denoted by Y: Score on the final. The data are summarized in Table 3-13.

We now perform the analysis as a stepwise regression based on a data-determined order of entry into the equation. It should be mentioned that as long as the complete

TABLE 3-13. Correlations among the variables

	1	2	3	4	5	6	7
1. High School GPA	—	0.666	0.556	− 0.038	− 0.141	0.076	0.644
2. Midterm 1		—	0.517	− 0.059	− 0.092	0.113	0.613
3. Midterm 2			—	− 0.130	− 0.034	0.065	0.589
4. Natural Science				—	− 0.383	− 0.269	− 0.057
5. Social Science					—	− 0.239	− 0.024
6. Humanities						—	0.061
7. Final							—

set of three covariates is entered before the group membership variable, the order in which individual covariates are entered makes no difference. That is, the results based on the three-covariate set will be invariant with respect to individual covariate reorderings. We begin by placing X_1: HSGPA into the regression equation since $r_{YX_1} = .64$ is largest. The results of this analysis, based on the standardized variables, are summarized in Table 3-14. In terms of standarized variables $\hat{Y} = b_1 X_1$. In this one-predictor variable case, $b_1 = r_{YX_1}$, so that:

$$\hat{R}^2_{YX_1} = r_{YX_1} b_1 = r_{YX_1}(r_{YX_1}) = r^2_{YX_1} = .6436^2 = .4142$$

Moreover:

$$\begin{aligned} SS_{\text{Reg}(Y \cdot X_1)} &= (N - 1)S_Y^2 r^2_{YX_1} \\ &= 215(28.1506)^2(.4142) \\ &= 70569.16 \end{aligned}$$

$$SS_{\text{Res}(Y \cdot X_1)} = (N - 1)S_Y^2(1 - r^2_{YX_1}) = 99809.47$$

These results are also summarized in Table 3-14.

At this point we see that $SS_{\text{Reg}(Y \cdot X_1)}$ relates to $B_{1(T)}$ and not $B_{1(W)}$ for X_1, or equivalently to $r_{YX_1(T)}$ and not $r_{YX_1(W)}$. This is readily apparent when placed in the multiple regression framework, inasmuch as the group membership has not even been specified in Step One. At the same time, we now see that the test of $\beta_{1(W)} = 0$ corresponds to a test of a partial correlation coefficient, or one that would follow had the group membership variable been entered in the equation first. As noted in Section 2-7, the test of $\beta_{1(T)} = 0$ must be interpreted with caution because of its confounding two sources of a relationship between X and Y, namely within and between groups. We also reiterate that the test of $\beta_{1(T)} = 0$, given by the F ratio of 151.31 in Table 3-14, is not a test of whether or not an analysis of covariance would be wise from a variance-reducing standpoint, since this test is uninformative concerning the locus of variance extraction. It could be extracted from the within-group variance, which generally would increase the power of the test for group differences. On the other hand, it could be extracted as well, or instead, from the variance associated with group centroid differences, which would serve to reduce the power of the test.

Proceeding now to Step Two, we note that M2 is added, since $r_{YX_3 \cdot X_1} = .363$ represents the larger of the two partial correlation coefficients. With this addition:

$$\hat{Y} = .4576X_1 + .3345X_3$$

TABLE 3-14. Analysis of covariance performed as a stepwise regression

Source	d/f		Sum of squares	Mean square	F	$\hat{R}^2$	Increment in $\hat{R}^2$
Step One							
Regression							
on HSGPA	1		70569.16	70569.16	151.31	.4142	—
Residual	214		99809.47	466.40			
Total	215		170378.63				
Note: $r_{YX_2 \cdot X_1} = .323$, $r_{YX_3 \cdot X_1} = .363$							
Step Two							
Regression on							
HSGPA and M2	2		83737.13			.4915	.0773
HSGPA		1	70569.16	—	—		
M2		1	13167.97	13167.97	32.37		
Residual	213		86641.52	406.77			
Total	215		170378.65				
Note: $r_{YX_2 \cdot X_1X_3} = .262$							
Step Three							
Regression on							
HSGPA, M1, and M2	3		89686.81			.5264	.0349
HSGPA and M2		2	83737.13	—	—		
M1		1	5949.68	5949.68	15.63		
Residual	212		80691.83	380.62			
Total	215		170378.64				
Step Four							
Regression on							
HSGPA, M1, M2,							
X_4, X_5, and X_6	6		90399.83			.5306	.0042
HSGPA, M1, and M2		3	89686.81	—	—		
College Major		3	713.02	237.67	.62		
Residual	209		79978.82	382.67			
Total	215		170378.65				

so that:

$$\hat{R}^2_{Y \cdot X_1X_3} = r_{YX_1}b_1 + r_{YX_3}b_3$$
$$= .6437(.4576) + .5889(.3345) = .4915$$

$$SS_{\text{Reg}(Y \cdot X_1X_3)} = (N - 1)S^2_Y\hat{R}^2_{Y \cdot X_1X_3}$$
$$= 215(28.1506)^2(.4915) = 83737.13$$

$$SS_{\text{Res}(Y \cdot X_1X_3)} = (N - 1)S^2_Y(1 - \hat{R}^2_{Y \cdot X_1X_3}) = 86641.52$$

We also note that the squared part correlation involving X_3 is given by:

$$r^2_{Y(X_3 \cdot X_1)} = \hat{R}^2_{Y \cdot X_1X_3} - r^2_{YX_1}$$
$$= .4915 - .4142 = .0773$$

At Step Three, M1 is added, since it is the only covariate remaining. With this addition:

$$\hat{Y} = .3166X_1 + .2796X_3 + .2577X_2$$

so that:

$$\hat{R}^2_{Y\cdot X_1X_2X_3} = r_{YX_1}b_1 + r_{YX_2}b_2 + r_{YX_3}b_3$$
$$= .6436(.3166) + .6130(.2577) + .5889(.2796)$$
$$= .5264$$

$$SS_{\text{Reg}(Y\cdot X_1X_2X_3)} = (N - 1)S^2_Y\hat{R}^2_{Y\cdot X_1X_2X_3}$$
$$= 215(28.1506)^2(.5264) = 89686.81$$

$$SS_{\text{Res}(Y\cdot X_1X_2X_3)} = (N - 1)S^2_Y(1 - \hat{R}^2_{Y\cdot X_1X_2X_3}) = 80691.83$$

We also note that the squared part correlation involving X_3 is given by:

$$r^2_{Y(X_2\cdot X_1X_3)} = \hat{R}^2_{Y\cdot X_1X_2X_3} - \hat{R}^2_{Y\cdot X_1X_3}$$
$$= .5264 - .4915 = .0349$$

Suppose we now wish to determine how much impact college major has on the distribution of final test scores. When this analysis of covariance hypothesis is viewed from a multiple regression perspective, another way to think of it is in terms of how much additional variance can be explained by the inclusion of the college major variable in an equation that already includes three individual difference measures. In terms of our example, we might expect students in the social sciences to earn higher scores on the sociology final in comparison to students in the other disciplines. If so, then college major would explain some extra part of the total final test score variance.

We can introduce the qualitative variable, college major, into the regression equation, by using the same dummy-coding scheme that was used in the previous analysis of variance example. Thus each student is represented in the regression equation as:

Major	X_4	X_5	X_6
Natural Science	1	0	0
Social Science	0	1	0
Humanities	0	0	1
Others and Unknowns	0	0	0

We now enter the set of three dummy variables into the regression equation. The results of this analysis are shown as Step Four in Table 3-14. The resulting standardized regression equation is given as:

$$\hat{Y} = .3270X_1 + .2577X_2 + .2806X_3 + .0181X_4 + .0757X_5 + .0413X_6$$

so that:

$$\hat{R}^2_{Y\cdot X_1X_2\ldots X_6} = r_{YX_1}b_1 + r_{YX_2}b_2 + \ldots + r_{YX_6}b_6$$
$$= .6436(.3270) + .6130(.2577) + \ldots + .0614(.0413)$$
$$= .5306$$

$$SS_{\text{Reg}(Y\cdot X_1X_2\ldots X_6)} = (N - 1)S^2_Y\hat{R}^2_{Y\cdot X_1\ldots X_6}$$
$$= 215(28.1506)^2(.5306) = 90399.83$$
$$SS_{\text{Res}(Y\cdot X_1X_2\ldots X_6)} = (N - 1)S^2_Y(1 - \hat{R}^2_{Y\cdot X_1\ldots X_6}) = 79978.82$$

We also see that the squared part correlation for X_4, X_5, and X_6 is given by:

$$r^2_{Y(X_4X_5X_6 \cdot X_1X_2X_3)} = \hat{R}^2_{Y \cdot X_1X_2 \ldots X_6} - \hat{R}^2_{Y \cdot X_1X_2X_3}$$
$$= .5306 - .5264 = .0042$$

The partial F test for this set of three variables is given by:

$$F = \frac{v_2}{v_1}\left(\frac{\hat{R}^2_{Y \cdot X_1X_2 \ldots X_6} - \hat{R}^2_{Y \cdot X_1X_2X_3}}{1 - \hat{R}^2_{Y \cdot X_1X_2 \ldots X_6}}\right) = \frac{209}{3}\left(\frac{.5306 - .5264}{1 - .5306}\right) = .62$$

which is very small and statistically not significant. Thus it would be concluded that college major is not significantly related to final test scores when high school grade point average and the two midterm scores are considered.

Although we have illustrated the model for only a single group membership variable or factor, it should be quite apparent that it can be used for multiple factors and more complex designs. In general, there should be little difficulty in performing a general analysis of covariance with many covariates and many analyses of variance factors, since many computer programs are designed to perform a stepwise regression. As cautioned earlier, however, our interpretation of such analyses must be conditioned by the extent to which the various assumptions associated with analysis of covariance are met.

For completeness, we provide directions for performing an analysis of covariance as a stepwise regression.

Procedure for performing an analysis of covariance as a stepwise regression.

Step 1. Perform a stepwise regression on the P covariates $X_1, X_2, \ldots, X_P$. Let the squared multiple correlation coefficient associated with these P variables be denoted:

$$\hat{R}^2_{Y \cdot X_1X_2 \ldots X_P}$$

Step 2. Consider a qualitative factor defined in terms of K unique levels. Introduce $v = K - 1$ dummy variables as:

Group	X_{P+1}	X_{P+2}	...	X_{P+K-1}
1	1	0	...	0
2	0	1	...	0
.	.	.	.	.
.	.	.	.	.
.	.	.	.	.
K	0	0	...	0

Step 3. Enter these dummy variables into the regression equation as a set of $K - 1$ variables. Let the squared multiple correlation associated with both covariates and dummy variables in the equation be denoted:

$$\hat{R}^2_{Y \cdot X_1X_2 \ldots X_{P+K-1}}$$

Step 4. Compute:

$$F = \frac{N - K - P}{K - 1}\left(\frac{\hat{R}^2_{Y \cdot X_1X_2 \ldots X_{P+K-1}} - \hat{R}^2_{Y \cdot X_1X_2 \ldots X_P}}{1 - \hat{R}^2_{Y \cdot X_1X_2 \ldots X_{P+K-1}}}\right)$$

Step 5. With chosen α level of significance, reject the hypothesis of no difference in intercepts or adjusted averages if:

$$F > F_{K-1, N-K-P:1-\alpha}$$

Even though our demonstration of dummy coding was performed within the context of testing the analysis of covariance (equal intercepts) hypothesis, it is a much more general procedure than that. For example, entering the set of covariates *after* the set of dummy variables is in the equation permits a test of the pooled within-group relationship between the covariates and the dependent variable. In particular:

$$F = \frac{N - K - P}{P}\left(\frac{\hat{R}^2_{Y\cdot X_1X_2\ldots X_{P+K-1}} - \hat{R}^2_{Y\cdot X_1X_2\ldots X_{K-1}}}{1 - \hat{R}^2_{Y\cdot X_1X_2\ldots X_{P+K-1}}}\right)$$

is referred to an F distribution with P and $N - K - P$ degrees of freedom. When $P = 1$, this reduces to the test of the within-group regression coefficient discussed in Section 2-6.

In addition to the inclusion of P covariates and $K - 1$ dummy-coded variables in the model, we can also define $P(K - 1)$ products in which each covariate is multiplied by each dummy variable. This will result in a total of $P + (K - 1) + (PK - P) = PK + K - 1$ variables. If we enter the $PK - P = P(K - 1)$ products after the $P + K - 1$ original variables are already in the regression equation, we can compute:

$$F = \frac{N - K(P + 1)}{P(K - 1)}\left(\frac{\hat{R}^2_{Y\cdot X_1X_2\ldots X_{PK+K-1}} - \hat{R}^2_{Y\cdot X_1X_2\ldots X_{P+K-1}}}{1 - \hat{R}^2_{Y\cdot X_1X_2\ldots X_{PK+K-1}}}\right)$$

to test for the presence of a covariate-by-treatment interaction. The reference F distribution is based on $P(K - 1)$ and $N - K(P + 1)$ degrees of freedom. With $P = 1$, this reduces to the equal slopes (parallelism) test of Section 2-4.

Finally, if the P covariates are entered first, followed by the $K - 1$ dummy variables and the $PK - P$ products jointly, we would obtain:

$$F = \frac{N - K(P + 1)}{(P + 1)(K - 1)}\left(\frac{\hat{R}^2_{Y\cdot X_1X_2\ldots X_{PK+K-1}} - \hat{R}^2_{Y\cdot X_1X_2\ldots X_P}}{1 - \hat{R}^2_{Y\cdot X_1X_2\ldots X_{PK+K-1}}}\right)$$

which would be referred to an F distribution based on $(P + 1)(K - 1)$ and $N - K(P + 1)$ degrees of freedom. This statistic can be used to determine whether K regression lines are identical, the specialization of which for $P = 1$ is the test of identity discussed in Section 2-8.

The situation in which there are only dummy variables in the equation, with no covariates, yields the analysis of variance situation discussed at the beginning of this section.

3-17. Rudiments of path analysis

In recent years, sociologists have made extensive use of *path analysis* in studying social systems. Similar models have been proposed by economists and are usually referred to as *structural equations models*. Although we cannot examine these models in detail, we can briefly consider some *nonreciprocal* (unidirectional) models of causation. The statistics for these models have been presented in some detail in some previous sections. As will be seen from the examples, the logic of path analysis is easy to comprehend and simple to execute. What is not so easy and simple is the generation of a path structure that truly represents cause-and-effect relationships. When the model was first proposed by Wright (1934), it was thought that path analysis would illuminate the nature of cause-and-effect relationships in biological systems. However, unlike biological systems, it must be stated at the start that many of the applications of path analysis in the social sciences do not, and cannot, represent true cause-and-effect models. We do not wish to enter the discussion as to whether or not statistical models prove cause and effect in social contexts. In fact, we have argued earlier that they probably do not have that property. We do wish to present the method, however, because of its widespread use. Even though our examples are mainly predictive or correlational in nature, we will describe them in cause-and-effect terms, knowing that they may not possess such characteristics. Our goal is the description of a methodology and not a justification of its use for sociological investigations. We will leave that discussion to others. In addition, because of space limitations, we will not provide an in-depth discussion of path analysis. Our purpose is to present the basic principles and rules concerning use of the method. With that in mind, let us consider the simplest path analysis based on one dependent variable and two predictor variables.

The simplest two-predictor path model is the one shown in Figure 3-7. In this model, it is hypothesized that Y is caused by X_1 and X_2 and by U_Y. X_1 and X_2 are two variables that are believed to have a direct influence on Y, whereas U_Y refers to all other variables in the environment that could influence Y. Obviously we are using U_Y to represent the unexplained factors, other than X_1 and X_2, that affect Y. Direct arrows to Y from X_1 and X_2 are used to represent direct effects. The curved double arrow between X_1 and X_2 represents a simple correlation between X_1 and X_2 that may or may not be causative in nature. When reading from left to right, the figure represents a temporal ordering, with X_1 and X_2 appearing in time before Y. The background variables X_1 and X_2 in this example are often referred to as *exogeneous* variables, although we will continue to call them predictor or independent variables. Three basic assumptions that we make for this discussion are:

1. The X variables are measured without error.
2. There are no reciprocal causations, such as X causing Y and Y causing X.
3. U_Y is uncorrelated with the X variables.

Models exist in which these assumptions are not made and which are considered more realistic by sociologists and economists. As indicated, however, we are only providing the flavor of path analysis.

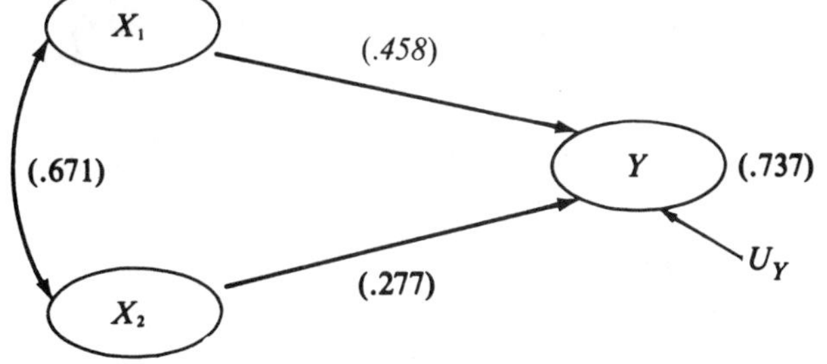

Figure 3-7. Path model for two direct predictors.

We have already provided a solution of this path model in our example of Section 3-1, where Y, X_1, and X_2 are given by Y: Final, X_1: Midterm 1, and X_2: Midterm 2. The theory specified by the path is that scores on the final are influenced by what is measured on the two midterms. By this we mean, for example, that a unit change in Midterm 1 scores is associated with some change in the final scores. Although this is not strictly a cause-and-effect statement, it represents what is referred to as a *weak causal ordering*. If there is a cause-and-effect relationship between Y and X_1, it must extend from Midterm 1 to the final and not from the final to Midterm 1, since Midterm 1 is measured, in time, prior to the final. Also note that we are not saying that Midterm 1 causes the final. Instead, we are saying that the variable measured by Midterm 1, knowledge early in the course, has a direct impact on final test scores, end-of-course knowledge. In this sense, a student who is doing well early in the course is expected to do better on the final in comparison to a student who is initially doing poorly. As we saw in Section 3-4, the standardized multiple regression equation for predicting Y from X_1 and X_2 is given by:

$$\begin{aligned}\hat{Z}_Y &= b_1 Z_{X_1} + b_2 Z_{X_2} \\ &= .458 Z_{X_1} + .277 Z_{X_2}\end{aligned}$$

The standardized beta weights of this equation are called the *path coefficients* of this model and reflect the relationship that X_1 and X_2 have to Y. The simple correlation coefficient between X_1 and X_2 represents the association between the predictor variables of the model. In this case $r_{X_1X_2} = .671$. These numbers appear in the path diagram of Figure 3-7. As we see, one standard deviation change in X_1 produces a .46 standard deviation change in Y, whereas one standard deviation change in X_2 produces a .28 standard deviation change in Y. Finally:

$$U_Y = \sqrt{1 - \hat{R}^2_{Y \cdot X_1X_2}} = \sqrt{1 - .457} = .737$$

As we saw in Section 3-8, B_1 or b_1 was significantly different from zero, while B_2 or b_2 was not. These findings are represented, respectively, by the italicized and nonitalicized numbers in Figure 3-7. In any case, we see that X_1 and X_2 are not the sole determinants of Y, since $U_Y = .737$ is so large.

A slightly more complicated path model for two predictors is shown in Figure 3-8. The difference between the paths shown in Figures 3-7 and 3-8 is that, in the latter

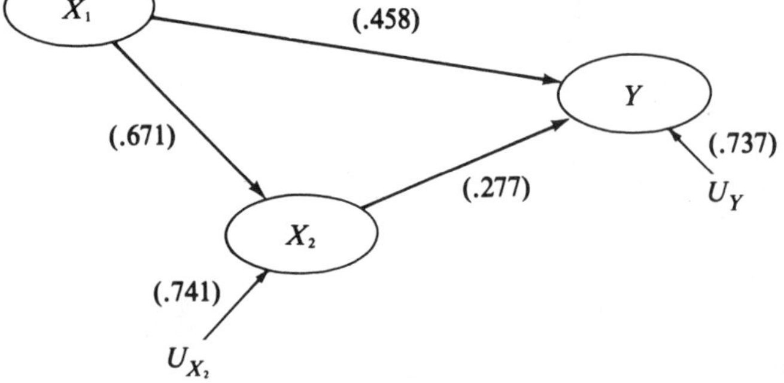

Figure 3-8. Path model for one direct and one indirect predictor.

figure, X_1 and X_2 are not just correlated but are postulated to exist in a cause-and-effect or time-ordered relationship in that scores on the second midterm are directly related to scores on the first midterm. Students doing well on the first midterm are expected to do well on the second midterm, while students doing poorly on the first midterm are expected to repeat their poor performance on the second midterm. Of the two models, this one makes more intuitive sense because of the time ordering in the two midterms.

Let us reconsider the same data using this model. Here there are two paths for X_1 leading to Y. They are the direct path of X_1 to Y and the indirect path of X_1 to Y, passing through X_2. On the other hand, X_2 has only one single, direct connection to Y. Since X_1 has a direct and an indirect path to Y, it has two different ways for influencing the outcomes of Y.

Recalling from Section 3-4 the special case where $p = 1$, we see that the path coefficient for X_2 regressed on X_1 is given simply by $r_{X_1X_2} = .671$, with:

$$U_{X_2} = \sqrt{1 - r^2_{X_1X_2}} = \sqrt{1 - .671^2} = .741$$

From the previous analysis, $U_Y = .737$, $b_{Y \cdot X_1} = .458$, and $b_{Y \cdot X_2} = .277$. With these pieces of information we can now decompose r_{YX_1} to measure the direct effect of X_1 on Y and the indirect effect of X_1 acting through X_2 on Y. In this case, the total effect of Midterm 1 acting through Midterm 2 is given by:

$$\begin{aligned} b_{Y \cdot X_1'} + r_{X_1X_2} b_{Y \cdot X_2} &= .458 + (.671)(.277) \\ &= .458 + .186 = .644 \\ &= r_{YX_1} \end{aligned}$$

a somewhat surprising result. The element $b_{Y \cdot X_1}$ is called the *direct effect* and $r_{X_1X_2} b_{Y \cdot X_2}$ is called the *indirect effect*. As indicated, we see that the simple correlation r_{YX_1} has been decomposed into two additive measures of explained variation. This relationship is demonstrated quite simply from the formulas of Section 3-4. Furthermore, this decomposition will always exist in the two-predictor model. Of course, the same total decomposition would occur in the three or higher order prediction model provided all indirect paths are included in the path analysis structure. However, not all path structures created by researchers are so complete. We will present an example in which the component parts do not sum to the total simple correlation. This happens in the example to be presented because a number of potential paths do not appear in the postulated path structure and so complete additivity is not achieved. In practice, this is of minor concern since path analysis is used to investigate and understand social systems and not just to balance numerical equations.

Some possible paths for three predictors are shown in Figure 3-9. Model A is solved by regressing Y on X_1, X_2, and X_3. For solution, Model B requires a regression of Y on X_1, X_2, and X_3 and a regression of X_3 on X_1 and X_2. Model C requires a regression of Y on X_1, X_2, and X_3 and a regression of X_3 on X_1. Finally, Model D requires a regression of Y on X_1, X_2, and X_3, along with a regression of X_2 on X_1, X_3 on X_1, and X_2 on X_3 or X_3 on X_2. As we see, a path analysis solution only involves a series of multiple regressions on variables that appear earlier in time or simultaneously in time. We now give directions for a path analysis.

Figure 3-9. Examples of path models for three predictors.

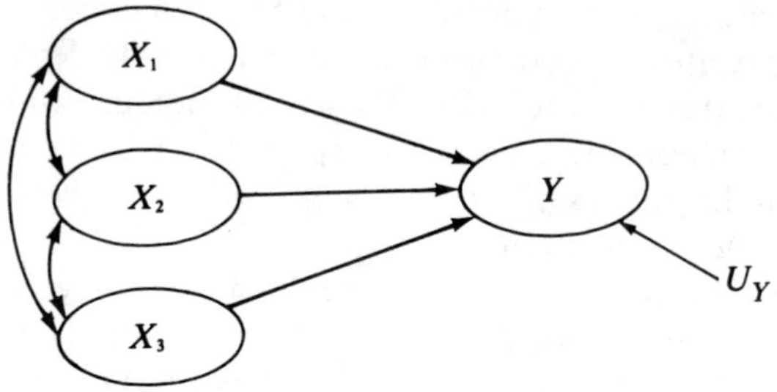

A. Three direct predictors

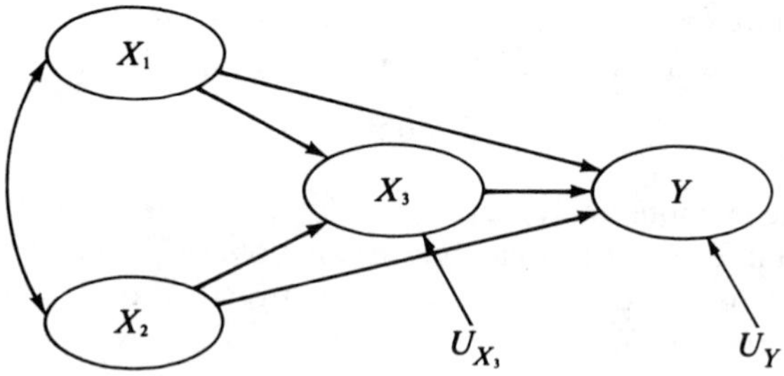

B. Two direct predictors and one indirect predictor associated with both direct predictors

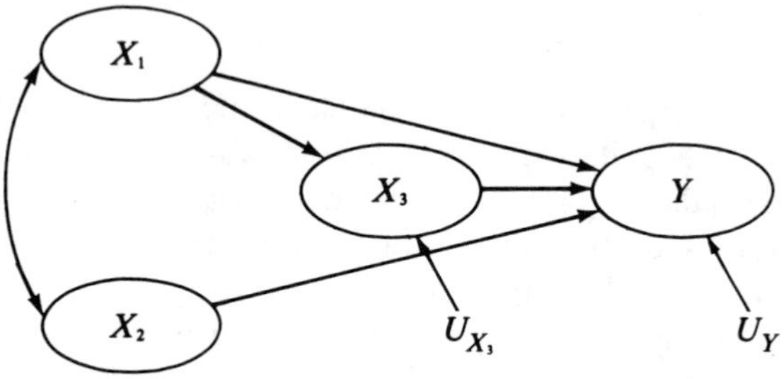

C. Two direct predictors and one indirect predictor associated with only one direct predictor

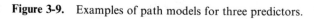

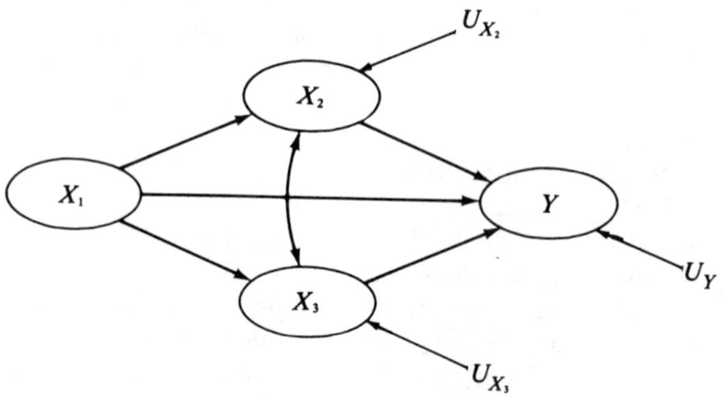

D. Three direct predictors, with one having an indirect effect on the other two.

Procedure for conducting a path analysis.

Step 1. Draw the path diagram with time extending from left to right. Use directed arrows to represent weak causal orderings or direct causation relationships. Use curved double arrowed lines to represent simple two-variable correlations.

Step 2. Regress Y on all of its predictors to obtain the path coefficients which are the beta weights of the resulting multiple regression equation. Estimate the effect of the unexplained factors by:

$$U_Y = \sqrt{1 - \hat{R}^2_{Y \cdot X_1 X_2 \ldots X_P}}$$

Step 3. Regress each predictor on the variables that precede it in time to obtain the corresponding beta weights and U_{X_p} values.

Step 4. Determine the simple correlation coefficients for the variables that appear as simple correlations.

Before we illustrate a path model with six predictors, we need to comment about the use of standardized or unstandardized variables. In practice, a researcher would like to relate variables to one another in the metric on which they were measured and so unstandardized variables would be preferred. Unfortunately, when describing the impact of one variable on another, standardized weights are more convenient because, as we saw in Section 3-5:

$$\hat{R}^2_{Y \cdot X_1 X_2 \ldots X_P} = \sum_{p=1}^{P} b_p^2 + 2 \sum_{p=1}^{P} \sum_{p'=1}^{P} b_p b_{p'} r_{X_p X_{p'}} \qquad p < p'$$

With unstandardized weights, this relationship is lost, but can be recaptured by computing $S^2_{\hat{Y}}$ in the manner to be described in Section 4-8. Unfortunately there seems to be little agreement in the literature concerning the use of standardized or unstandardized variables. In the following example, we have chosen to standardize each of the six predictor variables and to treat them as having equal importance. We also refrain from significance testing in this example.

As an example of a complicated path model, consider the diagram of Figure 3-10. In this model, we wish to predict for our sample of 40 students listed in Table 1-1,

Y: Final Test Score, from:
X_1: Midterm 2
X_2: Midterm 1
X_3: Pretest
X_4: College Board scores
X_5: Previous high school course in social studies, dummy coded as 1 (previous course) and 0 (no previous course)
X_6: High school grade point average

Missing data were estimated as described in Section 3-1 (see also Table 5-1). We treat X_4, X_5, and X_6 as independent variables that are correlated among themselves but that do not causally affect one another. For these variables, $r_{X_4X_5} = .226$, $r_{X_4X_6} = .465$, and $r_{X_5X_6} = .513$. We now postulate that pretest performance, X_3, is directly influenced by X_4, X_5, and X_6. From this association we have:

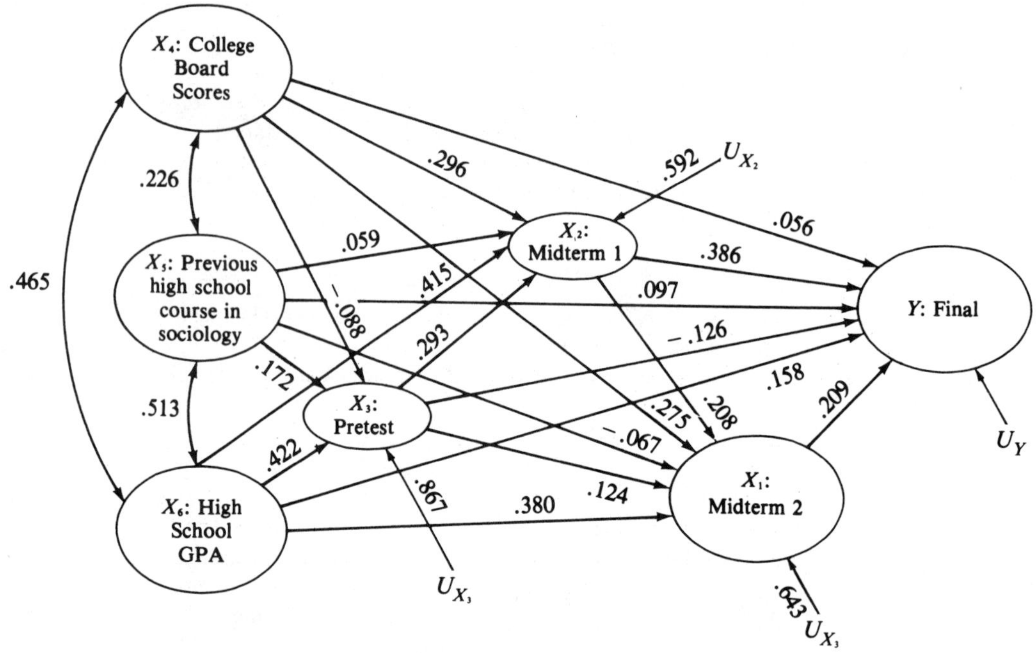

Figure 3-10. A path model for predicting final examination scores in sociology from six independent variables.

$$\hat{Z}_{X_3} = -.088Z_{X_4} + .172Z_{X_5} + .422Z_{X_6}$$

$$U_{X_3} = \sqrt{1 - \hat{R}^2_{X_3 \cdot X_4X_5X_6}} = \sqrt{1 - .249} = .867$$

Measures taken in the sociology course, such as X_1, X_2, and Y, are probably dependent upon X_3, in that the latter reflects a student's sociology-relevant knowledge prior to enrollment in the class. The coefficients leading to the first midterm, X_2, are read from:

$$\hat{Z}_{X_2} = .293Z_{X_3} + .296Z_{X_4} + .059Z_{X_5} + .415Z_{X_6}$$

$$U_{X_2} = \sqrt{1 - \hat{R}^2_{X_2 \cdot X_3X_4X_5X_6}} = \sqrt{1 - .650} = .592$$

Midterm 2, X_1, is clearly dependent on X_2, X_3, X_4, X_5, and X_6. The path coefficients for X_1 are read from:

$$\hat{Z}_{X_1} = .208Z_{X_2} + .124Z_{X_3} + .275Z_{X_4} - .067Z_{X_5} + .380Z_{X_6}$$

$$U_{X_1} = \sqrt{1 - \hat{R}^2_{X_1 \cdot X_2X_3X_4X_5X_6}} = \sqrt{1 - .587} = .643$$

If we want, we can measure the impact of each variable on the final score. For example, the impact of Midterm 1 is given by its direct effect on Y plus its indirect effect through Midterm 2, so that:

$$b_{Y \cdot X_2} + b_{X_1 \cdot X_2} b_{Y \cdot X_1} = .386 + .208(.209) = .429$$

The effect of the previous course in high school social studies is given by its direct effect on the final, as well as its indirect effects on the pretest and the two midterms.

This is represented by the eight paths in Figure 3-11 and is measured, going from right to left in Figure 3-11, by:

$$
\begin{aligned}
&b_{Y\cdot X_5} + b_{X_1\cdot X_5}b_{Y\cdot X_1} + b_{X_2\cdot X_5}b_{Y\cdot X_2} + b_{X_2\cdot X_5}b_{X_1\cdot X_2}b_{Y\cdot X_1} \\
&\quad + b_{X_3\cdot X_5}b_{Y\cdot X_3} + b_{X_3\cdot X_5}b_{X_1\cdot X_3}b_{Y\cdot X_1} + b_{X_3\cdot X_5}b_{X_2\cdot X_3}b_{Y\cdot X_2} \\
&\quad + b_{X_3\cdot X_5}b_{X_2\cdot X_3}b_{X_1\cdot X_2}b_{Y\cdot X_1} \\
&= .097 + (-.067)(.209) + .059(.386) + .059(.208)(.209) + .172(-.126) \\
&\quad + .172(.124)(.209) + .172(.293)(.386) + .172(.293)(.208)(.209) \\
&= .097 - .014 + .023 + .002 - .022 + .004 + .019 + .002 \\
&= .111
\end{aligned}
$$

As can be seen, having a previous course in social science has little impact on final scores. The largest contribution comes from the direct path and virtually none comes from the seven indirect paths leading to Y. Note also that the contributions do not sum to $r_{YX_5} = .386$. This happens because the paths involving X_4 and X_6 with X_5 are not considered in this path structure. If they had been included, the addition of component parts to .386 would be seen.

Finally, we have judiciously avoided the questions of significance testing and the risks of making type I errors in the testing of a path model. There seems to be little agreement as to how this problem should be solved. Many researchers test each coefficient at $\alpha = .05$ or .01. As might be expected, there exists an extensive literature on the methodology of path analysis. A good starting point on investigation into this complex model is provided by the text by Hanushek and Jackson (1977). We recommend that their chapter be examined for a more complete discussion of this frequently used multivariate model. A somewhat related

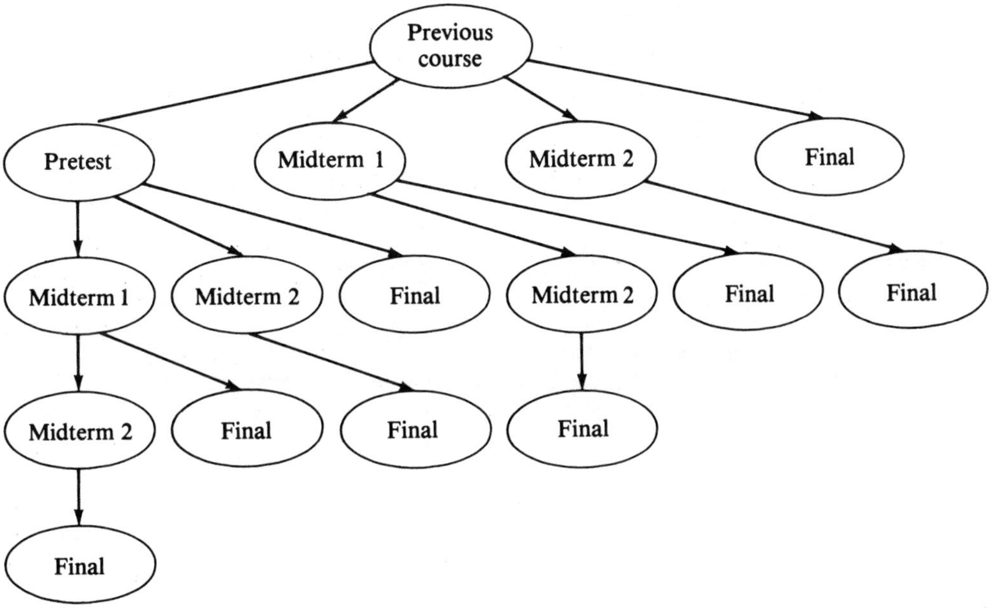

Figure 3-11. Eight possible paths leading from previous course in high school social studies to score on the final.

procedure for identifying the unique and joint contributions to $\hat{R}^2$ of the various independent variables is known as *commonality analysis*, and is described by Kerlinger and Pedhazur (1973).

3-18. Simplified statistics for multiple regression

As shown in Section 3-4, the regression equation for predicting final test performance from the two midterm scores is given by:

$$\hat{Y} = 31.5995 + .9027X_1 + .4184X_2$$

In Z score form, the equation is written as:

$$\hat{Z}_Y = .4583Z_{X_1} + .2772Z_{X_2}$$

Although it is definitely true that these weights will result in the maximum possible value of $\hat{R}^2 = .4574$ with the given data, a much simpler set of weights can be applied in many situations, which will not result in a great loss of predictability or explained variance. The argument has been articulated by Wainer (1976, 1978) who suggests that, in most practical situations, the application of equal weights to the P predictors will result in little information loss and indeed in some cases will even be advantageous, relative to data-derived unequal weights. For details of the argument, see Wainer's articles; for rejoinders, see Laughlin (1978) and Pruzek and Frederick (1978).

This suggestion may be viewed somewhat as the extension of our relative weighting scheme, as proposed in Section 1-11. There it was mentioned that in a single-predictor-variable case, the use of the simplified prediction rule:

$$\hat{Z}_Y = Z_X$$

would do just as well for rank ordering individuals as would the complete least squares rule:

$$\hat{Z}_Y = r_{XY}Z_X$$

The simplified rule is extended to the P-variable prediction problem as follows:

Procedure for using simple Z scores for multiple prediction.

Step 1. Compute Z scores for all predictor variables that are moderately to highly correlated with Y. As a rule of thumb, retain variables for which $r_{YX_p} \leq -.30$ or $r_{YX_p} \geq .30$ and disregard all predictors with negligible Y correlations for which $-.30 < r_{YX_p} < .30$. Statistical tests of $r_{YX_p} = 0$, using the procedure of Section 3-2, might also be applied here.

Step 2. For each of the p' nonnegligible predictors, reexamine r_{YX_p} to determine whether it is positive or negative. If positive, keep the associated Z scores as they are; if negative, reorient or *reflect* the associated Z scores by multiplying them by -1.

Step 3. Sum the Z scores and reflected Z scores to form the equally weighted composite variable:

$$Z_C = Z_{X_1} + Z_{X_2} + \ldots + Z_{X_{p'}}$$

Step 4. Compute the correlation between Z_C and Y. The square of this index, $r^2_{YZ_C}$, affords a simplified approximation to $\hat{R}^2_{Y \cdot X_1 X_2 \ldots X_{P'}}$.

When this simplified rule is applied to our two-predictor example, a correlation between predicted and actual scores is given by $r_{YZ_C} = .672$, yielding $r^2_{YZ_C} = .672^2 = .452$.

To determine r_{YZ_C}, we could either compute the correlation between Z_C and Y in the usual manner or take advantage of the algebraic shortcut to be developed here. Specifically, since $Z_C = Z_1 + Z_2$, it follows that:

$$S_{YZ_C} = \frac{1}{N-1}\sum_{i=1}^{N}(Y_i - \bar{Y})(Z_{1i} + Z_{2i} - \bar{Z}_1 - \bar{Z}_2)$$

Since $\bar{Z}_1 = \bar{Z}_2 = 0$, these terms can be dropped. Now, by substituting and multiplying numerator and denominator by S_Y, we obtain:

$$\begin{aligned} S_{YZ_C} &= \left[S_Y \sum_{i=1}^{N}\left(\frac{Y_i - \bar{Y}}{S_Y}\right)\left(\frac{X_{1i} - \bar{X}_1}{S_{X_1}}\right)\right] + \left[S_Y \sum_{i=1}^{N}\left(\frac{Y_i - \bar{Y}}{S_Y}\right)\left(\frac{X_{2i} - \bar{X}_2}{S_{X_2}}\right)\right] \\ &= S_Y(r_{YX_1} + r_{YX_2}) \end{aligned}$$

Since:

$$S^2_{Z_C} = S^2_{Z_1} + S^2_{Z_2} + 2S_{Z_1}S_{Z_2}r_{Z_1Z_2} = 1 + 1 + 2r_{X_1X_2}$$

it follows that:

$$r^2_{YZ_C} = \frac{(S_{YZ_C})^2}{S^2_Y S^2_{Z_C}} = \frac{S^2_Y(r_{YX_1} + r_{YX_2})^2}{S^2_Y(2 + 2r_{X_1X_2})} = \frac{(r_{YX_1} + r_{YX_2})^2}{2 + 2r_{X_1X_2}}$$

For our example:

$$r^2_{YZ_C} = \frac{(.64438 + .58482)^2}{2 + 2(.67120)} = .4520$$

In the more general case when there are $P'(\geq 2)$ predictors entering into the composite Z, this formula extends as:

$$r^2_{YZ_C} = \frac{(r_{YX_1} + r_{YX_2} + \cdots + r_{YX_{P'}})^2}{P' + 2(r_{X_1X_2} + r_{X_1X_3} + \cdots + r_{X_{P'-1}X_{P'}})}$$

It must be stated that the preceding formulas depend on all r_{YX_p} correlations being positive. When one or more r_{YX_p} correlations are negative and reflection must be employed, the intercorrelations among the X_p will undergo sign changes in the preceding formulas. Exactly what kind of changes occur will be discussed in more detail in Section 5-10.

In the present example, the $r^2_{YZ_C}$ value of .452 is virtually identical to the previously given exact value of $\hat{R}^2_{Y \cdot X_1X_2} = .457$, and thus we would conclude that there was little loss in predictability when the simplified sum-of-Z-scores rule was employed. It should not be concluded that the simplified approach will always do as well as the optimal multiple regression solution, however. What is particularly interesting here is that the examination of the partial correlation coefficients, $r_{YX_1 \cdot X_2} = .42$ and $r_{YX_2 \cdot X_1} = .27$, or the standardized partial regression coefficients, $b_1 = .46$ and $b_2 = .28$, suggests that Midterm 1 should count much more than Midterm 2. Yet, in the simplified rule with the two midterms counting equally, about the same degree of predictability is produced. This equal contributions notion is clearly more in accord with the comparable zero-order correlations which in this case are given by $r_{YX_1} = .64$ and $r_{YX_2} = .58$.

Thus, researchers who desire an easy-to-apply estimate of the proportion of variance in Y explained by the P predictors should consider the sum of Z scores approach. Its computational advantages are obvious, and its conceptual simplicity makes interpretation straightforward. As Wainer (1976, 1978) has suggested, this approach may have some additional advantages when it comes to assessing the stability of prediction rules on the basis of cross-validation. See also Dorans and Drasgow (1978).

3-19. Concluding comments

Two final comments will be included. First, in Section 3-1, it was indicated that nonlinear and interaction terms can be easily incorporated into a multiple regression equation based on quantitative variables. For directions on how this is done, see Cohen and Cohen (1975). For the specialized topic dealing with orthogonalizing nonlinear terms, see Serlin (1978). There is also the question of whether the interaction term should be defined by a product based on standardized, rather than unstandardized, components. Finn (1974) has proposed the former in correspondence with an analysis of variance interpretation of an interaction as discussed in Marascuilo and Levin (1970). Cohen (1978) has shown that the interaction term per se is statistically invariant under standardization of its components. However, the separate components of a simultaneous regression model are affected statistically by the particular kind of interaction term included. On the other hand, as long as a stepwise procedure is employed with the interaction terms entered last, the standardized and unstandardized interaction solutions will be statistically identical.

The second comment concerns multicollinearity, as it applies to multiple regression problems. Multicollinearity in the data can occur if X_1 and a constant multiple of X_1, such as $3X_1$ or $(1/10)X_1$, are included in the same analysis. The same problem could exist if, for example, X_1, X_2, and X_3 entered an analysis, along with $X_4 = a_1X_1 + a_2X_2 + a_3X_3$. Such collinearities make it impossible to estimate the beta weights and $\hat{R}^2_{Y \cdot X_1X_2\ldots X_P}$. The reason for this is described in Section 4-4, where the problem of singular matrices is discussed.

3-20. Summary

In this chapter, the underlying theory for part, partial, and multiple correlation and regression theory was presented, mostly in terms of two-predictor variables and one-criterion variable. For a three-variable model, a partial correlation between two variables X_1 and X_2, with the effects of a third variable X_3 removed is defined as the correlation between the unexplained deviations for X_1 regressed on X_3 and X_2 regressed on X_3. Thus, for X_1 regressed on X_3, the unexplained deviations are given by:

$$d_{U_{X_1}} = X_1 - [\bar{X}_1 + B_{1\cdot 3}(X_3 - \bar{X}_3)]$$

and for X_2 regressed on X_3, the corresponding deviations are given as:

$$d_{U_{X_2}} = X_2 - [\bar{X}_2 + B_{2\cdot 3}(X_3 - \bar{X}_3)]$$

When these deviations are correlated with one another and the algebra is worked out, it is seen that the correlation between X_1 and X_2, after the effects of X_3 on X_1 and X_2 are removed, is given by:

$$r_{X_1X_2\cdot X_3} = \frac{r_{X_1X_2} - r_{X_1X_3}r_{X_2X_3}}{\sqrt{1 - r^2_{X_1X_3}}\sqrt{1 - r^2_{X_2X_3}}}$$

Part correlation, on the other hand, refers to the correlation that exists between a variable X_1 and the unexplained deviation of a second variable X_2 regressed on a third variable X_3. Thus $r_{X_1(X_2\cdot X_3)}$ is defined as the correlation between X_1 and $d_{U_{X_2}}$. Upon completion of the algebra, it is seen that:

$$r_{X_1(X_2\cdot X_3)} = \frac{r_{X_1X_2} - r_{X_1X_3}r_{X_2X_3}}{\sqrt{1 - r^2_{X_2X_3}}} = r_{X_1X_2\cdot X_3}\sqrt{1 - r^2_{X_1X_2}}$$

With $r_{X_1X_2} \neq 0$, it follows that statistical tests about $r_{X_1X_2\cdot X_3}$ and $r_{X_1(X_2\cdot X_3)}$ and $r_{X_2(X_1\cdot X_3)}$ are identical. Thus, to test any of the three hypotheses:

H_{0_1}: $\rho_{X_1X_2\cdot X_3} = 0$

H_{0_2}: $\rho_{X_1(X_2\cdot X_3)} = 0$

H_{0_3}: $\rho_{X_2(X_1\cdot X_3)} = 0$

we compute:

$$t = \frac{r_{X_1X_2\cdot X_3}\sqrt{N - 3}}{\sqrt{1 - r_{X_1X_2\cdot X_3}}}$$

and reject H_{0_1}, H_{0_2}, and H_{0_3}, if $t < t_{v:\alpha/2}$ or if $t > t_{v:1-\alpha/2}$, where $v = N - 3$.

In practice, we may remove the effects of any number of variables from two variables and test the resulting partial correlation for significance. If V independent variables are each removed from X_1 and X_2, the test of H_0: $\rho_{X_1X_2\cdot X_3X_4\ldots X_{V+2}} = 0$ is given by:

$$t = \frac{r_{X_1X_2\cdot X_3X_4\ldots X_{V+2}}\sqrt{N - 2 - V}}{\sqrt{1 - r^2_{X_1X_2\cdot X_3X_4\ldots X_{V+2}}}}$$

H_0 is rejected if $t < t_{v:\alpha/2}$ or if $t > t_{v:1-\alpha/2}$, where $v = N - 2 - V$. Of course, the same statistic is used for testing the corresponding part correlations for significance from zero.

The assumptions for this test are the usual correlation theory assumptions:

1. There is independence of observations between subjects or sample elements.
2. All variables are measured with error.
3. The errors have a distribution that is multivariate normal (i.e., the extension of bivariate normality, and which will be discussed in detail in Section 5-8).

As a consequence, tests about these correlation coefficients are truly multivariate in form; however, this is not true for the tests of hypotheses associated with multiple regression theory. The reason for this is that in multiple regression theory, the independent variables $X_1, X_2, \ldots, X_P$ are assumed to be measured without error and only the dependent variable Y is measured with error. In most cases, the assumption is unrealistic for the same reasons as those described in the Summary of Chapter 2 for the bivariate regression model. Under the multiple regression model, each observation may be characterized as:

$$Y_i = \beta_0 + \beta_1 X_{1i} + \beta_2 X_{2i} + \cdots + \beta_P X_{Pi} + \varepsilon_{Y_i}$$

where:

1. The ε_{Y_i} are assumed to be independent of one another and normally distributed.
2. $E(\varepsilon_{Y_i}) = 0$.
3. $\text{Var}(\varepsilon_{Y_i}) = \sigma^2_{Y \cdot X_1 X_2 \ldots X_P}$

In this sense, multiple regression theory is a univariate model and again comes under the framework of the analysis of variance. Thus, in the sample of N subjects or elements:

$$\sum_{i=1}^{N} (Y_i - \bar{Y})^2 = \sum_{i=1}^{N} (\hat{Y}_i - \bar{Y})^2 + \sum_{i=1}^{N} (Y_i - \hat{Y}_i)^2$$

corresponds to:

$$SS_{\text{Total}} = SS_{\text{Regression}} + SS_{\text{Residual}}$$

with degrees of freedom given by:

$$N - 1 = P + (N - P - 1)$$

From these sums of squares, the squared multiple correlation coefficient is defined as:

$$\hat{R}^2 = \frac{SS_{\text{Regression}}}{SS_{\text{Total}}}$$

With $\hat{\theta} = \hat{R}^2$ and $1 - \hat{\theta}^2 = 1 - \hat{R}^2$ and $\nu_1 = P$ and $\nu_2 = N - P - 1$, the test statistic for testing H_0: $R^2 = 0$ is given by:

$$F = \frac{\nu_2}{\nu_1}\left(\frac{\hat{\theta}^2}{1 - \hat{\theta}^2}\right) = \frac{N - P - 1}{P}\left(\frac{\hat{R}^2}{1 - \hat{R}^2}\right)$$

H_0 is rejected if $F > F_{\nu_1, \nu_2: 1-\alpha}$. For this model, the residual variance is estimated as:

$$MS_{\text{Residual}} = \frac{N - 1}{N - P - 1}\left[S_Y^2(1 - \hat{R}^2)\right]$$

If $b_1, b_2, \ldots, b_P$ represent standardized regression weights, $\hat{R}^2$ can be computed as:

$$\hat{R}^2 = \sum_{p=1}^{P} b_p^2 + 2\sum_{p=1}^{P}\sum_{p'=1}^{P} b_p b_{p'} r_{X_p X_{p'}} \qquad p \neq p'$$

or as:

$$\hat{R}^2 = \sum_{p=1}^{P} r_{YX_p} b_p$$

Unfortunately this estimate possesses a positive bias since, if H_0 is true:

$$E(\hat{R}^2) = \frac{P}{N-1}$$

For this reason, a corrected estimate measured by:

$$\hat{R}^2_C = 1 - (1 - \hat{R}^2)\left(\frac{N-1}{N-P-1}\right)$$

is recommended.

The test of H_0: $R^2 = 0$ is identical to the test of:

$$H_0: \quad \beta_1 = \beta_2 = \ldots = \beta_P = 0$$

If H_0 is rejected, we might like to know which β_p values are different from zero. For a post hoc model, we examine each:

$$\psi_p = B_p \pm \mathbf{S}\, SE_{B_p}$$

to see whether or not zero is included in the interval. If zero is not in the interval, we conclude that $\beta_p \neq 0$. In this case:

$$B_p = r_{YX_p \cdot X_1X_2 \ldots X_{p-1}X_{p+1}\ldots X_P}\sqrt{\frac{MS_{\text{Res}(Y \cdot X_1X_2\ldots X_{p-1}X_{p+1}\ldots X_P)}}{MS_{\text{Res}(X_p \cdot X_1X_2\ldots X_{p-1}X_{p+1}\ldots X_P)}}}$$

with:

$$SE^2_{B_p} = \frac{MS_{\text{Res}}}{(N-1)S^2_{X_p}(1 - \hat{R}^2_{X_p \cdot X_1 \ldots X_{p-1}X_{p+1}\ldots X_P})}$$

$$\mathbf{S} = \sqrt{PF_{P,N-P-1:1-\alpha}}$$

To obtain a planned analysis, count the number of contrasts of interest and relate:

$$t = \frac{B_p}{SE_{B_p}}$$

to the critical values read from Table B-4. In Section 4-7 we will see how more complicated contrasts involving the beta weights can be tested for significance. In addition, we will take a second look at H_0: $R^2 = 0$, in terms of contrasts.

Researchers who use multiple regression models often would like to report on how much of the variance can be attributed to a specific independent variable. It was shown that this could never be done except in the case where the independent variables were pairwise uncorrelated. Unless this is the case, no procedure can be recommended that handles the problem perfectly. Because of this inability to partition explained variance into unique unrelated components, a number of approximate procedures were described and illustrated. They are the method of all possible regressions, backward elimination or backward selection of variables, and forward selection. Forward selection was based on the fact that any $\hat{R}^2_{Y \cdot X_1X_2\ldots X_P}$ could be decomposed as:

$$\hat{R}^2_{Y \cdot X_1X_2 \cdots X_P} = r^2_{YX_1} + r^2_{Y(X_2 \cdot X_1)} + r^2_{Y(X_3 \cdot X_1X_2)} + \cdots + r^2_{Y(X_p \cdot X_1X_2 \cdots X_{p-1})}$$

and that each part correlation could be tested for significance as described earlier in this summary.

An introduction to dummy coding was presented and used to show how qualitative variables can be incorporated into a regression model, thereby making the univariate analysis of variance a special case of univariate regression analysis. An introduction to path analysis was presented for the special case in which reciprocal causation was not defined and where $U_Y, U_{X_1}, U_{X_2}, \ldots, U_{X_P}$ were uncorrelated. In general, these assumptions are invalid for social science data, and so the model described has limited utility. As indicated, our goal was to present the flavor of path analysis and not a definitive description of the model.

Finally, we considered the utility of using standard scores and equal unit weights with $b_p = 1$ for all p in which $r_{YX_p} \leq -.3$ or $r_{YX_p} \geq .3$. For such a simplified procedure, based on $P' < P$ predictors:

$$Z_C = Z_{X_1} + Z_{X_2} + \cdots + Z_{X_{P'}}$$

with:

$$r^2_{YZ_C} = \frac{(r_{YX_1} + r_{YX_2} + \cdots + r_{YX_{P'}})^2}{P' + 2(r_{X_1X_2} + r_{X_1X_3} + \cdots + r_{X_{P'-1}X_{P'}})}$$

This value could be compared to $\hat{R}^2_{Y \cdot X_1X_2 \ldots X_{P'}}$ to see how well Z_C fits the data. If:

$$\Delta = \hat{R}^2_{Y \cdot X_1X_2 \ldots X_P} - r^2_{YZ_C}$$

is small, the use of equal weights on standard scores may indeed be of utility and is therefore recommended.

3-21. Exercises

***3-1.** In a study in which it was believed that performance on a standardized reading test, Y, could be related to:

X_1: IQ score and X_2: Need achievement

the following statistics were generated for a sample of 15 students.

Student	Y	X_1	X_2
1	52	83	18
2	50	84	15
3	47	90	20
4	53	95	16
5	55	96	18
6	56	97	23
7	49	100	14
8	72	103	15
9	68	103	10
10	39	110	9
11	55	115	15
12	80	122	23
13	79	127	27
14	83	129	26
15	82	139	32

a. Complete the data table for the interaction model:

$$\hat{Y} = B_0 + B_1X_1 + B_2X_2 + B_3X_1X_2$$

by adding a column titled $X_3 = X_1X_2$

b. Complete the data table for the quadratic model:

$$\hat{Y} = B_0 + B_1X_1 + B_2X_2 + B_3X_2^2$$

by adding a column titled $X_4 = X_1^2$

c. Complete the data for the fully quadratic model with interaction:

$$\hat{Y} = B_0 + B_1X_1 + B_2X_2 + B_3X_1X_2 + B_4X_1^2 + B_5X_2^2$$

by adding columns labeled:

$X_3 = X_1X_2$, $X_4 = X_1^2$, and $X_5 = X_2^2$

3-2. For your sample of $N = 40$ students, compute $r_{YX_2 \cdot X_1}$ for:

Y: Final examination
X_1: First midterm
X_2: Second midterm

Test the hypothesis ($\alpha = .05$, one-tailed),

$$\text{H}_0\text{:} \quad \rho_{YX_2 \cdot X_1} = 0$$

***3-3.** Estimate $\hat{R}^2_{Y \cdot X_1X_2}$ and $S^2_{Y \cdot X_1X_2}$ for your sample of 40 students.

3-4. For your sample, determine b_1, b_2, and $\hat{R}^2_{Y \cdot X_1X_2} = r_{YX_1}b_1 + r_{YX_2}b_2$ and set up the analysis of variance table for testing H$_0$: $R^2_{Y \cdot X_1X_2} = 0$. Recall that $SS_{\text{Tot}} = (N - 1)S^2_{Y}$.

3-5. For your sample of students, compute the two-variable prediction equation using standard scores, as $\hat{Z}_Y = b_1Z_{X_1} + b_2Z_{X_2}$. Show that $S^2_{\hat{Z}_Y} = \hat{R}^2_{Y \cdot X_1X_2}$.

3-6. **a.** Estimate β_1 and β_2 for your sample of students and use the Dunn-Bonferroni procedure with α equally divided to set up 95% confidence intervals for the unknown parameters.

b. Estimate β_0 and set up the corresponding 95% confidence interval.

3-7. Compare your estimates of β_1 and β_2 to those reported in Section 3-4. Use $\alpha_1 = \alpha_2 = .025$ for each t test.

3-8. For your sample of students, determine the part correlations $r_{Y(X_1 \cdot X_2)}$ and $r_{Y(X_2 \cdot X_1)}$, and use them to show that:

$$\hat{R}^2_{Y \cdot X_1X_2} = r^2_{YX_1} + r^2_{Y(X_2 \cdot X_1)}$$

$$\hat{R}^2_{Y \cdot X_1X_2} = r^2_{YX_2} + r^2_{Y(X_1 \cdot X_2)}$$

3-9. On the basis of the statistics of Exercise 3-8, what would be the order of entry in a data-determined stepwise regression? Set up the corresponding analysis-of-variance table.

3-10. Perform a hierarchical stepwise regression on your sample of students by:

a. placing X_1 into the regression equation first and X_2 second; and

b. placing X_2 into the regression equation first and X_1 second.

c. How much of the variance in Y can be attributed to X_1 and to X_2 individually? Defend your answer.

***3-11.** Use a computer program and complete a stepwise regression on the data of Exercise 3-1, Part a. Do the analysis according to the following orders:

a. X_1, X_2, and X_3 **d.** X_2, X_3, and X_1

b. X_1, X_3, and X_2 **e.** X_3, X_1, and X_2

c. X_2, X_1, and X_3 **f.** X_3, X_2, and X_1

g. Explain what is happening.

h. Redefine, or let the computer redefine, all X scores as standard Z scores.

***3-12.** Perform a stepwise regression on the data of Exercise 3-1, Part b. Enter the linear component first and the quadratic component second. Report the results in an analysis-of-variance table.

***3-13.** Perform a user-determined stepwise regression on the data of Exercise 3-1, Part c, with variables entered in the order X_1, X_2, X_3, X_4, and X_5.

3-14. For your sample of students, test the analysis of variance hypothesis on final test scores:

$$H_0: \quad \mu_1 = \mu_2 = \mu_3 = \mu_4$$

by dummy coding College Major as:
X_1: Natural Science
X_2: Social Science
X_3: Humanities
X_4: Others and Unknown
Let $\alpha = .05$.

3-15. Determine the regression equation for Exercise 3-14. Compute the mean scores for the four groups of students, showing that they equal the ordinary sample mean values.

3-16. For the data of Exercise 3-15, show that:

$$B_0 = \bar{Y}_4$$

$$B_1 = \bar{Y}_1 - \bar{Y}_4$$

$$B_2 = \bar{Y}_2 - \bar{Y}_4$$

$$B_3 = \bar{Y}_3 - \bar{Y}_4$$

***3-17.** Use a multiple regression approach to perform an analysis of covariance on the data of Exercise 2-14. Verify the result previously obtained.

3-18. Use a multiple regression approach to perform an analysis of covariance on the data of Exercise 3-14, where the pretest is the covariate. (Let $\alpha = .05$.) Now redo the analysis, adding high school unit in sociology as a second covariate. Are the results the same?

3-19. Use the simplified statistics model on your sample of students and determine r_{YZ_C} where Y is final test score and $Z_C = Z_1 + Z_2$ with X_1 as the first midterm and X_2 as the second midterm.

CHAPTER FOUR

MATRIX ALGEBRA AND MULTIPLE REGRESSION THEORY

4-1. Introduction

In the previous chapters, we were able to discuss P-variable prediction models in simple algebraic terms by generalizing from the well-known cases in which $P = 1$ and $P = 2$. In a certain sense, this kind of presentation is limiting, especially when we wish to study and learn about other multivariate procedures, such as canonical correlation theory, principal component analysis, discriminant analysis, and multivariate analysis of variance. These more advanced topics are best learned under the aegis of matrix algebra. For this reason, we must digress from our presently increasing level of multiple variate abstraction and provide the basic elements of matrix algebra that facilitate the learning of these higher order statistical models. We will do this in two steps. First, we will describe the required elements of matrix algebra. This description will be followed by connecting the matrix algebra results to the multiple regression model described in Chapter 3. The reader who is already familiar with matrix algebra may wish to completely pass over this chapter and proceed directly to Chapter 5, where the main thread developed in Chapters 1, 2, and 3 is continued and expanded. The only new substantive material in this chapter is that of Section 4-9, where matrix algebra is applied to testing the hypothesis that K independent variance-covariance matrices are identical.

4-2. Vectors and matrices

In multivariate analysis it is customary to refer to the data of a sample unit as a *data point* and to represent it as a *vector* of numbers. A vector is defined as follows.

Definition of a vector.
A vector of numbers is simply a listing of the numbers in a vertical column closed on each side by parentheses. It is usually denoted in bold type. Thus the vector of numbers $(a_1, a_2, \ldots, a_N)$ is denoted as:

$$\mathbf{A} = \begin{pmatrix} a_1 \\ a_2 \\ \cdot \\ \cdot \\ \cdot \\ a_N \end{pmatrix}$$

Vectors of numbers will usually be denoted by letters near the front of the alphabet, while vectors of variables will be denoted by letters near the end of the alphabet.

To save printing space, it is convenient to report a vector as a row of values, rather than a column. Such a row vector is called a *transposed* vector and is denoted for, say, a vector of variables, as:

$$\mathbf{X}' = (X_1 \ X_2 \ldots X_N)$$

For completeness, we define a transposed vector of numbers as follows.

Definition of a transposed vector.
The transposed vector, denoted $\mathbf{A}'$, of a column vector $\mathbf{A}$ is a row vector written as:

$$\mathbf{A}' = (a_1 \; a_2 \ldots a_N)$$

For the data of Table 3-1, the data point for Subject No. 003, written as a row vector, is given by:

$$\mathbf{X}_1' = (43 \;\; 61 \;\; 129)$$

while the data for Subject No. 211 is given by:

$$\mathbf{X}_{40}' = (20 \;\; 59 \;\; 91)$$

The totality of data points is referred to as a *data matrix* and is just a simple row by row listing of the observed values. In particular, the matrix $\mathbf{A}$, consisting of R rows and C columns, is defined as follows.

Definition of a matrix.
A matrix is a rectangular array of real numbers with R rows and C columns. In particular:

$$\mathbf{A} = \begin{bmatrix} a_{11} & a_{12} & \cdots & a_{1c} & \cdots & a_{1C} \\ a_{21} & a_{22} & \cdots & a_{2c} & \cdots & a_{2C} \\ \cdot & \cdot & \cdots & \cdot & \cdots & \cdot \\ \cdot & \cdot & \cdots & \cdot & \cdots & \cdot \\ \cdot & \cdot & \cdots & \cdot & \cdots & \cdot \\ a_{r1} & a_{r2} & \cdots & a_{rc} & \cdots & a_{rC} \\ \cdot & \cdot & \cdots & \cdot & \cdots & \cdot \\ \cdot & \cdot & \cdots & \cdot & \cdots & \cdot \\ \cdot & \cdot & \cdots & \cdot & \cdots & \cdot \\ a_{R1} & a_{R2} & \cdots & a_{Rc} & \cdots & a_{RC} \end{bmatrix}$$

With this notation, it follows that Table 3-1 represents a data matrix with $R = 40$ rows and $C = 3$ columns. Whenever we refer to the data matrix of Table 3-1, we will replace R by N, the sample size, and C by M, the number of variables. Thus, in our future discussion, $N = 40$ and $M = 3$. If there are multiple dependent variables, we will usually list them in the right-hand columns of the data matrix. The independent variables will appear in the left-hand columns. We will let the number of dependent variables be denoted by Q and the number of independent variables by P. Thus, in all cases, $P + Q = M$. For the data of Table 3-1, $P = 2$ and $Q = 1$. At times, it will be useful to refer to the three variables X_1, X_2, and Y as X_1, X_2, and X_3. In general, this should cause no confusion since the meaning will always be clear from the context.

Sometimes we need to denote the dimensions of a matrix. This is accomplished by denoting $\mathbf{X}$ by $\mathbf{X}_{R \times C}$. Thus $\mathbf{X}_{40 \times 3}$ refers to a matrix with 40 rows and 3 columns. Other times we want to emphasize the elements of a matrix in our discussion. This is accomplished by denoting **X** by (X_{rc}).

We can associate three very useful matrices with the matrix **X** of Table 3-1. They are the matrix of means, the matrix of standard deviations, and the matrix of correlation coefficients. For the data of Table 3-1, these matrices are:

$$\bar{\mathbf{X}}' = (\bar{X}_1 \; \bar{X}_2 \; \bar{Y}) = (46.0500 \quad 62.8750 \quad 99.4750)$$

$$\mathbf{S}' = (S_{X_1} \; S_{X_2} \; S_Y) = (15.3956 \quad 20.0872 \quad 30.3230)$$

$$\mathbf{R} = \begin{bmatrix} 1 & r_{X_1X_2} & r_{X_1Y} \\ r_{X_2X_1} & 1 & r_{X_2Y} \\ r_{YX_1} & r_{YX_2} & 1 \end{bmatrix} = \begin{bmatrix} 1.00000 & .67120 & .64438 \\ .67120 & 1.00000 & .58482 \\ .64438 & .58482 & 1.00000 \end{bmatrix}$$

The matrix **R** is called the *correlation matrix*. It is always a square matrix with M rows and M columns. It is also symmetric about the diagonal containing the unities. Since $r_{X_1X_1} = r_{X_2X_2} = r_{YY} = 1$, it follows that the unities represent the correlation coefficients for each variable with itself. A square matrix **A** is said to be *symmetric* about its *main diagonal* if $a_{rc} = a_{cr}$. As we see, the correlation matrix **R** is symmetric about its diagonal of unities. The sum of the main diagonal elements extending from the left upper row to the right lower row is called the *trace* of the matrix. For this example the trace is given by:

$$T = 1 + 1 + 1 = 3$$

We formalize this discussion with the following definition of a correlation matrix.

The definition of a correlation matrix.
Consider the variables $X_1, X_2, \ldots, X_M$ and their correlation coefficients $r_{11}, r_{12}, \ldots, r_{MM}$. The matrix of their correlation coefficients is called a correlation matrix and is written as follows:

$$\mathbf{R} = \begin{bmatrix} 1 & r_{12} & r_{13} & \cdots & r_{1M} \\ r_{21} & 1 & r_{23} & \cdots & r_{2M} \\ \cdot & \cdot & \cdot & \cdots & \cdot \\ \cdot & \cdot & \cdot & \cdots & \cdot \\ \cdot & \cdot & \cdot & \cdots & \cdot \\ r_{M1} & r_{M2} & r_{M3} & \cdots & 1 \end{bmatrix}$$

For completeness, we define the trace of a matrix as follows.

Definition of the trace of a square matrix.
The trace of a square matrix is given as the sum of the main diagonal elements. Thus:

$$T = a_{11} + a_{22} + a_{33} + \cdots + a_{MM}$$

For a correlation matrix of M variables:

$$T = 1 + 1 + 1 + \cdots + 1 = M$$

Sometimes it is convenient to separate the correlations involving Y from the remaining correlations. This is achieved by writing the matrix as a *partitioned matrix* which consists of four submatrices. For X_1, X_2, and Y, the partitioning is performed as follows and is indicated as shown:

$$\mathbf{R} = \left[\begin{array}{cc|c} 1 & r_{X_1X_2} & r_{X_1Y} \\ r_{X_2X_1} & 1 & r_{X_2Y} \\ \hline r_{YX_1} & r_{YX_2} & 1 \end{array}\right] = \left[\begin{array}{c|c} \mathbf{R}_{XX} & \mathbf{R}_{XY} \\ \hline \mathbf{R}_{YX} & \mathbf{R}_{YY} \end{array}\right]$$

The partitioning of $\mathbf{R}$ into the four submatrices may be used to represent any situation where $P \geq 1$ independent and $Q \geq 1$ dependent variables are being examined. As will be seen, the notation has considerable value since many of the statistics we will want to examine in detail come directly from $\mathbf{R}_{XX}$, the submatrix of intercorrelations among the independent variables, and not from $\mathbf{R}$ directly.

4-3. The algebra of vectors and matrices

Vectors can be added or subtracted as follows.

Definition of the addition of two vectors.
Let $\mathbf{A}' = (a_1 \ a_2 \ldots a_N)$ and let $\mathbf{B}' = (b_1 \ b_2 \ldots b_N)$.
The vector $(\mathbf{A} + \mathbf{B})'$ is defined to be:

$$(a_1 + b_1 \ \ a_2 + b_2 \ldots a_N + b_N)$$

As an example:

$$\mathbf{A} + \mathbf{B} = \begin{bmatrix} 2 \\ 6 \\ 1 \\ 4 \end{bmatrix} + \begin{bmatrix} -1 \\ 3 \\ 7 \\ -2 \end{bmatrix} = \begin{bmatrix} 2-1 \\ 6+3 \\ 1+7 \\ 4-2 \end{bmatrix} = \begin{bmatrix} 1 \\ 9 \\ 8 \\ 2 \end{bmatrix}$$

Sometimes it is useful to multiply vectors. This can be done whenever one of the vectors is a row vector and the remaining vector is a column vector. In addition, the row vector must have as many columns as the column vector has rows. When this happens, the product of two vectors is defined as follows.

Definition of the product of two vectors.
Let $\mathbf{A}'$ be a row vector with N columns and $\mathbf{B}$ be a column vector with N rows. Their product is defined as:

$$\mathbf{A}'\mathbf{B} = (a_1 \ a_2 \ldots a_N) \begin{pmatrix} b_1 \\ b_2 \\ \cdot \\ \cdot \\ \cdot \\ b_N \end{pmatrix}$$

$$= a_1b_1 + a_2b_2 + \cdots + a_Nb_N$$

$$= \sum_{i=1}^{N} a_ib_i$$

If $\mathbf{A}' = (2 \;\; 6 \;\; -1)$ and $\mathbf{B} = \begin{pmatrix} 3 \\ 0 \\ 7 \end{pmatrix}$, then:

$$\mathbf{A}'\mathbf{B} = (2 \;\; 6 \;\; -1)\begin{pmatrix} 3 \\ 0 \\ 7 \end{pmatrix}$$

$$= 2(3) + 6(0) + (-1)(7)$$

$$= 6 + 0 - 7$$

$$= -1$$

A vector can be multiplied by a real number called a *scalar*. The multiplication proceeds as follows.

Definition of the multiplication of a vector by a scalar.
Let $\mathbf{A}' = (a_1 \;\; a_2 \ldots a_N)$. Multiplication of $\mathbf{A}'$ by the real number c produces the vector:

$$c\mathbf{A}' = (a_1c \;\; a_1c \ldots a_Nc)$$

For example, let $\mathbf{A}' = (3 \;\; 6 \;\; 4 \;\; -6)$ and let $c = 2/5$.
Then:

$$c\mathbf{A}' = (6/5 \;\; 12/5 \;\; 8/5 \;\; -12/5)$$

Scalars are used to expand or compress the scale on which variables are observed. The most commonly encountered scalars in multivariate analysis are $1/N$ and $1/S_X$.

Sample means, variances, correlation coefficients, and regression equations can be denoted in vector notation.

Definition of sample statistics in vector notation.

1. Sample mean. If the column vector $\mathbf{X}$ is multiplied by the row vector:

$$\mathbf{1}' = (1 \;\; 1 \ldots 1)$$

then:

$$\mathbf{1}'\mathbf{X} = (1)X_1 + (1)X_2 + \cdots + (1)X_N = \sum_{i=1}^{N} X_i$$

so that a sample mean, in vector notation, is given simply as:

$$\bar{X} = \frac{1}{N}\mathbf{1}'\mathbf{X}$$

where $1/N$ is a scalar quantity.

2. *Sample variance.* If:

$$(\mathbf{X} - \bar{\mathbf{X}})' = [(X_1 - \bar{X})\ (X_2 - \bar{X}) \ldots (X_N - \bar{X})]$$

and we postmultiply this by $(\mathbf{X} - \bar{\mathbf{X}})$, then:

$$(\mathbf{X} - \bar{\mathbf{X}})'(\mathbf{X} - \bar{\mathbf{X}}) = \sum_{i=1}^{N} (X_i - \bar{X})^2$$

so that a sample variance, in vector notation, is given as:

$$S_X^2 = \frac{1}{N-1}(\mathbf{X} - \bar{\mathbf{X}})'(\mathbf{X} - \bar{\mathbf{X}})$$

where $1/(N-1)$ is a scalar quantity.
In terms of the computational formula, with $\mathbf{X}' = (X_1\ X_2\ \ldots\ X_N)$, if we let:

$$\mathbf{X}'\mathbf{X} = X_1^2 + X_2^2 + \cdots + X_N^2$$

then:

$$S_X^2 = \frac{N\mathbf{X}'\mathbf{X} - (\mathbf{1}'\mathbf{X})^2}{N(N-1)}$$

3. *Sample correlation coefficient.* A sample correlation coefficient, in vector notation, can be written as:

$$r_{XY} = \frac{(\mathbf{Y} - \bar{\mathbf{Y}})'(\mathbf{X} - \bar{\mathbf{X}})}{\sqrt{(\mathbf{X} - \bar{\mathbf{X}})'(\mathbf{X} - \bar{\mathbf{X}})}\sqrt{(\mathbf{Y} - \bar{\mathbf{Y}})'(\mathbf{Y} - \bar{\mathbf{Y}})}}$$

4. *Sample regression equation.* If $\mathbf{X}' = (1\ X_1\ X_2\ \ldots\ X_P)$ is postmultiplied by the column vector:

$$\mathbf{B} = \begin{pmatrix} B_0 \\ B_1 \\ B_2 \\ \cdot \\ \cdot \\ \cdot \\ B_P \end{pmatrix}$$

then the regression equation relating $\hat{Y}$ to $X_1, X_2, \ldots, X_P$ is given as:

$$\hat{Y} = \mathbf{X}'\mathbf{B}$$

For the data of Table 3-1:

$$\mathbf{B} = \begin{pmatrix} 31.60 \\ .90 \\ .42 \end{pmatrix}$$

so that:

$$\hat{Y} = \mathbf{X}'\mathbf{B} = (1 \;\; X_1 \;\; X_2)\begin{pmatrix} 31.60 \\ .90 \\ .42 \end{pmatrix}$$
$$= 31.60 + .90X_1 + .42X_2$$

The addition of matrices parallels that of the addition of vectors in that corresponding elements are added directly.

Definition of the addition of two matrices.
Let **A** and **B** be two matrices, each with R rows and C columns. The matrix $\mathbf{A} + \mathbf{B}$ has elements:

$(a_{rc} + b_{rc})$

As an example:

$$\mathbf{A} + \mathbf{B} = \begin{bmatrix} 2 & 6 & 7 \\ -1 & 3 & 4 \end{bmatrix} + \begin{bmatrix} -2 & 3 & -9 \\ -1 & 6 & 12 \end{bmatrix}$$
$$= \begin{bmatrix} 2-2 & 6+3 & 7-9 \\ -1-1 & 3+6 & 4+12 \end{bmatrix} = \begin{bmatrix} 0 & 9 & -2 \\ -2 & 9 & 16 \end{bmatrix}$$

Just as vectors can sometimes be multiplied, the same is true for matrices. In particular, two matrices can be multiplied if the matrix on the left has as many columns as the matrix on the right has rows. The multiplication proceeds as described in the following definition.

Definition of the product of two matrices.
Let $\mathbf{A}_{R_A \times C_A} = (a_{ij})$ and $\mathbf{B}_{R_B \times C_B} = (b_{jk})$. The product of **A** with **B** is defined as:

$\mathbf{C}_{R_A \times C_B} = (c_{ik})$

where:

$$c_{ik} = \sum_{j=1}^{n} a_{ij}b_{jk}$$

As an example, let:

$$\mathbf{A} = \begin{bmatrix} 2 & 3 & 7 & 3 \\ -1 & 0 & 6 & 0 \\ 5 & 8 & -7 & 4 \end{bmatrix}$$

$$\mathbf{B} = \begin{bmatrix} 3 & -6 \\ 4 & 1 \\ 3 & 7 \\ -9 & 2 \end{bmatrix}$$

The multiplication of **B** by **A** on the *left* proceeds as follows:

$$\mathbf{AB} = \begin{bmatrix} 2 & 3 & 7 & 3 \\ -1 & 0 & 6 & 0 \\ 5 & 8 & -7 & 4 \end{bmatrix} \begin{bmatrix} 3 & -6 \\ 4 & 1 \\ 3 & 7 \\ -9 & 2 \end{bmatrix}$$

$$= \begin{bmatrix} 2(3) + 3(4) + 7(3) + 3(-9) & 2(-6) + 3(1) + 7(7) + 3(2) \\ -1(3) + 0(4) + 6(3) + 0(-9) & -1(-6) + 0(1) + 6(7) + 0(2) \\ 5(3) + 8(4) + (-7)(3) + 4(-9) & 5(-6) + 8(1) + (-7)(7) + 4(2) \end{bmatrix}$$

$$= \begin{bmatrix} 12 & 46 \\ 15 & 48 \\ -10 & -63 \end{bmatrix}$$

In this example. it is not possible to multiply **A** by **B** on the left. **B** has only two columns, whereas **A** has three rows. As this example shows, order of multiplication is important in the multiplication of matrices.

Vectors of means and variances can be denoted as products of matrices, as follows.

Definition of a vector of means and the variance-covariance matrix.

1. Vector of means. Let **X** denote a data matrix with N rows and M columns. If it is multiplied by the vector $\mathbf{1}' = (1 \quad 1 \quad \ldots \quad 1)$, then:

$$\mathbf{1}'\mathbf{X} = (1 \quad 1 \quad \ldots \quad 1) \begin{bmatrix} X_{11} & X_{12} & \ldots & X_{1M} \\ X_{21} & X_{22} & \ldots & X_{2M} \\ \cdot & \cdot & & \cdot \\ \cdot & \cdot & & \cdot \\ \cdot & \cdot & & \cdot \\ X_{N1} & X_{N2} & \ldots & X_{NM} \end{bmatrix}$$

$$= \left[\sum_{i=1}^{N} X_{i1} \quad \sum_{i=1}^{N} X_{i2} \ldots \sum_{i=1}^{N} X_{iM} \right]$$

Thus the vector of means can be denoted as:

$$\bar{\mathbf{X}}' = \frac{1}{N} \mathbf{1}'\mathbf{X} = (\bar{X}_1 \ \bar{X}_2 \ \ldots \ \bar{X}_M)'$$

where $1/N$ is a scalar.

2. Variance-covariance matrix. If $\mathbf{X} - \bar{\mathbf{X}}$ denotes the matrix of deviations from the mean:

$$\mathbf{X} - \bar{\mathbf{X}} = \begin{bmatrix} X_{11} - \bar{X}_1 & X_{12} - \bar{X}_2 & \ldots & X_{1M} - \bar{X}_M \\ X_{21} - \bar{X}_1 & X_{22} - \bar{X}_2 & \ldots & X_{2M} - \bar{X}_M \\ \cdot & \cdot & & \cdot \\ \cdot & \cdot & & \cdot \\ \cdot & \cdot & & \cdot \\ X_{N1} - \bar{X}_1 & X_{N2} - \bar{X}_2 & \ldots & X_{NM} - \bar{X}_M \end{bmatrix}$$

then the *sample variance-covariance matrix* is defined as:

$$\hat{\Sigma}_{XX} = \frac{1}{N-1}(\mathbf{X} - \bar{\mathbf{X}})'(\mathbf{X} - \bar{\mathbf{X}})$$

$$= \begin{bmatrix} S^2_{X_1} & r_{X_1X_2}S_{X_1}S_{X_2} & \cdots & r_{X_1X_M}S_{X_1}S_{X_M} \\ r_{X_2X_1}S_{X_2}S_{X_1} & S^2_{X_2} & \cdots & r_{X_2X_M}S_{X_2}S_{X_M} \\ \vdots & \vdots & & \vdots \\ r_{X_MX_1}S_{X_M}S_{X_1} & r_{X_MX_2}S_{X_M}S_{X_2} & \cdots & S^2_{X_M} \end{bmatrix}$$

with diagonal elements:

$$S^2_{X_m} = \frac{1}{N-1}\sum_{i=1}^{N}(X_{im} - \bar{X}_m)^2 = S_{X_mX_m}$$

and off-diagonal elements:

$$r_{X_mX_{m'}}S_{X_m}S_{X_{m'}} = \frac{1}{N-1}\sum_{i=1}^{N}(X_{im} - \bar{X}_m)(X_{im'} - \bar{X}_{m'})$$

$$= S_{X_mX_{m'}}$$

Often we denote the sample variance-covariance matrix as the product of three matrices. We illustrate the determination of this matrix for $M = 3$. Consider the matrix:

$$\mathbf{S}' = \begin{bmatrix} S_{X_1} & 0 & 0 \\ 0 & S_{X_2} & 0 \\ 0 & 0 & S_Y \end{bmatrix}$$

used as a multiplier on the left for:

$$\mathbf{R} = \begin{bmatrix} 1 & r_{X_1X_2} & r_{X_1Y} \\ r_{X_2X_1} & 1 & r_{X_2Y} \\ r_{YX_1} & r_{YX_2} & 1 \end{bmatrix}$$

For this multiplication:

$$\mathbf{S}'\mathbf{R} = \begin{bmatrix} S_{X_1} & 0 & 0 \\ 0 & S_{X_2} & 0 \\ 0 & 0 & S_Y \end{bmatrix} \begin{bmatrix} 1 & r_{X_1X_2} & r_{X_1Y} \\ r_{X_2X_1} & 1 & r_{X_2Y} \\ r_{YX_1} & r_{YX_2} & 1 \end{bmatrix}$$

$$= \begin{bmatrix} S_{X_1} & r_{X_1X_2}S_{X_1} & r_{X_1Y}S_{X_1} \\ r_{X_2X_1}S_{X_2} & S_{X_2} & r_{X_2Y}S_{X_2} \\ r_{YX_1}S_Y & r_{YX_2}S_Y & S_Y \end{bmatrix}$$

As indicated, premultiplication by a diagonal matrix results in a multiplication of each row of the operated-upon matrix by the corresponding row element of the diagonal matrix.

If we now postmultiply $\mathbf{S'R}$ by $\mathbf{S}$, we have that:

$$\mathbf{S'RS} = \begin{bmatrix} S_{X_1} & r_{X_1X_2}S_{X_1} & r_{X_1Y}S_{X_1} \\ r_{X_2X_1}S_{X_2} & S_{X_2} & r_{X_2Y}S_{X_2} \\ r_{YX_1}S_Y & r_{YX_2}S_Y & S_Y \end{bmatrix} \begin{bmatrix} S_{X_1} & 0 & 0 \\ 0 & S_{X_2} & 0 \\ 0 & 0 & S_Y \end{bmatrix}$$

$$= \begin{bmatrix} S^2_{X_1} & r_{X_1X_2}S_{X_1}S_{X_2} & r_{X_1Y}S_{X_1}S_Y \\ r_{X_2X_1}S_{X_2}S_{X_1} & S^2_{X_2} & r_{X_2Y}S_{X_2}S_Y \\ r_{YX_1}S_YS_{X_1} & r_{YX_2}S_YS_{X_2} & S^2_Y \end{bmatrix}$$

As illustrated, postmultiplication by a diagonal matrix results in the column multiplication by the corresponding diagonal element.

Just as we can partition $\mathbf{R}$ into four submatrices, so can we partition $\hat{\Sigma}$ into four submatrices that serve to separate the X_1 and X_2 variables from Y. For this three-variable matrix:

$$\hat{\Sigma} = \left[\begin{array}{cc|c} S_{X_1X_1} & S_{X_1X_2} & S_{X_1Y} \\ S_{X_2X_1} & S_{X_2X_2} & S_{X_2Y} \\ \hline S_{YX_1} & S_{YX_2} & S_{YY} \end{array}\right] = \left[\begin{array}{c|c} \hat{\Sigma}_{XX} & \hat{\Sigma}_{XY} \\ \hline \hat{\Sigma}_{YX} & \hat{\Sigma}_{YY} \end{array}\right]$$

The same notation extends to a model with P predictor variables and Q dependent variables.

For the data of Table 3-1, the sample variance-covariance matrix is given as:

$$\hat{\Sigma} = \begin{bmatrix} 15.3956 & 0 & 0 \\ 0 & 20.0872 & 0 \\ 0 & 0 & 30.3230 \end{bmatrix} \begin{bmatrix} 1 & .67120 & .64438 \\ .67120 & 1 & .58482 \\ .64438 & .58482 & 1 \end{bmatrix} \begin{bmatrix} 15.3956 & 0 & 0 \\ 0 & 20.0872 & 0 \\ 0 & 0 & 30.3230 \end{bmatrix}$$

$$= \begin{bmatrix} 237.0231 & 207.5705 & 300.8218 \\ 207.5705 & 403.4968 & 356.2147 \\ 300.8218 & 356.2147 & 919.4865 \end{bmatrix}$$

As partitioned matrices:

$$\hat{\Sigma}_{XX} = \begin{bmatrix} 237.0231 & 207.5705 \\ 207.5705 & 403.4968 \end{bmatrix}$$

$$\hat{\Sigma}_{YY} = [919.4865]$$

$$\hat{\Sigma}'_{YX} = [300.8218 \quad 356.2147]$$

We note that the normal equations for determining estimates of $\beta_0, \beta_1, \ldots, \beta_P$ can be represented in matrix notation. For this, let the data matrix $\mathbf{X}$ be augmented by a column of ones in the first column. Let this augmented matrix be denoted by $\mathscr{X}$. Then:

$$\mathbf{Y} = \begin{bmatrix} Y_1 \\ Y_2 \\ \cdot \\ \cdot \\ \cdot \\ Y_N \end{bmatrix} = \begin{bmatrix} 1 & X_{11} & X_{12} & \dots & X_{1P} \\ 1 & X_{21} & X_{22} & \dots & X_{2P} \\ \cdot & \cdot & \cdot & \cdot & \cdot \\ \cdot & \cdot & \cdot & \cdot & \cdot \\ \cdot & \cdot & \cdot & \cdot & \cdot \\ 1 & X_{N1} & X_{N2} & \dots & X_{NP} \end{bmatrix} \begin{bmatrix} B_0 \\ B_1 \\ \cdot \\ \cdot \\ \cdot \\ B_P \end{bmatrix} = \mathscr{X}\mathbf{B}$$

If we now premultiply both sides of this equation by $\mathscr{X}'$, we have:

$$\mathscr{X}'\mathbf{Y} = \mathscr{X}'\mathscr{X}\mathbf{B}$$

This simple equation actually represents the following set of $(P + 1)$ equations which, when solved, provide the least square estimates of the βs.

Definition of the normal equations for P predictors.
The $(P + 1)$ normal equations for estimating the values of $\beta_0, \beta_1, \dots, \beta_P$ are as follows:

$$\begin{aligned} \sum_{i=1}^{N} Y_i &= NB_0 + \left(\sum_{i=1}^{N} X_{i1}\right)B_1 + \cdots + \left(\sum_{i=1}^{N} X_{iP}\right)B_P \\ \sum_{i=1}^{N} Y_i X_{i1} &= \left(\sum_{i=1}^{N} X_{i1}\right)B_0 + \left(\sum_{i=1}^{N} X_{i1}^2\right)B_1 + \cdots + \left(\sum_{i=1}^{N} X_{i1}X_{iP}\right)B_P \\ &\cdot \\ &\cdot \\ &\cdot \\ \sum_{i=1}^{N} Y_i X_{iP} &= \left(\sum_{i=1}^{N} X_{iP}\right)B_0 + \left(\sum_{i=1}^{N} X_{iP}X_{i1}\right)B_1 + \cdots + \left(\sum_{i=1}^{N} X_{iP}^2\right)B_P \end{aligned}$$

In matrix notation, this set of $(P + 1)$ equations is equivalent to:

$$\mathscr{X}'\mathbf{Y} = \mathscr{X}'\mathscr{X}\mathbf{B}$$

For $P = 1$, we have:

$$\mathscr{X}' = \begin{bmatrix} 1 & 1 & \dots & 1 \\ X_1 & X_2 & \dots & X_N \end{bmatrix}$$

so that:

$$\mathscr{X}'\mathscr{X} = \begin{bmatrix} N & \sum_{i=1}^{N} X_i \\ \sum_{i=1}^{N} X_i & \sum_{i=1}^{N} X_i^2 \end{bmatrix}$$

and:

$$\mathscr{X}'\mathscr{X}\mathbf{B} = \begin{bmatrix} N & \sum_{i=1}^{N} X_i \\ \sum_{i=1}^{N} X_i & \sum_{i=1}^{N} X_i^2 \end{bmatrix} \begin{bmatrix} B_0 \\ B_1 \end{bmatrix}$$

$$= \begin{bmatrix} NB_0 & +\left(\sum_{i=1}^{N} X_i\right)B_1 \\ \left(\sum_{i=1}^{N} X_i\right)B_0 & +\left(\sum_{i=1}^{N} X_i^2\right)B_1 \end{bmatrix}$$

Since:

$$\mathscr{X}'\mathbf{Y} = \begin{bmatrix} \sum_{i=1}^{N} Y_i \\ \sum_{i=1}^{N} Y_iX_i \end{bmatrix}$$

we see that:

$$\mathscr{X}'\mathbf{Y} = \mathscr{X}'\mathscr{X}\mathbf{B}$$

corresponds to the normal equations of Section 1-9.

For the data of Table 3-1, the normal equations are given by:

$$3979 = 40B_0 + 1842B_1 + 2515B_2$$

$$194965 = 1842B_0 + 94068B_1 + 123911B_2$$

$$264072 = 2512B_0 + 123911B_1 + 173867B_2$$

These equations may be solved using Cramer's rule, as illustrated in Section 1-9, but using determinants with three rows and three columns. In practice this is rarely done since computers can solve the system of equations with great ease. The method used requires the computation of a matrix called the *inverse* matrix. We examine these kinds of matrices in the next section.

4-4. Inverse matrices

The solution of the normal equations for P predictors requires the introduction of an important type of matrix which we will define, but not show how to compute except for $R = C = 2$. When the dimensions of the matrix exceed 2, electronic computers are generally employed. This matrix is called an *inverse* matrix and is analogous to a reciprocal in ordinary arithmetic. As we recall, the inverse of the number a is the reciprocal $1/a$. The important characteristic associated with a and $1/a$ is that $a(1/a) = 1/a(a) = 1$. Sometimes the reciprocal of a is denoted as a^{-1}, so that:

$$(a)a^{-1} = a^{-1}(a) = 1$$

For example, the inverse or reciprocal of the number 3 is 1/3, since

(3)1/3 = 1/3(3) = 1. In ordinary arithmetic, the number zero does not have an inverse. Thus division by zero is not permitted in ordinary arithmetic. A similar problem exists in finding the inverse of a matrix since, in the computation, division by zero may be required. If this should happen, an inverse cannot be obtained. In multiple regression and correlation analysis, inverses always exist, except in certain special cases. Later we will be forced to consider the properties of inverses in a little more depth.

In ordinary algebra, an equation such as:

$$7X = 12$$

is solved by multiplying each side of the equation by the inverse of 7. If we perform this multiplication, we have:

$$(7^{-1})\,(7X) = (7^{-1})12$$

or:

$$X = (7^{-1})12 = 12/7$$

so that we obtain a solution of the equation for X. As will be seen, the same process is used for solving matrix equations.

With this introduction, we define the inverse of the square matrix, **A**, as the matrix $\mathbf{A}^{-1}$ that has the property:

$$\mathbf{AA}^{-1} = \mathbf{A}^{-1}\mathbf{A} = \mathbf{I}$$

where **I** is a diagonal matrix with ones in the main diagonal and zeros elsewhere. The matrix **I** is called an *identity* matrix, and has the property that **AI** = **A** and **IA** = **A**. For completeness the definitions are as follows.

Definition of an inverse and identity matrix.
Let **A** be a square matrix. The inverse of **A** consists of the matrix $\mathbf{A}^{-1}$ that has the property:

$$\mathbf{AA}^{-1} = \mathbf{A}^{-1}\mathbf{A} = \mathbf{I}$$

where **I** is the identity matrix:

$$\mathbf{I} = \begin{bmatrix} 1 & 0 & \dots & 0 \\ 0 & 1 & \dots & 0 \\ \cdot & \cdot & \cdot & \cdot \\ \cdot & \cdot & \cdot & \cdot \\ \cdot & \cdot & \cdot & \cdot \\ 0 & 0 & \dots & 1 \end{bmatrix}$$

As an example, let us find the inverse matrix of:

$$\mathbf{A} = \begin{bmatrix} 5 & 2 \\ 1 & 4 \end{bmatrix}$$

Let the inverse be:

$$\mathbf{A}^{-1} = \begin{bmatrix} a_1 & a_2 \\ a_3 & a_4 \end{bmatrix}$$

By definition:

$$\mathbf{AA}^{-1} = \begin{bmatrix} 5 & 2 \\ 1 & 4 \end{bmatrix}\begin{bmatrix} a_1 & a_2 \\ a_3 & a_4 \end{bmatrix}$$

$$= \begin{bmatrix} 5a_1 + 2a_3 & 5a_2 + 2a_4 \\ a_1 + 4a_3 & a_2 + 4a_4 \end{bmatrix} = \begin{bmatrix} 1 & 0 \\ 0 & 1 \end{bmatrix}$$

so that:

$$5a_1 + 2a_3 = 1 \qquad 5a_2 + 2a_4 = 0$$

$$a_1 + 4a_3 = 0 \qquad a_2 + 4a_4 = 1$$

If each of these sets of equations is solved by means of Cramer's rule, it follows that:

$$a_1 = \frac{\begin{vmatrix} 1 & 2 \\ 0 & 4 \end{vmatrix}}{\begin{vmatrix} 5 & 2 \\ 1 & 4 \end{vmatrix}} = \frac{4 - 0}{20 - 2} = \frac{4}{18}$$

$$a_3 = \frac{\begin{vmatrix} 5 & 1 \\ 1 & 0 \end{vmatrix}}{\begin{vmatrix} 5 & 2 \\ 1 & 4 \end{vmatrix}} = \frac{0 - 1}{20 - 2} = -\frac{1}{18}$$

$$a_2 = \frac{\begin{vmatrix} 0 & 2 \\ 1 & 4 \end{vmatrix}}{\begin{vmatrix} 5 & 2 \\ 1 & 4 \end{vmatrix}} = \frac{0 - 2}{20 - 2} = -\frac{2}{18}$$

$$a_4 = \frac{\begin{vmatrix} 5 & 0 \\ 1 & 1 \end{vmatrix}}{\begin{vmatrix} 5 & 2 \\ 1 & 4 \end{vmatrix}} = \frac{5 - 0}{20 - 2} = \frac{5}{18}$$

so that:

$$\mathbf{A}^{-1} = \begin{bmatrix} \frac{4}{18} & -\frac{2}{18} \\ -\frac{1}{18} & \frac{5}{18} \end{bmatrix}$$

As this example illustrates, the inverse of:

$$\mathbf{A} = \begin{bmatrix} a_1 & a_2 \\ a_3 & a_4 \end{bmatrix}$$

is given simply as:

$$\mathbf{A}^{-1} = \begin{bmatrix} \dfrac{a_4}{|\mathbf{A}|} & \dfrac{-a_2}{|\mathbf{A}|} \\ \dfrac{-a_3}{|\mathbf{A}|} & \dfrac{a_1}{|\mathbf{A}|} \end{bmatrix} = \begin{bmatrix} \dfrac{a_4}{a_1a_4 - a_2a_3} & \dfrac{-a_2}{a_1a_4 - a_2a_3} \\ \dfrac{-a_3}{a_1a_4 - a_2a_3} & \dfrac{a_1}{a_1a_4 - a_2a_3} \end{bmatrix}$$

In addition, we see that the determination of $\mathbf{A}^{-1}$ is dependent on $|\mathbf{A}|$ being different from zero. If $|\mathbf{A}| = 0$, the inverse cannot be computed, since a_1, a_2, a_3, and a_4 all have $|\mathbf{A}|$ as a common denominator and, as mentioned previously, division by zero is not defined. If the determinant of a square matrix should be equal to zero, the determinant is said to be *singular*. Thus, implied in the definition of $\mathbf{A}^{-1}$ is that $\mathbf{A}$ is nonsingular.

Definition of a singular matrix.
If the determinant of a matrix $\mathbf{A}$ is equal to zero, the matrix is said to be singular. If the determinant is not equal to zero, the determinant is said to be nonsingular.

4-5. Estimation of the beta weights and associated standard errors for *P* predictors

Let us now use the idea of an inverse to solve the normal equations:

$$\mathcal{X}'\mathcal{X}\boldsymbol{\beta} = \mathcal{X}'\mathbf{Y}$$

If we premultiply each side of this matrix equation by $(\mathcal{X}'\mathcal{X})^{-1}$, we have that:

$$(\mathcal{X}'\mathcal{X})^{-1}(\mathcal{X}'\mathcal{X})\boldsymbol{\beta} = (\mathcal{X}'\mathcal{X})^{-1}\mathcal{X}'\mathbf{Y}$$

Since:

$$(\mathcal{X}'\mathcal{X})^{-1}(\mathcal{X}'\mathcal{X}) = \mathbf{I}$$

and:

$$\mathbf{I}\boldsymbol{\beta} = \boldsymbol{\beta}$$

it follows that the solution is given simply as:

$$\boldsymbol{\beta} = (\mathcal{X}'\mathcal{X})^{-1}\mathcal{X}'\mathbf{Y}$$

In practice these $(P + 1)$ normal equations are rarely solved in this fashion since the computations can be greatly reduced by ignoring the estimation of β_0. If we do not augment the matrix $\mathbf{X}$, we can obtain estimates of $\beta_1, \beta_2, \ldots, \beta_P$ directly from the variance-covariance matrix. In terms of the partitioned matrices $\hat{\Sigma}_{XX}$ and $\hat{\Sigma}_{XY}$, the normal equations reduce to P equations with solution given by:

$$\mathbf{B} = \hat{\boldsymbol{\beta}} = \hat{\Sigma}_{XX}^{-1}\hat{\Sigma}_{XY}$$

In this form, a solution is obtained for:

$$Y - \bar{Y} = B_1(X_1 - \bar{X}_1) + B_2(X_2 - \bar{X}_2) + \cdots + B_P(X_P - \bar{X}_P)$$

Once the $B_1, B_2, \ldots, B_P$ values are known, B_0 is computed as:

$$B_0 = \bar{Y} - B_1\bar{X}_1 - B_2\bar{X}_2 - \cdots - B_P\bar{X}_P$$

For completeness, we give directions for estimating $\beta_0, \beta_1, \ldots, \beta_P$ in terms of the augmented matrix $\mathscr{X}$ and the original data matrix **X**.

The solution of the normal equations for *P* predictors.
In terms of the augmented data matrix, the solution of the $(P + 1)$ normal equations for $B_0, B_1, B_2, \ldots, B_P$ is given as:

$$\mathbf{B} = (\mathscr{X}'\mathscr{X}')^{-1}(\mathbf{X'Y})$$

In terms of the original data matrix, the solution of the P normal equations for $B_1, B_2, \ldots, B_P$ is given as:

$$\mathbf{B} = \hat{\Sigma}_{XX}^{-1}\hat{\Sigma}_{XY}$$

with:

$$B_0 = \bar{Y}_1 - B_1\bar{X}_1 - B_2\bar{X}_2 - \cdots - B_P\bar{X}_P$$

For the original data matrix of Table 3-1, we will determine B_1 and B_2 directly, with B_0 determined by substitution. Thus:

$$\hat{\Sigma}_{XX} = \begin{bmatrix} 237.0231 & 207.5705 \\ 207.5705 & 403.4968 \end{bmatrix}$$

$$\hat{\Sigma}_{XX}^{-1} = \begin{bmatrix} .0076779 & -.0039497 \\ -.0039497 & .0045102 \end{bmatrix}$$

In addition:

$$\hat{\Sigma}_{XY} = \begin{bmatrix} 300.8218 \\ 356.2147 \end{bmatrix}$$

so that:

$$\begin{aligned} \mathbf{B} &= \begin{bmatrix} .0076779 & -.0039497 \\ -.0039497 & .0045102 \end{bmatrix}\begin{bmatrix} 300.8218 \\ 356.2147 \end{bmatrix} \\ &= \begin{bmatrix} .0076779(300.8218) - .0039497(356.2147) \\ -.0039497(300.8218) + .0045102(356.2147) \end{bmatrix} \\ &= \begin{bmatrix} .9027 \\ .4184 \end{bmatrix} = \begin{bmatrix} B_1 \\ B_2 \end{bmatrix} \end{aligned}$$

Finally:

$$\begin{aligned} B_0 &= \bar{Y} - B_1\bar{X}_1 - B_2\bar{X}_2 \\ &= 99.4750 - .9027(46.0500) - .4184(62.8750) \\ &= 31.5955 \end{aligned}$$

and as shown in Section 3-4:

$$\hat{Y} = 31.60 + .90X_1 + .42X_2$$

In addition to solving the system of normal equations, inverses also generate the standard errors for the beta weights. This is demonstrated with ease for simple regression. Consider the augmented data matrix $\mathscr{X}$ for $P = 1$ and:

$$\mathscr{X}'\mathscr{X} = \begin{bmatrix} N & \sum_{i=1}^{N} X_i \\ \sum_{i=1}^{N} X_i & \sum_{i=1}^{N} X_i^2 \end{bmatrix}$$

Since $\mathscr{X}'\mathscr{X}$ is a 2-by-2 matrix with:

$$|\mathscr{X}'\mathscr{X}| = N\sum_{i=1}^{N} X_i^2 - \left[\sum_{i=1}^{N} X_i\right]^2 = N(N-1)S_X^2 = NSS_X$$

we see that:

$$(\mathscr{X}'\mathscr{X})^{-1} = \begin{bmatrix} \dfrac{\sum_{i=1}^{N} X_i^2}{NSS_X} & \dfrac{-\sum_{i=1}^{N} X_i}{NSS_X} \\ \dfrac{-\sum_{i=1}^{N} X_i}{NSS_X} & \dfrac{N}{NSS_X} \end{bmatrix}$$

If this matrix is multiplied by the scalar $MS_{\text{Res}(Y\cdot X)}$, we have that:

$$MS_{\text{Res}(Y\cdot X)}(\mathscr{X}'\mathscr{X})^{-1} = \begin{bmatrix} \dfrac{\sum_{i=1}^{N} X_i^2}{NSS_X} MS_{\text{Res}(Y\cdot X)} & \dfrac{-\sum_{i=1}^{N} X_i}{NSS_X} MS_{\text{Res}(Y\cdot X)} \\ \dfrac{-\sum_{i=1}^{N} X_i}{NSS_X} MS_{\text{Res}(Y\cdot X)} & \dfrac{1}{NSS_X} MS_{\text{Res}(Y\cdot X)} \end{bmatrix}$$

$$= \frac{MS_{\text{Res}(Y\cdot X)}}{SS_X} \begin{bmatrix} \dfrac{\sum_{i=1}^{N} X_i^2}{N} & \dfrac{-\sum_{i=1}^{N} X_i}{N} \\ \dfrac{-\sum_{i=1}^{N} X_i}{N} & 1 \end{bmatrix}$$

We recall from Section 2-3 that:

$$\frac{MS_{\text{Res}(Y\cdot X)}}{SS_X} = SE_{B_1}^2$$

and:

$$\frac{MS_{\text{Res}(Y\cdot X)}}{SS_X}\left(\frac{\sum_{i=1}^{N} X_i^2}{N}\right) = SE_{B_0}^2 = \left(\frac{\sum_{i=1}^{N} X_i^2}{N}\right) SE_{B_1}^2$$

The off-diagonal element defines what we will term the squared *co-standard error* of B_0 and B_1. Thus:

$$CoSE^2_{B_0,B_1} = \frac{MS_{\text{Res}(Y \cdot X)}}{SS_X}\left(\frac{-\sum_{i=1}^{N} X_i}{N}\right)$$

This suggests that:

$$MS_{\text{Res}(Y \cdot X)}(\mathscr{X}'\mathscr{X})^{-1} = (\mathbf{SE}^2_B)$$

In terms of $MS_{\text{Res}(Y \cdot X)}(\mathscr{X}'\mathscr{X})^{-1}$ we see that the squared standard errors of B_0 and B_1 appear along the main diagonal and that the squared co-standard error of B_0 and B_1 is found in the off-diagonal positions. If we now generalize from this result to P variables, we see that the squared standard errors and co-standard errors for B_0, B_1, $B_2, \ldots, B_P$ are given by:

$$(\mathbf{SE}^2_B) = MS_{\text{Res}(Y \cdot X)}(\mathscr{X}'\mathscr{X})^{-1}$$

If the standard error of B_0 is of no interest, one can use the original data matrix directly and ignore the augmented data matrix entirely. For example, with $P = 1$ and the original data, $\hat{\Sigma}^{-1}_{XX}$ reduces to the single element $1/S^2_X$, so that

$$SE^2_{B_1} = \frac{MS_{\text{Res}(Y \cdot X)}}{N-1}\left(\frac{1}{S^2_X}\right).$$

This suggests that in the P-variable case the squared standard errors for B_1, $B_2, \ldots, B_P$ are given by:

$$(\mathbf{SE}^2_B) = \frac{MS_{\text{Res}(Y \cdot X_1 \ldots X_P)}}{N-1}\hat{\Sigma}^{-1}_{XX}$$

For completeness, we have the following.

Definition of the standard errors for *P* predictors.
In terms of the augmented data matrix, the $(P + 1)$ squared standard errors of B_0, $B_1, B_2, \ldots, B_P$ are given by the elements of:

$$MS_{\text{Res}(Y \cdot X_1 \ldots X_P)}(\mathscr{X}'\mathscr{X})^{-1}$$

In terms of the original data matrix, the P squared standard errors of $B_1, B_2, \ldots, B_P$ are given as the elements of:

$$\frac{MS_{\text{Res}(Y \cdot X_1 \ldots X_P)}}{N-1}\hat{\Sigma}^{-1}_{XX}$$

When the augmented data matrix is employed, we obtain the standard error of B_0 directly. When the original data matrix is used, we do not obtain the standard error of B_0. We now determine the standard errors associated with the data in Table 3-1, using the original data matrix. For these data, $MS_{\text{Res}(Y \cdot X_1 X_2)} = 525.84098$, so that:

$$\mathbf{SE}^2_B = \frac{525.84098}{39}\begin{bmatrix} .0076779 & -.0039497 \\ -.0039497 & .0045102 \end{bmatrix}$$
$$= \begin{bmatrix} .10352 & -.05325 \\ -.05325 & .06081 \end{bmatrix}$$

Thus:

$$SE_{B_1} = \sqrt{.10352} = .32175$$

$$SE_{B_2} = \sqrt{.06081} = .24660$$

Since the squared co-standard error of B_1 and B_2 is given by:

$$CoSE^2_{B_1B_2} = -.05325$$

the associated correlation is equal to:

$$r_{B_1B_2} = \frac{CoSE^2_{B_1B_2}}{SE_{B_1}SE_{B_2}}$$

$$= \frac{-.05325}{\sqrt{.10352}\sqrt{.06081}} = -.67113$$

Apart from permitting an inspection of the correlation between B_1 and B_2, the off-diagonal elements of $\mathbf{SE}^2_B$ also have practical significance. Thus, for example, the squared standard error of the difference in B_1 and B_2 is given by:

$$SE^2_{B_1-B_2} = SE^2_{B_1} - 2CoSE^2_{B_1B_2} + SE^2_{B_2}$$
$$= .10352 - 2(-.05325) + .06081$$
$$= .27083$$

so that:

$$SE_{B_1-B_2} = \sqrt{.27083} = .52042$$

The test of H_0: $\beta_1 - \beta_2 = 0$ could then be performed as a one-sample t test with:

$$t = \frac{B_1 - B_2}{SE_{B_1-B_2}} = \frac{.90273 - .41843}{.52042} = \frac{.48430}{.52042} = .93$$

With $v = N - P - 1 = 40 - 2 - 1 = 37$ and $\alpha = .05$, the hypothesis of equal beta weights would not be rejected. As a confidence interval with $\alpha = .05$, we have that $t_{37:.025} = -2.03$ and $t_{37:.975} = 2.03$, so that:

$$.48430 - 2.03(.52042) < \beta_1 - \beta_2 < .48430 + 2.03(.52042)$$
$$-.5721 < \beta_1 - \beta_2 < 1.5407$$

Since zero is in the interval, we conclude that $\beta_1 = \beta_2$.

As an aside, we note that B_0 and B_1 of simple regression theory are generally negatively related to one another. By definition, $\rho_{B_0B_1}$ can be estimated by:

$$r_{B_0B_1} = \frac{CoSE^2_{B_0B_1}}{SE_{B_0}SE_{B_1}}$$

$$= \frac{\dfrac{MS_{\text{Res}(Y\cdot X)}}{SS_X}\left(\dfrac{-\sum_{i=1}^{N} X_i}{N}\right)}{\sqrt{\dfrac{MS_{\text{Res}(Y\cdot X)}}{SS_X}\left(\dfrac{\sum_{i=1}^{N} X_i^2}{N}\right)}\sqrt{\dfrac{MS_{\text{Res}(Y\cdot X)}}{SS_X}}}$$

$$= \frac{\dfrac{-\sum_{i=1}^{N} X_i}{N}}{\sqrt{\dfrac{\sum_{i=1}^{N} X_i^2}{N}}} = \frac{-\bar{X}}{\sqrt{\dfrac{\sum_{i=1}^{N} X_i^2}{N}}}$$

For data with nonnegative values, obviously the numerator of this ratio will always be negative, thereby resulting in a negative correlation between B_0 and B_1.

The same negative correlation between B_0 and B_1 can be demonstrated intuitively by recalling that $B_0 = \bar{Y} - B_1\bar{X}$. Once again, note that for nonnegative values of $\bar{X}$, whenever B_1 is large, B_0 will tend to be small, and vice versa. Recognizing this mathematical truism may prove useful in various substantive applications. For example, certain learning psychologists record how long it takes a subject to make a yes/no decision (the subject's response *latency*) about stimuli of varying complexity or similarity. Thus Stimulus A may be briefly exposed, followed by a one-, two-, or three-stimulus array that either contains or does not contain Stimulus A as a member. The subject's task is to decide as rapidly as possible whether or not Stimulus A is included in the subsequent set. If each subject were administered trials at all three array sizes, X, it would be possible to compute the correlation between X and response latency, Y, on a subject-by-subject basis. From these computations, a slope and an intercept could be determined for each subject, and it would not be surprising to find that subjects with steep slopes have small intercepts and those with flat slopes have large intercepts. This result is expected from the negative correlation between B_0 and B_1 just developed, rather than from any genuine psychological or psychophysical process. As a result, our substantive interpretations of this expected phenomenon must be tempered accordingly.

4-6. The expected value and variance of linear combinations of variables

Many research questions in multivariate analysis can be specified in terms of linear combination of variables. In some special cases, we refer to such linear combinations as *linear contrasts.* Since these mathematical functions assume such an important role in multivariate data analysis, we consider them in detail.

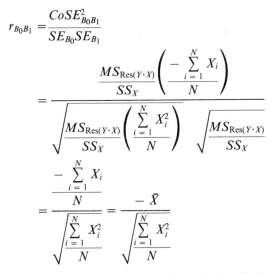

Definitions of a linear combination and a linear contrast.
Let $\theta_1, \theta_2, \ldots, \theta_P$ represent a set of population parameters. Let the sample estimates be denoted by $\hat{\theta}_1, \hat{\theta}_2, \ldots, \hat{\theta}_P$. A linear combination of the population parameters is defined as:

$$L = a_1\theta_1 + a_2\theta_2 + \cdots + a_P\theta_P = \mathbf{A}'\boldsymbol{\theta}$$

and is estimated as:

$$\hat{L} = a_1\hat{\theta}_1 + a_2\hat{\theta}_2 + \cdots + a_P\hat{\theta}_P = \mathbf{A}'\hat{\boldsymbol{\theta}}$$

If, in addition:

$$a_1 + a_2 + \cdots + a_P = \mathbf{A}'\mathbf{1} = 0$$

the linear combination, L, is called a linear contrast, and is denoted by:

$$\psi = \mathbf{A}'\boldsymbol{\theta}$$

and is estimated by:

$$\hat{\psi} = \mathbf{A}'\hat{\boldsymbol{\theta}}$$

The comparison of Section 4-5, $B_1 - B_2$, is an example of a linear contrast. It serves as an estimate of:

$$\psi = \beta_1 - \beta_2 = [1 \quad -1]\begin{bmatrix}\beta_1\\ \beta_2\end{bmatrix} = \mathbf{A}'\boldsymbol{\beta}$$

where:

$$\mathbf{A}' = [1 \quad -1]$$

$$\boldsymbol{\beta} = \begin{bmatrix}\beta_1\\ \beta_2\end{bmatrix}$$

Tests of hypothesis and confidence intervals for any linear combinations or linear contrasts are based on the sample estimator of the population variance.

As a familiar example, consider the contrast for the matched-pair t test:

$$\psi = \mu_1 - \mu_2$$

estimated as:

$$\hat{\psi} = \bar{Y}_1 - \bar{Y}_2.$$

The variance of this contrast is given as:

$$\sigma^2_{\hat{\psi}} = \sigma^2_{\bar{Y}_1} + \sigma^2_{\bar{Y}_2} - 2\rho_{Y_1Y_2}\sigma_{\bar{Y}_1}\sigma_{\bar{Y}_2}$$

and is estimated in the sample as:

$$SE^2_{\hat{\psi}} = \frac{S^2_{Y_1}}{N} + \frac{S^2_{Y_2}}{N} - 2r_{Y_1Y_2}\frac{S_{Y_1}S_{Y_2}}{N}$$

This latter form can be written in matrix notation as:

$$\mathbf{SE}^2_{\hat{\psi}} = [1 \quad -1] \begin{bmatrix} \dfrac{S^2_{Y_1}}{N} & r_{Y_1Y_2}\dfrac{S_{Y_1}S_{Y_2}}{N} \\ r_{Y_1Y_2}\dfrac{S_{Y_1}S_{Y_2}}{N} & \dfrac{S^2_{Y_2}}{N} \end{bmatrix} \begin{bmatrix} 1 \\ -1 \end{bmatrix}$$

$$= \mathbf{A}'\hat{\Sigma}_{\bar{Y}}\mathbf{A}$$

where $\mathbf{A}' = [1 \quad -1]$ and $\hat{\Sigma}_{\bar{Y}}$ equals the 2×2 matrix involving $S^2_{Y_1}$, $S^2_{Y_2}$, and $r_{Y_1Y_2}$.

The variance of any linear combination is defined as follows.

Definition of the variance of a linear combination of variables.

Let:

$$\hat{L} = a_1\hat{\theta}_1 + a_2\hat{\theta}_2 + \cdots + a_P\hat{\theta}_P = \mathbf{A}'\hat{\boldsymbol{\theta}}$$

The variance of $\hat{L}$ is defined as:

$$\text{Var}(\hat{L}) = \mathbf{A}'\hat{\Sigma}_{\hat{\theta}}\mathbf{A}$$

where $\hat{\Sigma}_{\hat{\theta}}$ is the variance-covariance matrix for the $\hat{\theta}$. If the population $\hat{\Sigma}_{\hat{\theta}}$ is unknown, it can be estimated from the sample as $\hat{\Sigma}_{\hat{\theta}}$. In terms of this estimator, the squared standard error of $\hat{L}$ is defined as:

$$SE^2_{\hat{L}} = \mathbf{A}'\hat{\Sigma}_{\hat{\theta}}\mathbf{A}$$

For $\hat{\psi} = B_1 - B_2$, we see that:

$$\mathbf{SE}^2_{\hat{\psi}} = [1 \quad -1] \begin{bmatrix} SE^2_{B_1} & CoSE^2_{B_1B_2} \\ CoSE^2_{B_1B_2} & SE^2_{B_2} \end{bmatrix} \begin{bmatrix} 1 \\ -1 \end{bmatrix}$$

$$= SE^2_{B_1} - 2\,CoSE^2_{B_1B_2} + SE^2_{B_2}$$

Other linear combinations and linear contrasts will appear in most of the examples given in later sections of this book.

4-7. The analysis of variance model for regression analysis

The analysis of variance table for a regression analysis can be obtained directly from the variance-covariance matrix and the least squares estimates of the betas. In this section, we consider some common computational methods in terms of matrix notation. For notational simplicity, as well as to parallel the computational approaches of most existing computer programs, we introduce the following matrices:

$$\mathbf{SS}_X = (N-1)\hat{\Sigma}_{XX}$$

$$\mathbf{SP}_{XY} = (N-1)\hat{\Sigma}_{XY}$$

$$\mathbf{SS}_Y = (N-1)\hat{\Sigma}_{YY}$$

Since in this chapter the Y matrix consists of only a single dependent variable, $\mathbf{SS}_Y$

can be represented simply as the scalar, SS_Y.

Let us begin by examining the predicted value of Y_i for the set of values $X_{i1}, X_{i2}, \ldots, X_{iP}$. By definition:

$$\begin{aligned}\hat{Y}_i &= B_0 + B_1X_{i1} + B_2X_{i2} + \cdots + B_PX_{iP} \\ &= (\bar{Y} - B_1\bar{X}_1 - B_2\bar{X}_2 - \cdots - B_P\bar{X}_P) + (B_1X_{i1} + B_2X_{i2} + \cdots + B_PX_{iP}) \\ &= \bar{Y} + B_1(X_{i1} - \bar{X}_1) + B_2(X_{i2} - \bar{X}_2) + \cdots + B_P(X_{iP} - \bar{X}_P)\end{aligned}$$

The explained deviation for the ith observation is given by:

$$\begin{aligned}d_{E_i} &= (\hat{Y}_i - \bar{Y}) \\ &= B_1(X_{i1} - \bar{X}_1) + B_2(X_{i2} - \bar{X}_2) + \cdots + B_P(X_{iP} - \bar{X}_P)\end{aligned}$$

Thus, across all N observations:

$$\sum_{i=1}^{N} d_{E_i}^2 = \sum_{i=1}^{N} [B_1(X_{i1} - \bar{X}_1) + B_2(X_{i2} - \bar{X}_2) + \cdots + B_P(X_{iP} - \bar{X}_P)]^2$$

If this expression were to be expanded, it would be found to be equal to:

$$\begin{aligned}\sum_{i=1}^{N} d_{E_i}^2 = (N-1)[&B_1^2S_{X_1X_1} + B_1B_2S_{X_1X_2} + \cdots + B_1B_PS_{X_1X_P} \\ &+ B_2B_1S_{X_2X_1} + B_2^2S_{X_2X_2} + \cdots + B_2B_PS_{X_2X_P} + \cdots \\ &+ B_PB_1S_{X_PX_1} + B_PB_2S_{X_PX_2} + \cdots + B_P^2S^2_{X_PX_P}]\end{aligned}$$

In matrix notation, this is identical to:

$$SS_E = (N-1)\mathbf{B}'\hat{\Sigma}_{XX}\mathbf{B} = \mathbf{B}'\mathbf{SS}_X\mathbf{B} = SS_{\text{Reg}}$$

Note that this is the same equation derived in Section 2-3 for simple regression. Since $\nu_{\text{Tot}} = N - 1$ and $\nu_{\text{Res}} = N - P - 1$, it follows that:

$$\nu_{\text{Reg}} = (N-1) - (N-P-1) = P$$

Thus, for $P = 1$, we see that:

$$\begin{aligned}SS_{\text{Reg}} = MS_{\text{Reg}} &= (N-1)\mathbf{B}'\hat{\Sigma}_{XX}\mathbf{B} \\ &= (N-1)B_1S_X^2B_1 \\ &= (N-1)S_X^2B_1^2 \\ &= SS_XB_1^2\end{aligned}$$

Note that when $P = 1$:

$$B_1 = r_{XY}\frac{S_Y}{S_X}$$

so that SS_{Reg} reduces to:

$$SS_{\text{Reg}} = (N-1)S_Y^2r_{XY}^2 = SS_Yr_{XY}^2$$

as was shown previously in Section 2-3.

For $P > 1$, extensions in terms of $\mathbf{B}$ are direct, whereas those in terms of the zero-order correlation matrix, $\mathbf{R}_{XY}$, are not, because of the need for partial correlations. For this reason, our subsequent developments are given in terms of **B**. Thus, for the data of Table 3-1 with $P = 2$:

$$SS_{\text{Reg}} = (N-1)\mathbf{B}'\hat{\Sigma}_{XX}\mathbf{B}$$

$$= (40-1)[.9027 \quad .4184]\begin{bmatrix}237.0231 & 207.5705\\ 207.5705 & 403.4968\end{bmatrix}\begin{bmatrix}.9027\\ .4184\end{bmatrix}$$

$$= 7533.0524 + 6115.6254 + 2755.1812$$

$$= 16403.8590$$

Thus:

$$MS_{\text{Reg}} = \frac{SS_{\text{Reg}}}{P} = \frac{16403.8590}{2} = 8201.9295$$

Since:

$$SS_{\text{Tot}} = (N-1)S_Y^2 = SS_Y$$

it follows that:

$$SS_{\text{Res}} = SS_Y - \mathbf{B}'\mathbf{SS}_X\mathbf{B}$$

For $P = 1$, this is identical to the results of Section 2-3, since:

$$\begin{aligned} SS_{\text{Res}} = (N-1)(S_Y^2 - B_1^2 S_X^2) &= (N-1)(S_Y^2 - r_{XY}^2 S_Y^2)\\ &= (N-1)S_Y^2(1 - r_{XY}^2)\\ &= SS_Y(1 - r_{XY}^2)\end{aligned}$$

For the data of Table 3-1:

$$SS_{\text{Res}} = (40-1)\left(30.32304^2 - \frac{16403.8590}{40-1}\right) = 19456.1250$$

Thus, since $\nu_{\text{Res}} = N - P - 1$, it follows that:

$$MS_{\text{Res}} = \frac{SS_{\text{Res}}}{N-P-1} = \frac{19456.1250}{40-2-1} = 525.8410$$

and $F = 15.60$, as were previously reported in Sections 3-6 and 3-8. The analysis of variance table associated with these data is given as Table 4-1. For completeness, we note the following.

TABLE 4-1. The analysis of variance table for the multiple linear regression of Table 3-1

Source	*d/f*	*Sum of squares*	*Mean square*	*F*
Regression	2	16403.86	8201.93	15.60
Residual	37	19456.12	525.84	
Total	39	35859.98		

Procedure for determining sums of squares for a multiple regression.

Step 1. Find the values of $B_1, B_2, \ldots, B_P$, and $\mathbf{SS}_X = (N-1)\hat{\Sigma}_{XX}$.

Step 2. SS_{Reg}, SS_{Res}, and SS_{Tot} are determined as:

$$SS_{\text{Reg}} = \mathbf{B}'\mathbf{SS}_X\mathbf{B}$$

$$SS_{\text{Res}} = SS_Y - \mathbf{B}'\mathbf{SS}_X\mathbf{B}$$

$$SS_{\text{Tot}} = SS_Y$$

Step 3. The degrees of freedom for the three sums of squares are given as:

$$\nu_{\text{Reg}} = P, \quad \nu_{\text{Res}} = N - P - 1, \quad \text{and} \quad \nu_{\text{Tot}} = N - 1$$

Step 4. The mean squares are given by:

$$MS_{\text{Reg}} = \frac{1}{P} SS_{\text{Reg}}$$

$$MS_{\text{Res}} = \frac{1}{N - P - 1} SS_{\text{Res}}$$

Step 5. The F ratio for testing H_0: $\beta_1 = \beta_2 = \cdots = \beta_P = 0$ against H_1: H_0 is false, is given by:

$$F = \frac{MS_{\text{Reg}}}{MS_{\text{Res}}}$$

Step 6. Reject H_0 if:

$$F > F_{\nu_{\text{Reg}}, \nu_{\text{Res}}:1-\alpha}$$

Note that the alternative hypothesis to H_0 states that H_0 is false. This is an alternative similar to the univariate analysis of variance model for which post hoc comparisons are needed. In the multiple regression situation, the hypothesis that all $\beta_p = 0$ can be better stated as:

H_0: All $L = 0$

where:

$$L = a_1\beta_1 + a_2\beta_2 + \cdots + a_P\beta_P = \mathbf{A}'\boldsymbol{\beta}$$

With direct analogy to the one-way analysis of variance, it is seen that H_0 is tested against the alternative:

H_1: At least one $L \neq 0$

Thus rejection of H_0 implies that at least one linear combination of the β_p is different from zero. A researcher can identify it by the application of the following model.

Procedure for performing a post hoc analysis on the β_p.

Step 1. Examine all linear combinations of interest in terms of the following simultaneous Scheffé confidence intervals:

$$\hat{L} - \mathbf{S}\, SE_{\hat{L}} < L < \hat{L} + \mathbf{S}\, SE_{\hat{L}}$$

where:

1. $L = a_1\beta_1 + a_2\beta_2 + \cdots + a_P\beta_P = \mathbf{A}'\boldsymbol{\beta}$
2. $\hat{L} = a_1B_1 + a_2B_2 + \cdots + a_PB_P = \mathbf{A}'B$
3. $SE_{\hat{L}}^2 = \mathbf{A}'\hat{\sum}_{B_1}\mathbf{A}$
4. $\hat{\sum}_{B_1} = \dfrac{MS_{\text{Res}(Y \cdot X_1X_2 \ldots X_P)}}{N-1}\hat{\sum}_{XX}^{-1} = \mathbf{SE}_{B_1}^2$
5. $\mathbf{S} = \sqrt{P\,F_{P,N-P-1:1-\alpha}}$

Step 2. If any confidence interval does not cover zero, conclude that a significant source of variance is identified with the contrast. The familywise type I error rate associated with all such confidence intervals is given by α.

Note that the post hoc procedure for rejecting H_0: All $\beta_p = 0$ is not restricted to contrasts, but also includes *any* linear combinations of the B_p.

For the data of Table 3-1:

$$\mathbf{S} = \sqrt{PF_{P,N-P-1:1-\alpha}} = \sqrt{2F_{2,37:.95}} = \sqrt{2(3.26)} = 2.55$$

and for the contrast between β_1 and β_2 examined earlier, we have:

$$.48430 - 2.55(.52040) < \beta_1 - \beta_2 < .48430 + 2.55(.52040)$$
$$-.84 < \beta_1 - \beta_2 < 1.81$$

Compared with the previous 95% t interval of:

$$-.57 < \beta_1 - \beta_2 < 1.54$$

we note immediately that the present interval is considerably wider. This is a direct consequence of $\mathbf{S} = 2.55$ being greater than $t = 2.03$. At first it may seem puzzling why these two critical values would differ in this case, since with $P = 2$ there appears to be only one contrast in the B_p. That is, when comparing *means* with $K = 2$, the only comparison possible is given by $\psi = \mu_1 - \mu_2$ and, since in that case $\mathbf{S} = \sqrt{(K-1)F_{K-1,N-K:1-\alpha}} = \sqrt{F_{1,N-K:1-\alpha}} = t_{N-K}$, the Scheffé and t critical values are identical.

The discrepancy in the case of $P = 2$ *regression coefficients* arises from the fact that the Scheffé method permits the simultaneous investigation of all linear combinations of the β_p and not just contrasts. That is, all linear combinations involving the β_p are subsumed by the Scheffé procedure defined by $\mathbf{S} = \sqrt{PF_{P,N-P-1:1-\alpha}}$. Exactly the same situation exists in the one-way analysis. If a researcher wished to determine whether all linear combinations of means and not just contrasts were equal to zero, the appropriate Scheffé coefficient is given by $\mathbf{S}^* = \sqrt{KF_{K,N-K:1-\alpha}}$, rather than the usual $\mathbf{S} = \sqrt{(K-1)F_{K-1,N-K:1-\alpha}}$. The additional degree of freedom is obtained from the typically ignored test that the grand mean differs from zero. Thus the t and $\mathbf{S}$ critical values differ in the case of $P = 2$ regression coefficients since with t only one contrast, $\beta_1 - \beta_2$, is possible, whereas with $\mathbf{S}$ an infinite number of linear combinations, $a_1B_1 + a_2B_2$, can be defined. Similar contrast versus combination arguments generalize to situations where $P > 2$.

Continuing with the present example, if the Scheffé procedure were adopted, we could build additional confidence intervals to determine whether β_1 or β_2, or any linear combination of them, differed significantly from zero. If the appropriate standard errors are applied individually to $B_1 = .9027$ and $B_2 = .4184$, the resulting simultaneous 95% Scheffé confidence intervals are given by:

$$.08 < \beta_1 < 1.72$$

and $-.21 < \beta_2 < 1.05$

As a result, we would conclude that β_1, though not β_2, was nonzero.

4-8. The multiple correlation coefficient

In simple regression theory, we saw that:

$$r^2_{XY} = \frac{SS_{\text{Reg}}}{SS_{\text{Tot}}} = \frac{SS_Y r^2_{XY}}{SS_Y} = \frac{SS_X B_1^2}{SS_Y} = \frac{1}{SS_Y} B_1\, SS_X\, B_1$$

In like manner:

$$\hat{R}^2_{Y\cdot X_1X_2\ldots X_P} = \frac{1}{SS_Y}\mathbf{B}'\mathbf{SS}_X\mathbf{B}$$

For completeness, we define $\hat{R}^2_{Y\cdot X_1X_2..X_P}$ as follows.

Definition of the squared multiple correlation coefficient.
Let SS_Y, $\mathbf{SS}_X$, and $\mathbf{B}$ be computed from the data. The value of $\hat{R}^2$ is given as:

$$\hat{R}^2_{Y\cdot X_1X_2\ldots X_P} = \frac{1}{SS_Y}\mathbf{B}'\mathbf{SS}_X\mathbf{B}$$

For the data of Table 3-1 and the figures of Table 4-1:

$$\hat{R}^2_{Y\cdot X_1X_2} = \frac{16403.86}{35859.98} = .457$$

Finally, we note that the test of H_0: $R^2_{Y\cdot X_1X_2\ldots X_P} = 0$ against H_1: $R^2_{Y\cdot X_1X_2\ldots X_P} \neq 0$ is identical to the analysis of variance test of H_0: $\beta_1 = \beta_2 = \cdots = \beta_P = 0$, since the only way R^2 could equal zero would be if:

$$R^2_{Y\cdot X_1X_2\ldots X_P} = \frac{\boldsymbol{\beta}'\sum_{XX}\boldsymbol{\beta}}{\sigma^2_Y} = 0$$

and this could only happen if $\beta_1 = \beta_2 = \cdots = \beta_P = 0$. This also helps to clarify our previous discussion of linear combinations, as applied to regression. If all β_p are equal to zero, it must be true that all linear combinations involving the β_p are also equal to zero.

We must point out another problem in multiple regression and correlation theory that was alluded to earlier. It is the problem of a singular $\boldsymbol{\Sigma}_{XX}$. If $\boldsymbol{\Sigma}_{XX}$ is singular, a unique solution for the $B_0, B_1, \ldots, B_P$ is not available. Most computer programs in use today do not provide solutions for singular matrices. For this reason, singularities should be avoided. Singularities can arise in a data matrix if any column of data is a linear combination of some of the other columns. When conducting a regression analysis, the creation of new variables from previously observed variables should be avoided since, in many cases, the analysis will prove uninterpretable, if not impossible. For example, if a researcher has two variables X_1 and X_2 in a regression model, a third variable should not be added if it has the form of a linear combination, such as $X_3 = a_1X_1 + a_2X_2$, where a_1 and a_2 are constants, nor should $\sqrt{X_1}$ or any other mathematical function of X_1 and X_2 be used if they produce a singularity.

Singular matrices or *near singular* matrices sometimes intrude into a study, undetected by a researcher. One of the most common situations in which this occurs is in the collection of a set of scores $X_1, X_2, \ldots, X_P$ that measure a highly similar characteristic. An example might be where:

X_1 = Stanford Binet IQ score

X_2 = Wechsler IQ score

X_3 = California Test of Mental Maturity

Clearly all three tests measure intellectual ability. Their intercorrelations are certain to be high. Although none of the variables may be a true linear combination of the others, they may be so highly intercorrelated that they may function as reliabilities and/or near equal values on each subject. If they do, they may well produce a singular matrix that renders the complete analysis uninterpretable.

4-9. Test of the hypothesis $\Sigma_1 = \Sigma_2 = \cdots = \Sigma_K$ in K independent samples

We close this chapter with a statistical test whose importance in multivariate behavioral research is often overlooked. As was mentioned in Chapter 2, it is often of interest to test the hypothesis that K independent correlation coefficients, $\rho_{XY(1)}, \rho_{XY(2)}, \ldots, \rho_{XY(K)}$ are equal. Note that for this two-variable situation, equality of correlations would be implied if, in the K populations under consideration, $\sigma^2_{X(1)} = \sigma^2_{X(2)} = \cdots \sigma^2_{X(K)}$, $\sigma^2_{Y(1)} = \sigma^2_{Y(2)} = \cdots = \sigma^2_{Y(K)}$, and $\sigma_{XY(1)} = \sigma_{XY(2)} = \cdots = \sigma_{XY(K)}$. In terms of our matrix notation, identical correlation matrices would be implicit if:

$$\Sigma_1 = \Sigma_2 = \cdots = \Sigma_K$$

where $\mathbf{\Sigma}$ represents a square $P \times P$ matrix containing P variances and $2\binom{P}{2} = P(P - 1)$ covariances, with half of the covariances being mirror images of the other half. The converse of this hypothesis is not implied; that is, equality of correlation matrices does not imply equality of variance-covariance matrices.

The test of H_0: $\mathbf{\Sigma}_1 = \mathbf{\Sigma}_2 = \cdots = \mathbf{\Sigma}_K$ is of special interest in the behavioral sciences because of the frequent need to make between-group comparisons with respect to variances and covariances. In certain applications, such as canonical correlation (discussed in Chapter 5) and principal component analysis (discussed in Chapter 6), it may be of substantive interest to a researcher to determine whether P variables are similarly structured in two or more independent populations. In other applications, such as discriminant analysis (discussed in Chapter 7) and multivariate analysis of variance (discussed in Chapters 8 and 9), variance-covariance matrix identity becomes an assumption that is inherent to the valid use of the techniques. Thus the question of identity of variance-covariance matrices remains a question, or an assumption, that could be pursued in many of the models to be described in the remaining chapters of this book.

The test we will describe was derived by Bartlett (1937), refined by Box (1950), and presented in Timm (1975). We describe the test as follows. Critical values are found from the Chi-square distribution presented in Table B-3.

Procedure for testing for the identity of K independent variance-covariance matrices.

Step 1. Obtain the $P \times P$ variance-covariance matrix of each sample $\hat{\Sigma}_1, \hat{\Sigma}_2, \ldots, \hat{\Sigma}_K$ and the usual estimate of the pooled variance-covariance matrix:

$$\hat{\Sigma}_0 = \frac{(N_1 - 1)\hat{\Sigma}_1 + (N_2 - 1)\hat{\Sigma}_2 + \cdots + (N_K - 1)\hat{\Sigma}_K}{(N_1 - 1) + (N_2 - 1) + \cdots + (N_K - 1)}$$

The diagonal entries of this matrix will consist of the P pooled variances, $MS_{W(p)} = S^2_{p(W)}$, and the off-diagonal entries will consist of the $P(P - 1)/2$ distinct pooled covariances $S_{pp'(W)}$, both of which were discussed previously.

Step 2. Compute:

$$L = (N - K)\log_e |\hat{\Sigma}_0| - \sum_{k=1}^{K} (N_k - 1)\log_e |\hat{\Sigma}_k|$$

where:

$$N = \sum_{k=1}^{K} N_k$$

Step 3. Compute:

$$C^* = 1 - \frac{2P^2 + 3P - 1}{6(P + 1)(K - 1)} \left(\sum_{k=1}^{K} \frac{1}{N_k - 1} - \frac{1}{N - K} \right)$$

Step 4. Compute:

$$\chi^2 = C^*L$$

and reject:

$$H_0: \Sigma_1 = \Sigma_2 = \cdots = \Sigma_K$$

in favor of:

H_1: H_0 is false

if $\chi^2 > \chi^2_{v:1-\alpha}$ where $v = \frac{1}{2}(K - 1) P(P + 1)$

In essence, the test is easy to carry out, provided it has been programmed for an electronic computer. Even so, it is difficult to justify, in that it is highly dependent on the assumption that all variables of the matrices have a multivariate normal distribution. Up to now we have been able to ignore this assumption since none of the methods we have described has depended on it. This luxury comes to an end in the next chapter, where it will appear as an assumption for the first time. We will consider this assumption only briefly here, but will discuss it in Section 5-8. Suffice it to say that the Bartlett test of identity of variance-covariance matrices is justified only if the variables are multivariate normal or close to multivariate normal. As with univariate analyses that depend on normality, it may be that large sample sizes, in the region of $N_k = 20$, will help to compensate for nonnormality, as a result of the Central Limit Theorem (see, for example, Glass et al., 1972). Similar compensations may apply in multivariate situations, although the confirming evidence is not too well documented. Because of the multivariate normality assumption associated with the Bartlett test, it cannot be used for dichotomous or dummy variables, nor for variables that can take on a small set of numerical values, such as 1, 2, and 3. Similarly, one or more 'outlying' observations in a given sample could possibly invalidate this test's use. Scatterplots, based on each pair of variables, are therefore recommended to detect potential invalidating influences.

We illustrate the use of this test for the four variance-covariance matrices associated with Tasks 2 and 3 of Table A-2, which are reported in Table 4-2, along with the pooled variance-covariance matrix. For these data, $N_1 = N_2 = N_3 = N_4 = 30$. Since natural logarithms, those to the base e, are somewhat unfamiliar and not readily available to most researchers, we may transform the data using logarithms with a base of 10. Under this transformation:

$$\log_e x = 2.3026 \log_{10} x$$

Tables of $\log_{10} x$ are given in Table B-8. In terms of these logarithms:

$$\log_e |\hat{\Sigma}_0| = 2.3026 \log_{10}(521.4651) = 2.3026(2.7172) = 6.2568$$

$$\log_e |\hat{\Sigma}_1| = 2.3026 \log_{10}(234.3333) = 2.3026(2.3698) = 5.4568$$

$$\log_e |\hat{\Sigma}_2| = 2.3026 \log_{10}(380.0855) = 2.3026(2.5799) = 5.9405$$

$$\log_e |\hat{\Sigma}_3| = 2.3026 \log_{10}(728.3810) = 2.3026(2.8623) = 6.5907$$

$$\log_e |\hat{\Sigma}_4| = 2.3026 \log_{10}(539.0590) = 2.3026(2.7316) = 6.2899$$

TABLE 4-2. Variance-covariance matrices associated with the data of Table A-2

Condition	*Variance-covariance matrix*		$\lvert\hat{\Sigma}_k\rvert$
1. Vocalization-Control	37.5769 12.7504	12.7504 10.5625	234.3333
2. Vocalization-Strategy	55.5025 3.1114	3.1114 7.0225	380.0855
3. Imagery-Control	75.1689 4.1812	4.1812 9.9225	728.3810
4. Imagery-Strategy	105.2676 19.2570	19.2570 8.6438	539.0590
Pooled Data	68.3790 9.8250	9.8250 9.0378	521.4651

In terms of these values:

$$L = (120 - 4)6.2568 - [(30 - 1)(5.4568 + 5.9405 + 6.5907 + 6.2899)]$$
$$= 21.7297$$

With $P = 2$ and $N_1 = N_2 = N_3 = N_4 = 30$:

$$C^* = 1 - \frac{2(2^2) + 3(2) - 1}{6(2 + 1)(4 - 1)}\left(\frac{1}{29} + \frac{1}{29} + \frac{1}{29} + \frac{1}{29} - \frac{1}{116}\right)$$
$$= 1 - .0311 = .9689$$

so that:

$$\chi^2 = (.9689)(21.7297) = 21.05$$

With:

$$\nu = \tfrac{1}{2}(4 - 1)(2)(3) = 9$$

and $\alpha = .05$, $\chi^2_{9:.95} = 16.92$, so that the hypothesis of identity of variance-covariance matrices is rejected. The largest difference seems to be associated with the S_{XY} values since:

$$\frac{S_{XY(\text{largest})}}{S_{XY(\text{smallest})}} = \frac{19.2570}{3.1114} = 6.19$$

The corresponding ratios for the S_X^2 and S_Y^2 are given by 2.80 and 1.50, respectively. More precise statements than this are not possible because of the nonexistence of all-inclusive Scheffé post hoc procedures.

As a final note, we mention that Jennrich (1970) has proposed a test for the equality of two correlation matrices. For the case of $K = 2$, Jennrich's test likely has greater statistical power than Bartlett's test.

4-10. Summary

In this chapter the rudiments of vector and matrix algebra needed for an understanding of multivariate methods were presented. Addition, subtraction, multiplication, and division of matrices were illustrated. It was seen that the single matrix equation:

$$\mathbf{Y} = \mathscr{X}\boldsymbol{\beta}$$

is identical to the set of N equations:

$$Y_1 = \beta_0 + \beta_1 X_{11} + \beta_2 X_{12} + \cdots + \beta_P X_{1P}$$
$$Y_2 = \beta_0 + \beta_1 X_{21} + \beta_2 X_{22} + \cdots + \beta_P X_{2P}$$
$$\vdots \qquad\qquad \vdots$$
$$Y_N = \beta_0 + \beta_1 X_{N1} + \beta_2 X_{N2} + \cdots + \beta_P X_{NP}$$

provided that:

$$\mathbf{Y} = \begin{bmatrix} Y_1 \\ Y_2 \\ \cdot \\ \cdot \\ \cdot \\ Y_N \end{bmatrix}$$

$$\mathscr{X} = \begin{bmatrix} 1 & X_{11} & X_{12} & \cdots & X_{1P} \\ 1 & X_{21} & X_{22} & \cdots & X_{2P} \\ \cdot & \cdot & \cdot & \cdot & \cdot \\ \cdot & \cdot & \cdot & \cdot & \cdot \\ \cdot & \cdot & \cdot & \cdot & \cdot \\ 1 & X_{N1} & X_{N2} & \cdots & X_{NP} \end{bmatrix}$$

$$\boldsymbol{\beta} = \begin{bmatrix} \beta_0 \\ \beta_1 \\ \cdot \\ \cdot \\ \cdot \\ \beta_P \end{bmatrix}$$

We saw that the normal equations needed to solve for $\beta_0, \beta_1, \ldots, \beta_P$ can be written simply as:

$$\mathscr{X}'\mathbf{Y} = \mathscr{X}'\mathscr{X}\boldsymbol{\beta}$$

where $\mathscr{X}'$ is the transposed matrix of $\mathscr{X}$. In general, if the elements of $\mathscr{X}$ are denoted as X_{rc}, the elements of the transposed $\mathscr{X}$ are defined as X_{cr}. We also saw that the least square estimators of the β_p value can be written in matrix notation as:

$$\mathbf{B} = (\mathscr{X}'\mathscr{X})^{-1}\,\mathscr{X}'\mathbf{Y}$$

where $(\mathscr{X}'\mathscr{X})^{-1}$ is the inverse of the matrix $\mathscr{X}'\mathscr{X}$. In general, the inverse matrix $\mathbf{A}^{-1}$ of a square matrix $\mathbf{A}$ is defined as the matrix with the property that:

$$\mathbf{AA}^{-1} = \mathbf{A}^{-1}\mathbf{A} = \mathbf{I}$$

where $\mathbf{I}$ is the identity matrix defined as:

$$\mathbf{I} = \begin{bmatrix} 1 & 0 & \ldots & 0 \\ 0 & 1 & \ldots & 0 \\ \cdot & \cdot & \cdot & \cdot \\ \cdot & \cdot & \cdot & \cdot \\ \cdot & \cdot & \cdot & \cdot \\ 0 & 0 & \ldots & 1 \end{bmatrix}$$

In practice, the B values are generated from the variance-covariance matrix defined as:

$$\hat{\Sigma} = \begin{bmatrix} S_1^2 & S_{12} & \cdots & S_{1P} & S_{1Y} \\ S_{21} & S_2^2 & \cdots & S_{2P} & S_{2Y} \\ \cdot & \cdot & \cdot & \cdot & \cdot \\ \cdot & \cdot & \cdot & \cdot & \cdot \\ \cdot & \cdot & \cdot & \cdot & \cdot \\ S_{P1} & S_{P2} & \cdots & S_P^2 & S_{PY} \\ S_{Y1} & S_{Y2} & \cdots & S_{YP} & S_Y^2 \end{bmatrix}$$

which is shown as a partitioned matrix:

$$\hat{\Sigma} = \left[\begin{array}{c|c} \hat{\Sigma}_{XX} & \hat{\Sigma}_{XY} \\ \hline \hat{\Sigma}_{YX} & \hat{\Sigma}_{YY} \end{array}\right]$$

In terms of these partitioned matrices:

$$\mathbf{B} = \hat{\Sigma}_{XX}^{-1}\hat{\Sigma}_{XY}$$

for $p = 1, 2, \ldots, P$. B_0 is defined as:

$$B_0 = \bar{Y}_1 - B_1\bar{X}_1 - B_2\bar{X}_2 - \cdots - B_P\bar{X}_P$$

Finally, the standard errors of B can be found in the diagonal of:

$$(\mathbf{SE}_B^2) = \frac{MS_{\text{Res}(Y \cdot X_1X_2\ldots X_P)}}{N-1}\hat{\Sigma}_{XX}^{-1}$$

The off-diagonal elements define the squared co-standard errors of these estimates.

Many multivariate procedures involve linear combinations of the form:

$$L = a_1\theta_1 + a_2\theta_2 + \cdots + a_P\theta_P = \mathbf{A}'\boldsymbol{\theta}$$

where $\boldsymbol{\theta}$ is estimated from the sample. The squared standard error of an estimated L is given by:

$$\mathbf{SE}_{\hat{L}}^2 = \mathbf{A}'\hat{\Sigma}_{\theta}\mathbf{A}$$

Linear regression was examined in matrix notation. It was seen that:

$$SS_{\text{Regression}} = \mathbf{B}'\,\mathbf{SS}_X\,\mathbf{B}$$

$$SS_{\text{Residual}} = SS_Y - \mathbf{B}'\,\mathbf{SS}_X\,\mathbf{B}$$

$$SS_{\text{Total}} = SS_Y$$

where:

$$SS_Y = (N-1)S_Y^2 \quad \text{and} \quad \mathbf{SS}_X = (N-1)\hat{\Sigma}_{XX}$$

so that:

$$\hat{R}^2_{Y \cdot X_1X_2\ldots X_P} = \frac{1}{SS_Y}\mathbf{B}'\,\mathbf{SS}_X\,\mathbf{B}$$

Finally, Bartlett's test for identity of K variance-covariance matrices was presented. The test statistic is defined as:

$$\chi^2 = C^*L$$

where:

$$C^* = 1 - \frac{2P^2 + 3P - 1}{6(P+1)(K-1)}\left(\sum_{k=1}^{K} \frac{1}{N_k - 1} - \frac{1}{N-K}\right)$$

$$L = (N-K)\log_e|\hat{\Sigma}_0| - \sum_{k=1}^{K}(N_k - 1)\log_e|\hat{\Sigma}_k|$$

The hypothesis:

$$H_0:\ \hat{\Sigma}_1 = \hat{\Sigma}_2 = \cdots = \hat{\Sigma}_K$$

is rejected if $\chi^2 > \chi^2_{v:1-\alpha}$, where $v = \frac{1}{2}(K-1)(P)(P+1)$.

4-11. Exercises.

4-1. Add the two matrices:

$$\mathbf{A}_1 = \begin{bmatrix} 2 & 0 & 5 & 1 \\ 3 & 6 & 4 & 2 \\ 1 & 6 & 7 & 5 \end{bmatrix} \quad \mathbf{A}_2 = \begin{bmatrix} 3 & -1 & 2 & -6 \\ 0 & 5 & -0 & -2 \\ 3 & 2 & 4 & 7 \end{bmatrix}$$

4-2. Can the matrices of Exercise 4-1 be multiplied? Why or why not?

4-3. Use matrix $\mathbf{A}_1$ of Exercise 4-1 and postmultiply it by:

$$\mathbf{A}_3 = \begin{bmatrix} 0 & 1 \\ 2 & 0 \\ 1 & 1 \\ 2 & 0 \end{bmatrix}$$

4-4. Is the product $\mathbf{A}_3\mathbf{A}_1$ defined? Why or why not?

4-5. Find $\bar{\mathbf{X}}'$, $\mathbf{S}'$, and $\mathbf{R}$ for your sample of 40 subjects.

4-6. Determine $\hat{\Sigma}$ for your sample of 40 subjects.

4-7. Does the following matrix have an inverse?

$$\mathbf{A}_4 = \begin{bmatrix} 2 & 6 & 3 & 11 \\ 3 & 2 & -9 & -4 \\ 7 & 0 & -7 & 0 \\ -1 & 4 & 6 & 9 \end{bmatrix}$$

See Exercise 1-16 for directions for finding the determinant of $\mathbf{A}_4$.

4-8. Find the inverse of:

$$\mathbf{A}_5 = \begin{bmatrix} 10 & 2 \\ 2 & 6 \end{bmatrix}$$

4-9. Use the data for your sample of 40 subjects and verify that:

$$B = \hat{\Sigma}_{XX}^{-1}\hat{\Sigma}_{XY}$$

4-10. Find the standard errors for the beta weights of Exercise 4-9.

4-11. Consider a study with X_1, X_2, X_3, and X_4, and:

$$\hat{\Sigma} = \begin{bmatrix} 10 & 2 & 7 & 6 \\ 2 & 8 & 3 & 4 \\ 7 & 3 & 15 & 1 \\ 6 & 4 & 1 & 20 \end{bmatrix}$$

Find the standard deviation of:

$$L = 3X_1 - 2X_2 - X_3 + X_4$$

4-12. Suppose that the data of Exercise 4-11 were drawn from distributions in which $\mu_1 = \mu_2 = \mu_3 = \mu_4 = 12$. How many standard deviations are there between $E(L)$ and L, based on a subject whose X values are given by $X' = (2 \quad 15 \quad 6 \quad 22)$?

4-13. For your sample of 40 subjects, show that:

$$SS_{\text{Total}} = SS_{\text{Explained}} + SS_{\text{Unexplained}}$$

where:

$$SS_{\text{Explained}} = \mathbf{B}'\hat{\Sigma}_{XX}\mathbf{B}$$

$$SS_{\text{Unexplained}} = SS_Y - \mathbf{B}'\hat{\Sigma}_{XX}\mathbf{B}$$

$$SS_{\text{Total}} = (N-1)S_Y^2$$

4-14. Complete the ANOVA Table for Exercise 4-13.

4-15. For your sample of 40 subjects, show that:

$$\hat{R}^2_{Y\cdot X_1X_2} = \frac{1}{S_Y^2}\mathbf{B}'\hat{\Sigma}_{XX}\mathbf{B}$$

4-16. Is there any reason to believe that $\Sigma_1 = \Sigma_2 = \Sigma_3$, if:

$$\hat{\Sigma}_1 = \begin{bmatrix} 2.12 & 0.86 \\ 0.86 & 1.71 \end{bmatrix}$$

$$\hat{\Sigma}_2 = \begin{bmatrix} 1.91 & 0.98 \\ 0.98 & 1.63 \end{bmatrix}$$

$$\hat{\Sigma}_3 = \begin{bmatrix} 2.09 & 1.03 \\ 1.03 & 1.41 \end{bmatrix}$$

and $N_1 = N_2 = N_3 = 40$.

CHAPTER FIVE

CANONICAL CORRELATION THEORY

5-1. Canonical correlation

As we saw in Chapter 3, multiple regression and correlation theory were based on an extension of the simple regression and correlation model for $P = 1$ independent and $Q = 1$ dependent variables. For $P = 1$ and $Q = 1$, we started with the model $Y = \beta_0 + \beta_1 X$ and found that we could find an estimate for ρ_{YX} by finding weights B_0 and B_1 that maximize the sample correlation coefficient between Y and its predicted value $\hat{Y}$. As we saw in Section 1-10, $r_{Y\hat{Y}} = r_{YX}$, where $\hat{Y} = B_0 + B_1 X$.

For $P = P$ and $Q = 1$, the multiple regression model was given as:

$$Y = \beta_0 + \beta_1 X_1 + \beta_2 X_2 + \cdots + \beta_P X_P$$

and it was again seen that $B_0, B_1, \ldots, B_P$ were determined so as to maximize $r_{Y\hat{Y}}$. In this case, we saw that, in terms of standardized weights:

$$r^2_{Y\hat{Y}} = \hat{R}^2_{Y\cdot X_1 X_2 \ldots X_P} = r_{YX_1} b_1 + r_{YX_2} b_2 + \cdots + r_{YX_P} b_P$$

Clearly the next step in this generalization process is to let Q increase and be a number greater than one. With Q dependent measures, $Y_1, Y_2, \ldots, Y_Q$, we can think of a correlation coefficient between the set of variables X and the set of variables Y. Let us formalize these ideas in some detail.

Let:

$$X = a_1 X_1 + a_2 X_2 + \cdots + a_P X_P = \mathbf{A'X}$$

be a linear combination in the X variables and let:

$$Y = b_1 Y_1 + b_2 Y_2 + \cdots + b_Q Y_Q = \mathbf{B'Y}$$

be a linear combination in the Y variables. If we now consider the correlation between X and Y, we are introducing the next logical extension of correlation theory. If we knew the values of the **A** and **B**, we could determine the correlation coefficient between X and Y. Since we do not know them, we can adopt the same model used for simple regression and multiple regression and ask for estimates of the **A** and **B** that maximize the correlation between X and Y. The values of **A** and **B** that achieve such a maximization define two constructs:

$$\hat{X} = \hat{a}_1 X_1 + \hat{a}_2 X_2 + \cdots + \hat{a}_P X_P = \mathbf{\hat{A}'X}$$

$$\hat{Y} = \hat{b}_1 Y_1 + \hat{b}_2 Y_2 + \cdots + \hat{b}_Q Y_Q = \mathbf{\hat{B}'Y}$$

$\hat{X}$ and $\hat{Y}$ are called *canonical variables* or *canonical variates*. The resulting correlation coefficient between $\hat{X}$ and $\hat{Y}$ is called the *sample canonical correlation coefficient*. We summarize this introduction in the following definition.

Definition of canonical variates and correlation.
Let $X_1, X_2, \ldots, X_P$ be a set of independent variables and let $a_1, a_2, \ldots, a_P$ be a set of constants. Also let:

$$X = a_1 X_1 + a_2 X_2 + \cdots + a_P X_P = \mathbf{A'X}$$

be a linear combination generated from the X set of variables. Let $Y_1, Y_2, \ldots, Y_Q$ be a set of dependent variables, and let $b_1, b_2, \ldots, b_Q$ be a set of constants.

Also let:

$$Y = b_1 Y_1 + b_2 Y_2 + \cdots + b_Q Y_Q = \mathbf{B'Y}$$

be a linear combination generated from the Y set of variables. The estimated constants $\hat{a}_1, \hat{a}_2, \ldots, \hat{a}_P$ and $\hat{b}_1, \hat{b}_2, \ldots, \hat{b}_Q$ that maximize the correlation coefficient between X and Y are called *canonical weights* and, when applied as multipliers to the variables, produce canonical variables or canonical variates $\hat{X}$ and $\hat{Y}$. The correlation coefficient between $\hat{X}$ and $\hat{Y}$ is called a canonical correlation coefficient.

Canonical correlation coefficients and canonical weights are closely tied to concepts from matrix algebra. They are best understood through their matrix associations. Because of this, we continue our digression into matrix algebra and then resume our discussion of canonical correlation theory.

5-2. Characteristic equations, eigen values, and eigen vectors

We begin with a definition of a *characteristic* equation.

Definition of a characteristic equation.
Let **A** be a square matrix and let **I** be the identity matrix with the same number of rows and columns as **A**. Consider the scalar λ used as a multiplier of **I**. The characteristic equation for **A** is the determinantal equation defined by:

$$|\mathbf{A} - \lambda\mathbf{I}| = 0$$

A solution to this equation is called an eigen value and is denoted by λ. This equation has as many solutions or *roots* as the dimensions of **A**.

As an example, let:

$$\mathbf{A} = \begin{bmatrix} 7 & 2 \\ 2 & 5 \end{bmatrix}$$

Since the present procedures are typically applied to variance-covariance matrices, the reader may find it helpful to make this example concrete, with $S_X^2 = 7$, $S_Y^2 = 5$, and $S_{XY} = 2$. Our objective is to find all possible values of λ that will make the determinant of:

$$\begin{bmatrix} 7-\lambda & 2 \\ 2 & 5-\lambda \end{bmatrix} = 0$$

Evaluating this determinant, it follows that:

$$(7 - \lambda)(5 - \lambda) - 2(2) = 0$$

or that:

$$\lambda^2 - 12\lambda + 31 = 0$$

This is a quadratic equation in λ which can be solved according to the general quadratic formula:

$$\lambda = \frac{-b \pm \sqrt{b^2 - 4ac}}{2a}$$

where $a\lambda^2 + b\lambda + c = 0$. In the present case, $a = 1$, $b = -12$, and $c = 31$, so that:

$$\lambda_1 = \frac{12 + \sqrt{20}}{2} = 8.236 \qquad \text{and} \qquad \lambda_2 = \frac{12 - \sqrt{20}}{2} = 3.764$$

As indicated, an eigen equation has multiple solutions. The number of solutions is equal to the number of rows in **A**, or the number of columns since **A** is a square matrix. Thus, if **A** has C columns and C rows, it has C λ values. In most applications the roots are unequal and positive in value. It is customary to denote them from largest to smallest by:

$$\lambda_1 \geq \lambda_2 \geq \lambda_3 \geq \cdots \geq \lambda_C$$

It can be shown that the trace of a square matrix with C columns is given by:

$$\text{Trace} = \lambda_1 + \lambda_2 + \cdots + \lambda_C$$

For the example, the trace of $\mathbf{A} = 7 + 5 = 12$. In like manner, $\lambda_1 + \lambda_2 = 8.236 + 3.764 = 12$.

If the determinant of **A** is a positive number, all eigen values are positive. For the example:

$$|\mathbf{A}| = \begin{vmatrix} 7 & 2 \\ 2 & 5 \end{vmatrix} = 7(5) - 2(2) = 31$$

and so both roots were positive.

For all multivariate applications $|\mathbf{A}|$ must be positive. While $|\mathbf{A}|$ is generally associated with variance-covariance matrices, it can also refer to correlation matrices and related inverses. Such matrices always have positive determinants unless they contain a singularity. As mentioned in Chapter 4, data matrices with singularities arising from linear dependencies among two or more variables must be corrected before any data analysis is begun. Since these corrections are assumed, it is not necessary to consider any cases in which $|\mathbf{A}|$ is negative, equal to zero, or close to zero in value. As was mentioned in Chapter 4, the close-to-zero situation is a problem, since dividing by a number close to zero can produce serious computational inaccuracies.

With every characteristic root, λ_i, of a square matrix, we can associate a vector of constants whose elements satisfy the *eigen equation*:

$$(\mathbf{A} - \lambda_i\mathbf{I})\mathbf{X} = 0$$

which represents a system of *homogeneous* equations. A system of homogeneous equations does not have a unique solution; rather, it has an infinite number of solutions that are all proportional to one another.

For our example with $\lambda_1 = 8.236$, we have:

$$\begin{bmatrix} 7 - 8.236 & 2 \\ 2 & 5 - 8.236 \end{bmatrix} \begin{bmatrix} X_1 \\ X_2 \end{bmatrix} = \begin{bmatrix} 0 \\ 0 \end{bmatrix}$$

If we perform the algebra, we generate the two homogeneous equations:

$$-1.236X_1 + 2X_2 = 0 \qquad \text{and} \qquad 2X_1 - 3.236X_2 = 0$$

From the first equation, it follows that:

$$X_1 = \frac{2}{1.236} X_2 = 1.618X_2$$

This equation has multiple solutions. If we let $X_2 = 1$, then one solution is that:

$$X_1 = 1.618 \qquad \text{and} \qquad X_2 = 1.000$$

Other solutions can be found by letting X_2 take on any other value of interest. Note that the indicated solution satisfies the second equation, since:

$$2(1.618) - 3.236(1) = 0$$

An example of another solution is found by letting $X_2 = 3.827$, so that $X_1 = (1.618)(3.827) = 6.192$.

The vectors $\mathbf{X}' = (1.618 \quad 1.000)$ and $\mathbf{X}' = (3.827 \quad 6.192)$ are called *eigen vectors*. They are associated with the eigen value $\lambda_1 = 8.236$. The eigen value $\lambda_2 = 3.764$ also has its set of associated eigen vectors. Each eigen value can have an infinite number of eigen vectors.

So as to avoid the ambiguity of multiple solutions, it is customary to place *side conditions* or *restrictions* on the vectors and determine their values under the restrictions. One model, used extensively in mathematical analysis to obtain a unique solution, is to restrict the eigen vectors $\mathbf{A}' = (a_1, a_2, \ldots, a_P)$ and $\mathbf{B}' = (b_1, b_2, \ldots, b_Q)$, so that:

$$\text{Var}(X) = \mathbf{A}' \textstyle\sum_{XX} \mathbf{A} = 1 \quad \text{and}$$

$$\text{Var}(Y) = \mathbf{B}' \textstyle\sum_{YY} \mathbf{B} = 1$$

The resulting weights are said to be standardized weights since the standard deviations of both the canonical variates are equal to one in value.

5-3. The algebra of canonical correlation theory for a sample

The model for canonical correlation theory is surprisingly simple. Given the two sets of variables:

$$X\text{:}\quad (X_1, X_2, \ldots, X_P) \qquad \text{and} \qquad Y\text{:}\quad (Y_1, Y_2, \ldots, Y_Q)$$

we can form the sample partitioned intercorrelation matrix:

$$\mathbf{R} = \left[\begin{array}{c|c} \mathbf{R}_{XX} & \mathbf{R}_{XY} \\ \hline \mathbf{R}_{YX} & \mathbf{R}_{YY} \end{array}\right]$$

Throughout this chapter we will focus on samples and change our definition of P and Q to let P refer to the number of variables in the smaller set and to let Q refer to the number of variables in the larger set. This is done simply for mathematical convenience. Moreover, as will be seen from the computations that follow, in canonical correlation analysis no true distinction between independent and dependent variables is made.

We start by examining the sample intercorrelation matrix, $\mathbf{R}_{XY}$, to see if any of the Y variables show some correlation with the X variables. If most of the correlations in $\mathbf{R}_{XY}$ are close to zero, we might be tempted to abandon the plans to perform a canonical correlation analysis, since the final results will most likely be ambiguous or unintelligible. If a number of the $\mathbf{R}_{XY}$ correlations are moderate to large (e.g., larger than .40), we could proceed to construct two variables:

$$\hat{X}^{(1)} = a_1X_1 + a_2X_2 + \cdots + a_PX_P = \mathbf{A}'\mathbf{X}$$

$$\hat{Y}^{(1)} = b_1Y_1 + b_2Y_2 + \cdots + b_QY_Q = \mathbf{B}'\mathbf{Y}$$

so that the correlation coefficient between $\hat{X}^{(1)}$ and $\hat{Y}^{(1)}$ is maximized. After we construct these specific linear combinations we define two new variables:

$$\hat{X}^{(2)} = c_1X_1 + c_2X_2 + \cdots + c_PX_P = \mathbf{C}'\mathbf{X}$$

$$\hat{Y}^{(2)} = d_1Y_1 + d_2Y_2 + \cdots + d_QY_Q = \mathbf{D}'\mathbf{Y}$$

such that the correlation coefficient between $\hat{X}^{(2)}$ and $\hat{Y}^{(2)}$ is maximized, but subject to the restriction that the correlation coefficients between $\hat{X}^{(1)}$ and $\hat{X}^{(2)}$, $\hat{X}^{(1)}$ and $\hat{Y}^{(2)}$, $\hat{Y}^{(1)}$ and $\hat{X}^{(2)}$, and $\hat{Y}^{(1)}$ and $\hat{Y}^{(2)}$ are all zero. We continue this process until P sets of canonical variates are generated. With $P \leq Q$, this is the maximum number of canonical variate pairs that can be constructed.

As indicated, the creation of canonical variates means that the matrix $\mathbf{R}$ is transformed to the following reduced matrix of correlations:

$$\boldsymbol{\lambda} = \left[\begin{array}{cccc|cccc}
1 & 0 & \cdots & 0 & R_{11} & 0 & \cdots & 0 \\
0 & 1 & \cdots & 0 & 0 & R_{22} & \cdots & 0 \\
\cdot & \cdot & \cdot & \cdot & \cdot & \cdot & \cdot & \cdot \\
\cdot & \cdot & \cdot & \cdot & \cdot & \cdot & \cdot & \cdot \\
\cdot & \cdot & \cdot & \cdot & \cdot & \cdot & \cdot & \cdot \\
0 & 0 & \cdots & 1 & 0 & 0 & \cdots & R_{PP} \\
\hline
R_{11} & 0 & \cdots & 0 & 1 & 0 & \cdots & 0 \\
0 & R_{22} & \cdots & 0 & 0 & 1 & \cdots & 0 \\
\cdot & \cdot & \cdot & \cdot & \cdot & \cdot & \cdot & \cdot \\
\cdot & \cdot & \cdot & \cdot & \cdot & \cdot & \cdot & \cdot \\
\cdot & \cdot & \cdot & \cdot & \cdot & \cdot & \cdot & \cdot \\
0 & 0 & \cdots & R_{PP} & 0 & 0 & \cdots & 1
\end{array}\right]$$

If we let $\mathbf{D}_{XY}$ represent the diagonal matrix:

$$\mathbf{D}_{XY} = \begin{bmatrix}
R_{11} & 0 & \cdots & 0 \\
0 & R_{22} & \cdots & 0 \\
\cdot & \cdot & \cdot & \cdot \\
\cdot & \cdot & \cdot & \cdot \\
\cdot & \cdot & \cdot & \cdot \\
0 & 0 & \cdots & R_{PP}
\end{bmatrix}$$

we see that the canonical analysis consists of taking a correlation matrix of size $(P + Q) \times (P + Q)$ and reducing it to a matrix of size $P \times P$. Thus we wish to transform:

$$\mathbf{R} = \left[\begin{array}{c|c} \mathbf{R}_{XX} & \mathbf{R}_{XY} \\ \hline \mathbf{R}_{YX} & \mathbf{R}_{YY} \end{array}\right] \quad \text{into} \quad \left[\begin{array}{c|c} \mathbf{I} & \mathbf{D}_{XY} \\ \hline \mathbf{D}_{YX} & \mathbf{I} \end{array}\right] = \boldsymbol{\lambda}$$

Under this model, we see that a reduction of a correlation matrix to a smaller size is being accomplished, not through the original variables and $\hat{\boldsymbol{\Sigma}}$, but through $\mathbf{R}$ and standard scores. However, we will still use X and Y to denote the variables under consideration, though we realize that all of the analysis is in terms of standard scores.

Since $\hat{X} = \mathbf{A}'\mathbf{X}$ is a linear combination, we know from Section 4-6 that the variance of $\hat{X}$ in the sample in standard score form is given by:

$$S^2_{\hat{X}} = \mathbf{A}'\mathbf{R}_{XX}\mathbf{A}$$

In like manner:

$$S^2_{\hat{Y}} = \mathbf{B}'\mathbf{R}_{YY}\mathbf{B}$$

In addition:

$$S_{\hat{X}\hat{Y}} = \mathbf{A}'\mathbf{R}_{XY}\mathbf{B}$$

Thus the correlation coefficient between X and Y, in standard score form, is defined as:

$$R = \frac{\mathbf{A}'\mathbf{R}_{XY}\mathbf{B}}{\sqrt{(\mathbf{A}'\mathbf{R}_{XX}\mathbf{A})\,(\mathbf{B}'\mathbf{R}_{YY}\mathbf{B})}}$$

We must emphasize at this time that $\mathbf{A}$ and $\mathbf{B}$ refer to weights in terms of standardized variables. If we were to remain in the metric of the originally observed variables, we would encounter both computational and interpretation problems. Because of this, we switch to standardized variables. The remainder of the discussion is in terms of such variables with means of zero and standard deviations of one.

While we have proceeded according to first principles, it turns out that the canonical correlation problem has no solution unless we place some restrictions on the model. The restrictions we make are that the resulting variables have a standard deviation of one, or that:

$$S^2_{\hat{X}} = \mathbf{A}'\mathbf{R}_{XX}\mathbf{A} = 1$$

and:

$$S^2_{\hat{Y}} = \mathbf{B}'\mathbf{R}_{YY}\mathbf{B} = 1$$

Under these restrictions, R reduces to:

$$R = \mathbf{A}'\mathbf{R}_{XY}\mathbf{B}$$

With these restrictions, the problem of determining maximizing values for **A** and **B** becomes one of simple calculus.

We consider the value of the correlation coefficient, R, that we wish to maximize, subject to the preceding two restrictions. This is accomplished by introducing two artificial variables, λ_1^* and λ_2^* which are called *Lagrange multipliers*. They are introduced by way of the mathematical function:

$$W = R^2 - \lambda_1^*(S_{\hat{X}}^2 - 1) - \lambda_2^*(S_{\hat{Y}}^2 - 1)$$

Since $S_{\hat{X}}^2 - 1 = 0$ and $S_{\hat{Y}}^2 - 1 = 0$, W actually equals R^2. We now maximize W by taking partial derivatives on the **A** and **B** values and setting the resulting equations equal to zero. We bypass this algebra and note that, in the end, the process generates the following characteristic equation:

$$|\mathbf{R}_{XX}^{-1}\mathbf{R}_{XY}\mathbf{R}_{YY}^{-1}\mathbf{R}_{XY}' - \lambda\mathbf{I}| = 0$$

which has the form:

$$|\mathbf{A} - \lambda\mathbf{I}| = 0$$

In almost all applications, this equation is solved by a computer. Since **A** has P rows and columns, the resulting equation has P roots. The roots prove to have a simple interpretation. In fact, for $\hat{X}^{(1)}$ and $\hat{Y}^{(1)}$, the first canonical variates of X and Y:

$$\lambda_1^* = \lambda_2^* = (\mathbf{A}'\mathbf{R}_{XY}\mathbf{B})^2 = R_{\hat{X}^{(1)}\hat{Y}^{(1)}}^2 = \lambda_1 = R_1^2$$

Thus the largest eigen value equals the square of the correlation coefficient between $\hat{X}^{(1)}$ and $\hat{Y}^{(1)}$, that is, the square of the first canonical correlation coefficient. As such, λ_1 or R_1^2 represents the percentage of variance in the linear combination $\hat{Y}^{(1)}$ that can be accounted for by the linear combination $\hat{X}^{(1)}$, and vice versa. The remaining canonical correlation coefficients decrease in value as:

$$\lambda_1 \geq \lambda_2 \geq \cdots \geq \lambda_P > 0$$

and each has a similar interpretation.

As we saw in Section 5-2, each eigen value has its own eigen vector. These can now be determined for each λ_p. As might be expected, they reduce to the estimates $\hat{a}_1, \hat{a}_2, \ldots, \hat{a}_P$ and $\hat{b}_1, \hat{b}_2, \ldots, \hat{b}_Q$ associated with the linear combinations of interest.

Definition of sample canonical variates.
The solutions to the characteristic equations:

$$|\mathbf{R}_{XX}^{-1}\mathbf{R}_{XY}\mathbf{R}_{YY}^{-1}\mathbf{R}_{XY}' - \lambda\mathbf{I}| = 0$$

define the squared correlation coefficients $\lambda_1, \lambda_2, \ldots, \lambda_P$ for the canonical variables:

$$\hat{X}^{(p)} = \hat{a}_1^p X_1 + \hat{a}_2^p X_2 + \cdots + \hat{a}_P^p X_P$$

$$\hat{Y}^{(p)} = \hat{b}_1^p Y_1 + \hat{b}_2^p X_2 + \cdots + \hat{b}_Q^p X_Q$$

where the coefficients are the eigen vectors associated with the eigen values and are found as solutions to the eigen equations:

$$(\mathbf{R}_{XY}\,\mathbf{R}_{YY}^{-1}\,\mathbf{R}'_{XY} - \lambda \mathbf{R}_{XX})\mathbf{A} = 0 \quad \text{and}$$

$$\mathbf{B} = \frac{1}{\sqrt{\lambda}}\mathbf{R}_{YY}^{-1}\,\mathbf{R}'_{XY}\,\mathbf{A}$$

5-4. Statistical tests for canonical correlation

Just as we can test the multiple regression hypothesis H_0: $\beta_1 = \beta_2 = \cdots = \beta_P = 0$ to determine whether $R^2_{Y\cdot X_1X_2\ldots X_P} = 0$, we can similarly assess the canonical correlation hypothesis H_0: $\lambda_1 = \lambda_2 = \cdots = \lambda_P = 0$ to determine whether the two sets of variables, X and Y, are statistically related. A test of the omnibus no-relationship hypothesis, based on P pairs of canonical variates, was developed by Bartlett (1938). It makes use of what is called *Wilks's lambda criterion.*

Definition of Wilks's lambda criterion.
Let $\lambda_1, \lambda_2, \ldots, \lambda_P$ be the eigen values of the determinantal equation $|\,\mathbf{A} - \lambda\mathbf{I}\,| = 0$. Wilks's lambda criterion is defined as follows:

$$\Lambda = (1 - \lambda_1)(1 - \lambda_2)\cdots(1 - \lambda_P) = \prod_{p=1}^{P}(1 - \lambda_p)$$

where Π represents the product of the P terms.

Note that if $P = 1$ and $Q = 1$, $\Lambda = (1 - \lambda_1) = 1 - r^2_{XY}$ is the amount of unexplained variance in a simple regression model. Also, if all eigen values equal zero, $\Lambda = 1$; and at the other extreme, if the largest eigen value is equal to one, $\Lambda = 0$. Thus Λ measures the strength or, more precisely, the weakness of the association. When Λ is close to zero, at least one eigen value is large; when Λ is close to one, all eigen values are small. The distribution of Λ has been tabled by Schatzoff (1966) and Wall (1968), and is given in Table IX of Timm (1975). However, the approximation developed by Bartlett will be used here for determining whether a significant relationship exists between the X and Y sets.

Procedure for testing the hypothesis that $\lambda_1 = \lambda_2 = \cdots \lambda_P = 0$, according to Bartlett's Chi-square approximation.

Step 1. Compute:

$$\Lambda = (1 - \lambda_1)(1 - \lambda_2)\cdots(1 - \lambda_P)$$

Step 2. Reject H_0 if:

$$\chi^2 = -\left[(N - 1) - \frac{1}{2}(P + Q + 1)\right]\log_e\Lambda$$

exceeds the $100(1 - \alpha)$ percentile of the Chi-square distribution with $\nu = PQ$.

An alternative, and generally better, approximation to the exact distribution of Λ was developed by Rao (1951) to test the same hypothesis. It relies on the F distribution and is given as follows.

Procedure for testing the hypothesis that $\lambda_1 = \lambda_2 = \cdots = \lambda_P = 0$, according to Rao's F approximation.

Step 1. Compute:

$$\Lambda = (1 - \lambda_1)(1 - \lambda_2)\cdots(1 - \lambda_P)$$

Step 2. Compute:

$$F = \frac{ab - \frac{1}{2}PQ + 1}{PQ}\left(\frac{1 - \Lambda^{1/b}}{\Lambda^{1/b}}\right)$$

where:

$$a = (N - 1) - \frac{1}{2}(P + Q + 1) \quad \text{and} \quad b = \sqrt{\frac{P^2Q^2 - 4}{P^2 + Q^2 - 5}}$$

except whenever $PQ = 2$, b is automatically set equal to 1.

Step 3. Reject H_0 if F exceeds the $100(1 - \alpha)$ percentile of the F distribution with $\nu_1 = PQ$ and $\nu_2 = ab - \frac{1}{2}PQ + 1$.

Rao's test is an approximation in more ways than one. Not only does it approximate the distribution of Λ via the F distribution, but it does so by, in most cases, yielding approximate noninteger denominator degrees of freedom. Consider, for example, the situation where $P = Q = 3$ and $N = 30$. For these values:

$$\nu_2 = [(29 - 3.5)\sqrt{77/13}] - 4.5 + 1 = 58.5603$$

Such solutions require interpolation or rounding down to the nearest integer. At the same time, two special situations should be noted. Whenever $P(\leq Q)$ is equal to either 1 or 2, Rao's statistic is distributed as an exact F variable. In the case where $P = 1$, we find through substituting into the formula that:

$$a = (N - 1) - \frac{1}{2}(Q + 2)$$

$$b = \sqrt{\frac{Q^2 - 4}{Q^2 - 4}} = 1$$

for $Q \neq 2$. If $Q = 2$, $b = 1$ by the preceding convention. Thus:

$$F = \frac{(N - 1) - \frac{1}{2}(Q + 2) - \frac{1}{2}Q + 1}{P}\left(\frac{1 - \Lambda^{1/1}}{\Lambda^{1/1}}\right) = \frac{N - Q - 1}{Q}\left(\frac{1 - \Lambda}{\Lambda}\right)$$

with $\nu_1 = Q$ and $\nu_2 = N - Q - 1$. The connection with our previous F test of $\hat{R}^2_{Y \cdot X_1X_2 \ldots X_P}$ should be apparent since, with $P = 1$, $1 - \Lambda = \hat{R}^2_{Y \cdot X_1X_2 \ldots X_Q}$.

The second exact F situation occurs when $P(\leq Q) = 2$. In this case:

$$a = (N - 1) - \frac{1}{2}(Q + 3) \quad \text{and} \quad b = \sqrt{\frac{4Q^2 - 4}{Q^2 - 1}} = \sqrt{\frac{4(Q^2 - 1)}{Q^2 - 1}} = 2$$

since Q cannot equal 1. This yields:

$$F = \frac{2[(N-1) - \frac{1}{2}(Q+3)] - Q + 1}{2Q}\left(\frac{1-\Lambda^{1/2}}{\Lambda^{1/2}}\right)$$

$$= \frac{2(N-1) - (Q+3) - Q + 1}{2Q}\left(\frac{1-\sqrt{\Lambda}}{\sqrt{\Lambda}}\right) = \frac{2(N-Q-2)}{2Q}\left(\frac{1-\sqrt{\Lambda}}{\sqrt{\Lambda}}\right)$$

with $\nu_1 = 2Q$ and $\nu_2 = 2(N - Q - 2)$. Thus, for any canonical correlation problem where the smaller of the two sets contains only two variables, an exact test of the hypothesis H_0: $\lambda_1 = \lambda_2 = 0$ is afforded by Rao's procedure. In contrast, no exact test is possible with the Bartlett procedure.

A few additional comments should be directed toward the Bartlett and Rao tests of Wilks's Λ. Keep in mind that rejection of the hypothesis of no relationship between the X and Y sets is quite unspecific as to how many canonical variate pairs are significantly related. From a logical standpoint, researchers may feel comfortable arguing that, since $\lambda_1 \geq \lambda_2 \geq \cdots \geq \lambda_P$, rejection of the hypothesis implies that at least $\lambda_1 = \hat{R}_1^2$ differs significantly from zero. The problem with this conclusion is that logical inference and statistical inference frequently do not match, since the latter is always influenced by sampling variability and sample size. Thus, because the two tests presented so far consider all of the λ_p simultaneously, it is quite possible to reject the hypothesis, H_0: $\lambda_1 = \lambda_2 = \cdots \lambda_P = 0$, even though no single λ_p would be judged significant when assessed individually. This is completely analogous to the situation that arises when testing the hypothesis H_0: $\beta_1 = \beta_2 = \cdots = \beta_P = 0$, where rejection implies only that $R^2_{Y \cdot X_1 X_2 \ldots X_P} > 0$. Post hoc comparisons involving the β_p may reveal that no single beta weight is statistically significant, even though some linear combinations of them must be. See our discussion in Section 4-7 regarding the kind of Scheffé post hoc assessments that are compatible with rejecting the omnibus $R^2_{Y \cdot X_1 X_2 \ldots X_P}$ hypothesis.

We therefore provide here a possible solution for deciding how many canonical variate pairs should be retained following a canonical correlation analysis. It is based on partitioning the Bartlett Chi-square statistic associated with Wilks's Λ. In many ways, the procedure is analogous to the backward elimination method of multiple regression, where reductions in $\hat{R}^2$ are examined as variables are dropped from the model. As applied to canonical correlation analysis, the partitioned Bartlett procedure affords a statistical basis for deciding how many canonical variate pairs can reasonably be disregarded.

Procedure for performing a sequential Bartlett analysis on the λ_p.

Step 1. Compute Λ which we will call Λ_1. Then perform the Bartlett Chi-square test as previously described. If the test is nonsignificant at the chosen α level, conclude that $\lambda_1 = \lambda_2 = \cdots = \lambda_P = 0$. If the test is significant, proceed to Step 2.

Step 2. Compute:

$$\Lambda_2 = (1 - \lambda_2)(1 - \lambda_3) \cdots (1 - \lambda_P)$$

$$\chi^2 = -\left[(N-1) - \frac{1}{2}(P + Q + 1)\right]\log_e \Lambda_2$$

based on $\nu = (P-1)(Q-1)$. Note that λ_1 has been dropped from these computations. If χ^2 is not significant at the chosen α level, conclude that $\lambda_2 = \lambda_3 = \cdots = \lambda_P = 0$ and that it is worth retaining $\hat{X}^{(1)}$ and $\hat{Y}^{(1)}$ as meaningful canonical variates. If χ^2 is significant, proceed to Step 3.

Step 3. Compute:

$$\Lambda_3 = (1 - \lambda_3)(1 - \lambda_4) \cdots (1 - \lambda_P)$$

$$\chi^2 = -\left[(N - 1) - \frac{1}{2}(P + Q + 1)\right]\log_e \Lambda_3$$

based on $v = (P - 2)(Q - 2)$. If χ^2 is not significant at the chosen α level, conclude that $\lambda_3 = \lambda_4 = \cdots = \lambda_P = 0$ and that both pairs, $\hat{X}^{(1)}$, $\hat{Y}^{(1)}$ and $\hat{X}^{(2)}$, $\hat{Y}^{(2)}$, should be retained as meaningful canonical variates. If χ^2 is significant, proceed to the next step, continuing in the same fashion. At Step p, the degrees of freedom associated with χ^2 are given by $v = (P - p + 1)(Q - p + 1)$.

In the preceding sequential procedure, the question of the specific α to be selected at each step was purposely avoided. Because of the data-dependent basis for determining how many tests will be performed, it is not possible to specify a familywise error rate in the usual manner. The problem is similar to that associated with the sequential multiple comparison procedures in analysis of variance designs, such as the Newman-Keuls and Duncan multiple range tests (see Kirk, 1982). Although these procedures purport to control the familywise error rate adequately, Monte Carlo investigations suggest that they do not, as shown by Petrinovich and Hardyck (1969). In the present context, we can offer some possible options for deciding upon α at each step, however. These options are intended as recommendations to think about, rather than as personal endorsements. In the final analysis, type I error decisions must be made and justified by the individual researcher.

1. The most obvious course of action is simply to perform each test using a traditional α of .05. Using α for each test may be worrisome to many researchers, however, especially if several tests are performed.

2. Each test could be performed at a reduced α, in a manner analogous to the Dunn-Bonferroni procedure. Here, $P(\leq Q)$ would be known before starting, and $\alpha' = \alpha/P$ would be allocated for each test. Thus, if $\alpha = .05$, with $P = 4$, each test would be planned for $\alpha' = .05/4 = .0125$. It should be clear that, when a sequential testing procedure is adopted, not all tests are likely to be performed, and since each test is dependent on the preceding one, the true familywise α is not easily specified.

3. Rather than an equal allocation of α, a researcher could make an a priori decision to apportion most of α to the first test, the next most to the second test, and so on. With $\alpha = .05$ and $P = 4$, for example, we might elect to perform the first test using $\alpha_1 = .02$, the second using $\alpha_2 = .015$, the third using $\alpha_3 = .01$, and the last using $\alpha_4 = .005$. In general, a reasonable α allocation for the Pth test is given by:

$$\alpha_p = \frac{2(P - p + 1)}{P(P + 1)}\alpha$$

In adopting this approach in preference to the preceding equal α allocation approach, a researcher would be less likely to commit a type II error when performing the first test. If it is important to find any relationship, then the largest α_p should be allocated to the first test since, if that test is not significant, no more tests are performed.

4. The final approach is exactly the opposite of the preceding one. Here, the least of the apportioned α is allocated to the first test and the most to the Pth test. For $\alpha = .05$ and $P = 4$, we might choose to allocate $\alpha_1 = .005$, $\alpha_2 = .01$, $\alpha_3 = .015$, and $\alpha_4 = .02$. In general:

$$\alpha_p = \frac{2p}{P(P + 1)}\alpha$$

In adopting this approach, a researcher would be operating under the assumption that if any relationship were present, it would be most likely to emerge on the first test and thus only a small amount of α is necessary for that test. If it is important that more than one pair of canonical variates be retained, this approach might be recommended.

In practice, this last option may be the one that is most reasonable when we wish to retain more than one pair of canonical variates. Successive tests in the sequential procedure become more and more conservative in that they are made with an increasing risk of a type II error (see Timm, 1975, p. 351; and Chou and Muirhead, 1979). To reduce the risk of this error we can always increase the risk of a type I error.

In addition to the sequential Bartlett procedure for deciding how many pairs of canonical variates should be retained, there is a test that focuses on just λ_1, the eigen value associated with the first pair of canonical variates. The test has much to recommend it when we suspect that the relationship between X and Y is concentrated mainly in one dimension; that is, in one pair of linear combinations. The test was suggested by Roy (1957), who obtained the sampling distribution of λ_1. Charts of this distribution were prepared by Heck (1960) and are presented in the Appendix as Table B-6. The Heck charts are entered with the following four parameters:

1. $\alpha = .05$ or $.01$.
2. $s =$ minimum (P, Q) which, according to our convention, will always be P here.
3. $m = \frac{1}{2}(|P - Q| - 1)$.
4. $n = \frac{1}{2}(N - P - Q - 2)$.

A few words about reading the Heck charts are in order. The charts are defined only for $\alpha = .05, .025$, and $.01$, and for $s = 2, 3, 4$, and 5. The vertical column of the charts is associated with n, while the curves are associated with values of m. In particular, the curves are defined only for $m = -1/2, 0, 1, 2, \ldots, 10$. This means that eyeball interpolation will generally have to suffice. More about reading these charts will be considered in Section 5-5.

Critical values for $\alpha = .05$ and $.01$, and for selected values of $s > 5$ have been prepared by Pillai (1960). These tables appear in the Appendix as Table B-7. They are entered with the same four parameters used to enter the Heck charts. When these tables are employed, more accurate interpolation is possible.

In addition, note that whenever these charts or tables are called upon, adjustments are frequently required since they are defined only for the largest eigen value, which Heck denoted θ. In the case of canonical correlations, however, θ and λ_1 are identical, and so the charts may be used with no modification necessary.

Charts for $s = 1$ are not required since critical values can be read directly from the F table. The relationship between θ and F is given by:

$$F = \frac{\dfrac{\theta}{m+1}}{\dfrac{1-\theta}{n+1}} = \frac{n+1}{m+1}\left(\frac{\theta}{1-\theta}\right) = \frac{v_2}{v_1}\left(\frac{\theta}{1-\theta}\right)$$

with $v_1 = 2m + 2$ and $v_2 = 2n + 2$.

For simple regression, as discussed in Chapters 2 and 3, $P = 1$ and $Q = 1$, so that $s = \min(1, 1) = 1$, $m = -1/2$, and $n = (1/2)(N - 4)$. In addition, $\theta = r^2_{XY}$, $v_1 = 2(-1/2) + 2 = 1$, and $v_2 = 2[1/2(N - 4)] + 2 = N - 2$, so that:

$$F = \frac{\dfrac{r^2_{XY}}{1}}{\dfrac{1 - r^2_{XY}}{N-2}} = \frac{(N-2)r^2_{XY}}{1 - r^2_{XY}} = \frac{v_2}{v_1}\left(\frac{r^2_{XY}}{1 - r^2_{XY}}\right)$$

the familiar formula for testing H_0: $\rho^2_{XY} = 0$.

For multiple regression, as discussed in Chapters 3 and 4, P referred to the number of independent variables and Q referred to the number of dependent variables. In that case, $P = P$ and $Q = 1$, so that $s = \min(P, 1) = 1$, $m = (1/2)(P - 2)$, and $n = (1/2)(N - P - 3)$. For multiple regression, $\theta = \hat{R}^2_{Y\cdot X_1X_2\ldots X_P}$. In addition, we see that $v_1 = 2(1/2)(P - 2) + 2 = P$, and $v_2 = 2(1/2)(N - P - 3) + 2 = N - P - 1$, so that:

$$F = \frac{\dfrac{\hat{R}^2_{Y\cdot X_1X_2\ldots X_P}}{P}}{\dfrac{1 - \hat{R}^2_{Y\cdot X_1X_2\ldots X_P}}{N-P-1}} = \frac{v_2}{v_1}\left(\frac{\hat{R}^2_{Y\cdot X_1X_2\ldots X_P}}{1 - \hat{R}^2_{Y\cdot X_1X_2\ldots X_P}}\right)$$

which is the familiar formula for testing H_0: $R^2_{Y\cdot X_1X_2\ldots X_P} = 0$.

The Roy test of H_0: $\lambda_1 = 0$ against H_1: $\lambda_1 > 0$ is performed as follows.

Procedure for testing the hypothesis that $\lambda_1 = 0$ according to Roy's test.

Step 1. Compute λ_1 and:

$$s = \min(P, Q) \qquad m = \frac{1}{2}(|P - Q| - 1) \qquad n = \frac{1}{2}(N - P - Q - 2)$$

Step 2. Choose $\alpha = .05$ or $\alpha = .01$ as a level of significance.

Step 3. Enter the Heck charts or Pillai tables to determine the critical value for rejecting H_0: $\lambda_1 = 0$. Let this value be denoted as $\lambda_{1:1-\alpha}$.

Step 4. Reject H_0 if $\lambda_1 > \lambda_{1:1-\alpha}$.

Other statistical criteria for assessing the significance of canonical variates are available, but they will not be discussed here. The interested reader is referred to Timm (1975, Chapter 4) or to our Chapter 8 where we present selected alternative criteria in the context of multivariate analysis of variance.

5-5. An example

As an example of canonical correlation analysis, consider the data of Table 5–1, listed by code number, with missing data estimated according to Method 1 of Section 2-10 and partitioned into the two sets:

Y_1: Score on first midterm
Y_2: Score on second midterm
Y_3: Score on final examination
Y_4: Course evaluation

X_1: Social class
X_2: Sex
X_3: Grade point average
X_4: College Board test scores
X_5: Previous high school unit in sociology
X_6: Score on pretest

which we wish to relate to one another as sets. In particular, let us examine the relationship between the sociology course measures Y and the predictor variables X. For these two sets, let $P = 4$ be associated with the Y set and $Q = 6$ be associated with the X set. Under this model, the number of paired canonical variates and correlations is given by $P = 4$.

Note that the X set contains the dummy variable X_2: Sex. Other dummy variables, such as college major, could also be used if desired. The same coding procedure described in Section 3-16 could be used in this case. Also note that X_1: Social class represents an ordered qualitative variable. Since it has been coded quantitatively as 1, 2, and 3, it is acceptable as a variable for canonical analysis. If desired, social class could instead be entered into the model as two dummy variables.

As we see, the matrix of intercorrelations reported in Table 5-2 is reduced to the matrix of intercorrelations reported in Table 5-3. Examination of Table 5-2 shows that the canonical analysis should prove successful since a number of the correlations in $\mathbf{R}_{XY}$ are large in absolute value. For example, $r_{Y_1X_3} = .721$, $r_{Y_2X_3} = .682$, $r_{Y_3X_3} = .596$, $r_{Y_2X_4} = .569$, $r_{Y_1X_6} = .553$, $r_{Y_1X_4} = .546$, $r_{Y_4X_1} = -.521$, $r_{Y_3X_4} = .463$, $r_{Y_1X_5} = .447$, $r_{Y_2X_6} = .433$, and $r_{Y_3X_5} = .386$. This conjecture is supported by examination of the canonical correlations in Table 5-3, which are equal to $\hat{R}_1 = .924$, $\hat{R}_2 = .718$, $\hat{R}_3 = .289$, and $\hat{R}_4 = .229$. Note that $\hat{R}_1 = .924 > r_{Y_1X_3} = .721$. This inequality illustrates a basic property of canonical correlation. The largest canonical, $\hat{R}_1$, always exceeds the largest correlation in $\mathbf{R}_{XY}$. This happens because we can always attain a correlation at least as large as the maximum $r_{X_pY_q}$ simply by applying weights of 1.00 to the respective X_p and Y_q variables and weights of .00 to all other X and Y variates.

The standardized weights and correlation coefficients for the data of Table 5-1 are summarized in Table 5-4. The four vectors listed in the upper part of Table 5-4 are sometimes referred to as the *pattern matrix* for the canonical variates $\hat{X}^{(1)}$, $\hat{X}^{(2)}$, $\hat{X}^{(3)}$, and $\hat{X}^{(4)}$. Similarly, the second set of four vectors listed below the X set may be termed the pattern matrix for the canonical variates $\hat{Y}^{(1)}$, $\hat{Y}^{(2)}$, $\hat{Y}^{(3)}$, and $\hat{Y}^{(4)}$.

TABLE 5-1. Original data for the canonical analysis

Subject	X_1	X_2	X_3	X_4	X_5	X_6	Y_1	Y_2	Y_3	Y_4
003	2	1	3.55	410	0	17	43	61	129	3
004	2	1	2.70	390	0	20	50	47	60	1
010	2	1	3.50	510	0	22	47	79	119	1
014	3	1	2.91	430	0	13	24	40	100	1
018	2	1	3.10	600	0	16	47	60	79	2
020	3	1	3.49	610	0	28	57	59	99	1
032	1	0	3.17	610	0	14	42	61	92	3
040	2	1	3.57	560	0	10	42	79	107	2
050	3	1	3.76	700	1	28	69	83	156	1
052	2	0	3.81	460	1	30	48	67	110	1
055	2	0	3.60	590	1	28	59	74	116	1
070	3	0	3.10	500	1	15	21	40	49	1
072	1	1	3.08	410	0	24	52	71	107	5
076	2	1	3.50	470	1	15	35	40	125	1
080	2	1	3.43	210	1	26	35	57	64	5
083	2	0	3.39	610	0	16	59	58	100	1
089	2	0	3.76	510	1	25	68	66	138	2
091	3	0	3.71	600	0	3	38	58	63	1
103	2	1	3.00	470	1	5	45	24	82	3
104	2	0	3.47	460	0	16	37	48	73	3
106	2	1	3.69	800	1	28	54	100	132	2
108	1	1	3.24	610	0	13	45	83	87	2
117	2	1	3.46	490	0	9	31	70	89	2
118	2	0	3.39	470	0	13	39	48	99	1
128	2	0	3.90	610	1	30	67	85	119	2
143	1	0	2.76	580	0	10	30	14	100	1
150	2	1	2.70	410	0	13	19	55	84	2
166	1	1	3.77	630	1	8	71	100	166	3
171	2	1	4.00	790	1	29	80	94	111	2
174	3	1	3.40	490	0	17	47	45	110	1
179	2	0	3.09	400	0	15	46	58	93	1
183	2	1	3.80	610	1	16	59	90	141	2
188	1	1	3.28	610	1	13	48	84	99	2
193	1	1	3.70	500	1	30	68	81	114	5
195	2	1	3.42	430	1	17	43	49	96	1
196	3	1	3.09	540	0	17	31	54	39	1
199	1	1	3.70	610	0	25	64	87	149	4
207	2	1	2.69	400	0	10	19	36	53	3
208	3	1	3.40	390	0	23	43	51	39	1
211	1	0	2.95	490	0	18	20	59	91	1

TABLE 5-2. Correlation matrix for the data of Table 5-1. Upper portion only is given since matrix is symmetric

Variable	X_1	X_2	X_3	X_4	X_5	X_6	Y_1	Y_2	Y_3	Y_4
X_1	1.000	0.055	0.064	− 0.090	− 0.047	0.037	− 0.161	− 0.285	− 0.321	− 0.521
X_2		1.000	− 0.033	− 0.035	0.022	0.019	0.087	0.219	0.089	0.287
X_3			1.000	0.465	0.513	0.469	0.721	0.682	0.596	0.089
X_4				1.000	0.226	0.147	0.546	0.569	0.463	− 0.196
X_5					1.000	0.369	0.447	0.329	0.386	0.121
X_6						1.000	0.553	0.433	0.296	0.139
Y_1							1.000	0.671	0.644	0.189
Y_2								1.000	0.585	0.249
Y_3									1.000	0.129
Y_4										1.000

TABLE 5-3. Canonical correlations for the correlation matrix of Table 5-1

Variable	$\hat{X}^{(1)}$	$\hat{X}^{(2)}$	$\hat{X}^{(3)}$	$\hat{X}^{(4)}$	$\hat{Y}^{(1)}$	$\hat{Y}^{(2)}$	$\hat{Y}^{(3)}$	$\hat{Y}^{(4)}$
$\hat{X}^{(1)}$	1.000	0.000	0.000	0.000	0.924	0.000	0.000	0.000
$\hat{X}^{(2)}$	0.000	1.000	0.000	0.000	0.000	0.718	0.000	0.000
$\hat{X}^{(3)}$	0.000	0.000	1.000	0.000	0.000	0.000	0.289	0.000
$\hat{X}^{(4)}$	0.000	0.000	0.000	1.000	0.000	0.000	0.000	0.229
$\hat{Y}^{(1)}$	0.924	0.000	0.000	0.000	1.000	0.000	0.000	0.000
$\hat{Y}^{(2)}$	0.000	0.718	0.000	0.000	0.000	1.000	0.000	0.000
$\hat{Y}^{(3)}$	0.000	0.000	0.289	0.000	0.000	0.000	1.000	0.000
$\hat{Y}^{(4)}$	0.000	0.000	0.000	0.229	0.000	0.000	0.000	1.000

TABLE 5-4. Standardized weights and associated statistics for the canonical variates based on the data of Table 5-1

	Set one		*Set two*		*Set three*		*Set four*	
Variable	$\hat{X}^{(1)}$	$\hat{Y}^{(1)}$	$\hat{X}^{(2)}$	$\hat{Y}^{(2)}$	$\hat{X}^{(3)}$	$\hat{Y}^{(3)}$	$\hat{X}^{(4)}$	$\hat{Y}^{(4)}$
X_1	0.410		− 0.764		0.188		− 0.118	
X_2	− 0.265		0.351		− 0.110		− 0.606	
X_3	− 0.634		0.153		− 0.270		0.065	
X_4	− 0.264		− 0.681		− 0.460		− 0.192	
X_5	0.029		0.021		0.226		0.829	
X_6	− 0.231		− 0.134		0.898		− 0.430	
Y_1		− 0.358		− 0.561		1.302		0.271
Y_2		− 0.516		− 0.115		− 0.706		− 1.115
Y_3		− 0.222		0.333		− 0.784		1.035
Y_4		− 0.124		0.968		0.339		− 0.031
λ_p	0.854		0.516		0.084		0.052	
$\hat{R}_p$	0.924		0.718		0.289		0.229	
Λ	0.061		0.420		0.868		0.948	
χ^2	93.56		29.05		4.73		1.80	
d/f	24		15		8		3	

Let us illustrate hypothesis testing according to both Roy's and the sequential Bartlett procedure. For the Roy test, we have that:

$$\lambda_1 = .854$$

$$s = \min(4, 6) = 4$$

$$m = \frac{1}{2}(|4 - 6| - 1) = \frac{1}{2} \quad \text{and}$$

$$n = \frac{1}{2}(40 - 4 - 6 - 2) = 14$$

We enter the Heck charts with $\alpha = .05$ and find the critical value of X_α given by $\lambda_{1:.95} \simeq .480$. Looking at the Heck charts, we see two sets of curves. Actually the lower set is an extension of the upper set, but to save space they are plotted together. The upper row of X_α values refers to the upper curves, and the lower row to the lower set of curves. Finally, a curve for $m = 1/2$ is not depicted since, from left to right, $m = -1/2, 0, 1, 2, \ldots, 10$. As a result, we must interpolate between $m = 0$ and $m = 1$ in the upper set of curves to obtain the required critical value of about .480. Since $\lambda_1 = .854 > .480$, we may reject H_0: $\lambda_1 = 0$ and conclude that the first pair of canonical variates are statistically related.

The preceding test does not permit a specification of how many canonical variate pairs should be retained. If this were of interest, we would have instead adopted Bartlett's sequential test of Wilks's Λ. We illustrate this procedure for the present data using the unequal α allocation according to our previous Option 4, where:

$$\alpha_p = \frac{2p}{P(P+1)}\alpha$$

Here, with $P = 4$ and $\alpha = .10$, we have:

$$\alpha_1 = .01, \quad \alpha_2 = .02, \quad \alpha_3 = .03, \quad \text{and} \quad \alpha_4 = .04$$

As indicated earlier, the Bartlett test is based on logarithms computed to the base e. Since this logarithmic base is unfamiliar to most researchers, we will use logarithms to the base 10, which are reported in Table B-8. To transform $\log_{10}$ to $\log_e$, simply multiply $\log_{10}$ by 2.3026.

Let us examine the four λ_p in order to test the initial hypothesis, H_{0_1}: $\lambda_1 = \lambda_2 = \lambda_3 = \lambda_4 = 0$. For this test:

$$\begin{aligned}\Lambda_1 &= (1 - .854)(1 - .516)(1 - .084)(1 - .052)\\ &= .061\end{aligned}$$

Now:

$$\begin{aligned}\chi^2 &= -[(N-1) - \tfrac{1}{2}(P+Q+1)]\log_e\Lambda_1\\ &= -[(40-1) - \tfrac{1}{2}(4+6+1)]\log_e(.061)\\ &= -33.5\log_e(.061)\\ &= (-33.5)(2.3026)\log_{10}(.061)\\ &= (-77.1371)(-1.2147) = 93.70\end{aligned}$$

and with $\nu_1 = PQ = 4(6) = 24$ and $\alpha = .01$, we reject H_0 since $\chi^2 = 93.70 > \chi^2_{24:.99} = 42.98$. As an aside, for the Rao approximation for testing the same hypothesis, we must compute:

$$a = (40 - 1) - \tfrac{1}{2}(4 + 6 + 1) = 33.5 \quad \text{and}$$

$$b = \sqrt{\frac{4^2(6)^2 - 4}{4^2 + 6^2 + 5}} = 3.4886$$

As a result:

$$\begin{aligned}F &= \frac{33.5(3.4886) - \frac{1}{2}(4)(6) + 1}{4(6)}\left(\frac{1 - .061^{(1/3.4886)}}{.061^{(1/3.4886)}}\right)\\ &= 4.4112(1.229) = 5.42\end{aligned}$$

For the Rao approximation:

$$\nu_1 = PQ = 4(6) = 24 \quad \text{and}$$

$$\begin{aligned}\nu_2 &= ab - \tfrac{1}{2}PQ + 1 = (33.5)(3.4886) - \tfrac{1}{2}(4)(6) + 1\\ &= 105.8681 \simeq 105\end{aligned}$$

Since $F = 5.42 > F_{\nu_1,\nu_2:1-\alpha} = F_{24,105:.99} \simeq 1.99$, we would reject the hypothesis of no association between the two sets using the same α as with the Bartlett χ^2 test of Λ_1.

Returning, then, to the latter procedure we now conclude that the X and Y sets are statistically related, and therefore proceed to Step 2. Here we test the hypothesis H_{0_2}: $\lambda_2 = \lambda_3 = \lambda_4 = 0$. For this test:

$$\Lambda_2 = (1 - .516)\,(1 - .084)\,(1 - .052) = .420$$

Now:

$$\chi^2 = (-\,77.1371)\log_{10}\Lambda_2 = (-\,77.1371)\,(-.3768) = 29.06$$

and with $\nu_2 = (P - 1)(Q - 1) = 15$ and $\alpha = .02$, we reject H_0 since $\chi^2 = 29.06 > \chi^2_{15:.98} \simeq 28.5$. As a result, we continue our examination of the remaining λ_p in Step 3. At this step, we test the hypothesis H_0: $\lambda_3 = \lambda_4 = 0$. For this test:

$$\Lambda_3 = (1 - .084)\,(1 - .052) = .868$$

Now:

$$\chi^2 = (-\,77.1371)\log_{10}\Lambda_3 = (-\,77.1371)\,(-\,.0615) = 4.74$$

and with $\nu_3 = (P - 2)(Q - 2) = 8$ and $\alpha = 0.03$, we cannot reject H_0 since $\chi^2 = 4.74 < \chi^2_{8:.97} \simeq 17.1$. Thus we decide to retain the first two canonical variate pairs, and now attempt to determine what they are measuring.

The first canonical correlation is given by $\hat{R}_1 = \sqrt{\lambda_1} = .924$. Clearly, $\hat{R}_1^2 = \lambda_1 = .854$ indicates that 85.4% of the variance in $\hat{Y}^{(1)}$ is explained by the linear relationship between $\hat{X}^{(1)}$ and $\hat{Y}^{(1)}$. The two canonical variates are written in standard score form as:

$$\hat{Y}^{(1)} = -\,.358Z_{Y_1} - .516Z_{Y_2} - .222Z_{Y_3} - .124Z_{Y_4}$$

and

$$\hat{X}^{(1)} = .410Z_{X_1} - .265Z_{X_2} - .634Z_{X_3} - .264Z_{X_4} + .029Z_{X_5} - .231Z_{X_6}$$

We should warn users that different computer programs use different bases for attaching algebraic signs within a pair of canonical variates. For example, a given program may define $\hat{Y}^{(1)}$ as $.358Z_{Y_1} + .516Z_{Y_2} + .222Z_{Y_3} + .124Z_{Y_4}$ and $\hat{X}^{(2)}$ as $-.0410Z_{X_1} + .265Z_{X_2} + \cdots + .231Z_{X_6}$. It should be clear, however, that these weights are thoroughly in agreement with the first set. They are said to be reversed or *reflected* forms of what has just been given. Fortunately interpretation of the canonical variates is not affected by such reflections.

According to Darlington, Weinberg, and Walberg (1973), there are two recommended ways to interpret the influence of a given variable on a given canonical variate. In one technique, the researcher focuses on each variable's contribution to the canonical variate by examining the relative magnitudes of the standardized weights obtained. Consistent with the preceding usage, this might be termed a *pattern interpretation*. As we see for the present example, $\hat{Y}^{(1)}$ appears to contain a large component of Y_2 and Y_1, a smaller component of Y_3, and a negligible component of Y_4. Since the three highest weighted variates are all achievement variables that enter with the same algebraic sign, it follows that $\hat{Y}^{(1)}$ is related to total learning in the sociology course. The meaning we might give to $\hat{X}^{(1)}$ is a bit more problematical. It appears to be defined mostly by X_3, grade point average. This is not surprising since $r_{Y_1X_3} = .721$. Furthermore, we would expect high school grade point average to be a good predictor of college performance in general. The next largest variable defining $\hat{X}^{(1)}$ is X_1, social class. This might not be expected on the basis of the relatively low zero-order correlations between social class and performance in the sociology course, since $r_{Y_1X_1} = -.161$, $r_{Y_2X_1} = -.285$, and $r_{Y_3X_1} = -.321$. However, this demonstrates that simply 'eyeballing' zero-order correlations does not tell us everything to expect from a canonical correlation analysis.

Since social class appears with a positive sign in $\hat{X}^{(1)}$ and since all achievement variables in $\hat{Y}^{(1)}$ have negative signs, high values of social class are related to low values of $\hat{Y}^{(1)}$, and vice versa. Thus students from Social Class 1, high social class, tend to obtain high total scores as measured by $\hat{Y}^{(1)}$, and students from Social Class 3, low social class, tend to obtain low total scores. This relationship might be expected since college performance seems to show some relationship to social class in that students from the upper social classes seem to perform better, as a group, than do students from the lower social classes. It is generally believed that they have been primed to succeed.

Variables X_2, X_4, and X_6 are next and about equal in weight. Certainly the results for X_4 and X_6 would be expected. High school achievement, X_4, is known to be related to performance in a college level class. Also, as we saw in Table 5-2, $r_{Y_1X_4} = .546$, $r_{Y_2X_4} = .569$, and $r_{Y_3X_4} = .463$. That X_6, score on the pretest, would be positively related to $\hat{Y}^{(1)}$ is not surprising, since prior knowledge in a particular subject matter area is known to predict later performance in the same area. Variable X_2, sex, shows a similar relationship to $\hat{Y}^{(1)}$. Since $X_2 = 0$ is associated with males and $X_2 = 1$ is associated with females and since the weight applied to X_2 is negative, it appears that females perform at a higher level than males. Finally, a previous high school unit in sociology, X_5, contributes very little to $\hat{X}^{(1)}$. In sum, $\hat{X}^{(1)}$ appears to be defined by variables that are known to predict college performance. Therefore it might be convenient to label $\hat{X}^{(1)}$ and $\hat{Y}^{(1)}$ as:

$\hat{X}^{(1)}$ = predictor of college performance

and

$\hat{Y}^{(1)}$ = overall performance in beginning college sociology

The significant value of $\hat{R}_2 = \sqrt{\lambda_2} = .718$ allowed us to retain the second pair of canonical variates, in addition to the first. The standard score definitions of $\hat{Y}^{(2)}$ and $\hat{X}^{(2)}$ are given, respectively, by:

$$\hat{Y}^{(2)} = -.561Z_{Y_1} - .115Z_{Y_2} + .333Z_{Y_3} + .968Z_{Y_4}$$

$$\hat{X}^{(2)} = -.764Z_{X_1} + .351Z_{X_2} + .153Z_{X_3} - .681Z_{X_4} + .021Z_{X_5} - .134Z_{X_6}$$

According to these weights, $\hat{Y}^{(2)}$ seems to be defined primarily by Y_4, course evaluation, and to a lesser extent by Y_1, first midterm score. At the same time, $\hat{X}^{(2)}$ is defined primarily by X_1, social class, and X_4, College Board scores. If we ignore the lesser contribution of Y_1 to $\hat{Y}^{(2)}$, we might be tempted to account for the second dimension on attitudinal or affective grounds, in contrast to the strong cognitive component apparent in the first pair of canonical variates. Thus, considering the manner in which course evaluation and social class were coded, we find that since Y_4 and X_1 are opposite in sign, lower-class students tended to have more positive attitudes toward the college sociology course in comparison to upper-class students. This is further supported by discovering that $r_{Y_4X_1} = -.521$. It also appears that students with higher College Board scores evaluated the course more favorably. The zero-order correlation of $r_{Y_4X_4}$ is only equal to $-.196$, however, in contrast to that between College Board scores and the lesser defining variable of Midterm 1, where $r_{Y_1X_4} = .546$. Thus the second dimension does not appear to be clean with respect to its interpretation, at least when attempting to do so on the basis of standard score weights. Consequently, we do not offer labels for $\hat{X}^{(2)}$ and $\hat{Y}^{(2)}$ at this point.

5-6. Correlation between canonical variates and the original variables

In the previous section, we said that there were two primary methods for interpreting canonical variates. In particular, we illustrated how we might attempt to characterize canonical variates in terms of their standardized weights or pattern. A second method, and one that is often preferable, is to examine the correlation between a given canonical variate and each of the original variables. At first, though, this may seem to require tedious computations in order to obtain canonical variate scores, such as $\hat{Y}^{(1)}$, for each student. Having done this, we could then compute the correlation between each Y_p and $\hat{Y}^{(1)}$, across all N students. Thus for the student with code number 003, the value of the first canonical variate, $\hat{Y}^{(1)}$, based on the reported standardized weights, is given by:

$$\begin{aligned}
\hat{Y}_1^{(1)} &= b_1^{(1)}\left(\frac{Y_1 - \bar{Y}_1}{S_{Y_1}}\right) + b_2^{(1)}\left(\frac{Y_2 - \bar{Y}_2}{S_{Y_2}}\right) \\
&\quad + b_3^{(1)}\left(\frac{Y_3 - \bar{Y}_3}{S_{Y_3}}\right) + b_4^{(1)}\left(\frac{Y_4 - \bar{d}_4}{S_{Y_4}}\right) \\
&= -.358\left(\frac{43 - 46.05}{15.40}\right) - .516\left(\frac{61 - 62.88}{20.09}\right) \\
&\quad - .222\left(\frac{129 - 99.48}{30.32}\right) - .124\left(\frac{3 - 1.95}{1.20}\right) \\
&= -.358(-.1980) - .516(-.0936) - .222(.9736) - .124(.8750) \\
&= -.2054
\end{aligned}$$

The remaining 39 values could be computed in a similar fashion. These $\hat{Y}^{(1)}$ values could then be correlated with the corresponding Y_1 scores to see how highly related Y_1, Midterm 1, is to the first canonical variate. The same could be done for Y_2, Y_3, and Y_4 with respect to $\hat{Y}^{(1)}$, as well as for $X_1, X_2, \ldots, X_6$, with respect to the $\hat{X}^{(1)}$ values that could be similarly computed. It would also be possible to compute the correlation between each individual X variable and $\hat{Y}^{(1)}$ or between each individual Y variable and $\hat{X}^{(1)}$ to gain additional information about the structure of the data.

Fortunately these lengthy computations are unnecessary since there is an easier method that can be used.

By definition:

$$r_{Y_1\hat{Y}^{(1)}} = \frac{1}{N-1}\sum_{i=1}^{N}\left(\frac{Y_1 - \bar{Y}_1}{S_{Y_1}}\right)\left(\frac{\hat{Y}^{(1)} - \bar{\hat{Y}}^{(1)}}{S_{\hat{Y}^{(1)}}}\right)$$

Since $\hat{Y}^{(1)}$ is defined in standard score form, it follows that:

$$\bar{\hat{Y}}^{(1)} = 0 \qquad \text{and} \qquad S_{\hat{Y}^{(1)}} = 1$$

so that $r_{Y_1\hat{Y}^{(1)}}$ reduces to:

$$r_{Y_1\hat{Y}^{(1)}} = \frac{1}{N-1}\sum_{i=1}^{N}\left(\frac{Y_1 - \bar{Y}_1}{S_{Y_1}}\right)\hat{Y}^{(1)}$$

Since, by definition:

$$\hat{Y}^{(1)} = b_1^{(1)}\left(\frac{Y_1 - \bar{Y}_1}{S_{Y_1}}\right) + b_2^{(1)}\left(\frac{Y_2 - \bar{Y}_2}{S_{Y_2}}\right) + b_3^{(1)}\left(\frac{Y_3 - \bar{Y}_3}{S_{Y_3}}\right) + b_4^{(1)}\left(\frac{Y_4 - \bar{Y}_4}{S_{Y_4}}\right)$$

it follows that:

$$\begin{aligned} r_{Y_1\hat{Y}^{(1)}} = {} & b_1^{(1)}\left[\frac{1}{N-1}\sum_{i=1}^{N}\left(\frac{Y_1 - \bar{Y}_1}{S_{Y_1}}\right)\left(\frac{Y_1 - \bar{Y}_1}{S_{Y_1}}\right)\right] \\ & + b_2^{(1)}\left[\frac{1}{N-1}\sum_{i=1}^{N}\left(\frac{Y_1 - \bar{Y}_1}{S_{Y_1}}\right)\left(\frac{Y_2 - \bar{Y}_2}{S_{Y_2}}\right)\right] \\ & + b_3^{(1)}\left[\frac{1}{N-1}\sum_{i=1}^{N}\left(\frac{Y_1 - \bar{Y}_1}{S_{Y_1}}\right)\left(\frac{Y_3 - \bar{Y}_3}{S_{Y_3}}\right)\right] \\ & + b_4^{(1)}\left[\frac{1}{N-1}\sum_{i=1}^{N}\left(\frac{Y_1 - \bar{Y}_1}{S_{Y_1}}\right)\left(\frac{Y_4 - \bar{Y}_4}{S_{Y_4}}\right)\right] \\ = {} & b_1^{(1)} r_{Y_1Y_1} + b_2^{(1)} r_{Y_1Y_2} + b_3^{(1)} r_{Y_1Y_3} + b_4^{(1)} r_{Y_1Y_4} \\ = {} & b_1^{(1)} + b_2^{(1)} r_{Y_1Y_2} + b_3^{(1)} r_{Y_1Y_3} + b_4^{(1)} r_{Y_1Y_4} \end{aligned}$$

For the example:

$$\begin{aligned} r_{Y_1\hat{Y}^{(1)}} &= (-.358) + (-.516)(.6712) + (-.222)(.6444) + (-.124)(.1893) \\ &= -.871 \end{aligned}$$

as is reported to two decimal places in Table 5-5. Thus:

$$r_{Y_2\hat{Y}^{(1)}} = b_1^{(1)} r_{Y_2Y_1} + b_2^{(1)} + b_3^{(1)} r_{Y_2Y_3} + b_4^{(1)} r_{Y_2Y_4}$$

and so forth. In addition:

$$r_{Y_1\hat{Y}^{(2)}} = b_1^{(2)} + b_2^{(2)} r_{Y_1Y_2} + b_3^{(2)} r_{Y_1Y_3} + b_4^{(2)} r_{Y_1Y_4}$$

and

$$r_{X_1\hat{X}^{(1)}} = a_1^{(1)} + a_2^{(1)} r_{X_1X_2} + a_3^{(1)} r_{X_1X_3} + a_4^{(1)} r_{X_1X_4} + a_5^{(1)} r_{X_1}X_5 + a_6^{(1)} r_{X_1X_6}$$

Finally, if we wanted to compute between-set correlations with the canonical variates $r_{X\hat{Y}^{(p)}}$ and $r_{Y\hat{X}^{(p)}}$, it could be done in in the same manner. For example:

TABLE 5-5. Correlation coefficients between the significant canonical variates and the original variables

Variable	$\hat{X}^{(1)}$	$\hat{Y}^{(1)}$	$\hat{X}^{(2)}$	$\hat{Y}^{(2)}$
X_1: Social class	0.37	—*	− 0.68	—
X_2: Sex	− 0.22	—	0.32	—
X_3: High school grade point average	− 0.82	—	− 0.28	—
X_4: College Board score	− 0.61	—	− 0.57	—
X_5: Previous high school sociology unit	− 0.47	—	− 0.06	—
X_6: Pretest score	− 0.55	—	− 0.18	—
Y_1: Midterm 1 score	—	− 0.87	—	− 0.24
Y_2: Midterm 2 score	—	− 0.92	—	− 0.06
Y_3: Final score	—	− 0.77	—	0.03
Y_4: Course evaluation	—	−0.35	—	0.88

* Note that $r_{X\hat{Y}^{(p)}}$ and $r_{Y\hat{X}^{(p)}}$ were computed according to the procedure of Section 5-6, but they are not included in this table.

$$r_{X_1\hat{Y}^{(1)}} = b_1^{(1)} r_{X_1Y_1} + b_2^{(1)} r_{X_1Y_2} + b_3^{(1)} r_{X_1Y_3} + b_4^{(1)} r_{X_1Y_4}$$

and

$$r_{Y_1\hat{X}^{(1)}} = a_1^{(1)} r_{X_1Y_1} + a_2^{(1)} r_{X_2Y_1} + a_3^{(1)} r_{X_3Y_1} + a_4^{(1)} r_{X_4Y_1} + a_5^{(1)} r_{X_1Y_1} + a_6^{(1)} r_{X_6Y_1}$$

Note that the derivations are based on the $\hat{Y}^{(p)}$ and $\hat{X}^{(p)}$ being defined in standard score form. Since not all computer programs available to researchers in the social sciences standardize the canonical weights, caution must be exercised. Thus the algorithm as presented here works only for standardized canonical variates.

Procedure for computing the correlation between canonical variates and the original variables.

Step 1. Determine the following matrices:

$\mathbf{R}_{XX}$, $\mathbf{R}_{XY}$, $\mathbf{R}_{YY}$, $\mathbf{A}$, and $\mathbf{B}$

Step 2. The correlations are given as the column vectors resulting from the following matrix multiplications:

1. Correlations of the Xs with the pth canonical X variable:

$$r_{X\hat{X}^{(p)}} = \mathbf{R}_{XX}\mathbf{A}^{(p)}$$

2. Correlation of the Ys with the pth canonical Y variable:

$$r_{Y\hat{Y}^{(p)}} = \mathbf{R}_{YY}\mathbf{B}^{(p)}$$

3. Correlation of the Ys with the pth canonical X variable:

$$r_{Y\hat{X}^{(p)}} = \mathbf{R}_{YX}\mathbf{A}^{(p)}$$

4. Correlation of the Xs with the pth canonical Y variable:

$$r_{X\hat{Y}^{(p)}} = \mathbf{R}_{XY}\mathbf{B}^{(p)}$$

We illustrate the computation of these correlation coefficients for the first pair of canonical variates in our example. We use three-decimal-place accuracy only to avoid excessive arithmetic.

$$r_{X\hat{X}^{(1)}} = \mathbf{R}_{XX}\mathbf{A}^{(1)} = \begin{bmatrix} 1.000 & 0.055 & 0.064 & -0.090 & -0.047 & 0.037 \\ 0.055 & 1.000 & -0.033 & -0.035 & 0.022 & 0.019 \\ 0.064 & -0.033 & 1.000 & 0.465 & 0.513 & 0.469 \\ -0.090 & -0.035 & 0.465 & 1.000 & 0.226 & 0.147 \\ -0.047 & 0.022 & 0.513 & 0.226 & 1.000 & 0.369 \\ 0.037 & 0.019 & 0.469 & 0.147 & 0.369 & 1.000 \end{bmatrix} \begin{bmatrix} 0.410 \\ -0.265 \\ -0.634 \\ -0.264 \\ 0.029 \\ -0.231 \end{bmatrix} = \begin{bmatrix} 0.37 \\ -0.22 \\ -0.82 \\ -0.61 \\ -0.47 \\ -0.55 \end{bmatrix}$$

$$r_{Y\hat{Y}^{(1)}} = \mathbf{R}_{YY}\mathbf{B}^{(1)} = \begin{bmatrix} 1.000 & 0.671 & 0.644 & 0.189 \\ 0.671 & 1.000 & 0.585 & 0.249 \\ 0.644 & 0.585 & 1.000 & 0.129 \\ 0.189 & 0.249 & 0.129 & 1.000 \end{bmatrix} \begin{bmatrix} -0.358 \\ -0.516 \\ -0.222 \\ -0.124 \end{bmatrix} = \begin{bmatrix} -0.87 \\ -0.92 \\ -0.77 \\ 0.35 \end{bmatrix}$$

$$r_{Y\hat{X}^{(1)}} = \mathbf{R}'_{YX}\mathbf{A}^{(1)} = \begin{bmatrix} -0.161 & 0.087 & 0.721 & 0.546 & 0.447 & 0.553 \\ -0.285 & 0.219 & 0.682 & 0.569 & 0.329 & 0.433 \\ -0.321 & 0.089 & 0.596 & 0.463 & 0.386 & 0.296 \\ -0.521 & 0.287 & 0.089 & -0.196 & 0.121 & 0.139 \end{bmatrix} \begin{bmatrix} 0.410 \\ -0.265 \\ -0.634 \\ -0.264 \\ 0.029 \\ -0.231 \end{bmatrix} = \begin{bmatrix} -0.80 \\ -0.85 \\ -0.71 \\ -0.32 \end{bmatrix}$$

$$r_{X\hat{Y}^{(1)}} = \mathbf{R}_{XY}\mathbf{B}^{(1)} = \begin{bmatrix} -0.161 & -0.285 & -0.321 & -0.521 \\ 0.087 & 0.219 & 0.089 & 0.287 \\ 0.721 & 0.682 & 0.596 & 0.089 \\ 0.546 & 0.569 & 0.463 & -0.196 \\ 0.447 & 0.329 & 0.386 & 0.121 \\ 0.553 & 0.433 & 0.296 & 0.139 \end{bmatrix} \begin{bmatrix} -0.358 \\ -0.516 \\ -0.222 \\ -0.124 \end{bmatrix} = \begin{bmatrix} 0.34 \\ -0.20 \\ -0.75 \\ -0.57 \\ -0.43 \\ -0.50 \end{bmatrix}$$

The four resulting vectors of correlation coefficients for each canonical variate constitute what is sometimes referred to as the *structure* matrices. We focus on the $r_{X\hat{X}^{(p)}}$ and $r_{Y\hat{Y}^{(p)}}$ matrices, given in Table 5-5, to characterize the canonical variates. In doing this, we present the second method for interpreting canonical variates as the structure interpretation. The two terms, pattern and structure, as used here, are derived from the corresponding terms of psychometric factor analysis, a variant of which is described in Chapter 6. As just noted, the structure of the first pair of canonical variates is represented in Table 5-5. Sometimes correlations are also computed for the nonsignificant canonical variates; however, we do not follow that model since we regard such correlations as chance deviations about zero. When more than one canonical correlation is found to be statistically significant, as was the case here, a very nice interpretive strategy is to draw a scatterplot in which the weights for two canonical X variates, or two canonical Y variates, constitute the entries. See Darlington et al. (1973) for a description of this procedure.

Among the X variables, the largest correlations with $\hat{X}^{(1)}$ are X_3, high school GPA, with $r_{\hat{X}^{(1)}X_3} = -.82$; X_4, College Board test scores, with $r_{\hat{X}^{(1)}X_4} = -.61$; X_6, pretest score, with $r_{\hat{X}^{(1)}X_6} = -.55$; and X_5, previous high school unit in sociology with $r_{\hat{X}^{(1)}X_5} = -.47$. Clearly these variables measure preparation to do well in a college-level sociology course. With the appearance of X_5 and the reduced importance of X_1, social class, in the structure, as compared to the pattern approach, it is reasonable to change the title of $\hat{X}^{(1)}$, predictor of college performance, to the more specific *predictor of performance in sociology*. Concerning

$\hat{Y}^{(1)}$, we see that among the Y set, $r_{\hat{Y}^{(1)}Y_2} = -.92$ for the second midterm score, $r_{\hat{Y}^{(1)}Y_1} = -.87$ for the first midterm score, and $r_{\hat{Y}^{(1)}Y_3} = -.77$ for the final. Together these appear to measure performance in sociology. Thus it makes sense to call $\hat{Y}^{(1)}$, *performance in sociology*. Note that not all canonical variate interpretation is as simple as it is for the first pair of canonical variates. The names we have given to $\hat{X}^{(1)}$ and $\hat{Y}^{(1)}$ were based on common-sense notions and an examination of R_{XY}. A comparable simple interpretation cannot be given to $\hat{X}^{(2)}$ and $\hat{Y}^{(2)}$, however, which confirms the previous pattern interpretation. Although attitude toward sociology may characterize what is being defined by $\hat{Y}^{(2)}$ here, note that it is still the case that lower-class students and those with higher College Board scores evaluated the course more favorably. Neither will there always be a consistent relationship between the pattern and structure matrices, and for this reason it may be wise to examine each before assigning canonical variate names.

5-7. Tests of mean difference in canonical variates

One use of canonical correlation analysis is to study the interrelationships and structure that exist between two sets of variables. In this sense, canonical correlation analysis is allied with psychometric factor analysis which is designed to examine how variables hold together as an entity, factor, or hypothetical construct. Just as factor scores can be used for further analysis, so can canonical variate scores. This second use of canonical correlation analysis suggests that we can perform statistical analyses, such as mean comparisons, on a smaller, easier-to-handle set of variables than is afforded by the original variables themselves. For additional uses of canonical correlation analysis that will not be discussed here, see Weinberg and Darlington (1976). In the example of Section 5-5, six independent variables were reduced to two new variables, $\hat{X}^{(1)}$ and $\hat{X}^{(2)}$, and four dependent variables were reduced to two new variables, $\hat{Y}^{(1)}$ and $\hat{Y}^{(2)}$. Thus this analysis reduced ten variables to four more manageable constructs. Actually a total of eight new variables were created, but four of these were subsequently discarded when statistical criteria were applied.

As an example of how canonical variates can be used, let us compare the four college major groups with respect to $\hat{Y}^{(1)}$, performance in the sociology course. This can be tested by planned comparisons or by an analysis of variance on $\hat{Y}^{(1)}$, performance in beginning sociology. Although analysis of variance conducted here could be based strictly on the canonical variate scores, we have opted to employ scores with a mean of 50 and a standard deviation of 10. These scores will be immediately recognized as T scores. This transformation removes negative signs and permits a comparison to a mean score of 50. Under this model, the $\hat{Y}^{(1)}$ score for student No. 003 is transformed from $\hat{Y}^{(1)} = -.2054$ to $T = 48$. The remaining T scores are reported in Table 5-6. For these data:

$$MS_{\text{Between}} = 5.69 \quad \text{and} \quad MS_{\text{Within}} = 107.97$$

so that:

$$F = \frac{MS_B}{MS_W} = \frac{5.69}{107.97} = .05$$

TABLE 5-6. *T* scores for the $\hat{Y}^{(1)}$ scores of Table 5-4, reported by college major

	Natural Sciences	*Social Sciences*	*Humanities*	*Other and Unknown*
	48	57	44	45
	62	49	46	52
	36	36	38	51
	49	52	67	46
	66	56	34	43
	49	59	66	58
	41	36		54
	57	56		60
	37	59		57
	44			29
	61			33
				55
				53
				59
N	11	9	6	14
Mean	50.00	51.11	49.17	49.64
SD	10.28	9.14	14.09	9.48

With $\nu_1 = 3$ and $\nu_2 = 36$, H_0 is not rejected using $\alpha = .05$, since $F = .05 < F_{3,36:.95} = 2.81$. We therefore conclude that all college majors have equal mean scores on $\hat{Y}^{(1)}$.

Finally, it should be mentioned that in situations where an analysis of covariance could be justified, we might consider choosing $\hat{X}^{(p)}$ as a covariate when comparing groups with respect to $\hat{Y}^{(p)}$, or vice versa.

5-8. The assumptions underlying canonical correlation analysis

The assumptions required for an efficient use of canonical correlation analysis are quite extensive and not always easy to satisfy. These assumptions are essentially the same as those required of the independent variables in regression analysis as described in Chapters 2 and 3. The first assumption to be satisfied is that we are sampling from the entire population. Truncations on either the dependent or independent set should not be permitted. Thus we should cover the full range of the variables. As a second condition, a researcher must ensure that no collinearities or near collinearities appear in either the dependent or independent variable set. For example, if X_1, X_2, and X_3 are included in the analysis, $X_4 = 2X_1 - 3X_2 + 4X_3$ cannot be included and neither can any other linear function of X_1, X_2, and X_3. Also, variables that are very highly correlated with other variables within the same set should not be included. The third condition is that the sample size N should be large relative to the total number of variables, $P + Q$, to help ensure that the resulting solution is stable; that is, that conclusions about each variable's contribution will hold up under cross-validation. To minimize the influence of sampling variability in canonical correlation analysis, a common rule of thumb is that $N/(P + Q) > 10$. Note in this context that Weinberg and Darlington (1976) have recently proposed a stagewise analog to canonical correlation analysis that appears to perform well, especially when the rule of thumb is not satisfied. In general, these three conditions must be satisfied so that stable canonical correlation estimates and canonical variate interpretations will result.

To test for significance by means of statistical procedures such as Bartlett's and Rao's tests, we must assume that the $P + Q$ variates have a joint multivariate normal distribution and that a random sample has been selected from the population. In practice these assumptions are almost impossible to justify, however. In our example, the multivariate normality assumption cannot be justified, since sex was a dichotomous variable and social class was trichotomous. We might be able to justify the use of statistical procedures for such variables, however, provided that the sample size were large enough for the multivariate analog to the Central Limit Theorem to come into play.

For completeness, we note that the multivariate normal density function for the variables $X_1, X_2, \ldots, X_P$ has the form:

$$f(X_1, X_2, \ldots, X_P) = \frac{1}{(2\Pi)^{P/2}\,|\Sigma|^{1/2}}\, e^{-\frac{1}{2}(X - \boldsymbol{\mu})'\boldsymbol{\Sigma}^{-1}(X - \boldsymbol{\mu})}$$

where $\boldsymbol{\Sigma}$ is the variance-covariance matrix of $X_1, X_2, \ldots, X_P$, and where $\boldsymbol{\mu}$ is the corresponding vector of means. When $P = 1$, $f(X_1)$ reduces to the density of the familiar univariate normal distribution. All conditional and all marginal distributions of $f(X_1, X_2, \ldots, X_P)$ are multivariate normal except for the $f(X_P)$, which are univariate normal. The mean value of X_1 conditioned on $X_2, X_3, \ldots, X_P$ is given by the regression equation:

$$X_1 = \beta_0^{(1)} + \beta_2^{(1)} X_2 + \beta_3^{(1)} X_3 + \cdots + \beta_P^{(1)} X_P$$

with the residual variance defined by:

$$\sigma^2_{X_1 \cdot X_2 X_3 \ldots X_P} = \sigma^2_{X_1}(1 - R^2_{X_1 \cdot X_2 X_3 \ldots X_P})$$

Corresponding relations hold for $X_2, X_3, \ldots,$ and X_P. One important property of $f(X_1, X_2, \ldots, X_P)$ is that:

$$Y = (\mathbf{X} - \boldsymbol{\mu})'\Sigma^{-1}(\mathbf{X} - \boldsymbol{\mu})$$

is distributed as Chi-square with $v = P$. In Chapter 7, we will see that Y is directly related to Hotelling's T^2, a multivariate extension of the one- and two-sample t test. In addition, in Chapters 7, 8, and 9 we will use $f(X_1, X_2, \ldots, X_P)$ to establish criteria for grouping individuals on the basis of linear combinations called discriminant functions.

The multivariate normal distribution is somewhat hidden throughout multivariate methods. It is not required in the estimation and data description aspects of the theory. Its impact and role, however, are basic to the inference procedures of multivariate analysis and it is here that it must be assumed. There are no satisfactory tests of its truth in any one situation. About the closest one can come to verifying its existence is to make all two-variable scatter diagrams and single-variable histograms. If the two-variable plots graph as ellipses and if the histograms appear as bell shapes, the assumption of multivariate normality has empirical support.

Finally, we should note that like the univariate case, there is a multivariate Central Limit Theorem. It states that as sample sizes are allowed to increase without limit the sampling distribution of the vector:

$$\bar{\mathbf{X}}' = (\bar{X}_1, \bar{X}_2, \ldots, \bar{X}_P)$$

approaches a multivariate normal form. Since most of the multivariate methods are based on $\bar{\mathbf{X}}'$, a researcher should use large samples so that reliance on the multivariate Central Limit Theorem can be assured. It is our recommendation that $N > 10(P + Q)$. Thus, in our example, we would feel satisfied if N had exceeded $10(4 + 6) = 100$, instead of the insufficient $N = 40$ that we used for illustrative purposes.

As a research tool, canonical correlation analysis has not been overly successful. One of the reasons for this failure is that researchers are not often careful enough when defining the X or Y sets or when selecting variables to be included. In particular, the number of resulting canonical variate pairs is, in large part, dependent on the researcher's particular selection of variables to be included in the analysis. If the object is to create a small set of explanatory constructs, then we should select variables that are correlated to a fair degree both between and within the sets to be studied. The latter recommendation means that redundant within-set variables should be selected in preference to variables with low within-set correlations. This strategy will likely produce at least one pair of highly correlated canonical variates. If, on the other hand, a researcher wishes to establish large number of new exploratory constructs, then a more efficient strategy would be to select subsets of variables that are correlated across the domains of the independent and dependent variables, but that are only weakly correlated or uncorrelated within each domain of variables. This strategy will likely produce several pairs of moderately correlated canonical variates. For example, a canonical correlation analysis based on a set of X variables that are all related to achievement in elementary school arithmetic and a set of Y variables that all relate to general intellectual ability has a higher probability of producing a small set of canonical variates than does an analysis in which the X variables include measurements on achievement in and attitude toward arithmetic, reading, and social studies, and where the Y variables include measures of intellectual ability, as well as demographic, psychological, and affective characteristics. This means that either few or many canonical variate pairs can be anticipated simply as a function of how the constituent variables correlate with one another between and within the sets.

A second situation in which canonical correlation analysis will fail to yield interpretable results is when the correlations between the X and Y variables are low, for example, less than .3 or .4. When this occurs, very peculiar connections are generated between the canonical variates because the determination of the coefficients is strictly a mathematical problem, rather than a substantive one. That is, the arithmetic operations in canonical correlation analysis, as in all statistical procedures, are independent of the conceptual interpretation of the variables themselves. The scores and the measurements are simply numbers and are treated as such according to the rules of arithmetic. Thus there is no built-in guarantee that a particular solution will be meaningful. There are exceptions to this general view, however. Consider, for example, the situation where both the P and Q sets contain a large number of variables, as might be true when *individual items* from one test are related to those from another test. Because individual-item correlations are generally low, the use of canonical correlation analysis may be advisable as a means of uncovering item combinations that will increase the inter-test relationships.

A final reason for the failure of canonical correlation is related to the previously discussed need for maintaining a large N to $(P + Q)$ ratio. As we saw in Chapter 2, correlation coefficients have large standard errors associated with them. Thus, by sampling error alone, a researcher could obtain a correlation coefficient that appears to be considerably different from zero. If N is small, there could be many of these in $\mathbf{R}_{XY}$. Since the determination of the λ_p is based on a maximization process, these spuriously large correlations might be drawn together to give a spuriously large value to λ_1 or even λ_2. There is good empirical evidence to support such an unpleasant state of affairs.

Sweet (1973) performed a Monte Carlo investigation of the bias in canonical correlation analysis. In one part of his study, he created a multivariate distribution with $P = 5$, $Q = 5$, and $\mathbf{R} = \mathbf{I}$. With $\mathbf{R} = \mathbf{I}$ it follows that all variables are uncorrelated and that no statistical associations exist among any of the variables. He then superimposed normal distributions on the model, so that not only were the variables uncorrelated but they were also statistically independent. He then proceeded to draw 1000 random samples of size $N = 25$ and had λ_1 computed for each sample. Note that for these simulations, $N/(P + Q) = 2.5$ is well below the rule-of-thumb ratio of 10. As a result of this procedure, he found that 25% of the largest eigen values were less than .38, 50% were less than .44, and 75% were less than .51. The process was repeated for uniformly distributed and double exponentially distributed variables with similar results. With no correlations in the system, the median correlation associated with the first canonical variates was $\sqrt{\lambda_1} = \sqrt{.44} = .66$. The moral is that a careful researcher will not attempt to interpret seemingly large sample canonical correlations without first assessing whether they represent real departures from chance relationships, according to formal statistical criteria such as Bartlett's or Roy's test, discussed in Section 5-4.

5-9. The relationship of canonical correlation analysis to other statistical procedures

A little reflection about canonical correlation analysis indicates that it is closely connected to many other statistical models. In this section, we draw from Knapp's (1978) useful integration of these models and discuss them briefly.

Special case one: If $P = 1$ and $Q = 1$, canonical correlation analysis reduces to a simple correlation or regression model. In this case, $\lambda_1 = r^2_{XY}$, $\hat{Y}^{(1)} = Y$, and $\hat{X}^{(1)} = B_0 + B_1 X$. The test of H_0: $\lambda_1 = 0$ is identical to the test of H_0: $\rho_{XY} = 0$, which is given by $F = (N - 2)r^2_{XY}/(1 - r^2_{XY})$, where $\nu_1 = 1$ and $\nu_2 = N - 2$.

Special case two: If, in addition to $P = 1$ and $Q = 1$, it is also known that X_1 assumes the values X_1: $\{0, 1\}$, then λ_1 is identical to the square of the point biserial correlation coefficient, r_{pb}. In addition, the test of H_0: $\lambda_1 = 0$ is identical to the test of H_0: $\rho_{pb} = 0$ and its equivalent two-sample t test of H_0: $\mu_1 - \mu_2 = 0$. In this case:

$$\sqrt{F} = t = \frac{\bar{Y}_1 - \bar{Y}_2}{\sqrt{MS_W\left(\dfrac{1}{N_1} + \dfrac{1}{N_2}\right)}}$$

is related to the t distribution with $\nu = N_1 + N_2 - 2$.

Special case three: If $P = P$ and $Q = 1$, canonical correlation analysis reduces to multiple regression theory, as discussed in Chapter 4. As indicated, $\lambda_1 = \hat{R}^2_{Y \cdot X_1 X_2 \ldots X_P}$, and the test of H_0: $R^2 = 0$ reduces to:

$$F = \frac{\dfrac{\hat{R}^2}{P}}{\dfrac{1 - \hat{R}^2}{N - P - 1}} = \frac{N - P - 1}{P} \frac{\hat{R}^2}{1 - \hat{R}^2}$$

with $\nu_1 = P$ and $\nu_2 = N - P - 1$.

Special case four: If $P = P' + (K - 1)$ and $Q = 1$, where P' = the number of covariates and K = the number of independent groups, then canonical correlation analysis reduces to the analysis of covariance, with the independent variable dummy coded as:

	$X_{P'+1}$	$X_{P'+2}$	...	$X_{P'+(K-1)}$
Group 1	1	0	...	0
Group 2	0	1	...	0
.	.	.	.	.
.	.	.	.	.
.	.	.	.	.
Group K	0	0	...	0

The analysis of covariance hypothesis of equal adjusted means is tested with:

$$F = \frac{\dfrac{\hat{R}^2_{Y \cdot X_1 X_2 \ldots X_{P'+(K-1)}} - \hat{R}^2_{Y \cdot X_1 X_2 \ldots X_{P'}}}{K - 1}}{\dfrac{1 - \hat{R}^2_{Y \cdot X_1 X_2 \ldots X_{P'+(K-1)}}}{N - [P' + (K - 1)] - 1}}$$

based on $\nu_1 = K - 1$ and $\nu_2 = N - [P' + (K - 1)] - 1$. This model was described in Section 3-16, as a special case of multiple regression.

Special case five: If $P = K - 1$ and $Q = 1$ refers to the K groups of an analysis of variance design where H_0: $\mu_1 = \mu_2 = \cdots = \mu_K$, we can use the canonical correlation model if $X_1, X_2, \ldots, X_{K-1}$ are dummy coded with:

	X_1	X_2	...	X_{K-1}
Group 1	1	0	...	0
Group 2	0	1	...	0
.	.	.	.	.
.	.	.	.	.
.	.	.	.	.
Group K	0	0	...	0

This model was also described in Section 3–16 as a special case of multiple regression.

Special case six: If $P = (R - 1) + (C - 1) + (R - 1)(C - 1)$ and $Q = 1$, then canonical correlation analysis can be adapted to test the two-factor analysis of variance model described in Section 9-1.

H_{0_1}: $\alpha_1 = \alpha_2 = \cdots = \alpha_R$

H_{0_2}: $\beta_1 = \beta_2 = \cdots = \beta_C$

H_{0_3}: $\gamma_{11} = \gamma_{12} = \cdots = \gamma_{RC}$

where:

$$X_{rci} = \mu + \alpha_r + \beta_c + \gamma_{rc} + \varepsilon_{rci}$$

by introducing two sets of dummy variables for the row, *R*, and column, *C*, factors. For the row factor, we introduce:

	X_1	X_2	$\cdots$	X_{R-1}
Row 1	1	0	$\cdots$	0
Row 2	0	1	$\cdots$	0
.	.	.	.	.
.	.	.	.	.
.	.	.	.	.
Row *R*	0	0	$\cdots$	0

For the column factor, we introduce:

	$X_{(R-1)+1}$	$X_{(R-1)+2}$	$\cdots$	$X_{(R-1)+(C-1)}$
Column 1	1	0	$\cdots$	0
Column 2	0	1	$\cdots$	0
.	.	.	.	.
.	.	.	.	.
.	.	.	.	.
Column *C*	0	0	$\cdots$	0

Interactions are introduced with:

	$X_1X_{(R-1)+1}$	$X_2X_{(R-1)+1}$	$\cdots$	$X_{(R-1)}X_{(R-1)+(C-1)}$
Cell 1×1	1	0	$\cdots$	0
Cell 2×1	0	1	$\cdots$	0
.	.	.	.	.
.	.	.	.	.
.	.	.	.	.
Cell $R \times C$	0	0	$\cdots$	0

Special case seven: If $P = P$ and $Q = 1$ and Y is scored as $\{1, -1\}$, canonical correlation analysis reduces to two-group discriminant analysis, a model we examine in Chapter 7. This model is identical to Hotelling's T^2 described in Section 7-6.

Special case eight: If $P = P$ and $Q = K - 1$ refers to K independent groups that are dummy coded, we obtain the multivariate analysis of variance described in Chapter 8.

Special case nine: If $P = P$ and $Q = (R - 1) + (C - 1) + (R - 1)(C - 1)$ and dummy coding is employed, we obtain factorial multivariate analysis of variance designs as described in Section 9-2.

Special case ten: If $P = J - 1$ and $Q = K - 1$ are both dummy coded, canonical correlation analysis reduces to the Karl Pearson Chi-square test of independence, as described in Section 10-9.

Special case eleven: Knapp (1978) also describes the form of canonical correlation analysis that reduces to the matched pair t test as applied to testing for the difference between correlated means.

As indicated, the canonical correlation model is tremendously versatile. At the same time, we concur with Knapp's remarks on the nonessentiality of applying the model in all situations:

> The fact that each of several popular statistical techniques can be regarded as a special case of canonical correlation analysis raises two very interesting questions:
> 1. Should they be taught that way?
> 2. Should they be run that way?
>
> The answer to both questions is, probably not. Students who study canonical correlation analysis should surely be told that a wide variety of statistical procedures is subsumed under the canonical model, and some time should be spent in showing them why this is, using arguments and examples similar to [these]. This is not to say, however, that all students should start with canonical correlation analysis and then go on to study its special cases (although the idea is indeed tempting), since there is so much matrix algebra that one must know before one can study canonical analysis. Nor does it necessarily follow that students should study canonical analysis only and forget about all of the special jargon and formulas that are associated with t tests, analyses of variance and covariance, chi-square, and so on. They will still have to read the research literature in which such things abound and will be at a distinct disadvantage if they have not been exposed to these matters in their statistics courses. (Knapp, 1978, pp. 414–415)

5.10. Simplified statistics for canonical correlation analysis

To obtain a ballpark estimate of the magnitude of the first canonical correlation coefficient, $\sqrt{\lambda_1}$, a simplified approach may be adopted as a direct extension of the *sum of Z scores* model that was described for multiple regression analysis. In the canonical correlation context, two sums of Z variables are created, one corresponding to the X set and one to the Y set. These two sums, if properly constructed by reflecting each variable according to its within- and between-set correlations, can be subsequently correlated to yield a convenient estimate of $\sqrt{\lambda_1}$. The steps for this procedure follow.

Procedure for approximating λ_1 without solving a characteristic equation.

Step 1. Examine the between-set correlations as revealed by $\mathbf{R}_{XY}$. Using the rule of thumb to disregard any correlations less than .30 in absolute value, include in the sets of P' and Q' variables, $P' \leq P$, $Q' \leq Q$, and $P' \leq Q'$, only those variables with at least one $r_{X_pY_q}$ greater than .30 in absolute value.

Step 2. Now examine the within-set correlations associated with the P' variables in the smaller, or equal-sized, set. Reflect variables within that set such that as many large correlations as possible are in the positive direction. This is accomplished by applying weights of -1 to selected variables. For each reflected variable, change the signs attached to all correlations involving that variable for both the between- and within-set correlations.

Step 3. Convert each of the P' and Q' retained variables to standardized variables, Z scores, as was done for multiple regression simplified statistics.

Step 4. Reexamine the $\mathbf{R}_{XY}$ portion of the correlation matrix, with respect to each of the Q' variables in the larger, second set. For each variable in the Q' variable set, determine whether most of the large correlations between that variable and variables in the smaller, first, set are positive or negative. If positive, leave the variable in the Q' variable set as it is. If negative, reflect it; that is, multiply the Z scores for that variable by -1.

Step 5. Add the original and reflected Z scores within each set and correlate the two sums. This correlation provides an estimate of the degree of relationship between the X and Y sets, and will always be less than or equal to $\sqrt{\lambda_1}$.

Before reworking the example of Section 5-5 according to this simplified canonical correlation approach, we will first demonstrate the double reflection process as just described in Steps 2 and 4. Consider the hypothetical correlation matrix in Table 5-7. In this example, since all intercorrelations exceed .30 in absolute value, all will be retained. Also, since $P' = Q' = 4$, we will arbitrarily call the X set the P' variable set.

Step 2 requires that variables in the P' variable set be reoriented to maximize the number of large positive within-set correlations. Note that if variable X_3 is reflected, the matrix in Table 5-8 would result. If, in addition, variable X_4 is reflected, the matrix in Table 5-9 is produced, which satisfies perfectly the conditions of Step 2.

Now, the two sets of variables should be standardized, as indicated in Step 3. At this point, each reflected variable from the P' variable set has a negative weight of -1 applied to its standardized scores, here, X_3 and X_4. Finally, since the XY correlations involving Y_3 and Y_4 are all negative, in the final correlation matrix of Table 5-9 these two variables in the Q' variable set should also have -1 weights applied to their standardized scores. The two composite variables P'_C and Q'_C, are

TABLE 5-7. Hypothetical correlation matrix to demonstrate reflection process for canonical correlation

	X_1	X_2	X_3	X_4	Y_1	Y_2	Y_3	Y_4
X_1	1.00	0.60	− 0.60	− 0.60	0.40	0.40	− 0.40	− 0.40
X_2		1.00	− 0.60	− 0.60	0.40	0.40	− 0.40	− 0.40
X_3			1.00	0.60	− 0.40	− 0.40	0.40	0.40
X_4				1.00	− 0.40	− 0.40	0.40	0.40
Y_1					1.00	0.60	− 0.60	− 0.60
Y_2						1.00	− 0.60	− 0.60
Y_3							1.00	0.60
Y_4								1.00

TABLE 5-8. Table 5-7 with variable X_3 reflected

	X_1	X_2	X_3	X_4	Y_1	Y_2	Y_3	Y_4
X_1	1.00	0.60	0.60	− 0.60	0.40	0.40	− 0.40	− 0.40
X_2		1.00	0.60	− 0.60	0.40	0.40	− 0.40	− 0.40
X_3			1.00	− 0.60	0.40	0.40	− 0.40	− 0.40
X_4				1.00	− 0.40	− 0.40	0.40	0.40
Y_1					1.00	0.60	− 0.60	− 0.60
Y_2						1.00	− 0.60	− 0.60
Y_3							1.00	0.60
Y_4								1.00

TABLE 5-9. Table 5-7 with variables X_3 and X_4 reflected

	X_1	X_2	X_3	X_4	Y_1	Y_2	Y_3	Y_4
X_1	1.00	0.60	0.60	0.60	0.40	0.40	− 0.40	− 0.40
X_2		1.00	0.60	0.60	0.40	0.40	− 0.40	− 0.40
X_3			1.00	0.60	0.40	0.40	− 0.40	− 0.40
X_4				1.00	0.40	0.40	− 0.40	− 0.40
Y_1					1.00	0.60	− 0.60	− 0.60
Y_2						1.00	− 0.60	− 0.60
Y_3							1.00	0.60
Y_4								1.00

therefore given by:

$$P'_C = Z_{X_1} + Z_{X_2} - Z_{X_3} - Z_{X_4}$$

$$Q'_C = Z_{Y_1} + Z_{Y_2} - Z_{Y_3} - Z_{Y_4}$$

which can then be correlated to yield the degree of relationship between the X and Y composites based on equally weighted constituents.

Let us now apply this simplified canonical correlation procedure to the data of Section 5-5. Examining the R_{XY} portion of the correlation matrix given in Table 5-2, we note:

1. Variable X_2, sex, should be eliminated from further consideration, since the correlation with any Y variable is less than .30.
2. Within the set of $P' = 4$ Y variables, all are positively intercorrelated, so no reflection is required at this point.
3. Converting each variable to a standardized variable proceeds in the usual manner.
4. Each of the $Q' = 5$ X variables correlates positively with the Y variables, with the exception of X_1, social class, for which $r_{X_1Y_1} = -.16$, $r_{X_1Y_2} = -.28$, $r_{X_1Y_3} = -.32$, and $r_{X_1Y_4} = -.52$. Thus the standardized scores for X_1 are reflected by multiplying them by a factor of -1. The one negative correlation involving X_4, College Board scores, $r_{X_4Y_4} = -.20$, is low and in the minority, and therefore should be left alone. Thus the standardized X_3, X_4, X_5, and X_6 variables stay as they are.
5. Finally, the sum of the five standardized X variables, including the reflected standardized X_1, is correlated with the sum of the four standardized Y variables, to yield $r_{P'_CQ'_C} = .81$. This figure may be arrived at by first computing:

$$Q'_C = -Z_{X_1} + Z_{X_3} + Z_{X_4} + Z_{X_5} + Z_{X_6}$$

$$P'_C = Z_{Y_1} + Z_{Y_2} + Z_{Y_3} + Z_{Y_4}$$

for each student, and then correlating the two across students. On the other hand, a simpler computational formula is given by:

$$r_{P'_CQ'_C} = \frac{a'\mathbf{R}_{XY}b}{\sqrt{a'\mathbf{R}_{XX}a}\sqrt{b'\mathbf{R}_{YY}b}}$$

where a represents the vector of $+1$s and -1s associated with the retained X set, and b the vector of the $+1$s and -1s associated with the retained Y set.

For the correlations given in Table 5-2:

$$a'\mathbf{R}_{XY}b = [-1 \quad 1 \quad 1 \quad 1 \quad 1]\begin{bmatrix} -0.161 & -0.285 & -0.321 & -0.521 \\ 0.721 & 0.682 & 0.596 & 0.089 \\ 0.546 & 0.569 & 0.463 & -0.196 \\ 0.447 & 0.329 & 0.386 & 0.121 \\ 0.553 & 0.433 & 0.296 & 0.139 \end{bmatrix}\begin{bmatrix}1\\1\\1\\1\end{bmatrix} = 7.462$$

$$a'\mathbf{R}_{XX}a = [-1 \quad 1 \quad 1 \quad 1 \quad 1]\begin{bmatrix} 1.000 & 0.064 & -0.090 & -0.047 & 0.037 \\ 0.064 & 1.000 & 0.465 & 0.513 & 0.469 \\ -0.090 & 0.465 & 1.000 & 0.226 & 0.147 \\ -0.047 & 0.513 & 0.226 & 1.000 & 0.369 \\ 0.037 & 0.469 & 0.147 & 0.369 & 1.000 \end{bmatrix}\begin{bmatrix}-1\\1\\1\\1\\1\end{bmatrix} = 9.450$$

$$b'\mathbf{R}_{YY}b = [1 \quad 1 \quad 1 \quad 1]\begin{bmatrix} 1.000 & 0.671 & 0.644 & 0.189 \\ 0.671 & 1.000 & 0.585 & 0.249 \\ 0.644 & 0.585 & 1.000 & 0.129 \\ 0.189 & 0.249 & 0.129 & 1.000 \end{bmatrix}\begin{bmatrix}1\\1\\1\\1\end{bmatrix} = 8.934$$

so that:

$$r_{P'_C Q'_C} = \frac{7.462}{\sqrt{9.450(8.934)}} = .812$$

Thus the correlation based on the two Z composites is not too bad when compared with the maximally created correlation between the two sets, given by $\sqrt{\lambda_1} = .92$. Although we should not expect the simplified procedure always to yield results comparable to those obtained by exact canonical correlation analysis, in many practical applications the smaller amount of computational labor and expense afforded by the simpler procedure may be worth the losses. Note that if there exists more than one significant canonical correlation, reporting the correlation in this simplified fashion will not convey all of the relevant information in the data. At the same time, the procedure should be regarded for what it is: an arithmetically simple-to-compute, easy-to-interpret index of relationship. That is, if all retained X and Y variables are equally weighted, the correlation between the two sets will be $r_{P'_C Q'_C}$ according to our simplified approach. Moreover, we can do further analyses in terms of the simpler P'_C and Q'_C score functions, instead of the more complexly defined $\hat{X}^{(1)}$ and $\hat{Y}^{(1)}$ variates. We can expect these further analyses to be quite comparable in what they portray.

5-11. Summary

In this chapter, canonical correlation theory was described in considerable detail. Starting with the partitioned matrix:

$$\mathbf{R} = \left[\begin{array}{c|c} \mathbf{R}_{XX} & \mathbf{R}_{XY} \\ \hline \mathbf{R}_{YX} & \mathbf{R}_{YY} \end{array}\right]$$

the canonical correlation problem is to define two linear combinations:

$$\hat{X}^{(1)} = \mathbf{A}'\,\mathbf{X} \qquad \text{and} \qquad \hat{Y}^{(1)} = \mathbf{B}'\,\mathbf{Y}$$

with correlation coefficient:

$$R = \frac{\mathbf{A}' \mathbf{R}_{XY} \mathbf{B}}{\sqrt{\mathbf{A}' \mathbf{R}_{XX} \mathbf{A}} \sqrt{\mathbf{B}' \mathbf{R}_{YY} \mathbf{B}}}$$

The problem is solved when $\mathbf{A}'$ and $\mathbf{B}'$ are specified or estimated from the data. This is accomplished by choosing $\mathbf{A}'$ and $\mathbf{B}'$ so that they maximize R. This solution is achieved by solving the eigen equation:

$$| \mathbf{R}_{XX}^{-1} \mathbf{R}_{XY} \mathbf{R}_{YY}^{-1} \mathbf{R}_{XY}' - \lambda \mathbf{I} | = 0$$

which leads to the set of homogeneous equations:

$$(\mathbf{R}_{XY} \mathbf{R}_{YY}^{-1} \mathbf{R}_{XY}' - \lambda \mathbf{R}_{XX})\mathbf{A} = 0$$

$$\mathbf{B} = \frac{1}{\sqrt{\lambda}} \mathbf{R}_{YY}^{-1} \mathbf{R}_{XY} \mathbf{A}$$

for solution.

The eigen equation has P roots where P is the smaller of P and Q, where P is the number of variables in the Y set, and where Q is the number of variables in the X set. The ordered roots are generally denoted as:

$$\lambda_1 > \lambda_2 > \lambda_3 > \cdots > \lambda_P > 0$$

With each root, we have a pair of canonical variates which are pairwise uncorrelated with one another. As a result:

$$\mathbf{R} = \left[\begin{array}{c|c} \mathbf{R}_{XX} & \mathbf{R}_{XY} \\ \hline \mathbf{R}_{YX} & \mathbf{R}_{YY} \end{array}\right]$$

can be viewed as being reduced to:

$$\mathbf{R} = \left[\begin{array}{c|c} \mathbf{I} & \mathbf{D}_{XY} \\ \hline \mathbf{D}_{YX} & \mathbf{I} \end{array}\right]$$

where:

$$\mathbf{D}_{XY} = \begin{bmatrix} \lambda_1 & 0 & \cdots & 0 \\ 0 & \lambda_2 & \cdots & 0 \\ \cdot & \cdot & \cdot & \cdot \\ \cdot & \cdot & \cdot & \cdot \\ \cdot & \cdot & \cdot & \cdot \\ 0 & 0 & \cdots & \lambda_P \end{bmatrix}$$

where $\lambda_p = R_{pp}^2$, the correlation coefficient between the paired canonical variates.

The statistical test of:

$$\mathrm{H}_0\colon \ \lambda_1 = \lambda_2 = \cdots = \lambda_P = 0$$

can be made according to a method described by Bartlett or by Rao. Both tests are based on Wilks's criterion, which is defined as:

$$\Lambda = \prod_{p=1}^{P} (1 - \lambda_p)$$

When $P = Q = 1, \Lambda = 1 - r^2_{XY}$, suggesting that Λ measures unexplained variance. Bartlett's test is performed with:

$$\chi^2 = -\left[(N-1) - \frac{1}{2}(P + Q + 1)\right] \log_e \Lambda$$

H_0 is rejected if $\chi^2 > \chi^2_{PQ:1-\alpha}$. Rao's test is performed with:

$$F = \frac{ab - \frac{1}{2}PQ + 1}{PQ}\left(\frac{1 - \Lambda^{1/b}}{\Lambda^{1/b}}\right)$$

where:

$$a = (N-1) - \frac{1}{2}(P + Q + 1)$$

$$b = \sqrt{\frac{P^2Q^2 - 4}{P^2 + Q^2 - 4}}$$

$$v_1 = PQ \quad \text{and}$$

$$v_2 = ab - \frac{1}{2}PQ + 1$$

H_0 is rejected if $F > F_{v_1,v_2:1-\alpha}$. Bartlett's test can be modified to provide tests of significance for $\lambda_1, \lambda_2, \ldots$, and so on. Procedures for doing this stepwise test were described and strategies for controlling type I errors were discussed.

Like psychometric factor analysts, researchers tend to name canonical variates. Two procedures were described for doing this. One is to make subjective descriptions of the pattern matrices $\mathbf{A}'$ and $\mathbf{B}'$ for the canonical variates. A second procedure is to examine the structure matrices, $\mathbf{R}_{XX}\,\mathbf{A}$, $\mathbf{R}_{YY}\,\mathbf{B}$, $\mathbf{R}_{YX}\,\mathbf{A}$, and $\mathbf{R}_{XY}\,\mathbf{B}$, which are simply the matrices of correlation coefficients of each canonical variate with the original set of variables X and Y.

For our simplified procedure, it was suggested that $\mathbf{A}'$ and $\mathbf{B}'$ be replaced by unit weights when canonical variates are clearly defined. Finally, we described a number of special cases of canonical correlation theory and saw that they include simple regression, multiple regression, the one-way analysis of variance, the two-way analysis of variance with interaction, contingency table analysis, and other multivariate procedures described in later chapters.

Successful canonical variate analyses are few in number. One of the reasons for this failure is that researchers are not often careful enough when defining the X or Y sets that are to be examined. To maximize success, the X set as well as the Y set should be redundant as much as possible. For example, an analysis based on a highly intercorrelated set of arithmetic tests, X, and cognitive measures, Y, is bound to be more fruitful than would be an analysis that included language tests, personality tests, and attitude inventories, provided a researcher wished to generate a small set of canonical variates. With many constructs included in the X and Y set, many canonical variates will be generated. Thus researchers should consider the final outcome when concerned with many or few canonical variates, since this will certainly influence the composition of the two sets of variables. In any case, collinearities will need to be avoided and the sample size should be as large as possible relative to $P + Q$. A sample based on 100 observations is twice as good as one based on 50 observations, and, as far as that goes, a sample based on 200 observations is even better.

5-12. Exercises

***5-1.** Take your sample of 40 students and define two sets of variables X and Y according to the example of Section 5-5. Perform a canonical correlation analysis on the two sets. Compare your results to the example of Section 5-5.

5-2. Test your canonical variates for statistical significance ($\alpha = .05$), using:
1. Roy's criterion.
2. Rao's test of Wilks's Λ.
3. Bartlett's sequential procedure with the risks of a type I error specified by

$$\alpha_p = \frac{2p}{P(P + 1)}\alpha$$

5-3. Use the pattern matrix and try to name your variates. Compare your results to the description provided in Section 5-5.

5-4. Obtain the structure matrices for your data and provide descriptions for the significant canonical variates. Compare your results to those in the text.

5-5. Score your sample on the first canonical variates and test for:
1. Program differences.
2. Major differences.

5-6. Compute the approximate correlation between the first pair of canonical variates, using the procedure of Section 5-10.

5-7. The data of Table A-4 are based on information obtained from a sample of medical students. The variables are:

Variable	*Class Code*
1	2 (2nd year of medical school)
	3 (3rd year of medical school)
	4 (4th year of medical school)
2	ID number (3 digits)
3	Social class
	1 (High), . . . ,4 (Low)
4	Miller Analogy Test Score
5	Psychological Need for Order
6	Psychological Need for Nurturance
7	Knowledge of Medicine
8	Knowledge of Psychiatry
9	Knowledge of Obstetrics-Gynecology
10	Knowledge of Pediatrics
11	Knowledge of Public Health
12	Knowledge of Surgery
13	Type of Specialty
	1. (Primary Care practice)
	2. (Sub-specialty such as cardiology, psychiatry, and nephrology)
	3. (Surgical specialties)
	4. (Miscellaneous)
	5. (None or unknown)

Transfer the data to IBM cards and perform a canonical analysis in which X: (X_4, X_5, and X_6) and Y: (Y_7, Y_8, Y_9, Y_{10}, Y_{11}, and Y_{12})

5-8. Test the canonical variates of Exercise 5-7 for statistical significance, using:

1. Roy's criterion
2. Rao's test of Wilks's Λ
3. Bartlett's sequential procedure, with the risk of a Type I error specified by

$$\alpha_p = \frac{2p}{P(P + 1)}\alpha, \quad \text{where } \alpha = .05$$

5-9. Use the pattern matrix and try to explain what is happening for the analysis of Exercise 5-8.

5-10. Obtain the structure matrix for the analysis of Exercise 5-8. Explain what is happening.

5-11. Score the entire sample on the first canonical variates and test for differences by:

a. Specialties
b. Social Class
c. Year in Medical School

CHAPTER SIX

PRINCIPAL COMPONENT ANALYSIS

6-1. The nature of principal component analysis

The methods of Chapters 1 through 5 are based on the distinction between two sets of variables, X and Y, with one or more variables in each set. In simple regression theory, Y is treated as a criterion variable measured with error, whereas X is assumed to be a predictor variable measured without error. In correlation theory, both X and Y are measured with error and are believed to be interdependent. In multiple regression theory, Y is again treated as a criterion variable, whereas $X_1, X_2, \ldots, X_P$ are interrelated predictor variables. In canonical correlation analysis, the set of variables $Y_1, Y_2, \ldots, Y_Q$ is examined in relation to the set $X_1, X_2, \ldots, X_P$.

Many research investigations in the behavioral sciences exist where the relationships among variables within a single set are of interest. Consider, for example, a survey in which a sample of adults in a particular community is asked to complete a questionnaire related to their attitudes toward the election of a minority group member to a public school board. The questionnaire could easily contain 20 interrelated items that measure those attitudes. Since a clearly defined dependent variable may not exist, the methods of Chapters 1 through 5 are of little value. Yet, a reduction of the 20 items to two or three specific attitude characteristics could be useful for comparing responses across social class, sex, race, religion, and so on. Such a reduction can be achieved through a variety of multivariate procedures, the best known of which is *principal component analysis*.

In this sense, principal component analysis should be regarded as the reduction of a single multiple-variable set to a smaller, more manageable set. This represents a simpler alternative to canonical correlation analysis, where two correlated multiple-variable sets were reduced to two smaller, more manageable uncorrelated sets. We now present the model for principal component analysis.

Consider a set of variables $X_1, X_2, \ldots, X_P$ measured on N observational units. Assume that the X variables can be put together to form a linear combination:

$$Y_1 = a_1^{(1)}X_1 + a_2^{(1)}X_2 + \cdots + a_P^{(1)}X_P$$

which is referred to as the first principal component of the P variables. If the values of $\mathbf{A}_1' = [a_1^{(1)}, a_2^{(1)}, \ldots, a_P^{(1)}]$ were known, each observation could be scored on the Y_1 scale and then this derived set of numbers could be used for future analyses. According to the principal component model, the coefficients $\mathbf{A}_1$ are selected so as to maximize the variance of Y_1. This corresponds, in a way, to the canonical correlation model, where the weights were determined so that the covariance or, more precisely, the correlation, between sets was maximized.

If, for example, we consider the set of X variables as a profile on each of N subjects, we see that maximizing the variance of Y_1 is like maximally separating the subjects along the Y_1 scale. For example, for two variables in which we seek a_1 and a_2 that maximize the variance of $Y = a_1X_1 + a_2X_2$, consider the geometry of Figure 6-1 and the family of straight lines defined by changing the values of a_1 and a_2. Of the possible set of infinite lines, only five are shown in Figure 6-1. Superimposed on each line is the resulting distribution of the proportion of the subjects represented by the scatter diagram. As we see, the variances of the distribution extend from a minimum value on the line Y_2 to the maximum value on line Y_1. Our task is to select the correct

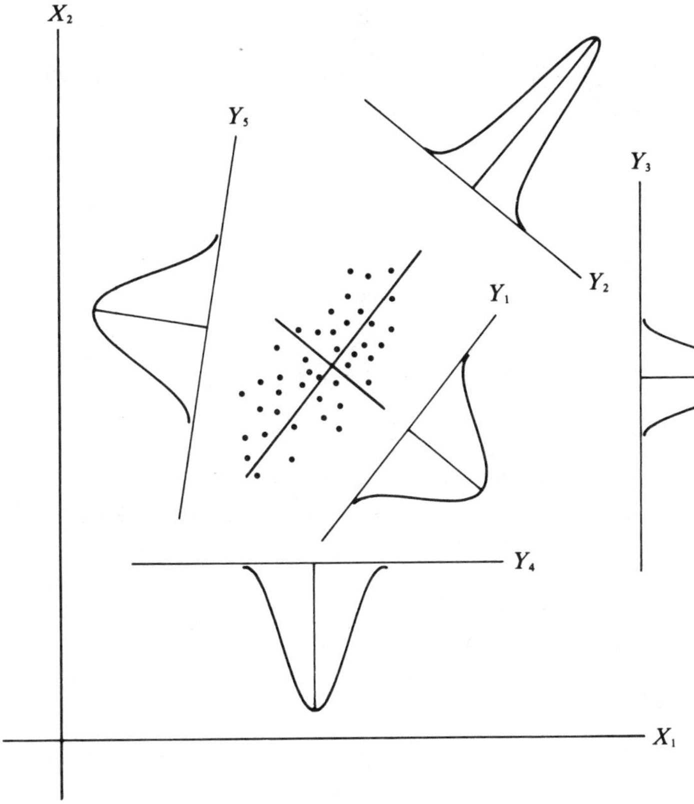

Figure 6-1. Possible Y_1 scales determined from $Y = a_1X_1 + a_2X_2$ showing various degrees of separation of subjects, with Y_1 representing the maximum discrimination and Y_2 the minimum.

a_1 and a_2 that produce this maximum separation.

In essence, this means that the $\mathbf{A}_1$ values are really being selected so as to maximize the distance between subjects so as to facilitate discrimination between similar, though not necessarily identical, profiles. The mathematical reasoning for choosing the constants so as to maximize $\text{Var}(Y_1) = \mathbf{A}_1' \mathbf{\Sigma}_{XX} \mathbf{A}_1$ is easy to understand by examining the geometry associated with principal components, which we will do in Section 6-2. Before we do so, however, we will complete the discussion of principal component analysis.

As was the case with canonical correlation analysis, the exact determination of the vector of constants, $\mathbf{A}_1$, is not possible since the multiplication of $\mathbf{A}_1$ by a scalar also produces a set of constants that will satisfy the condition of maximization. To overcome this difficulty, the set of possible solutions is restricted by requiring that $\mathbf{A}_1$ be normalized. This means that $\text{Var}(Y_1)$ is maximized subject to the restriction that $\mathbf{A}_1'\mathbf{A}_1 = 1$. The problem now reduces to one of differential calculus in which we want to maximize the mathematical function:

$$\phi = \mathbf{A}_1' \sum\nolimits_{XX} \mathbf{A}_1 + \lambda_1(\mathbf{A}_1'\mathbf{A}_1 - 1)$$

where λ_1 is a LaGrange multiplier. Since $(\mathbf{A}_1'\mathbf{A}_1 - 1) = 0$, we see that maximizing ϕ is identical to maximizing Var(Y_1).

Once the values of λ_1 and $\mathbf{A}_1$ are determined, the process is repeated for a new linear combination:

$$Y_2 = a_1^{(2)}X_1 + a_2^{(2)}X_2 + \cdots + a_P^{(2)}X_P$$

but with the constants for Y_2 being selected so that Y_1 and Y_2 are uncorrelated. This means that the vector $\mathbf{A}_2$ is selected so that:

$$\mathbf{A}_2'\mathbf{A}_2 = 1 \qquad \text{and} \qquad \mathbf{A}_2'\mathbf{A}_1 = 0$$

Because there is no need to stop at Y_2, the entire process is repeated until Y_P components have been obtained such that:

$$\mathbf{A}_p'\mathbf{A}_p = 1 \qquad \text{and} \qquad \mathbf{A}_p'\mathbf{A}_{p'} = 0 \qquad \text{for } p' = 1, 2, 3, \ldots, P-1 \quad (p \neq p')$$

In practice, the determination of the $\mathbf{A}_p$ need not be performed in discrete steps, since the entire process can be completed by using a general LaGrange multiplier λ. With a general parameter, one begins with:

$$\phi = \mathbf{A}' \textstyle\sum_{XX} \mathbf{A} - \lambda(\mathbf{A}'\mathbf{A} - 1)$$

Applying standard calculus procedures, we are eventually led to the eigen equation:

$$|\textstyle\sum_{XX} - \lambda\mathbf{I}| = 0$$

for solution. As with canonical correlation analysis, this equation has P ordered roots:

$$\lambda_1 \geq \lambda_2 \geq \cdots \geq \lambda_P \geq 0$$

The first root, λ_1, gives rise to the vector of coefficients, $\mathbf{A}_1$, since, upon substitution into the matrix equation, one can generate the set of homogeneous equations:

$$(\textstyle\sum_{XX} - \lambda_1\mathbf{I})\mathbf{A}_1 = 0$$

to solve for $\mathbf{A}_1$.

As might be expected, the remaining eigen values have some statistical import. In particular, λ_2 is associated with the second principal component:

$$Y_2 = a_1^{(2)}X_1 + a_2^{(2)}X_2 + \cdots + a_P^{(2)}X_P$$

This second new variable has the desired property of being uncorrelated with Y_1, since the coefficients were chosen so that:

$$\mathbf{A}_2'\mathbf{A}_1 = 0$$

As a result:

$$\text{Cov}(Y_1, Y_2) = \mathbf{A}_2' \textstyle\sum_{XX} \mathbf{A}_1 = 0$$

In like manner, $\lambda_3, \lambda_4, \ldots, \lambda_P$ are associated with other principal components, all of which are mutually orthogonal. The importance of this specific transformation of the X set to the Y set should be appreciated. Operationally it means that a researcher uses a set of P mutually correlated observable variables to explain the variance in a derived set of mutually uncorrelated hypothetical variables (or 'components'). On the other hand, in psychometric factor analysis a researcher derives a set of $Q(< P)$ hypothetical variables (or 'factors') and uses these to explain the variance in the original set of observable variables. A cursory description of factor analysis is given in Section 6-9; for extensive coverage of that topic, refer to specialized books such as those of Harman (1967) and Mulaik (1972).

Finally, we should note that the eigen values have a very simple statistical meaning similar, though not identical, to that of canonical correlation analysis. Consider the first eigen value, λ_1, and the set of homogeneous equations used to generate $\mathbf{A}_1$. In particular, consider:

$$(\Sigma_{XX} - \lambda_1 \mathbf{I})\mathbf{A}_1 = 0$$

from which it follows that:

$$\Sigma_{XX} \mathbf{A}_1 - \lambda_1 \mathbf{I} \mathbf{A}_1 = 0$$

so that:

$$\Sigma_{XX} \mathbf{A}_1 = \lambda_1 \mathbf{A}_1$$

If we now premultiply each side of this equation by $\mathbf{A}_1'$, we obtain:

$$\mathbf{A}_1' \Sigma_{XX} \mathbf{A}_1 = \lambda_1(\mathbf{A}_1'\mathbf{A}_1) = \lambda_1 \mathbf{A}_1'\mathbf{A}_1$$

Since $\mathbf{A}_1'\mathbf{A}_1 = 1$, it follows that:

$$\mathbf{A}_1' \Sigma_{XX} \mathbf{A}_1 = \lambda_1$$

But:

$$\mathbf{A}_1' \Sigma_{XX} \mathbf{A}_1 = \mathrm{Var}(Y_1)$$

Therefore:

$$\mathrm{Var}(Y_1) = \lambda_1$$

Thus, in addition to generating the eigen vector $\mathbf{A}_1$, λ_1 has the surprising property that it is equal to $\mathrm{Var}(Y_1)$. In like manner, λ_2 is equal to $\mathrm{Var}(Y_2)$, and so on. The contrast in interpreting the λ_p here, as opposed to in canonical correlation analysis, should now be apparent. With principal component analysis, each λ_p is regarded as the *amount* of Y variance explained by a particular component, whereas in canonical correlation analysis each λ_p is regarded as the *proportion* of a particular Y variate's variance explained by its corresponding X variate. Thus principal component analysis results in a reduction of $\mathbf{\Sigma}_{XX}$ to a diagonal matrix with diagonal elements representing variances equal to $\lambda_1, \lambda_2, \ldots, \lambda_P$. We summarize our discussion as follows, not for $\mathbf{\Sigma}_{XX}$, but for the sample estimator, $\hat{\mathbf{\Sigma}}_{XX}$.

Procedure for performing a principal component analysis on $\hat{\Sigma}_{XX}$.

Step 1. Obtain the sample variance-covariance matrix:

$$\hat{\Sigma}_{XX}$$

Step 2. Solve the characteristic equation:

$$|\hat{\Sigma}_{XX} - \lambda\mathbf{I}| = 0$$

Step 3. Find the eigen vectors for each solution represented by $\lambda_1 \geq \lambda_2 \geq \cdots \geq \lambda_P$ by solving the system of equations:

$$(\hat{\Sigma}_{XX} - \lambda_p\mathbf{I})\mathbf{A}'_p = 0 \qquad \text{with } \mathbf{A}'_p\mathbf{A}_p = 1$$

Step 4. Score each observation as:

$$Y_1 = \mathbf{A}'_1X,\ Y_2 = \mathbf{A}'_2X, \ldots, Y_P = \mathbf{A}'_PX$$

Step 5. The variance for each principal component is:

$$S^2_{Y_1} = \lambda_1,\ S^2_{Y_2} = \lambda_2, \ldots, S^2_{Y_P} = \lambda_P$$

Step 6. The mean for each principal component is:

$$\bar{Y}_1 = \mathbf{A}'_1\bar{X},\ \bar{Y}_2 = \mathbf{A}'_2\bar{X}, \ldots, \bar{Y}_P = \mathbf{A}'_P\bar{X}$$

Note: While we have given directions for finding the principal components based on the variance-covariance matrix, $\hat{\Sigma}_{XX}$, it should be noted that in practice, $\hat{\Sigma}_{XX}$ is replaced by the correlation matrix, $\mathbf{R}_{XX}$. In using $\mathbf{R}_{XX}$ in place of $\hat{\Sigma}_{XX}$, each variable is given equal weight in the analysis so that each has a variance of unity.

There are three things to note about principal component analysis:

1. If P is large, each Y_p has an asymptotic normal distribution with the approximation to normality improving with increasing P. This approach to normality comes about because of the Central Limit Theorem. Thus the joint distribution of $X_1, X_2, \ldots, X_P$ can be of any nature since the resulting distributions of $Y_1, Y_2, \ldots, Y_P$ will tend to be normal and independently distributed. Of course, the convergence to normality will be a function of the kinds of distributions possessed by the individual observed variables. Variables with unusual distributions are certain to generate perturbations in the convergence to normality. However, in most cases encountered in the social sciences, this should not happen. If P is small, the convergence to normality should not be expected unless the observed variables are close to normal in their distributions.

2. We must avoid overdetermination of the solution of the eigen equations because of small sample size. This problem can be avoided by requiring, as a rule of thumb, that N exceed $10P$. Thus a principal component analysis based on five variables should employ at least 50 subjects; otherwise it would be prudent to bypass the analysis.

3. As has been noted in canonical correlation analysis, eigen values represented proportions of explained variance. In principal component analysis, on the other hand, eigen values represent variances themselves, and not proportions of explained variance. In particular, as we will see in Section 6-4 where we introduce standard

scores for which each $S^2_{X_p} = 1$, the sum of the eigen values is given by:

$$\lambda_1 + \lambda_2 + \cdots + \lambda_P = P$$

With standard scores, P equals the total variance of the model, so that the variance explained by Y_1 is given by $(1/P)\ \lambda_1$, the amount explained by Y_2 is $(1/P)\ \lambda_2$, etc.

6-2. The geometry of principal component analysis

In this section, we describe the geometry and algebra of principal components. The discussion is fairly technical and the uninterested reader can skip it with little loss in continuity. We note that the geometry of principal component analysis is best understood in terms of only two variables, X_1 and X_2, both of which have been previously reduced to means of zero by subtracting $\bar{X}_1$ and $\bar{X}_2$ from all observed values. Once having made these subtractions, prepare the scatter diagram of $x_1 = X_1 - \bar{X}_1$ and $x_2 = X_2 - \bar{X}_2$. Let the scatter diagram be as illustrated in Figure 6-2. Superimposed on the scatter diagram are four straight lines that pass through $\bar{x}_1 = 0$ and $\bar{x}_2 = 0$. The heavy lines represent the coordinate system based on X_1 and X_2. The lighter lines represent the principal components Y_1 and Y_2. Like X_1 and X_2, the angle between Y_1 and Y_2 is equal to 90°, or a right angle. Note the visual impression gained from looking at the scatter diagram with respect to the coordinate system defined by Y_1 and Y_2. The variation in the values on the Y_1 axis is clearly larger than it is along either the X_1 or X_2 axes. In addition, whereas it can be seen that the original variables X_1 and X_2 are positively correlated, the transformed variables Y_1 and Y_2 are uncorrelated or orthogonal.

Actually a set of concentric ellipses is associated with the centroid of a scatter diagram, three of which are later shown for the scatter diagram of Figure 6-2. The mathematical equation of all such ellipses can be written as:

$$\frac{x_1^2}{a_{11}} + \frac{2x_1x_2}{a_{12}} + \frac{x_2^2}{a_{22}} = 1$$

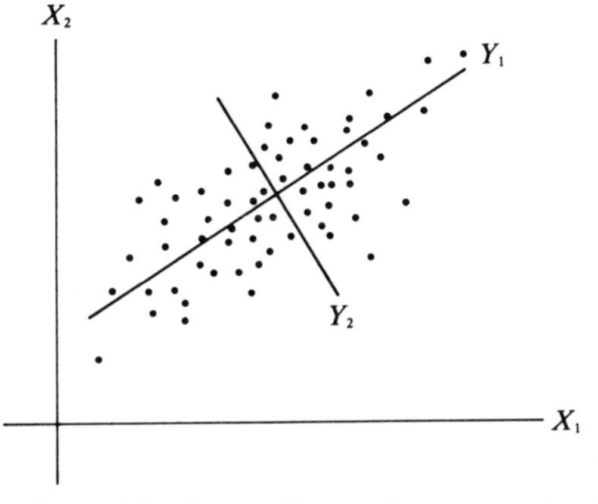

Figure 6-2. Scatter diagram for two correlated variables X_1 and X_2. Shown are the principal components $Y_1 = a_1^{(1)}X_1 + a_2^{(1)}X_2$ and $Y_2 = a_1^{(2)}X_1 + a_2^{(2)}X_2$.

where a_{11}, a_{12}, and a_{22} are constants that define each ellipse. As can be seen, the equation can be defined in terms of the original variables X_1 and X_2, but it can also be defined in terms of the reference system denoted by Y_1 and Y_2, which are called the *principal axes* of the ellipse. In terms of this second reference system, the equation of the ellipses can be written as:

$$\frac{y_1^2}{b_{11}} + \frac{y_2^2}{b_{22}} = 1$$

In this form, it is seen that no cross-product term in y_1y_2 is required and so the equation has a simpler mathematical form. When it is written in this form, the equation is said to be in *canonical form*. To obtain a canonical form, we must relate the a_{11}, a_{12}, and a_{22} values to b_{11} and b_{22}. As it happens, the b_{11} and b_{22} values are easily described, whereas a_{11}, a_{12}, and a_{22} are difficult to define. In particular, $\sqrt{b_{11}}$ equals the distance from the point (0, 0) to the curve along the principal axis defined by y_1. Also, $\sqrt{b_{22}}$ equals the corresponding distance from (0, 0) to the curve along the principal axis defined by y_2. If $b_{11} > b_{22}$, then y_1 is called the major axis, the longer axis of the ellipse, and y_2 is called the secondary, or shorter, axis. Note that if $|r_{X_1X_2}|$ is large, the secondary axis will be short in length. In the extreme case where $|r_{X_1X_2}| = 1.00$, we could replace the pair of scores for each subject (x_1, x_2) by a single score that represents the distance along the Y_1. At the other extreme, if $|r_{X_1X_2}| = 0$, the principal axes will be of equal length and parallel to X_1 and X_2. In that case, no single measure can be used for each observation as a substitute for each point of the original scatter diagram.

As might be expected, the relationship between (x_1 and x_2) and (y_1 and y_2) is easily specified. If θ represents the angle between y_1 and x_1, then:

$$y_1 = (\cos\theta)x_1 + (\sin\theta)x_2$$

$$y_2 = (-\sin\theta)x_1 + (\cos\theta)x_2$$

where $\sin\theta$ and $\cos\theta$ are as defined in Figure 6-3. If we consider a right triangle with the angle θ placed on the (0, 0) point of the coordinate system (U, V), the sine and cosine of θ are defined by the ratios:

$$\sin\theta = \frac{V}{R}$$

and

$$\cos\theta = \frac{U}{R}$$

where:

$$R = \sqrt{U^2 + V^2}$$

As θ ranges from 0° to 90°, $\sin\theta$ ranges from 0 to 1, while $\cos\theta$ ranges from 1 to 0. As an aside, we also note that:

$$\cos^2\theta + \sin^2\theta = \frac{U^2}{R^2} + \frac{V^2}{R^2} = \frac{U^2 + V^2}{U^2 + V^2} = 1$$

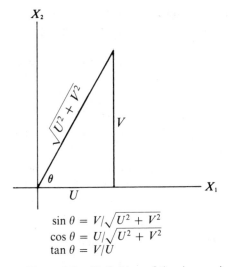

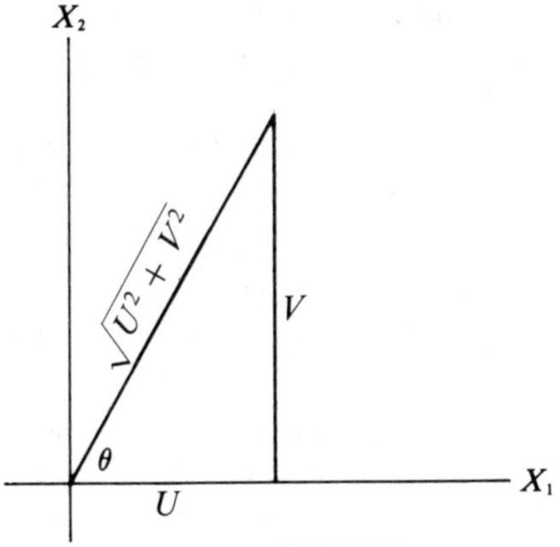

$\sin\theta = V/\sqrt{U^2 + V^2}$
$\cos\theta = U/\sqrt{U^2 + V^2}$
$\tan\theta = V/U$

Figure 6-3. Definition of the sine, cosine, and tangent of the angle θ.

Later we will need to consider the tangent of θ. This trigonometric function is defined as:

$$\tan\theta = \frac{V}{U}$$

and it ranges from a low of zero at $\theta = 0°$ to an undefined quantity at $\theta = 90°$, usually referred to as infinity and denoted as ∞. This latter equation is generally used to determine θ. In particular, if we know the values of V and U, we can enter the body of a tan θ table and read the value of θ. The value of θ so obtained is called the arctan and is represented by:

$$\theta = \arctan\frac{V}{U}$$

In any case, the determination of the principal axes requires only the simple determination of θ. This means that the definition of y_1 and y_2 reduces to a trigonometric problem which fortunately can be solved algebraically. We illustrate both the trigonometric and algebraic solutions in Section 6-3.

Note that:

$$\mathbf{AA}' = \begin{bmatrix} \cos\theta & \sin\theta \\ -\sin\theta & \cos\theta \end{bmatrix}\begin{bmatrix} \cos\theta & -\sin\theta \\ \sin\theta & \cos\theta \end{bmatrix}$$

$$= \begin{bmatrix} \cos^2\theta + \sin^2\theta & -\sin\theta\ \cos\theta + \sin\theta\ \cos\theta \\ -\sin\theta\ \cos\theta + \sin\theta\ \cos\theta & \cos^2\theta + \sin^2\theta \end{bmatrix}$$

$$= \begin{bmatrix} 1 & 0 \\ 0 & 1 \end{bmatrix}$$

$$= \mathbf{I}$$

In like manner, it can be shown that $\mathbf{A}'\mathbf{A} = \mathbf{I}$. This means that $\mathbf{A}' = \mathbf{A}^{-1}$, since $\mathbf{A}\mathbf{A}^{-1} = \mathbf{A}^{-1}\mathbf{A} = \mathbf{I}$. The matrix **A** also has the property that for any row or column $\cos^2\theta + \sin^2\theta = 1$, and between any two rows or two columns, $\cos\theta \sin\theta - \sin\theta\cos\theta = 0$. A matrix that has these properties is called an *orthogonal matrix* or, more precisely, an *orthonormal matrix*, since the diagonal elements are all equal to unity. An orthonormal matrix has three important properties:

1. The transpose of an orthonormal matrix is its inverse.
2. The sum of the squares of the elements in any column or row is one.
3. Any two rows or two columns are orthogonal to one another.

As the geometry of Figure 6-2 indicates, we can turn the discussion on its side and use the y_1, y_2 axis as the reference system and then find the transformation that takes y_1, y_2 to x_1, x_2. By solving these two trigonometric equations which define y_1 and y_2 for x_1 and x_2, it follows that:

$$x_1 = (\cos\theta)y_1 + (-\sin\theta)y_2$$

$$x_2 = (\sin\theta)y_1 + (\ \ \cos\theta)y_2$$

Note that the matrix of trigonometric coefficients associated with Y and X are simply transposes of one another. This means that principal component coefficients have the unusual property summarized in the following matrix equations:

$$\mathbf{Y} = \mathbf{AX} \qquad \text{and} \qquad \mathbf{X} = \mathbf{A}'\mathbf{Y}$$

Thus:

$$Y_p = a_1^{(p)}X_1 + a_2^{(p)}X_2 + \cdots + a_P^{(p)}X_P$$

and

$$X_p = a_p^{(1)}Y_1 + a_p^{(2)}Y_2 + \cdots + a_p^{(P)}Y_P$$

While Y_p has been created as a linear combination from $X_1, X_2, \ldots, X_P$, it also follows that X_p is a linear combination of $Y_1, Y_2, \ldots, Y_P$. Because of simple transformation processes, it is often said that the original observable variables X_p can be decomposed into its principal components Y_p. The reverse process is one of the basic assumptions of psychometric factor analysis.

Let us resume our geometric and algebraic discussion on principal components and concentric ellipses and note that the matrix product:

$$[x_1 \quad x_2]\begin{bmatrix} \dfrac{1}{a_{11}} & \dfrac{1}{a_{12}} \\ \dfrac{1}{a_{21}} & \dfrac{1}{a_{22}} \end{bmatrix}\begin{bmatrix} x_1 \\ x_2 \end{bmatrix} = 1$$

is identical to:

$$\frac{x_1^2}{a_{11}} + \frac{2x_1x_2}{a_{12}} + \frac{x_2^2}{a_{22}} = 1$$

If we let:

$$\mathbf{x}' = [x_1 \; x_2] \qquad \text{and} \qquad \mathbf{Q} = \begin{bmatrix} \frac{1}{a_{11}} & \frac{1}{a_{12}} \\ \frac{1}{a_{21}} & \frac{1}{a_{22}} \end{bmatrix}$$

then the equation of an ellipse can be written as:

$$\mathbf{x}'\,\mathbf{Q}\,\mathbf{x} = 1$$

Explicit definitions of a_{11}, a_{12}, a_{21}, and a_{22} are provided in Exercise 6-3.
For P variables:

$$\mathbf{x}' = [x_1 \quad x_2 \quad \cdots \quad x_P], \quad \text{and}$$

$$\mathbf{Q} = \begin{bmatrix} \frac{1}{a_{11}} & \frac{1}{a_{12}} & \cdots & \frac{1}{a_{1P}} \\ \frac{1}{a_{21}} & \frac{1}{a_{22}} & \cdots & \frac{1}{a_{2P}} \\ \cdot & \cdot & \cdot & \cdot \\ \cdot & \cdot & \cdot & \cdot \\ \cdot & \cdot & \cdot & \cdot \\ \frac{1}{a_{P1}} & \frac{1}{a_{P2}} & \cdots & \frac{1}{a_{PP}} \end{bmatrix}$$

we still have that:

$$\mathbf{x}'\mathbf{Q}\mathbf{x} = 1$$

If all off-diagonal elements are equal to zero:

$$\frac{x_1^2}{a_{11}} + \frac{x_2^2}{a_{22}} + \cdots + \frac{x_P^2}{a_{PP}} = 1$$

If we consider the two-dimensional ellipses drawn on the scatter diagram, we might suspect that the equations should be related in some fashion to $\bar{X}_1$, $\bar{X}_2$, $S_{X_1}^2$, $S_{X_2}^2$, and $r_{X_1X_2}$. The suspicion is correct, and the connection is quite simple. Let:

$$\mathbf{x}' = [X_1 - \bar{X}_1 \quad X_2 - \bar{X}_2] = (\mathbf{x} - \bar{\mathbf{x}})'$$

and let:

$$\mathbf{Q} = \Sigma_{XX}^{-1} = \begin{bmatrix} S_{X_1}^2 & rS_{X_1}S_{X_2} \\ rS_{X_1}S_{X_2} & S_{X_2}^2 \end{bmatrix}^{-1}$$

then the set of concentric ellipses can be represented by:

$$(\mathbf{X} - \bar{\mathbf{X}})'\,\hat{\Sigma}_{XX}^{-1}\,(\mathbf{X} - \bar{\mathbf{X}}) = C_X^2$$

where C_X^2 is given various values to generate the contours of the ellipses. When $C^2 = 0$, the ellipse degenerates to the point (0, 0). Larger and larger values of C^2

generate ellipses with longer and longer axes. As might be expected, the matrix definition of the ellipses for X_1 and X_2 also holds for:

$$(\mathbf{X} - \bar{\mathbf{X}})' = (X_1 - \bar{X}_1 \;\; X_2 - \bar{X}_2 \;\cdots\; X_P - \bar{X}_P)$$

As we now note, principal component analysis really consists of transforming the set of equations:

$$(\mathbf{X} - \bar{\mathbf{X}})' \hat{\Sigma}_{XX}^{-1} (\mathbf{X} - \bar{\mathbf{X}}) = C_X^2$$

to the set of equations:

$$(\mathbf{Y} - \bar{\mathbf{Y}})' \hat{\Sigma}_{YY}^{-1} (\mathbf{Y} - \bar{\mathbf{Y}}) = C_Y^2$$

where:

$$\hat{\Sigma}_{YY}^{-1} = \begin{bmatrix} \frac{1}{\lambda_1} & 0 & \cdots & 0 \\ 0 & \frac{1}{\lambda_2} & \cdots & 0 \\ \vdots & \vdots & \ddots & \vdots \\ 0 & 0 & \cdots & \frac{1}{\lambda_P} \end{bmatrix}$$

If the original variables are normally distributed or if P is large, we can use the normal distribution values to draw ellipses of interest. For example, the ellipse on $Y_1, Y_2, \ldots, Y_P$ that contains 68% of the distribution is defined by $C_Y = 1$. The 90% contour is defined for $C_Y = 1.645$, with the 95% contour defined by $C_Y = 1.96$. $C_Y = 2.58$ is associated with the 99% ellipse. For all practical purposes, the 100% concentration ellipse is associated with $C_Y = 3.00$. As indicated, these values are valid only for $Y_1, Y_2, \ldots, Y_P$ and not $X_1, X_2, \ldots, X_P$.

6-3. A numerical example

Let us illustrate the model for a simple case in which:

$$\bar{\mathbf{X}}' = [3 \quad 7] \qquad \text{and} \qquad \hat{\Sigma}_{XX} = \begin{bmatrix} 9 & 3 \\ 3 & 16 \end{bmatrix}$$

For this example $\bar{X}_1 = 3$, $\bar{X}_2 = 7$, $S_{X_1}^2 = 9$, $S_{X_2}^2 = 16$, and $r_{X_1X_2} = 3/\sqrt{9(16)} = .25$. For these sample values:

$$|\hat{\Sigma}_{XX}| = \begin{vmatrix} 9 & 3 \\ 3 & 16 \end{vmatrix} = [9(16)] - [3(3)] = 135$$

so that:

$$\hat{\Sigma}_{XX}^{-1} = \begin{bmatrix} \frac{16}{135} & -\frac{3}{135} \\ -\frac{3}{135} & \frac{9}{135} \end{bmatrix} = \begin{bmatrix} \frac{1}{a_{11}} & \frac{1}{a_{12}} \\ \frac{1}{a_{21}} & \frac{1}{a_{22}} \end{bmatrix}$$

Thus the system of concentric ellipses is defined by:

$$[X_1 - 3 \quad X_2 - 7] \begin{bmatrix} \frac{16}{135} & -\frac{3}{135} \\ -\frac{3}{135} & \frac{9}{135} \end{bmatrix} \begin{bmatrix} X_1 - 3 \\ X_2 - 7 \end{bmatrix} = C_X^2$$

$$\frac{16}{135}(X_1 - 3)^2 - \frac{2(3)}{135}(X_1 - 3)(X_2 - 7) + \frac{9}{135}(X_2 - 7)^2 = C_X^2$$

or in standard form as:

$$\frac{(X_1 - 3)^2}{\frac{135}{16} C_X^2} - \frac{2(X_1 - 3)(X_2 - 7)}{\frac{135}{3} C_X^2} + \frac{(X_2 - 7)^2}{\frac{135}{9} C_X^2} = 1$$

The 68%, 95%, and near 100% ellipses of concentration are shown in Figure 6-4. A simple method for constructing these ellipses is discussed later in this section after Y_1 and Y_2 are determined.

We begin by solving the characteristic equation:

$$|\hat{\Sigma}_{XX} - \lambda \mathbf{I}| = \begin{vmatrix} 9 - \lambda & 3 \\ 3 & 16 - \lambda \end{vmatrix} = 0$$

or:

$$(9 - \lambda)(16 - \lambda) - 3(3) = 0$$
$$\lambda^2 - 25\lambda + 135 = 0$$

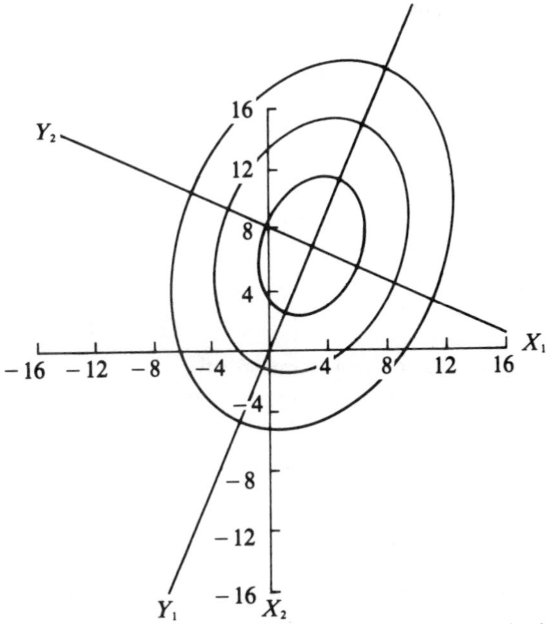

Figure 6-4. Graphic representation of the principal components and the 68%, 95%, and near 100% ellipses of concentration for the example of Section 6-3.

This quadratic equation has two solutions. With $a = +1$, $b = -25$, and $c = +135$, we have from the quadratic formula of Section 5-2:

$$\lambda_1 = \frac{25 + \sqrt{625 - 4(135)}}{2} = 17.11$$

$$\lambda_2 = \frac{25 - \sqrt{625 - 4(135)}}{2} = 7.89$$

We now know that the variance of the observations along the major principal axis is given by $S^2_{Y_1} = \lambda_1 = 17.11$. The variance along the second principal axis is given by $S^2_{Y_2} = \lambda_2 = 7.89$. Note that $S^2_{Y_1}$ is larger than either $S^2_{X_1}$ or $S^2_{X_2}$. Thus Y_1 is better able to discriminate among values than either X_1 or X_2 alone. Also note that:

$$\lambda_1 + \lambda_2 = 17.11 + 7.89 = 25 = S^2_{X_1} + S^2_{X_2}$$
$$= \text{trace of } \hat{\Sigma}_{XX}$$

Since the total variance is equal to $S^2_{X_1} + S^2_{X_2} = 25$, we see that Y_1 accounts for $(\lambda_1/25)(100) = (17.11/25)(100) = 68.4\%$ of the variance. In like manner, Y_2 accounts for $(\lambda_2/25)(100) = (7.89/25)(100) = 31.6\%$ of the variance. Note that in principal component analysis, total variance has a meaning different from that used in regression analysis and ANOVA. In these models, total variance is associated with:

$$S^2_{X_1+X_2} = S^2_{X_1} + S^2_{X_2} + 2r_{12}S_{X_1}S_{X_2}$$

When we speak of total variance in principal component analysis, we are referring to the more restricted definition based on $S^2_{X_1} + S^2_{X_2}$ only.

From calculus and analytic geometry, we can show that the angle θ that exists between X_1 and Y_1 can be determined from the trigonometric equation:

$$\theta = \frac{1}{2}\arctan\left(\frac{2r_{X_1X_2}S_{X_1}S_{X_2}}{S^2_{X_1} - S^2_{X_2}}\right) \qquad \text{if } S^2_{X_1} \neq S^2_{X_2}$$

whereas if $S^2_{X_1} = S^2_{X_2}$, $\theta = 45°$. For our example:

$$\theta = \frac{1}{2}\arctan\left(\frac{2(.25)(3)(4)}{9 - 16}\right) = \frac{1}{2}\arctan(6/-7) = \frac{1}{2}\arctan(-.8571)$$

Referring to a table of trigonometric functions, we find that arctan(−.8571) is approximately equal to 140°, so that:

$$\theta = \frac{1}{2}(140°) = 70°$$

Finally, to two decimal places:

$$Y_1 = (\cos 70°)\, X_1 + (\sin 70°)\, X_2 = .34X_1 + .94X_2 \quad \text{and}$$

$$Y_2 = (-\sin 70°)\, X_1 + (\cos 70°)X_2 = -.94X_1 + .34X_2$$

Furthermore, if we wish to rotate back to the original variables, the transforming equations are given by:

$$X_1 = .34Y_1 - .94Y_2$$

and

$$X_2 = .94Y_1 + .34Y_2$$

In either case, we see that:

$$(.34)^2 + (.94)^2 = 1$$

$$(.34)^2 + (-.94)^2 = 1$$

and

$$(.34)(.94) + (-.94)(.34) = 0$$

For P variables, the eigen vectors are usually found directly from the eigen equation by successive substitutions of $\lambda_1, \lambda_2, \ldots, \lambda_P$. We demonstrate this process here for the present $P = 2$ variable case. For $\lambda_1 = 17.11$, we have that:

$$(\hat{\Sigma}_{XX} - \lambda_1 \mathbf{I})\mathbf{A}_1 = 0$$

or that:

$$\begin{bmatrix} 9 - 17.11 & 3 \\ 3 & 16 - 17.11 \end{bmatrix} \begin{bmatrix} a_1^{(1)} \\ a_2^{(1)} \end{bmatrix} = \begin{bmatrix} 0 \\ 0 \end{bmatrix}$$

This matrix equation is equivalent to the set of homogeneous equations:

$$-8.11a_1^{(1)} + 3a_2^{(1)} = 0$$

$$3a_1^{(1)} - 1.11a_2^{(1)} = 0$$

From the first of these equations, it follows that:

$$a_1^{(1)} = \frac{3}{8.11} a_2^{(1)} = .3699a_2^{(1)}$$

As we see, there are an infinite set of solutions to this one equation, but if we now add the restriction:

$$\mathbf{A}_1'\mathbf{A}_1 = a_1^{(1)2} + a_2^{(1)2} = 1$$

we can obtain a unique solution. In this case, we have that:

$$(.3699a_2^{(1)})^2 + a_2^{(1)2} = 1$$

or that:

$$(.3699^2 + 1)a_2^{(1)2} = 1$$

so that:

$$a_2^{(1)2} = \frac{1}{.3699^2 + 1} = \frac{1}{1.1368} = .8796$$

As a result:

$a_2^{(1)} = .9379$

Thus:

$a_1^{(1)} = .3699a_2^{(1)} = .3699(.9379) = .3469$

so that:

$Y_1 = .3469X_1 + .9379X_2$

Finally, the coefficients for Y_2 can be found by starting the analysis with $\lambda_2 = 7.89$. (These four-decimal-place results differ from the previous two-decimal-place values because of the approximation made in reading arctan 70°.)

As we have seen, the variance on the longest axis is given by $\lambda_1 = S_{Y_1}^2 = 17.11$. Another way to determine $S_{Y_1}^2$ is to recall that $S_{Y_1}^2 = \mathbf{A}_1'\hat{\mathbf{\Sigma}}_{XX}\mathbf{A}_1$. In this case:

$$S_{Y_1}^2 = [.3469 \quad .9379]\begin{bmatrix} 9 & 3 \\ 3 & 16 \end{bmatrix}\begin{bmatrix} .3469 \\ .9376 \end{bmatrix}$$

$$= (.3469)^2(9) + 2(.3469)(.9379)(3) + (.9379)^2(16)$$

$$= 17.11$$

so that $S_{Y_1} = 4.14$. In like manner, the variance on the shorter axis is determined from $(-\ .9379 \quad .3469)$. In this case, $S_{Y_2}^2 = 7.89$, so that $S_{Y_2} = 2.81$.

The equations that serve to define the principal components are plotted in Figure 6-4. In this diagram, ellipses have been drawn, relative to the Y_1 component at $1.00S_{Y_1} = \pm 4.14$, $1.96S_{Y_1} = \pm 8.11$, and $3.00S_{Y_1} = \pm 12.42$ and the Y_2 component at $1.00S_{Y_2} = \pm 2.81$, $1.96S_{Y_2} = \pm 5.51$, and $3.00S_{Y_2} = \pm 8.43$. If the joint distribution of X_1 and X_2 were bivariate normal, about 68% of the distribution would be concentrated in the inner ellipse, 95% of the distribution within the middle ellipse, and almost 100% of the distribution within the outermost ellipse. As a result, these ellipses are frequently termed the 68%, 95%, and 100% ellipses of concentration.

Finally, we would be hesitant to replace X_1 and X_2 by Y_1 alone, since the correlation between X_1 and X_2, $r_{X_1X_2} = .25$, is quite small. In any case, note that Y_1 and Y_2 are not correlated, even though X_1 and X_2 are. It is this latter property that makes Y_1 and Y_2 so important for model building and data analysis. The variables Y_1 and Y_2 are orthogonal and if, in addition, the joint distribution of X_1 and X_2 is bivariate normal, then Y_1 and Y_2 are statistically independent as well. We recall that orthogonality does not imply independence, but rather only that the correlation coefficient is equal to zero. Bivariate normality is required to justify independence. The reader is cautioned against falling into this potential trap!

6-4. A substantive example

As an example, let us reconsider the 10 variables and the 40 subjects used in the canonical correlation analysis. In this case, we will not separate the 10 variables into two sets as we did previously. Instead we will treat the following $P = 10$ variables as one set.

X_1: Social class
X_2: Sex
X_3: High school grade point average
X_4: College Board test scores
X_5: Previous high school unit in sociology
X_6: Pretest score
X_7: Midterm 1 score
X_8: Midterm 2 score
X_9: Final test score
X_{10}: Evaluation of the course

Variables X_2 and X_5 are dichotomous, taking on the values 0 or 1. Variables X_1 and X_{10} are qualitative ordered variables. Social class is scored as 1, 2, or 3, whereas the evaluation item is scored 1, 2, 3, 4, or 5. Variables such as race or religious preference cannot be used in principal component analysis unless they are dummy coded as they were for the multiple-regression approach to the analysis of variance (Section 3-16). In the present example a score of 0 was assigned to males and 1 to females.

Sample means and standard deviations are presented in Table 6-1. The mean social class value is given by $\bar{X} = 1.98$, indicating that the average student comes from the middle social class category, since the variable has been scored 1 = low, 2 = middle, and 3 = high. Similarly, about 68% of the students are females since 0 = male and 1 = female; mean GPA is 3.38, and so on. Corresponding standard deviations are also presented in Table 6-1.

The sample correlation matrix of Table 6-2 is a simple rearrangement of that previously given as Table 5-2. The rearrangement comes from the variables being listed in a different order. The largest correlation is between X_3, high school grade point average, and X_7, first midterm score. For these variables, $r_{X_3X_7} = .72$. The other correlations are self-explanatory. Although we previously described principal component analysis in terms of $\hat{\boldsymbol{\Sigma}}_{XX}$, we could have alternatively described it in terms of $\mathbf{R}_{XX}$. In fact, almost all principal component solutions are based on $\mathbf{R}_{XX}$, with the reason for this easy to understand. Consider the standard deviations of Table 6-1. They range from a low of $S_{X_3} = .35$ to a high of $S_{X_4} = 114.66$. Thus the largest variance is about $114.66^2/.35^2 = 107{,}322$ times larger than the smallest variance. As we saw in describing the geometry of ellipses, the variables with large variances are going to be associated with the longest or major principal axes. Thus we would expect that variable X_4 would have a tremendously large effect on the

TABLE 6-1. Sample means and standard deviations

Variable	$\bar{X}$	S_X
1	1.975	0.660
2	0.675	0.474
3	3.376	0.353
4	524.250	114.665
5	0.400	0.496
6	18.125	7.426
7	46.050	15.396
8	62.875	20.087
9	99.475	30.323
10	1.950	1.197

TABLE 6-2. Sample correlation matrix for the principal component analysis

Variable	X_1	X_2	X_3	X_4	X_5	X_6	X_7	X_8	X_9	X_{10}
X_1	1.00	0.06	0.06	− 0.09	− 0.05	0.04	− 0.16	− 0.28	− 0.32	− 0.52
X_2		1.00	− 0.03	− 0.04	0.02	0.02	0.09	0.22	0.09	0.29
X_3			1.00	0.47	0.51	0.47	0.72	0.68	0.60	0.09
X_4				1.00	0.23	0.15	0.55	0.57	0.46	− 0.20
X_5					1.00	0.37	0.45	0.33	0.39	0.12
X_6						1.00	0.55	0.43	0.30	0.14
X_7							1.00	0.67	0.64	0.19
X_8								1.00	0.58	0.25
X_9									1.00	0.13
X_{10}										1.00

coefficients that define Y_1. On the other hand, X_3 would have a small effect. If we wished to treat each variable equally in the analysis, we should make sure that each has the same variance. An easy solution to this problem is to replace everyone's set of observed raw scores by standard scores, each with a mean of zero and a standard deviation of one. Clearly $\mathbf{R}_{XX}$ would be the resulting variance-covariance matrix for the standardized scores, and so it makes perfectly good sense to use it for the reduction. Even so, we will continue to denote the standardized variables $X_1, X_2, \ldots, X_{10}$ and not $Z_1, Z_2, \ldots, Z_{10}$.

The 10 eigen values associated with each of the principal components are reported in Table 6-3, along with the coefficients used to define $Y_1, Y_2, \ldots, Y_{10}$. These coefficients are sometimes referred to as *loadings*. As we see, the eigen values decrease in magnitude from $\lambda_1 = 4.05$ to $\lambda_{10} = .11$. As a check, we note that:

$$\sum_{p=1}^{P} \lambda_p = 4.05 + 1.62 + \cdots + .11 = 10 = P$$

From Table 6-3, it can also be seen that the first three principal components account

TABLE 6-3. Table of principal component weights and eigen values: the pattern matrix

Variable	Y_1	Y_2	Y_3	Y_4	Y_5	Y_6	Y_7	Y_8	Y_9	Y_{10}
X_1: Social Class	− 0.12	0.57	0.52	0.16	− 0.01	− 0.18	0.25	0.16	0.27	0.41
X_2: Sex	0.06	− 0.31	0.54	0.67	0.16	0.06	− 0.22	0.00	− 0.09	− 0.27
X_3: HS GPA	0.42	0.20	0.09	− 0.08	0.02	− 0.32	0.51	− 0.14	− 0.02	− 0.62
X_4: College Board	0.31	0.26	− 0.39	0.38	− 0.02	0.50	0.04	0.27	0.42	− 0.12
X_5: Previous unit	0.29	0.07	0.23	− 0.36	0.75	0.35	− 0.07	− 0.07	− 0.02	0.09
X_6: Pretest	0.29	0.08	0.40	− 0.37	− 0.54	0.21	− 0.43	− 0.09	0.25	− 0.15
X_7: Midterm 1	0.44	0.04	0.02	− 0.00	− 0.15	− 0.06	− 0.03	0.62	− 0.60	0.21
X_8: Midterm 2	0.42	− 0.09	− 0.05	0.23	− 0.21	0.15	0.24	− 0.62	− 0.18	0.47
X_9: Final	0.39	− 0.05	− 0.21	0.10	0.21	0.63	− 0.43	− 0.02	0.34	0.18
X_{10}: Attitude	0.12	− 0.67	0.16	− 0.18	− 0.05	0.00	0.43	0.31	0.43	0.18
Variance of $Y_p(\lambda_p)$	4.05	1.62	1.13	0.99	0.68	0.46	0.45	0.30	0.20	0.11
Cumulative percentage	40.5	56.8	68.1	78.0	84.7	89.3	93.8	96.9	98.9	100.0

for 68.1% of the total variance. The remaining 31.9% of the total variance is associated with the components whose eigen values are all less than 1.00. Each of these components has a variance that is on the average less than that of the original observable variables. As a result, interpreting such components is generally not recommended.

The first principal component, Y_1, is defined as:

$$Y_1 = -.12X_1 + .06X_2 + .42X_3 + .31X_4 + .29X_5 + .29X_6 + .44X_7 + .42X_8 + .39X_9 + .12X_{10}$$

This variable has the following properties. Its mean and variance are given by $\bar{Y}_1 = 0$ and $S^2_{Y_1} = \lambda_1 = 4.05$. Furthermore:

$$\sum_{p=1}^{P} a_p^{(1)2} = -.12^2 + .06^2 + \cdots + .39^2 + .12^2 = 1.00$$

In addition, Y_1 is orthogonal to $Y_2, Y_3, \ldots, Y_{10}$. Corresponding relationships exist for the remaining principal components, so that for any two components, Y_p and $Y_{p'}$:

$$r_{Y_pY_{p'}} = 0$$

Another interesting property of the matrix of Table 6-3 is illustrated in the coefficients for the first row. Note that:

$$\sum_{p=1}^{P} a_1^{(p)2} = -.12^2 + .57^2 + \cdots + .41^2 = 1.00$$

As noted previously, these coefficients can be alternatively used to relate X_1 to $Y_1, Y_2, \ldots, Y_{10}$. Under this model, X_1 can be expressed as:

$$X_1 = -.12Y_1 + .57Y_2 + .52Y_3 + .16Y_4 - .01Y_5 - .18Y_6 + .25Y_7 + .16Y_8 + .27Y_9 + .41Y_{10}$$

Since $\bar{Y}_1 = \bar{Y}_2 = \cdots = \bar{Y}_{10} = 0$, it follows that $\bar{X}_1 = 0$. Since $Y_1, Y_2, \ldots, Y_P$ are mutually orthogonal, we see that to two-decimal-point accuracy:

$$\begin{aligned} \text{Var}(X_1) &= \sum_{p=1}^{P} a_1^{(p)2}\,\text{Var}(Y_p) = \sum_{p=1}^{P} a_1^{(p)2}\lambda_p \\ &= -.12^2(4.05) + .57^2(1.62) + \cdots + .41^2(.11) \\ &= .06 + .53 + .31 + .02 + .00 + .01 + .03 + .01 + .01 + .02 \\ &= 1.00 \end{aligned}$$

We already knew this, but what is more important is that, according to this partitioning, we can clearly see that the variance in X_1 is associated mostly with Y_2 and Y_3, the former accounting for 53% of the variance in X_1. The remaining partitioning of the variances for each of the individual variables is reported in Table 6-4. These results are reported to two-place accuracy.

As just noted, we see that the variance of X_1 is associated mainly with Y_2, as is the variance of X_{10}. The amounts involved are 53% for X_1 and 73% for X_{10}. The variance of X_2 is associated mainly with Y_4. The variance of X_3 is associated mainly with Y_1,

TABLE 6-4. Distribution of the variance of each observable variable across the ten principal components

Variable	Y_1	Y_2	Y_3	Y_4	Y_5	Y_6	Y_7	Y_8	Y_9	Y_{10}	Var(X_p)
X_1	0.06	0.53	0.31	0.03	0.00	0.01	0.03	0.01	0.01	0.02	1.00
X_2	0.01	0.16	0.33	0.44	0.02	0.00	0.02	0.00	0.00	0.01	1.00
X_3	0.71	0.06	0.01	0.01	0.00	0.05	0.12	0.01	0.00	0.04	1.00
X_4	0.39	0.11	0.17	0.14	0.00	0.11	0.00	0.02	0.04	0.00	1.00
X_5	0.34	0.01	0.06	0.13	0.38	0.06	0.00	0.00	0.00	0.00	1.00
X_6	0.34	0.01	0.18	0.13	0.20	0.02	0.08	0.00	0.01	0.00	1.00
X_7	0.78	0.00	0.00	0.00	0.02	0.00	0.00	0.12	0.07	0.00	1.00
X_8	0.71	0.01	0.00	0.05	0.03	0.01	0.03	0.12	0.01	0.03	1.00
X_9	0.62	0.00	0.05	0.01	0.03	0.18	0.08	0.00	0.02	0.00	1.00
X_{10}	0.06	0.73	0.03	0.03	0.00	0.00	0.08	0.03	0.04	0.00	1.00
λ_p	4.05	1.62	1.13	0.99	0.68	0.46	0.45	0.30	0.20	0.11	10.00

which is also true for X_4, X_5, X_6, X_7, X_8, and X_9. The amounts involved are .71, .39, .34, .34, .78, .71, and .62. Note that 7 of the 10 variables have most of their variance associated with Y_1, the first principal component. This is a basic property of principal component analysis. The first principal component is the one that takes up the largest part of the total variance in the set of the X variables. It picks up this largest share by extracting the maximum possible from each X variable that is associated with Y_1. From the remainder, Y_2 is then defined by the maximum it can extract from the residual X variance. This process is repeated until the last bit of the X variance is placed on the final component, Y_P. Often we read in a scientific research article that the extraction process was terminated when $p\%$ of the total X variance had been extracted. All this means is that the researcher considered as meaningful components the ordered eigen values that accounted for $p\%$ of P. Thus, if in this sample, we should decide to retain only the principal components whose eigen values exceed 1.00 (i.e., the first three), we would say that components were extracted until 68.1% of the total X variance was utilized.

6-5. Interpreting principal components

If one of the objectives of principal component analysis is to reduce the number of observed variables $X_1, X_2, \ldots, X_P$ to a smaller set of $Y_1, Y_2, \ldots, Y_Q$, an obvious question is what value of Q should be selected. One possible solution, described in Section 6-4, is to extract components until we have accounted for $p\%$ (for example, 60%, 70%, 80% or any other percentage) of the total X variance. The percentage value to use is a subjective decision for which no universally accepted mode has been established. Often the decision is based on data such as those summarized in Table 6-5. In this table, cumulative variances are summarized for each X variable across the P principal components. For X_1, for example, the increasing cumulative variances, derived from Table 6-4, are .06, .06 + .53 = .59, .06 + .53 + .31 = .90, and so on. It can be seen that Y_1, Y_2, and Y_3 account for 90% of the variance of X_1. For X_2, only 50% is extracted. For the remaining X variables, the amounts extracted by the first three principal components are given by 78%, 67%, 41%, 53%, 78%, 72%, 67%, and 82%. As can be seen from the bottom row of Table 6-3, more than 68% of the total X variance is extracted by Y_1, Y_2, and Y_3.

TABLE 6-5. Cumulative variances for each observable variable across the ten principal components

Variable	Y_1	Y_2	Y_3	Y_4	Y_5	Y_6	Y_7	Y_8	Y_9	Y_{10}
X_1	0.06	0.59	0.90	0.93	0.93	0.94	0.97	0.98	0.99	1.01
X_2	0.01	0.17	0.50	0.94	0.96	0.96	0.98	0.98	0.98	0.99
X_3	0.71	0.77	0.78	0.79	0.79	0.84	0.96	0.97	0.97	1.01
X_4	0.39	0.50	0.67	0.81	0.81	0.92	0.92	0.94	0.98	0.98
X_5	0.34	0.35	0.41	0.54	0.92	0.98	0.98	0.98	0.98	0.98
X_6	0.34	0.35	0.53	0.66	0.86	0.88	0.96	0.96	0.97	0.97
X_7	0.78	0.78	0.78	0.78	0.80	0.80	0.80	0.92	0.99	0.99
X_8	0.71	0.72	0.72	0.77	0.80	0.81	0.84	0.96	0.97	1.00
X_9	0.62	0.62	0.67	0.68	0.71	0.89	0.97	0.97	0.99	0.99
X_{10}	0.06	0.79	0.82	0.85	0.85	0.85	0.93	0.96	1.00	1.00

Recall that each of the first three principal components in this example has an associated eigen value greater than or equal to 1.00. The argument against including components with variances less than 1.00 is that they have even less discrimination power than any of the original X variables, for which the variances were set equal to 1.00. This procedure was followed here and, consequently, components Y_1, Y_2, and Y_3 have been retained. The percentage of total X variance extracted by these three components is given by 68.1%. Retaining only those principal components with associated eigen values greater than 1.00 was originally proposed by Kaiser (1960) and hence is often referred to as Kaiser's rule.

Kaiser's rule.
Only components with eigen values greater than 1.00 should be retained when interpreting the results of a principal component analysis.

In most cases, Kaiser's rule is quite workable, but one disadvantage is that it is a function of P, the number of original X variables. In many practical applications, we can expect that the number of eigen values greater than 1.00 is approximately $\frac{1}{3}P$ (Kaiser, personal communication). Thus 30 variables could be expected to reduce to about 10 principal components.

Another disadvantage of applying Kaiser's rule is that it ignores the fact that $\mathbf{R}_{XX}$ is based on a set of random variables that could vary with repeated samplings. In the same vein, it makes no distinction between analyses based on 40 subjects, 400 subjects, 4000 subjects, and so on. Consequently we may wish to apply inferential statistical procedures in deciding how many components to retain. In the present application, we would wish to determine how many eigen values are statistically greater than 1.00. A test was proposed by Girshick (1939), but this is only appropriate for a principal component analysis based on $\hat{\mathbf{\Sigma}}_{XX}$, rather than on $\mathbf{R}_{XX}$. As mentioned previously, modern-day solutions are based on $\mathbf{R}_{XX}$, so Girshick's test is not particularly helpful to us. A sequential Chi-square procedure, developed by Bartlett (1950, 1951), is associated with $\mathbf{R}_{XX}$, however, and is described by Mulaik (1972).

Once the number of retained principal components has been decided on (three here) according to Kaiser's rule, it is of interest to assign labels to the new constructs. As with canonical correlation analysis, we can attempt to interpret principal components by computing the correlation between a given component Y_q and each original variable X. Those X variables that are highly correlated with a given Y then serve as definers of that principal component. For example, if $r_{X_1Y_1} = .90$, it would be said that X_1 'loads' heavily on Y_1 and is a variable that helps to define Y_1. On the other hand, if $r_{X_1Y_1} = .10$, it would be said that X_1 does not load on Y_1 and it should not be used to define Y_1.

Surprisingly, the values of the correlation coefficients are exceedingly simple to obtain, even simpler than in the canonical correlation situation. As we saw earlier, if **A** is the matrix of principal component coefficients, it follows that **Y** = **AX** and that **X** = **A′Y**. Let us begin with this latter equation. In particular, consider the first row of coefficients of **A′** and the expansion of X_1 in terms of $Y_1, Y_2, \ldots, Y_P$. This expansion is defined as:

$$X_1 = a_1^{(1)}Y_1 + a_1^{(2)}Y_2 + \cdots + a_1^{(P)}Y_P = \sum_{p=1}^{P} a_1^{(p)}Y_p$$

Now consider the correlation between X_1 and Y_1. First, recall that all X variables are represented in standard score form, so that $\bar{X}_1 = 0$ and $S_{X_1} = 1$. In addition, it was previously shown that:

$$\bar{Y}_1 = \bar{Y}_2 = \cdots = \bar{Y}_P = 0$$

with:

$$S_{Y_1} = \sqrt{\lambda_1},\ S_{Y_2} = \sqrt{\lambda_2}, \ldots, S_{Y_P} = \sqrt{\lambda_P}$$

Under these conditions:

$$\begin{aligned}
r_{X_1Y_1} &= \frac{1}{N-1}\sum_{i=1}^{N}\left(\frac{X_{1i}-\bar{X}_1}{S_{X_1}}\right)\left(\frac{Y_{1i}-\bar{Y}_1}{S_{Y_1}}\right) \\
&= \frac{1}{N-1}\sum_{i=1}^{N}\frac{X_{1i}Y_{1i}}{S_{Y_1}} = \frac{1}{(N-1)S_{Y_1}}\sum_{i=1}^{N} X_{1i}Y_{1i} \\
&= \frac{1}{(N-1)S_{Y_1}}\sum_{i=1}^{N}(a_1^{(1)}Y_{1i} + a_1^{(2)}Y_{2i} + \cdots + a_1^{(P)}Y_{Pi})Y_{1i} \\
&= \frac{1}{S_{Y_1}}\left(a_1^{(1)}\frac{1}{N-1}\sum_{i=1}^{N}Y_{1i}^2 + a_1^{(2)}\frac{1}{N-1}\sum_{i=1}^{N}Y_{1i}Y_{2i} + \cdots + a_1^{(P)}\frac{1}{N-1}\sum_{i=1}^{N}Y_{1i}Y_{Pi}\right) \\
&= \frac{1}{S_{Y_1}}(a_1^{(1)}S_{Y_1}^2 + a_1^{(2)}r_{Y_1Y_2} + \cdots + a_1^{(P)}r_{Y_1Y_P})
\end{aligned}$$

From the preceding, $S_{Y_1}^2 = \lambda_1$ and since the Y_p are mutually uncorrelated, it follows that:

$$r_{Y_1Y_2} = r_{Y_1Y_3} = \cdots = r_{Y_1Y_P} = 0$$

so that:

$$r_{X_1Y_1} = a_1^{(1)}S_{Y_1} = a_1^{(1)}\sqrt{\lambda_1}$$

Clearly, the remaining correlation coefficients satisfy a similar equation. Thus, in general, we have the following simple way to compute $r_{X_pY_q}$.

The correlation between X_p and Y_q.
The correlation between any standardized observable variable X_p and any principal component Y_q is given simply as:

$$r_{X_pY_q} = a_p^{(q)}\sqrt{\lambda_q}$$

A little reflection immediately shows that the correlation coefficients with the originally observable variables are obtainable from the numbers reported in Table 6-3. All we need do is multiply each table entry by the square root of its corresponding eigen value. From our previous discussion in Section 6-4, also note that the correlations can also be found by taking the square roots of the values reported in Table 6-4. Thus:

1. $r_{X_1Y_1} = -.12\sqrt{4.05} = -.25 = -\sqrt{.06}$
2. $r_{X_2Y_1} = -.06\sqrt{4.05} = -.12 = \sqrt{.01}$
3. $r_{X_3Y_1} = -.42\sqrt{4.05} = -.84 = \sqrt{.71}$
4. $r_{X_4Y_1} = -.31\sqrt{4.05} = -.63 = \sqrt{.39}$
5. $r_{X_5Y_1} = -.29\sqrt{4.05} = -.59 = \sqrt{.34}$
6. $r_{X_6Y_1} = -.29\sqrt{4.05} = -.59 = \sqrt{.34}$
7. $r_{X_7Y_1} = -.44\sqrt{4.05} = -.89 = \sqrt{.78}$
8. $r_{X_8Y_1} = -.42\sqrt{4.05} = -.85 = \sqrt{.71}$
9. $r_{X_9Y_1} = -.39\sqrt{4.05} = -.78 = \sqrt{.62}$
10. $r_{X_{10}Y_1} = -.12\sqrt{4.05} = -.25 = \sqrt{.06}$

The remaining correlations are reported in Table 6-6. In psychometric factor analysis, Table 6-6 is referred to as the *structure matrix*, and that terminology is retained here.

It is also worth mentioning that within each column of Y_1, the signs attached to the entries of Table 6-6 may vary from one computer solution to the next. For example, a different computer program may show, for Y_1, a positive sign for X_1 and negative signs for X_2 through X_{10}. Within-column reflections will be consistent, however, and will not affect the interpretation of the resulting solution.

TABLE 6-6. Table of correlations between each Y and each original X variable: the structure matrix

Variable	Y_1	Y_2	Y_3	Y_4	Y_5	Y_6	Y_7	Y_8	Y_9	Y_{10}
X_1	– 0.25	0.72	0.55	0.16	– 0.01	– 0.12	0.17	0.09	0.12	0.14
X_2	0.12	– 0.39	0.57	0.67	0.13	0.04	– 0.15	– 0.00	– 0.04	– 0.09
X_3	0.84	0.25	0.10	– 0.08	0.02	– 0.22	0.34	– 0.08	– 0.01	– 0.21
X_4	0.62	0.33	– 0.42	0.38	– 0.02	0.34	0.03	0.15	0.19	– 0.04
X_5	0.59	0.09	0.24	– 0.36	0.62	0.24	– 0.05	– 0.04	– 0.01	0.03
X_6	0.60	0.10	0.43	– 0.37	– 0.44	0.14	– 0.29	– 0.05	0.11	– 0.05
X_7	0.89	0.05	0.03	– 0.00	– 0.12	– 0.04	– 0.02	0.34	– 0.26	0.06
X_8	0.85	– 0.11	– 0.05	0.23	– 0.17	0.10	0.16	– 0.34	– 0.08	0.16
X_9	0.78	– 0.06	– 0.22	0.10	0.17	– 0.43	– 0.29	– 0.01	0.15	0.06
X_{10}	0.25	– 0.85	0.17	– 0.18	– 0.04	0.00	0.29	0.17	0.19	0.06

The largest correlations with Y_1 are found for X_7: Midterm 1, X_8: Midterm 2, X_3: High school grade point average, X_9: Final exam score, X_4: College Board score, X_6: Pretest score, and X_5: Previous high school unit in sociology. These correlations are .89, .85, .84, .78, .62, .60, and .59, respectively. The low correlations are associated with X_2: Sex, X_1: Social class, and X_{10}: Course evaluation. These correlations are given by .12, − .25, and .25, respectively. For the most part, this outcome seems reasonable. Scores on midterms and finals are expected to correlate highly with one another. Previous courses in social studies should help students to achieve higher grades in related subject matter. Since high school grade point average and College Board scores seem to be reliable predictors of school success, we would expect them to cluster with test grades. None of these variables should be associated with sex and, perhaps, not with students' evaluation of the course. It may be somewhat surprising that social class is also excluded, although it is likely that, in a self-selected college population, socioeconomic background variables are not as predictive of academic achievement as they are in grade school. Since Y_1 is defined by variables that predict school success and that actually measure achievement in sociology, Y_1 might be labeled *scholastic achievement*. Another way of stating this is that variables X_3 through X_9 all seem to load on the first principal component, which therefore might reasonably be called a scholastic achievement component. Note that, because of the previously indicated one-to-one correspondence between the entries of Tables 6-3 and 6-6, the former factor pattern matrix could also be used to identify the primary definers of each component.

The second principal component has as its major loaders, X_{10}: Course evaluation and X_1: Social class. The correlations are − .85 and .72, respectively. Thus X_1 and X_{10} relate to Y_2 in opposite fashions. Because of the way in which these two X variables were coded, this suggests that students from higher social classes would be more likely *not* to have liked the course in comparison to students from lower social classes. Since the course dealt with many urban and low-income family issues and since lower social class students tended to like the course more, this may reflect a *social class identification* component.

The correlations between individual X variables and Y_3 are not too large. Those with loadings above .40 in absolute value include X_2: Sex, X_1: Social class, X_6: Pretest score, and X_4: College Board score, with corresponding correlations of .47, .55, .43, and − .42, respectively. Coming up with an appropriate label for this third component is difficult, especially since the academic achievement measures, pretest and College Board scores, are opposite in sign. The way in which the variables were coded, however, indicates that at one end of the scale this component groups together females, lower socioeconomic students, high pretest scores, and low College Board scores or, alternatively, at the opposite end of the scale males, higher socioeconomic students, low pretest scores, and high College Board scores. Several sterotypical labels could be applied to this component, but we choose not to do so.

As this example shows, our ability to ascribe meaningful names to principal components decreases very quickly. In many cases it cannot even be done since often no reasonable explanation can be offered as to why certain variables cluster together. Finally, components beyond the third will not be examined here, based on our decision to ignore Ys with associated eigen values of 1.00 or less, following Kaiser's rule. As mentioned previously, this decision rule for deciding on the number of principal components to retain is based on the commonsense notion of retaining only those variables for which the variance exceeds that of the original standardized variables.

Finally, once the number of retained components has been decided on, a researcher can examine the amount of each original variable's variance that is distributed across the set of these components, referred to here as the *cumulative variances* retained. These are analogous to what are called *communalities* in factor analysis. Thus, if three components are retained, the cumulative variances retained can be read from Table 6-5 to be equal to .90 for X_1, .50 for X_2, .78 for X_3, .67 for X_4, .41 for X_5, .53 for X_6, .78 for X_7, .72 for X_8, .67 for X_9, and .82 for X_{10}. In addition, this information can be combined with that in Table 6-4 to show that $.53/.90(100) = 59\%$ of the X_1 cumulative variance retained is accounted for by Y_2, $.33/.50(100) = 66\%$ of the X_2 cumulative variance retained is accounted for by Y_3, and so on.

6-6. Rotation to simple structure

As suggested in the previous sections, researchers in the social sciences would like to name the resulting components $Y_1, Y_2, \ldots, Y_Q$. In most cases, a successful or meaningful naming of the components is doomed to failure, mainly because the coefficients $\mathbf{A}_p$ are generated from mathematical considerations and not from psychological or sociological theory. The $\mathbf{A}_p$ are mathematical entities and not real-world constructs. Yet the desire to relate mathematics to reality persists. In the late forties, L. L. Thurstone (1947) specified a number of conditions that should be satisfied if we wish to give meaning to the principal components. Actually, he specified requirements for psychometric factor analysis and not for principal components. These conditions give rise to the notion of *simple structure*. The primary conditions associated with simple structure are as follows, with a more complete description provided by Guilford (1954).

The nature of simple structure.

The variables $Y_1, Y_2, \ldots, Y_Q$ are said to have simple structure if:

1. There is at least one zero or, in practice, near-zero, correlation for each X with the set of Y variables.
2. There are substantial numbers of zero correlations between each Y and the original X variables.
3. For each pair of Y components there exists a small number of X variables that load on either of the Y components, but not on both.

In most cases, these conditions are impossible to attain, though they can be approximated reasonably well for most purposes. As an example, consider the structure matrix of Table 6-6 for the components with eigen values greater than 1.00.

The first condition of simple structure is fairly well satisfied, in that it holds for every X except X_4. Within the first three components, the smallest correlation with

X_4 is found for Y_2, where $r_{X_4Y_2} = .33$. For the remaining X variables, each has at least one near-zero correlation, given by:

$r_{X_1Y_1} = -.25$, $r_{X_2Y_1} = .12$, $r_{X_3Y_3} = .10$,

$r_{X_5Y_2} = .09$, $r_{X_6Y_2} = .10$, $r_{X_7Y_3} = .03$,

$r_{X_8Y_3} = -.05$, $r_{X_9Y_2} = -.06$, and $r_{X_{10}Y_3} = .17$

The second condition seems to be satisfied for Y_2 and Y_3, but not for Y_1 since, for Y_1, there are only three X variables whose loadings are less than .30 in absolute value, that is, X_1, X_2, and X_{10}. This should not be surprising since, as might be deduced from Section 6-2, a general property of principal component analysis is that as many variables as possible are aligned on the principal axis, that is, on the first principal component. The third condition seems to be satisfied for the pairs (Y_1, Y_2), but not for (Y_1, Y_3) and (Y_2, Y_3). In the case of (Y_1, Y_3), variables X_4 and X_6 have loadings in excess of .30 on both; and for (Y_2, Y_3), variables X_1, X_2, and X_4 also have loadings in excess of .30 on both. Thus the structure matrix of Table 6-6 does not appear to have the property of simple structure.

One way to achieve a near-simple structure is to *rotate* the component structure to the desired structure. This is illustrated in Figure 6-5, which shows a freehand, or eyeball, rotation of the structures for Y_1, Y_2, and Y_3 of Table 6-6. In making these graphs we are attempting to force as many variables as possible to load on only one component and not more than one. These graphs are made by plotting the correlations of Table 6-6 on the two-dimensional grids defined by the paired components. As indicated, the rotation to near-simple structure requires a small angle, especially for (Y_1, Y_2), but the problem is to put the three separate rotations together so as to make sense. This is next to impossible to achieve in the manner illustrated. Furthermore this manual rotation is exceedingly unreliable since one person's rotations may not be another's.

To overcome this difficulty, a number of objective criteria have been proposed. The one in greatest use is Kaiser's (1958) *varimax rotation*. This method of rotation is based on the criterion of maximizing the variance of the loadings for each component. We do not describe the method because of its mathematical complexity, but we illustrate the result of a varimax rotation for the three components of Table 6-3 that have eigen values greater than 1.00. The resulting rotated structure matrix is reported in Table 6-7. Let us examine this matrix for simple structure.

Condition 1 is satisfied. Near-zero correlations are found for every X variable, each of which displays at least one correlation less than .20 in absolute value. Condition 2 is satisfied for each Y^R, again with the possible exception of the first component, Y_1^R, which shows only three out of ten near-zero correlations, these involving X_1, X_2, and X_{10}, as before. In contrast Y_2^R is uncorrelated with X_2, X_3, X_4, X_5, X_6, and X_7. Finally, Y_3^R is uncorrelated with X_1, X_3, X_5, X_7, X_8, and X_9. Condition 3 is essentially satisfied, since only two variables, X_4 and X_6, appear to load on the same two components, Y_1^R and Y_3^R.

Variable Y_1^R is correlated with X_3: High school grade point average, X_4: College Board test score, X_5: Previous high school unit in sociology, X_6: Pretest score, X_7: First midterm, X_8: Second midterm, and X_9: Final exam score. This suggests that Y_1^R measures scholastic achievement, just as did Y_1 of the unrotated structure.

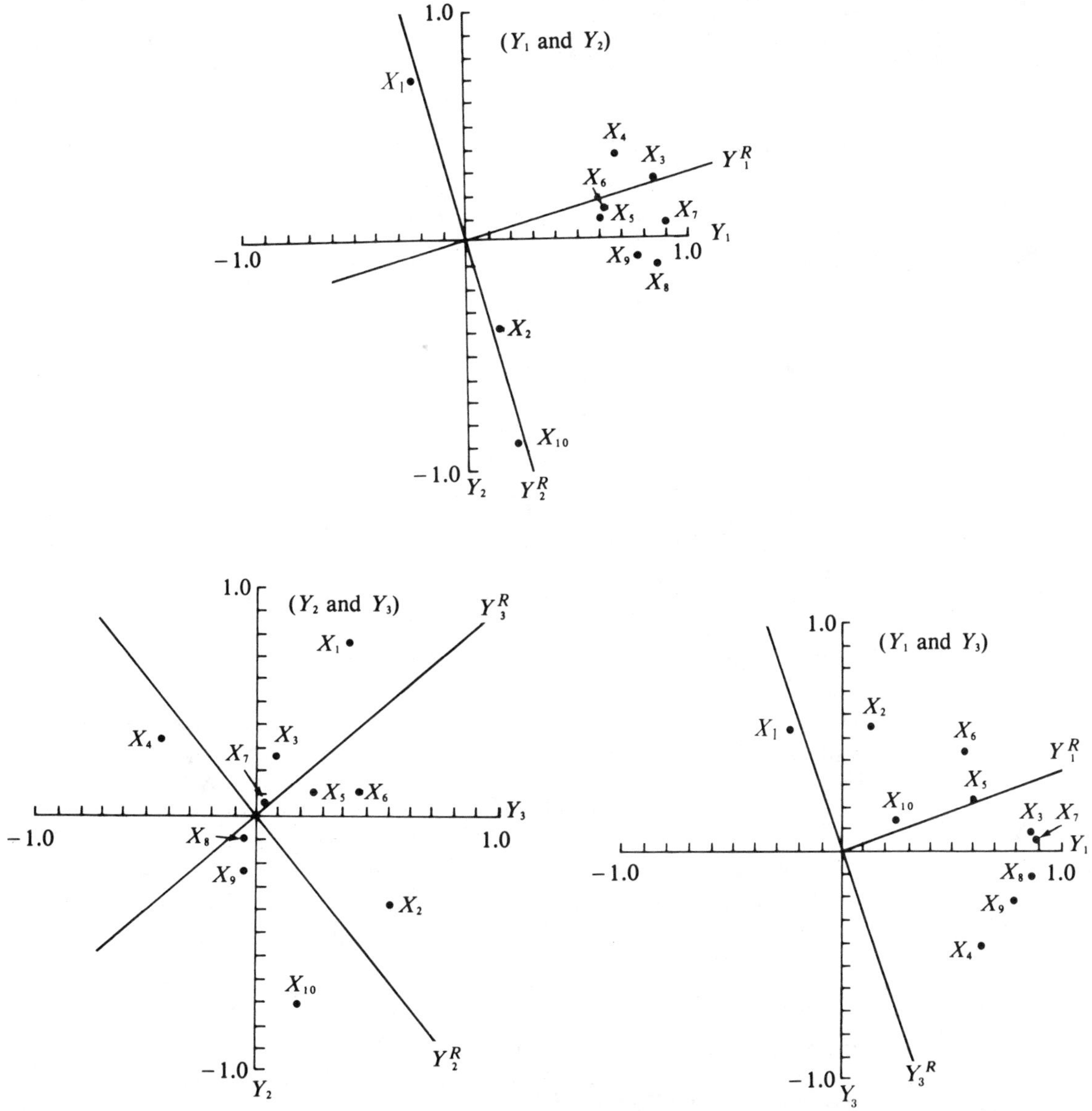

Figure 6-5. Freehand rotations of the structures of Table 6-6 to a near simple structure.

Variable Y_2^R is correlated primarily with X_1: Social class and, to a lesser extent, with X_{10}: Course evaluation. It, therefore, appears to be basically a social class identification component, similar to that found for Y_2.

Variable Y_3^R is correlated with X_2: Sex, X_4: College Board test score, and X_{10}: Course evaluation. A clear description of this variable is hard to make, just as it was for Y_3.

TABLE 6-7. The structure matrix and variance distribution for the varimax rotation of the first three largest eigen vectors of Table 6-3

	Correlation coefficients			*Percent of variance*			
Variable	Y_1^R	Y_2^R	Y_3^R	Y_1^R	Y_2^R	Y_3^R	*Communality*
X_1	− 0.04	− 0.94	0.02	0.00	0.88	0.00	0.88
X_2	0.10	0.01	0.70	0.01	0.00	0.49	0.50
X_3	0.88	− 0.07	− 0.04	0.77	0.00	0.00	0.77
X_4	0.63	− 0.12	− 0.51	0.40	0.01	0.26	0.67
X_5	0.62	− 0.08	0.16	0.38	0.01	0.03	0.42
X_6	0.64	− 0.19	0.31	0.41	0.04	0.10	0.55
X_7	0.88	0.14	0.02	0.77	0.02	0.00	0.79
X_8	0.80	0.30	0.05	0.64	0.09	0.00	0.73
X_9	0.73	0.35	− 0.12	0.53	0.12	0.01	0.66
X_{10}	0.09	0.63	0.64	0.01	0.40	0.41	0.82
Eigen value (variance)				3.95	1.57	1.30	

Thus, for the present example, nothing new has been learned from the rotated solution in comparison to the unrotated one. Note, however, that the fuzzy distinction between social class and sex in unrotated components 2 and 3 is cleared up in rotated components 2 and 3. Social class, but not sex, loads on the second rotated component, whereas the opposite is true on the third rotated component. As indicated, simple structure seems to have been more nearly achieved, and yet interpreting the new rotated components was not facilitated. In many applications, however, it will be found that rotating to simple structure does assist a researcher in naming and interpreting components, relative to unrotated ones. Of course, this depends on the particular input variables selected and the degree to which they can be conceptualized as representing logically interpretable sets.

Another property of varimax rotation is that it takes the total variance associated with the retained unrotated components and redistributes it more equally across the new rotated ones. In this example, we began with $\lambda_1 + \lambda_2 + \lambda_3 = 6.81$. As may be seen from Table 6-7, this variance has been distributed across the new rotated components with:

$$S_{Y_1}^2 = (-.04)^2 + (.10)^2 + (.88)^2 + \cdots + (.08)^2 = 3.95 = \lambda_1^R$$

$$S_{Y_2}^2 = (-.94)^2 + (.01)^2 + (-.07)^2 + \cdots + (.63)^2 = 1.57 = \lambda_2^R \quad \text{and}$$

$$S_{Y_3}^2 = (.02)^2 + (.70)^2 + (-.04)^2 + \cdots + (.64)^2 = 1.30 = \lambda_3^R$$

Note that the previously largest variance, $\lambda_1 = 4.05$, has been reduced to $\lambda_1^R = 3.95$ and the previously smallest variance, $\lambda_3 = 1.13$, has been increased to $\lambda_3^R = 1.30$. This redistribution to a more equal set of variances is a basic property of varimax rotation and is one of the reasons it is preferred by researchers in the social sciences.

Many researchers have the mistaken belief that principal component analysis is a form of psychometric factor analysis. Although principal component analysis may often constitute the first step of a factor analysis, it is important not to confuse it with factor analysis per se. Many factor analyses are based on the use of communalities, the total explained or shared variances associated with each variable. For example, a researcher who believed that the ten variables of our example really measured four unobservable variables would replace the entries of Table 6-2 with the figures of Column 4 of Table 6-5. Thus the unities would be replaced by .93, .94, .79, . . . , .85, and a solution would be sought from these diagonal elements. Other factor analytic models would replace each diagonal unity with a squared multiple correlation coefficient determined by regressing X_1 on $X_2, X_3, \ldots, X_{10}$ for the r_{11} spot in Table 6-2. The r_{22} spot would be replaced by the squared multiple correlation coefficient for X_2 regressed on $X_1, X_3, \ldots, X_{10}$, and so on. Still other models would use individual *X reliabilities* as the diagonal entries. By using communalities, squared multiple correlation coefficients, or reliabilities, the factor extraction procedure is said to proceed on the explained portion of the variance and not on the total variance which is known to contain error of one kind or another. Obviously there are many factor analytic models, and the interested reader should consult the many fine books that are available about this complex psychometric model. We include a brief description of factor analysis in Section 6-9.

6-7. Principal component scores and group differences

If the unrotated principal components with eigen values exceeding 1.00 have interpretable and/or theoretical interest, they can be used for further research and analysis with subjects being assigned principal component scores using the coefficients of Table 6-3. If the rotated components are retained, the derivation of scores is slightly more complex.

One way to generate rotated principal component scores is to consider the estimation problem as a regression problem based on standard scores. This means that if we want to predict Y_1^R, we begin by assuming:

$$Y_1^R = \beta_1 X_1 + \beta_2 X_2 + \cdots + \beta_P X_P$$

As we know from multiple regression theory in Section 4-5:

$$\hat{\boldsymbol{\beta}} = (\mathbf{X}'\mathbf{X})^{-1}(\mathbf{X}'\mathbf{Y})$$

For standard score measures, $(\mathbf{X}'\mathbf{X})^{-1}$ corresponds to $\mathbf{R}_{XX}^{-1}$ and $(\mathbf{X}'\mathbf{Y})$ corresponds to the partitioned matrix $\mathbf{R}_{XY}$ reported in the structure matrix of the rotated factors.

For the three retained rotated components of the present example, $\mathbf{R}_{XX}^{-1}$ is identical to the inverse of the correlation matrix reported in Table 6-2, whereas $\mathbf{R}_{XY}$ is identical to the structure matrix reported in Table 6-7. In terms of these matrices:

$$\hat{\boldsymbol{\beta}} = \mathbf{R}_{XX}^{-1}\mathbf{R}_{XY}$$

The results of this matrix multiplication are summarized in Table 6-8. We see that, to two decimal places:

$$\begin{aligned} Y_1^R = {} & .08X_1 + .03X_2 + .24X_3 + .15X_4 + .18X_5 \\ & + 19X_6 + .22X_7 + .19X_8 + .16X_9 - .03X_{10} \end{aligned}$$

Since the X values are in standard score form, it follows that:

$$\bar{Y}_1^R = 0$$

Further, it can be shown that:

$$S^2_{Y^R_1} = 1.00$$

The two other sets of weights are reported in Table 6-8, with means and variances given by $\bar{Y}^R_2 = \bar{Y}^R_3 = 0$ and $S^2_{Y^R_2} = S^2_{Y^R_3} = 1.00$. These equations can now be used to obtain Y^R_1, Y^R_2, and Y^R_3 for each subject of the study.

Once each subject is scored on the basis of the three regression equations, we can use the resulting scores as variables for further investigation, as was done with canonical variate scores in Section 5-7. Recall that students were divided according to whether or not they subsequently chose a sociology-related career:

Group 1: Sociology-related career
Group 2: Nonsociology-related career

A question of potential interest is whether or not these two groups differ with respect to the variables included here. Mean scores and variances for each group of students on the three standardized rotated components are reported in Table 6-9 as T scores, as was done in Section 5-7. For Y^R_1, the test of H_0: $\mu_1 = \mu_2$ against H_1: H_0 is false, is given by:

$$t_1 = \frac{\bar{T}_1 - \bar{T}_2}{\sqrt{\frac{MS_W}{N_1} + \frac{MS_W}{N_2}}} = \frac{53.6 - 45.1}{\sqrt{\frac{84.0}{23} + \frac{84.0}{17}}} = 2.90$$

TABLE 6-8. The pattern matrix for the three rotated components

Variable	Y^R_1	Y^R_2	Y^R_3
X_1	0.08	− 0.64	0.13
X_2	0.03	− 0.09	0.55
X_3	0.24	− 0.13	− 0.01
X_4	0.15	0.08	− 0.41
X_5	0.18	− 0.13	0.14
X_6	0.19	− 0.23	0.28
X_7	0.22	0.01	0.01
X_8	0.19	0.13	0.01
X_9	0.16	0.19	− 0.13
X_{10}	− 0.03	0.34	0.43

TABLE 6-9. Comparison of students in the two career groups on the basis of the three rotated component scores

	Y^R_1	Y^R_2	Y^R_3
$\bar{T}_1$	53.6	49.4	52.1
$\bar{T}_2$	45.1	50.9	47.2
S^2_1	100.7	93.0	78.7
S^2_2	77.5	111.1	120.0
MS_W	84.0	102.0	96.5
N_1	23	23	23
N_2	17	17	17
t	2.90	− 0.46	− 1.56

The remaining t values for Y_2^R and Y_3^R are $t_2 = -.46$ and $t_3 = -1.56$. If we were to set $\alpha = .05$ for the analysis of each Y variable, with $v = N_1 + N_2 - 2 = 23 + 17 - 2 = 38$, the critical t values would be given by $\pm t_{38:.975} = \pm 2.02$. On the other hand, we could employ the Dunn-Bonferroni procedure in this situation and set $\alpha = .05/3 = .0167$ for the analysis of each of the three Y variables. By so doing, we would preserve the familywise type I error probability at .05. With $C = 3$ comparisons, the critical values based on 38 degrees of freedom are given in Appendix B-4 as ± 2.50. Thus, according to either procedure, $\alpha = .05$ or $\alpha = .0167$, it is seen that the two groups differ significantly on Y_1^R, and only on Y_1^R, which was previously labeled as scholastic achievement. Since the groups differ on this variable, we can estimate the proportion of explained variance in terms of the squared point biserial correlation coefficient. Because the point biserial correlation coefficient r_{pb} is related to the t distribution as:

$$t = \frac{r_{pb}\sqrt{N-2}}{\sqrt{1 - r_{pb}^2}}$$

it follows that:

$$r_{pb}^2 = \frac{t^2}{t^2 + (N-2)} = \frac{2.90^2}{2.90^2 + 38} = .18$$

The weights in Table 6-8 for the rotated components associated with the seven defining variables, given in Section 6-6 as variables 3–9, are all positive. Since for each variable, a high score is indicative of better performance, it is evident that subjects who selected sociology-related careers had higher achievement scores, on the average, in comparison to students who did not select sociology-related careers. This may be seen more clearly from the information reported to two decimal places in Table 6-10. In this table, summary data are presented for the two career groups on the seven achievement-defining variables. Mean differences between groups, expressed in within-group standard deviation units, $(\bar{X}_1 - \bar{X}_2)/\sqrt{MS_W}$, for purposes of across-variable equating, are also included. Comparisons of these standardized differences provide a researcher with a rough idea as to which of the constituent variables are contributing most to group differences on the particular rotated principal component, as long as it can be assumed that all defining variables

TABLE 6-10. Means and standard deviations of each career group on the original X variables that define Y_1^R

Variable	*Group 1 (N = 23)*	*Group 2 (N = 17)*	MS_W	*Difference, in pooled standard deviation units*
X_3	3.47	3.24	0.11	0.67
X_4	565.65	468.24	11052.97	0.93
X_5	0.56	0.18	0.21	0.84
X_6	19.00	16.94	55.50	0.28
X_7	52.48	37.35	184.41	1.11
X_8	66.83	57.53	391.88	0.47
X_9	104.78	92.29	903.56	0.42

have approximately the same weight in absolute value. This assumption is not unreasonable here since Table 6-8 reveals that the weights associated with variables 3–9 range only from .15 to .24. From the data in Table 6-10, we might conclude that the two career groups differed most with respect to X_7: Midterm 1 and X_4: College Board score; they appear to have differed least with respect to X_6: Pretest, X_9: Final score, and X_8: Midterm 2 score. Statistical bases for inferring which of several variables differentiate among two or more groups will be discussed in detail in the remaining chapters. For completeness, we provide directions for obtaining factor scores.

Procedure for obtaining factor scores for principal components.

Step 1. Determine how many components should be retained. Let this number be denoted by Q.

Step 2. Find the structure matrix for these Q components. Denote it by $\mathbf{R}_{XY}$.

Step 3. From the original correlation matrix, determine $\mathbf{R}_{XX}^{-1}$ and obtain the beta weights, $\hat{\boldsymbol{\beta}}$, for a multiple regression model as:

$$\hat{\boldsymbol{\beta}} = \mathbf{R}_{XX}^{-1}\mathbf{R}_{XY}$$

Step 4. Score each subject as:

$$Y_Q^R = \hat{\boldsymbol{\beta}}'\mathbf{X}$$

where $\mathbf{X} = (X_1 \; X_2 \; \ldots \; X_P)$ are in standard score form.

Step 5. Verify that:

$$\bar{Y}_1^R = \bar{Y}_2^R = \cdots = \bar{Y}_Q^R = 0$$

$$S^2_{Y_1^R} = S^2_{Y_2^R} = \cdots = S^2_{Y_Q^R} = 1$$

6-8. Multiple regression based on principal component scores

An interesting and often useful application of principal component scores is to use them as predictor variables for a multiple regression equation (see Kendall, 1961). Actually the material in Section 6-7 could have been discussed in these terms, but it was not. A similar connection will be made in Chapter 7. The best way to describe the model is by means of an example. Suppose we wished to predict final examination scores, Y_C, from the following $P = 9$ independent variables; X_1: Social class, X_2: Sex, X_3: High school grade point average, X_4: College Board score, X_5: Previous high school unit in sociology, X_6: Pretest score, X_7: First midterm score, X_8: Second midterm score, and X_9: Course evaluation. The first step is to perform a principal component analysis on the independent variables. The pattern matrix associated with these variables, based on components with eigen values exceeding 1.00, is reported in Table 6-11. The second step is to determine the beta weights for each of the $Q(\leq P)$ retained components in the regression equation:

$$Y_C = \hat{\beta}_1 Y_1 + \hat{\beta}_2 Y_2 + \cdots + \hat{\beta}_Q Y_Q$$

where the $\hat{\beta}_q$ and Y_q are standardized regression weights and principal component scores, respectively. Since the $Y_1, Y_2, \ldots, Y_Q$ are mutually orthogonal, it is known

TABLE 6-11. Pattern matrix for the unrotated components of Section 6-8

Variable	Y_1	Y_2	Y_3
X_1	0.15	− 0.83	0.24
X_2	0.10	− 0.11	0.67
X_3	0.50	− 0.12	− 0.03
X_4	0.31	0.08	− 0.45
X_5	0.37	− 0.11	0.12
X_6	0.41	− 0.20	0.24
X_7	0.47	0.06	− 0.03
X_8	0.40	0.20	− 0.03
X_9	− 0.03	0.53	0.37
Variance	3.52	1.62	1.10

that all correlations are equal to zero and, as a result, the normal equations for determining the $\hat{\beta}_1, \hat{\beta}_2, \ldots, \hat{\beta}_Q$ are very simple in form. In particular, if all variables are standardized:

$$\hat{\beta}_1 = \frac{S_{Y_1 Y_C}}{S^2_{Y_1}} = \frac{\dfrac{1}{N-1}\sum_{i=1}^{N} Y_{1i} Y_{Ci}}{\dfrac{1}{N-1}\sum_{i=1}^{N} Y^2_{1i}}$$

Since:

$$S^2_{Y_1} = \frac{1}{N-1}\sum_{i=1}^{N} Y^2_{1i} = \lambda_1$$

it follows that:

$$\hat{\beta}_1 = \frac{1}{\lambda_1}\left(\frac{1}{N-1}\sum_{i=1}^{N} Y_{1i} Y_{Ci}\right)$$

$$= \frac{1}{\lambda_1}\left[\frac{1}{N-1}\sum_{i=1}^{N} Y_{Ci}\,(a_1^{(1)} X_{1i} + a_2^{(1)} X_{2i} + \cdots + a_P^{(1)} X_{Pi})\right]$$

$$= \frac{1}{\lambda_1}(a_1^{(1)} r_{Y_C X_1} + a_2^{(1)} r_{Y_C X_2} + \cdots + a_P^{(1)} r_{Y_C X_P})$$

Thus, in general:

$$\hat{\beta}_p = \frac{1}{\lambda_p}(a_1^{(p)} r_{Y_C X_1} + a_2^{(p)} r_{Y_C X_2} + \cdots + a_P^{(p)} r_{Y_C X_P})$$

This means that we can determine the final regression equation in a stepwise fashion by first computing $\hat{\beta}_1$, then $\hat{\beta}_2$, and so on. Because the principal components are orthogonal:

$$\hat{R}^2_{Y_C \cdot X_1 X_2 \ldots X_P} = \hat{\beta}_1^2 \lambda_1 + \hat{\beta}_2^2 \lambda_2 + \cdots + \hat{\beta}_P^2 \lambda_P$$

As a result, the decision to stop can be based on sequential inspections of the increment in $\hat{R}^2$.

For this example, the correlations of Y_C with $X_1, X_2, \ldots, X_P$ are reported in

Table 6-2 as $r_{Y_9X_1} = -.32$, $r_{Y_9X_2} = .09$, $r_{Y_9X_3} = .60$, $r_{Y_9X_4} = .46$, $r_{Y_9X_5} = .39$, $r_{Y_9X_6} = .30$, $r_{Y_9X_7} = .64$, $r_{Y_9X_8} = .58$, and $r_{Y_9X_{10}} = .13$. With these correlations:

$$\begin{aligned}\hat{\beta}_1 &= \frac{1}{3.52}[(-.32)(.15) + (.09)(.10) + (.60)(.50) + (.46)(.31) + (.39)(.37) \\ &\qquad + (.30)(.41) + (.64)(.47) + (.58)(.40) + (.13)(-.03)] \\ &= \frac{1.1998}{3.52} = .3408\end{aligned}$$

so that, in terms of the first principal component, Y_1:

$$\hat{R}^2_{Y_C \cdot Y_1} = (.3408)^2 3.52 = .4090$$

In addition:

$$\begin{aligned}\hat{Y}_C &= \hat{\beta}_1 Y_1 \\ &= (.3408)(.15X_1 + .10X_2 + .50X_3 + .31X_4 + .37X_5 + .41X_6 + .47X_7 \\ &\qquad + .40X_8 + .03X_9) \\ &= .05X_1 + .03X_2 + .17X_3 + .11X_4 + .13X_5 + .14X_6 + .16X_7 + .14X_8 \\ &\qquad - .01X_9\end{aligned}$$

These represent the optimal weights applied to the nine standardized independent variables in order to predict final examination scores.

For the second principal component, Y_2, it follows that:

$$\begin{aligned}\hat{\beta}_2 &= \frac{1}{1.62}[(-.32)(-.83) + (.09)(-.11) + (.60)(-.12) + (.46)(.08) \\ &\qquad + (.39)(-.11) + (.30)(-.20) + (.64)(.06) + (.58)(.20) + (.13)(.53)] \\ &= \frac{.3409}{1.62} = .2104\end{aligned}$$

so that in terms of Y_1 and Y_2:

$$\begin{aligned}\hat{R}^2_{Y_C \cdot Y_1 Y_2} &= .3408^2(3.52) + .2104^2(1.62) \\ &= .4090 + .0717 = .4807\end{aligned}$$

With the addition of Y_2, we have that:

$$\begin{aligned}\hat{Y}_C &= \hat{\beta}_1 Y_1 + \hat{\beta}_2 Y_2 \\ &= .3408(.05X_1 + .03X_2 + .17X_3 + .11X_4 + .13X_5 + .14X_6 + .16X_7 + .14X_8 \\ &\qquad - .01X_9) \\ &\quad + .2104(-.83X_1 - .11X_2 - .12X_3 + .08X_4 - .11X_5 - .20X_6 + .06X_7 \\ &\qquad + .20X_8 + .53X_9) \\ &= -.12X_1 + .01X_2 + .15X_3 + .13X_4 + .11X_5 + .10X_6 + .17X_7 + .18X_8 \\ &\qquad + .10X_9\end{aligned}$$

It should be noted that separate regressions of Y_C on each of the preceding principal components could just as easily have been justified.

For Y_3 we have:

$$\hat{\beta}_3 = \frac{1}{1.10}[(-.32)(.24) + (.09)(.67) + (.60)(-.03) + (.46)(-.45) + (.39)(.12)$$

$$+ (.30)(.24) + (.64)(-.03) + (.58)(-.03) + (.13)(.31)]$$

$$= \frac{-.1112}{1.10} = -.1011$$

so that in terms of Y_1, Y_2, and Y_3:

$$\hat{R}^2_{Y_C \cdot Y_1 Y_2 Y_3} = .3408^2(3.52) + .2104^2(1.62) + (-.1011)^2(1.10)$$
$$= .4909 + .0717 + .0112 = .4919$$

Because the increase in explained variance, from 48% to 49% is negligible, we can ignore Y_3. Thus it appears that the regression equation based on just Y_1 and Y_2 is convenient for present purposes. Note that $\hat{R}^2_{Y_C \cdot X_1 X_2 \ldots X_9} = .5777$. Thus $\hat{R}^2_{Y_C \cdot Y_1 Y_2} = .4807$ captures most of the explained variance.

In terms of the original unstandardized variables, the equation is given by:

$$\hat{Y}_C = -.12\left(\frac{X_1 - 1.98}{.66}\right) + .01\left(\frac{X_2 - .68}{.47}\right) + .15\left(\frac{X_3 - 3.38}{.35}\right)$$
$$+ .13\left(\frac{X_4 - 524.25}{114.67}\right) + .11\left(\frac{X_5 - .40}{.50}\right) + .10\left(\frac{X_6 - 18.20}{7.41}\right)$$
$$+ .17\left(\frac{X_7 - 46.05}{15.40}\right) + .18\left(\frac{X_8 - 57.88}{22.58}\right) + .10\left(\frac{X_9 - 1.95}{1.20}\right)$$

Three interesting final points deserve mention. First, because the varimax-rotated components are also orthogonal, the same model can be applied to the rotated pattern. In most cases, the interpretation based on the rotated solution should be clearer because of its simple structure property. Second, if the regression equation were to involve all P of the principal components, the resulting equation would reduce to the familiar multiple regression equation. In this case, $\hat{R}^2_{Y_C \cdot Y_1 Y_2 \ldots Y_P}$ would be exactly equal to $\hat{R}^2_{Y_C \cdot X_1 X_2 \ldots X_P}$. And third, a potential commendable feature of using these principal component scores as multiple regression predictors is their ability to stand up under cross-validation, as mentioned in Chapter 4. Morris and Guertin (1977) have provided some preliminary evidence to suggest that a subset of Q such composites can perform as well as, and perhaps better than, all P original variables in multiple regression replication samples.

Rather than provide explicit directions in a Procedure box, we suggest that the reader follow the procedures of this section if a regression on principal components is of interest.

6-9. Psychometric factor analysis

Even though factor analysis is based on multivariate data, it must be noted that from a strict psychometric point of view, factor analysis does not belong in a book that focuses on *statistical* multivariate models. Many psychometricians believe that factor analysis belongs only in books dealing with *measurement* theory. We agree with this position, but at the same time feel obliged to provide a cursory description of psychometric factor analysis, since we have used the terminology of this measurement model repeatedly in our discussion of principal components.

As a starting point, we recall that principal components represent geometric abstractions that serve as reference axes for mathematically defined curves such as ellipses. They become a part of statistical theory when they are used to define the axes of a cluster of data points in a multidimensional space of random variables, $X_1, X_2, \ldots, X_P$. In this sense, principal components represent simple geometrical and statistical abstractions or constructs. This is contrary to their counterparts that exist in psychometric factor analysis. In this unique measurement model, factors are conceptualized, not as mathematical and statistical entities, but as real-world human characteristics, such as intelligence, fear, self-concept, locus of control, anxiety, androgyny, verbal ability, musical aptitude, as well as many other psychological variables that cannot be measured in the same direct manner as physical characteristics such as age, weight, height, temperature, and blood pressure.

To help understand what makes psychometric factor analysis different from principal component analysis, assume that a large number of subjects, N, have been given a battery of P paper and pencil tests that are believed to measure intelligence. If indeed intelligence were a unitary human quality and if each of the tests measured intelligence with no errors in the measurement, we would find that all the correlation coefficients of the correlation matrix would be equal to one in value. Unfortunately intelligence may not be unitary in nature, since psychometricians have not been too successful in designing tests that are perfectly correlated with one another. Instead, they are typically correlated in the range of about .5 to .9. This suggests that the commonly used tests of intelligence are measuring characteristics other than *general* intelligence. Certainly error is one of these components.

It is because of these imperfect correlation coefficients between tests of a single unifying characteristic, such as intelligence, that factor analysis was conceived. The goal of factor analysis is to take a hypothetical construct and relate it to a set of tests by determining how much of the variance of the construct contributes to the variance of each of the tests. If most of the variance of the construct is distributed among the tests, a secondary task is to determine weights that can be assigned to the tests so that collectively they can be used as a measure of one or more factors being measured by each of the tests.

Whereas principal component analysis involves a decomposition of the matrix, $\mathbf{R}$, into a diagonal matrix, $\lambda\mathbf{I}$, factor analysis involves a decomposition of a different matrix, $\mathbf{R} - \mathbf{U}$, to be described later, into a nonsquare matrix that ideally has the form:

$$\begin{bmatrix} \lambda_1 & 0 & \ldots & 0 \\ 0 & \lambda_2 & \ldots & 0 \\ \cdot & \cdot & \cdot & \cdot \\ \cdot & \cdot & \cdot & \cdot \\ \cdot & \cdot & \cdot & \cdot \\ 0 & 0 & \ldots & \lambda_{P'} \\ \cdot & \cdot & \cdot & \cdot \\ \cdot & \cdot & \cdot & \cdot \\ \cdot & \cdot & \cdot & \cdot \\ 0 & 0 & \ldots & 0 \end{bmatrix}$$

with P rows and P' columns. More specifically, the $a_1^{(1)}, a_2^{(1)}, \ldots, a_{P'}^{(1)}$ of factor analysis are chosen so that the matrix $\mathbf{A}_1\mathbf{A}_1'$ reproduces $(\mathbf{R} - \mathbf{U})$. Thus, from a stepwise point of view, we determine Y_1 and the matrix $\mathbf{A}_1\mathbf{A}_1'$, and then determine:

$$\mathbf{\Delta}_1 = (\mathbf{R} - \mathbf{U}) - \mathbf{A}_1\mathbf{A}_1'$$

If the elements of $\mathbf{\Delta}_1$ differ from zero, then $\mathbf{A}_2$, usually determined orthogonal to $\mathbf{A}_1$, is found. Then:

$$\mathbf{\Delta}_2 = \mathbf{\Delta}_1 - \mathbf{A}_2\mathbf{A}_2'$$

is examined for elements that differ from zero. This process is continued until:

$$\mathbf{\Delta}_{p-1} - \mathbf{A}_p\mathbf{A}_p' = \mathbf{0}$$

or is as close to $\mathbf{0}$ as possible.

In a sense, this stepwise extraction of factors can be followed in principal component analysis and is indeed the same process, provided we use $\mathbf{R}$ in place of $(\mathbf{R} - \mathbf{U})$. Thus a major difference between factor analysis and principal components is in the nature of $\mathbf{U}$. In principal components, it is assumed that the $X_1, X_2, \ldots, X_P$ are measured without error. Thus the variances in these measures are completely explainable. This was seen in Tables 6-4 and 6-5, where we saw that $\sum a_p^2 \text{Var}(Y_p) = 1.00$ for all X_p. This is not the case in factor analysis since it is assumed that each X_p contains measurement error. This measurement error gives rise to two interrelated problems of factor analysis. They are:

1. The communality problem.
2. The number of factors problem.

We have touched on both of these problems in our presentation of principal component analysis. Let us examine these problems, using the results of our principal component analysis to aid our deliberations.

Consider the variances and cumulative variances of Table 6-4 and Table 6-5. As we see:

$$\lambda_1 = 4.05 = .06 + .01 + .71 + \cdots + .62 + .06$$

We can now evaluate how the variance of Y_1 is shared by each of the observed variables: .06 of the total variance of X_1 comes from Y_1; .01 of the X_2 variance is in common with the Y_1 variance; .71 of the variance of X_3 is explained by Y_1; and so on.

As we see in Table 6-5, Y_1, Y_2, and Y_3 account for 90% of the variance of X_1; 50% of the variance of X_2; 78% of the variance of X_3; and so on. As was mentioned in Section 6-5, these cumulative variances are called *communalities*. Because these are measures of explained, or true variance, factor analysts prefer to use them when extracting factors, rather than using measures that contain both true and error variance. The problem is that the values of these true variances are unknown and so they are estimated from the data. A number of solutions have been proposed for the estimation process.

The first solution is to examine the correlation matrix and identify the largest correlations for each variable. These largest correlations are listed in Table 6-12, along with their squared values. The matrix $\mathbf{U}$ is defined from these values. It is a square matrix with diagonal elements $U_p = 1 -$ maximum r_p^2, and off-diagonal elements of value zero, so that the diagonal elements of (**R** – **U**) are simply the maximum r_p^2. The factor analysis now proceeds on this reduced matrix.

One of the problems with this solution is that some of the individual r^2s may be small, as they are in our example. For the illustration, this is expected since the 10 variables are not measuring a single factor. Because of this, use of maximum r^2 values is rarely encountered.

A second solution is to replace the unities of the **R** matrix by the squared multiple correlation coefficients of each X_p predicted on all of the others, since it is known that $\hat{R}_p^2 >$ maximum r_p^2. These values are listed in Table 6-12 for our example. As can be seen, they are all larger than the maximum r_p^2.

A third solution is to perform a principal component analysis on **R** itself, count the number of eigen values that exceed one, determine the communalities for those specific components, use these communalities to replace the unities of **R**, and extract as many factors as there are principal components used to compute the communalities. For completeness, we have shown what these values are for three and four factors for the example of this chapter. We include communalities for four factors since $\lambda_4 = .99$ is essentially equal to 1.00.

Regardless of which method is used, the remaining factor analytic procedures parallel those described in Sections 6-5, 6-6, 6-7, and 6-8. Since matrix inversion may become impossible because the determinant of $|\mathbf{R} - \mathbf{U}|$ may be close to zero or negative, it may happen that the extraction of factors is not possible. In any case, canned computer programs are required. If the analysis cannot proceed, most programs will so inform the user.

6-10. Simplified statistics for principal component analysis

As is apparent from the material covered in this chapter, principal component analysis is not the kind of thing that we are likely to undertake on our own; that is, without the assistance of an electronic computer. Although the theory behind the procedure is straightforward enough, the associated matrix algebra is sufficiently formidable that it could effectively dissuade us from attempting to conduct a principal component analysis with only a simple calculator at hand. This becomes more and more true as the number of variables in our data set increases from $P = 2$,

TABLE 6-12. Possible measures of communality

			Communalities for	
Variate p	*Maximum* r_p^2	$\hat{R}_p^2$	*3 factor*	*4 factor*
X_1	$-0.52^2 = 0.27$	0.62	0.90	0.93
X_2	$0.29^2 = 0.08$	0.36	0.50	0.94
X_3	$0.72^2 = 0.52$	0.77	0.78	0.79
X_4	$0.57^2 = 0.32$	0.55	0.67	0.81
X_5	$0.51^2 = 0.26$	0.32	0.41	0.54
X_6	$0.55^2 = 0.30$	0.43	0.53	0.66
X_7	$0.72^2 = 0.52$	0.71	0.78	0.78
X_8	$0.68^2 = 0.46$	0.73	0.72	0.77
X_9	$0.64^2 = 0.41$	0.58	0.67	0.68
X_{10}	$-0.52^2 = 0.27$	0.54	0.82	0.85

as in Section 6-3, to a larger number. Fortunately for the researcher, however, alternative techniques exist that enable us to get a feel for the structure of our data without undue labor, expense, or frustration.

Just as was done in the preceding chapters, we will describe here a simple-to-use data reduction procedure that in many cases yields solutions that approximate those obtained according to the more sophisticated principal component and factor analytic methods. As we have cautioned in the past, however, our simplified approach is not meant to supplant the more formal approaches, but rather to give a researcher a quick-and-dirty lay of the land in cases when that is all that is desired. Other advocates of the method to be presented would go even further and, in many cases, prescribe it as an efficient, more interpretable competitor to the other more sophisticated data reduction procedures. Following our discussion of the simplified data reduction procedure, we will mention briefly another simplified approach that can be used to generate scores corresponding to the first unrotated principal component.

Simplified data reduction technique. This is one of a number of *hierarchical clustering* techniques, and the discussion that follows draws heavily from the writings of Hubert and his colleagues. See Hubert and Baker (1976) for a very readable account of this method. The idea behind clustering is one of grouping variables together on the basis of a systematic, a priori, plan or algorithm that is optimal in some sense. We hope that the resulting variable groupings will resemble those represented by the principal components. The algorithm we will apply here is known as the *complete link* method, although many other labels have also been ascribed to the method.

It will become apparent that the most appealing feature of clustering is its simplicity. This refers to both:

1. The kind of input data operated upon, since all that is required in the present context is a correlation matrix.
2. The amount of computational labor involved, since not even a calculator is needed. For up to about seven or eight variables, a solution can be obtained with less than 15 minutes of work.

To illustrate, consider the correlation matrix in Table 6-2, for which a principal component analysis of the 10 constituent variables was previously presented in Tables 6-3 and 6-8.

The complete link clustering algorithm consists of two basic steps. The first is to arrange all $P(P-1)/2$, here 45, correlations according to their sign and magnitude. Variables that are most highly correlated positively are regarded as most similar, and those that are most highly correlated negatively are regarded as least similar. Such an arrangement of the 45 pairs of variables is made in Table 6-13, where it may be seen that variables 3 and 7, High school GPA and First midterm score, are the most similar with $r_{X_3X_7} = .72$, while variables 1 and 10, Social class and Course evaluation, are the least similar with $r_{X_1X_{10}} = -.52$. A useful practical recommendation that will greatly simplify subsequent steps is to list each pair of variables and its associated correlation on a separate 3×5 card. A card can also be used for each of the P variables. The latter cards would be laid out on a table, and the former would be in a stack in order of their similarities. Cards are then sorted and moved in each of the following steps.

TABLE 6-13. Rank-ordered similarities of the 10 variables

Rank	*Variables*	*r*	*Rank*	*Variables*	*r*
1	{3, 7}	0.72	23	{2, 8}	0.22
2	{3, 8}	0.68	24	{7, 10}	0.19
3	{7, 8}	0.67	25	{4, 6}	0.15
4	{7, 9}	0.64	26	{6, 10}	0.14
5	{3, 9}	0.60	27	{9, 10}	0.13
6	{8, 9}	0.58	28	{5, 10}	0.12
7	{4, 8}	0.57	29	{2, 9}	0.0894
8	{6, 7}	0.553	30	{3, 10}	0.0886
9	{4, 7}	0.546	31	{2, 7}	0.086
10	{3, 5}	0.51	32	{1, 3}	0.064
11	{3, 6}	0.469	33	{1, 2}	0.055
12	{3, 4}	0.465	34	{1, 6}	0.04
13	{4, 9}	0.463	35	{2, 5}	0.022
14	{5, 7}	0.45	36	{2, 6}	0.019
15	{6, 8}	0.43	37	{2, 3}	− 0.033
16	{5, 9}	0.39	38	{2, 4}	− 0.035
17	{5, 6}	0.37	39	{1, 5}	− 0.05
18	{5, 8}	0.33	40	{1, 4}	− 0.09
19	{6, 9}	0.30	41	{1, 7}	− 0.16
20	{2, 10}	0.29	42	{4, 10}	− 0.20
21	{8, 10}	0.25	43	{1, 8}	− 0.28
22	{4, 5}	0.23	44	{1, 9}	− 0.32
			45	{1, 10}	− 0.52

The second step of the algorithm involves setting up what is called a *partition hierarchy*, as represented in Table 6-14. This hierarchy contains P levels, with the first level labeled Level 0 and the last labeled Level $P - 1$. As may be seen from Levels 0 and 9 of Table 6-14, these two levels are always composed of trivial partitionings of the input variables, consisting, respectively, of P sets of one variable apiece and one set of all P variables.

Starting at Level 0 with P sets of one variable apiece, we apply the clustering algorithm in a sequential fashion to unite, or link, variables that are most similar, as defined by the similarity rankings of Step 1. The *complete* link aspect of this procedure refers to the fact that two variables (A and B, for instance) cannot be linked, that is, put into the same set, until all other variables linked with A have also been linked with B. This will be illustrated shortly for Level 2 and elsewhere in Table 6-14. First, however, variables 3 and 7 are linked at Level 1 since they are the most similar in that they represent Rank 1 of Table 6-13. Now, according to Table 6-13, the next most similar variables are variables 3 and 8, Rank 2. However, according to the complete link rule, variable 3 now occupies the same set as variable 7, and variable 8 cannot be linked with variable 3 until variable 8 is also linked with variable 7. Fortunately this happens at the next level of the partition hierarchy, Rank 3, at which time it is permissible to form a three-variable set consisting of variables 3, 7, and 8, as indicated by Level 2 of Table 6-14. The same arguments apply to variables 9 and 4, which become completely linked with variables 3, 7, and 8, respectively, by Ranks 6 and 13 of Table 6-14. Next, note that at Level 5 of Table 6-14, variables 5 and 6 are linked to form their own set before any other complete links have been formed with the large set containing variables 3, 4, 7, 8, and 9.

TABLE 6-14. Partition hierarchy associated with the similarities of Table 6-13

Level	*Linking Rank*	*Partition*
0	—	{1}, {2}, {3}, {4}, {5}, {6}, {7}, {8}, {9}, {10}
1	1	{3, 7}, {1}, {2}, {4}, {5}, {6}, {8}, {9}, {10}
2	3	{3, 7, 8}, {1}, {2}, {4}, {5}, {6}, {9}, {10}
3	6	{3, 7, 8, 9}, {1}, {2}, {4}, {5}, {6}, {10}
4	13	{3, 4, 7, 8, 9}, {1}, {2}, {5}, {6}, {10}
5	17	{3, 4, 7, 8, 9}, {5, 6}, {1}, {2}, {10}
6	20	{3, 4, 7, 8, 9}, {5, 6}, {2, 10}, {1}
7	25	{3, 4, 5, 6, 7, 8, 9}, {2, 10}, {1}
8	42	{2, 3, 4, 5, 6, 7, 8, 9, 10}, {1}
9	45	{1, 2, 3, 4, 5, 6, 7, 8, 9, 10}

The algorithm continues according to this complete link rule, as represented in Table 6-14.

What does all this mean? At each partition level, there is a potential solution corresponding to what might have been obtained via a full-blown principal component analysis. The mutually exclusive sets that are formed can be viewed as components, and the elements within a particular set are viewed as the variables that load on that component. For example, at Level 6, three or four components are apparent, depending on whether the single element set consisting of variable 1 is viewed as a component. At Level 7, two or three components are apparent. The partition level selected by a researcher for interpretation can be based on either statistical criteria, substantive criteria, or both. A statistical basis for deciding which partition level is best is given by Hubert and Baker (1976), and this will not be discussed here. Rather, we consider the substantive basis for arriving at a reasonable solution.

Such considerations lead us directly to a reasonable choice between the Level 6 and Level 7 partitions. First, let us consider the Level 7 partition. It is important to note that this duplicates almost exactly the rotated three-factor solution of Table 6-7. Note that variables 3–9 all load on the previously termed scholastic achievement first component; variables 2 and 10 are the primary definers of the previously unclear third component; and variable 1 is the predominant contributor to the previously termed social class identification second component. Level 6 of the partition hierarchy is in essential agreement with this breakdown, with the extraction of a fourth component from the first. In this partition, variables 5 and 6, Previous unit in sociology and Pretest score, respectively, define a potentially interesting and substantively meaningful component apart from scholastic achievement, as defined by variables 3, 4, 7, 8, and 9. This appears to reflect *readiness* for the sociology course, which might be viewed by some as an important construct in and of itself.

Thus, although perhaps not as precise as principal component analysis, clustering is an easy-to-employ procedure that will frequently yield solutions quite similar to those obtained by the 'real thing.' In many cases, the amount of time saved by clustering is well worth the potential loss in precision. It should be noted, however, that with this procedure, only the relative, rather than absolute, magnitudes of the correlations are examined. This means that even with very weakly correlated variables, solutions will be obtained. This is clearly a drawback of clustering and is analogous to interpreting components with eigen values less than 1.00.

Procedure for performing a cluster analysis, according to the complete link procedure.

Step 1. List each pair of variables and the associated correlations on 3 × 5 cards. Also, list the P variables on cards.

Step 2. Stack the first set of cards in order of similarity, that is, from the highest to the lowest correlation. Lay out the second set of cards on a table.

Step 3. Sort the cards into piles according to the algorithm described in the text. Basically this consists of linking variables that are most similar, as defined by higher correlations. Each time a card on the table is linked with another card on the table, record this as a level of the partition hierarchy, as recorded in Table 6-14.

Step 4. When all cards on the table have been sorted, examine the nontrivial $P - 2$ levels of the partition hierarchy to obtain a substantively meaningful solution, or rely on more formal statistical criteria as described by Hubert and Baker (1976).

Simplified principal component scores. As was discussed in the context of multiple regression and canonical correlation analysis, a simplified linear combination of variables can be effected by selecting $Q(\leq P)$ variables and then standardizing, reflecting, and summing them. These procedures will not be detailed here, since they closely parallel what was done for the within-set correlations in canonical correlation analysis shown in Steps 2, 3, and 5 in the procedural description of Section 5-10. Thus the reflected z scores for all P, or all Q moderately intercorrelated, variables could be summed. This resulting Z score composite could then be used as a dependent variable for analyses involving between-group comparisons, such as that presented in Section 6-7. This Z score composite approximates the scores on the first unrotated principal component.

6-11. Summary

In this chapter, a description of principal component analysis was presented. It was pointed out that the main use of principal components is to take a set of P interdependent variables and reduce it to a smaller set $Q < P$, where, for each $q = 1, 2, \ldots, Q$:

$$Y_q = a_1^{(q)}X_1 + a_2^{(q)}X_2 + \cdots + a_P^{(q)}X_P$$

and where:

$$r_{Y_qY_{q'}} = 0 \text{ for } q \neq q'$$

and where:

$$\text{Var}(Y_1) \geq \text{Var}(Y_2) \geq \cdots \geq \text{Var}(Y_Q) > 1$$

and where:

$$\text{Var}(Y_1) + \text{Var}(Y_2) + \cdots + \text{Var}(Y_Q)$$

is as close in numerical value to P as is possible to attain with the data.

In practice, the $Y_1, Y_2, \ldots, Y_Q$ are defined by solving the following characteristic equation:

$$|\mathbf{R}_{XX} - \lambda \mathbf{I}| = 0$$

and then finding the $\mathbf{A}_p$ as solutions to the set of homogeneous equations:

$$(\mathbf{R}_{XX} - \lambda_p \mathbf{I})\,\mathbf{A}'_p = 0$$

In terms of this solution:

$$\text{Var}(Y_p) = \mathbf{A}'_p\,\mathbf{R}_{XX}\,\mathbf{A}_p = \lambda_p$$

If P is large, each Y_p has a probability distribution that is approximately normal in form with:

$$\bar{Y}_p = \mathbf{A}'_p\,\bar{\mathbf{X}}_p$$

$$\text{Var}(Y_p) = \lambda_p$$

In addition, the amount of the total variance in the set $X_1, X_2, \ldots, X_P$ that can be attributed to Y_p is given by $(1/P)\,\lambda_p$.

An unusual property of principal components is that if all P principal components are used, it is possible to reproduce the original X variates through the simple transformation:

$$\mathbf{X} = \mathbf{A}'\,\mathbf{Y}$$

Thus, for example, if:

$$\begin{bmatrix} Y_1 \\ Y_2 \\ Y_3 \end{bmatrix} = \begin{bmatrix} a_1^{(1)} & a_1^{(2)} & a_1^{(3)} \\ a_2^{(1)} & a_2^{(2)} & a_2^{(3)} \\ a_3^{(1)} & a_3^{(2)} & a_3^{(3)} \end{bmatrix} \begin{bmatrix} X_1 \\ X_2 \\ X_3 \end{bmatrix}$$

then:

$$\begin{bmatrix} X_1 \\ X_2 \\ X_3 \end{bmatrix} = \begin{bmatrix} a_1^{(1)} & a_2^{(1)} & a_3^{(1)} \\ a_1^{(2)} & a_2^{(2)} & a_3^{(2)} \\ a_1^{(3)} & a_2^{(3)} & a_3^{(3)} \end{bmatrix} \begin{bmatrix} Y_1 \\ Y_2 \\ Y_3 \end{bmatrix}$$

An important outcome of this property is that:

$$\begin{aligned} \text{Var}(X_p) &= \sum_{p=1}^{P} a_p^{(p)^2}\text{Var}(Y_p) \\ &= a_p^{(1)^2}\lambda_1 + a_p^{(2)^2}\lambda_2 + \cdots + a_p^{(P)^2}\lambda_P \\ &= 1 \end{aligned}$$

so that:

$$a_p^{(p)^2}\lambda_p$$

represents the proportion of the variance of X_p that is assigned to Y_p. The quantities:

$$a_p^{(1)^2}\lambda_1,\quad a_p^{(1)^2}\lambda_1 + a_p^{(2)^2}\lambda_2,\quad a_p^{(1)^2}\lambda_1 + a_p^{(2)^2}\lambda_2 + a_p^{(3)^2}\lambda_3, \ldots$$

are termed communalities. They refer to the amount of variance in Y_p that is attributed to the original observed variables. They play a very important role in psychometric factor analysis as described briefly in Section 6-9.

The distribution of the Var(X_p) to the Y_p variables is a basic property of principal components. The first principal component is the one that takes up the largest part of the total variance in the set of X variables. Y_1 picks up the largest share of the variance by extracting the maximum possible from each X variable that is associated with Y_1. From the remaining variance in each X, Y_2 is then defined through the extraction of the maximum variance possible in each X that is associated with Y_2. The process terminates in the residual variance going to Y_P.

Since the goal of principal component analysis is to reduce P variables to Q, where $Q < P$, we are faced with the problem of deciding on the value of Q. A number of solutions have been proposed. One solution is to extract components until a predetermined percentage of the total variance, $\lambda_1 + \lambda_2 + \cdots + \lambda_P = P$ is attained. One disadvantage of this procedure is that we might extract components whose variance is less than one, the variance of each of the standardized variables in the original $\mathbf{R}_{XX}$ matrix. Kaiser suggested that only components with $\lambda_p > 1$ be retained. This suggestion is generally referred to as Kaiser's rule and is the procedure in greatest use today. It is one we recommend. It is simple, and it is based on the rational argument that each component should explain more variance than each of the original variables.

Many researchers like to name principal components that are retained. One way to simplify the naming process is to determine the correlation between each X_p and the Y_q to be named. The correlations are given simply as:

$$r_{X_p Y_q} = a_p^{(q)} \sqrt{\lambda_q}$$

These correlations are called *structure* coefficients and should be distinguished from the $a_p^{(q)}$ values which are called *pattern* coefficients. In principal components, the correlations are proportional to the coefficients. This is not always true for psychometric factor analysis.

In most situations, the naming of principal components is unsuccessful since the Y_q are really mathematical constructs and not psychometrically meaningful variables. To overcome this problem, many researchers rotate the axes so as to produce a set of Y_q^R variables that are said to have simple structure. According to Guilford, simple structure means that:

1. Each row of the rotated component matrix should have at least one zero.
2. Each column of the rotated component matrix should have at least Q zeros.
3. For every pair of columns in the rotated component matrix, there should be a number of rows having zeros in one column matched with nonzeros in the other.
4. For every pair of columns, there should be a number of pairs of zero loadings.
5. For every pair of columns, there should be very few pairs of loadings of substantial size.

A number of procedures have been proposed to achieve simple structure. The method in greatest use today is Kaiser's varimax rotation. This method of rotation is based on the criterion of maximizing the variance of the loadings for each component. In general, it seems to complete the task quite effectively and is, therefore, recommended. An interesting property of varimax rotated components is that the variance of the unrotated components is distributed more equally across the rotated components. Thus the variance of $\lambda_1^R, \lambda_2^R, \ldots, \lambda_Q^R$ is less than the variance of $\lambda_1, \lambda_2, \ldots, \lambda_Q$.

Unrotated principal component scores can be used as independent or dependent variables in both univariate or multivariate contexts because of their normal distribution form. Rotated factors cannot be used directly because the loadings are not weighting factors. To obtain the correct values, a multiple regression analysis is applied to the standard scores to obtain:

$$\hat{\beta} = \mathbf{R}_{XX}^{-1}\mathbf{R}_{XY}$$

where $\mathbf{R}_{XX}^{-1}$ is the inverse of the correlation matrix and where $\mathbf{R}_{XY}$ is the matrix of rotated structure loadings.

Finally, this chapter closed with a brief discussion of three specialized topics. They are:

1. Regression on principal components.
2. Hierarchical clustering.
3. Factor analysis.

Regression on principal components is a useful, interpretable data-reduction procedure, being based on the creation of a small uncorrelated set of prediction variables. Hierarchical cluster analysis is an alternative to principal components, based on a simple procedure for grouping together similar variables. Factor analysis is a psychometric model about the latent nature of observable variables. Its main difference from principal component analysis is that it is based on using the best estimate we have about the true variance contained in the X set of variables about the Y set.

6-12. Exercises

6-1. Find the principal axes for:

$$\hat{\Sigma}_{XX} = \begin{bmatrix} 256 & 64 \\ 64 & 100 \end{bmatrix}$$

if $\bar{X}_1 = 100$ and $\bar{X}_2 = 50$.

6-2. Using the data of Exercise 6-1, draw the five concentric ellipses for $C_Y = 1$, 1.645, 1.96, 2.58, and 3. Note that approximately two-thirds of the distribution is contained in the ellipse defined by $C_Y = 1$.

6-3. Find the inverse of:

$$\begin{bmatrix} S_{X_1} & rS_{X_1}S_{X_2} \\ rS_{X_1}S_{X_2} & S_{X_2} \end{bmatrix}$$

and show that:

$$a_{11} = \frac{1}{S_{X_1}^2(1 - r^2)}$$

$$a_{12} = a_{21} = \frac{-r}{S_{X_1}S_{X_2}(1 - r^2)}$$

$$a_{22} = \frac{1}{S_{X_2}^2(1 - r^2)}$$

where:

$$\frac{(X_1 - \bar{X}_1)^2}{a_{11}} + \frac{2(X_1 - \bar{X}_1)(X_2 - \bar{X}_2)}{a_{12}} + \frac{(X_2 - \bar{X}_2)^2}{a_{22}} = 1$$

***6-4.** Find the principal components of your sample of 40 subjects.

***6-5.** For the data of Exercise 6-4, examine the pattern and structure matrices for the components with eigen values greater than 1.00. How well do your results agree with those in the text?

***6-6.** Rotate your principal components with eigen values greater than 1.00 to simple structure using a varimax rotation. Compare the rotated components to the unrotated components of Exercise 6-5. Which set seems to make more sense?

***6-7.** Find the factor scores for your rotated components generated in Exercise 6-6. Compare:
1. The two career groups.
2. The majors categorized as:
   a. Natural Science
   b. Social Science
   c. Humanities
   d. Other

***6-8.** Let the two midterms in your sample of 40 students serve as predictor variables, and submit them to a principal component analysis. Let the final exam serve as a criterion variable. Carry out a regression on principal components. Compare your results to those of Exercises 4-9 and 4-13. What do you observe? Explain what has happened.

6-9. Apply the method of Section 6-9 to your sample of 40 subjects. Compare the results to those of Exercises 6-4 and 6-6.

6-10. Perform a principal component analysis with varimax rotation on
a. 2nd year medical students
b. 3rd year medical students
c. 4th year medical students
on the six Y variables of Exercise 5-7. Compare the three sets of results.

6-11. Score the 2nd year students on the first rotated principal component and test for differences among social class groups.

CHAPTER SEVEN

TWO-GROUP LINEAR DISCRIMINANT ANALYSIS

7-1. What is discriminant analysis?

> 'Why Me?' That's the first question often asked by taxpayers when they are informed by the Internal Revenue Service that their tax returns are being audited . . . The IRS audited more than 2 million of the 83 million individual returns filed in 1976 in two ways: manually and by a sophisticated and somewhat mysterious computer technique known as Discriminant Function, or DIF . . . For its part, DIF produces a composite score for each return on computer tapes and pinpoints those that show significant variations from the norm. Certain data profiles that are far out of line are thereby brought to the attention of audit managers for follow-through. (Sloane, 1977).

This excerpt from a popular news weekly captures the essence of discriminant analysis, that is, to determine which of two or more groups a given individual should be assigned to, based on a linear composite of P input variables. In terms of the preceding two-group problem, an overly high composite score would cause the Internal Revenue Service to have the individual assigned to an 'audit' group, whereas any score below the specified cutoff composite would cause the IRS to have the individual assigned to a 'no-audit' group. Procedures for determining composite scores and points where cutoffs should be made, will be discussed in this chapter.

It should also be mentioned that two-group linear discriminant analysis is merely a special case of multiple linear regression. In particular, with discriminant analysis, the purpose is to predict which of *K discrete groups* an individual belongs to, rather than to predict an individual's *score* on some continuous variable Y. As stated in Section 5-9, multiple regression is subsumed by canonical correlation, where the number of variables predicted need not be just one. Like the previously discussed regression procedures, discriminant analysis may also be regarded as serving two primary functions. The first is a *forecasting function*, where the objective is to predict accurately the group membership for individuals not included in the original equation-determining sample. In the tax audit problem, equations and cutoffs are determined on the basis of prior tax returns of honest tax payers and those of known tax evaders and then are applied to subsequent returns. It is, thus, hoped that what has happened before will accurately predict what will happen again with regard to the kind of tax returns associated with known and assumed tax evaders. The second use of discriminant analysis is an *evaluative function* which addresses the question of how well the equation fits the data from which it was derived. In this sense, estimated and observed results can be compared to determine the accuracy of the equation, in a manner similar to that of determining R^2 and goodness of fit in regression models.

The relationship between multiple regression and two-group discriminant analysis is considered explicitly in the following section.

7-2. Linear prediction of a dichotomous variable

When multiple regression was introduced and described, we purposely avoided the question of the measurement nature of Y, the dependent variable. Frequently it is reported that Y should be a continuous variable and, in some cases, it is often explicitly stated that Y must have a normal distribution. Such heavy restrictions are not necessary, provided that we only want to estimate $\beta_1, \beta_2, \ldots, \beta_P, \sigma^2_{Y \cdot X_1 X_2 \ldots X_P}$, and $R^2_{Y \cdot X_1 X_2 \ldots X_P}$. In theory, normality is required for tests of H_0: $\beta_p = 0$ and H_0: $R^2_{Y \cdot X_1 X_2 \ldots X_P} = 0$. Otherwise it is not needed. In particular, if the number of independent variables P is large (and N is much larger still, as required for all the multivariate procedures discussed in this book), normality of Y ceases to be of importance, since the sampling distribution of $\hat{Y}$, the predicted values, approaches a normal form as a result of the Central Limit Theorem. This last characteristic is easy to demonstrate, as will be seen in the following example.

For the example, consider the 40 students taking the beginning class in sociology. As was indicated previously, some of these students, $N_1 = 23$, ended up in a sociology-related career and others, $N_2 = 17$, did not. Suppose we attempted to predict the nature of each student's career by quantifying it as:

$$Y = \begin{cases} 1, & \text{if student selects a sociology-related career} \\ 2, & \text{if student selects a nonsociology-related career} \end{cases}$$

With Y as a dependent variable, let its prediction be based on the 10 independent variables:

X_1: Social class
X_2: Sex
X_3: High school grade point average
X_4: College Board scores
X_5: Previous high school unit in sociology
X_6: Pretest score
X_7: Midterm 1
X_8: Midterm 2
X_9: Final examination
X_{10}: Course evaluation

The results of the regression analysis are summarized in Table 7-1. Let $\hat{p}$ represent the proportion of students selecting a sociology-related career and let $\hat{q} = 1 - \hat{p}$

TABLE 7-1. Multiple regression analysis for the example of Section 7-2

Analysis of variance table

Source	*d/f*	*Sum of squares*	*Mean square*	*F*	*Explained variance*
Regression	10	4.4881	0.44881	2.4618	0.4591
Residual	29	5.2869	0.18231		
Total	39	9.7750			

Summary statistics

	Variable	B_p	SE_{B_p}
X_1:	Social class	− 0.11910	0.16867
X_2:	Sex	0.23020	0.18071
X_3:	High school grade point average	0.37457	0.40210
X_4:	College Board	− 0.00079	0.00089
X_5:	High school sociology unit	− 0.33513	0.16663
X_6:	Pretest	0.01599	0.01217
X_7:	Midterm 1	− 0.02322	0.00826
X_8:	Midterm 2	− 0.00084	0.00656
X_9:	Final	0.00300	0.00347
X_{10}:	Evaluation	0.01921	0.08411
	Constant (B_0)	1.28344	0.97558

represent the proportion of students selecting a nonsociology-related career. Since Y is binomially distributed, we note that the total sum of squares associated with Y is given by $N\hat{p}\hat{q} = 40(23/40)(17/40) = 9.775$. Of the total sum of squares, $SS_{\text{reg}} = 4.4881$. As can be seen, $\hat{R}^2_{Y \cdot X_1 X_2 \ldots X_{10}} = .4591$, and its associated regression equation is statistically significant since $F = 2.46$ is larger than $F_{10,29:.95} = 2.17$. Using the individual beta weights also given in Table 7-1, we could proceed to determine each student's composite score in terms of the best-fitting linear regression equation. The results are reported in Table 7-2 and graphed in Figure 7-1 in terms of career groups.

The mean predicted score for the $N_1 = 23$ subjects in sociology-related careers is equal to $\bar{\hat{Y}} = 1.23$, a number larger than the observed mean of $\bar{Y} = 1.00$. The mean predicted score for the $N_2 = 17$ subjects in nonsociology-related careers is equal to $\bar{\hat{Y}} = 1.69$, a number smaller than the observed mean of $\bar{Y} = 2.00$. As an aside, we note that this provides an interesting example of regression to the mean. In this case, the mean of all Y scores is given by $\bar{Y} = (1/23)(1) + (1/17)(2) = 1.425$. However, since $r_{\hat{Y}Y} = \sqrt{.4591} = .6776 \neq 1.00$, each predicted score is regressed away from its observed value of either 1 or 2, and toward the grand mean of 1.425. In fact, it turns out that:

TABLE 7-2. Estimated regression scores for students selecting the two career types

Student Number	*Sociology-related careers*	*Student Number*	*Nonsociology-related careers*
004	1.2984	003	1.9494
010	1.7554	014	1.8441
018	1.3537	040	1.6496
020	1.3743	052	1.4334
032	1.4025	072	1.7594
050	0.9418	080	1.9032
055	0.9770	117	1.8565
070	1.2432	118	1.5233
076	1.6692	143	1.5122
083	0.9912	150	1.9750
089	0.9351	174	1.5362
091	1.1684	188	1.1660
103	1.0125	196	1.5314
104	1.6159	199	1.6649
106	1.2370	207	1.8732
108	1.5206	208	1.5855
128	0.9389	211	1.9497
166	0.9268		
171	0.7153		
179	1.3092		
183	1.1554		
193	1.3227		
195	1.4224		
Sample size	23		17
Mean	1.2299		1.6890
Variance	0.0734		0.0508
Standard deviation	0.2709		0.2254

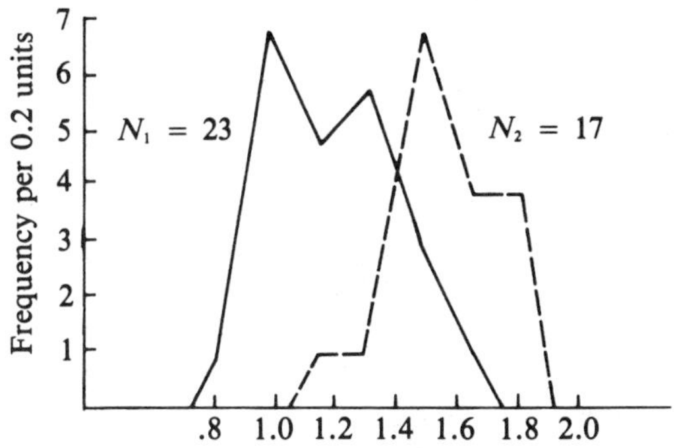

Figure 7-1. Distribution of L for the two career groups.

$$\bar{\hat{Y}}_1 = r^2_{\hat{Y}Y}\bar{Y}_1 + (1 - r^2_{\hat{Y}Y})\bar{Y}$$
$$= .4591(1) + .5409(1.425) = 1.2299 \simeq 1.23 \quad \text{and}$$
$$\bar{\hat{Y}}_2 = r^2_{\hat{Y}Y}\bar{Y}_2 + (1 - r^2_{\hat{Y}Y})\bar{Y}$$
$$= .4591(2) + .5409(1.425) = 1.6890 \simeq 1.69$$

The important point, however, is that the distributions of $\hat{Y}$ for Career Groups 1 and 2 are essentially bell shaped and separated from one another. They possess little overlap. This is reflected also in the test of hypothesis, for the predicted scores:

$$\text{H}_0\text{: } \mu_1 = \mu_2 \qquad \text{versus} \qquad \text{H}_1\text{: } \mu_1 \neq \mu_2$$

Since the value of the pooled variance is given by:

$$S_p^2 = \frac{(N_1 - 1)S_1^2 + (N_2 - 1)S_2^2}{(N_1 - 1) + (N_2 - 1)}$$
$$= \frac{(23 - 1)(.0734) + (17 - 1)(.0503)}{(23 - 1) + (17 - 1)} = .0639$$

it follows that:

$$t = \frac{\bar{\hat{Y}}_1 - \bar{\hat{Y}}_2}{\sqrt{\dfrac{S_p^2}{N_1} + \dfrac{S_p^2}{N_2}}} = \frac{1.2299 - 1.6890}{\sqrt{\dfrac{.0639}{23} + \dfrac{.0639}{17}}} = \frac{-.4591}{.0808} = -5.68$$

so that the hypothesis of equal mean values for the predicted values is rejected at $\alpha = .05$.

We can estimate the strength of association for the two-sample t test by computing the sample point biserial correlation coefficient. For this model, the point biserial correlation coefficient is a familiar Pearson product correlation measure where the dependent variable is dichotomous and the independent variable is quantitative. As was shown in Section 6-7, the point biserial correlation coefficient r_{pb} is related to the t distribution as:

$$t = \frac{r_{pb}\sqrt{N - 2}}{\sqrt{1 - r_{pb}^2}}$$

It follows that:

$$r^2_{pb} = \frac{t^2}{(N-2)+t^2}$$

For these data:

$$r^2_{pb} = \frac{-5.68^2}{(40-2)+(-5.68)^2} = \frac{32.2624}{70.2624} = .4592$$

which is identical, within rounding errors, to the value of $\hat{R}^2_{Y \cdot X_1 X_2 \ldots X_{10}}$ reported in Table 7-1. The value of the point biserial correlation coefficient is given by:

$$r_{pb} = \sqrt{.4592} = .6776 = \hat{R}_{Y \cdot X_1 X_2 \ldots X_{10}}$$

This analysis has shown that $\hat{R}_{Y \cdot X_1 X_2 \ldots X_{10}}$ has a simple interpretation if Y is a dichotomous variable. It is the simple point biserial correlation coefficient between Y and the predicted $\hat{Y}$ values and agrees with the finding of Section 1-10, namely that $r_{XY} = r_{\hat{Y}Y}$. As we will see, these same notions extend to the K-group discriminant analysis problem. In that case, the obtained correlation coefficient follows from our previous discussion of canonical correlation in Chapter 5.

7-3. Fisher's discriminant function

The object of two-group discriminant analysis is to create a linear combination $\hat{Y}$ that maximizes the distance between the centers of the two populations under consideration. This was the approach taken by Sir R. A. Fisher (1936) and discussed here. For the K-group discrimination problem, more than one linear combination must be created, as will be described in Chapter 8.

The geometry for the two-group, two-variable model is shown in Figure 7-2. Y_1 is the combination producing maximum discrimination, whereas Y_2 provides the minimum. Note that Y_1 is parallel to the line joining the centroids of each distribution.

Let us now return to the two-group, P-variable model. We begin by considering P interdependent variables, $X_1, X_2, \ldots, X_P$, which we wish to pool together to form a linear combination:

$$L = a_1 X_1 + a_2 X_2 + \cdots + a_P X_P = \mathbf{A}'\mathbf{X}$$

Consider two groups of subjects, N_1 and N_2, whose expected values are denoted by the vectors:

$$\boldsymbol{\mu}_1' = [\mu_{11} \quad \mu_{12} \quad \cdots \quad \mu_{1P}] \quad \text{and}$$

$$\boldsymbol{\mu}_2' = [\mu_{21} \quad \mu_{22} \quad \cdots \quad \mu_{2P}]$$

and are estimated as:

$$\bar{\mathbf{X}}_1' = [\bar{X}_{11} \quad \bar{X}_{12} \quad \cdots \quad \bar{X}_{1P}] \quad \text{and}$$

$$\bar{\mathbf{X}}_2' = [\bar{X}_{21} \quad \bar{X}_{22} \quad \cdots \quad \bar{X}_{2P}]$$

with the grand mean given by:

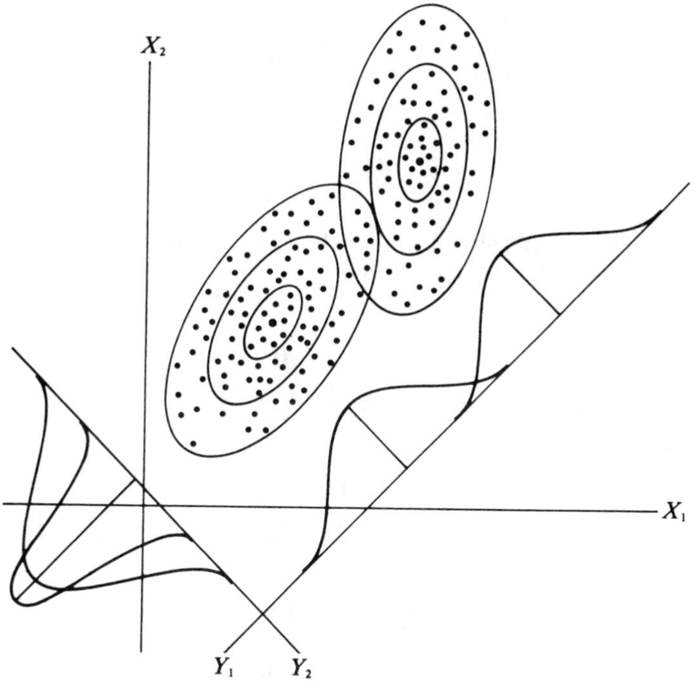

Figure 7-2. Possible Y_1 scales determined from $Y = a_1X_1 + a_2X_2$ showing various degrees of separation of subjects, with Y_1 representing the maximum discrimination and Y_2 the minimum.

$$\bar{\mathbf{X}}' = [\bar{X}_{\cdot 1} \quad \bar{X}_{\cdot 2} \quad \cdots \quad \bar{X}_{\cdot P}]$$

In terms of these estimates, the mean values for the two groups are given by:

$$\bar{L}_1 = a_1\bar{X}_{11} + a_2\bar{X}_{12} + \cdots + a_P\bar{X}_{1P} = \mathbf{A}'\bar{\mathbf{X}}_1 \quad \text{and}$$

$$\bar{L}_2 = a_1\bar{X}_{21} + a_2\bar{X}_{22} + \cdots + a_P\bar{X}_{2P} = \mathbf{A}'\bar{\mathbf{X}}_2$$

with the grand mean given by:

$$\bar{L} = a_1\bar{X}_{\cdot 1} + a_2\bar{X}_{\cdot 2} + \cdots + a_P\bar{X}_{\cdot P} = \mathbf{A}'\bar{\mathbf{X}}$$

The difference in the mean values is given by:

$$\begin{aligned}\bar{L}_1 - \bar{L}_2 &= \mathbf{A}'\bar{X}_1 - \mathbf{A}'\bar{X}_2 \\ &= a_1(\bar{X}_{11} - \bar{X}_{21}) + a_2(\bar{X}_{12} - \bar{X}_{22}) + \cdots + a_P(\bar{X}_{1P} - \bar{X}_{2P}) \\ &= \mathbf{A}'(\bar{\mathbf{X}}_1 - \bar{\mathbf{X}}_2)\end{aligned}$$

The variance of $\bar{L}_1 - \bar{L}_2$ is equal to:

$$\begin{aligned}\text{Var}(\bar{L}_1 - \bar{L}_2) &= \text{Var}(\mathbf{A}'\bar{\mathbf{X}}_1) + \text{Var}(\mathbf{A}'\bar{\mathbf{X}}_2) \\ &= \mathbf{A}'\frac{\Sigma_1}{N_1}\mathbf{A} + \mathbf{A}'\frac{\Sigma_2}{N_2}\mathbf{A}\end{aligned}$$

where $\mathbf{\Sigma}_1$ and $\mathbf{\Sigma}_2$ are the variance-covariance matrices for the two populations. If we now assume that:

$$\Sigma_1 = \Sigma_2 = \Sigma_{XX}$$

then:

$$\text{Var}(\bar{L}_1 - \bar{L}_2) = \mathbf{A}'\Sigma_{XX}\mathbf{A}\left(\frac{1}{N_1} + \frac{1}{N_2}\right)$$

Since $\mathbf{\Sigma}$ is, in general, unknown, it can be estimated from the data as $\hat{\mathbf{\Sigma}}_{XX}$ where the diagonal elements are defined by:

$$MS_{W_p} = \frac{(N_1 - 1)S_{1p}^2 + (N_2 - 1)S_{2p}^2}{(N_1 - 1) + (N_2 - 1)}$$

and the off-diagonal elements are defined by:

$$MS_{W_{pp'}} = \frac{(N_1 - 1)r_{1pp'}S_{1p}S_{1p'} + (N_2 - 1)r_{2pp'}S_{2p}S_{2p'}}{(N_1 - 1) + (N_2 - 1)}$$

With these estimates, $\text{Var}(\bar{L}_1 - \bar{L}_2)$ is estimated as:

$$SE^2_{\bar{L}_1 - \bar{L}_2} = \mathbf{A}'\hat{\Sigma}_{XX}\mathbf{A}\left(\frac{1}{N_1} + \frac{1}{N_2}\right) = \mathbf{A}'(\mathbf{MS}_W)\mathbf{A}\left(\frac{1}{N_1} + \frac{1}{N_2}\right)$$

Under this model, the square of the two-sample t test statistic is given by:

$$t^2 = \frac{(\bar{L}_1 - \bar{L}_2)^2}{SE^2_{\bar{L}_1 - \bar{L}_2}} = \frac{\mathbf{A}'(\bar{\mathbf{X}}_1 - \bar{\mathbf{X}}_2)'(\bar{\mathbf{X}}_1 - \bar{\mathbf{X}}_2)\mathbf{A}}{\mathbf{A}'\hat{\Sigma}_{XX}\mathbf{A}\left(\frac{1}{N_1} + \frac{1}{N_2}\right)}$$

To achieve maximum separation between the two sample distributions, we wish to maximize the difference, $\bar{L}_1 - \bar{L}_2$. As we see, maximizing $\bar{L}_1 - \bar{L}_2$ is identical to maximizing t^2, but R. A. Fisher was able to show there is no unique solution to the problem. However, there exists an infinite set of solutions, all of which are proportional to the *classical* solution:

$$\mathbf{A} = \hat{\Sigma}_{XX}^{-1}(\bar{\mathbf{X}}_1 - \bar{\mathbf{X}}_2)$$

For this reason, not all canned computer programs generate the same coefficients. However, this is of no major importance since the solutions are proportional. Nonetheless, knowledge of each particular computer program's estimation procedure is needed to avoid errors in interpretation. Thus it is important to read computer program manuals carefully to determine exactly what estimation procedures are being used. It is important that the reader know that none of the programs used here and later summarized in Table 7-5 provide the values defined by the R. A. Fisher model. Thus the reader should not attempt to show that any of the solutions of Table 7-5 can be reproduced as $\mathbf{A} = \hat{\mathbf{\Sigma}}_{XX}^{-1}(\bar{\mathbf{X}}_1 - \bar{\mathbf{X}}_2)$.

For the 40 students employed in the regression model of Section 7-2, the basic matrices are as reported in Tables 7-3 and 7-4. These tables contain the vector $(\bar{\mathbf{X}}_1 - \bar{\mathbf{X}}_2)$ and the matrix $\hat{\mathbf{\Sigma}}_{XX}$ which are used to estimate the $\mathbf{A}$ values. The last column of Table 7-3 will be discussed in Section 7-7. For these data, the equation of

TABLE 7-3. Sample means and standard deviations for the two career groups

Variable	*Sociology-related careers*		*Nonsociology-related careers*					
	Mean	*S.D.*	*Mean*	*S.D.*	$\sqrt{MS_T}$	$\sqrt{MS_W}$	$(\bar{X}_1 - \bar{X}_2)$	*D*
X_1	2.0000	0.6030	1.9412	0.7475	0.6597	0.6677	0.0588	0.0881
X_2	0.6087	0.4990	0.7647	0.4372	0.4743	0.4740	− 0.1560	− 0.3291
X_3	3.4722	0.3299	3.2453	0.3506	0.3532	0.3388	0.2269	0.6697
X_4	565.6522	109.3712	468.2353	99.0098	114.6653	105.1330	97.4169	0.9266
X_5	0.5652	0.5069	0.1765	0.3930	0.4961	0.4623	0.3887	0.8408
X_6	19.0000	8.0735	16.9412	6.4949	7.4255	7.4497	2.0588	0.2764
X_7	52.4783	14.1128	37.3529	12.8108	15.3956	13.5798	15.1254	1.1138
X_8	66.8261	20.7203	57.5294	18.4497	20.0872	19.7960	9.2967	0.4697
X_9	104.7826	30.4496	92.2941	29.5143	30.3230	30.0593	12.4885	0.4155
X_{10}	1.8261	1.0292	2.1176	1.4090	1.1972	1.2038	− 0.2915	− 0.2421

TABLE 7-4. Within-sample variance-covariance matrix

Variable	X_1	X_2	X_3	X_4	X_5	X_6	X_7	X_8	X_9	X_{10}
X_1	0.4458	0.0201	0.0120	− 8.4675	− 0.0217	0.1563	− 1.9121	− 4.0124	− 6.7818	− 0.4180
X_2		0.2247	0.0034	1.9425	0.0209	0.1517	1.2557	2.5146	1.8216	0.1554
X_3			0.1148	13.6584	0.0696	1.1431	3.1412	4.4225	5.8167	0.0555
X_4				11052.9666	3.4686	77.0592	610.7485	1111.8016	1338.6104	− 20.3644
X_5					0.2138	1.1888	1.9926	2.4386	4.7087	0.1038
X_6						55.4985	56.8775	61.4084	61.7445	1.4241
X_7							184.4112	176.8612	260.1483	4.7159
X_8								391.8828	335.7234	6.8484
X_9									903.5647	5.7510
X_{10}										1.4492

TABLE 7-5. The discriminant function for predicting career groups

	X_1	X_2	X_3	X_4	X_5	X_6	X_7	X_8	X_9	X_{10}
Raw score weights with $S_p^2 = 1.00$	0.4712	− 0.9108	− 1.4820	0.0031	1.3259	− 0.0633	0.0919	0.0033	− 0.0119	− 0.0760
Raw score weights with leading coefficient set equal to 1	1.0000	− 1.9329	− 3.1452	0.0066	2.8139	− 0.1343	0.1950	0.0070	− 0.0252	− 0.1613
Raw score weights normalized	0.2102	− 0.4063	− 0.6612	0.0014	0.5915	− 0.0282	0.0410	0.0015	− 0.0053	− 0.0339
Standardized score weights based on $\sqrt{MS_W}$.	0.3146	− 0.4317	− 0.5021	0.3278	0.6130	− 0.4714	1.2475	0.0657	− 0.3572	− 0.0915
Standardized score weights based on $\sqrt{MS_T}$.	0.3109	− 0.4320	− 0.5234	0.3576	0.6579	− 0.4698	1.4143	0.0666	− 0.3603	− 0.0910

the discriminant function, for which the pooled variance is equal to 1.00, is as reported in the first row of Table 7-5. In terms of raw scores, the equation may be given as:

$$L = \mathbf{A}'\mathbf{X} = .4712X_1 - .9108X_2 - 1.4820X_3 + .0031X_4 + 1.3259X_5 - .0633X_6 + .0919X_7 + .0033X_8 - .0119X_9 - .0760X_{10}$$

For the sociology-related career group:

$$\bar{L}_1 = \mathbf{A}'\bar{X}_1 = .4712(2.00) - .9108(.6087) + \cdots - .0760(1.8261)$$
$$= .2118$$

whereas for the nonsociology-related career group:

$$\bar{L}_2 = \mathbf{A}'\bar{X}_2 = .4712(1.9412) - .9108(.7647) + \cdots - .0760(2.1176)$$
$$= -1.6048$$

Furthermore:

$$S^2_{L_1} = \mathbf{A}'\hat{\sum}_1\mathbf{A} = 1.1484$$

and

$$S^2_{L_2} = \mathbf{A}'\hat{\sum}_2\mathbf{A} = .7955$$

The discriminant scores for each subject are as reported in Table 7-6, along with the sample means and standard deviations. It is worth mentioning that the mean of all

TABLE 7-6. Discriminant scores for the subjects of Table 1-1

Sociology-related careers		*Nonsociology-related careers*	
Student Number	*L*	*Student Number*	*L*
004	− 0.059	003	− 2.635
010	− 1.867	014	− 2.218
018	− 0.278	040	− 1.449
020	− 0.359	052	− 0.593
032	− 0.471	072	− 1.883
050	1.352	080	− 2.452
055	1.212	117	− 2.267
070	0.159	118	− 0.949
076	− 1.526	143	− 0.905
083	1.156	150	− 2.736
089	1.378	174	− 1.000
091	0.455	188	0.465
103	1.072	196	− 0.981
104	− 1.315	199	− 1.509
106	0.184	207	− 2.333
108	− 0.938	208	− 1.195
128	1.363	211	− 2.636
166	1.411		
171	2.258		
179	− 0.102		
183	0.507		
193	− 0.155		
195	− 0.550		
Sample size	23		17
Mean	0.212		− 1.604
Variance	1.150		0.796
Standard deviation	1.072		0.892

40 discriminant scores, $\bar{L}$, is equal to $-.560$. Most computer programs in use today would add .560 to every score in order that $\bar{L} = 0$. In terms of these sample statistics:

$$S_p^2 = \frac{22(1.1484) + 16(.7955)}{38} = .9998 \simeq 1.$$

Note that S_p^2 is equal to 1.00, within rounding errors, which is the criterion used by several current computer programs in determining the particular **A** vector generated. With the constant added, as just noted, this would result in a set of discriminant scores L for which the mean $\bar{L}$, is equal to zero and the pooled variance of L, S_p^2 or MS_W, is equal to 1. Now:

$$t = \frac{.2118 - (-1.6048)}{\sqrt{\frac{1}{23} + \frac{1}{17}}} = \frac{1.8166}{.3198} = 5.68$$

the same value reported in Section 7-2 for testing H_0: $\mu_1 = \mu_2$.

7-4. Eigen equations and discriminant functions

The original model of discriminant analysis that was presented in Section 7-3 is somewhat outdated. Its main value is that it shows how discriminant functions were originally conceived and used. In recent times, a different approach based on eigen values and eigen vectors has become widely adopted. Although the newer matrix development is mathematically elegant, it has the disadvantage that it conceals more than it reveals. By this we mean that an intuitive understanding of discriminant analysis is sacrificed in favor of mathematical theory. However, since it leads directly into other statistical procedures by simple generalizations, it is prudent to examine it in some detail.

As we know from univariate theory:

$$t_{v2}^2 = F_{1,v2}$$

so that the test of H_0: $\mu_1 = \mu_2$ versus H_1: $\mu_1 \neq \mu_2$ can be tested as:

$$F = \frac{MS_B}{MS_W}$$

Let us consider the model for the discrimination of two groups. In terms of the notation of Section 7-3:

$$\begin{aligned} MS_B &= \frac{1}{2-1}[N_1(\bar{L}_1 - \bar{L})^2 + N_2(\bar{L}_2 - \bar{L})^2] \\ &= N_1\mathbf{A}'(\bar{\mathbf{X}}_1 - \bar{\mathbf{X}})(\bar{\mathbf{X}}_1 - \bar{\mathbf{X}})'\mathbf{A} + N_2\mathbf{A}'(\bar{\mathbf{X}}_2 - \bar{\mathbf{X}})(\bar{\mathbf{X}}_2 - \bar{\mathbf{X}})'\mathbf{A} \\ &= \mathbf{A}'(\mathbf{MS_B})\mathbf{A} \end{aligned}$$

where $\mathbf{MS_B}$ is a $P \times P$ square matrix with diagonal elements:

$$MS_{B_p} = N_1(\bar{X}_{1p} - \bar{X}_p)^2 + N_2(\bar{X}_{2p} - \bar{X}_p)^2$$

and off-diagonal elements:

$$MS_{B_{pp'}} = N_1(\bar{X}_{1p} - \bar{X}_p)(\bar{X}_{1p'} - \bar{X}_{p'}) + N_2(\bar{X}_{2p} - \bar{X}_p)(\bar{X}_{2p'} - \bar{X}_{p'})$$

In addition:

$$MS_W = \mathbf{A}' \hat{\Sigma}_{XX} \mathbf{A} = \mathbf{A}'(\mathbf{MS_W})\mathbf{A}$$

With this notation:

$$F = \frac{\mathbf{A}'(\mathbf{MS_B})\mathbf{A}}{\mathbf{A}'(\mathbf{MS_W})\mathbf{A}}$$

The problem now is to discover the **A** vector that maximizes *F*. As indicated in Section 7-3, there is no unique solution, so the following restriction is usually imposed:

$$\mathbf{A}'\mathbf{MS_W}\mathbf{A} = 1$$

With this restriction, the mathematical function to be maximized is:

$$\mathbf{Q} = \mathbf{A}'\mathbf{MS_B}\mathbf{A} - \lambda(\mathbf{A}'\mathbf{MS_W}\mathbf{A} - 1)$$

If this function is now differentiated with respect to the **A** values, we are led to the characteristic equation:

$$|(\mathbf{MS_W})^{-1}(\mathbf{MS_B}) - \lambda\mathbf{I}| = 0$$

Although we could use this form of the equation to generate a solution, most available computer programs solve a simpler equation. This results from replacing $\mathbf{MS_W}$ and $\mathbf{MS_B}$ with $\mathbf{SS_W}$ and $\mathbf{SS_B}$, respectively, to yield the following equation:

$$|(\mathbf{SS_W})^{-1}(\mathbf{SS_B}) - \lambda\mathbf{I}| = 0$$

which has the basic form:

$$|\mathbf{A} - \lambda\mathbf{I}| = 0$$

Once λ is determined, the **A** values are found as solutions to the set of homogeneous equations:

$$[(\mathbf{SS_W})^{-1}(\mathbf{SS_B}) - \lambda\mathbf{I}]\mathbf{A} = 0$$

As an example, consider the statistics reported in Tables 7-3 and 7-4 which are based on the data used in Section 7-2 for the regression analysis.

The vector of **A** values is reported in Table 7-5. Three different computer programs in common use today each determine the **A** values from the preceding set of equations, as applied to the raw, unstandardized data. These programs are the *BMDP* program (Dixon and Brown, 1979), the *Multivariance* program (Finn, 1972), and the *SPSS* program (Nie et al., 1975). These three programs determine the weights based on the restriction that:

$$\mathbf{A}'\mathbf{MS_W}\,\mathbf{A} = 1$$

and the resulting solution may be found in the first row of Table 7-5. Other programs may replace the first coefficient by 1. This is obtained by dividing each weight by the leading value, in this case, .4712. The result is reported in the second row of Table 7-5. Still another approach is to normalize the weights by dividing each by the square root of the sum of the squared coefficients. Here:

$$\sum_{i=1}^{P} a_p^2 = (.4712)^2 + (-.9108)^2 + \cdots + (-.0760)^2$$
$$= 5.0243$$

With this sum, the normalized weights are given by:

$$\frac{.4712}{\sqrt{5.0243}}, \frac{-.9108}{\sqrt{5.0243}}, \ldots, \frac{-.0760}{\sqrt{5.0243}} = .2102, -.4063, \ldots, -.0339$$

with the resultant property that the sum of their squares is equal to 1. These normalized weights are reported in the third row of Table 7-5.

Most computer programs also supply weights that can be applied to the standardized data. That is, they are to be applied to each individual's set of Z scores. For both the *BMDP* and *Multivariance* programs, the square root of the pooled within-group variance, $\sqrt{MS_{W_p}}$, is used to standardize each variable. In contrast, for the current version of *SPSS*, the across-group standard deviation, S_X or $\sqrt{MS_{T_p}}$, is used in the standardization, although a change to $\sqrt{MS_{W_p}}$ is planned for the next version. The corresponding weights for the present data are found in rows 4 and 5 of Table 7-5.

Although all three computer programs generated identical coefficients for the raw weights, the standardization procedures for the *SPSS* and *Multivariance* programs are different. *SPSS* standardizes the coefficients relative to the total sample standard deviation as given in Table 7-3. Thus, for example, the standardized coefficient for X_1 is given by:

$$a_1\sqrt{MS_{T_1}} = .47122(.6597) = .3109$$

whereas the standardized coefficient for X_{10} is given by:

$$a_{10}\sqrt{MS_{T_{10}}} = -.07600(1.1972) = -.0910$$

On the other hand, *Multivariance* standardizes the coefficients relative to the within-sample standard deviation. Thus:

$$a_1\sqrt{MS_{W_1}} = .47122(.6677) = .3146$$

and

$$a_{10}\sqrt{MS_{W_{10}}} = -.07600(1.2038) = -.0915$$

Note that this latter standardization procedure implies that:

$\mathbf{A}_S' \mathbf{R_W} \mathbf{A}_S = 1$ (where $\mathbf{A}_S'$ is the vector of standardized weights)
since $\mathbf{A}'$ $(\mathbf{MS_W})$ $\mathbf{A}$ can be written as:

$$\mathbf{A}' (\mathbf{S_W'} \mathbf{R_W} \mathbf{S_W}) \mathbf{A}$$

which, in turn, is equal to:

$$(\mathbf{A} \mathbf{S_W})' \mathbf{R_W} (\mathbf{A} \mathbf{S_W})$$

Finally, this can be written as:

$$\mathbf{A}'_S \mathbf{R_W} \mathbf{A}_S$$

Procedure for obtaining the linear discriminant function for comparing two groups with $\mathbf{A}'\ \mathbf{MS_W}\ \mathbf{A} = 1$.

Step 1. Determine the matrix $\mathbf{SS_B}$, whose diagonal and off-diagonal elements are given, respectively, by:

$$SS_{B_p} = \sum_{k=1}^{2} N_k(\bar{X}_{kp} - \bar{X}_p)^2$$

$$SS_{B_{pp'}} = \sum_{k=1}^{2} N_k(\bar{X}_{kp} - \bar{X}_p)(\bar{X}_{kp'} - \bar{X}_{p'})$$

Step 2. Determine the matrix $\mathbf{SS_W}$ whose diagonal and off-diagonal elements are given, respectively, by:

$$SS_{W_p} = \sum_{k=1}^{2} (N_k - 1)S^2_{kp}$$

$$SS_{W_{pp'}} = \sum_{k=1}^{2} (N_k - 1)r_{kpp'}S_{kp}S_{kp'}$$

Step 3. Solve the characteristic equation:

$$|(\mathbf{SS_W})^{-1}(\mathbf{SS_B}) - \lambda\mathbf{I}| = 0$$

Step 4. The coefficients $a_1, \ldots, a_P$ are found as solutions to the set of homogeneous equations:

$$[(\mathbf{SS_W})^{-1}(\mathbf{SS_B}) - \lambda\mathbf{I}]\mathbf{A} = 0$$

Step 5. Weights can be standardized to suit the researcher. A useful standardization is to divide the pth weight by $\sqrt{MS_{W_p}}$.

7-5. Interpretation of λ

As indicated in Section 7-4, the vector of coefficients **A** is determined for the set of homogeneous equations:

$$[(\mathbf{SS_W})^{-1}(\mathbf{SS_B}) - \lambda\mathbf{I}]\ \mathbf{A} = 0$$

under the restriction that:

$$\mathbf{A}'\ (\mathbf{MS_W})\ \mathbf{A} = 1.$$

With this method of standardization, $\mathbf{A}'\ (\mathbf{MS_W})\ \mathbf{A}$, the within-group variance of L, the discriminant function, is equal to unity. With this as the model, let us examine the data of Table 7-6 to see what we can learn about the nature of λ, the eigen value associated with the preceding set of homogeneous equations. For these data:

$$\begin{aligned} SS_B &= N_1(\bar{L}_1 - \bar{L})^2 + N_2(\bar{L}_2 - \bar{L})^2 \\ &= 23[.212 - (-.560)]^2 + 17[-1.604 - (-.560)]^2 \\ &= 32.24 \end{aligned}$$

Except for rounding errors, this is equal to:

$$t^2 = (-\ 5.68)^2 = 32.26$$

as computed in Section 7-2. In addition, this between-group sum of squares has a direct connection to λ, the eigen value for the two-group discrimination model. Specifically,

$$SS_B = \nu_2\lambda = (N_1 + N_2 - 2)\lambda = (N - 2)\lambda$$

In this case, $\lambda = .8489$ so that, except for rounding errors,

$$SS_B = (40 - 2)(.8489) = 32.26$$

This relationship is not unexpected. It can be derived from mathematical considerations since the eigen values of the general K-group model

$$|\ (\mathbf{SS_W})^{-1}(\mathbf{SS_B}) - \lambda\mathbf{I}\ | = 0$$

are directly related to the eigen values of the corresponding model based on mean square statistics. If we denote the eigen values of

$$|\ (\mathbf{MS_W})^{-1}(\mathbf{MS_B}) - \lambda^*\mathbf{I}\ | = 0$$

as:

$$\lambda_1^* > \lambda_2^* > \cdots > \lambda_s^*$$

the relationship to $\lambda_1 > \lambda_2 > \cdots > \lambda_s$ is given by:

$$\lambda_1^* + \lambda_2^* + \cdots + \lambda_s^* = \frac{\nu_2}{\nu_1}(\lambda_1 + \lambda_2 + \cdots + \lambda_s)$$

In the two-group case, $s = 1$, $\nu_1 = 1$, and $\nu_2 = N - 2$ so that:

$$\lambda_1^* = (N - 2)\lambda_1$$

If we continue our examination of the data of Table 7-6, we see that:

$$\begin{aligned} SS_W &= (N_1 - 1)S_1^2 + (N_2 - 1)S_2^2 \\ &= 22(1.072)^2 + 16(.892)^2 \\ &= 38.04 \end{aligned}$$

Except for rounding errors, this agrees with the restriction that $\mathbf{A}'\ \mathbf{MS_W}\ \mathbf{A} = 1$ since for univariate models:

$$MS_W = \frac{SS_W}{N - 2} = \frac{38.04}{38} \simeq 1.00$$

Thus it follows that:

$$SS_W = (N - 2)$$

Let us now summarize what we have shown. For $\mathbf{A}'\ \mathbf{MS_W}\ \mathbf{A} = 1$, we know that:

$$SS_B = (N - 2)\lambda$$

$$SS_W = (N - 2)$$

so that in terms of univariate ANOVA statistics:

$$SS_B + SS_W = SS_T$$

can be represented for L by:

$$(N - 2)\lambda + (N - 2) = (N - 2)(1 + \lambda)$$

with degrees of freedom given by:

$$1 + (N - 2) = (N - 1)$$

In addition:

$$MS_B = (N - 2)\lambda$$

$$MS_W = 1$$

Furthermore the proportion of variance that is associated with group membership is given by the univariate correlation ratio:

$$\hat{\eta}^2 = \frac{SS_B}{SS_T} = \frac{(N - 2)\lambda}{(N - 2)(1 + \lambda)} = \frac{\lambda}{1 + \lambda}$$

In the univariate case, $\hat{\eta}^2 = 0$ when $\bar{L}_1 = \bar{L}_2$. Thus $\hat{\eta}^2$ and λ are directly related to the truth of the hypothesis:

$$H_0: \quad E(L_1) = E(L_2).$$

If H_0 is true, $\lambda = 0$. If H_0 is false, λ will be significantly different from zero. In fact, as will be seen in Section 7-8,

$$MS_B = (N - 2)\lambda = \frac{N_1 N_2}{N_1 + N_2}(\bar{L}_1 - \bar{L}_2)^2$$

so that it provides a measure of the distance between the centroids of the two distributions. It equals zero when $\bar{L}_1 = \bar{L}_2$.

In canonical correlation, as described in Chapter 5, λ_i may be thought of as the proportion of variance accounted for in one canonical variate by its companion. In principal component analysis, as described in Chapter 6, λ_i may be thought of as the amount of variance in a standardized set of variables accounted for by a particular factor. In discriminant analysis as described in this chapter and in multivariate analysis of variance as described in the next chapters, λ may be thought of as the variance between the sample centroids. In the present two-group problem, λ can be associated with the SS_B, since $\lambda/(1 + \lambda)$ may be thought of as a proportion of variance explained. We now begin with this latter ratio, and summarize some important properties for $K = 2$.

1. *Roy's criterion* is defined as:

$$\theta = \frac{\lambda}{1 + \lambda}$$

For the example of Section 7-3, $\lambda = .8489$ is obtained from the computer printout and thus:

$$\theta = \frac{.8489}{1 + .8489} = .4591$$

which is recognized as the squared multiple correlation coefficient of Table 7-1. It is also the squared point biserial correlation coefficient between dichotomous independent variable, group membership, and the discriminant function L. For $K = 2$:

$$\hat{R}^2_{Y \cdot X_1 X_2 \ldots X_P} = \theta = \frac{\lambda}{1 + \lambda}$$

and represents the proportion of variance accounted for by group membership. Finally, based on our discussion in Section 5-9, θ could also be properly regarded as a squared canonical correlation in the two-group problem.

2. *Hotelling's trace criterion* is defined as:

$$\text{Trace} = \lambda$$

For this example:

$$\text{Trace} = .8489$$

As is apparent from our previous interpretation of λ, for $K = 2$, Hotelling's trace criterion may be regarded as the variance between group centroids.

3. *Wilks's lambda criterion* is defined as:

$$\Lambda = 1 - \theta = \frac{1}{1 + \lambda}$$

and corresponds to the proportion of unexplained variance. The careful reader may wonder why $\Lambda = 1 - \theta$ and not $1 - \lambda$ as it did for canonical correlation. The reason is that a different form of the characteristic equation is solved for this situation, and so the eigen values have a different meaning. Even though we have solved the equation $|(\mathbf{SS_W})^{-1}(\mathbf{SS_B}) - \lambda \mathbf{I}| = 0$, the Heck charts and the Pillai tables are based on solutions to $|(\mathbf{SS_B}) - \theta(\mathbf{SS_B} + \mathbf{SS_W})| = 0$. We now show that the two solutions are related to each other by $\theta = \lambda/(\lambda + 1)$. From the latter equation, we have that

$$|(1 - \theta)\,\mathbf{SS_B} - \theta \mathbf{SS_W}| = 0$$

so that upon division by $(1 - \theta)$ we have

$$\left|\mathbf{SS_B} - \frac{\theta}{1 - \theta}\mathbf{SS_W}\right| = 0$$

If we now multiply through by $(\mathbf{SS_W})^{-1}$, we see that

$$\left|(\mathbf{SS_W})^{-1}(\mathbf{SS_B}) - \frac{\theta}{1 - \theta}\mathbf{I}\right| = 0$$

so that

$$\lambda = \frac{\theta}{1 - \theta}$$

Solving this equation for θ, we have that

$$\theta = \frac{\lambda}{\lambda + 1}.$$

As can be seen, whenever $\theta = 0$, Λ must equal 1. Thus, in the case of $K = 2$, the hypothesis H_0: $\Lambda = 1$ is identical to the hypothesis H_0: $\theta = 0$. These equivalent hypotheses may be tested by the same F test. Specifically, both Rao's F approximation for testing the former hypothesis and the test of the latter hypothesis that normally requires the Heck charts or Pillai tables reduce to the following exact F ratio whenever $K = 2$ or, more generally, whenever $s = \min(K - 1, P) = 1$:

$$F = \frac{\dfrac{1 - \Lambda}{P}}{\dfrac{\Lambda}{N - P - 1}} = \frac{N - P - 1}{P}\left(\frac{1 - \Lambda}{\Lambda}\right)$$

$$= \frac{N - P - 1}{P}\left(\frac{\theta}{1 - \theta}\right)$$

with $\nu_1 = P$ and $\nu_2 = N - P - 1$. Since θ corresponds to $\hat{R}^2$ in this case, note that the preceding expressions may also be written in the familiar form:

$$F = \frac{\nu_2}{\nu_1}\left(\frac{\hat{R}^2}{1 - \hat{R}^2}\right)$$

For the example of Section 7-3:

$$\Lambda = 1 - .4591 = \frac{1}{1.8489} = .5409$$

with $\nu_1 = 10$ and $\nu_2 = 40 - 10 - 1 = 29$, so that:

$$F = \frac{29}{10}\left(\frac{.4591}{.5409}\right) = 2.4614$$

which agrees, within rounding errors, with the F value reported in Table 7-1.

Bartlett's Chi-square approximation for testing the same hypotheses when $K = 2$ is given by:

$$\chi^2 = -\left[(N - 1) - \left(\frac{P + 2}{2}\right)\right] \log_e \Lambda$$

with $\nu = P$. For the present example:

$$\chi^2 = -\left[(40 - 1) - \left(\frac{10 + 2}{2}\right)\right] \log_e (.5409) = 20.28$$

With $\nu = 10$, the hypothesis H_0: $\lambda = 0$ is rejected at $\alpha = .05$, since $\chi^2_{10:.95} = 18.31$ which agrees with our decision based on the preceding F test, since $F_{10,29:.95} = 2.17$.

We have already noted that for $K = 2$, both Roy's θ criterion and Wilks's Λ criterion can be tested for significance with an exact F test based on $\nu_1 = P$ and $\nu_2 = N - P - 1$. In the next section, we show yet another correspondence.

Procedure for testing the two-group discriminant function for statistical significance.

Step 1. Determine the value of λ.

Step 2a. In terms of Wilks's Λ, compute:

$$\Lambda = 1 - \theta = \frac{1}{1+\lambda} \quad \text{and} \quad F = \frac{N-P-1}{P}\left(\frac{1-\Lambda}{\Lambda}\right)$$

and reject H_0: $\lambda = 0$ if:

$F > F_{P,N-P-1:1-\alpha}$

Step 2b. In terms of Roy's θ, compute:

$$\theta = \frac{\lambda}{1+\lambda} \quad \text{and} \quad F = \frac{N-P-1}{P}\left(\frac{\theta}{1-\theta}\right)$$

and reject H_0: $\lambda = 0$, if:

$F > F_{P,N-P-1:1-\alpha}$

Step 2c. In terms of Hotelling's trace criterion, compute λ and:

$$F = \frac{N-P-1}{P}\lambda$$

and reject H_0: $\lambda = 0$, if:

$F > F_{P,N-P-1:1-\alpha}$

Step 2d. In terms of Bartlett's Chi-square approximation, compute:

$$\Lambda = 1 - \theta = \frac{1}{1+\lambda}$$

and:

$$\chi^2 = -\left[(N-1) - \left(\frac{P+2}{2}\right)\right]\log_e \Lambda$$

and reject H_0: $\lambda = 0$, if:

$\chi^2 > \chi^2_{P:1-\alpha}$

7-6. Hotelling's T^2

Let us review the univariate case of the test of H_0: $\mu_1 = \mu_2$ against the alternative H_1: $\mu_1 \neq \mu_2$. The classical two-sample t statistic is given by:

$$t = \frac{\bar{X}_1 - \bar{X}_2}{\sqrt{\dfrac{S_p^2}{N_1} + \dfrac{S_p^2}{N_2}}}$$

which is distributed as t with $v = N_1 + N_2 - 2$ degrees of freedom. Since $t^2_{v2} = F_{1,v2}$, we have:

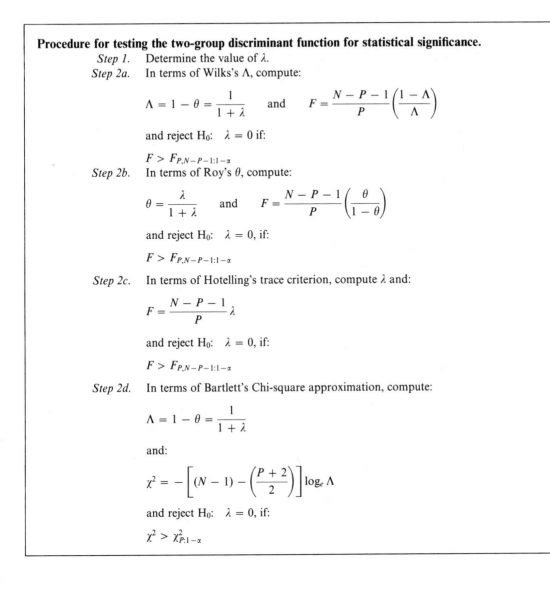

$$t^2 = F = \frac{(\bar{X}_1 - \bar{X}_2)^2}{\frac{S_p^2}{N_1} + \frac{S_p^2}{N_2}} = \frac{(\bar{X}_1 - \bar{X}_2)^2}{S_p^2\left(\frac{1}{N_1} + \frac{1}{N_2}\right)}$$

Moreover, because:

$$\frac{1}{\frac{1}{N_1} + \frac{1}{N_2}} = \frac{N_1 N_2}{N_1 + N_2}$$

t^2 can be written as:

$$t^2 = \frac{N_1 N_2}{N_1 + N_2} (\bar{X}_1 - \bar{X}_2)'(S_p^2)^{-1}(\bar{X}_1 - \bar{X}_2)$$

which is distributed as F with $v_1 = 1$ and $v_2 = N_1 + N_2 - 2$.

Let us now consider the hypothesis:

$$\text{H}_0: \begin{bmatrix} \mu_{11} \\ \mu_{12} \\ \cdot \\ \cdot \\ \cdot \\ \mu_{1P} \end{bmatrix} = \begin{bmatrix} \mu_{21} \\ \mu_{22} \\ \cdot \\ \cdot \\ \cdot \\ \mu_{2P} \end{bmatrix}$$

against the alternative H_1: H_0 is false. If we replace $\bar{X}_1$ by the vector of means $\bar{\mathbf{X}}_1$, $\bar{X}_2$ by the vector of means $\bar{\mathbf{X}}_2$, and S_p^2 by the pooled variance-covariance matrix $\hat{\mathbf{\Sigma}}_{XX}$ and if we write t^2 as T^2, we have:

$$T^2 = \frac{N_1 N_2}{N_1 + N_2} (\bar{\mathbf{X}}_1 - \bar{\mathbf{X}}_2)' \hat{\Sigma}_{XX}^{-1} (\bar{\mathbf{X}}_1 - \bar{\mathbf{X}}_2)$$

which serves as the P-variate analog to t^2. Hotelling (1931) has shown that this statistic produces the most powerful test of H_0 against H_1. In addition, Hotelling showed that T^2 is related to the F distribution by the following simple relationship:

$$F = \frac{(N - P - 1)}{P(N - 2)} T^2$$

where, once again, F is based on $v_1 = P$ and $v_2 = N - P - 1$. Note also that when $P = 1$ (the univariate case), $F = (N - 2)/(N - 2)\, T^2 = T^2 = t^2$.

Definition of Hotelling's T^2.
Hotelling's T^2 is defined as:

$$T^2 = \frac{N_1 N_2}{N_1 + N_2} (\bar{\mathbf{X}}_1 - \bar{\mathbf{X}}_2)' \hat{\Sigma}_{XX}^{-1} (\bar{\mathbf{X}}_1 - \bar{\mathbf{X}}_2)$$

Interestingly, T^2 can be related to the Λ and θ measures discussed in Section 7-5.

Recall that:

$$F = \frac{N - P - 1}{P}\left(\frac{1 - \Lambda}{\Lambda}\right)$$

and since, as just noted:

$$F = \frac{N - P - 1}{P}\left(\frac{T^2}{N - 2}\right)$$

it follows that:

$$\frac{T^2}{N - 2} = \frac{1 - \Lambda}{\Lambda}$$

Thus:

$$T^2 = \frac{(N - 2)(1 - \Lambda)}{\Lambda} = \frac{(N - 2)\theta}{1 - \theta}$$

Note also from Section 7-2, that if $P = 1$:

$$t^2 = \frac{(N - 2)r_{pb}^2}{1 - r_{pb}^2}$$

When $P = 1$, it follows that $v_1 = 1$, $v_2 = N - 2$, and $r_{pb}^2 = \theta = \hat{R}^2$, so that, once again, the familiar relationship:

$$F = \frac{v_2}{v_1}\left(\frac{\hat{R}^2}{1 - \hat{R}^2}\right)$$

holds. In addition:

$$T^2 = (N - 2)\frac{1 - \dfrac{1}{1 + \lambda}}{\dfrac{1}{1 + \lambda}} = (N - 2)\lambda$$

For the example of Section 7-4:

$$T^2 = (40 - 2)(.8489) = 32.2582 \simeq 32.26$$

so that:

$$\sqrt{T^2} = \sqrt{32.2582} = 5.68 = |\,t\,|$$

the value reported in Section 7-2 for testing H_0: $E(\bar{L}_1) = E(\bar{L}_2)$. This means that T itself has the simple interpretation of a t test for which the dependent variable is L.

Procedure for testing H_0: $E(L_1) = E(L_2)$ in terms of Hotelling's T^2.

Step 1. Compute:
λ and $T^2 = (N - 2)\lambda$

Step 2. Compute:

$$F = \frac{(N - P - 1)}{P(N - 2)} T^2$$

and reject H_0: $E(L_1) = E(L_2)$ if:

$$F > F_{P,N-P-1:1-\alpha}$$

Note that testing H_0: $E(L_1) = (E(L_2)$ is the same as testing $\Lambda = 1$, or that $\lambda = 0$. Thus we have another way of testing the significance of a discriminant function. To say that L is a significant discriminator is the same as saying that the expected mean scores for the two distributions based on L are statistically different from one another. This particular correspondence was previously shown in Section 7-3.

Although we have described in considerable detail Hotelling's two-sample model, for completeness we should note that a one-sample procedure exists for comparing an observed mean vector against an a priori specified mean vector. In particular:

$$H_0: \begin{bmatrix} \mu_1 \\ \mu_2 \\ \cdot \\ \cdot \\ \cdot \\ \mu_P \end{bmatrix} = \begin{bmatrix} \mu_{1_0} \\ \mu_{2_0} \\ \cdot \\ \cdot \\ \cdot \\ \mu_{P_0} \end{bmatrix}$$

can be tested with:

$$T^2 = N(\bar{\mathbf{X}} - \boldsymbol{\mu}_0)'\hat{\Sigma}_{XX}^{-1}(\bar{\mathbf{X}} - \boldsymbol{\mu}_0)$$

where:

N = Sample size

$\bar{\mathbf{X}}' = [\bar{X}_1, \bar{X}_2, \ldots, \bar{X}_P]$

and

$\hat{\Sigma}_{XX}$ = sample variance-covariance matrix

This statistic can be referred to the F distribution via the transformation:

$$F = \frac{v_2}{v_1}\left(\frac{T^2}{N - 1}\right)$$

where $v_1 = P - 1$ and $v_2 = N - P + 1$.

In practice, this form of the test is rarely encountered since $\boldsymbol{\mu}_0' = [\mu_{1_0}, \mu_{2_0}, \ldots, \mu_{P_0}]$ is generally not known. However, a common form of the test is encountered when the original variables represent difference scores. For this case, $\boldsymbol{\mu}_0' = [0, 0, \ldots, 0]$, so that:

$$T^2 = N\bar{\mathbf{X}}'\hat{\Sigma}_{XX}^{-1}\bar{\mathbf{X}}$$

An important application of this model arises in repeated measures designs, which are examined in Sections 9-4 and 9-5.

7-7. Post hoc comparisons for Hotelling's T^2

Rejection of the hypothesis H_0: $\boldsymbol{\mu}_1 = \boldsymbol{\mu}_2$ does not identify which particular means in the two populations are different. Fortunately, simultaneous post hoc comparisons, based on a multivariate extension of Scheffé's procedure, can be used in conjunction with the omnibus Hotelling T^2 test. The appropriate coefficient is given by:

$$\mathbf{S} = \sqrt{\frac{\nu_1(N-K)}{\nu_2} F_{\nu_1,\nu_2:1-\alpha}} = \sqrt{\frac{P(N-2)}{N-P-1} F_{P,N-P-1:1-\alpha}}$$

$$= \sqrt{T^2_{P,N-P-1:1-\alpha}}$$

The latter representation is useful when tabled values of T^2 are available, as for instance in Timm (1975). The reason for including $N - K$ in the numerator is given in the next chapter. In any case, using this coefficient we can simultaneously investigate, with familywise type I error probability α, all contrasts of the form:

$$\psi = b_1(a_1\mu_{11} + a_2\mu_{12} + \cdots + a_P\mu_{1P}) + b_2(a_1\mu_{21} + a_2\mu_{22} + \cdots + a_P\mu_{2P})$$

where:

$$b_1 + b_2 = 0$$

Since $b_1 + b_2 = 0$, it follows that $b_1 = -b_2$, so that all contrasts reduce to the form:

$$\psi = a_1(\mu_{11} - \mu_{21}) + a_2(\mu_{12} - \mu_{22}) + \cdots + a_P(\mu_{1P} - \mu_{2P})$$

Thus we see that, if $(a_1, a_2, \ldots, a_P)$ are the coefficients of the linear discriminant function, ψ is a simple test of $E(L_1) = E(L_2)$. Since the hypothesis H_0: $\boldsymbol{\mu}_1 = \boldsymbol{\mu}_2$ may be alternatively written as H_0: All $\psi = 0$, or H_0: Max $\psi = 0$, it turns out that Hotelling's T^2 in this case is also a test of the discriminant analysis hypothesis:

$$H_0\text{:}\quad E(L_1) = E(L_2)$$

If the discriminant function is not significant at the preassigned α level, all contrasts involving the sample means will prove to be nonsignificant. Thus, if H_0 is not rejected, it is known that no statistically significant contrast among the sample means will be found. This includes the maximum possible contrast, namely that based on the linear discriminant function coefficients.

For the data of Table 7-1:

$$\mathbf{S} = \sqrt{\frac{10(40-2)}{40-10-1} F_{10,40-10-1:.95}} = \sqrt{\frac{10(38)}{29}(2.17)}$$

$$= 5.33$$

As many contrasts as desired may be examined in conjunction with the **S** coefficient. The particular contrasts selected can be based on substantive considerations or on the data themselves. In terms of the latter approach, we could consider the standardized difference in means for each variable. Such an index is defined as:

$$D_p = \frac{\bar{X}_{1p} - \bar{X}_{2p}}{\sqrt{MS_{W_p}}}$$

Values of D for each of the 10 variables are reported in the last column of Table 7-3. Those variables with the largest D, in absolute value, should be examined first since they are most likely to result in a statistically significant contrast. According to Table 7-3, the two career groups differ most with respect to X_7, Midterm 1. On this variable, students selecting sociology-related careers outdistanced students not selecting sociology-related careers by an average of 1.11 within-group standard deviations.

To test for the statistical significance of this difference, we would define:

$$\hat{\psi} = \bar{X}_{17} - \bar{X}_{27} = 52.4783 - 37.3529 = 15.1254$$

We would then use this contrast to estimate ψ, as follows:

$$\begin{aligned}\psi &= \hat{\psi} \pm \mathbf{S}\sqrt{\frac{MS_{W_7}}{N_1} + \frac{MS_{W_7}}{N_2}} \\ &= 15.1254 \pm 5.33\sqrt{\frac{184.4112}{23} + \frac{184.4112}{17}} \\ &= 15.12 \pm 23.15\end{aligned}$$

Thus:

$$-8.03 < \psi < 38.27$$

Since zero is in this interval, the contrast is reported as not being statistically different from zero. Since this contrast represented the largest standardized difference in means, it may also be concluded that no other single-variable contrast will be statistically significant either. Consequently, if we wished to identify a significant contrast, linear combinations of variables of the form:

$$\hat{\psi} = \sum_{p=1}^{P} a_p(\bar{X}_{1p} - \bar{X}_{2p})$$

would have to be considered. Once again, Table 7-3 is helpful in selecting the most likely candidates. Note that, in addition to Midterm 1, variables X_4, College Board scores, and X_5, High school sociology unit, both seem to differentiate between the two career groups, as evidenced by the standardized mean differences of $D = .93$ and $D = .84$, respectively. As a result, we might wish to combine these with X_7 to define:

$$\hat{\psi} = (\bar{X}_{14} - \bar{X}_{24}) + (\bar{X}_{15} - \bar{X}_{25}) + (\bar{X}_{17} - \bar{X}_{27})$$

or the statistically equivalent:

$$\hat{\psi} = \frac{1}{3}(\bar{X}_{14} - \bar{X}_{24}) + \frac{1}{3}(\bar{X}_{15} - \bar{X}_{25}) + \frac{1}{3}(\bar{X}_{17} - \bar{X}_{27})$$

Note also that the a_p chosen need not be equal to one another, as they were here.

Although the preceding contrasts appear to be weighting X_4, X_5, and X_7 equally in the linear combination, it is important to point out that this impression is false because of the very different standard deviations associated with the three variables. If we did in fact wish to weight the three variables equally in the contrast, we would choose:

$$a_4 = \frac{1}{\sqrt{MS_{W_4}}} = \frac{1}{105.1331} = .00951$$

$$a_5 = \frac{1}{\sqrt{MS_{W_5}}} = \frac{1}{.4623} = 2.16310$$

and

$$a_7 = \frac{1}{\sqrt{MS_{W_7}}} = \frac{1}{13.5798} = .07364$$

and then compute:

$$\begin{aligned}\hat{\psi} &= a_4(\bar{X}_{14} - \bar{X}_{24}) + a_5(\bar{X}_{15} - \bar{X}_{25}) + a_7(\bar{X}_{17} - \bar{X}_{27}) \\ &= .00951(565.6522 - 468.2353) + 2.16310(.5652 - .1765) \\ &\qquad + .07364(52.4783 - 37.3529) \\ &= 2.8811\end{aligned}$$

which in this case is simply the sum of the respective D_p given in Table 7-3. Now an estimate of the variance of this contrast is given by:

$$SE^2_{\hat{\psi}} = \left(\sum_{p=1}^{P} a_p^2 MS_{W_p} + 2\sum_{p=1}^{P}\sum_{p'=1}^{P} a_p a_{p'} MP_{W_{pp'}}\right)\left(\frac{1}{N_1} + \frac{1}{N_2}\right) \quad \text{where} \quad p < p'$$

Whenever standardization is employed, this formula simplifies to:

$$SE^2_{\hat{\psi}} = \left(\sum_{p=1}^{P} a_p^2 + 2\sum_{p=1}^{P}\sum_{p'=1}^{P} a_p a_{p'} r_{pp'(W)}\right)\left(\frac{1}{N_1} + \frac{1}{N_2}\right) \quad \text{where} \quad p < p'$$

where a_p represents the numerator of the standardized a_p, and $r_{pp'(W)}$ is the pooled correlation coefficient involving variables p and p'. This index was described in earlier chapters and is given by:

$$r_{pp'(W)} = \frac{MP_{pp'(W)}}{\sqrt{MS_{W_p} MS_{W_{p'}}}}$$

where MP represents the mean crossproducts. Values of $r_{pp'(W)}$ for the present example are presented in Table 7-7, where it may be seen that:

$$r_{45(W)} = .0714$$

$$r_{47(W)} = .4278$$

and

$$r_{57(W)} = .3174$$

TABLE 7-7. The within-sample correlation matrix for the example of Section 7-1

Variable	X_1	X_2	X_3	X_4	X_5	X_6	X_7	X_8	X_9	X_{10}
X_1	1.0000	0.0636	0.0530	− 0.1206	− 0.0702	0.0314	− 0.2108	− 0.3036	− 0.3379	− 0.5200
X_2		1.0000	0.0214	0.0390	0.0952	0.0430	0.1951	0.2680	0.1278	0.2724
X_3			1.0000	0.3835	0.4446	0.4529	0.6827	0.6594	0.5712	0.1360
X_4				1.0000	0.0714	0.0984	0.4278	0.5342	0.4236	− 0.1609
X_5					1.0000	0.3452	0.3174	0.2665	0.3388	0.1848
X_6						1.0000	0.5622	0.4164	0.2757	0.1588
X_7							1.0000	0.6579	0.6373	0.2885
X_8								1.0000	0.5642	0.2874
X_9									1.0000	0.1589
X_{10}										1.0000

As a result:

$$SE^2_{\hat{\psi}} = \{(1)^2 + (1)^2 + (1)^2 + 2[(1)(1)(.0714)$$
$$+ (1)(1)(.4278) + (1)(1)(.3174)]\}\left(\frac{1}{23} + \frac{1}{17}\right)$$
$$= 4.6332(.1023) = .4740$$

The associated confidence interval for ψ is given by:

$$\psi = 2.8811 \pm 5.33\sqrt{.4740}$$
$$= 2.88 \pm 3.67$$

which once again is not statistically significant.

We could continue in this fashion, defining other linear combinations suggested by the data. Standardization of each mean difference, that is, defining contrasts in terms of the D_p, is recommended if we wish to offer an appropriate interpretation of the coefficients selected for the linear combination. From the preceding formulas it can be seen that variables with large mean differences and small correlations with the other variables selected are the best candidates for inclusion in the linear combination. An alternative approach for identifying discriminating variables will be included in the simplified statistics section of this chapter.

For now, however, we wish to offer some clarifications relevant to the simultaneous post hoc procedure associated with Hotelling's T^2. First, it should be understood that the defined linear combinations can consist of differences among variables, in addition to sums. In the case of a simple difference, $\bar{X}_p - \bar{X}_{p'}$, the associated weights become $a_p = +1$ and $a_{p'} = -1$. The preceding formulas then apply to these weights. Second, although implied in our preceding discussion, we wish to emphasize that raw and standardized weights entering into the linear combination can often lead to different statistical conclusions. This is most likely to occur when the within-group standard deviations differ considerably from one variable to the next. We will illustrate each of these points in the following hypothetical example, and an actual research example will be provided in Chapter 9.

Consider a two-group problem in which, following different treatments, two different achievement measures, X_1 and X_2, are taken. Suppose further that these

TABLE 7-8. Data to illustrate post hoc comparisons in T^2

	Group 1		Group 2
n	6		6
$\bar{X}_1$	15		10
S_1		$\sqrt{MS_{W_1}} = 2$	
$\bar{X}_2$	125		130
S_2		$\sqrt{MS_{W_2}} = 20$	
r_{12}		$r_{12(W)} = .50$	

two measures are scaled quite differently, resulting in grossly unequal standard deviations, and that Group 1 students appear to have higher average scores on X_1, whereas the reverse is true on X_2. Relevant statistics are given in Table 7-8.

If we wished to determine whether the treatments produced different effects on the two achievement measures, we could examine between-group differences on the linear combination $\bar{X}_1 - \bar{X}_2$. Note that this is equivalent to asking whether treatments and dependent variables interact, or whether the treatment effects are identical from one measure to the next. More about interactions will be included in the remaining chapters. In the present situation, it can be seen that in terms of raw scores, Group 1 exceeds Group 2 by an average of five points on X_1, whereas Group 2 exceeds Group 1 by an average of five points on X_2. Clearly, however, these differences are not of equal importance, in that the X_1 effect represents a two and one-half standard deviation difference in favor of Group 1, $D_1 = (15 - 10)/2 = 2.5$; whereas the X_2 effects amount to only one-quarter of a standard deviation difference in favor of Group 2, $D_2 = (125 - 130)/20 = -.25$. In terms of raw difference weights in the contrast:

$$\begin{aligned}\hat{\psi} &= +1(\bar{X}_{11} - \bar{X}_{21}) + (-1)(\bar{X}_{12} - \bar{X}_{22}) \\ &= (15 - 10) - (125 - 130) = 10\end{aligned}$$

with:

$$\begin{aligned}SE^2_{\hat{\psi}} &= [(+1)^2(2)^2 + (-1)^2(20)^2 + 2(1)(-1)(.50)(2)(20)][2/6] \\ &= 364(2/6) = 121.3333\end{aligned}$$

The $\alpha = .05$ squared Scheffé value in this case is given by:

$$\begin{aligned}\mathbf{S}^2 &= \frac{2(10)}{9} F_{2,9:.95} \\ &= \frac{20}{2}(4.26) = 9.47\end{aligned}$$

Consequently:

$$\mathbf{S}\, SE_{\hat{\psi}} = \sqrt{9.47(121.3333)} = 33.90$$

and the preceding contrast would not be statistically significant.

Using standardized difference weights in the contrast, however, we find that:

$$\hat{\psi} = \frac{+1}{2}(\bar{X}_{11} - \bar{X}_{21}) + \left(\frac{-1}{20}\right)(\bar{X}_{12} - \bar{X}_{22})$$
$$= \frac{1}{2}(15 - 10) - \frac{1}{20}(125 - 130)$$
$$= 2.75$$

with:

$$SE^2_{\hat{\psi}} = [(+1)^2 + (-1)^2 + 2(1)(-1)(.50)][2/6]$$
$$= 1(2/6) = .3333$$

The squared Scheffé value is still equal to 9.47 and, as a result:

$$\mathbf{S}\, SE_{\hat{\psi}} = \sqrt{9.47(.3333)} = 1.78$$

In this case, the contrast would be declared statistically significant, and its interpretation is straightforward: when the two dependent variables are weighted equally, there is an interaction between treatments and measures. The mean difference between Group 1 and Group 2 is relatively larger on X_1 than it is on X_2. Additional post hoc comparisons could be conducted using the Scheffé procedure, and it would be found that in fact the two groups differ significantly with respect to X_1, but not with respect to X_2. This underscores the fact that a misleading impression of the data is obtained by simply examining the mean raw score differences and/or formulating statistical contrasts in terms of these unstandardized variables.

Procedure for testing contrasts following the rejection of H_0: $\lambda = 0$.

Step 1. Determine the value of:

$$\mathbf{S} = \sqrt{\frac{P(N-2)}{N-P-1} F_{P,N-P-1:1-\alpha}}$$

Step 2. Define a contrast as:

$$\psi = a_1(\mu_{11} - \mu_{21}) + a_2(\mu_{12} - \mu_{22}) + \cdots + a_P(\mu_{1P} - \mu_{2P})$$

and estimate it in the sample by:

$$\hat{\psi} = a_1(\bar{X}_{11} - \bar{X}_{21}) + a_2(\bar{X}_{12} - \bar{X}_{22}) + \cdots + a_P(\bar{X}_{1P} - \bar{X}_{2P})$$

Step 3. Determine the squared standard error of the contrast as:

$$SE^2_{\hat{\psi}} = \mathbf{A}'\, \mathbf{MS}_W\, \mathbf{A}\left(\frac{1}{N_1} + \frac{1}{N_2}\right)$$

Step 4. Determine the $1 - \alpha$ percent confidence interval for ψ as:

$$\psi = \hat{\psi} \pm \mathbf{S}\, SE_{\hat{\psi}}$$

Notes:

1. If $(a_1, a_2, \ldots, a_P)$ are the P discriminant coefficients, then $\psi = E(L_1) - E(L_2)$.

2. If we wish to make standardized comparisons and the $(a_1, a_2, \ldots, a_P)$ are not standardized, define ψ as:

$$\psi = a_1\left(\frac{\mu_{11} - \mu_{21}}{\sqrt{MS_{W_1}}}\right) + a_2\left(\frac{\mu_{12} - \mu_{22}}{\sqrt{MS_{W_2}}}\right) + \cdots + a_P\left(\frac{\mu_{1P} - \mu_{2P}}{\sqrt{MS_{W_P}}}\right)$$

so that $SE^2_{\hat{\psi}}$ becomes:

$$SE^2_{\hat{\psi}} = \mathbf{A}'\,\mathbf{R}_W\,\mathbf{A}\left[\frac{1}{N_1} + \frac{1}{N_2}\right]$$

where $\mathbf{R}_W$ is the pooled within-group correlation matrix.

3. The $(a_1, a_2, \ldots, a_P)$ of Step 2 do not represent contrast coefficients. The contrast coefficients are given by $b_1 = +1$ and $b_2 = -1$, which are implicit in Step 2. Thus pairwise comparisons in each variable can be made with:

$$\psi = (\mu_{1p} - \mu_{2p})$$

$$SE^2_{\hat{\psi}} = MS_{W_p}\left(\frac{1}{N_1} + \frac{1}{N_2}\right)$$

4. For a planned Dunn-Bonferroni analysis, replace **S** by the value read from Table B-4. In most cases, it will be smaller than **S**.

7-8. Mahalanobis's D^2

Closely allied with the material in the preceding section are descriptive measures of the difference and standardized distance between two population centroids. As we recall from elementary geometry, the Euclidean distance between two points (X_1, Y_1) and (X_2, Y_2), as shown in Figure 7-3, is given simply as:

$$d = \sqrt{(X_2 - X_1)^2 + (Y_2 - Y_1)^2}$$

This follows directly from the Pythagorean theorem.

For a P-dimensional space with points $(X_{11}, X_{12}, \ldots, X_{1P})$ and $(X_{21}, X_{22}, \ldots, X_{2P})$, the Euclidean distance, often referred to as a generalized distance, between the points is given simply as:

$$d = \sqrt{(X_{21} - X_{11})^2 + (X_{22} - X_{12})^2 + \cdots + (X_{2P} - X_{1P})^2}$$

so that:

$$d^2 = (\mathbf{X}_2 - \mathbf{X}_1)'(\mathbf{X}_2 - \mathbf{X}_1)$$

If we consider two sample centroids:

$$\bar{\mathbf{X}}_1' = [\bar{X}_{11}, \bar{X}_{12}, \ldots, \bar{X}_{1P}] \qquad \text{and} \qquad \bar{\mathbf{X}}_2' = [\bar{X}_{21}, \bar{X}_{22}, \ldots, \bar{X}_{2P}]$$

then the squared generalized distance between them is given as:

$$d^2 = (\bar{\mathbf{X}}_2 - \bar{\mathbf{X}}_1)'(\bar{\mathbf{X}}_2 - \bar{\mathbf{X}}_1) = (\bar{\mathbf{X}}_1 - \bar{\mathbf{X}}_2)'(\bar{\mathbf{X}}_1 - \bar{\mathbf{X}}_2)$$

More usually, we wish to take into consideration the effects that the standard

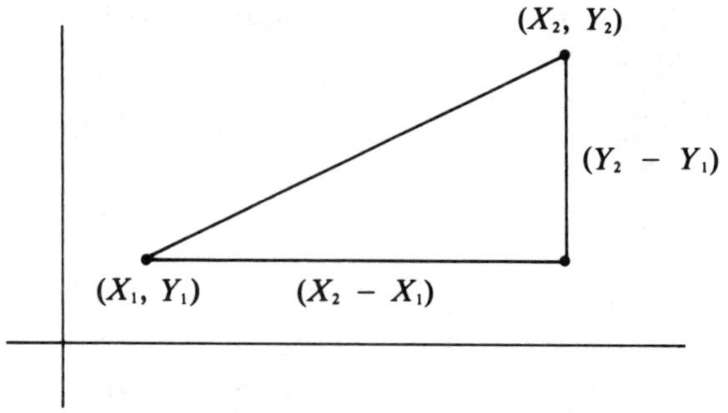

Figure 7-3. The Euclidean distance between two points.

deviations have on the distance. In that case, we can use the following squared standardized generalized distance measure:

$$D^2 = (\bar{\mathbf{X}}_1 - \bar{\mathbf{X}}_2)'\hat{\Sigma}_{XX}^{-1}(\bar{\mathbf{X}}_1 - \bar{\mathbf{X}}_2)$$

which is called Mahalanobis's D^2. Note that D^2 takes into account the correlations among the P variables, in addition to the standard deviations.

Definition of Mahalanobis's D^2.
Consider the two centroids $\bar{\mathbf{X}}_1$ and $\bar{\mathbf{X}}_2$. We define the standardized generalized distance between the two centroids as:

$$D = \sqrt{(\bar{\mathbf{X}}_1 - \bar{\mathbf{X}}_2)'\hat{\Sigma}_{XX}^{-1}(\bar{\mathbf{X}}_1 - \bar{\mathbf{X}}_2)}$$

where $\hat{\mathbf{\Sigma}}_{XX}^{-1}$ is the inverse of the within-group variance-covariance matrix with elements:

$$MS_{W_p} = \frac{\sum_{k=1}^{2} (N_k - 1)S_{kp}^2}{N_1 + N_2 - 2}$$

and

$$MS_{pp'(W)} = \frac{\sum_{k=1}^{2} (N_k - 1)r_{pp'(k)}S_{kp}S_{kp'}}{N_1 + N_2 - 2}$$

Note that when $P = 1$, D^2 represents the square of the standardized mean difference index used for interpretation in Section 7-7. As we see, D^2 and T^2 are intimately connected. In particular, from Section 7-6:

$$T^2 = \frac{N_1N_2}{N_1 + N_2}D^2$$

so that:

$$D^2 = \frac{N_1 + N_2}{N_1N_2}T^2 = \left(\frac{1}{N_1} + \frac{1}{N_2}\right)T^2$$

In terms of λ:

$$D^2 = \frac{N_1 + N_2}{N_1 N_2}(N - 2)\lambda = \left(\frac{1}{N_1} + \frac{1}{N_2}\right)(N - 2)\lambda$$

For the data of Table 7-1:

$$D^2 = \frac{23 + 17}{23(17)}(38)(.8489) = 3.3001 = 1.817^2$$

It is worth noting that D^2 is also closely tied to the two-sample t test of H_0: $E(L_1) = E(L_2)$. As shown in Section 7-3:

$$D = \bar{L}_1 - \bar{L}_2 = .212 - (-1.605) = 1.817$$

In terms of the regression approach:

$$D = \frac{\bar{\bar{Y}}_1 - \bar{\bar{Y}}_2}{S_p} = \frac{1.2299 - 1.6890}{\sqrt{.0639}} = -1.816$$

Thus the further apart the centroid means are, the greater is the value of D^2 and the ability to discriminate between the two groups.

7-9. Naming discriminant functions

Just as some researchers like to name principal components or canonical variates, others like to name discriminant functions. The same problems that exist in naming the principal components and canonical variates also exist in the naming of linear discriminant functions. One method that seems to show some utility is that of finding the correlation between each variable and the resulting linear discriminant function. A formula for computing these correlations more simply is given in Section 8-5. The correlations for the example of Section 7-2 are summarized in Table 7-9.

As will be seen in Section 8-5:

$$r_{LX_p} = \mathbf{R}_p\mathbf{A}_S$$

where R_p is the pth row of the within-sample correlation matrix and $\mathbf{A}_S$ is the vector of standardized linear discriminant coefficients where the standardization is in terms of the $\sqrt{MS_{W_p}}$ for each variable. Thus, from the correlations of Table 7-7 and the standardized weights given by the *Multivariance* program and reported in Table 7-5, we see that:

$$r_{LX_1} = (.3146)(1.0000) + (-.4317)(.0636) + \cdots + (-.0915)(-.5200) = .05$$

The remaining correlations are found in a similar fashion.

The highest correlation with L is found for X_7: Midterm 1. Next in line is X_4: College Board test scores. Other large correlations are found for X_5: Previous high school unit in sociology and X_3: High school grade point average. Except for X_7, the largest correlations are associated with college readiness variables. If X_7 were replaced by X_6: Pretest, then L could certainly be considered a measure of readiness. As can be seen, it is not an easy job to label L appropriately.

7.10. Classification via two-group discriminant analysis

Thus far, we have concentrated on the linear discriminant function L and, in particular, on how it is determined and examining its components. Another point of interest is how well the function discriminates between the two groups under consideration, and for this purpose measures such as $\hat{R}^2$, or equivalently θ, could be examined. In the present data, for example, $\hat{R}^2 = \theta = .4591$, which indicates that almost 46% of the total variance in $\hat{Y}$ or in L can be explained by group membership. For a related measure, see Levy (1967).

Recall, though, from the IRS example given in Section 7-1, that an important use of discriminant functions is to make decisions about group membership on the basis of discriminant scores. Thus, on the basis of discriminant function weights, discriminant scores can be computed for each subject. Similarly a criterion or cutoff score can be established such that any new or unknown score falling below the cutoff would be predicted to belong to one of the groups and any unknown score at or above the cutoff would be predicted to belong to the other group. In this section, we provide a variety of rules that have traditionally been proposed for deciding exactly where the cutoff should be made. We do not include rules that take into consideration various a priori or Bayesian probability information. For a related discussion, see Birnbaum and Maxwell (1960).

TABLE 7-9. Correlation between each of the ten variables and L of Section 7-2

Variable	*Correlation*
X_1	0.05
X_2	− 0.18
X_3	0.37
X_4	0.51
X_5	0.46
X_6	0.15
X_7	0.61
X_8	0.26
X_9	0.23
X_{10}	− 0.13

1. A simple rule that can be applied internally to see how well predicted and actual classifications match is first to determine which of the two groups has the higher mean discriminant score, and then to predict that the highest N_1 (or N_2) scores belong to that group. For example, here we found that the mean discriminant score of Group 1, sociology-related careers, was higher than that of Group 2, nonsociology-related careers, as shown in Table 7-6. Since $N_1 = 23$, Rule 1 would be to predict that the 23 students with the highest discriminant scores belong to Group 1. Predicted and actual classifications are summarized in the first 2 × 2 contingency table of Table 7-10. An evaluation of the goodness of this rule will be described shortly.

2. Suppose we set C, the cutoff score, equal to the mean of the 40 discriminant scores. According to this rule, anyone with a discriminant score greater than

TABLE 7-10. 2 × 2 Contingency tables showing predicted and actual classifications for a variety of rules

		Predicted		
Rule 1		*Program 1*	*Program 2*	
Actual:	*Program 1*	20	3	23
	Program 2	3	14	17
		23	17	40
		Predicted		
Rule 2		*Program 1*	*Program 2*	
Actual:	*Program 1*	19	4	23
	Program 2	1	16	17
		20	20	40
		Predicted		
Rule 3		*Program 1*	*Program 2*	
Actual:	*Program 1*	19	4	23
	Program 2	2	15	17
		21	19	40
		Predicted		
Rule 4		*Program 1*	*Program 2*	
Actual:	*Program 1*	19	4	23
	Program 2	2	15	17
		21	19	40

$\bar{L} = -.560$ would be predicted to be in Group 1 since $\bar{L}_1 > \bar{L}_2$, and anyone with a discriminant score less than $-.560$ would be predicted to be in Group 2. The results associated with this procedure are given by Rule 2 in Table 7-10. Huberty and Holmes (1978) describe a variation of this procedure.

3. Since P is large, there is reason to believe that L has a normal distribution, according to the Central Limit Theorem. A procedure for establishing C in a manner analogous to equalizing type I and type II errors in hypothesis testing results in:

$$C = \frac{\dfrac{\bar{L}_1}{S_{L_1}} + \dfrac{\bar{L}_2}{S_{L_2}}}{\dfrac{1}{S_{L_1}} + \dfrac{1}{S_{L_2}}} = \frac{\dfrac{.212}{1.0716} + \dfrac{-1.604}{.8919}}{\dfrac{1}{1.0716} + \dfrac{1}{.8919}} = -.779$$

With two equally populous normal distributions, the use of this rule will result in $\alpha = \beta$, where α represents the probability of incorrectly classifying a given L_1 as L_2 and β represents the probability of incorrectly classifying a given L_2 as L_1. For the present data, see Rule 3 in Table 7-10.

4. Whenever $N_1 \neq N_2$, as in the present example, Rule 3 can be modified to weight the various components of C differentially. According to this procedure:

$$C = \frac{N_1 \dfrac{\bar{L}_1}{S_{L_1}} + N_2 \dfrac{\bar{L}_2}{S_{L_2}}}{N_1 \dfrac{1}{S_{L_1}} + N_2 \dfrac{1}{S_{L_2}}}$$

Here:

$$C = \frac{23\left(\frac{.212}{1.072}\right) + 17\left(\frac{-1.604}{.892}\right)}{23\left(\frac{1}{1.072}\right) + 17\left(\frac{1}{.892}\right)} = -.642$$

Classifications according to this model are summarized as Rule 4 in Table 7-10.

The goodness of each of the rules can be evaluated according to various measures appropriate for contingency tables, two of the more common being the classical ϕ coefficient, which is actually a Pearson correlation coefficient in the 2×2 case, and Goodman and Kruskal's λ, or predictive efficiency index; see Hays (1973). Yet another measure, appropriate for the present situation is Cohen's (1960) κ, which is a percentage agreement measure. That is to say, it will reveal how close the agreement is between predicted and actual classifications beyond that which can be expected by chance. For 2×2 tables, ϕ and κ and, for that matter, χ^2 are closely related to one another; see Cohen (1960). But κ generalizes very nicely to larger classification tables. For the present example, $\kappa = .693$, .750, .698, and .698 for Rules 1–4, respectively. Accordingly we would conclude that Rule 2 is best in this case.

One other classification rule, based on normal distribution theory, will be included here. In univariate distribution theory, the equation that represents the likelihood of a normally distributed random variable is given by:

$$f(x) = \frac{1}{\sqrt{2\pi}\,\sigma} e^{-1/2[(X-\mu)/\sigma]^2}$$

In standard score form, the likelihood is given by:

$$f(Z) = \frac{1}{\sqrt{2\pi}} e^{(-1/2)Z^2}$$

where:

$$Z = \frac{X - \mu}{\sigma}$$

Thus, if X is distributed normally with $\mu = 50$ and $\sigma = 10$, then the likelihood of $X = 50$ is given by:

$$f(Z) = f\left(\frac{x-\mu}{\sigma}\right) = f\left(\frac{50-50}{10}\right) = f(0) = \frac{1}{\sqrt{2\pi}} e^{(-1/2)0^2} = .3989$$

A little reflection shows that $f(Z)$ is simply the ordinate or height of the normal curve at the value Z. Tables of the ordinates of the standard normal distribution are reported in Table B-9. As an example of the use of this table, suppose that $X_1 = 45$, with $\mu = 50$ and $\sigma = 10$. For these numbers:

$$Z_1 = \frac{X_1 - 50}{10} = \frac{45 - 50}{10} = -.5$$

so that:

$f(-.5) = .3521$

In like manner, for $X_2 = 54$, we can show that $Z_2 = .4$ and $f(.4) = .3683$. These numbers are not probabilities, but they are proportional to probabilities. Thus, if we know that X is either equal to $X_1 = 45$ or $X_2 = 54$, the relative probability that $X = 45$ is given by:

$$P(X = 45 \mid X_1 = 45 \text{ and } X_2 = 54) = \frac{f(-.50)}{f(-.50) + f(.40)}$$

$$= \frac{.3521}{.3521 + .3683} = .4888$$

Similarly, the relative probability that $X = 54$ is given by:

$$P(X = 54 \mid X_1 = 45 \text{ and } X_2 = 54) = \frac{f(.40)}{f(-.50) + f(.40)}$$

$$= \frac{.3683}{.3521 + .3683} = .5112$$

Thus, if we knew that X were either 45 or 54, we would guess that $X = 54$, since $p_{54} > p_{45}$.

The model based on relative probabilities is best illustrated by an example. For the example, consider the data summarized in Table 7-6, which has the discriminant scores for each subject. Let us consider the likelihood that Student No. 004 is a member of Group 1 or Group 2. The Z scores for Student No. 004 under classification as a member of Group 1 or Group 2 are given by:

$$Z_1 = \frac{L - \bar{L}_1}{S_{L_1}} = \frac{.059 - .212}{1.0716} = -.25$$

and

$$Z_2 = \frac{L - \bar{L}_2}{S_{L_2}} = \frac{.059 - (-1.604)}{.8919} = 1.73$$

The corresponding likelihoods read from Table B-9 are:

$f(-.25 \mid \text{Group 1}) = .387$ and

$f(1.73 \mid \text{Group 2}) = .089$

so that the relative probabilities are:

$$p_1 = \frac{.387}{.476} = .813 \qquad \text{and} \qquad p_2 = \frac{.089}{.476} = .187$$

On the basis of these probabilities, we would conclude that Student No. 004 is a member of Group 1. In this case, the decision would be correct.

If we believed that the variances of the two samples were equal, we could replace S_{L_1} and S_{L_2} by their pooled estimate:

$$\sqrt{MS_{W_L}} = \sqrt{\frac{(N_1 - 1)S_{L_1}^2 + (N_2 - 1)S_{L_2}^2}{N_1 + N_2 - 2}}$$
$$= \sqrt{\frac{22(1.0716)^2 + 16(.8919)^2}{38}}$$
$$= .9998 \simeq 1.0000$$

In terms of the pooled estimate the Z score for Student No. 004 under classification as a member of Group 1 or Group 2 is given by:

$$Z_1 = \frac{L - \bar{L}_1}{\sqrt{MS_{W_L}}} = \frac{-.059 - .212}{1} = -.271$$

and

$$Z_2 = \frac{L - \bar{L}_2}{\sqrt{MS_{W_L}}} = \frac{-.059 - (-1.604)}{1} = 1.545$$

The corresponding likelihoods, read from Table B-9 are:

$f(-.271 \mid \text{Group 1}) = .385$ and

$f(1.545 \mid \text{Group 2}) = .121$

so that the relative probabilities are:

$$p_1 = \frac{.385}{.506} = .761 \qquad \text{and} \qquad p_2 = \frac{.121}{.505} = .239$$

On the basis of these probabilities, we would conclude that Student No. 004 is in Group 1. As before, the decision would be correct, since we actually know that this student is a member of Group 1.

As indicated, the assumptions for this model are quite simple. The basic assumption is that L_1 and L_2 have normal distributions whose parameters can be estimated by the corresponding sample statistics. The probabilities for the remaining 39 students are reported in Table 7-11. As can be seen, Students 010, 052, 076, 104, 108, and 188 are misclassified. These are the same students misclassified in Table 7-10 by Rule 3. This particular classification procedure is the one employed by many of the current social sciences computer programs.

How to classify subjects in terms of their likelihoods.

Step 1. Obtain the discriminant function:

$$L = a_1\left(\frac{X_1 - \bar{X}_1}{S_1}\right) + a_2\left(\frac{X_2 - \bar{X}_2}{S_2}\right) + \cdots + a_P\left(\frac{X_P - \bar{X}_P}{S_P}\right)$$

Step 2. Consider a subject with data values:

$$X = (X_1, X_2, \ldots, X_P)$$

and determine the value of L.

Step 3. Compute $\bar{L}_1$, $\bar{L}_2$, and S_{L_1} and S_{L_2}.

Step 4. For the subject being classified, determine:

$$Z_1 = \frac{L - \bar{L}_1}{\sqrt{MS_{W_L}}} \quad \text{and} \quad Z_2 = \frac{L - \bar{L}_2}{\sqrt{MS_{W_L}}}$$

Step 5. Determine the likelihoods:

$f(Z_1)$ and $f(Z_2)$

and the conditional probabilities:

$$p_1 = \frac{f(Z_1)}{f(Z_1) + f(Z_2)} \quad \text{and} \quad p_2 = \frac{f(Z_2)}{f(Z_1) + f(Z_2)}$$

Step 6. Assign the subject to the group having the larger conditional probability.

7-11. Simplified statistics for two-group discriminant analysis

In this section, we propose simplified procedures for approximating two of the techniques discussed in this chapter. The first is an approximation for determining the linear discriminant function L; the second is a simplified procedure for determining which of the P variables statistically differentiate between the two groups.

Approximating the discriminant function. The procedure here is simply to standardize the group mean difference on each of the P variables, as defined by the D

TABLE 7-11. Probabilities of group membership for the 40 students

Student Number	Group 1 $P(X \mid 1)$	Group 1 $P(X \mid 2)$	Student Number	Group 2 $P(X \mid 1)$	Group 2 $P(X \mid 2)$
004	0.761	0.239	003	0.029	0.971
010*	0.106	0.894	014	0.059	0.941
018	0.681	0.319	040	0.203	0.797
020	0.648	0.352	052*	0.547	0.453
032	0.601	0.399	072	0.104	0.896
050	0.976	0.024	080	0.040	0.960
055	0.970	0.030	117	0.054	0.946
070	0.825	0.175	118	0.387	0.613
076*	0.181	0.819	143	0.406	0.594
083	0.967	0.033	150	0.024	0.976
089	0.977	0.023	174	0.366	0.634
091	0.890	0.110	188*	0.892	0.108
103	0.961	0.039	196	0.374	0.626
104*	0.245	0.755	199	0.186	0.814
106	0.832	0.168	207	0.049	0.951
108*	0.392	0.608	208	0.288	0.712
128	0.977	0.023	211	0.029	0.971
166	0.979	0.021			
171	0.995	0.005			
179	0.747	0.253			
183	0.899	0.101			
193	0.728	0.272			
195	0.566	0.434			

* Subject is misclassified

measure in the last column of Table 7-3. Those variables with moderate to large D values should be retained, whereas those close to zero should be dropped. The sum-of-Z-scores approach is then applied to the P' nonnegligible discriminators, as has been done in previous chapters. In this sum, variables with negative mean differences would be subtracted, thereby resulting in reflection which was also previously discussed. For the present example, suppose it were decided to retain all variables with $|D| > .30$. From Table 7-4, it can be seen that:

$$\hat{L} = -Z_2 + Z_3 + Z_4 + Z_5 + Z_7 + Z_8 + Z_9$$

Alternatively, we could weight each $Z_{p'}$ by its $D_{p'}$, in which case not all of the P' variables would be seen as contributing equally to $\hat{L}$. In either case, the resulting $\hat{L}$ scores should serve to differentiate between the two groups. Note that if it is decided on an a priori basis that all P standardized variables will be included in $\hat{L}$, then a single statistical test of the difference between $\bar{\hat{L}}_1$ and $\bar{\hat{L}}_2$ would be appropriate. If elimination of certain variables, based on examination of the data, takes place, then a statistical test of the resulting $\bar{\hat{L}}_1 - \bar{\hat{L}}_2$ difference is not strictly appropriate.

Testing variables for significance. If our sole interest is in determining which individual variables discriminate best between the two groups, it is easy to show that the procedures discussed in this chapter are not the wisest ones to apply. Rather, bypassing discriminant analysis (or Hotelling's T^2) and Scheffé-type multiple comparisons in favor of a more direct approach is advised. The approach is a straightforward multivariate extension of the Dunn-Bonferroni model discussed throughout the book. In particular, for any number C of planned comparisons conducted with $\alpha_1, \alpha_2, \ldots, \alpha_C$, the familywise type I error probability is at most $\alpha_1 + \alpha_2 + \cdots + \alpha_C$. When α' is selected for each comparison, the maximum familywise type I error probability is given by $C\alpha'$. Note that there are no restrictions on this statement whatsoever. It applies to both pairwise and complex comparisons alike, or to combinations of the two. It also applies to both orthogonal and nonorthogonal comparisons, although it should be mentioned that an exact familywise type I error probability can be determined if the C statistical tests are independent. Finally, the statement applies as well to comparisons based on two or more dependent variables. That is to say, there is no distinction between multiple comparisons involving the same dependent variable and those involving several dependent variables. It is this latter feature that is of importance to us in the present situation.

Recall from Section 7-7 that the critical $\alpha = .05$ familywise Scheffé value for our example was given by $\mathbf{S} = 5.33$. If, on the other hand, researchers could specify prior to data collection which particular variables or linear combinations thereof they wished to examine for between-group differentiation, the Dunn-Bonferroni procedure should certainly be considered. Here, if it were decided that $C = 10$, based on the ten variable-by-variable comparisons, the Dunn-Bonferroni $\alpha \leq .05$ familywise critical value is given by $t = 2.98$, based on $\nu = 38$, as shown in Table B-4. Note that ν does not depend on C, only on N; in particular, for the two-group problem, $\nu = N_1 + N_2 - 2$. Surprisingly, we can see from Table B-4 that for up to and including *250* planned comparisons (for example, the 10 variable-by-variable comparisons and 240 other linear combinations of variables), the Dunn-Bonferroni procedure will yield narrower confidence intervals in comparison to the Scheffé-type procedure, since the standard errors associated with the two procedures are identical. Schluck (1971) has made the same point in a different context. In the present illustration, with C equal to the 10 variable-by-variable comparisons, the confidence interval associated with variable 7, Midterm 1, would be given by:

$$2.18 < \psi < 28.06$$

In contrast to the previously given Scheffé-type interval, zero is not included in the Dunn-Bonferroni interval. As a result, we could conclude that Group 1 students, $\bar{X}_{17} = 52.48$, outperformed Group 2 students, $\bar{X} = 37.35$, on the first midterm. No other mean differences are statistically significant according to this procedure.

7-12. Summary

In this chapter an introduction to linear discriminant analysis was presented. What was conceived originally as a classification model was later seen to have close ties to canonical correlation analysis, multiple regression, and multivariate analysis of variance. These connections were illustrated in this chapter. As was shown, linear discriminant analysis can be conceived as a special case of each of these three statistical models.

For the two-group case in which group membership is coded as (0, 1), (1, 2), or any set of values (Y_1, Y_2), the regression equation given by $\hat{Y} = B_0 + B_1X_1 + \cdots + B_PX_P$ can be used to discriminate between the two groups by choosing an appropriate cutoff point $\hat{Y}_C$. The determination of four different cutoff points and corresponding classification procedures were illustrated in Section 7-10. In addition, we saw that the squared multiple correlation coefficient $R^2_{Y \cdot X_1X_2 \ldots X_P}$ is identical in value to the squared point biserial correlation coefficient of Y with $\hat{Y}$. This completely agrees with the relationship established in Section 1-10, where it was shown that for univariate X and Y, $r^2_{Y\hat{Y}} = r^2_{YX}$. In the multivariate model, $X = \hat{Y}$ is a linear combination that is still single valued, but is structurally more complex than a simple univariate independent variable.

It was also pointed out that a linear discriminant function plays a role similar to principal components. In principal components, the coefficients on the first principal component are selected so as to maximize the separation or discrimination among the individual elements. On the other hand, the coefficients for the first linear discriminant function are selected so as to maximize the separation between the centroids of the two groups under study. In the K-group case, discussed in Chapter 8, $K - 1$ multiple discriminant functions will be generated which, collectively, will maximize distances between K group centroids. For principal components, maximum discrimination among individuals is desired, whereas for discriminant analysis, maximum discrimination among groups is desired.

Under the R. A. Fisher approach, we consider P interdependent variables $X_1, X_2, \ldots, X_P$, which we wish to combine to form a linear combination, $L = a_1X_1 + a_2X_2 + \cdots + a_PX_P$. Under the assumption of common variance-covariance matrix $\boldsymbol{\Sigma}$, the square of the two sample t test statistic for comparing $\bar{L}_1$ to $\bar{L}_2$ can be written in matrix notation as:

$$t^2 = \left(\frac{\bar{L}_1 - \bar{L}_2}{SE_{\bar{L}_1 - \bar{L}_2}}\right)^2 = \frac{\mathbf{A}'(\bar{\mathbf{X}}_1 - \bar{\mathbf{X}}_2)(\bar{\mathbf{X}}_1 - \bar{\mathbf{X}}_2)'\mathbf{A}}{\mathbf{A}'\hat{\Sigma}_{XX}\mathbf{A}\left(\frac{1}{N_1} + \frac{1}{N_2}\right)}$$

where N_1 and N_2 are the sample sizes of the two groups to be maximally separated, $\hat{\Sigma}_{XX}$ is the pooled variance-covariance matrix, and $\bar{\mathbf{X}}_1$ and $\bar{\mathbf{X}}_2$ are the vectors of means for the two groups. The object under this formulation is to maximize t^2. This occurs when:

$$\mathbf{A} = \hat{\Sigma}_{XX}^{-1}(\bar{\mathbf{X}}_1 - \bar{\mathbf{X}}_2)$$

so that:

$$L = \hat{\Sigma}_{XX}^{-1}(\bar{\mathbf{X}}_1 - \bar{\mathbf{X}}_2)\mathbf{X}$$

serves as the desired discriminating function.

Unfortunately the determination of the **A** vector is not as clearcut as suggested. In point of fact, there is no unique set of **A** values that give rise to L, but there exists an infinite set of values that are all proportional to **A**. Because of this, a user must pay close attention to the manual of the computer program employed, so as to know how the **A** values are determined. Most computer programs available today scale the resulting coefficients so that the mean of the discriminant scores $\bar{L} = 0$, and so that the variance of the discriminant scores $S_L^2 = 1$. Under this condition:

$$t^2 = \frac{(L_1 - L_2)^2}{\frac{1}{N_1} + \frac{1}{N_2}} = \frac{N_1 N_2}{N_1 + N_2}(\bar{L}_1 - \bar{L}_2)^2$$

can be used to test H_0: $E(L_1) = E(L_2)$.

Another way to view the linear discriminant analysis is via characteristic equations and resulting eigen values. For this approach, we create a univariate F ratio of MS_B/MS_W which, in matrix notation, is given by:

$$F = \frac{\mathbf{A}'(\mathbf{MS_B})\mathbf{A}}{\mathbf{A}'(\mathbf{MS_W})\mathbf{A}}$$

The problem for this model is one of maximizing F. Again there is no unique solution, but we can obtain one by requiring that $\mathbf{A}'(\mathbf{MS_W})\mathbf{A} = 1$. Under this restriction, we are led to the characteristic equation:

$$|(\mathbf{MS_W})^{-1}(\mathbf{MS_B}) - \lambda\mathbf{I}| = 0$$

for solution. This equation, however, is not the one that is usually solved. Rather, the **A** vector is found as a solution to:

$$[(\mathbf{SS_W})^{-1}(\mathbf{SS_B}) - \lambda\mathbf{I}]\mathbf{A} = 0$$

Under this approach, λ has a very simple interpretation. It measures the standardized variance between the sample centroids. For the two-group situation:

$$(N - 2)\lambda + (N - 2) = (N - 2)(1 + \lambda)$$

corresponds to the univariate analysis of variance model:

$$SS_B + SS_W = SS_T$$

so that:

$$\theta = \frac{SS_B}{SS_T} = \frac{(N-2)\lambda}{(N-2)(1+\lambda)} = \frac{\lambda}{1+\lambda}$$

is equal to the proportion of explained variance in L that is due to the difference in the two groups and is identical to Roy's θ criterion defined in Chapter 5. In addition, $\theta = \hat{R}^2_{Y\cdot X_1X_2\ldots X_P}$ so that θ is interpretable as a squared multiple correlation coefficient in which Y is a univariate dummy coded variable and X corresponds to the set $X_1, X_2, \ldots, X_P$. Obviously the proportion of unexplained variance is given by:

$$1 - \theta = \frac{1}{1+\lambda} = \Lambda$$

which is identical to Wilks's Λ defined in Chapter 5. As indicated, this differs from the Λ of canonical theory in that $\theta = \lambda/(\lambda + 1)$ is a measure of explained variance. The difference arises from the way in which the characteristic equations are generated.

The statistical test of H_0: $\theta = 0$ or H_0: $\Lambda = 1$ is given by:

$$F = \frac{v_2}{v_1}\left(\frac{\theta}{1-\theta}\right) = \frac{v_2}{v_1}\left(\frac{\hat{R}^2_{Y\cdot X_1X_2\ldots X_P}}{1 - \hat{R}^2_{Y\cdot X_1X_2\ldots X_P}}\right) = \frac{v_2}{v_1}\left(\frac{1-\Lambda}{\Lambda}\right)$$

where $v_1 = P$ and $v_2 = N - P - 1$. In addition, Bartlett's Chi-square approximation for testing $\theta = 0$ or $\Lambda = 1$ is given by:

$$\chi^2 = -\left[(N-1) - \left(\frac{P+2}{2}\right)\right]\log_e \Lambda$$

with $v = P$.

Closely allied to R. A. Fisher's discriminant function theory is Hotelling's multivariate t test theory. Hotelling generated a test of:

$$H_0: \begin{bmatrix} \mu_{11} \\ \mu_{12} \\ \cdot \\ \cdot \\ \cdot \\ \mu_{1P} \end{bmatrix} = \begin{bmatrix} \mu_{21} \\ \mu_{22} \\ \cdot \\ \cdot \\ \cdot \\ \mu_{2P} \end{bmatrix}$$

in terms of the statistic:

$$T^2 = \frac{N_1N_2}{N_1 + N_2}(\bar{\mathbf{X}}_1 - \bar{\mathbf{X}}_2)'\hat{\Sigma}^{-1}_{XX}(\bar{\mathbf{X}}_1 - \bar{\mathbf{X}}_2)$$

which can be related to the F distribution by means of:

$$F = \frac{v_2}{v_1}\left(\frac{T^2}{N-2}\right)$$

The Hotelling hypothesis of identical mean vectors is rejected when $\theta = 0$ and $\Lambda = 1$ are rejected. Thus Hotelling's T^2 is another way to view a linear discriminant analysis. If Hotelling's hypothesis of identity of mean vectors is rejected, then the centroids are statistically different from one another and so L has discriminatory power. With the rejection of H_0, we can examine contrasts of the form:

$$\psi = a_1(\mu_{11} - \mu_{21}) + a_2(\mu_{12} - \mu_{22}) + \cdots + a_P(\mu_{1P} - \mu_{2P})$$

for being statistically different from zero. In particular, the $a_1, a_2, \ldots, a_P$ can be the constants that define the discriminant function. In this special case, $(\hat{\psi}/SE_{\hat{\psi}})^2$ equals Hotelling's T^2. This shows that Hotelling's T^2 provides a test of the contrast that generates maximum separation between the two centroids. If it is significant, other less discriminating contrasts may also be significant. A researcher can look for them. For any post hoc comparison, critical values are defined by:

$$\mathbf{S} = \sqrt{\frac{\nu_1}{\nu_2}(N - 2)F_{\nu_1,\nu_2:1-\alpha}}$$

with $\nu_1 = P$ and $\nu_2 = N - P - 1$ and with squared standard errors defined as:

$$SE^2_{\hat{\psi}} = \mathbf{A}'\hat{\Sigma}_{XX}\mathbf{A}\left(\frac{1}{N_1} + \frac{1}{N_2}\right)$$

$$= \left(\sum_{p=1}^{P} a_p^2\, MS_{W_p} + 2\sum_{p=1}^{P}\sum_{p'=1}^{P} a_p a_{p'}\, MS_{W_{pp'}}\right)\left(\frac{1}{N_1} + \frac{1}{N_2}\right) \qquad p < p'$$

In practice, we can simplify post hoc comparisons by using standardized mean differences:

$$D_p = \frac{\bar{X}_{1p} - \bar{X}_{2p}}{\sqrt{MS_{W_p}}}$$

in place of simple mean differences, $\bar{X}_{1p} - \bar{X}_{2p}$. For standardized mean differences:

$$SE^2_{\hat{\psi}} = \left(\sum_{p=1}^{P} a_p^2 + 2\sum_{p=1}^{P}\sum_{p'=1}^{P} a_p a_{p'} r_{pp'(W)}\right)\left(\frac{1}{N_1} + \frac{1}{N_2}\right) \qquad p < p'$$

where:

$$r_{pp'(W)} = \frac{MP_{pp'(W)}}{\sqrt{MS_{W_p} MS_{W_{p'}}}}$$

If H_0 is rejected, a useful strategy for identifying significant contrasts is to look for variables with large D_p values and small correlations for likely reasons for the rejection of the Hotelling hypothesis of identical mean vectors.

Once it is known that two centroids differ from one another, interest may exist concerning the magnitude of the difference. One measure of the distance between two multivariate distributions is provided in terms of Mahalanobis's D^2 which is defined as:

$$D^2 = (\bar{\mathbf{X}}_1 - \bar{\mathbf{X}}_2)'\hat{\Sigma}^{-1}_{XX}(\bar{\mathbf{X}}_1 - \bar{\mathbf{X}}_2)$$

This measure is related to T^2 in that:

$$D^2 = \frac{N_1 + N_2}{N_1 N_2} T^2$$

Thus $D^2 = 0$ whenever $T^2 = 0$. When $T^2 \neq 0$, $D^2 = (\bar{L}_1 - \bar{L}_2)^2$

provided the **A** vector is defined with $\mathbf{A}' \, (\mathbf{MS_W}) \, \mathbf{A} = 1$.

Just as canonical variates and principal components sometimes can be named, so can discriminant functions. The model is identical to that used earlier in that the correlation coefficients of each X_p with L are computed simply as:

$$r_{LX_p} = \mathbf{R}_p \mathbf{A}_S$$

where $\mathbf{R}_p$ is the pth row of the within-sample correlation matrix and where $\mathbf{A}_S$ is the vector of standardized linear discriminant coefficients where the standardization is in terms of the $\sqrt{MS_{W_p}}$ for each variable.

Finally, this chapter concluded with methods for classifying individuals into two groups on the basis of the generated discriminant function. The use of unit weights applied to standardized variables was presented. In addition, it was pointed out that a planned analysis using the Dunn-Bonferroni model was almost certain to be more powerful than a post hoc procedure based on a Scheffé model and for that reason is recommended.

7-13. Exercises

***7-1.** Perform a multiple regression analysis on your sample of 40 students. Use the 10 predictor variables employed in Section 7-2. Score the career variable as 1 and 2, with:

$$Y = \begin{cases} 1, & \text{if student selects a sociology-related career} \\ 2, & \text{if student selects a nonsociology-related career} \end{cases}$$

Compare your results to those in the text.

***7-2.** Find the predicted values for each of your 40 students on the basis of the results to Exercise 7-1. Perform a t test on the predicted scores and show that $\hat{R}^2_{Y \cdot X_1 \ldots X_{10}} = r^2_{pb}$ where r_{pb} is the point biserial correlation coefficient between Y and the predicted Y.

7-3. Graph the predicted scores for the two career groups and determine the cutoff point so that the probabilities of misclassification are the same for each group.

7-4. Find the coefficients for the R. A. Fisher model which are given by:

$$\mathbf{A} = \hat{\Sigma}^{-1}_{XX} (\bar{\mathbf{X}}_1 - \bar{\mathbf{X}}_2)$$

Score your 40 subjects and repeat Exercise 7-3. What do you observe? Explain what it means.

***7-5.** Find the coefficients for the linear discriminant function where $\mathbf{A}' \, \mathbf{MS_W} \, \mathbf{A} = 1$ and repeat Exercise 7-3.

7-6. What is the value of Roy's criterion for your data? What relationship does it have to the answer of Exercise 7-2?

7-7. Use Bartlett's test ($\alpha = .05$) to see if $\lambda = 0$.

***7-8.** Determine Hotelling's T^2 for your data. Use it to test the hypothesis ($\alpha = .05$) that $\lambda = 0$.

7-9. If H_0 of Exercise 7-8 is rejected, perform a post hoc analysis to determine possible reasons for the rejection.

7-10. Under what conditions will the Dunn-Bonferroni approach be better than the Scheffé model for analyzing the data for your 40 subjects?

***7-11.** Determine the value of Mahalanobis's D^2 for your sample of 40 subjects. Show that $D = \bar{L}_1 - \bar{L}_2$ where $\bar{L}_1$ and $\bar{L}_2$ are determined from Exercise 7-5. Also, show that:

$$D^2 = \left(\frac{1}{N_1} + \frac{1}{N_2}\right) T^2$$

where T^2 is determined from Exercise 7-8.

7-12. Find the correlation between L and each X_p and try to name your discriminant function.

7-13. Use the model based on the normal distribution described in Section 7-10 to classify your 40 subjects into their career groups. How good is the classification?

7-14. Approximate your discriminant function with unit weights. Find the correlation of the resulting function, $\hat{L}$ with Y. See Section 3-18 for a simple formula for this correlation.

CHAPTER EIGHT

MULTIPLE-GROUP DISCRIMINANT ANALYSIS AND THE ONE-WAY MULTIVARIATE ANALYSIS OF VARIANCE

8-1. An example

The material in this chapter represents a simple extension of the models of Chapter 7 to more than two groups. In particular, we will generalize the concepts and terminology related to the two-group discriminant analysis problem to situations in which we wish to separate or classify individuals into K groups, where $K \geq 3$. Similarly the extension of Hotelling's T^2, in which we test the hypothesis that two mean vectors are the same, becomes the one-way multivariate analysis of variance, commonly abbreviated MANOVA. In that case, we wish to test the hypothesis that $K \geq 3$ mean vectors are the same. We will illustrate the procedures relevant to these problems, both from a traditional multivariate perspective as well as from our own less formal simplified statistics point of view.

We begin the presentation by means of an example taken from a longitudinal study on language development conducted by Professor Walter Loban at the University of California, Berkeley. The dependent variables for the study were obtained by asking children to tell a story related to a series of pictures. Their spoken words were recorded on tape and scored by trained listeners. Whenever a child hesitated or lost track of the story, gentle hints were provided to make the story advance to a conclusion. Fluency relates to the ease with which children speak. A highly fluent child has a speech rich in communication units, low in mazes and speech loops, high in the use of dependent clauses, and given to excesses in elaboration. A nonfluent speaker represents the opposite pole of this scale. The terms just used will now be defined.

Communication unit (fluency): A communication unit may be defined semantically as a group of words that cannot be further segmented or divided without the loss of its essential meaning. Grammatically, a communication unit is any independent predication and all of its relevant modification. Thus, "I saw a man wearing a red hat" is a single unit of communication because if "wearing a red hat" were omitted, the essential meaning of that unit would have been changed and grammatically the participial modifier of "man" would be missing. Furthermore, "with a red hat" does not constitute a complete predication and it cannot stand alone. However, "I saw a girl and she was wearing a green hat" results in two communication units: (1) "I saw a girl;" and (2) "[and] she was wearing a green hat." Dividing the sentence into two communication units does not result in loss of meaning of either unit and grammatically each is an independent unit. It is well known that the average length of these communication units increases with age, beginning with the brief sentences of very young children and progressing to the complex, elaborated sentences of adults.

Examples of communication units used by subjects in the oral language transcripts are as follows:

1. Short units

Lower grades: She is outside. (3 words)
Upper grades: He is plowing. (3 words)

2. Medium units

Lower grades: They don't have very many clothes. (7 words)
Upper grades: And it is just about a father and his four boys. (11 words)

3. Long units

Lower grades: Or we might play some games that I have in my house, some games that are in a box like that. (21 words)

Upper grades: And they're all working together to try to get her husband into this high political office to set him up for bigger and better things and maybe to become president or whatever he's got his mind on. (39 words)

Maze words as a percentage of total words: A maze may be defined as a group of words or initial parts of words not resulting in a meaningful communication unit, that is, a confused tangle of language not necessary to the communication unit. Most communication units contain no mazes whatsoever; thus the following examples are designed to illustrate the extent to which mazes can occur in a given communication unit.

1. Minor maze problem

Lower grades: [and] and it looks like a cute little dog. (1 maze in a total of 9 words)

Upper grades: I think maybe the one that is running, the girl that is running, [knows] apparently knows something that the other one doesn't know because she's got sort of a puzzled look on her face. (1 maze in a total of 36 words)

2. Moderate maze problem

Lower grades: [probably] probably [going] they're going back to their house. (2 mazes in a total of 10 words)

Upper grades: So what does Trina do but tell him to give her the money [which his last payoff] his last payroll because the company before firing him [had] of course [given him] had paid him off that money which he had deserved. (7 mazes in a total of 41 words)

3. Major maze problem

Lower grades: I got [one of my favorite toys a type] my favorite type in the garage. (7 mazes in a total of 15 words)

Upper grades: [and then and and] and [it's it's very] it's written effectively [so that] so that you think that [Leon-] Leonard's going to come in [and] and sort of you know [r-] release [his his] his love for Tolson [and his] and his need for Tolson [in] in this kind of weird relationship. (19 mazes in a total of 56 words)

Dependent clause ratio: A communication unit consists of an independent clause that may or may not be modified by one or more dependent clauses. Thus, 'I saw a man' is an independent clause, as well as a complete communication unit, that may stand alone. One could also elaborate this with a dependent clause and produce 'I saw a man who was wearing a scarlet hat' or with two dependent clauses and produce 'I saw a man who was wearing a scarlet hat that was made of feathers.' Actual examples from the oral transcripts of the subjects are as follows:

1. No use of dependent clauses

Lower grades: I know that.
Upper grades: That's all.

2. Medium use of dependent clauses

Lower grades: I don't know what that is. (1 dependent clause)
Upper grades: And it ended up the way she thought it would, somehow. (2 dependent clauses)

3. Large use of dependent clauses

Lower grades: I think they're going home after a long day's work because it looks like it's getting to be night because the stars are out. (4 dependent clauses)
Upper grades: Well, it was an illustration of how a man can be brainwashed to the point where he knows nothing but what he is told and does what he's told to do by a special person whose been set aside as his controller or master, however you'd like to put it. (6 dependent clauses)

Conventional English usage: Standard English is defined as the type of language usage typically spoken in the social, political, economic, educational, and religious life of this country. This set of language habits is standard, not because it is any more correct or capable than other varieties of English, but rather because it is the type of English most frequently used in the conduct of the most important affairs of this country. Standard English ranges from informal to formal styles with many usages that are disputed or in transition. In this research, the investigator was concerned with obvious departures from standard English usage, such as the deviant forms following:

Lower grades: She ain't got no dress on or nothing.
And the boy have a shirt on.
She don't know nothing.
And he brung it over.
And her is trying it.
Upper grades: And this man and the horse was plowing.
Once upon a time there was two girls.
And then when they move into it, Marlene found out that she didn't like it because it too far from school.
And her mother and them liked it, too.

Weighted index of elaboration: The weighted index of elaboration assigns specific numerical weights to the component syntactic elements within a communication unit. Thus a unit with simple adjectives and adverbs as modifiers will receive fewer points than a unit containing more elaborated phrases or clauses. Clauses or phrases embedded within other elaborated structures will receive still additional weight in this index. The following examples range from short, nonelaborated communication units to units containing a variety of embedded structures.

1. No elaboration

Lower grades: We play house. (0 points)
Upper grades: She was nineteen. (0 points)

2. Medium elaboration

Lower grades: On Thursdays there's Deputy Dave again. ($2\frac{1}{2}$ points)
Upper grades: And she's running towards it to see what's happening. ($14\frac{1}{2}$ points)

3. Extensive elaboration

Lower grades: Well that looks like there's an Eskimo traveling in a sleigh with a whole bunch of dogs pulling it. (22 points)
Upper grades: Well this isn't a plot so much as a situation where we'll say that the girl that's running beneath the tree is the daughter of the woman who's holding clothes or something in her hands. ($27\frac{1}{2}$ points)

In the present example, we discuss the performance of $N = 211$ schoolchildren in Oakland, California. The children were scored with respect to these five variables, longitudinally, in each of several school grades. In the present example, we focus on the first set of five measurements taken when the children were in the first grade. The independent variable is the race of the child, with three levels: 1 = Asian, 2 = Black, and 3 = White. A typical observation is denoted:

$$X_{kpi} = \mu_{kp.} + \varepsilon_{kpi} = \mu_{.p.} + \alpha_{kp.} + \varepsilon_{kpi}$$

where:

$$k = 1, 2, \ldots, K$$

$$p = 1, 2, \ldots, P$$

$$i = 1, 2, \ldots, N_k$$

$\mu_{.p.}$ = population mean of the pth variable

$\alpha_{kp.}$ = treatment effect for the pth variable in group k

$\mu_{kp.} = \mu_{.p.} + \alpha_{kp.}$ = population mean of the pth variable in group k

ε_{kpi} = error for the ith subject in group k on variable p

In the example, $P = 5$, $K = 3$, $N_1 = 17$, $N_2 = 86$, and $N_2 = 108$. It is assumed that the errors are selected from a multivariate normal distribution for which the mean errors on each variable are zero. (See Section 5-8 for a discussion of multivariate normality.) In addition, it is assumed that the variance-covariance matrix of the errors is the same for the K levels of the independent variable, here, racial groups, and may be represented by:

$$\Sigma_{XX} = \begin{bmatrix} \sigma_1^2 & \rho_{12}\sigma_1\sigma_2 & \rho_{13}\sigma_1\sigma_3 & \cdots & \rho_{1P}\sigma_1\sigma_P \\ & \sigma_2^2 & \rho_{23}\sigma_2\sigma_3 & \cdots & \rho_{2P}\sigma_2\sigma_P \\ & & & \cdot & \cdot \\ & & & \cdot & \cdot \\ & & & \cdot & \cdot \\ & & & & \sigma_P^2 \end{bmatrix}$$

The hypothesis to be tested is that the mean vectors of the K groups are identical:

H_0: $\boldsymbol{\mu}_1 = \boldsymbol{\mu}_2 = \cdots = \boldsymbol{\mu}_K$

or:

$$H_0: \begin{bmatrix} \mu_{11} \\ \mu_{12} \\ \cdot \\ \cdot \\ \cdot \\ \mu_{1P} \end{bmatrix} = \begin{bmatrix} \mu_{21} \\ \mu_{22} \\ \cdot \\ \cdot \\ \cdot \\ \mu_{2P} \end{bmatrix} = \cdots = \begin{bmatrix} \mu_{K1} \\ \mu_{K2} \\ \cdot \\ \cdot \\ \cdot \\ \mu_{KP} \end{bmatrix}$$

The alternative hypothesis is that H_0 is false. The sample statistics for the example are summarized in Tables 8-1, 8-2, 8-3, and 8-4.

A preliminary comment about these data is in order. An important assumption underlying MANOVA and discriminant analysis is that the distribution of each dependent variable is normal within each of the K populations under investigation. Moreover it is assumed that the variance-covariance matrix of the dependent variables is the same for each of the K populations. Although the separate variance-covariance matrices are not presented in full here, information relating to variance homogeneity can be found in Table 8-2. There it may be seen that, for conventional usage in particular, the three standard deviations appear to be quite discrepant. The great variance in the Asian group may be attributed to the fact that a large number of the Asian students spoke mainly Chinese when entering school. Their exposure to standard English in the home and community was very limited. Since children were scored in the use of contemporary English, they appeared as a rather heterogeneous group of children.

TABLE 8-1. First-grade means and sample sizes for the three racial groups

	Racial group			
Variable	*Asian*	*Black*	*White*	*Across groups*
1. Fluency	4.5082	5.9523	6.2313	5.9788
2. Mazes	0.0674	0.0828	0.0654	0.0727
3. Dependent clauses	0.0906	0.1767	0.1828	0.1729
4. Conventional usage	677.4118	535.7791	232.3056	391.8578
5. Elaboration index	50.8235	74.7791	79.7870	75.4123
Sample size	17	86	108	211

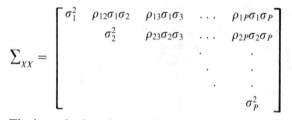

TABLE 8-2. First-grade standard deviations for the three racial groups

	Racial group			
Variable	*Asian*	*Black*	*White*	$\sqrt{MS_W}$
1. Fluency	1.5186	1.3898	1.2371	1.3244
2. Mazes	0.0522	0.0424	0.0345	0.0395
3. Dependent clauses	0.0857	0.1265	0.1079	0.1144
4. Conventional usage	565.6930	263.2880	146.9756	253.0941
5. Elaboration index	24.8451	26.9288	26.8088	26.7123

TABLE 8-3. First-grade within-sample variance-covariance matrix

Variable	1	2	3	4	5
1. Fluency	1.7539				
2. Mazes	0.0169	0.0016			
3. Dependent clauses	0.0863	0.0009	0.0131		
4. Conventional usage	− 62.6018	1.7489	− 7.0121	64056.6426	
5. Elaboration index	27.3156	0.2902	2.3984	− 1479.4131	713.5451

TABLE 8-4. First-grade within-sample correlation matrix

Variable	1	2	3	4	5
1. Fluency	1.0000				
2. Mazes	0.3237	1.0000			
3. Dependent clauses	0.5696	0.1904	1.0000		
4. Conventional usage	− 0.1868	0.1751	− 0.2422	1.0000	
5. Elaboration index	0.7712	0.2753	0.7848	− 0.2188	1.0000

Olson (1974) has shown that variance and/or covariance heterogeneity can have a serious inflationary effect on type I error probabilities in MANOVA, even when the K sample sizes are equal. If principles from univariate ANOVA can be generalized, the problem may well be exacerbated when the sample sizes are widely disparate, as in the present example. As a result, MANOVA hypothesis testing using conventional procedures may not be appropriate in this situation. In practice, we might consider dropping the conventional usage variable from the analysis or consider applying some of the more recent developments in nonparametric MANOVA. Alternatively, nonlinear transformations of the conventional usage variable could be attempted in an effort to reduce variance heterogeneity; see, for example, Kirk (1982). With the preceding cautions in mind, we proceed here with standard MANOVA and discriminant analysis procedures for purposes of illustration only.

8-2. MANOVA according to Wilks's criterion

As noted in Chapter 7, the two-sample Hotelling T^2 model and two-group discriminant analysis are one and the same, both leading to an evaluation of Wilks's Λ criterion. A similar parallel holds in the K-sample model. In this case, one can show that Wilks's criterion reduces to:

$$\Lambda = \left(\frac{1}{1+\lambda_1}\right)\left(\frac{1}{1+\lambda_2}\right)\cdots\left(\frac{1}{1+\lambda_s}\right) = \prod_{p=1}^{s} \frac{1}{1+\lambda_p}$$

where $s = \min[(K-1), P]$ and $\lambda_1, \lambda_2, \ldots, \lambda_s$ are the eigen values of:

$$|(\mathbf{SS_W})^{-1}(\mathbf{SS_B}) - \lambda\mathbf{I}| = 0$$

If eigen values are determined from:

$$|(\mathbf{SS_B}) - \theta(\mathbf{SS_B} + \mathbf{SS_W})| = 0$$

then $\Lambda = (1-\theta_1)(1-\theta_2)\cdots(1-\theta_s)$.

An interpretation of Wilks's Λ will be offered in Section 8-5.

The matrices $\mathbf{SS_B}$ and $\mathbf{SS_W}$ are generated directly from the original data. For example, the first diagonal element of $\mathbf{SS_B}$ is defined as:

$$SS_{B_1} = N_1(\bar{X}_{11.} - \bar{X}_{.1.})^2 + N_2(\bar{X}_{21.} - \bar{X}_{.1.})^2 + \cdots + N_K(\bar{X}_{K1.} - \bar{X}_{.1.})^2$$

while the first off-diagonal element is defined as:

$$SS_{B_{12}} = SS_{B_{21}} = N_1(\bar{X}_{11.} - \bar{X}_{.1.})(\bar{X}_{12.} - \bar{X}_{.2.}) + N_2(\bar{X}_{21.} - \bar{X}_{.1.})(\bar{X}_{22.} - \bar{X}_{.2.}) + \cdots + N_K(\bar{X}_{K1.} - \bar{X}_{.1.})(\bar{X}_{K2.} - \bar{X}_{.2.})$$

The first diagonal element of $\mathbf{SS_W}$ is defined as:

$$SS_{W_1} = (N_1 - 1)S_{11}^2 + (N_2 - 1)S_{21}^2 + \cdots + (N_K - 1)S_{K1}^2$$

while the first off-diagonal element is defined as:

$$SS_{W_{12}} = SS_{W_{21}} = (N_1 - 1)S_{11}S_{12}r_{12(1)} + (N_2 - 1)S_{21}S_{22}r_{12(2)} + \cdots + (N_K - 1)S_{K1}S_{K2}r_{12(K)}$$

For the Loban data, $s = \min(3-1, 5) = 2$, so that two eigen values are generated. In particular, the two eigen values are equal to:

$\lambda_1 = .4905$ and $\lambda_2 = .0632$

so that Wilks's criterion is equal to:

$$\Lambda = \left(\frac{1}{1+.4905}\right)\left(\frac{1}{1+.0632}\right) = .6709(.9405) = .6310$$

The exact sampling distribution of Λ has proved to be intractable, except for some special cases, namely, $s = 1$ or 2. However, the Rao (1951) approximation based on the F distribution may be used here, as was done for testing canonical variates in Section 5-4. Bartlett's χ^2 approximation for testing successively defined Λ_p follows directly from the material in Section 5-4, but will be reserved for our discussion of multiple-group discriminant analysis in Section 8-5.

Procedure for performing a MANOVA, in terms of the Rao approximation.

Step 1. Compute the eigen values of the characteristic equation:

$$|(\mathbf{SS_W})^{-1}(\mathbf{SS_B}) - \lambda\mathbf{I}| = 0$$

Let the ordered eigen values be:

$$\lambda_1, \lambda_2, \ldots, \lambda_s$$

Step 2. Compute Wilks's Λ as:

$$\Lambda = \left(\frac{1}{1+\lambda_1}\right)\left(\frac{1}{1+\lambda_2}\right)\cdots\left(\frac{1}{1+\lambda_s}\right)$$

Step 3. Compute:

$$F = \frac{\nu_2}{\nu_1}\left(\frac{1-(\Lambda)^{1/b}}{(\Lambda)^{1/b}}\right)$$

where:

$$\nu_1 = P(K-1)$$

$$\nu_2 = ab - \left(\frac{1}{2}P(K-1)\right) + 1$$

with:

$$a = (N-K) + (K-1) - \frac{1}{2}(P+K)$$

$$= (N-1) - \frac{1}{2}(P+K) \quad \text{and}$$

$$b = \sqrt{\frac{P^2(K-1)^2 - 4}{P^2 + (K-1)^2 - 5}}$$

Step 4. Reject H_0 with a type I error probability of α if F exceeds:

$$F_{\nu_1,\nu_2:1-\alpha}$$

The identity to the Rao formula in Section 5-4 should be noted, where $K - 1 = Q$. As was true in that context, whenever $s = 1$ or 2, the Rao statistic is distributed as an exact F variate. Moreover, whenever $s = 1$ or 2, then $b = 2$ in the preceding formula.

For the language development example, since:

$$s = \min[(3-1), 5] = 2$$

Rao's statistic will be distributed exactly as F, assuming independence between and within samples, multivariate normality (as described in Section 5-8), and homogeneity of the separate variance-covariance matrices; however, see our previous caveats related to the present example. Thus:

$$\nu_1 = 5(3-1) = 10$$

With:

$$a = (211 - 1) - \frac{1}{2}(5 + 3) = 210 - 4 = 206$$

$$b = s = 2$$

Then:

$$\nu_2 = 206(2) - \left(\frac{1}{2}(5)(2)\right) + 1 = 412 - 5 + 1 = 408$$

Since $\Lambda = .6310$, it follows that:

$$F = \frac{408}{10}\left(\frac{1 - (.6310)^{1/2}}{(.6310)^{1/2}}\right) = \frac{408}{10}\left(\frac{1 - .7944}{.7944}\right) = 10.56$$

With $\alpha = .05$, H_0 is rejected, since:

$$F = 10.56 > F_{10,408:.95} \simeq 1.84$$

Thus, for the present example, it would be concluded that the three mean vectors are not equal.

8-3. Other MANOVA criteria based on all *s* eigen values

From the previous section, it should be apparent that in assessing H_0: $\boldsymbol{\mu}_1 = \boldsymbol{\mu}_2 = \cdots = \boldsymbol{\mu}_K$, Wilks's Λ criterion focuses on all s eigen values simultaneously. This can be seen from the formula for Wilks's Λ, which is derived from a product involving all s eigen values. Although Wilk's Λ is probably the most frequently used MANOVA simultaneous criterion in the social sciences, it should be noted that there are others. Two of the most common are the Hotelling-Lawley and Pillai-Bartlett trace criteria, as described by Olson (1974).

The Hotelling-Lawley criterion is defined by the simple sum of the eigen values, that is:

$$T = \sum_{p=1}^{s} \lambda_p$$

which for the present example would yield a value of $.4905 + .0632 = .5537$. Special tables exist for assessing the statistical significance of this criterion (Pillai, 1960), although Morrison (1976) notes that for reasonable sample sizes, the χ^2 distribution provides a decent approximation.

In contrast, the Pillai-Bartlett trace criterion involves taking the sum:

$$V = \sum_{p=1}^{s} \frac{\lambda_p}{1 + \lambda_p}$$

with tables once again available in Pillai (1960). For the present example, the obtained Pillai-Bartlett trace criterion equals .3885. This less commonly used criterion may well be the most desirable in many applied situations, as mentioned by Olson (1974) and as will be discussed in Section 8-7.

8-4. MANOVA according to Roy's criterion

Unlike the MANOVA criteria discussed in the two preceding sections, Roy's criterion does not consider all s eigen values simultaneously. Rather, only the largest eigen value is considered. Since $\lambda_1 \geq \lambda_2 \geq \lambda_3 \geq \cdots \geq \lambda_s$, this implies that the criterion is defined solely in terms of the first eigen value λ_1.

In particular, Roy's criterion is given by:

$$\theta = \frac{\lambda_1}{1 + \lambda_1}$$

which, for the present example, is equal to:

$$\theta = \frac{.4905}{1 + .4905} = .3291$$

The statistical significance of θ can be assessed using the Heck charts of Table B-6. Pillai's (1960) tables (Table B-7) should be used for $s>5$. The Heck charts were previously described in Section 5-4. For MANOVA, the three parameters of the charts are defined by:

$$s = \min(K - 1, P)$$

$$m = \frac{|P - (K - 1)| - 1}{2}$$

and

$$n = \frac{N - P - K - 1}{2}$$

When $s = 1$, the F distribution is used, as illustrated in Sections 7-5 and 8-2. In that case, all four MANOVA criteria discussed in this chapter will lead to identical results.

For the present example:

$$s = \min(3 - 1, 5) = 2$$

$$m = \frac{|5 - (3 - 1)| - 1}{2} = 1$$

and

$$n = \frac{211 - 5 - 3 - 1}{2} = 101$$

The values read from the charts may be denoted by $\theta^{\alpha}_{(s,m,n)}$. For the present data, $\theta^{.05}_{(2,1,101)} = .07$. Since $\theta = .3291$ exceeds this critical value, we would reject the hypothesis H_0: $\lambda_1 = 0$ and conclude that mean differences among the three groups do exist. In Section 8-5 we show that $\theta_1 = .3291$ represents the proportion of explained variance associated with the first discriminant function.

Procedure for performing a MANOVA in terms of Roy's criterion

Step 1. Determine the largest eigen value, λ_1, of:

$$|(\mathbf{SS_W})^{-1}(\mathbf{SS_B}) - \lambda \mathbf{I}| = 0$$

Step 2. Determine:

$$\theta = \frac{\lambda_1}{1 + \lambda_1}$$

$$s = \min(K - 1, P)$$

$$m = \frac{|P - (K - 1)| - 1}{2}$$

$$n = \frac{N - P - K - 1}{2}$$

Step 3. Enter the Heck charts or the Pillai tables and determine for α, the value of:

$$\theta^{\alpha}_{(s,m,n)}$$

Step 4. Reject H_0: $\lambda_1 = 0$ if:

$$\theta > \theta^{\alpha}_{(s,m,n)}$$

8-5. Multiple-group discriminant analysis

As noted in earlier discussions, each eigen value is associated with an eigen vector. In Chapter 7, we saw that the linear combination using the eigen vector values as weights was called the linear discriminant function. A similar situation exists for the K-sample model in that multiple discriminant functions are encountered, with the number being equal to the number of eigen values, $s = \min(K - 1, P)$. For the present example, $s = 2$. The discriminant functions in the *Multivariance* computer program of Finn (1972), associated with λ_1 and λ_2, are reported in Table 8-5. It should be noted that the coefficients in Table 8-5 will yield discriminant scores L_1 and L_2 that are orthogonal, that is, for which $r_{L_1L_2} = 0$. This means that information obtained from L_1 is unrelated to the information obtained from L_2.

As we have noted in other contexts, the naming of discriminant functions is not easy. Perhaps the easiest way to achieve a rational naming is to compute the correlation of each variable with the discriminant function. A simple way to obtain each correlation coefficient is as demonstrated for the correlation of L_1 with X_1. In terms of standardized Z scores and standardized discriminant coefficients:

$$r_{L_1X_1} = \frac{1}{N - 1} \sum_{i=1}^{N} \left(\frac{L_{1i} - \bar{L}_1}{S_{L_1}}\right)\left(\frac{X_{1i} - \bar{X}_1}{S_1}\right)$$

With $\bar{L}_1 = 0$, and $S^2_{L_1} = \mathbf{A'MS_WA} = 1$ as required by the solution described in Section 7-4, it follows that:

TABLE 8-5. The two discriminant functions for contrasting the three racial groups

	Function 1		*Function 2*	
Variable	*Raw*	*Standardized*	*Raw*	*Standardized*
1. Fluency	0.2245	0.2974	− 0.5968	− 0.7904
2. Mazes	− 3.8385	− 0.1515	− 6.9010	− 0.2723
3. Dependent clauses	− 2.5449	− 0.2912	− 3.3754	− 0.3862
4. Conventional usage	− 0.0036	− 0.9035	− 0.0010	− 0.2593
5. Elaboration index	0.0061	0.1627	0.0077	0.2065
Eigen value	0.4905		0.0632	

$$
\begin{aligned}
r_{L_1X_1} &= \frac{1}{N-1}\sum_{i=1}^{N} L_{1i}Z_{1i} \\
&= \frac{1}{N-1}\sum_{i=1}^{N}(a_1Z_{1i} + a_2Z_{2i} + \cdots + a_PZ_{Pi})Z_{1i} \\
&= \frac{1}{N-1}\sum_{i=1}^{N}(a_1Z_{1i}^2 + a_2Z_{1i}Z_{2i} + \cdots + a_PZ_{1i}Z_{Pi}) \\
&= a_1\left(\frac{\sum_{i=1}^{N} Z_{1i}^2}{N-1}\right) + a_2\left(\frac{\sum_{i=1}^{N} Z_{1i}Z_{2i}}{N-1}\right) + \cdots + a_P\left(\frac{\sum_{i=1}^{N} Z_{1i}Z_{Pi}}{N-1}\right) \\
&= a_1\,(1) + a_2r_{Z_1Z_2} + \cdots + a_Pr_{Z_1Z_P} \\
&= a_1 + a_2r_{X_1X_2} + \cdots + a_Pr_{X_1X_P} \\
&= \mathbf{R}_1\mathbf{A}_1
\end{aligned}
$$

where $\mathbf{R}_1$ is equal to the first row of $\mathbf{R}_W$. If standardized weights are not used, then:

$$r_{L_1X_1} = \frac{\mathbf{R}_1\mathbf{A}_1}{\sqrt{\mathbf{A}_1'\mathbf{R}_w\mathbf{A}_1}}$$

In a similar fashion, it can be shown that with standardized variables:

$$r_{L_sX_P} = \mathbf{R}_p\mathbf{A}_s$$

where $\mathbf{R}_p$ is the pth row of $\mathbf{R}_W$. If the unstandardized weights are used, then:

$$r_{L_sX_P} = \frac{\mathbf{R}_p\mathbf{A}_s}{\sqrt{\mathbf{A}_s'\mathbf{R}_W\mathbf{A}_s}}$$

For the present data with standardized weights, we see that:

$$\mathbf{R}_1 = [1.0000 \quad .3237 \quad .5696 \quad -.1868 \quad .7721]$$

and:

$$\mathbf{A}_1' = [.2974 \quad -.1515 \quad -.2912 \quad -.9035 \quad .1627]$$

As a result:

$$\begin{aligned}\mathbf{R}_1\mathbf{A}_1 &= r_{L_1X_1}\\ &= (1.0000)(.2974) + (.3237)(-.1515) + \cdots + (.7721)(.1627)\\ &= .3769\end{aligned}$$

Since not all discriminant function computer programs provide standardized weights, we provide instructions for the general situation.

Procedure for computing the correlation between each dependent variable X_p and the linear discriminant function L_s

Step 1. Compute:

$$\sqrt{\mathbf{A}_s'\mathbf{R}_W\mathbf{A}_s}$$

where $\mathbf{R}_W$ is the pooled within-sample correlation matrix and $\mathbf{A}_s$ is the vector of weights for the sth linear discriminant function.

Step 2. Compute:

$$\mathbf{R}_p\mathbf{A}_s$$

where $\mathbf{R}_p$ is the pth row of $\mathbf{R}_W$.

Step 3. The correlation coefficient of X_p with L_s is given as:

$$r_{X_pL_s} = \frac{\mathbf{R}_p\mathbf{A}_s}{\sqrt{\mathbf{A}_s'\mathbf{R}_W\mathbf{A}_s}}$$

If standardized weights are used:

$$r_{X_pL_s} = \mathbf{R}_p\mathbf{A}_s$$

For the example, the correlation coefficients have the values reported in Table 8-6. From these values, we see that the first discriminant function is defined almost exclusively by Conventional Usage, whereas the second discriminant function is defined essentially by the four other language measures.

Recall from Chapter 7 that:

$$(N-2)\,\lambda_1 + (N-2) = (N-2)(\lambda_1 + 1)$$

corresponds to the univariate ANOVA model of:

$$SS_B + SS_W = SS_T$$

Under this model, it follows that our previously introduced Roy's criterion:

$$\theta_1 = \frac{\lambda_1}{1+\lambda_1} = \frac{SS_B}{SS_T}$$

represents the proportion of the total variation, as defined by SS_T, in the first discriminant function that can be accounted for by between-group differences. For the present example, $\theta = .3291$, which suggests that nearly one-third of the total sum of squares associated with L_1 is due to between-group mean differences.

TABLE 8-6. Correlation between each dependent variable X_p with the two discriminant functions L_1 and L_2

Variable	L_1	L_2
1. Fluency	0.3769	− 0.8906
2. Mazes	− 0.2241	− 0.5902
3. Dependent clauses	0.1959	− 0.6634
4. Conventional usage	− 0.9506	− 0.1110
5. Elaboration index	0.3198	− 0.7251

Two-thirds of the total sum of squares associated with L_1 is unexplained or due to within-group variation.

As a result of the preceding developments, an interpretation of Wilks's criterion can now be given. Since:

$$\theta_1 = \frac{\lambda_1}{1 + \lambda_1}$$

represents the proportion of explained variation for the first discriminant function, it is clear that:

$$1 - \theta_1 = \frac{1}{1 + \lambda_1}$$

represents the proportion of unexplained variation for the same function. Analogously, if:

$$\theta_2 = \frac{\lambda_2}{1 + \lambda_2}$$

represents the proportion of explained variation for the second discriminant function, then:

$$1 - \theta_2 = \frac{1}{1 + \lambda_2}$$

represents the proportion of unexplained variation for the second discriminant function.

Since the source of θ_2 must come from the residual unexplained variation associated with θ_1, the addition to θ_1 is given by:

$$(1 - \theta_1)\theta_2$$

so that the total proportion of explained variation is equal to:

$$\begin{aligned} E &= \theta_1 + (1 - \theta_1)\theta_2 \\ &= \theta_1 + \theta_2 - \theta_1\theta_2 \end{aligned}$$

which corresponds to the union of θ_1 with θ_2. At this point, note that:

$$\Lambda = \left(\frac{1}{1 + \lambda_1}\right)\left(\frac{1}{1 + \lambda_2}\right)$$
$$= (1 - \theta_1)(1 - \theta_2)$$
$$= 1 - \theta_1 - \theta_2 + \theta_1\theta_2$$
$$= 1 - (\theta_1 + \theta_2 - \theta_1\theta_2)$$
$$= 1 - E$$

which suggests that Λ corresponds to the total proportion of unexplained variation in the two discriminant functions. For $s > 2$, Λ generalizes directly as a proportion unexplained measure.

It is also the case that testing the hypothesis, H_0: $\lambda_1 = 0$, as was done in Section 8-4, using Roy's criterion, is equivalent to testing the hypothesis:

$$H_0: \quad E(L_1^{(1)}) = E(L_2^{(1)}) = \cdots = E(L_K^{(1)})$$

using the same criterion. This hypothesis states that the mean scores on the first discriminant function are equal from one group to the next. Concluding that $\lambda_1 \neq 0$ is equivalent to concluding that there are group mean differences on L_1. As usual, once H_0 is rejected, it is of interest to determine the locus of the difference, that is, which groups differ from which others and/or which dependent variables differentiate among the K groups. That is the topic of the next section.

First, however, we describe the Bartlett sequential tests of Wilks's Λ to determine how many discriminant functions should be retained. The rationale, including the type I error specification for each successive test, parallels our earlier discussion in the context of canonical variates in Section 5-4.

To test the hypothesis:

$$H_0: \quad \lambda_1 = \lambda_2 = \cdots = \lambda_s = 0$$

compute:

$$\Lambda_1 = \prod_{p=1}^{s} \frac{1}{1 + \lambda_p}$$

$$\chi^2 = -\left[(N - 1) - \left(\frac{P + K}{2}\right)\right]\log_e \Lambda_1$$

The preceding test statistic has an approximate Chi-square distribution with $\nu = P(K - 1)$.

If the test is not significant at the chosen α level, conclude that all $\lambda_p = 0$. On the other hand, if the test is significant, test the hypothesis:

$$H_0: \quad \lambda_2 = \lambda_3 = \cdots = \lambda_s = 0$$

using:

$$\Lambda_2 = \prod_{p=2}^{s} \frac{1}{1 + \lambda_p}$$

$$\chi^2 = -\left[(N - 1) - \left(\frac{P + K}{2}\right)\right]\log_e \Lambda_2$$

based on $v = (P - 1)(K - 2)$.

If this test is not significant at the chosen alpha level, decide to retain only the first discriminant function. If the test is significant, continue testing Λ_3, based on $v = (P - 2)(K - 3)$, and so on.

We illustrate this test for the present example, with Procedure 4 of Section 5-4. In this case $\alpha_p = 2p\alpha/P(P + 1)$ is distributed so that $\alpha_1 = 2(1)(.05)/2(2 + 1) = .0167$ and $\alpha_2 = 2(2)(.05)/2(2 + 1) = .0333$ with a familywise type I error rate given by $\alpha \leq .05$. Here, Λ_1 was previously computed to be $\Lambda_1 = .6310$ in Section 8-2. Consequently:

$$\begin{aligned}\chi^2 &= -\left[(211 - 1) - \frac{5 + 3}{2}\right]\log_e(.6310)\\ &= -206(-.4604)\\ &= 94.84\end{aligned}$$

which is significant, since $\chi^2_{5(3-1):.9833} = \chi^2_{10:.9833} \simeq 22.00$. In addition, in this case:

$$\Lambda_2 = \frac{1}{1 + \lambda_2} = \frac{1}{1 + .0632} = .9405$$

yielding:

$$\chi^2 = -206 \log_e(.9405) = 12.62$$

based on $v = (5 - 1)(3 - 2) = 4$. This test is also significant since $\chi^2_{4:.9667} \simeq 10.61$. Thus, for this example, we would decide to retain both discriminant functions L_1 and L_2.

Procedure for determining how many discriminant functions to retain according to Bartlett's test.

Step 1. Determine $\lambda_1, \lambda_2, \ldots, \lambda_s$ and test:

$$H_{0_1}: \lambda_1 = \lambda_2 = \cdots = \lambda_s = 0$$

by computing:

$$\chi_1^2 = -\left[(N - 1) - \left(\frac{P + K}{2}\right)\right]\log_e\Lambda_1$$

where:

$$\Lambda_1 = \prod_{p=1}^{s} \frac{1}{1 + \lambda_s}$$

Step 2. Reject H_{0_1} if $\chi^2 > \chi^2_{P(K-1):1-\alpha}$.

Step 3. If H_{0_1} is not rejected, stop testing, but if H_{0_1} is rejected, test:

$$H_{0_2}: \lambda_2 = \lambda_3 = \cdots = \lambda_s = 0$$

by computing:

$$\chi_2^2 = -\left[(N - 1) - \left(\frac{P + K}{2}\right)\right]\log_e\Lambda_2$$

where:

$$\Lambda_2 = \prod_{p=2}^{s} \frac{1}{1 + \lambda_s}$$

Step 4. Reject H_{0_2} if $\chi_2^2 > \chi^2_{(P-1)(K-2):1-\alpha}$.

Step 5. If H_{0_2} is not rejected, stop testing, but if H_{0_2} is rejected, continue testing, but drop λ_3 and use the Chi-square distribution with $v = (P - 2)(K - 3)$.

Step 6. Continue the testing until a hypothesis is not rejected or until the last eigen value is examined, whichever occurs first.

8-6. Multiple comparisons for MANOVA and discriminant analysis problems

Given that significant mean differences among the groups exist, how can the differences be interpreted? A simultaneous multiple comparison procedure proposed by Roy and Bose (1953) follows directly from the Roy criterion, as was discussed in Section 8-4. In particular, just as detecting a significant univariate F ratio guarantees that at least one significant contrast will be identified according to Scheffé's multiple comparison procedure, the same relationship holds between the multivariate test based on Roy's criterion and the multiple comparison procedure to be discussed here. Keep in mind, however, that in the multivariate case, we must determine not only which groups differ from one another, but also on which dependent variables. As Timm (1975) has indicated, even though other multivariate post hoc comparison procedures are available, the Roy-Bose procedure is to be recommended because of its narrower intervals. More will be said about this in Section 8-10.

Given these remarks, the following three statements can be made:

1. If the multivariate test based on Roy's criterion is significant, any between-group contrast involving the first discriminant function may be investigated. At least one such contrast must be statistically significant.

2. Any other variable combinations and between-group contrasts are legitimately subsumed by this model. There is no guarantee that such a contrast will be significant, however.

3. There is no necessary correspondence between the other multivariate test criteria, for instance Wilks's Λ and the two trace criteria, and the multiple comparison procedure discussed here. In particular, rejecting H_0 using the other criteria does not guarantee a significant Roy-Bose contrast; and a Roy-Bose contrast can be significant even though a test based on the other criteria is not.

Each of these statements will be further elaborated and illustrated in this section. We begin with Statement 1, regarding between-group contrasts in the first discriminant function. Such a contrast is defined as:

$$\psi = b_1 E(L_1) + b_2 E(L_2) + \cdots + b_K E(L_K)$$

with:

$$b_1 + b_2 + \cdots + b_K = 0$$

Contrasts are estimated as:

$$\begin{aligned}\hat{\psi} &= b_1\bar{L}_1 + b_2\bar{L}_2 + \cdots + b_K\bar{L}_K \\ &= \sum_{k=1}^{K} b_k\bar{L}_k\end{aligned}$$

with:

$$SE^2_{\hat{\psi}} = SE^2_L\left(\frac{b_1^2}{N_1} + \frac{b_2^2}{N_2} + \cdots + \frac{b_K^2}{N_K}\right)$$

where:

$$SE^2_L = \mathbf{A}_1' \hat{\Sigma}_{XX} \mathbf{A}_1 = \mathbf{A}_1' \mathbf{MS_W} \mathbf{A}_1$$

with:

$\mathbf{A}_1$ = the vector of weights associated with L_1

If each variable is standardized and the standardized discriminant function weights are employed, then:

$$\mathbf{A}_1' \mathbf{MS_W} \mathbf{A}_1 = 1$$

and $SE^2_{\hat{\psi}}$ simplifies to:

$$SE^2_{\hat{\psi}} = \sum_{k=1}^{K} \frac{b_k^2}{N_k}$$

The Roy-Bose critical value is a generalization of Scheffé's **S**, and is defined in this context as:

$$\mathbf{S} = \sqrt{\left(\frac{\theta^{\alpha}_{(s,m,n)}}{1 - \theta^{\alpha}_{(s,m,n)}}\right)(N - K)}$$

yielding simultaneous intervals given by:

$$\psi = \hat{\psi} \pm \mathbf{S}\ SE_{\hat{\psi}}$$

We note that other writers such as Morrison (1976) omit the $N - K$ in the preceding critical value. This is because they describe the procedure in terms of $\mathbf{SS_W}$, rather than in terms of $\mathbf{MS_W}$, as we do. Obviously both approaches will yield identical results.

For the present example:

$$\mathbf{S} = \sqrt{\frac{\theta^{.05}_{(2,1,101)}}{1 - \theta^{.05}_{(2,1,101)}}(N - K)} = \sqrt{\frac{.07}{.93}(211 - 3)} = 3.96$$

Mean standardized discriminant scores may be computed using the values reported in Tables 8-2, 8-3, and 8-5. In particular, the mean standardized discriminant score for the first group is given by:

$$\bar{L}_1 = a_1\left(\frac{\bar{X}_{11} - \bar{X}_1}{\sqrt{MS_{W_1}}}\right) + a_2\left(\frac{\bar{X}_{12} - \bar{X}_2}{\sqrt{MS_{W_2}}}\right) + \cdots + a_5\left(\frac{\bar{X}_{15} - \bar{X}_5}{\sqrt{MS_{W_5}}}\right)$$

where:

a_p = the weight associated with the first standardized discriminant function on the pth variable

$\bar{X}_{kp}$ = the mean of the pth variable in Group k

$\bar{X}_p$ = the across-groups mean on the pth variable

and

$\sqrt{MS_{W_p}}$ = the pooled within-group standard deviation on the pth variable

For the present data:

$$\bar{L}_1 = .2974\left(\frac{4.5082 - 5.9788}{1.3244}\right) - .1515\left(\frac{.0674 - .0726}{.0395}\right) + \cdots + .1627\left(\frac{50.8235 - 75.4123}{26.7123}\right)$$
$$= -1.2699$$

In similar fashion:

$\bar{L}_2 = -.5724$ and $\bar{L}_3 = .6553$

The three pairwise comparisons of the mean standardized discriminant scores are given by:

$$\psi_1 = (\bar{L}_1 - \bar{L}_2) \pm \mathbf{S}\sqrt{\frac{1}{N_1} + \frac{1}{N_2}}$$
$$= [-1.2699 - (-.5724)] \pm 3.96\sqrt{\frac{1}{17} + \frac{1}{86}} = -.70 \pm 1.05$$

$$\psi_2 = (\bar{L}_1 - \bar{L}_3) \pm \mathbf{S}\sqrt{\frac{1}{N_1} + \frac{1}{N_3}}$$
$$= [-1.2699 - (.6553)] \pm 3.96\sqrt{\frac{1}{17} + \frac{1}{108}} = -1.92 \pm 1.03$$

$$\psi_3 = (\bar{L}_2 - \bar{L}_3) \pm \mathbf{S}\sqrt{\frac{1}{N_2} + \frac{1}{N_3}}$$
$$= [-.5724 - (.6553)] \pm 3.96\sqrt{\frac{1}{86} + \frac{1}{108}} = -1.23 \pm .57$$

As a result, we would conclude that the mean discriminant score of the White children was higher than that of either Asian children or Black children. Since the first discriminant function is defined chiefly by Conventional Usage, as shown in Table 8-6, we could interpret these contrasts by focusing on the mean differences with respect to Conventional Usage, as in Table 8-1. Since larger scores are associated with departures from conventional English usage, as in Section 8-1, it is clear that the Asian and Black children tend to produce more deviant forms in comparison to the White children. This statement will be assessed more directly in a short time.

We might also wish to combine the Asian and Black groups to be compared with the Whites. Either the weighted contrast:

$$\hat{\psi}_4 = \frac{N_1\bar{L}_1 + N_2\bar{L}_2}{N_1 + N_2} - \bar{L}_3$$

or the unweighted contrast:

$$\hat{\psi}_{4'} = \frac{1}{2}(\bar{L}_1 + \bar{L}_2) - \bar{L}_3$$

could be legitimately investigated using the Roy-Bose procedure. Considering the first combination, we have:

$$\hat{\psi}_4 = \frac{17(-1.2699) + 86(-.5724)}{103} - .6553$$

$$= -.6875 - .6553 = -1.3428$$

Since:

$$SE^2_{\hat{\psi}_4} = \frac{(17/103)^2}{17} + \frac{(86/103)^2}{86} + \frac{(-1)^2}{108} = \frac{17 + 86}{103^2} + \frac{1}{108}$$

$$= \frac{1}{103} + \frac{1}{108} = \frac{1}{N_1 + N_2} + \frac{1}{N_3} = .01897$$

so that:

$$\mathbf{S}\ SE_{\hat{\psi}_4} = 3.96\sqrt{.01897} = .54$$

Consequently this contrast is also statistically significant.

For completeness, we report how to test contrasts in the first discriminant function for significance.

Procedure for testing contrasts on the first discriminant function.

Step 1. Determine the mean value of $L^{(1)}$ for each group. Let the mean values be denoted as:

$$\bar{L}_1, \bar{L}_2, \ldots, \bar{L}_K$$

Step 2. Define the contrasts of interest and estimate them as:

$$\hat{\psi} = b_1\bar{L}_1 + b_2\bar{L}_2 + \cdots + b_K\bar{L}_K$$

where:

$$b_1 + b_2 + \cdots + b_K = 0$$

Step 3. Estimate the standard deviation of a contrast as:

$$SE_{\hat{\psi}} = \sqrt{\mathbf{A}'\mathbf{MS_W}\mathbf{A}\left(\frac{b_1^2}{N_1} + \frac{b_2^2}{N_2} + \cdots + \frac{b_K^2}{N_K}\right)}$$

If the standardized discriminant function weights are used, then:

$$\mathbf{A}'\mathbf{MS_W}\mathbf{A} = 1$$

Step 4. Determine the value of:

$$\mathbf{S} = \sqrt{\frac{\theta^{\alpha}_{(s,m,n)}}{1 - \theta^{\alpha}_{(s,m,n)}}(N - K)}$$

Step 5. Determine the simultaneous $100(1-\alpha)$ percent confidence intervals for the set of $\hat{\psi}$ by:

$\psi = \hat{\psi} \pm \mathbf{S}\, SE_{\hat{\psi}}$

Note: See the notes attached to the Procedure box in Section 7-7. The comments made there apply in this situation. The only difference is that $b_1 + b_2 + \cdots + b_K = 0$.

In addition to contrasts defined in terms of the optimally determined a_p of the first discriminant function, any user-specified linear combination of variables is subsumed by the Roy-Bose procedure. In the present example, if we wished to focus just on X_1, Fluency, we could define $a_1 = 1$ and $a_2 = a_3 = a_4 = a_5 = 0$. Note that there is no restriction on these values, as in $\Sigma_{k=1}^{K} b_k = 0$. As indicated previously, a likely variable that differentiates among the three racial groups is X_4, Conventionality. Thus, with $a_1 = a_2 = a_3 = 0$, $a_4 = 1$, and $a_5 = 0$, we could investigate the three pairwise comparisons that were examined previously. Here:

$$\psi_5 = (\bar{X}_{14} - \bar{X}_{24}) \pm \mathbf{S}\sqrt{\frac{MS_{W_4}}{N_1} + \frac{MS_{W_4}}{N_2}}$$

$$= (677.4118 - 535.7791) \pm 3.96\sqrt{\frac{64056.6470}{17} + \frac{64056.6470}{86}}$$

$$= 141.63 \pm 266.02$$

$$\psi_6 = (\bar{X}_{14} - \bar{X}_{34}) \pm \mathbf{S}\sqrt{\frac{MS_{W_4}}{N_1} + \frac{MS_{W_4}}{N_3}}$$

$$= (677.4118 - 232.3056) \pm 3.96\sqrt{\frac{64056.6470}{17} + \frac{64056.6470}{108}}$$

$$= 445.11 \pm 261.51$$

$$\psi_7 = (\bar{X}_{24} - \bar{X}_{34}) \pm \mathbf{S}\sqrt{\frac{MS_{W_4}}{N_2} + \frac{MS_{W_4}}{N_3}}$$

$$= (535.7791 - 232.3056) \pm 3.96\sqrt{\frac{64056.6470}{86} + \frac{64056.6470}{108}}$$

$$= 303.47 \pm 144.85$$

Thus we would conclude that White children produced significantly fewer deviations from conventional English usage in comparison to either Asian or Black children. As many other complex contrasts as desired (for instance, White versus Asian and Black combined) could be conducted on this variable, as could simple and complex comparisons on any other variable or combination of variables. With respect to variable combinations, sums or differences based on either raw or standardized (using $\sqrt{MS_{W_p}}$) means could certainly be investigated, see Section 7-7, and are subsumed by the Roy-Bose simultaneous comparison procedure. An interesting possibility is discussed in Chapter 9.

For completeness, we describe the general form of the simultaneous Roy-Bose procedure.

Procedure for testing general contrasts using the Roy-Bose procedure.

Step 1. Define:

$$\bar{C} = a_1\bar{X}_1 + a_2\bar{X}_2 + \cdots + a_P\bar{X}_P$$

where C represents the particular variable combination of interest. If one-variable-at-a-time comparisons are of interest, say $\bar{X}_p$, then $a_p = +1$ and all other $a_{p'} = 0$. Note that the $(a_1\ a_2, \ldots, a_P)$ values are not restricted to discriminant function coefficients. They can be any meaningful set of coefficients of interest to the researcher.

Step 2. Determine $\bar{C}_k$ for each group. Define a contrast in the $\bar{C}_k$ values by:

$$\hat{\psi} = b_1\bar{C}_1 + b_2\bar{C}_2 + \cdots + b_K\bar{C}_K$$

where:

$$b_1 + b_2 + \cdots + b_K = 0$$

Step 3. Estimate the standard deviation of a contrast as:

$$SE_{\hat{\psi}} = \sqrt{\mathbf{A}'\mathbf{MS}_W\mathbf{A}\left(\frac{b_1^2}{N_1} + \frac{b_2^2}{N_2} + \cdots + \frac{b_K^2}{N_K}\right)}$$

If standardization based on $\sqrt{MS_{W_p}}$ is employed, then this becomes:

$$SE_{\hat{\psi}} = \sqrt{\mathbf{A}'\mathbf{R}_W\mathbf{A}\left(\frac{b_1^2}{N_1} + \frac{b_2^2}{N_2} + \cdots + \frac{b_K^2}{N_K}\right)}$$

where, in the latter case, **A** represents the original unstandardized weights. That is, the division by $\sqrt{MS_{W_p}}$ is ignored.

Step 4. Determine the value of:

$$\mathbf{S} = \sqrt{\frac{\theta^\alpha_{(s,m,n)}}{1 - \theta^\alpha_{(s,m,n)}}(N - K)}$$

Step 5. Determine the simultaneous $100(1 - \alpha)$ percent confidence intervals for all ψ by:

$$\psi = \hat{\psi} \pm \mathbf{S}\ SE_{\hat{\psi}}$$

8-7. Considerations in choosing among MANOVA and discriminant analysis criteria

As can be seen from Sections 8-2, 8-3, and 8-4, unlike univariate ANOVA where there is a single F test for assessing the simultaneous equality of K means, with multivariate ANOVA there exist several statistical test criteria for assessing the simultaneous equality of K mean vectors. A very clear discussion of the question of which criterion is best is given by Olson (1976), based on his earlier (1974) investigation of the null and nonnull behaviors of various test criteria. First of all, it is easily demonstrated that there is no uniformly best criterion, at least as far as statistical power is concerned. This is because multivariate mean vectors can differ in many respects; that is, groups can differ in different ways on different dependent variables.

A useful distinction to represent this notion may be found in the terms *concentrated* versus *diffuse noncentrality structures*, as discussed in Olson (1976) and Schatzoff (1966). The basic idea is that in certain situations, the nature of group differences may be described with reference to only one underlying dimension, as reflected by a single nonzero eigen value. Whenever group mean differences are concentrated in one dimension, it is possible to order the groups in terms of a single linear discriminant function along a straight line. In contrast, in other situations, two or more dimensions (nonzero eigen values) are required to characterize group differences. With this type of diffuse noncentrality structure, a two-, three-, or, in general, an $(s > 1)$-dimensional grid would be needed to reveal accurately the nature of between-group differences. In this case, two or more linear discriminant functions would have to be constructed, as was done in Section 8-5.

To illustrate some of these notions, we provide a simple example. Suppose that 36 students are randomly assigned in equal numbers to three experimental conditions. In Condition 1, the students are given special instruction in arithmetic skills; in Condition 2, the students are given special instruction in reading skills; and in Condition 3, the students are given either no special instruction or some type of 'placebo' instruction. Following this, performance on four dependent variables is assessed. To summarize thus far, $N = 36$, $K = 3$, and $P = 4$.

Now let us consider two different situations. In Situation 1, suppose that the $P = 4$ dependent variables represented four different arithmetic achievement measures. Were this the case, it might turn out that a single discriminant function would serve to characterize between-group differences. That is, L_1 might represent a general arithmetic achievement construct, and the three groups might be linearly ordered as in Example 1 of Figure 8-1. If left-to-right corresponds to low-to-high scores on L_1, it can be seen that the students who received special arithmetic instruction outperformed the other two groups of students.

In contrast, for Situation 2, suppose that the $P = 4$ dependent variables represented two arithmetic achievement tests and two reading achievement tests. As a result, two discriminant functions might be required to characterize between-group differences. In this case, L_1 might be defined by the two arithmetic variables and L_2 by the two reading variables, with different patterns of group differences on each. In Example 2 of Figure 8-1, a hypothetical outcome is depicted. There it can be seen that Condition 1, special arithmetic instruction, resulted in superior performance on the arithmetic dimension L_1 just as in Example 1; but, in addition, Condition 2, special reading instruction, resulted in superior performance on the reading dimension L_2. On the second dimension, Condition 1 and Condition 3 students performed comparably.

To illustrate that no one multivariate test criterion is uniformly best, suppose that the eigen values associated with Example 1 were $\lambda_1 = .60$ and $\lambda_2 = 0$, thereby reflecting the single dimension or concentrated structure. On the other hand, the eigen values associated with Example 2 might be $\lambda_1 = \lambda_2 = .30$, which reflect two equally important dimensions or a diffuse structure. It is easy to show that using the present information, Roy's test conducted on the data of Example 1 would be statistically significant, with $\alpha = .05$, $\theta = .375$, and $\theta^{.05}_{(2,1/2,14)} = .335$, whereas the F test based on Wilks's Λ would not be, with $F = 1.99$, $F_{8,60:.95} = 2.10$. Exactly the reverse is true for Example 2, where Roy's test would not be significant, with $\theta = .231$, whereas the test of Wilks's Λ would be, with $F = 2.25$.

An important generalization to be learned from this simple example is that for situations in which it is believed that the pattern of between-group differences is

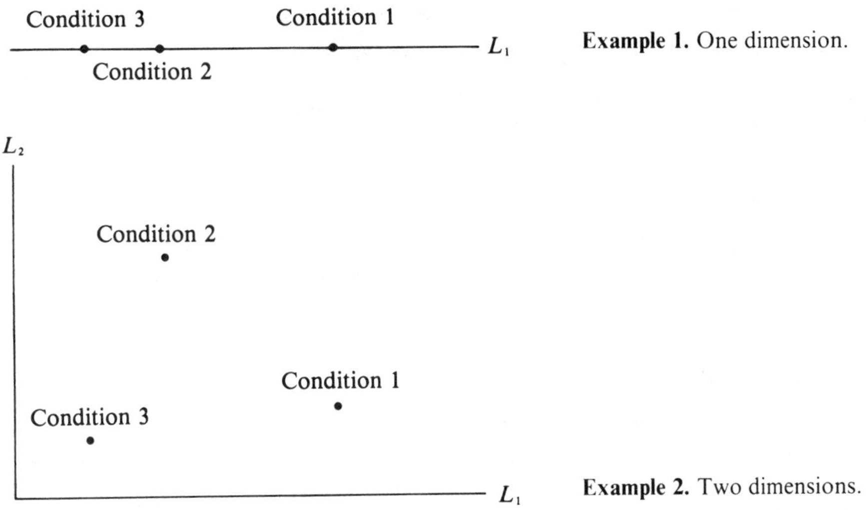

Figure 8-1. Examples of one- and two-dimension between-group differences.

concentrated in the first discriminant function, that is, $\lambda_1 > 0$, $\lambda_2 = \lambda_3 = \cdots = \lambda_s = 0$, then Roy's criterion is a wise selection. In contrast, for situations in which it is suspected that the pattern of between-group differences is diffuse, that is, more than one $\lambda_p > 0$, then Wilks's criterion or one of the others that considers all λ_p simultaneously (see Section 8-3) is preferred.

The preceding generalizations hold when the assumptions underlying MANOVA are met, specifically, multivariate normality and variance-covariance matrix homogeneity across groups. When such assumptions are violated, Olson (1974) has shown that the Pillai-Bartlett trace criterion of Section 8-3 is a wise choice, and that Roy's criterion is definitely not to be recommended as a result of a vastly inflated type I error probability. Unfortunately not much more in the way of recommendations can be given at present, and the interested reader is referred to Olson (1976) for more details.

8-8. Classification based on the multivariate normal distribution

In Section 7-10, classification of subjects into one of two groups was illustrated in terms of the univariate normal distribution. Since there was only one discriminant function associated with the two groups, the univariate normal distribution was a natural model. For the present example based on the Loban data, two discriminant functions have been retained. If we were so inclined, classification of each student into Asian, Black, or White could be performed for each discriminant function separately. In practice, this could cause problems since it is possible to assign a student to one group on the basis of the first discriminant function and to a different group on the basis of the second discriminant function. To avoid this embarrassing situation, classification can be achieved by using both discriminant functions together. This procedure is based on the likelihoods generated from the multivariate normal distribution (see Section 5-8).

In matrix notation, the univariate normal distribution can be written as:

$$f(x) = (\text{Constant}) \times e^{-\frac{1}{2}(\mathbf{X} - \boldsymbol{\mu})'(\sigma^2)^{-1}(\mathbf{X} - \boldsymbol{\mu})}$$

Since the constant is of no immediate interest, we denote it simply as C. For the vector of variables:

$$\mathbf{X}' = (X_1 \ X_2 \ \ldots \ X_P)$$

the corresponding density can be written as:

$$f(X_1, X_2, \ldots, X_P) = Ce^{-\frac{1}{2}(\mathbf{X}-\boldsymbol{\mu})'\Sigma_{XX}^{-1}(\mathbf{X}-\boldsymbol{\mu})}$$
$$= Ce^{-\frac{1}{2}Q}$$

where:

$$Q = (\mathbf{X} - \boldsymbol{\mu})'\Sigma_{XX}^{-1}(\mathbf{X} - \boldsymbol{\mu})$$

Clearly this function can be used to determine the likelihood of an observed unit, if it is believed that the vector of variables $\mathbf{X}'$ has a multivariate normal distribution. This model is used in the same manner as that described in Section 7-10 for $K = 2$. Since $\boldsymbol{\mu}$ and $\boldsymbol{\Sigma}_{XX}$ are unknown, they are replaced by the centroids of each distribution, $\bar{\mathbf{X}}_1, \bar{\mathbf{X}}_2, \ldots, \bar{\mathbf{X}}_K$, and the sample variance-covariance matrix. At this point, the procedures of Section 7-10 are involved. The likelihoods for a given subject are determined on the basis of $\bar{\mathbf{X}}_1, \bar{\mathbf{X}}_2, \ldots, \bar{\mathbf{X}}_K$, using the pooled sample variance-covariance matrix. Then, for a particular subject's discriminant scores, here L_1 and L_2, we determine likelihoods of belonging to a particular group. In our example, $S_{L_1}^2 = S_{L_2}^2 = 1$ and $r_{L_1L_2} = 0$, so that the likelihood reduces to:

$$f(L_1, L_2 \mid \text{Group } k) = \frac{1}{2\pi} e^{-(1/2)[(L_1 - \bar{L}_{k1})^2 + (L_2 - \bar{L}_{k2})^2]}$$
$$= \left[\frac{1}{\sqrt{2\pi}} e^{-(1/2)(L_1 - \bar{L}_{k1})^2}\right]\left[\frac{1}{\sqrt{2\pi}} e^{-(1/2)(L_2 - \bar{L}_{k2})^2}\right]$$
$$= [f(L_1 \mid \text{Group } k)][f(L_2 \mid \text{Group } k)]$$

where it will be recalled from Section 7-10 that each likelihood, $f(L \mid \text{Group } k)$, represents an ordinate of the normal distribution. For standardized discriminant functions based on a grand mean of 0 and a within-group standard deviation of 1, we need only compute the likelihood with respect to each group based on $f(L_1 - \bar{L}_{k1})$ and $f(L_2 - \bar{L}_{k2})$, and then simply multiply the resulting values.

Let us illustrate this procedure for the 17 Asian students in the Loban data. Each student's discriminant score may be computed in one of two equivalent ways, using the weights in Table 8-5. The two methods are as follows:

1. Standardize each variable, X_p, so that for subject i in group k:

$$Z_{kpi} = \frac{Y_{kpi} - \bar{Y}_{\cdot p \cdot}}{\sqrt{MS_{W_p}}}$$

To determine the values of the disciminant scores, apply the Z_{kpi} to the standardized weights.

2. Do not standardize each variable, but use the X_{kpi} as they are observed or reported. Since the mean values of the discriminant functions will differ from zero, subtract the mean discriminant score from each value.

Let us use the second method to classify Subject 1 in the Asian group. In terms of the notation of Section 8-1 the raw scores, X_{kpi}, for this subject are given by the vector:

$$[X_{111} \quad X_{121} \quad X_{131} \quad X_{141} \quad X_{151}] = [8.24 \quad .0712 \quad .13 \quad 201 \quad 90]$$

Across all subjects $\bar{L}_1 = -.3159$ and $\bar{L}_2 = -4.4718$. The values of L_1 and L_2, determined relative to these mean values, are given for Subject 1 as:

$$L_{11} = [.2245(8.24) - 3.8385(.0712) - 2.5449(.13) - .0036(201) + .0061(90)] - [-.3159]$$
$$= 1.39$$

and:

$$L_{12} = [-.5968(8.24) - 6.9010(.0712) - 3.3754(.13) - .0010(201) + .0077(90)] - [-4.4718]$$
$$= -.89$$

The mean discriminant scores for the $N_1 = 17$ Asians are $\bar{L}_{11} = -1.27$ and $\bar{L}_{12} = .71$, those for the $N_2 = 86$ Blacks are $\bar{L}_{21} = -.57$ and $\bar{L}_{22} = -.22$, and those for the $N_3 = 108$ Whites are $\bar{L}_{31} = .66$ and $\bar{L}_{32} = .06$. The corresponding likelihoods associated with the first Asian student are computed as follows:

$$f(L_{11} \mid k = 1) = f[1.39 - (-1.27)] = f(2.66) = .0116$$

$$f(L_{12} \mid k = 1) = f[-.89 - (.71)] = f(-1.60) = .1109$$

so that P_{11} is equal to:

$$P_{11} = f(L_{11}, L_{12} \mid \text{Asian}) = .0116(.1109) = .0013$$

This represents the likelihood that the first Asian student is, in fact, Asian. The corresponding likelihood that the student is Black is determined as follows:

$$f(L_{11} \mid k = 2) = f[1.39 - (-.57)] = f(1.96) = .0584$$

$$f(L_{12} \mid k = 2) = f[-.89 - (-.22)] = f(-.67) = .3187$$

so that P_{21} is equal to:

$$P_{21} = f(L_{11}, L_{12} \mid \text{Black}) = .0584(.3187) = .0186$$

Finally, for the White assignment,

$$f(L_{11} \mid k = 3) = f[1.39 - (.66)] = f(.74) = .3034$$

$$f(L_{12} \mid k = 3) = f[-.89 - (.06)] = f(-.95) = .2541$$

so that P_{31} is equal to:

$$P_{31} = f(L_{11}, L_{12} \mid \text{White}) = .3034(.2541) = .0771$$

The sum of the likelihood products is equal to .0970, so that the probabilities of classification are:

$P_{11} = P(\text{Subject is Asian}) = .0013/.0970 = .010 \simeq .01$

$P_{21} = P(\text{Subject is Black}) = .0186/.0970 = .192 \simeq .19$

and:

$P_{31} = P(\text{Subject is White}) = .0771/.0970 = .795 \simeq .80$

For this particular student, an Asian, a predicted classification of White would be made, which would be in error. The remaining discriminant scores (rounded to two decimal places), and corresponding probabilities and predicted classifications, are reported in Table 8-7 for the 17 Asian students. As can be seen from these data, 10 of the Asians were correctly classified, 2 were classified as Blacks, and 5 were classified as Whites. Note that the procedure used here does not incorporate a priori information relating to the very different actual group sizes, 17, 86, and 108. Such a procedure is possible, however.

For the present classification system, the total number of students correctly classified may be found in the main diagonal of Table 8-8. The percentage correctly classified is given by (147/211) (100) = 69.7%. The resulting Cohen's κ associated

TABLE 8-7. Likelihood values, associated probabilities, and predicted group membership for the 17 Asian students

Student Number	L_1	L_2	*Probability of* Asian	Black	White	*Predicted classification*
1	1.39	−0.89	0.01	0.19	0.80	White
2	−0.37	−0.28	0.21	0.50	0.29	Black
3	−1.29	1.38	0.74	0.20	0.06	Asian
4	−0.37	1.86	0.60	0.20	0.21	Asian
5	0.09	1.86	0.44	0.20	0.36	Asian
6	−6.90	−0.46	0.97	0.03	0.00	Asian
7	−2.60	0.26	0.76	0.23	0.01	Asian
8	−3.29	0.57	0.87	0.12	0.00	Asian
9	0.47	1.44	0.24	0.21	0.55	White
10	−1.41	−0.48	0.38	0.54	0.08	Black
11	−3.84	−0.07	0.85	0.15	0.00	Asian
12	0.25	−0.85	0.07	0.46	0.47	White
13	−1.98	0.97	0.79	0.19	0.02	Asian
14	0.56	1.82	0.27	0.17	0.56	White
15	0.09	0.28	0.19	0.37	0.44	White
16	−3.04	1.33	0.92	0.08	0.00	Asian
17	0.65	3.33	0.48	0.08	0.44	Asian

TABLE 8-8. Prediction of group membership on the basis of L_1 and L_2 for the Loban data

Predicted group	*Actual group* Asian	*Black*	*White*	*Total*
Asian	10	19	9	38
Black	2	42	4	48
White	5	25	95	125
Total	17	86	108	211

with these data may be computed to be .49. For completeness, we now provide directions for classifications based on discriminant scores, using the standardized approach mentioned earlier. (The interested reader should verify the equivalence of this and the raw score approach.)

Procedure for classifying subjects in terms of their likelihoods.

Step 1. Determine the number of retained discriminant functions. Let that number be Q, with any particular function designated q.

Step 2. Consider a subject with data values $(X_{k1i}, X_{k2i}, \ldots, X_{kpi}, \ldots, K_{kPi})$ where X_{kpi} is the value of variable X_p for subject i in Group k. For this subject determine $(L_{ki1}, L_{1i2}, \ldots, L_{kiq}, \ldots, L_{kiQ})$ where L_{kiq} is the value of discriminant function L_q for subject i of Group k. If raw scores are used, correct each L_{kiq} by subtracting $\bar{L}_q$ from each L_{kiq}. If standardized weights are used with Z scores, do not perform the subtracting adjustment.

Step 3. Determine the centroid of the discriminant functions for each group. Denote the centroid of Group k by:

$$(\bar{L}_{k1}, \bar{L}_{k2}, \ldots, \bar{L}_{kq}, \ldots, \bar{L}_{kQ})$$

Step 4. Since $MS_{W_{L1}} = MS_{W_{L2}} = \cdots = MS_{W_{Lq}} = \cdots = MS_{W_{LQ}} = 1$,

determine the standardized difference of the L_{kiq} values from each of the K centroids as $Z_{kiq} = L_{kiq} - \bar{L}_{kq}$. Denote the standardized values for subject i in group k by:

$$(Z_{ki1}, Z_{ki2}, \ldots, Z_{kiq}, \ldots, Z_{kiQ})$$

Step 5. From the table of normal distribution ordinates, determine the likelihoods for each Z_{kiq}. Denote them by:

$$f(L_{iq} \mid k) = f(Z_{kiq})$$

and find for each k:

$$P_{ki} = f(L_{i1}, L_{i2}, \ldots, L_{iq}, \ldots, L_{iQ}) = f(Z_{ki1})f(Z_{ki2}) \cdots f(Z_{kiq}) \cdots f(Z_{kiQ})$$

Denote these values by:

$$P_{1i}, P_{2i}, \ldots, P_{ki}, \ldots, P_{Ki}$$

Step 6. Determine the conditional probabilities for Subject i as:

$$(p_{1i}, p_{2i}, \ldots, p_{ki}, \ldots, p_{Ki})$$

where:

$$p_{ki} = \frac{P_{ki}}{P_{1i} + P_{2i} + \cdots + P_{Ki}}$$

Step 7. Assign Subject i of Group k to the group having the largest p_{ki}. If Step 6 is not carried out, assign Subject i of Group k to the group having the largest P_{ki}.

8-9. The topology of discriminant scores

It is sometimes useful to examine the results of a discriminant analysis in terms of a graphic presentation. With two retained discriminant functions, a two-dimensional grid is required, as in Example 2 of Figure 8-1. Since L_1 and L_2 are orthogonal to one another, they can be used as a right angle coordinate system with center at (0, 0). An example of the kind of graphic picture entailed in plotting joint discriminant scores for each group of students is shown in Figure 8-2.

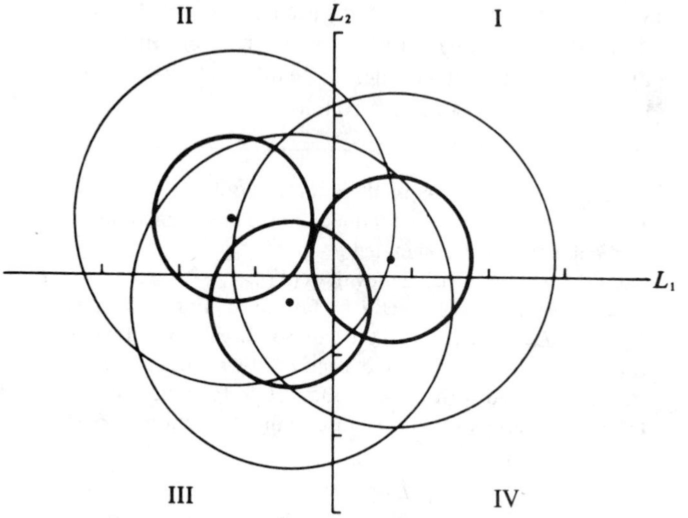

Figure 8-2. The topology of L_1 and L_2 for Asians, Blacks, and Whites. Dark contours represent one standard deviation. Circles with light lines represent two standard deviations.

As indicated, Asians tend to score 1.27 standard deviations below zero on the first discriminant function and .71 standard deviations above zero on the second discriminant function. They tend to occupy points represented by Quadrant II of the two-dimensional grid. Blacks, on the other hand, tend to center .57 standard deviations below average on the first discriminant function and .22 standard deviations below zero on the second function and congregate in Quadrant III. Finally, Whites are seen to cluster about .66 standard deviations above zero on the first discriminant function and .06 standard deviations above zero on the second function and to appear in Quadrants I and IV.

8-10. Simplified statistics for one-way MANOVA

As has been shown in this chapter, MANOVA is used to test the hypothesis that K mean vectors are equal. As is further evident from Section 8–6, in many if not most multivariate investigations, the conclusion of mean vector inequality is only of incidental interest. Rather, the researcher wishes to learn which groups differ on which variables or linear combinations of variables. This is the very reason why simultaneous post hoc comparison procedures such as the Roy-Bose method are employed. They allow us to investigate between-group comparisons, while having the desirable property of controlling the type I error probability familywise, that is, for the entire set of comparisons investigated.

Suppose, on the other hand, that instead of being able to look at an infinite number of variable combinations and between-group comparisons, as is permissible using the Roy-Bose procedure, a researcher were able to define on an a priori basis a finite set of variable combinations and/or between-group comparisons that were of interest. In such cases, and as will be demonstrated here, MANOVA may not be advisable, since the same degree of type I error control can be exercised with some much simpler alternative approaches. More importantly, these alternative approaches will often yield confidence intervals that are narrower than the corresponding Roy-Bose intervals, thereby making these alternatives more powerful. The procedures to be discussed here derive from the versatile Bonferroni equality that has been incorporated into Dunn's procedure throughout this text.

The important principle, for present purposes, is that if we perform C comparisons using α_1 for the first, α_2 for the second, up to α_C for the last, our maximum error for the set of comparisons is:

$$\alpha_1 + \alpha_2 + \cdots + \alpha_C$$

In the special case where all α_C are equal to, for instance, α', the total α is at most $C\alpha'$. The validity of these statements does not depend on comparisons being orthogonal, nor on their being restricted to only one dependent variable. All that is relevant is the number of contrasts examined, C, and the particular values of α_c chosen for each contrast.

For example, suppose a researcher analyzing the Loban data of this chapter wished to perform only the pairwise comparisons with respect to each of the five language measures. In that case, $C = 3$ (possible pairwise comparisons on each variable) $\times$ 5(variables) $= 15$. If we wished α for the set of these 15 comparisons not to exceed .05, and if equal allocation of α to each comparison were acceptable, then $\alpha' = .05/15 = .0033$. Each contrast would be tested using the univariate t distribution based on $v = N - K$, here $v = 211 - 3 = 208$.

Regular t tables with $t_{208:.9967}$ or $t_{208:.99835}$ would be used for directional and nondirectional tests, respectively. The tables in Appendix B-4 would yield the necessary values. Here, from Appendix B-4 we find that for 15 nondirectional comparisons, $t \simeq 2.96$. When compared with the previous Roy-Bose value of $\mathbf{S} = 3.96$ in Section 8-6, the present critical value is seen to be considerably smaller. Since $\hat{\psi}$ and $SE_{\hat{\psi}}$ are defined in exactly the same way according to each procedure, the confidence interval associated with the planned Dunn-Bonferroni approach would be narrower. Therefore, a MANOVA followed by Roy-Bose confidence intervals would not be recommended in this case. Bypassing the MANOVA and instead constructing the $C = 15$ Dunn-Bonferroni confidence intervals is clearly preferable. Directional, that is, one-tailed, comparisons would make the Dunn-Bonferroni advantage even greater.

Suppose instead that complex comparisons, such as $(1/2)\bar{X}_{11} + (1/2)\bar{X}_{21} - \bar{X}_{31}$, or variable combinations, such as $\bar{X}_1 + \bar{X}_2$, were of interest. These could be planned as well and easily subsumed by the Dunn-Bonferroni model. From Appendix B-4 it can be seen that, for the present example, over 250 such comparisons could be performed and still $t < \mathbf{S}$. As a result, we wonder why MANOVA would ever be considered in this, and in most other, research investigations. All a researcher need do is say that he or she will investigate all pairwise comparisons within each variable, which is given by $PK(K - 1)/2$. In addition, all pairwise comparisons on Q specified variable combinations, for instance, $X_1 + X_2$ or $X_3 + X_4 - X_5$, could be planned, yielding a total of $(P + Q)K(K - 1)/2$ comparisons. Finally, any complex comparisons of interest would be added to this total. If the t value associated with this C-comparison set is smaller than $\mathbf{S}$, based on the same α level, as will typically be the case, then MANOVA should be bypassed in favor of the Dunn-Bonferroni approach. On the other hand, if $\mathbf{S}$ is smaller than t, then MANOVA would be recommended. MANOVA would also be recommended in situations in which we wish to compare groups with respect to data-determined discriminant functions. Here the contrast weights cannot be specified on an a priori basis by the investigator.

Finally, it should be mentioned that another variation of the Dunn-Bonferroni approach is possible, one that mixes ANOVA with planned analyses. We could decide to perform, for instance, P univariate ANOVAs, each at an α level of $\alpha' = \alpha/P$. Any univariate F that is significant would be followed up with post hoc comparisons using the Scheffé procedure with $\alpha' = \alpha/P$. Tukey's (1953) procedure could be used as an alternative to ANOVA if only pairwise comparisons were of interest. In the present example, the Scheffé value associated with five univariate ANOVAs, each at $\alpha' = .01$, so that $\alpha \leq .05$, is given by:

$$\begin{aligned} \mathbf{S} &= \sqrt{v_1 F_{v_1,v_2:1-\alpha'}} \\ &= \sqrt{2F_{2,208:.99}} \\ &\simeq \sqrt{2(4.63)} \\ &= 3.04 \end{aligned}$$

which, for this example, is also less than $\mathbf{S}$, and almost as low as t with $C = 15$. With $\mathbf{S}$, an unlimited number of within-variable contrasts could be investigated. Once again, since $\hat{\psi}$ and $SE_{\hat{\psi}}$ are defined in the same way here, t and $\mathbf{S}$ critical values may be compared directly to determine which is preferable for a given problem. A modification is required for comparing Tukey's critical value with these.

It should be clear from the examples in this section that the Dunn-Bonferroni approach affords a very versatile, and often more powerful, approach to hypothesis testing than omnibus MANOVA hypotheses. Since the approach, with its user-specified weights, is easier to understand as well, we hope that more multivariate researchers will get into the habit of employing the Dunn-Bonferroni technique, as applied either to contrasts or to separate univariate ANOVAs.

8-11. Summary

This chapter extended the presentation of the two-sample models of the previous chapter to three or more samples. No new theory was presented. Basic concepts were elaborated upon and examples were provided to help understand the theory involved in the models to be presented in the next chapter.

In the K-sample case, we have P variables measured on K groups. The hypothesis of interest is that the mean vectors across the K groups are identical:

$$\text{H}_0\text{:} \quad \boldsymbol{\mu}_1 = \boldsymbol{\mu}_2 = \cdots = \boldsymbol{\mu}_K$$

where:

$$\boldsymbol{\mu}'_k = [\mu_{k1} \ \ \mu_{k2} \ \ \ldots \ \ \mu_{kP}]$$

Analysis of this hypothesis is based on whether or not the mean vectors can be viewed as representing a *concentrated* or *diffuse noncentrality structure*. Whenever the mean vectors give rise to a single discriminant function, it is said that the centroids of the distribution are concentrated on a single dimension. If many discriminant functions must be used to summarize or describe the complete set of variables, the structure is said to be diffused. If the structure is concentrated, the Roy criterion is the preferred model for testing H_0; whereas if the structure is diffuse, procedures based on Wilks's criterion are recommended because of their greater statistical power.

If the structure is diffuse, a topological examination of discriminant scores is advised. For this study, we let each discriminant function serve as a hypothetical dimension. Centroids are plotted on the grid defined by the functions and they are examined with regard to separation and overlap. For example, in a two-dimensional grid defined by a right angle coordinate system defined by L_1 and L_2, the discriminant functions associated with λ_1 and λ_2, we determine the values of $\bar{L}_{k1}$ and $\bar{L}_{k2}$ for each group. These paired values are plotted on the grid defined by L_1 and L_2. Since $\mathbf{A}' \mathbf{MS_W} \mathbf{A} = 1$ and $r_{L_1 L_2} = 0$, circles of radius 1, 2, and 3 can be drawn around each centroid so that group differences and overlap can be seen visually and related to the findings that come from making comparisons such as:

$$\hat{\psi}_{kk'}^{(1)} = \bar{L}_{k1} - \bar{L}_{k'1}$$

$$\hat{\psi}_{kk'}^{(2)} = \bar{L}_{k2} - \bar{L}_{k'2}$$

With a planned analysis and a graphing of the resulting data, a researcher has two powerful tools that aid in understanding the similarities and differences in K multivariate populations.

To simplify the computation of contrasts such as $\hat{\psi}_{kk'}^{(1)}$ and $\hat{\psi}_{kk'}^{(2)}$ and the determination of their corresponding standard errors, use of standardized discriminant scores is advisable. In standardized score form, with:

$$\bar{L}_{k1} = a_1^{(1)}\left(\frac{\bar{X}_{k1} - \bar{X}_1}{\sqrt{MS_{W_1}}}\right) + a_2^{(1)}\left(\frac{\bar{X}_{k2} - \bar{X}_2}{\sqrt{MS_{W_2}}}\right) + \cdots + a_P^{(1)}\left(\frac{\bar{X}_{kP} - \bar{X}_P}{\sqrt{MS_{W_P}}}\right)$$

the squared standard error of $\bar{L}_{k1}$ is given simply as:

$$SE^2_{\bar{L}_{k1}} = \frac{1}{N_k}$$

The advantage in using such estimators is obvious.

One of the problems that a researcher must face in the case of a diffuse structure is that of determining how many dimensions are covered by the set of P variables in terms of group differences and similarities. Unfortunately there is no direct answer to the question, but an operational answer can be had by using Bartlett's test in a stepwise fashion. Since the number of discriminant functions is equal to $\min(K - 1, P)$, we can always partition the risk of a type I error across the possible set of discriminant functions, or the models described in Section 5-4 can also be used. The final choice is up to the researcher and, if possible, should be based on a rational argument concerning the relationships expected between independent and dependent variables.

Finally, it was recommended that most multivariate analysis of variance designs could be improved upon by replacement of an analysis based on planned comparisons. In almost all cases, a planned analysis will exhibit greater statistical power than either the Roy or Wilks procedures because the number of contrasts examined under these specialized omnibus tests is exceedingly large. Most research studies can be reduced to a small set of questions and if a researcher can focus on them, a statistically tighter study can be had by using a Dunn-Bonferroni approach.

8-12. Exercises

***8-1.** Take your sample of 40 subjects and divide them according to major:
1. Natural Science
2. Social Science
3. Humanities
4. Other

Perform a one-way MANOVA using as dependent measures:
1. Pretest
2. Midterm
3. Final

8-2. Should you use Wilks's criterion or Roy's criterion for testing the hypothesis of Exercise 8-1? Why?

8-3. If you were to perform a planned analysis on the data of Exercise 8-1, how many pairwise contrasts would you examine? What would you use for your critical value? Would your planned analysis be more powerful than either of the methods of Exercise 8-2? Why?

***8-4.** Classify your 40 subjects in terms of the two discriminant functions generated under Exercise 8-1. Use the method of Section 8-8.

8-5. Make a topological map of the four majors and provide a brief description of what is shown.

8-6. Perform three one-way MANOVAs on the nine X and Y variables of Exercise 5-7. Use as independent variables
a. Social Class
b. Medical Specialty
c. Year of Medical School

8-7. Perform a post hoc analysis on the significant effects of Exercise 8-6.

8-8. Score the subjects on the first discriminant function of Exercise 8-6a and perform a univariate ANOVA. Compare the results of this analysis with that of Exercise 8-6a.

8-9. Using the methods of Section 8-8, classify the subjects of Exercise 8-6 according to
a. Social Class
b. Medical Specialty
c. Year of Medical School

Which classification scheme produces the lowest proportion of misclassified subjects?

8-10. Construct a topological map of the medical specialties.

CHAPTER NINE

OTHER MULTIVARIATE ANALYSIS OF VARIANCE DESIGNS

9-1. Factorial designs

Designs that include two or more independent qualitative variables are very common in the social sciences. Such designs are useful inasmuch as they permit a researcher to assess the effects of several factors within a single study. Even more importantly, in such designs it is possible to assess the joint effect or *interaction* of two or more factors simultaneously, something that cannot be done on the basis of successive one-factor designs. In this section, we distinguish between two different statistical models that are designed to answer different questions in factorial designs. These are referred to as *interaction* and *simple effects* models. An easy way to distinguish between the two models is in the context of an example.

Consider a 2 × 2 factorial design in which the two factors are sex of the student (male or female) and treatment (experimental or control). We say that the two independent variables, sex and treatment, do not interact if the treatment-control difference in mean scores for males is equal to the treatment-control difference in mean scores for females. If, on the other hand, the two treatment-control differences are not equal, an interaction is present. In this sense, an interaction may be thought of as a differential effect. If we denote the four group means as:

μ_{11} = mean score for the males in the control group

μ_{12} = mean score for the males in the experimental group

μ_{21} = mean score for the females in the control group

and

μ_{22} = mean score for the females in the experimental group

then the appearance of no interaction implies that:

$$(\mu_{12} - \mu_{11}) = (\mu_{22} - \mu_{21})$$

As a contrast statement, we can state that no interaction implies that:

$$\psi = (\mu_{12} - \mu_{11}) - (\mu_{22} - \mu_{21}) = 0$$

If $\psi \neq 0$, this implies a differential effect, and thus we would conclude that sex and treatment interact.

Another way to view an interaction is to consider the difference in mean values for males under the two treatment conditions. Let that difference be denoted by:

$$\Delta_1 = (\mu_{12} - \mu_{11})$$

Now consider the difference between the males and females in the control condition only. Let that difference be denoted by:

$$\Delta_2 = (\mu_{21} - \mu_{11})$$

We say there is no interaction if the mean score for the females in the experimental condition is given simply as:

$$\mu_{22} = \mu_{11} + \Delta_1 + \Delta_2$$

This is illustrated in the leftmost portion of Figure 9-1. As indicated, no interaction implies that the mean score for the females in the experimental condition is equal to the mean value for males in the experimental condition plus the difference in mean

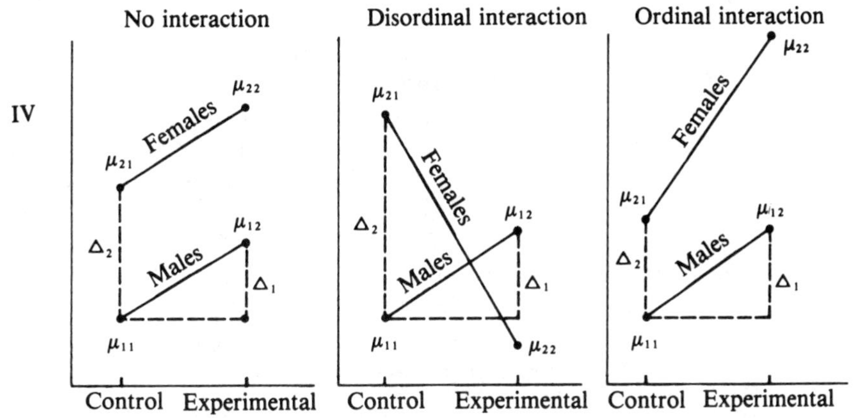

Figure 9-1. The geometry of a two-factor interaction.

scores that exists between males and females in the control condition alone.

Examination of Figure 9-1 shows that no interaction implies that the line segments joining the mean scores for males is parallel to the corresponding line segment for females. If the lines cross, the interaction is said to be *disordinal*, whereas, if the lines deviate from parallelism but do not cross, the interaction is said to be *ordinal*. Both types of interactions are illustrated in Figure 9-1.

If an interaction were to exist, we would be hard pressed to specify an exact mathematical form of its nature. However, it is instructive to think of the presence of an interaction as:

$$\mu_{22} = \mu_{11} + \Delta_1 + \Delta_2 + C\Delta_1\Delta_2$$

where C is an unknown constant. The important part of this conceptualization of an interaction is that it suggests that an interaction actually represents a multiplication of effects and not just a simple addition. This meaning is best illustrated by another example.

Consider the fictitious study in which subjects are randomly assigned to one of four experimental conditions:

Group 1. Subjects drink a glass of water containing a tablespoon of sugar.

Group 2. Subjects drink a glass of water containing a tablespoon of a potent barbiturate.

Group 3. Subjects drink a glass of alcohol containing a tablespoon of sugar.

Group 4. Subjects drink a glass of alcohol containing a tablespoon of a potent barbiturate.

Certainly, nothing out of the ordinary should happen to the subjects of Group 1. Members of Group 2 should feel quite relaxed and some should fall asleep. Members of Group 3 should get drunk; but members of Group 4 might experience death if no one were around to attend to their anticipated respiratory and circulatory difficulties. For subjects in Group 4, the joint effect of alcohol and barbiturates is not simply a combination of sleep and drunkenness. Instead, the outcome is precarious to their continued health. The two drugs interact explosively to produce a multiplicative or synergistic effect, that is, a total effect that surpasses the sum of its constituent effects.

Even though interactions represent joint effects of two or more factors operating simultaneously, researchers frequently do not interpret interactions that way. Rather, they are interpreted on the basis of comparing each cell mean with another, or by comparing cell means within levels of a given factor. Comparisons of the latter type have been variously referred to as *treatment within level* comparisons, *nested* comparisons, and *simple effect* comparisons. In other writings, we have cautioned researchers to be aware of the difference between interaction and simple effect comparisons, since confusing the two can often lead to anomalous statistical conclusions. See Marascuilo and Levin (1970, 1976) for a discussion of this problem in the context of what we have termed *type IV errors.*

For the present sex by treatment example, there exist four possible simple effect comparisons, two representing treatment differences within sex:

$\psi_1 = \mu_{12} - \mu_{11}$ (experimental vs. control males)

$\psi_2 = \mu_{22} - \mu_{21}$ (experimental vs. control females)

and two representing sex differences within treatment:

$\psi_3 = \mu_{11} - \mu_{21}$ (males vs. female control)

$\psi_4 = \mu_{22} - \mu_{12}$ (male vs. female experimental)

At the simplest level of abstraction it can be seen that each simple effect question can be answered by comparing only two cell means. On the other hand, the previous interaction question required that all four cell means be considered simultaneously in the contrast. Thus comparing only two means at a time can never be interpreted as getting at an interaction directly. The interested reader is referred to Marascuilo and Levin (1970) where more complicated comparisons are considered.

Let us now differentiate between the interaction and simple effects models in terms of the data presented in Table 9-1. These data represent the reading scores of six groups of fourth-grade students following 20 weeks of instruction. Students in the first column of the table were instructed in regular reading classes. Students in the second column were individually removed from their class for one hour of

TABLE 9-1. Data used to illustrate the interaction and simple effects models

	Treatment group		
Sex of student	*Regular classes*	*Eighth-grade tutor*	*College-trained tutor*
Male	30	32	41
	37	39	42
	44	49	50
	46	55	61
	51	57	63
Female	32	40	60
	38	46	61
	47	49	65
	48	55	70
	53	62	74

tutoring per week by an eighth-grade student who was reading at or above grade level. Students in the third column were also individually removed for one hour, but were tutored by college students specializing in the teaching of reading. Half of the fourth graders were male and half were female. Children in the two experimental groups were given same-sex tutors. Let the sex of the student be Factor A and the reading treatment variable be Factor B. The row, column, and cell means associated with the data of Table 9-1 are given in Table 9-2.

The interaction or differential effect model. We now define the components of the interaction model, using standard "dot" notation. A dot in the first subscript position represents an averaging over the I rows of the design, while a dot in the second subscript position represents an averaging over the J columns. For the two-way ANOVA interaction model, we assume each observation has the following latent structure:

$$Y_{ijk} = \mu_{..} + \alpha_i + \beta_j + \gamma_{ij} + \varepsilon_{ijk}$$

where:

$\mu_{..}$ = a standardizing constant that is estimated in the data by $\hat{\mu}_{..} = \bar{Y}_{..}$

$\alpha_i = \mu_{i.} - \mu_{..}$ = the effect of the ith level of the variable represented by rows in the data table, Factor A, and estimated by $\hat{\alpha}_i = \bar{Y}_{i.} - \bar{Y}_{..}$

$\beta_j = \mu_{.j} - \mu_{..}$ = the effect of the jth level of the variable represented by columns in the data table, Factor B, and estimated by $\hat{\beta}_j = \bar{Y}_{.j} - \bar{Y}_{..}$

$\gamma_{ij} = \mu_{ij} - \mu_{i.} - \mu_{.j} + \mu_{..}$ = the joint effect of the ith level of the row variable and the jth level of the column variable and estimated by $\hat{\gamma}_{ij} = \bar{Y}_{ij} - \bar{Y}_{i.} - \bar{Y}_{.j} + \bar{Y}_{..}$

ε_{ijk} = a random error estimated by $\hat{\varepsilon}_{ijk} = Y_{ijk} - \bar{Y}_{ij}$

We assume that each ε_{ijk} is selected independently from a normal distribution for which the mean value is zero and for which the unknown within-cell (residual) variance is estimated by MS_W. Because of the way α_i, β_j, and γ_{ij} are defined, it can be shown that:

$$\sum_{i=1}^{I} \alpha_i = \sum_{j=1}^{J} \beta_j = \sum_{i=1}^{I} \gamma_{ij} = \sum_{j=1}^{J} \gamma_{ij} = \sum_{i=1}^{I}\sum_{j=1}^{J} \gamma_{ij} = 0$$

In addition, it can be shown that $\nu_A = I - 1$, $\nu_B = J - 1$, $\nu_{AB} = (I - 1)(J - 1)$, and $\nu_{\text{Res}} = \nu_R = IJ(n - 1)$, where:

TABLE 9-2. Means associated with the data of Table 9-1

	Treatment group			
Sex of student	*Regular classes*	*Eighth-grade tutor*	*College-trained tutor*	*Across treatments*
Male	41.60	46.40	51.40	46.4667
Female	43.60	50.40	66.00	53.3333
Across sex	42.60	48.40	58.70	49.90

I = number of levels of the row variable

J = number of levels of the column variable

n = number of observations for each cell of the data table

ν_R = number of degrees of freedom associated with MS_W.

In the interaction model based on equal n's, three mutually orthogonal families are represented by the following hypotheses:

H_{0_A}: All $\alpha_i = 0$

or:

H_{0_A}: All $\psi_A = 0$

where ψ_A represents a contrast involving two or more row means and:

H_{0_B}: All $\beta_j = 0$

or:

H_{0_B}: All $\psi_B = 0$

where ψ_B represents a contrast involving two or more column means and:

$H_{0_{AB}}$: All $\gamma_{ij} = 0$

or:

$H_{0_{AB}}$: All $\psi_{AB} = 0$

where ψ_{AB} represents a specially defined contrast involving four or more cell means.

We now proceed to test for the presence of main effects of Factor A, H_{0_A}, and Factor B, H_{0_B}, as well as for the differential effect represented by the interaction $H_{0_{AB}}$.

Procedure for testing for the presence of a main effect in a two-factor design, and for assessing the significance of main effect contrasts.

Step 1. Compute the values:

$$\bar{Y}_{i.},\quad \bar{Y}_{.j},\quad \text{and}\quad \bar{Y}_{..}$$

Step 2. For the A factor, compute:

$$SS_A = Jn \sum_{i=1}^{I} (\bar{Y}_{i.} - \bar{Y}_{..})^2$$

$$= Jn \sum_{i=1}^{I} \bar{Y}_{i.}^2 - IJn\, \bar{Y}_{..}^2$$

For the B factor, compute:

$$SS_B = In \sum_{j=1}^{J} (\bar{Y}_{.j} - \bar{Y}_{..})^2$$

$$= In \sum_{j=1}^{J} \bar{Y}_{.j}^2 - IJn\, \bar{Y}_{..}^2$$

Step 3. Determine the values of:

$$MS_A = \frac{SS_A}{\nu_A} = \frac{SS_A}{I - 1}$$

$$MS_B = \frac{SS_B}{\nu_B} = \frac{SS_B}{J - 1}$$

Step 4. Determine the random variance of each cell, $S_{11}^2, S_{12}^2, \ldots, S_{IJ}^2$, and pool these estimates to obtain:

$$MS_W = \frac{1}{IJ} \sum_{i=1}^{I} \sum_{j=1}^{J} S_{ij}^2$$

Step 5. Determine the F ratios:

$$F_A = \frac{MS_A}{MS_W} \quad \text{and} \quad F_B = \frac{MS_B}{MS_W}$$

Step 6. For the A main effect, reject H_{0_A} at the alpha significance level if $F_A > F_{\nu_A,\nu_R:1-\alpha}$, where $\nu_A = I - 1$ and $\nu_R = IJ(n - 1)$. For the B main effect, reject H_{0_B} at the alpha significance level if $F_B > F_{\nu_B,\nu_R:1-\alpha}$, where $\nu_B = J - 1$ and $\nu_R = IJ(n - 1)$. The critical values are read from Table B-1.

Step 7. For post hoc Scheffé comparisons based on a familywise type I error probability of α, conclude that the contrast ψ_A or ψ_B is significant if, respectively:

$$\hat{\psi}_A - \mathbf{S}_A\, SE_{\hat{\psi}_A} < \psi_A < \hat{\psi}_A + \mathbf{S}_A\, SE_{\hat{\psi}_A} \quad \text{or} \quad \hat{\psi}_B - \mathbf{S}_A\, SE_{\hat{\psi}_B} < \psi_B < \hat{\psi}_B + \mathbf{S}_A\, SE_{\hat{\psi}_B}$$

does not cover zero, where:

$$\hat{\psi}_A = \sum_{i=1}^{I} a_i \bar{Y}_{i.} \quad \text{with} \sum_{i=1}^{I} a_i = 0$$

$$\hat{\psi}_B = \sum_{j=1}^{J} a_j \bar{Y}_{.j} \quad \text{with} \sum_{j=1}^{J} a_j = 0$$

$$SE_{\hat{\psi}_A} = \sqrt{\frac{MS_W}{Jn} \sum_{i=1}^{I} a_i^2}$$

$$SE_{\hat{\psi}_B} = \sqrt{\frac{MS_W}{In} \sum_{j=1}^{J} a_j^2}$$

$$\mathbf{S}_A = \sqrt{\nu_A F_{\nu_A,\nu_R:1-\alpha}}$$

$$\mathbf{S}_B = \sqrt{\nu_B F_{\nu_B,\nu_R:1-\alpha}}$$

with:

$\nu_A = I - 1$, $\nu_B = J - 1$, and $\nu_R = IJ(n - 1)$.

For planned Dunn-Bonferroni comparisons, conclude that the contrast is significant at the decided on reduced α level if:

$$\hat{\psi} - t\, SE_{\hat{\psi}} < \psi < \hat{\psi} + t\, SE_{\hat{\psi}}$$

where the appropriate value of t, based on $\nu = IJ(n - 1)$ comes from Table B-4 once C, the number of contrasts planned, has been set.

Applying these directions to the summary data of Table 9-2, we find that:

$$SS_A = 15[(46.4667)^2 + (53.3333)^2] - 30(49.90)^2$$
$$= 353.6265$$

and, since $v_A = 1$:

$$MS_A = SS_A = 353.6265$$

From Table 9-1, we can compute:

$$S_{11}^2 = \frac{5(8922) - 208^2}{5(4)} = 67.30$$

$$S_{12}^2 = \frac{5(11220) - 232^2}{5(4)} = 113.80$$

$$S_{13}^2 = \frac{5(13635) - 257^2}{5(4)} = 106.30$$

$$S_{21}^2 = \frac{5(9790) - 218^2}{5(4)} = 71.30$$

$$S_{22}^2 = \frac{5(12986) - 252^2}{5(4)} = 71.30$$

and

$$S_{23}^2 = \frac{5(21922) - 330^2}{5(4)} = 35.50$$

As a result:

$$MS_W = \frac{1}{2(3)}(67.30 + 113.80 + \cdots + 35.50) = 77.5833$$

Accordingly:

$$F_A = \frac{353.6265}{77.5833} = 4.56$$

which, with $\alpha = .05$, is statistically significant, since $F_{1,24:.95} = 4.26$. On the basis of the present data, we would conclude that the mean reading performance of the females is higher by about 6.9 points than that of the males. Note that since $v_A = 1$, no post hoc Scheffé comparisons are necessary. The overall F test being significant implies that the difference just mentioned is also significant.

We now assess the B main effect, according to the same directions. Thus:

$$SS_B = 10(42.60^2 + 48.40^2 + 58.70^2) - 30(49.90^2) = 1329.80$$

With $v_B = 2$, $MS_B = 1329.80/2 = 664.90$, and:

$$F_B = \frac{664.9000}{77.5833} = 8.57$$

Since $F_B > F_{2,24:.95} = 3.40$, we would conclude that, with $\alpha = .05$, significant differences exist among the three reading treatments. Post hoc Scheffé contrasts could be conducted to determine the locus of the differences. This would be done by defining contrasts in terms of the J column means and checking to see whether $\psi_B = 0$ is contained in:

$$\psi_B = \sum_{j=1}^{J} a_j \bar{Y}_{.j} \pm \sqrt{\nu_B F_{\nu_B,\nu_R:1-\alpha}} \sqrt{\frac{MS_W}{In} \sum_{j=1}^{J} a_j^2}$$

If $\psi_B = 0$ is not in this interval, the contrast is significant.

We now present the appropriate procedures for assessing the significance of an $A \times B$ interaction.

Procedure for testing for the presence of a two-factor interaction.

Step 1. Determine the values of each:

$$\hat{\gamma}_{ij} = \bar{Y}_{ij} - \bar{Y}_{i.} - \bar{Y}_{.j} + \bar{Y}_{..}$$

Step 2. As a computational check, show for each i and j that

$$\sum_{i=1}^{I} \hat{\gamma}_{ij} = 0 \qquad \text{and} \qquad \sum_{j=1}^{J} \hat{\gamma}_{ij} = 0$$

Step 3. Compute:

$$SS_{AB} = n \sum_{i=1}^{I} \sum_{j=1}^{J} \hat{\gamma}_{ij}^2$$

Step 4. Determine the value of:

$$MS_{AB} = \frac{SS_{AB}}{\nu_{AB}} = \frac{n \sum_{i=1}^{I} \sum_{j=1}^{J} \hat{\gamma}_{ij}^2}{(I-1)(J-1)}$$

Step 5. Find the previously computed MS_W.

Step 6. Compute:

$$F_{AB} = \frac{MS_{AB}}{MS_W}$$

Step 7. Reject $H_{0_{AB}}$ at the α significance level, if:

$$F_{AB} > F_{\nu_{AB},\nu_R:1-\alpha}$$

where:

$$\nu_{AB} = (I-1)(J-1) \qquad \text{and} \qquad \nu_R = IJ(n-1)$$

The critical F value is read from Table B-1.

From the data in Table 9-2, we have:

$$\hat{\gamma}_{11} = 41.6000 - 46.4667 - 42.6000 + 49.9000 = 2.4333$$

$$\hat{\gamma}_{12} = 46.4000 - 46.4667 - 48.4000 + 49.9000 = 1.4333$$

$$\hat{\gamma}_{13} = 51.4000 - 46.4667 - 58.7000 + 49.9000 = -3.8666$$

$$\hat{\gamma}_{21} = 43.6000 - 53.3333 - 42.6000 + 49.9000 = -2.4333$$

$$\hat{\gamma}_{22} = 50.4000 - 53.3333 - 48.4000 + 49.9000 = -1.4333$$

and

$$\hat{\gamma}_{23} = 66.0000 - 53.3333 - 58.7000 + 49.9000 = 3.8666$$

As computational checks, note that:

$$\sum_{i=1}^{I} \hat{\gamma}_{ij} = 0 \quad \text{and} \quad \sum_{j=1}^{J} \hat{\gamma}_{ij} = 0$$

According to Step 3:

$$SS_{AB} = 5(2.4333^2 + 1.4333^2 + \cdots + 3.8666^2) = 229.2667$$

Thus:

$$MS_{AB} = \frac{229.2667}{(2-1)(3-1)} = 114.6334$$

and, using:

$$MS_W = 77.5833$$

we obtain:

$$F_{AB} = \frac{114.6334}{77.5833} = 1.48$$

With $\alpha = .05$, $H_{0_{AB}}$ would not be rejected, since $F_{2,24:.95} = 3.40$. Thus the conclusion follows that the pattern of treatment differences is the same for males as it is for females.

Had the interaction been statistically significant, differential effect comparisons could have been investigated via Scheffé's procedure. Recall from the beginning of this section that differential effect comparisons have the basic form:

$$\begin{aligned}\hat{\psi}_{AB} &= (\bar{Y}_{ij} - \bar{Y}_{ij'}) - (\bar{Y}_{i'j} - \bar{Y}_{i'j'}) \\ &= (\bar{Y}_{ij} - \bar{Y}_{i'j}) - (\bar{Y}_{ij'} - \bar{Y}_{i'j'})\end{aligned}$$

where i and i' represent two different rows and j and j' represent two different columns.

In terms of the present data, three such *tetrad* differences, based on four means, can be defined. These are:

$$\begin{aligned}\hat{\psi}_1 &= (\bar{Y}_{11} - \bar{Y}_{12}) - (\bar{Y}_{21} - \bar{Y}_{22}) \\ &= (41.60 - 46.40) - (43.60 - 50.40) = 2.00\end{aligned}$$

$$\begin{aligned}\hat{\psi}_2 &= (\bar{Y}_{11} - \bar{Y}_{13}) - (\bar{Y}_{21} - \bar{Y}_{23}) \\ &= (41.60 - 51.40) - (43.60 - 66.00) = 12.60\end{aligned}$$

and

$$\begin{aligned}\hat{\psi}_3 &= (\bar{Y}_{12} - \bar{Y}_{13}) - (\bar{Y}_{22} - \bar{Y}_{23}) \\ &= (46.40 - 51.40) - (50.40 - 66.00) = 10.60\end{aligned}$$

with standard errors given by:

$$SE_{\hat{\psi}_1} = SE_{\hat{\psi}_2} = SE_{\hat{\psi}_3} = \sqrt{\frac{4MS_W}{n}} = \sqrt{\frac{4(77.5833)}{5}} = 7.8782$$

In defining interaction contrasts, we must be very careful in the selection of cell means and corresponding coefficients. That is, a difference within a given row or column must be compared with the same difference in a different row or column. According to this principle, $\hat{\psi} = (\bar{Y}_{11} - \bar{Y}_{12}) - (\bar{Y}_{22} - \bar{Y}_{23})$ is not acceptable since different columns are being compared in the two rows. At the same time, it is possible to define other than tetrad differences that satisfy the conditions of a differential effect comparison. We will refer to these as *complex* interaction comparisons. Thus, in the present example, we might wish to compare the male-female difference in the regular class with the same difference in the two tutoring conditions combined. This would be represented symbolically as:

$$\hat{\psi} = (\bar{Y}_{11} - \bar{Y}_{21}) - \left[\frac{1}{2}(\bar{Y}_{12} + \bar{Y}_{13}) - \frac{1}{2}(\bar{Y}_{22} + \bar{Y}_{23})\right]$$
$$= \left[\bar{Y}_{11} - \frac{1}{2}(\bar{Y}_{12} + \bar{Y}_{13})\right] - \left[\bar{Y}_{21} - \frac{1}{2}(\bar{Y}_{22} + \bar{Y}_{23})\right]$$

As in the one-way ANOVA and with main effects in the two-way ANOVA, an infinite number of such complex interaction contrasts exists, but only a small set of these makes sense. Scheffé's theorem guarantees that if the interaction F test is significant, one or more significant interactions can be found. If F_{AB} is not significant, however, no interaction contrast, neither tetrad nor complex, will be significant. Recall that $H_{0_{AB}}$ can be alternatively stated as $H_{0_{AB}}$: All $\psi_{AB} = 0$. For any interaction contrast within the same family, the Scheffé critical value is defined as:

$$S_{AB} = \sqrt{\nu_{AB} F_{\nu_{AB},\nu_R:1-\alpha}}$$

Note, however, that just as planned analyses are frequently preferable to post hoc analyses in the one-way ANOVA, the same is true in the two-way ANOVA, for both main effects and interactions. We conclude this subsection by giving directions for assessing the significance of interaction comparisons, either as an infinite set using the Scheffé procedure or as a finite set using the Dunn-Bonferroni procedure.

Procedure for performing a post hoc or planned analysis for two-factor interactions.

Step 1. Define a legitimate interaction comparison:

$$\hat{\psi} = \sum_{i=1}^{I} \sum_{j=1}^{J} a_{ij}\bar{Y}_{ij}$$

where:

$$\sum_{i=1}^{I} \sum_{j=1}^{J} a_{ij} = 0$$

and where the coefficients are balanced with respect to rows and columns, as explained in the text.

Step 2. Compute:

$$SE_{\hat{\psi}} = \sqrt{\frac{MS_W}{n} \sum_{i=1}^{I} \sum_{j=1}^{J} a_{ij}^2}$$

which, in the special case of tetrad differences, reduces to:

$$SE_{\hat{\psi}} = \sqrt{\frac{4MS_W}{n}}$$

Step 3. For post hoc Scheffé comparisons based on a familywise type I error probability of α, conclude that the contrast is significant if:

$$\hat{\psi} - \mathbf{S}_{AB}\, SE_{\hat{\psi}} < \psi < \hat{\psi} + \mathbf{S}_{AB}\, SE_{\hat{\psi}}$$

does not cover zero, where:

$$\mathbf{S}_{AB} = \sqrt{\nu_{AB} F_{\nu_{AB}, \nu_R : 1-\alpha}}$$

with $\nu_{AB} = (I-1)(J-1)$ and $\nu_R = IJ(n-1)$. For planned Dunn-Bonferroni comparisons, conclude that the contrast is significant at the decided on reduced α level if:

$$\hat{\psi} - t\, SE_{\hat{\psi}} < \psi < \hat{\psi} + t\, SE_{\hat{\psi}}$$

where the appropriate value of t, based on $\nu = IJ(n-1)$ comes from Table B-4 once C, the number of contrasts planned, has been set.

The simple effects model. In the two-factor simple effects model, it is possible to define either of two orthogonal families that differ from those of the interaction model: the A main effect and the simple effect of B within A; or the B main effect and the simple effect of A within B. In the present example, we choose to look at sex differences (the A main effect) and treatment within sex effects (B within A effects). The model associated with these questions is given by:

$$Y_{ijk} = \mu_{..} + \alpha_i + \beta_{j(i)} + \varepsilon_{ijk}$$

where all terms are as defined previously, with the exception of:

$\beta_{j(i)} = \mu_{ij} - \mu_{i.}$ = the simple effect associated with the ijth cell, B within levels of A, and is estimated by $\hat{\beta}_{j(i)} = \bar{Y}_{ij} - \bar{Y}_{i.}$

The corresponding hypothesis tested is given by $H_{0_{B(A)}}$: All $\beta_{j(i)} = 0$. We now give directions for performing a simple effects analysis based on this model.

Procedure for performing a simple effects analysis, *B* within *A*, for a two-factor design.

Step 1. Compute MS_A and MS_W, as in the interaction model.

Step 2. Compute $SS_{B(A_i)}$

where:

$$SS_{B(A_i)} = n \sum_{j=1}^{J} \bar{Y}_{ij}^2 - Jn\bar{Y}_{i.}^2$$

Note that this is operationally equivalent to viewing each level of A as a separate one-way ANOVA, and computing $SS_{B(A_i)}$ using one-way formulas.

Step 3. Within each level of A, $\nu_{B(A_i)} = J - 1$. Therefore, with $MS_{B(A_i)} = SS_{B(A_i)}/J - 1$, the simple effect of B within each level of A may be tested for significance, using:

$$F_{B(A_i)} = \frac{MS_{B(A_i)}}{MS_W}$$

Step 4. With the risk of a type I error controlled at $\alpha_{B(A_i)}$ for each B within A test performed, reject the hypothesis of no effect of B within a given level of A if:

$$F_{B(A_i)} > F_{\nu 1,\nu 2:1-\alpha B(A_i)}$$

where $\nu_1 = J - 1$ and $\nu_2 = IJ(n - 1)$.

Step 5. For those hypotheses rejected, conduct post hoc comparisons using:

$$\mathbf{S}_{B(A_i)} = \sqrt{\nu_1 F_{\nu 1,\nu 2:1-\alpha B(A_i)}}$$

For a planned analysis, replace $\mathbf{S}_{B(A_i)}$ with a t value, based on ν_2, taken from Appendix B-4.

The question of the particular type I error probability to accompany the preceding directions is a debatable one, since no universally accepted practice exists currently. Our own preference is to hold the *experimentwise* type I error probability constant from the interaction model to the simple effects model. Here experimentwise refers to the probability of committing at least one type I error in the entire set of tests conducted. As was true in the familywise error rate situation, the Bonferroni equality applies here. Thus, in the interaction model, if the A main effect is tested at α_A, the B main effect at α_B, and the interaction at α_{AB}, then the total experimentwise type I error probability is given by:

$$\alpha_T \leq \alpha_A + \alpha_B + \alpha_{AB}$$

If $\alpha_A = \alpha_B = \alpha_{AB} = .05$, for example, then $\alpha_T \leq .15$.

Consider now, the simple effects model, B within A. For this design, the corresponding experimentwise type I error probability is given by:

$$\alpha_T \leq \alpha_A + \alpha_{B(A_1)} + \alpha_{B(A_2)} + \cdots + \alpha_{B(A_I)}$$

We now invoke a basic principle of statistical theory which states that if a researcher has a choice to make among two or more models for analyzing the same data, the experimentwise type I error probability should be held constant from one model to the next. Only under this restriction can two or more models be appropriately compared. With this principle and noting that α_A is common to the interaction and the simple effects model, it follows that:

$$\alpha_B + \alpha_{AB} = \alpha_{B(A_1)} + \alpha_{B(A_2)} + \cdots + \alpha_{B(A_I)}$$

Thus the problem reduces to finding values for $\alpha_{B(A_1)}, \alpha_{B(A_2)}, \ldots, \alpha_{B(A_I)}$ in terms of the values for α_B and α_{AB}. If, in addition, we require that $\alpha_{B(A_1)} = \alpha_{B(A_2)} = \cdots = \alpha_{B(A_I)}$, then we have:

$$\alpha_B + \alpha_{AB} = I\alpha_{B(A_i)}$$

so that:

$$\alpha_{B(A_i)} = \frac{1}{I}(\alpha_B + \alpha_{AB})$$

As an example, suppose $I = 7$, $J = 3$, and $n = 10$, with $\alpha_A = \alpha_B = \alpha_{AB} = .05$. For a simple effects analysis, each $B(A_i)$ should be tested with:

$$\alpha_{B(A_i)} = \frac{1}{7}(.05 + .05) = .01428$$

The corresponding decision rules for each are to reject the hypothesis if $F > F_{6,189:.98572}$. Unfortunately tables of F with $\alpha = .01428$ do not exist. The table in this book has significance values only for $\alpha = .05$ and $\alpha = .01$. If these tables were used, each row would have to be investigated with $\alpha = .01$. In some cases, a researcher can use the proposed method provided the analysis has been performed with a computer package program, such as *BMD*, *SPSS*, or *Multivariance*, since each of these programs reports significance probabilities, p values, for each computed F value. Using these programs, a researcher need only change the decision rule to read:

D.R.: Reject the hypothesis under test if the reported significance probability,

$$p_{B(A_i)} \leq \frac{1}{I}(\alpha_B + \alpha_{AB})$$

For our example, we would reject the hypothesis, if the reported $p_{B(A_i)} \leq .01428$.

Let us now return to our sex-by-training example and suppose that we decided to test the three hypotheses of the interaction design with $\alpha_A = \alpha_B = \alpha_{AB} = .05$. Since $I = 2$, we would test each of the $B(A_i)$ hypotheses at $\alpha_{B(A_i)} = (1/2)(.05 + .05) = .05$, so that we would reject the level-by-level hypotheses if the row $F_{B(A_i)} > F_{2,24:.95} = 3.40$. For our data:

$$SS_{B(A_1)} = 5(41.60)^2 + 5(46.40)^2 + 5(51.40)^2 - 15(46.4667)^2$$
$$= 240.0869$$

$$SS_{B(A_2)} = 5(43.60)^2 + 5(50.40)^2 + 5(66.00)^2 - 15(53.3333)^2$$
$$= 1318.9867$$

Since $MS_W = 77.5833$, it follows that:

$$F_{B(A_1)} = \frac{120.0435}{77.5833} = 1.55 \quad \text{and} \quad F_{B(A_2)} = \frac{659.4934}{77.5833} = 8.50$$

Thus we conclude that there exist significant treatment differences for female, but not for male, students. A post hoc analysis within the female sample is now in order. For this post hoc analysis, conducted using t ratios in conjunction with the Scheffé method:

$$\hat{\psi}_1 = \bar{Y}_{21} - \bar{Y}_{22} = 43.60 - 50.40 = -6.8$$
$$\hat{\psi}_2 = \bar{Y}_{21} - \bar{Y}_{23} = 43.60 - 66.00 = -22.4$$
$$\hat{\psi}_3 = \bar{Y}_{22} - \bar{Y}_{23} = 50.40 - 66.00 = -15.6$$

$$SE_{\hat{\psi}_1} = SE_{\hat{\psi}_2} = SE_{\hat{\psi}_3} = \sqrt{77.5833(2/5)} = 5.5708$$

$$t_1 = \frac{-6.8}{5.5708} = -1.22$$

$$t_2 = \frac{-22.4}{5.5708} = -4.02$$

and

$$t_3 = \frac{-15.6}{5.5708} = -2.80$$

Since $S_{B(A_i)} = \sqrt{2(3.40)} = 2.61$, we conclude that among the female students, the college-trained tutoring groups differ from the group taught by the regular instructor alone or that taught by student tutors.

This example also demonstrates that decisions about interactions and simple effects need not necessarily coincide. According to the interaction model, no significant interaction was detected, yet different effects of treatment were detected within the female group when the simple effects model was applied.

For completeness, we provide ANOVA tables for each of the designs illustrated in this section. These appear as Tables 9-3 and 9-4, and agree within rounding errors. As can be seen for this example, the training effect of the interaction model (Table 9-3) was pretty much localized within the female sample (Table 9-4).

The problem of unequal cell frequencies. In the preceding example, an equal number of students appeared in each of the cells defined by the 2 × 3 factorial design. The attainment of equal cell frequencies in factorial designs is generally not an accidental process, but rather stems from a deliberate effort on the part of a researcher. To be sure, alternative data analysis strategies exist to handle situations in which a researcher willfully or accidentally ends up with a factorial design containing unequal cell frequencies. However, we provide here several reasons why striving for equal cell frequencies is desirable. The philosophy of matching cell sizes and the kind of analysis performed to the nature of the researcher's questions is a

TABLE 9-3. ANOVA table for the interaction model

Source	*d/f*	*Sum of squares*	*Mean square*	*F*	*Decision rule for* $\alpha = .05$
Sex of student (A)	1	353.6265	353.6265	4.56	Reject if $F > 4.26$
Training (B)	2	1329.8000	664.9000	8.57	Reject if $F > 3.40$
$A \times B$	2	229.2667	114.6334	1.48	Reject if $F > 3.40$
Within cells	24	1861.9992	77.5833		
Total	29	3774.6924			

TABLE 9-4. ANOVA table for the simple effects model

Source	*d/f*	*Sum of squares*	*Mean square*	*F*	*Decision rule for* $\alpha = .05$
Sex of student (A)	1	353.6265	353.6265	4.56	Reject if $F > 4.26$
Training in males (B in A_1)	2	240.0869	120.0435	1.55	Reject if $F > 3.40$
Training in females (B in A_2)	2	1318.9867	659.4934	8.50	Reject if $F > 3.40$
Within cells	24	1861.9992	77.5833		
Total	29	3774.6993			

broader issue that is beyond the scope of this book.

First, though not a terribly compelling reason, designs based on equal cell frequencies are *aesthetically pleasing* to the person reading or reviewing a research report. When the cell sizes are unequal, the reader may wonder why they are unequal and may attribute sloppiness, or worse, deception, to the researcher.

Second, and possibly also along noncompelling lines, the establishment of equal n's leads to greatly *simplified analysis of variance computations*. This reason may have been important at one time, but with the advent of computers and canned computer programs, it can no longer be offered as the major justification for the selection of equal cell frequencies.

Third, when cell sizes are equal and either the interaction model or the simple effects model is employed, we are guaranteed that all sources of variance, or contrast families, tested are *mutually orthogonal*. That is, the data are partitioned into nonoverlapping pieces so that each effect is meaningfully separated from all others. Unfortunately, with unequal cell frequencies, this separation of effects is not always easily accomplished; when it is, the separation may not be a meaningful one. See, for example, Carlson and Timm (1974) and Overall and Spiegel (1969).

Fourth, an often overlooked justification for striving for equal n's is that, in that case, the variance of any comparison based on two row, column, or cell means will be at its minimum. As a result, the *statistical power* associated with such comparisons will be at its maximum, if all else is held constant.

Finally, there is the important issue of analysis of variance assumptions. Regarding the *homogeneity of variance assumption* in particular, it is well known that this assumption can be violated, even severely violated, with little or no effect on the resulting type I and type II error probabilities, as long as the cell frequencies are equal or nearly equal. In the unequal n situation, we must be very concerned about the homogeneity of variance assumption, at least if we want to derive appropriate hypothesis testing probabilities from the F distribution. See Glass et al. (1972).

It is for these reasons that we have based the example of the preceding section on equal cell frequencies. We do so again in the factorial MANOVA example of the next section. We emphasize again, however, that there are ways of getting around the unequal n problem computationally and, depending on a researcher's questions and desired scope of inference, there may indeed be times when a purposeful unequal n design would be the most appropriate one.

9-2. Multivariate factorial designs

We now extend our discussion to factorial designs in which two or more dependent variables are considered simultaneously, but for simplicity, we restrict our attention to the multivariate model based on an equal number of observations per cell. To illustrate this multivariate factorial design, we use the Loban data described in Chapter 8. The independent variables or factors of the design are sex and social class. Sex, of course, has two levels (male and female), whereas social class is broken down into three levels (high, medium, and low). To simplify the presentation, only the third-grade results are reported. Since the sample sizes were quite variable, a table of random numbers was used to provide samples of 22 subjects in each of the six cells of the design. The resulting total sample size is given by $N = 6(22) = 132$ subjects. We recall that the five dependent variables consist of fluency, mazes, dependent clauses, conventional usage, and elaboration index. Mean scores, standard deviations, and within-cell correlation coefficients for the data under examination are reported in Tables 9-5, 9-6, and 9-7.

Main effect hypothesis in a two-factor MANOVA design (interaction model). In mathematical terms, we assume that each dependent variable, Y_1: fluency, Y_2: mazes, Y_3: dependent clauses, Y_4: conventional usage, and Y_5: elaboration index, can each be described by the latent structure model:

$$Y_{ijkp} = \mu_{...p} + \alpha_{i..p} + \beta_{.j.p} + \gamma_{ij.p} + \varepsilon_{ijkp}$$

TABLE 9-5. Table of means for the interaction design of Section 9-2

Group identification: Sex	Social class	Cell size	Y_1: Fluency	Y_2: Mazes	Y_3: Dependent clauses	Y_4: Conventional usage	Y_5: Elaboration index
	High	22	6.47	0.055	0.216	184.00	90.68
Males	Medium	22	6.77	0.062	0.260	288.82	88.64
	Low	22	6.41	0.085	0.178	610.41	89.36
	Total	66	6.55	0.067	0.218	361.10	89.56
	High	22	7.11	0.043	0.228	159.73	91.36
Females	Medium	22	6.79	0.058	0.211	311.50	78.27
	Low	22	7.19	0.063	0.238	382.41	99.27
	Total	66	7.03	0.055	0.226	284.50	89.64
	High	44	6.79	0.049	0.222	171.90	91.02
Across sex	Medium	44	6.78	0.060	0.236	300.20	83.45
	Low	44	6.80	0.074	0.208	496.40	94.32
Grand mean		132	6.79	0.061	0.222	322.81	89.60

TABLE 9-6. Table of standard deviations for the interaction design of Section 9-2

Group identification: Sex	Social class	Y_1: Fluency	Y_2: Mazes	Y_3: Dependent clauses	Y_4: Conventional usage	Y_5: Elaboration index
	High	1.01	0.029	0.105	214.02	24.52
Males	Medium	1.34	0.032	0.205	194.77	31.08
	Low	1.68	0.053	0.112	236.74	25.73
	High	1.01	0.023	0.119	52.93	25.73
Females	Medium	1.68	0.038	0.181	211.71	29.24
	Low	1.05	0.044	0.132	162.00	28.36
Within-cell SD ($\sqrt{MSw_p}$)		1.33	0.038	0.147	188.70	27.54

TABLE 9-7. Table of within-cell correlation coefficients for the interaction design of Section 9-2

	Y_1: Fluency	Y_2: Mazes	Y_3: Dependent clauses	Y_4: Conventional usage	Y_5: Elaboration index
Y_1	1.000	0.184	0.638	−0.258	0.718
Y_2	0.184	1.000	0.066	0.244	0.009
Y_3	0.638	0.066	1.000	−0.252	0.756
Y_4	−0.258	0.244	−0.252	1.000	−0.285
Y_5	0.718	0.009	0.756	−0.285	1.000

with:

$$\sum_{i=1}^{I} \alpha_{i..p} = \sum_{j=1}^{J} \beta_{.j.p} = \sum_{i=1}^{I} \gamma_{ij.p} = \sum_{j=1}^{J} \gamma_{ij.p} = 0$$

and where the ε_{ijkp} are distributed according to the multivariate normal distribution with mean values of zero and variance-covariance matrices $\sum_{11}, \sum_{12}, \ldots, \sum_{IJ}$, all equal to one another. Our task is to determine which parameters of the model can be set equal to zero. While we could test each variable for significance individually, giving rise to $3P$ statistically interrelated tests, the multivariate approach reduces the $3P$ tests to only 3; one for the vector of $\alpha_{i..p}$ parameters, one for the vector of $\beta_{.j.p}$ parameters, and one for the matrix of $\gamma_{ij.p}$ parameters. In particular, we will test for the A factor:

$$H_{0_A}: \begin{bmatrix} \alpha_{1..1} \\ \alpha_{1..2} \\ \cdot \\ \cdot \\ \cdot \\ \alpha_{1..P} \end{bmatrix} = \begin{bmatrix} \alpha_{2..1} \\ \alpha_{2..2} \\ \cdot \\ \cdot \\ \cdot \\ \alpha_{2..P} \end{bmatrix} = \cdots = \begin{bmatrix} \alpha_{I..1} \\ \alpha_{I..2} \\ \cdot \\ \cdot \\ \cdot \\ \alpha_{I..P} \end{bmatrix} = \begin{bmatrix} 0 \\ 0 \\ \cdot \\ \cdot \\ \cdot \\ 0 \end{bmatrix}$$

for the B factor:

$$H_{0_B}: \begin{bmatrix} \beta_{.1.1} \\ \beta_{.1.2} \\ \cdot \\ \cdot \\ \cdot \\ \beta_{.1.P} \end{bmatrix} = \begin{bmatrix} \beta_{.2.1} \\ \beta_{.2.2} \\ \cdot \\ \cdot \\ \cdot \\ \beta_{.2.P} \end{bmatrix} = \cdots = \begin{bmatrix} \beta_{.J.1} \\ \beta_{.J.2} \\ \cdot \\ \cdot \\ \cdot \\ \beta_{.J.P} \end{bmatrix} = \begin{bmatrix} 0 \\ 0 \\ \cdot \\ \cdot \\ \cdot \\ 0 \end{bmatrix}$$

and for the $A \times B$ interaction, stated, not in matrix form, but in vector form:

$$H_{0_{AB}}: \begin{bmatrix} \gamma_{11.1} \\ \gamma_{11.2} \\ \cdot \\ \cdot \\ \cdot \\ \gamma_{11.P} \end{bmatrix} = \begin{bmatrix} \gamma_{12.1} \\ \gamma_{12.2} \\ \cdot \\ \cdot \\ \cdot \\ \gamma_{12.P} \end{bmatrix} = \cdots = \begin{bmatrix} \gamma_{IJ.1} \\ \gamma_{IJ.2} \\ \cdot \\ \cdot \\ \cdot \\ \gamma_{IJ.P} \end{bmatrix} = \begin{bmatrix} 0 \\ 0 \\ \cdot \\ \cdot \\ \cdot \\ 0 \end{bmatrix}$$

If any of these hypotheses are rejected, simultaneous post hoc comparisons similar to those of a univariate analysis can then be performed to identify sources for the rejection. Of course, a planned Dunn-Bonferroni analysis could be performed where contrasts are counted and where critical values are selected from Table B-4. For present purposes, we describe a post hoc analysis only.

Before proceeding to the analysis, we should consider the assumptions placed on the model. We assume that the univariate analysis assumptions of normality, common variance, and independence of errors between and within groups hold for each of the P variables. In addition, we make the stringent assumption that the covariances for the variables across groups are identical. This latter assumption is important, in that a pooled variance-covariance matrix is used for all three statistical tests. Violating the assumption is known to have inflationary type I error consequences (see, for example, Olson, 1974). As indicated, the basic assumptions are multivariate normality as described in Section 5-4, equal variance-covariance matrices from one sample to the next, and independence between and within samples.

The first multivariate hypothesis of our example states that:

1. The mean vectors for males and females are identical.
2. The mean scores on the discriminant function associated with the sex factor are identical.
3. The point biserial correlation coefficient between sex and the discriminant function is zero, that is, $\theta_A = 0$.

In terms of the one-way multivariate test described in Section 8-2:

$$s = \min(\nu_A, P) = \min(1, 5) = 1$$

so that there will be only one solution to the characteristic equation:

$$|(\mathbf{SS_A})(\mathbf{SS_W})^{-1} - \lambda \mathbf{I}| = 0$$

The matrix $\mathbf{SS_A}$ for this equation is computed directly from the five means for the males, the five means for the females, and the across-group means. The matrix $\mathbf{SS_W}$ is computed from the five pooled within-cell standard deviations and the pooled within-cell correlations as defined in Section 2-6. This matrix is used for testing all three hypotheses of this design, the A main effect, the B main effect, and the $A \times B$ interaction.

The results of the analysis are summarized in Table 9-8, along with the corresponding univariate F ratios. Concerning the first hypothesis for which $s = 1$,

TABLE 9-8. MANOVA table for the interaction model of Section 9-2

Source of variance	ν_1	ν_2	*F ratio*
Sex	5	122	3.68
Y_1: Fluency	1	126	4.33
Y_2: Mazes	1	126	3.97
Y_3: Dependent clauses	1	126	0.09
Y_4: Conventional usage	1	126	5.43
Y_5: Elaboration index	1	126	0.00
Social class	10	244	8.33
Y_1: Fluency	2	126	0.00
Y_2: Mazes	2	126	5.07
Y_3: Dependent clauses	2	126	0.39
Y_4: Conventional usage	2	126	33.01
Y_5: Elaboration index	2	126	1.80
Sex $\times$ Social class	10	244	1.24
Y_1: Fluency	2	126	1.00
Y_2: Mazes	2	126	0.64
Y_3: Dependent clauses	2	126	1.49
Y_4: Conventional usage	2	126	5.49
Y_5: Elaboration index	2	126	1.49

we know that all of the various multivariate test criteria will lead to identical numerical results and, therefore, identical statistical conclusions. In terms of Wilks's Λ, for example, an exact F test is given by:

$$F = \frac{\nu_2}{\nu_1}\left(\frac{1 - \Lambda_A^{1/b}}{\Lambda_A^{1/b}}\right)$$

With:

$$\nu_A = I - 1 \qquad \text{and} \qquad \nu_{\text{Res}} = \nu_R = N - IJ$$

then:

$$\nu_1 = \nu_A P \qquad \text{and} \qquad \nu_2 = s(\nu_R + \nu_A - P)$$

For this hypothesis, $P = 5$, $I = 2$, $IJ = 2(3) = 6$, and $N = 132$

As a result:

$$\nu_1 = (2 - 1)5 = 5 \qquad \text{and} \qquad \nu_2 = (132 - 6) + (2 - 1) - 5 = 122$$

In general, Rao's approximate F test based on Wilks's Λ is given by:

$$F = \frac{\nu_2}{\nu_1}\left(\frac{1 - \Lambda_A^{1/b}}{\Lambda_A^{1/b}}\right)$$

as defined in Section 8-2. For the A main effect, the degrees of freedom are defined as follows:

$$\nu_1 = \nu_A P \qquad \text{and} \qquad \nu_2 = ab - \left(\frac{1}{2}\nu_A P\right) + 1$$

where:

$$a = \nu_R + \nu_A - \frac{1}{2}(P + \nu_A + 1)$$

and

$$b = \sqrt{\frac{\nu_A^2 P^2 - 4}{\nu_A^2 + P^2 - 5}}$$

Thus, for this first main effect hypothesis:

$$a = (132 - 6) + 1 + \frac{1}{2}(5 + 1 + 1) = 126 + 1 - 3.5 = 123.5$$

and

$$b = \sqrt{\frac{1^2(5)^2 - 4}{1^2 + 5^2 - 5}} = \sqrt{21/21} = 1$$

As a result:

$$\nu_1 = 1(5) = 5$$

and

$$\nu_2 = 123.5(1) - \left[\frac{1}{2}(1)(5)\right] + 1 = 123.5 - 2.5 + 1 = 122$$

which, since $b = s = 1$, agrees with the earlier computations.

For the present data, the eigen value associated with the sex effect is given by $\lambda_A = .1509$. To test H_0: $\lambda_A = 0$, we follow the model described in Section 8-2. Under this model:

$$\Lambda_A = \frac{1}{1 + \lambda_A} = \frac{1}{1.1509} = .8689$$

so that:

$$F = \frac{122}{5}\left(\frac{1 - .8689}{.8689}\right) = 3.68$$

is statistically significant using alpha equal to .05, since $F_{5,122:.95} = 2.29$.

The sex factor is seen to account for $1 - \Lambda_A = \theta_A = .1311$, or 13% of the variation in the associated discriminant function. Similar to the one-way MANOVA with $K = 2$, whenever $\nu_A = 1$, θ_A can be regarded as a squared point biserial correlation.

As we recall, coefficients for a linear discriminant function cannot be uniquely determined and so a number of procedures have been proposed. In what follows, we use standardized coefficients determined so that:

$$\mathbf{A}' \, (\mathbf{MS}_W) \, \mathbf{A} = 1$$

The standardization is achieved by replacing mean values by their corresponding Z values, but where the Z values are computed relative to the appropriate $\sqrt{MS_W}$. The standardized discriminant function for sex is defined in Table 9-9 as:

$$L^{(A)} = 1.16Z_1 - .57Z_2 - .06Z_3 - .36Z_4 - .88Z_5$$

In terms of the Z values reported in Table 9-10, where each variable is standardized relative to its associated $\sqrt{MS_W}$, the mean discriminant score for males is:

$$\bar{L}_M^{(A)} = 1.16(-.18) - .57(.16) - .06(-.03) - .36(.20) - .88(-.01) = -.36$$

and for females:

$$\bar{L}_F^{(A)} = 1.16(.18) - .57(-.16) - .06(.03) - .36(-.20) - .88(.01) = .36$$

In within-cell standard deviation units on the scale of $L^{(A)}$, the mean scores of the males and females are .72 units apart. The $100(1 - \alpha)$ percent confidence interval for the mean difference in standardized units is given by:

$$\psi = \bar{L}_M^{(A)} - \bar{L}_F^{(A)} \pm \mathbf{S}_A \sqrt{\mathbf{A}' \, \mathbf{MS}_W \, \mathbf{A} \left(\frac{1}{N_M} + \frac{1}{N_F}\right)}$$

For $s = 1$, charts or tables of the Roy-Bose critical $\mathbf{S}_A$ value are not needed, because $\mathbf{S}_A$ can be written in terms of F as:

$$\mathbf{S}_A = \sqrt{\frac{\nu_1 \nu_R}{\nu_2} F_{\nu_1,\nu_2:1-\alpha}} = \sqrt{\frac{5(126)}{122} F_{5,122:.95}}$$

$$= \sqrt{5.16(2.29)} = 3.44$$

Since $\mathbf{A}' \, \mathbf{MS}_W \, \mathbf{A} = \mathbf{A}' \, \mathbf{R}_W \, \mathbf{A} = 1$

the 95% confidence interval reduces to:

TABLE 9-9. Standardized linear discriminant functions for the interaction model of Section 9-2

Source of variance	*Function one*	*Function two*
Sex	$\lambda = 0.1509$	
	$\theta = 0.1311$	
Y_1: Fluency	1.16	
Y_2: Mazes	− 0.57	
Y_3: Dependent clauses	− 0.06	
Y_4: Conventional usage	− 0.36	
Y_5: Elaboration index	− 0.88	
Social class	$\lambda_1 = 0.6387$	$\lambda_2 = 0.0983$
	$\theta = 0.3898$	
Y_1: Fluency	0.04	− 0.47
Y_2: Mazes	− 0.13	0.04
Y_3: Dependent clauses	0.29	− 1.14
Y_4: Conventional usage	− 0.96	− 0.30
Y_5: Elaboration index	− 0.63	1.57
Sex × social class	$\lambda_1 = 0.0942$	$\lambda_2 = 0.0093$
	$\theta = 0.0861$	
Y_1: Fluency	− 0.12	− 0.99
Y_2: Mazes	− 0.10	0.53
Y_3: Dependent clauses	0.23	− 0.28
Y_4: Conventional usage	− 0.87	− 0.55
Y_5: Elaboration index	0.14	0.22

TABLE 9-10. Mean values of Table 9-5 reported as standard scores, based on $\sqrt{MS_W}$

Group identification				Y_3:	Y_4:	Y_5:
Sex	*Social class*	Y_1: *Fluency*	Y_2: *Mazes*	*Dependent clauses*	*Conventional usage*	*Elaboration index*
	High	− 0.24	− 0.16	− 0.04	− 0.74	0.04
Males	Medium	− 0.02	0.03	0.26	− 0.18	− 0.03
	Low	− 0.29	0.63	− 0.30	1.52	− 0.01
	Total	− 0.18	0.16	− 0.03	0.20	− 0.01
	High	0.24	− 0.47	0.04	− 0.86	0.06
Females	Medium	0.00	− 0.08	− 0.07	− 0.06	− 0.41
	Low	0.30	0.05	0.11	0.32	0.35
	Total	0.18	− 0.16	0.03	− 0.20	0.01
	High	0.00	− 0.32	0.00	− 0.80	0.05
Across sex	Medium	− 0.01	− 0.03	0.10	− 0.12	− 0.22
	Low	0.01	0.34	− 0.10	0.92	0.17

$$\psi = [-.36 - (.36)] \pm 3.44\sqrt{\frac{1}{66} + \frac{1}{66}}$$
$$= -.72 \pm .60$$

It is interesting to note that even though the difference in mean scores on the discriminant function is significant at the .05 level, none of the univariate mean differences is significant if the same simultaneous procedure is employed on each variable. This is seen in the variable-by-variable confidence intervals which all cover zero. While the confidence intervals could be based on the mean values on the original metric, we have chosen to use the standardized measure reported in Table 9-10. With standardized values, $\mathbf{A}'\,\mathbf{MS}_W\,\mathbf{A}$ is replaced by:

$$\frac{1}{\sqrt{MS_{W_p}}} MS_{W_p} \frac{1}{\sqrt{MS_{W_p}}}$$

which also equals one. Thus:

$$\psi_{Y_1} = [-.18 - (.18)] \pm 3.44\sqrt{2/66} = -.36 \pm .60$$

$$\psi_{Y_2} = [.16 - (-.16)] \pm 3.44\sqrt{2/66} = .32 \pm .60$$

$$\psi_{Y_3} = [-.03 - (.03)] \pm 3.44\sqrt{2/66} = .06 \pm .60$$

$$\psi_{Y_4} = [.20 - (-.20)] \pm 3.44\sqrt{2/66} = .40 \pm .60$$

$$\psi_{Y_5} = [-.01 - (.01)] \pm 3.44\sqrt{2/66} = -.02 \pm .60$$

Of course, several univariate F ratios are significant at the .05 level, as shown in Table 9-8, where a critical value of 3.92 is required. However, the familywise type I error probability associated with the five univariate tests is somewhere between .05 and .25.

The pooled within-cell correlation between each variable and $L^{(A)}$ is given by $\mathbf{R}_W\mathbf{A}$. For these data:

$$\mathbf{R}_W\mathbf{A} = \begin{bmatrix} 1.00 & .18 & .64 & -.26 & .72 \\ .18 & 1.00 & .07 & .24 & .01 \\ .64 & .07 & 1.00 & -.25 & .76 \\ -.26 & .24 & -.25 & 1.00 & -.29 \\ .72 & .01 & .76 & -.29 & 1.00 \end{bmatrix} \begin{bmatrix} 1.16 \\ -.57 \\ -.06 \\ -.36 \\ -.88 \end{bmatrix} = \begin{bmatrix} .48 \\ -.46 \\ .06 \\ -.53 \\ .01 \end{bmatrix}$$

As indicated, the correlations are given by:

$$r_{Y_1L^{(A)}} = .48$$

$$r_{Y_2L^{(A)}} = -.46$$

$$r_{Y_3L^{(A)}} = .06$$

$$r_{Y_4L^{(A)}} = -.53$$

and

$$r_{Y_5L^{(A)}} = .01$$

so that $L^{(A)}$ appears to be defined mainly in terms of fluency, mazes, and conventional usage. As is apparent in the data of Table 9-5, in comparison to males, females are more fluent, they utter fewer mazes, and their speech is more conventional. Thus third-grade females use standard English more adeptly than do males. This suggests that $L^{(A)}$ is a variable that measures general use of standard English. Note also that in this particular example, the three variables identified as definers were associated with the largest standardized sex differences (as in Table 9-10) and therefore univariate F ratios (as in Table 9-8).

The second multivariate hypothesis in the interaction model refers to differences among the three social class groups, the B main effect. The hypothesis tested is that:

1. The three social class mean vectors are identical.
2. The three social class groups have identical discriminant function means.
3. All possible between-social class contrasts in the five dependent variables are equal to zero.

For this main effect hypothesis:

$$s = \min(\nu_B, P) = \min(2, 5) = 2$$

so that, once again, an exact F test based on Wilks's Λ is possible. This time, the test statistic is defined as:

$$F = \frac{\nu_2}{\nu_1}\left(\frac{1 - \sqrt{\Lambda_B}}{\sqrt{\Lambda_B}}\right)$$

With

$$\nu_B = J - 1 \qquad \text{and} \qquad \nu_R = N - IJ$$

then:

$$\nu_1 = \nu_B P \qquad \text{and} \qquad \nu_2 = s(\nu_R + \nu_B - P - 1)$$

Thus, for the present example:

$$\nu_1 = (3 - 1)5 = 10 \qquad \text{and} \qquad \nu_2 = 2(126 + 2 - 5 - 1) = 244$$

For the more general statistic derived by Rao, recall that:

$$F = \frac{\nu_2}{\nu_1}\left(\frac{1 - \Lambda_B^{1/b}}{\Lambda_B^{1/b}}\right)$$

Adapting the formulas provided earlier, we have:

$$a = \nu_R + \nu_B - \frac{1}{2}(P + \nu_B + 1)$$

$$= 126 + 2 - \frac{1}{2}(5 + 2 + 1)$$

$$= 124$$

$$b = \sqrt{\frac{\nu_B^2 P^2 - 4}{\nu_B^2 + P^2 - 5}} = \sqrt{\frac{2^2(5)^2 - 4}{2^2 + 5^2 - 5}} = \sqrt{\frac{96}{24}} = \sqrt{4} = 2$$

yielding:

$$\nu_1 = \nu_B P = 2(5) = 10$$

and

$$\nu_2 = ab - \left(\frac{1}{2}\nu_B P\right) + 1 = 124(2) - \frac{1}{2}[2(5)] + 1 = 244$$

These results agree with the special case computations. Note also that $b = s = 2$ and $\Lambda_B^{1/b} = \Lambda_B^{1/2} = \sqrt{\Lambda_B}$, as is given in the special case formula.

For the B main effect, $\lambda_1 = .6387$ and $\lambda_2 = .0983$.

Thus:

$$\Lambda_B = \prod_{p=1}^{2} \frac{1}{1+\lambda_p} = \left(\frac{1}{1+.6387}\right)\left(\frac{1}{1+.0983}\right)$$
$$= (1/1.6387)(1/1.0983) = .5556$$

and

$$F = \frac{244}{10}\left(\frac{1-\sqrt{.5556}}{\sqrt{.5556}}\right) = 8.33$$

With a critical $\alpha = .05$ given by $F_{10,244:.95} = 1.83$, the multivariate hypothesis is rejected according to Wilks's Λ criterion. Similarly, were Roy's largest root criterion the one selected, the hypothesis that $\theta_B = 0$ would also be rejected. In this case:

$$\theta_B = \frac{\lambda_1}{1+\lambda_1} = \frac{.6387}{1+.6387} = .3898$$

exceeds the critical $\alpha = .05$ value, based on:

$$s = 2$$

$$m = \frac{|\nu_B - P| - 1}{2} = \frac{|2-5|-1}{2} = 1 \quad \text{and}$$

$$n = \frac{\nu_R - P - 1}{2} = \frac{126-5-1}{2} = 60$$

and given in Appendix B-6 by $\theta^{.05}_{2,1,60} = .115$. Note that social class accounts for 39% of the variance in the first discriminant function.

Tests based on the Hotelling-Lawley and Pillai-Bartlett trace criteria could also be performed, as was indicated in Section 8-3. Recall that the particular criterion selected should depend on the researcher's beliefs regarding the kind of non-centrality structure and associated distributional characteristics underlying the data. For a review of this topic, see Section 8-7. The distinction adopted for the present example is simply in terms of the researcher's belief in a diffuse structure on the one hand (Wilks's criterion), as opposed to a concentrated structure on the other (Roy's criterion). In either case, if our major concern is to identify significant between-group contrasts, following an omnibus test, then the Roy-Bose procedure described in Section 8-6 with its narrower intervals should be the one selected. We make this recommendation realizing that this procedure depends heavily on the twin assumptions of multivariate normality (or large sample sizes) and variance and covariance homogeneity across groups, as discussed by Olson (1976).

The pooled within-cell correlation of each variable with $L^{(B_1)}$ is obtained from Tables 9-7 and 9-9 as follows:

$$\mathbf{R}_W\mathbf{A} = \begin{bmatrix} 1.00 & .18 & .64 & -.26 & .72 \\ .18 & 1.00 & .07 & .24 & .01 \\ .64 & .07 & 1.00 & -.25 & .76 \\ -.26 & .24 & -.25 & 1.00 & -.29 \\ .72 & .01 & .76 & -.29 & 1.00 \end{bmatrix} \begin{bmatrix} .04 \\ -.13 \\ .29 \\ -.96 \\ -.63 \end{bmatrix} = \begin{bmatrix} -.00 \\ -.34 \\ .07 \\ -.89 \\ -.10 \end{bmatrix}$$

Thus the discriminant function that separates third-grade students on the basis of social class is defined mainly by X_4: Conventional usage and, to a lesser extent by X_2: Mazes.

Roy-Bose simultaneous comparisons could be performed, using as a critical value:

$$\mathbf{S}_B = \sqrt{\frac{\theta^{.05}_{2,1,60}\ \nu_R}{1 - \theta^{.05}_{2,1,60}}} = \sqrt{\frac{.115(126)}{.885}} = 4.05$$

Such comparisons would be of the form: $\psi = \hat{\psi} \pm \mathbf{S}_B\ SE_{\hat{\psi}}$ and could encompass any linear combinations of dependent variables that were of interest, including the maximum group-differentiating linear combination, $L^{(B_1)}$, and variable-by-variable comparisons as well.

As soon as the number of groups exceeds two, contrasts are defined in terms of more complex linear combinations. Contrasts of this kind were described in Section 8-6. As an example, consider a linear function of the five Loban variables, but measured on the high SES group. Such a function would have the form:

$$\bar{C}_1 = a_1\bar{Y}_{11} + a_2\bar{Y}_{12} + a_3\bar{Y}_{13} + a_4\bar{Y}_{14} + a_5\bar{Y}_{15}$$

where there are no restrictions on the nature of the $a_1, \ldots, a_5$ values. They do not have to sum to zero or any other constant. This linear combination can be evaluated for the medium SES group and for the low SES group. These three values, $\bar{C}_1$, $\bar{C}_2$, and $\bar{C}_3$ can then be compared by assigning constants b_1, b_2, and b_3 such that $b_1 + b_2 + b_3 = 0$ and $\hat{\psi} = b_1\bar{C}_1 + b_2\bar{C}_2 + b_3\bar{C}_3$. As an example, consider the a_1, $a_2, \ldots, a_5$ values as discriminant function coefficients and b_1, b_2, and b_3 defined as $(1, -1, 0)$, $(1, 0, -1)$, or $(0, 1, -1)$. With these values and with the appropriate standard errors, we can make pairwise comparisons across socioeconomic status.

In terms of $L^{(B_1)}$ the three social class means, using the standardized values in Table 9-10, are given by:

$$\bar{L}_1^{(B_1)} = .04(.00) - .13(-.32) + .29(.00) - .96(-.80) - .63(.05) = .78$$

$$\bar{L}_2^{(B_1)} = .04(-.01) - .13(-.03) + .29(.10) - .96(-.12) - .63(-.22) = .29 \quad \text{and}$$

$$\bar{L}_3^{(B_1)} = .04(.01) - .13(.34) + .29(-.10) - .96(.92) - .63(.17) = -1.06$$

and since $\mathbf{A}'\ \mathbf{MS_W}\ \mathbf{A} = 1$:

$$\psi_1 = (\bar{L}_1^{(B_1)} - \bar{L}_2^{(B_1)}) \pm \mathbf{S}_B\sqrt{\frac{1}{N_1} + \frac{1}{N_2}}$$
$$= (.78 - .29) \pm 4.05\sqrt{2/44} = .49 \pm .86$$

$$\psi_2 = (\bar{L}_1^{(B_1)} - \bar{L}_3^{(B_1)}) \pm \mathbf{S}_B\sqrt{\frac{1}{N_1} + \frac{1}{N_3}}$$
$$= (.78 + 1.06) \pm 4.05\sqrt{2/44} = 1.84 \pm .86 \quad \text{and}$$

$$\psi_3 = (\bar{L}_2^{(B_1)} - \bar{L}_3^{(B_1)}) \pm \mathbf{S}_B\sqrt{\frac{1}{N_2} + \frac{1}{N_3}}$$
$$= (.29 + 1.06) \pm 4.05\sqrt{2/44} = 1.35 \pm .86$$

These contrasts reveal that both high and medium social class third graders differ from low social classes with respect to the first discriminant function. The difference between high and low is not statistically significant.

Consider conventional usage and mazes, but in terms of the individual standardized variables in Table 9-10 or conventional usage, Y_4:

$$\psi_1 = (-.80 + .12) \pm .86 = -.68 \pm .86$$

$$\psi_2 = (-.80 - .92) \pm .86 = -1.72 \pm .86$$

$$\psi_3 = (-.12 - .92) \pm .86 = -1.04 \pm .86$$

which leads to the same conclusion as that found on the first discriminant function. For mazes, Y_2, the three pairwise constrasts are given by:

$$\psi_1 = (-.32 + .03) \pm .86 = -.29 \pm .86$$

$$\psi_2 = (-.32 - .34) \pm .86 = -.66 \pm .86$$

$$\psi_3 = (-.03 - .34) \pm .86 = -.37 \pm .86$$

None of these contrasts is statistically significant according to the simultaneous Roy-Bose procedure, suggesting that conventional usage has the stronger effect on the first discriminant function. We now provide instructions for analyzing the main effects in a two-factor MANOVA design.

Procedure for analyzing the main effects in a two-factor multivariate analysis of variance design based on equal cell sizes.

Step 1. Denote the three sources of variance by A, B, and AB. Let the levels of A be denoted by $1, 2, \ldots, I$ and those of B by $1, 2, \ldots, J$. With N representing the total number of subjects, let:

Y_{ijkp} = observation on the pth variable for the kth subject in the (i, j)th cell of the design

$\bar{Y}_{i..p}$ = mean on the pth variable for the ith level of Factor A

$\bar{Y}_{.j.p}$ = mean on the pth variable for the jth level of Factor B

$\bar{Y}_{ij.p}$ = mean on the pth variable for cell (i, j)

$S^2_{p(ij)}$ = variance on the pth variable for cell (i, j)

$r_{pp'(ij)}$ = correlation coefficient between variable p and p' in cell (i, j)

$N_A = N/J$

$N_B = N/I$ and

$N_{AB} = N/IJ$

Step 2. To test the multivariate hypothesis on the A factor, find the eigen values for the characteristic equation:

$$|(\mathbf{SS_A})(\mathbf{SS_W})^{-1} - \lambda \mathbf{I}| = 0$$

where $\mathbf{SS_A}$ has as diagonal elements:

$$N_A \sum_{i=1}^{I} (\bar{Y}_{i..p} - \bar{Y}_{...p})^2$$

and as off-diagonal elements:

$$N_A \sum_{i=1}^{I} (\bar{Y}_{i..p} - \bar{Y}_{...p})(\bar{Y}_{i..p'} - \bar{Y}_{...p'})$$

and where $\mathbf{SS_W}$ has as diagonal elements:

$$(N_{AB} - 1) \sum_{i=1}^{I} \sum_{j=1}^{J} S^2_{p(ij)}$$

and as off-diagonal elements:

$$(N_{AB} - 1) \sum_{i=1}^{I} \sum_{j=1}^{J} r_{pp'(ij)} S_{p(ij)} S_{p'(ij)}$$

Step 3. For Roy's procedure, reject H_{0_A}: $\theta_A = 0$, if:

$$\theta_A > \theta^{\alpha}_{s,m,n}$$

where:

$$s = \min(I - 1, P)$$

$$m = \frac{|\nu_A - P| - 1}{2}$$

$$n = \frac{\nu_R - P - 1}{2}$$

$$\nu_A = I - 1$$

and

$$\nu_R = N - IJ$$

If H_{0_A} is rejected, examine contrasts on the first discriminant function, as well as any other linear compounds of interest (see the following), using as a critical value:

$$\mathbf{S}_A = \sqrt{\nu_R \frac{\theta^{\alpha}_{s,m,m}}{1 - \theta^{\alpha}_{s,m,n}}}$$

and standardized means so that:

$$\mathbf{A}' \, \mathbf{MS_W} \, \mathbf{A} = 1$$

One is *guaranteed* of finding at least one significant contrast using this procedure. For procedures based on Wilks's criterion, use Rao's F approximation:

$$F = \frac{\nu_2}{\nu_1}\left(\frac{1 - \Lambda_A^{1/b}}{\Lambda_A^{1/b}}\right)$$

where:

$$\nu_1 = \nu_A P = (I - 1)P$$

$$\nu_2 = ab - \left(\frac{1}{2}\nu_A P\right) + 1$$

$$a = \nu_R + \nu_A - \frac{1}{2}(P + \nu_A + 1)$$

and

$$b = \sqrt{\frac{v_A^2 P^2 - 4}{v_A^2 + P^2 - 5}}$$

If the hypothesis of identical mean vectors is rejected, examine contrasts on the standardized means. The most general contrast in this model is a linear combination with coefficients not necessarily summing to zero in each group, and then weighted to sum to zero across groups. Let a_p represent the coefficients within a group and b_i represent the coefficients across the group, with:

$$b_1 + b_2 + \cdots + b_I = 0$$

Then, the most general contrast is defined by:

$$\psi = b_1(a_1\mu_{1..1} + a_2\mu_{1..2} + \cdots + a_P\mu_{1..P}) + b_2(a_1\mu_{2..1} + a_2\mu_{2..2} + \cdots + a_P\mu_{2..P}) + \cdots + b_I(a_1\mu_{I..1} + a_2\mu_{I..2} + \cdots + a_P\mu_{I..P})$$

With standardized means:

$$SE_{\hat{\psi}}^2 = \frac{IJ}{N} \mathbf{A}' \, \mathbf{MS}_\mathbf{W} \, \mathbf{A} \, (b_1^2 + b_2^2 + \cdots + b_I^2)$$

Examination of these linear combinations using the preceding **S** critical value will yield the narrowest simultaneous post hoc confidence intervals, but does not guarantee finding a significant contrast following a significant Rao F test.

Step 4. Repeat Steps 2 and 3 for the B factor by interchanging the letters A and B, and I and J.

Interaction hypothesis in a two-factor MANOVA design. The third hypothesis to be tested is the one stating that all interaction contrasts are simultaneously zero. For this hypothesis:

$$v_{AB} = (I - 1)(J - 1) = 1(2) = 2$$

$$v_R = 126$$

$$s = \min(v_{AB}, P) = 2$$

As a result, the F test based on Wilks's Λ is once again exact, with degrees of freedom equal to those for the B main effect, where $v_B = 2$. In particular:

$$F = \frac{v_2}{v_1}\left(\frac{1 - \Lambda_{AB}^{1/b}}{\Lambda_{AB}^{1/b}}\right)$$

with:

$$a = v_R + v_{AB} - \frac{1}{2}(P + v_{AB} + 1)$$

$$b = \sqrt{\frac{v_{AB}^2 P^2 - 4}{v_{AB}^2 + P^2 - 5}}$$

$$v_1 = v_{AB}P$$

and

$$v_2 = ab - \left(\frac{1}{2}v_{AB}P\right) + 1$$

For the interaction hypothesis:

$$a = 126 + 2 - \frac{1}{2}(5 + 2 + 1) = 124$$

$$b = \sqrt{\frac{2^2(5)^2 - 4}{2^2 + 5^2 - 5}} = 2$$

$v_1 = 2(5) = 10$ and

$$v_2 = 124(2) - \left(\frac{1}{2}(2)(5)\right) + 1 = 244$$

In addition:

$\lambda_1 = .0942$ and $\lambda_2 = .0093$

so that:

$$\Lambda_{AB} = \left(\frac{1}{1 + .0942}\right)\left(\frac{1}{1 + .0093}\right) = .9055$$

$$F = \frac{244}{10}\left(\frac{1 - \sqrt{.9055}}{\sqrt{.9055}}\right) = 1.24$$

Since the critical $\alpha = .05$ F value is given by $F_{v_1,v_2:\alpha} = F_{10,244:.95} = 1.83$, the interaction, as defined by Wilks's Λ_{AB} is not statistically significant.

According to Roy's criterion:

$$\theta_{AB} = \frac{\lambda_1}{1 + \lambda_1} = \frac{.0942}{1 + .0942} = .0861$$

does not exceed the critical $\alpha = .05$ value given by $\theta^{\alpha}_{s,m,n}$. In this case, and as with the B factor:

$s = 2$

$$m = \frac{|\,v_{AB} - P\,| - 1}{2} = \frac{|\,2 - 5\,| - 1}{2} = 1 \quad \text{and}$$

$$n = \frac{v_R - P - 1}{2} = \frac{126 - 5 - 1}{2} = 60$$

so that $\theta^{.05}_{2,1,60} = .115$. Therefore, the multivariate interaction hypothesis based on the largest root is not statistically significant.

Even though $H_{0_{AB}}$ was not rejected, we illustrate the kind of contrasts that would be legitimately subsumed under this model. Recall that the simplest kind of interaction contrast has the form of a tetrad difference defined as:

$$\psi = (\mu_{ij} - \mu_{ij'}) - (\mu_{i'j} - \mu_{i'j'})$$

with the estimated means defined by the $\bar{Y}_{ij.p}$, linear combinations of them. For the present data, applying the first discriminant function weights of Table 9-9 to the standardized cell means of Table 9-10 yields:

$$\bar{L}_{M1}^{(AB_1)} = -.12(-.24) - .10(-.16) + .23(-.04) - .87(-.74) + .14(.04)$$
$$= .68$$

$$\bar{L}_{M2}^{(AB_1)} = -.12(-.02) - .10(.03) + .23(.26) - .87(-.18) + .14(-.03)$$
$$= .21$$

$$\bar{L}_{M3}^{(AB_1)} = -.12(-.29) - .10(.63) + .23(-.30) - .87(1.52) + .14(-.01)$$
$$= -1.42$$

$$\bar{L}_{F1}^{(AB_1)} = -.12(.24) - .10(-.47) + .23(.04) - .87(-.86) + .14(.06)$$
$$= .78$$

$$\bar{L}_{F2}^{(AB_1)} = -.12(.00) - .10(-.08) + .23(-.07) - .87(-.06) + .14(-.41)$$
$$= -.01$$

and

$$\bar{L}_{F3}^{(AB_1)} = -.12(.30) - .10(.05) + .23(.11) - .87(.32) + .14(.35)$$
$$= -.24$$

For example, consider the contrast:

$$\hat{\psi} = (\bar{L}_{M1}^{(AB_1)} - \bar{L}_{M3}^{(AB_1)}) - (\bar{L}_{F1}^{(AB_1)} - \bar{L}_{F3}^{(AB_1)})$$
$$= [.68 - (-1.42)] - [.78 - (-.24)]$$
$$= 2.10 - 1.02 = 1.08$$

with:

$$\mathbf{S}_{AB} = \sqrt{\frac{\theta^{\alpha}_{s,m,m}}{1 - \theta^{\alpha}_{s,m,n}}\nu_R} = \sqrt{\frac{.115}{.885}(126)} = 4.05$$

and, since $\mathbf{A}'\ \mathbf{MS_W}\ \mathbf{A} = 1.00$, we have that:

$$SE_{\hat{\psi}} = \sqrt{4(IJ/N)} = \sqrt{4(6/132)} = .4264$$

As a result:

$$\psi = 1.08 \pm 4.05(.4264) = 1.08 \pm 1.73$$

which is not statistically significant.

The same tetrad difference procedure could be applied to other linear combinations of the dependent variables, as well as to variable-by-variable comparisons. However, since the overall interaction test, based on Roy's criterion, was not statistically significant, no interaction contrasts based on the same familywise α value will be significant either.

Procedure for analyzing the interaction in a two-factor multivariate analysis of variance design based on equal cell sizes.

Step 1. Find the eigen values for the characteristic equation:

$$|\,(\mathbf{SS}_{AB})(\mathbf{SS}_W)^{-1} - \lambda\mathbf{I}\,| = 0$$

where SS_{AB} has as diagonal elements:

$$N_{AB} \sum_{i=1}^{I} \sum_{j=1}^{J} (\bar{Y}_{ij.p} - \bar{Y}_{i..p} - \bar{Y}_{.j.p} + \bar{Y}_{...p})^2$$

and as off-diagonal elements:

$$N_{AB} \sum_{i=1}^{I} \sum_{j=1}^{J} (\bar{Y}_{ij.p} - \bar{Y}_{i..p} - \bar{Y}_{.j.p} + \bar{Y}_{...p})(\bar{Y}_{ij.p'} - \bar{Y}_{i..p'} - \bar{Y}_{.j.p'} + \bar{Y}_{...p'})$$

and where $\mathbf{SS}_W$ is as defined earlier.

Step 2. Follow the directions of Step 3 for the main effect, but replace ν_A by:

$$\nu_{AB} = (I - 1)(J - 1)$$

If $H_{0_{AB}}$ is rejected, examine contrasts that can be reduced to a tetrad difference of the form:

$$\hat{\psi} = (\mu_{ij} - \mu_{ij'}) - (\mu_{i'j} - \mu_{i'j'})$$

and use the Roy-Bose simultaneous multiple comparison procedure.

It should be mentioned that the procedure described in this section generalizes directly to factorial designs with more than two factors. However, we do not provide directions or examples since they involve considerable repetition of the material presented in this chapter. In any case, we should be able to generalize to more complicated designs, such as those described by Kirk (1982). In addition, simple effects designs can be analyzed following the model of Section 9-1 in conjunction with the principles illustrated for two-factor interactions.

9-3. Analysis of covariance designs

In Chapter 3, we described how an analysis of covariance could be performed using the multiple regression model. Given that the very restrictive assumptions associated with the analysis of covariance model are met (Elashoff, 1969), the design is a desirable one indeed. This is because differences among means on a dependent variable Y are examined on an adjusted measure with reduced error variance. In particular, the within-cell variance associated with Y is reduced proportionally to the size of the pooled within-cell squared correlation between the covariate, X, and Y. For moderate to large values of r_{YX}, increased statistical precision is achieved. In the case where two or more covariates, $X_1, X_2, \ldots X_Q$, are included, the within-cell Y variance is reduced proportionally to the size of the pooled within-cell $R^2_{Y.X_1X_2\ldots X_Q}$.

With multiple dependent variables, $Y_1, Y_2, \ldots, Y_P$, the canonical correlation model of Chapter 5 adequately represents the multivariate analysis of covariance analog, in that the most efficient linear combination of the covariates is used to reduce the variance in the best linear combination of the dependent variables. Under this model, group differences are examined on these variance-reduced Y composites, following the MANOVA procedures described in this and the preceding chapters. Because of the substantial overlap with material already presented, no specific example of the use of a MANCOVA design is included here. Instead, we believe that a researcher should be able to generalize from the univariate analysis of covariance model to the multivariate model on the basis of the material presented in Chapters 3 and 8.

9-4. One-group within-subject designs

It is often the case that a researcher wishes to compare the mean performance of the same subjects on a single variable that is measured on P different occasions or under P different treatment conditions. Such designs are commonly referred to as within-subject designs or repeated measures designs. These designs differ in one important respect from the multivariate analysis of variance designs discussed in Chapter 8 and Section 9-2. With classical multivariate analysis of variance designs, the dependent variables may consist of apples, oranges, and bananas. This means that direct comparisons across the dependent variables in each group are not possible or of interest. Rather, independent groups are compared with respect to their dependent variable vectors, with between-group comparisons defined in terms of selected dependent variables or dependent variable combinations. In contrast, in repeated measures multivariate analysis of variance, the dependent variables are directly comparable within groups, because they are measured on the same scale. In Morrison's (1976) terms, the dependent variables are *commensurable*. The researcher's main interest, in this case, is in making direct comparisons of the repeated measures within groups and between groups. When a single group is measured on P commensurable dependent variables, we refer to the situation as a completely within-subject design, since there is no between-group variation in performance. Alternatively, when $K \geq 2$ groups are measured on P commensurable dependent variables, the situation becomes a combined between- and within-subject design. In that case, there is systematic variation associated with the K groups, with the P measures, and with their interaction. We illustrate the combined between- and within-subject design in the next section. In this section, the completely within-subject design is illustrated.

In a study by Pressley et al. (1980), 16 sixth-grade students were given a list of 12 Spanish vocabulary items to study. The students were later tested for their recall of the Spanish words when presented with the English equivalents. Since four alternating study and test trials were provided, four recall scores were obtained from each student. The associated within-subject hypothesis is that the mean recall scores are the same on each of the four trials, or:

$$H_0: \quad \mu_1 = \mu_2 = \mu_3 = \mu_4$$

where the μ_p are based on correlated observations, inasmuch as the same students are contributing to each trial. If the variances at each trial were equal and if all $\binom{P}{2}$ covariances were equal, we could use a univariate ANOVA repeated measures analysis to evaluate the data. Fulfillment of this *compound symmetry* assumption is a sufficient (though not necessary) condition to render the univariate F test valid. (The necessary and sufficient condition is known as *circularity* or *sphericity*, which can be shown to reduce to all $\binom{P}{2}$ pairwise differences in the repeated measures having the same variance; see Huynh and Feldt, 1970.) The important point to be made here, however, is that if the compound symmetry assumption is not met, the regular univariate analysis may well be invalid. It should also be noted that the to-be-described multivariate analysis is justified, though less powerful than the corresponding univariate procedure, when variances and covariances are equal. For additional discussion, see Romaniuk, Levin, and Hubert (1977).

For this repeated measures model, we assume that each observation can be written as:

$$X_{ip} = \mu_{..} + s_i + \alpha_p + \varepsilon_{ip}$$

where:

$$\alpha_1 + \alpha_2 + \cdots + \alpha_P = 0$$

and where the s_i and ε_{ip} have multivariate normal distributions with mean values of zero and where the s_i are independently and identically distributed with variances σ_S^2 and where the variances and covariances of the ε_{ip} are given by Σ with respective elements $\sigma_{\varepsilon_p}^2$ and $\sigma_{\varepsilon_{pp'}}$. It is this latter assumption that differs from the more familiar univariate model where, as just noted, the sufficient condition is that the diagonal elements are all equal to σ_ε^2 and all off-diagonal elements are equal to $\rho\sigma_\varepsilon^2$, where ρ is the common correlation between each pair of measures. These restrictions are not required for the multivariate approach.

Testing the hypothesis of equal mean values across the repeated measures variable is achieved by transforming the P repeated measures into $P - 1$ new variables, $Y_1, Y_2, \ldots, Y_{P-1}$, that capture all the information regarding the differences among the original variables, $X_1, X_2, \ldots, X_P$. It can be shown mathematically that unlimited transformation possibilities for accomplishing this are available. A particularly simple one is generated by treating one measure as a standard. With X_P as the standard, we can create new variables, $Y_1, Y_2, \ldots, Y_{P-1}$, as:

$$\begin{aligned} Y_1 &= X_1 - X_P \\ Y_2 &= X_2 - X_P \\ &\vdots \\ Y_{P-1} &= X_{P-1} - X_P \end{aligned}$$

With X_1 as a standard, we can use:

$$\begin{aligned} Y_1 &= X_1 - X_2 \\ Y_2 &= X_1 - X_3 \\ &\vdots \\ Y_{P-1} &= X_1 - X_P \end{aligned}$$

Other common transformations include:

$$\begin{aligned} Y_1 &= X_1 - X_2 \\ Y_2 &= X_2 - X_3 \\ &\vdots \\ Y_{P-1} &= X_{P-1} - X_P \end{aligned}$$

and

$$Y_1 = X_1 - \frac{1}{P-1}(X_2 + X_3 + \cdots + X_P)$$

$$Y_2 = X_2 - \frac{1}{P-2}(X_3 + X_4 + \cdots + X_P)$$

$$\vdots \qquad \vdots$$

$$Y_{P-1} = X_{P-1} - X_P$$

Whichever one is used, the resulting variables are then analyzed as a one-sample Hotelling T^2, as described in Section 7-6. It should be mentioned that T^2 is invariant with respect to the particular differencing transformation selected, so that a researcher is free to select one that aids in the interpretation of the data.

If H_0: $\mu_1 = \mu_2 = \cdots = \mu_P$ is true, then: $E(Y_1) = E(Y_2) = \cdots = E(Y_{P-1}) = 0$

so that the one-sample Hotelling T^2 hypothesis can be stated as:

$$H_0: \begin{bmatrix} \mu_{Y_1} \\ \mu_{Y_2} \\ \cdot \\ \cdot \\ \cdot \\ \mu_{Y_{P-1}} \end{bmatrix} = \begin{bmatrix} 0 \\ 0 \\ \cdot \\ \cdot \\ \cdot \\ 0 \end{bmatrix}$$

and is tested with:

$$T^2 = N\,\bar{\mathbf{Y}}'\,\Sigma_{YY}^{-1}\,\bar{\mathbf{Y}}$$

This value can be transformed into an F statistic using:

$$F = \frac{v_2}{v_1}\left(\frac{T^2}{N-1}\right)$$

where $v_1 = P - 1$ and $v_2 = N - P + 1$. When $P = 2$, Hotelling's T^2 reduces to the single-sample matched pair t test, since $v_1 = 1$ and $v_2 = N - 1$, so that $F = T^2$. In this case, T reduces to:

$$T = \frac{\bar{X}_1 - \bar{X}_2}{SE_{\bar{X}_1 - \bar{X}_2}} = \frac{\bar{X}_1 - \bar{X}_2}{\sqrt{\dfrac{S_1^2 + S_2^2 - 2S_{12}}{N}}}$$

with $v = N - 1$. As developed in Section 7-5, we can relate T^2 to Wilks's Λ as:

$$T^2 = \frac{(N-1)(1-\Lambda)}{\Lambda}$$

and, therefore, to F, using:

$$F = \frac{N - P + 1}{P - 1}\left(\frac{1-\Lambda}{\Lambda}\right)$$

Since $K = 1$, it follows that $s = \min(K, P - 1) = 1$, so that there is only one eigen value, λ, so that:

$$\Lambda = \frac{1}{1 + \lambda}$$

Returning to the example, consider the summary data for the 16 subjects presented in Tables 9-11 and 9-12. As we see, the variances and covariances increase over trials, suggesting that a univariate repeated measures analysis of variance may not be justified. For our multivariate repeated measures analysis of variance, let us define:

$$Y_1 = X_2 - X_1, \qquad Y_2 = X_3 - X_2, \qquad \text{and} \qquad Y_3 = X_4 - X_3$$

This transformation produces a vector of three mean adjacent trial differences which will be inspected later. If H_0 is true, then

$$E(Y_1) = E(Y_2) = E(Y_3) = 0.$$

For these data, it can be shown that $\lambda = 3.0562$, so that:

$$\Lambda = \frac{1}{1 + 3.0562} = .2465$$

As a result:

$$T^2 = \frac{(16 - 1)(1 - .2465)}{.2465} = 45.85$$

$$F = \frac{16 - 4 + 1}{(4 - 1)(16 - 1)} 45.85 = 13.24$$

Since $F = 13.24$ exceeds $F_{3,13:.95} = 3.41$, we would reject the hypothesis of equal trial means based on a type I error probability of .05. The proportion of variance explained is given by:

$$\theta = 1 - \Lambda = 1 - .2465 = .7535$$

In this case, θ is directly comparable to the correlation ratio $\hat{\eta}^2$, which in a one-way

TABLE 9-11. Mean number of correct recalls on each of the four trials for Group 1 of the study

Trial	1	2	3	4
	4.3125	6.3750	7.3125	7.9375

TABLE 9-12. Variance-covariance matrix associated with the data of Table 9-11

	Trial number			
	1	2	3	4
1	6.3625	5.7417	6.9625	7.2875
2	5.7417	9.3167	10.6750	10.1583
3	6.9625	10.6750	12.7625	12.1542
4	7.2875	10.1583	12.1542	13.2625

ANOVA is defined as $\hat{\eta}^2 = SS_B/SS_T$.

Once the hypothesis has been rejected, simultaneous $100(1 - \alpha)$ percent confidence intervals follow from the procedures outlined in Section 7-7. The appropriate coefficient associated with such intervals is given by:

$$\mathbf{S} = \sqrt{\frac{\nu_1 \nu_R}{\nu_2} F_{\nu_1, \nu_2 : 1-\alpha}} = \sqrt{\frac{(P-1)(N-1)}{N-P+1} F_{P-1, N-P+1:1-\alpha}}$$

Even though the test has been performed in terms of $Y_1, Y_2, \ldots, Y_{P-1}$, contrasts can be defined directly in terms of the original variables, $X_1, X_2, \ldots, X_P$, since any contrast in the Y_p reduces to a contrast in the X_p. For our example:

$$\begin{aligned}
\hat{\psi}_Y &= a_1 \bar{Y}_1 + a_2 \bar{Y}_2 + a_3 \bar{Y}_3 \\
&= a_1(\bar{X}_2 - \bar{X}_1) + a_2(\bar{X}_3 - \bar{X}_2) + a_3(\bar{X}_4 - \bar{X}_3) \\
&= -a_1 \bar{X}_1 + (a_1 - a_2)\bar{X}_2 + (a_2 - a_3)\bar{X}_3 + a_3 \bar{X}_4 \\
&= \hat{\psi}_X
\end{aligned}$$

since: $-a_1 + (a_1 - a_2) + (a_2 - a_3) + a_3 = 0$

Thus:

$$\hat{\psi} = \sum_{p=1}^{P} a_p \bar{X}_p$$

can be defined, and when used in conjunction with:

$$\begin{aligned}
SE^2_{\hat{\psi}} &= \frac{1}{N} \mathbf{A}' (\mathbf{MS_W}) \mathbf{A} \\
&= \frac{1}{N}\left(\sum_{p=1}^{P} a_p^2 MS_{W_p} + 2 \sum_{p=1}^{P} \sum_{p'=1}^{P} a_p a_{p'} MS_{W_{pp'}} \right) \qquad p < p'
\end{aligned}$$

would produce the familiar confidence interval:

$$\psi = \hat{\psi} \pm \mathbf{S}\, SE_{\hat{\psi}}$$

For the present example, let us consider the three temporally adjacent trial differences, obtained from Table 9-11.

$$\hat{\psi}_1 = \bar{X}_2 - \bar{X}_1 = 6.3750 - 4.3125 = 2.0625$$

$$\hat{\psi}_2 = \bar{X}_3 - \bar{X}_2 = 7.3125 - 6.3750 = .9375$$

and

$$\hat{\psi}_3 = \bar{X}_4 - \bar{X}_3 = 7.9375 - 7.3125 = .6250$$

with corresponding estimated variances obtained from the values in Table 9-12:

$$SE^2_{\hat{\psi}_1} = \frac{1}{16}[9.3167 + 6.3625 - 2(5.7417)] = .2622$$

$$SE^2_{\hat{\psi}_2} = \frac{1}{16}[12.7625 + 9.3167 - 2(10.6750)] = .0456 \quad \text{and}$$

$$SE^2_{\hat{\psi}_3} = \frac{1}{16}[13.2625 + 12.7625 - 2(12.1542)] = .1073$$

(Note that these three variances—out of 6 possible—do not appear to be equal, thereby casting doubt on the circularity assumption required for univariate repeated measures ANOVA.)

With:

$$\mathbf{S}^2 = \frac{(4-1)(16-1)}{16-4+1}(3.41) = 11.80$$

the three intervals are defined as:

$$\psi_1 = 2.0625 \pm \sqrt{11.80(.2622)}$$
$$= 2.06 \pm 1.76$$

$$\psi_2 = .9375 \pm \sqrt{11.80(.0456)}$$
$$= .94 \pm .73$$

and

$$\psi_3 = .6250 \pm \sqrt{11.80(.1073)}$$
$$= .62 \pm 1.12$$

Thus, on the basis of these intervals we would conclude that subjects' performance improved significantly between Trials 1 and 2, and between Trials 2 and 3, but not between Trials 3 and 4.

Other contrasts could certainly be investigated as well, but these contrasts provide a trial-by-trial analysis of the learning process. One parsimonious contrast is that which seeks to determine whether there is a general increase or decrease in performance going from X_1, Trial 1 here, to X_P, Trial 4. If the amount of change is constant from one level of the within-subject factor to the next, such that successive differences are all equal to the same nonzero value, we say that the change between X_1 and X_P is *linear*. Methods for defining contrasts that examine linear trends, as well as curvilinear trends, in the data are described in books on experimental design, such as Kirk (1982), and will be further illustrated in Chapter 10. Tables of what are called *orthogonal polynomial coefficients* are also found in such sources and in our Table B-10. With $P = 4$, the contrast defining a linear trend is given by:

$$\hat{\psi}_4 = -3\bar{X}_1 + (-1)\bar{X}_2 + 1\bar{X}_3 + 3\bar{X}_4$$

Note that $-3 + (-1) + 1 + 3 = 0$, which means that such a contrast is legitimately subsumed by the present model. If there is a systematic increase or decrease over trials, use of these coefficients would be sensitive to it. For the present data:

$$\hat{\psi}_4 = -3(4.3125) + (-1)(6.3750) + (1)(7.3125) + (3)(7.9375)$$
$$= 11.8125$$

with:

$$
\begin{aligned}
SE^2_{\hat{\psi}_4} &= \frac{1}{16}[(-3)^2(6.3625) + (-1)^2(9.3167) + (1)^2(12.7625) + (3)^2(13.2625) \\
&\quad + 2\{(-3)(-1)(5.7417) + (-3)(1)(6.9625) + (-3)(3)(7.2875) \\
&\quad + (-1)(1)(10.6750) + (-1)(3)(10.1583) + (1)(3)(12.1542)\}] \\
&= 3.1769
\end{aligned}
$$

Therefore:

$$
\begin{aligned}
\psi_4 &= 11.8125 \pm \sqrt{11.80(3.1769)} \\
&= 11.81 \pm 6.12
\end{aligned}
$$

We may therefore conclude that there is a significant linear trend in the data. In particular, there appears to be a steady improvement in performance between Trial 1 and Trial 4. This conclusion is based on a simultaneous post hoc confidence interval procedure. If, instead, this contrast were of primary interest by itself, or with selected others defined on an a priori basis, then the planned Dunn-Bonferroni approach discussed throughout this book could be adapted to the present design. We now provide directions for conducting a one-sample multivariate repeated measures analysis.

Procedure for performing a within-subject analysis on a single group of subjects.

Step 1. Let:

$$X_{ip} = \mu + s_i + \alpha_p + \varepsilon_{ip}$$

represent the latent structure for the ith subject observed at time p, but where the dependent variables are commensurable.

Step 2. To test:

$$H_0: \ \alpha_1 = \alpha_2 = \cdots = \alpha_p = 0$$

transform the data by, for example, letting measure P serve as a standard. Let the transformed variables be

$$
\begin{aligned}
Y_{i1} &= X_{i1} - X_{ip} \\
Y_{i2} &= X_{i2} - X_{iP} \\
&\ \ \vdots \\
Y_{i(P-1)} &= X_{i(P-1)} - X_{iP}
\end{aligned}
$$

and test the hypothesis:

$$H_0: \ \mu_{.1} - \mu_{.P} = \mu_{.2} - \mu_{.P} = \cdots = \mu_{.P-1} - \mu_P = 0$$

by use of the one-sample Hotelling T^2 test.

Step 3. Compute:

$$T^2 = \mathbf{N}\,\bar{\mathbf{Y}}'\,\hat{\Sigma}^{-1}_{YY}\,\bar{\mathbf{Y}}$$

and:

$$F = \frac{v_2}{v_1}\left[\frac{T^2}{N-1}\right]$$

and reject

H_0 if $F > F_{\nu_1,\nu_2:1-\alpha}$ where $\nu_1 = P - 1$ and $\nu_2 = N - P + 1$.

Step 4. Perform post hoc comparisons with:

$$\mathbf{S} = \sqrt{\frac{(P-1)(N-1)}{(N-P+1)} F_{\nu_1,\nu_2:1-\alpha}}$$

on:

$$\hat{\psi} = \sum_{p=1}^{P} a_p \bar{X}_p$$

with:

$$a_1 + a_2 + \cdots + a_P = 0 \quad \text{and:}$$

$$SE_{\hat{\psi}}^2 = \frac{1}{N} \mathbf{A}' (\mathbf{MS_W}) \mathbf{A}$$

$$= \frac{1}{N}\left(\sum_{p=1}^{P} a_p^2 MS_{W_p} + 2 \sum_{p=1}^{P} \sum_{p'=1}^{P} a_p a_{p'} MS_{W_{pp'}} \right) \qquad p < p'$$

Four final comments about the multivariate within-subject design are in order. First, the design can easily accommodate two or more within-subject factors. Suppose, for instance, that the students of the present example were given four recall trials on each of three consecutive days. By taking appropriate sets of differences, the effects of both trials and days could be investigated in a manner analogous to the analysis of two factors in a completely between-subject design. One could define the difference variables in accordance with either the interaction or the simple effects model discussed in Section 9-1. The choice would be left to the researcher.

The second comment is that any time a within-subject factor consists of only two levels, only one difference per subject is possible. In that case, the problem is no longer multivariate, but rather it follows the model of the univariate correlated sample t test. The same statement can be made for any multilevel factor, for which only a single contrast is of interest. In that case, the linear combination of the variables again results in but a single difference for each subject and, thus, the univariate model applies there as well.

Third, there is a vast literature in the social sciences pertaining to the univariate analog to the multivariate repeated measures test described here. As stated earlier, there exists a univariate model for handling repeated measures data based on $P > 2$ commensurable responses. As might be expected, the univariate model is a great deal simpler computationally than the corresponding multivariate model. Of what utility, then, is the multivariate model? The answer boils down to one concerning the distributional assumptions associated with the two models. Both assume that each response variable is normally distributed, or that nonnormality is compensated for by large sample sizes, so that this assumption is not a distinguishing criterion. In addition, however, recall the previously stated compound symmetry assumption, namely that all P variances are equal and all $\binom{P}{2}$ covariances are equal. This assumption is often difficult to meet in practice, and violating it has been found to have an inflationary effect on the stated type I error probability, in that we will be incorrectly rejecting H_0 too often in most instances when the compound symmetry assumption is not met. With regard to the data of Table 9-12, the sample variances range from a low of 6.36 on Trial 1 to a high of 13.26 on Trial 4, and the covariances range from a low of 5.74 to a high of 12.15. Should either the four variances or the six covariances prove not to be homogeneous, we may be treading on dangerous ground in conducting a univariate repeated measures analysis. Although certain modifications of the classical univariate analysis are possible, most available computer programs do not attend to the problem. Because of its significant importance, we reiterate that the multivariate test described here does not depend on the variances being equal or the covariances being equal and, because of this, the multivariate model is recommended in most applications. As long as $N \geq P$, the multivariate test can be applied, and as long as N is large, it can be applied with a good deal of confidence. For more information about these issues, see Davidson (1972), Romaniuk et al. (1977), and Mandeville (1979).

Finally, another type of correlated sample design that is frequently adopted in social science research can be subsumed by the statistical model discussed here. The design is the K-sample extension of the two-group matched pair problem, and is referred to in the literature as a *randomized block* design. The rationale behind blocking is quite similar to that behind including a covariate in the analysis, that is, to make the statistical test more sensitive by reducing the error variance. The same multivariate test, Hotelling's T^2 or the F-transformed T^2, that is described in this section, can be directly applied to the randomized block situation as well, with *subjects* being replaced by *blocks*. It should be mentioned, however, that compound symmetry may not be as difficult to justify in the case when the P responses are associated with different subjects (randomized blocks) as it is when the responses are associated with the same subjects (repeated measures). Thus the univariate model may well be appropriate in many randomized block situations. There is, however, a related assumption which specifies that blocks and treatments (measures here) do not interact. See Kirk (1982) for additional discussion of this design.

9-5. Combined between- and within-subject designs

In the example presented in the previous section, one group of $N_1 = 16$ subjects was observed on $P = 4$ trials. The hypothesis of interest in that presentation was that the mean performance was equal on each trial. Suppose that a second group of N_2 subjects were included in the design, in that a second factor is added to the design which represents a between-subject classification where subjects are either in Group 1 or Group 2, but not both. Even though our presentation is based on equal sample sizes, it should be noted that in the tests of hypothesis that follow, it is not essential that sample sizes be equal. Unequal sample designs are nonetheless orthogonal due to proportionality properties and, as a result, alternative unequal sample size solutions need not be considered.

In the present example, 32 subjects were randomly assigned in equal numbers to two groups to learn the foreign vocabulary. Group 1 subjects, consisting of the 16 students considered in the preceding section, were allowed to study the vocabulary items in any manner they wished. In contrast, the $N_2 = 16$ subjects of Group 2 were instructed to use a new method of foreign vocabulary learning, the *keyword method* developed by Atkinson (1975). Of course, it would be of interest to know whether there are performance differences associated with the two different vocabulary learning conditions. This matter will be discussed shortly. Of immediate concern, however, is the question of whether there are trial differences, when averaged across the two experimental conditions. This, of course, is analogous to a main effect in a two-factor design. We examine the three hypotheses of this model in considerable detail, but with a change in notation from that of Section 9-2. The A factor will range from $k = 1, 2, \ldots, K$ and not from $i = 1, 2, \ldots, I$, as it did in the completely between-subjects design. In addition, the B factor, which is now treated as a multivariate response variable will range from $p = 1, 2, \ldots, P$, instead of from $j = 1, 2, \ldots, J$. Also, the repeated measures observation will be denoted by s_{ki} and, in most applications, will refer to the ith subject in the kth group. In particular, we assume that:

$$X_{kpi} = \mu_{\ldots} + \alpha_k + \beta_p + \gamma_{kp} + s_{ki} + \varepsilon_{kpi}$$

where:

1. $k = 1, 2, \ldots, K$ represents independent groups
2. $p = 1, 2, \ldots, P$ represents repeated measures
3. $i = 1, 2, \ldots, N_k$
4. $\sum_{k=1}^{K} \alpha_k = \sum_{p=1}^{P} \beta_p = \sum_{k=1}^{K} \gamma_{kp} = \sum_{p=1}^{P} \gamma_{kp} = 0$
5. mean of the $s_{ki} = 0$
6. mean of the $\varepsilon_{kpi} = 0$
7. variance of the $s_{ki} = \sigma_S^2$
8. variance-covariance matrix of the ε_{kpi} is equal from one level of k to the next; that is:

$$\Sigma_1 = \Sigma_2 = \cdots = \Sigma_K = \Sigma_0$$

9. s_{ki} and ε_{kpi} are completely independent of one another
10. s_{ki} are normally distributed
11. ε_{kpi} are multivariately normally distributed.

With this model, let us consider testing the two main effects, treatments and trials, and their interaction for statistical significance. We begin by testing the main effect for trials.

Test of the repeated measures hypothesis. Since trials are represented by the B factor, consider the hypothesis of no effect across trials; that is:

$$H_{0_B}: \; \mu_{.1.} = \mu_{.2.} = \mu_{.3.} = \mu_{.4.}$$

Testing this hypothesis follows the same differencing procedure described in the preceding section. That is, within each group, the same $P - 1 = 3$ trial differences are defined as Y_1, Y_2, and Y_3. In this case, the data for Group 2 are combined with those of Group 1 to create a single sample. Because pooling across groups will always allow the repeated measures to be represented as a *single* vector of differences, s will always equal 1 and an exact test of the hypothesis is possible. The means and variance-covariance information of Group 2 are summarized in Tables 9-13 and 9-14. The corresponding pooled Group 1 and Group 2 data appear in Tables 9-15 and 9-16.

To justify the pooling of the variances and covariances of Tables 9-12 and 9-14 to yield Table 9-16 requires the same assumption as in any between-group design, namely that the population variance-covariance matrices of the groups involved are identical. This general condition is required for all designs involving two or more groups of subjects. In the absence of variance-covariance homogeneity in the population—which appears suspect in this example since Group 1's variances and covariances appear uniformly larger than those of Group 2—the adoption of equal sample sizes will help to circumvent this strong multivariate ANOVA assumption. For the present example, $N_1 = N_2 = 16$. The assumption of homogeneous variance-covariance matrices from one between-subject population to the next is required for both the multivariate repeated measures analysis and the corresponding univariate repeated measures analysis mentioned in the preceding section. Note, however, that as before, within each population no assumption of equal variances and equal covariances is required for the multivariate analysis, even though it may be needed for the univariate analysis.

The actual analysis proceeds as in Section 9-4, but based on the pooled information contained in Tables 9-15 and 9-16, and the associated degrees of

TABLE 9-13. Mean number of correct recalls on each of the four trials for Group 2 of the study

Trial number			
1	2	3	4
3.4375	6.3125	7.8750	9.7500

TABLE 9-14. Variance-covariance matrix associated with the data of Table 9-13

	Trial number			
	1	2	3	4
1	2.9292	1.1208	1.8583	1.7833
2	1.1208	7.4292	4.9083	3.0167
3	1.8583	4.9083	5.3167	3.1667
4	1.7833	3.0167	3.1667	3.4000

TABLE 9-15. Mean number of correct recalls on each of the four trials, averaged across groups

Trial number			
1	2	3	4
3.8750	6.3438	7.5938	8.8438

TABLE 9-16. Pooled variance-covariance matrix associated with the data of Table 9-15

	Trial number			
	1	2	3	4
1	4.6458	3.4312	4.4104	4.5354
2	3.4312	8.3729	7.7917	6.5875
3	4.4104	7.7917	9.0396	7.6604
4	4.5354	6.5875	7.6604	8.3312

freedom. For K groups, the test of equal responses, $\mu_{.1.} = \mu_{.2.} = \cdots = \mu_{.P.}$, is based on:

$$T^2 = \frac{(N - K)(1 - \Lambda_B)}{\Lambda_B}$$

which can be transformed into:

$$F = \frac{v_2}{v_1}\left(\frac{T^2}{N - K}\right)$$

with $v_1 = P - 1$ and $v_2 = N - P - K + 2$. In terms of Wilks's Λ:

$$F = \frac{v_2}{v_1}\left(\frac{1 - \Lambda_B}{\Lambda_B}\right)$$

Since s always equals 1 for this test, there will only be one eigen value for the $N = N_1 + N_2 = 16 + 16 = 32$ subjects. In this case, $\lambda = 7.7347$. Therefore:

$$\Lambda_B = \frac{1}{1 + \lambda} = \frac{1}{1 + 7.7347} = .1145$$

As a result:

$$F = \frac{32 - 4 - 2 + 2}{4 - 1}\left(\frac{1 - .1145}{.1145}\right) = \frac{28}{3}(7.7336) = 72.18$$

With $v_1 = 4 - 1 = 3$ and $v_2 = 32 - 4 - 2 + 2 = 28$, we see that $F = 72.18$ exceeds $F_{3,28:.95} = 2.95$, so that the hypothesis of equal trial means within subjects would be rejected at an alpha level of .05. Simultaneous post hoc comparisons among the $P = 4$ trial means of Table 9-15 would follow the procedures of the previous section, with:

$$S_B = \sqrt{\frac{v_1 v_R}{v_2} F_{v_1, v_2:1-\alpha}} = \sqrt{\frac{(P - 1)(N - K)}{N - P - K + 2} F_{P-1, N-P-K+2:1-\alpha}}$$

and standard errors determined from the pooled variance-covariance matrix of Table 9-16. We now provide directions for testing the repeated measures variables in a split plot design.

Procedure for analyzing the repeated measures main effect in a split plot ANOVA design as a multivariate ANOVA.

Step 1. Let the variances and covariances of the ε_{kpi} be denoted by Σ_k and assume that they are all equal to a common value, Σ_0, which is estimated by $\mathbf{MS_W}$.

Step 2. To test the repeated measures hypothesis, make a differencing transformation by, for example, letting the pth measure serve as the standard. Test the hypothesis:

$$H_{0B}: \quad \mu_{.1.} = \mu_{.2.} = \cdots = \mu_{.P.}$$

or

$$H_{0B}: \quad \mu_{.1.} - \mu_{.P.} = \mu_{.2.} - \mu_{.P.} = \cdots = \mu_{.P-1.} - \mu_{.P.} = 0$$

by applying the F-transformed Hotelling's T^2 based on these differences and the pooled within-sample variance-covariance matrix associated with these differences.

Step 3. Compute:

$$\Lambda_B = \frac{1}{1+\lambda}$$

$$T^2 = \frac{(N-K)(1-\Lambda_B)}{\Lambda_B}$$

$$F = \frac{v_2}{v_1}\left(\frac{T^2}{N-K}\right)$$

based on $v_1 = P - 1$ and $v_2 = N - P - K + 2$.

Step 4. Reject:

$$\text{H}_{0_B}\text{:}\quad \mu_{.1.} = \mu_{.2.} = \cdots = \mu_{.P.}$$

if:

$$F > F_{P-1,N-P-K+2:1-\alpha}$$

Step 5. If H_{0_B} is rejected, perform simultaneous $100(1-\alpha)$ percent post hoc comparisons among the $\mu_{.p.}$, using the standard errors derived from the original pooled variance-covariance matrix and:

$$\mathbf{S}_B = \sqrt{\frac{(P-1)(N-K)}{N-P-K+2}F_{P-1,N-P-K+2:1-\alpha}}$$

Test for between-group differences. In addition to testing for the equality of the P measures in this design, we may wish to ascertain whether or not there are between-group differences in performance. What is meant by group differences is ambiguous, however, as will become apparent in the following discussion.

At first thought, it would seem that the most direct way to look for between-group differences on the P measures would be to test the multivariate hypothesis of Chapter 8 or, in the case of only two groups, of Chapter 7. That is, we might test:

$$\text{H}_{0_A}\text{:}\quad \begin{bmatrix} \mu_{11} \\ \mu_{12} \\ \cdot \\ \cdot \\ \cdot \\ \mu_{1P} \end{bmatrix} = \begin{bmatrix} \mu_{21} \\ \mu_{22} \\ \cdot \\ \cdot \\ \cdot \\ \mu_{2P} \end{bmatrix}$$

If this hypothesis were tested for the present example with $K = 2$, $P = 4$, and $s = 1$, it would be found that $\Lambda_A = .5702$ and $F = 5.09$, based on $v_1 = 4$ and $v_2 = 27$, leading to rejection of H_{0_A} at $\alpha = .05$. We could subsequently investigate between-group differences on the trial means, either one at a time, or in combination. As has been illustrated throughout this book, such combinations could take the form of whatever sums or differences, weighted or unweighted, were of interest to the researcher. In this regard, note that a group main effect contrast could be defined under this model by taking the simple average or sum of the P

measures. Similarly, condition by trial interaction contrasts could be investigated by comparing the groups with respect to selected trial differences. That is, if H_{0_A} were rejected here, it could be due to overall differences between the two groups (main effects), to differential effects associated with group by trial interactions, both of these, or something else, such as uninterpretable sum and difference combinations. Thus, even though the usual multivariate analysis of variance seems to be the most parsimonious way to investigate between-group differences, it is neither the most direct nor the most efficient for the specific kinds of questions usually of interest in combined between- and within-subject designs. In particular, in addition to focusing on response differences as measured on the repeated variable, a researcher typically wants to know whether there are overall group differences and whether groups and responses interact. Tests that separate out these two hypotheses are preferred to those that confound these two different research questions.

The question of overall group differences is most directly answered by comparing groups using the simple sum of the P measures, $X_1 + X_2 + \cdots + X_P$, which turns this multivariate question into a univariate question. For the present example, the overall performance for the two groups, summed over four trials, is 25.9375 for Group 1 and 27.3750 for Group 2. These figures may be obtained by adding together the four trial means in Table 9-11 and those in Table 9-13. With $MS_W = 99.2229$, a univariate test of the difference yields an F ratio of .17 based on $\nu_1 = K - 1 = 1$ and $\nu_2 = N - K = 30$ degrees of freedom. Thus we cannot reject the hypothesis of overall, or total, performance difference between the two groups. We now provide directions for testing the group effect in a split-plot design.

Procedure for assessing main effects for groups in a split-plot design treated as a multivariate problem.

Step 1. Sum the observations across the repeated measures, converting the data to a one-way univariate ANOVA problem. Denote the summed values as:

$$X_{k.i} = X_{k1i} + X_{k2i} + \cdots + X_{kPi}$$

Step 2. Reject:

$$H_{0_A}: \mu_{X1..} = \mu_{X2..} = \cdots = \mu_{XK..}$$

if:

$$F = \frac{MS_B}{MS_W} > F_{\nu_1,\nu_2:1-\alpha}$$

where:

$$\nu_1 = K - 1 \qquad \text{and} \qquad \nu_2 = N - K$$

with:

$$N = \sum_{k=1}^{K} N_k$$

(Note: N_k represents the number of *independent units* per group.)

Step 3. Conduct post hoc comparisons between groups with:

$$\mathbf{S}_A = \sqrt{v_1 F_{v1,v2:1-\alpha}}$$

$$\hat{\psi} = \sum_{k=1}^{K} a_k \bar{X}_{k..}$$

$$SE^2_{\hat{\psi}} = MS_W \frac{\sum_{k=1}^{K} a_k^2}{N_k}$$

Test of interaction in the multivariate split-plot design. The interaction between groups and trials is examined directly by comparing the two groups with respect to the $P - 1 = 3$ adjacent differences, $Y_1 = X_2 - X_1$, $Y_2 = X_3 - X_2$, and $Y_3 = X_4 - X_3$, for the within-subjects trials factor. (It should be noted that the compound symmetry and circularity statements made for the univariate test of the repeated measures main effect are relevant here as well.) To test for an interaction the Y mean vectors associated with two samples are compared, relative to the pooled variance-covariance matrix associated with the Y means. That is, the groups by measures interaction hypothesis on the X variable is tested in the general case by the main effects hypothesis on the Y variable as:

$$\text{H}_{0_{AB}}: \begin{bmatrix} \mu_{Y_{11}} \\ \mu_{Y_{12}} \\ \cdot \\ \cdot \\ \cdot \\ \mu_{Y_{1(P-1)}} \end{bmatrix} = \begin{bmatrix} \mu_{Y_{21}} \\ \mu_{Y_{22}} \\ \cdot \\ \cdot \\ \cdot \\ \mu_{Y_{2(P-1)}} \end{bmatrix} = \cdots = \begin{bmatrix} \mu_{Y_{K1}} \\ \mu_{Y_{K2}} \\ \cdot \\ \cdot \\ \cdot \\ \mu_{Y_{K(P-1)}} \end{bmatrix}$$

For the present example with $s = \min(K - 1, P - 1) = \min(2 - 1, 4 - 1) = 1$, there exists one eigen value, $\lambda = .6574$ and, therefore, $\Lambda_{AB} = 1/(1 + \lambda) = .6033$. In this case, we can use Hotelling's two-sample procedure of Section 7-6. Thus:

$$T^2 = \frac{(N - K)(1 - \Lambda_{AB})}{\Lambda_{AB}} = \frac{(32 - 2)(1 - .6033)}{.6033} = 19.73$$

and

$$F = \frac{v_2}{v_1}\left(\frac{T^2}{N - K}\right) = \frac{N - P}{P - 1}\left(\frac{T^2}{N - K}\right) = \frac{32 - 4}{4 - 1}\left(\frac{19.73}{32 - 2}\right) = 6.14$$

With $v_1 = P - 1 = 4 - 1 = 3$ and $v_2 = N - P = 32 - 4 = 28$, and with $\alpha = .05$:

$$\text{H}_{0_{AB}}: \begin{bmatrix} \mu_{Y_{11}} \\ \mu_{Y_{12}} \\ \mu_{Y_{13}} \end{bmatrix} = \begin{bmatrix} \mu_{Y_{21}} \\ \mu_{Y_{22}} \\ \mu_{Y_{23}} \end{bmatrix}$$

would be rejected since $F = 6.14$ exceeds $F_{P-1,N-P:1-\alpha} = F_{3,28:.95} = 2.95$. Thus we would conclude that there was a significant conditions by trials interaction.

In our example, direct use of the two-sample Hotelling T^2 statistic was possible, since $s = \min(K - 1, P - 1) = \min(2 - 1, 4 - 1) = \min(1, 3) = 1$. Whenever $s \geq 2$, the factorial MANOVA procedures of Section 9-2 must be used and a decision has to be made concerning which of the previously described test criteria are to be employed. As before, the decision should be based on the notion of concentrated or diffuse relationships expected among the group centroids.

Post hoc comparisons between conditions can be examined directly in terms of the original X variables and not necessarily in terms of the constructed Y variables. This is possible because all possible interaction contrasts in the X variable reduce to valid contrasts in the Y variable that do not necessarily resemble interaction contrasts. For example, the tetrad difference in the original variable, $\hat{\psi}_1 = (\bar{X}_{22} - \bar{X}_{21}) - (\bar{X}_{12} - \bar{X}_{11})$, reduces to the simple difference $\hat{\psi}_1 = \bar{Y}_{21} - \bar{Y}_{11}$, a simple pairwise comparison. On the other hand, the interaction contrast used to test parallelism of the linear components:

$$\hat{\psi}_2 = -3(\bar{X}_{11} - \bar{X}_{21}) - 1(\bar{X}_{12} - \bar{X}_{22}) + 1(\bar{X}_{13} - \bar{X}_{23}) + 3(\bar{X}_{14} - \bar{X}_{24})$$

reduces to:

$$\hat{\psi}_2 = 4(\bar{Y}_{12} - \bar{Y}_{22}) + 3[(\bar{Y}_{11} - \bar{Y}_{21}) + (\bar{Y}_{13} - \bar{Y}_{23})]$$

which is rather difficult to define, even though it is a contrast in Y.

As we see, $\hat{\psi}_1$ represents a tetrad difference, whereas $\hat{\psi}_2$ represents the difference between the linear components for Groups 1 and 2. More directly, $\hat{\psi}_2 = \bar{X}_{1(\text{Linear})} - \bar{X}_{2(\text{Linear})} = \bar{X}_{L_1} - \bar{X}_{L_2}$. As was seen previously, the linear trend component for Group 1 was equal to $\bar{X}_{L_1} = 11.8125$. The same contrast for Group 2 is given by $\bar{X}_{L_2} = -3(3.4375) + (-1)(6.3125) + 1(7.8750) + 3(9.7500) = 20.5000$. To determine whether the linear trends are statistically different requires the computation of the standard error of $\hat{\psi}_2 = \bar{X}_{L_1} - \bar{X}_{L_2}$. In this case:

$$SE^2_{\hat{\psi}} = \left(\frac{1}{N_1} + \frac{1}{N_2}\right)\left(\sum_{p=1}^{P} a_p^2 MS_{W_p} + 2\sum_{p=1}^{P}\sum_{p'=1}^{P} a_p a_{p'} MP_{pp'(W)}\right) \qquad p < p'$$

This formula for the squared standard error could be applied to any between-group contrast of linearly combined X_p.

For the present example:

$$\hat{\psi}_2 = \bar{X}_{L_1} - \bar{X}_{L_2} = 11.8125 - 20.5000 = -8.6875$$

and

$$\begin{aligned} SE^2_{\hat{\psi}_2} &= \frac{2}{16}\{(-3)^2(4.6458) + (-1)^2(8.3729) + (1)^2(9.0396) + (3)^2(8.3312) \\ &\quad + 2[(-3)(-1)(3.4312) + (-3)(1)(4.4104) + (-3)(3)(4.5354) \\ &\quad + (-1)(1)(7.7917) + (-1)(3)(6.5875) + (1)(3)(7.6604)]\} \\ &= 4.6934 \end{aligned}$$

Since:

$$\begin{aligned} \mathbf{S}_{AB} &= \sqrt{\frac{\nu_1\nu_R}{\nu_2}F_{\nu_1,\nu_2:1-\alpha}} = \sqrt{\frac{(P-1)(N-K)}{N-P}F_{P-1,N-P:1-\alpha}} \\ &= \sqrt{\frac{(4-1)(32-2)}{32-4}F_{3,28:.95}} \\ &= \sqrt{3.21(2.95)} = 3.08 \end{aligned}$$

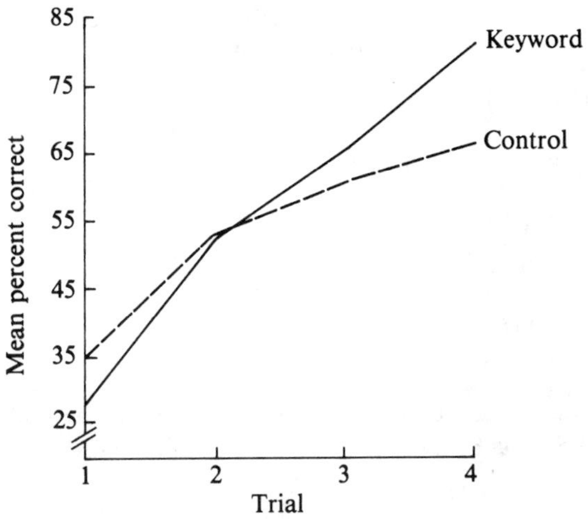

Figure 9-2. Examination of the groups by trials interaction for the data of Tables 9-11 and 9-13.

it follows that:

$$\begin{aligned}\psi_2 &= -8.6875 \pm 3.08\sqrt{4.6934} \\ &= -8.69 \pm 6.67\end{aligned}$$

Note that the contrast is significant, since zero is not in the interval. The direction of the contrast, which represents the difference between the two conditions with respect to the size of the linear change over trials, reveals that Group 2 subjects' linear trend is more pronounced than that of Group 1 subjects. This is graphically portrayed in Figure 9-2, where it may now be concluded that the keyword subjects, Group 2, showed a greater linear increase over trials in comparison to control subjects, Group 1.

The procedures discussed here readily extend to the case where $K > 2$, as well as to the case where more than one between-subject classification, for instance, a factorial structure, is imposed on the design. We now provide directions for testing the groups by repeated measures interaction.

Procedure for testing the interaction of a split-plot design treated as a multivariate problem in which $s \geq 2$.

Step 1. Select, for example, the Pth trial as a standard and compute the corresponding differences:

$$\begin{bmatrix} Y_{k1i} \\ Y_{k2i} \\ \cdot \\ \\ \cdot \\ Y_{k(P-1)i} \end{bmatrix} = \begin{bmatrix} X_{k1i} - X_{kPi} \\ X_{k2i} - X_{kPi} \\ \cdot \\ \\ \cdot \\ X_{k(P-1)i} - X_{kPi} \end{bmatrix}$$

for each subject in each group, and perform a one-way MANOVA on the resulting Y_{kpi} values.

Step 2. For a presumed diffuse structure on the group centroids, use Wilks's criterion and Rao's approximation procedure of Section 8-2, with:

$$v_1 = (P - 1)(K - 1)$$

$$v_2 = ab - \frac{1}{2}[(P - 1)(K - 1)] + 1$$

$$a = (N - 1) - \frac{1}{2}(P - 1 + K)$$

$$b = \sqrt{\frac{(P - 1)^2(K - 1)^2 - 4}{(P - 1)^2 + (K - 1)^2 - 5}}$$

For a presumed concentrated structure on the group centroids, use Roy's criterion procedure of Section 8-4, with:

$$s = \min(K - 1, P - 1)$$

$$m = \frac{|(P - 1) - (K - 1)| - 1}{2}$$

$$n = \frac{N - (P - 1) - K - 1}{2}$$

Step 3. Use the methods of Section 8-6 for analyzing post hoc or planned comparisons.

9-6. Simplified statistics for other multivariate analysis of variance designs

The simplified statistics strategies described in Chapters 7 and 8 can be incorporated into any multivariate analysis of variance design. The two basic approaches consist of: variable-by-variable comparisons, perhaps with partitioned type I error probabilities via Scheffé's and/or the Bonferroni procedure; and selected sums and differences of the dependent variables. The idea of defining selected differences, including those representing linear and higher order trend components, fits very nicely with the questions of concern in repeated measures designs. But taking meaningful differences in the dependent variables is not restricted to such designs, as will be illustrated in a study by Readence and Baldwin (1978b). We are grateful to Scott Baldwin for making the data of that study available to us.

Readence and Baldwin (1978b) classified 170 second-grade students according to whether their *conceptual tempo* was either *reflective* or *impulsive* (Factor A). Reflective subjects are defined as those who take a relatively long time to respond to a problem and make fewer errors, whereas impulsive subjects respond relatively quickly and make more errors. It was believed that the two types of students might profit differently from two different types of reading instruction, *synthetic* versus an *analytic* phonics approach (Factor B). In particular, little difference in the two approaches was expected for reflective students, but the synthetic approach was posited to be more effective for impulsive students, since that approach presumably forces attention to details that might otherwise be missed. Two dependent variables were employed in the analysis: raw scores on the vocabulary, X_1, and comprehension, X_2, sections of the Gates-MacGinitie Reading Test.

TABLE 9-17. Means and cell sizes of the original Readence and Baldwin data (1978b)

			Factor A	
			Impulsive students	*Reflective students*
Factor B	Synthetic Approach	V	37.5400	41.3333
		C	24.5800	26.7556
	Sample size		50	45
	Analytic Approach	V	36.7949	37.1667
		C	22.7692	25.7222
	Sample size		39	36

Note: V = Vocabulary raw score
C = Comprehension raw score

TABLE 9-18. Pooled within-cell variance-covariance matrix associated with data of Table 9-17

	Vocabulary X_1	*Comprehension* X_2
X_1	49.7579	33.6920
X_2	33.6920	37.6669

The data for the 2 × 2 multivariate factorial design are summarized in Tables 9-17 and 9-18. Even though these data are associated with unequal and disproportional cell frequencies, this will not affect the present discussion which focuses on the $A \times B$ interaction.

Using the interaction model discussed in Section 9-2, we will obtain for these data, $\lambda = .0554$ and $\Lambda_{AB} = 1/(1 + .0554) = .9475$. Since $s = 1$, the exact F ratio associated with these data is given by:

$$F = \frac{v_2}{v_1} \cdot \frac{1 - \Lambda_{AB}}{\Lambda_{AB}}$$

where:

$$v_1 = v_{AB}P$$

$$v_2 = v_R + v_{AB} - P$$

$$v_R = N - AB$$

Since:

$$v_R = 170 - 2(2) = 166$$

$$v_1 = (2 - 1)(2 - 1)2 = 2$$

$$v_2 = 166 + (2 - 1)(2 - 1) - 2 = 165$$

then:

$$F = \frac{165}{2}\left(\frac{.0525}{.9475}\right) = 4.57$$

Since $F_{2,165:.95} = 3.06$ we would reject the multivariate interaction hypothesis, using $\alpha = .05$.

As Readence and Baldwin (1978b) were interested in variable-by-variable comparisons, they looked at the interaction contrast associated with vocabulary, X_1, and comprehension, X_2, separately. They discovered that neither of the univariate interaction contrasts was statistically significant, even using separate α levels of .10. The example readily points out the nonnecessary correspondence between multivariate and univariate tests of hypothesis. In particular, it is possible for a multivariate test to be significant, and yet none of the variable-by-variable univariate tests will be significant. The converse is also true. See Finn (1974) for a pictorial representation of these situations.

In terms of Readence and Baldwin's interaction hypothesis, we would expect to find a more pronounced effect of teaching approach on the achievement scores of impulsives than on the scores of reflectives. The means in Table 9-17 show that for vocabulary scores X_1, if anything, the reverse is true—there appears to be a larger synthetic-analytic difference for reflectives, an average of 4.17 points, than for impulsives, an average of .74 points. The effect is in the predicted direction on the comprehension measure X_2, but it is relatively small, an average difference of 1.03 for reflectives as compared to one of 1.81 for impulsives, resulting in a negligible t ratio. The fact that the two interaction contrasts are in the opposite direction, that is, a descriptively larger effect of the synthetic approach for reflectives on the vocabulary measure and for impulsives on the comprehension measure, suggests that the interaction contrast might itself interact with the particular dependent variable considered. If so, this would result in what might be termed a three-way interaction of conceptual tempo, teaching approach, and reading measure.

To get at this three-way interaction, a difference score Y could be computed for each subject, where $Y = X_1 - X_2$ or vocabulary score minus comprehension score. Since X_1 and X_2 are not necessarily commensurable, however, inasmuch as they are raw scores of different subtests with possibly different variances, as shown in Table 9-18, standardized rather than raw differences should probably be taken. Thus, as has been done throughout this book, suppose we put each variable on the same scale by incorporating $\sqrt{MS_{W_p}}$ into the difference. As a result, we could define:

$$Y = \frac{1}{\sqrt{MS_{W_1}}} X_1 - \frac{1}{\sqrt{MS_{W_2}}} X_2$$

and the interaction contrast:

$$\hat{\psi} = (\bar{Y}_{11} - \bar{Y}_{12}) - (\bar{Y}_{21} - \bar{Y}_{22})$$

could be investigated according to the simultaneous Roy-Bose procedure. In terms of the data in Tables 9-17 and 9-18:

$$\bar{Y}_{11} = \frac{1}{\sqrt{49.7579}}(37.5400) - \frac{1}{\sqrt{37.6669}}(24.5800) = 1.3169$$

$$\bar{Y}_{12} = \frac{1}{\sqrt{49.7579}}(36.7949) - \frac{1}{\sqrt{37.6669}}(22.7692) = 1.5063$$

$$\bar{Y}_{21} = \frac{1}{\sqrt{49.7579}}(41.3333) - \frac{1}{\sqrt{37.6669}}(26.7556) = 1.5001 \quad \text{and}$$

$$\bar{Y}_{22} = \frac{1}{\sqrt{49.7579}}(37.1667) - \frac{1}{\sqrt{37.6669}}(25.7222) = 1.0778$$

Then:

$$\hat{\psi} = (1.3169 - 1.5063) - (1.5001 - 1.0778) = -.6117$$

The estimated variance of this contrast is given by:

$$SE^2_{\hat{\psi}} = MS_{W(Y)} \sum_{k=1}^{4} \frac{a_k^2}{N_k}$$

It has been shown previously that under standardization of this kind:

$$MS_{W(Y)} = 1 + 1 - 2r_{X_1X_2(W)} = 2(1 - r_{X_1X_2(W)})$$

For the present example $r_{X_1X_2(W)}$ is obtained from Table 9-18 as:

$$r_{X_1X_2(W)} = \frac{33.6920}{\sqrt{49.7579(37.6669)}} = .7782$$

and, thus:

$$MS_{W(Y)} = 2(1 - .7782) = .4436$$

Accordingly:

$$SE^2_{\hat{\psi}} = .4436\left[\frac{(+1)^2}{50} + \frac{(-1)^2}{39} + \frac{(-1)^2}{45} + \frac{(+1)^2}{36}\right] = .0424$$

With:

$$\mathbf{S}_{AB} = \sqrt{\frac{\nu_1\nu_R}{\nu_2}F_{\nu_1,\nu_2:1-\alpha}} = \sqrt{\frac{2(166)}{165}F_{2,165:.95}}$$

$$= \sqrt{2.012(3.05)} = 2.48$$

we finally obtain:

$$\psi = \hat{\psi} \pm \mathbf{S}_{AB}\, SE_{\hat{\psi}}$$

$$= -.61 \pm 2.48\sqrt{.0424}$$

$$= -.61 \pm .51$$

which reveals a statistically significant contrast. It appears that the effect of teaching approach on the two types of students differs from one dependent variable to the next. Although this does not provide overall support for the researchers' interaction hypothesis, it does suggest that such a hypothesis might be quite dependent on the particular dependent measure chosen to validate it.

From a simplified statistics point of view, a potentially difficult to compute or interpret multivariate test could be bypassed altogether. In its place, a simple univariate analysis could be performed. For the present example, once again one could define:

$$Y = \frac{1}{\sqrt{MS_{W_1}}} X_1 - \frac{1}{\sqrt{MS_{W_2}}} X_2$$

Also, as before:

$$\hat{\psi} = (\bar{Y}_{11} - \bar{Y}_{12}) - (\bar{Y}_{21} - \bar{Y}_{22}) = -.6117$$

with:

$$SE^2_{\hat{\psi}} = MS_{W(Y)} \sum_{k=1}^{4} \frac{a_k^2}{N_k} = .0424$$

To test the interaction contrast for statistical significance, we merely compute the univariate F ratio given by:

$$F = \frac{\hat{\psi}^2}{SE^2_{\hat{\psi}}}$$

based on $v_1 = 1$ and $v_2 = N - AB = 170 - 4 = 166$. Thus:

$$F = \frac{(-.6117)^2}{.0424} = 8.82$$

which exceeds $F_{1,166:.95} = 3.90$.

Consequently the derived three-way univariate interaction would be significant using $\alpha = .05$, with the same interpretation as given previously. Exactly this procedure was followed by Readence and Baldwin (1978a) in a reanalysis of their original data with precisely the same result. A graph of the standardized differences, depicting the three-way interaction, allowed these authors to understand their data more fully.

We do not provide directions for this procedure because of its specificity to the research question under investigation. Our purpose in presenting this example has been to illustrate that once again, complex multivariate methods can be closely approximated by simpler univariate methods.

9-7. Summary

In this chapter, an introduction to factorial multivariate analysis of variance designs was presented. To set the stage, a description of univariate interaction and univariate simple effects designs were presented. The purpose of this review was to show that interaction hypotheses always involved four or more mean values, while simple effects could be examined in terms of simple pairwise differences. The easiest way to view the difference in these two models is to consider a two-factor design in which each factor is measured at two levels. Let the factors and their levels be denoted by (A_1 and A_2) and (B_1 and B_2). An interaction is said to exist between A and

B if the contrast:

$$\psi_{AB} = \mu_{11} - \mu_{12} - \mu_{21} + \mu_{22}$$

is statistically significant from zero. Another way to view ψ_{AB} is to see that:

$$\psi_{AB} = (\mu_{11} - \mu_{12}) - (\mu_{21} - \mu_{22})$$

or that:

$$\psi_{AB} = (\mu_{11} - \mu_{21}) - (\mu_{12} - \mu_{22})$$

In these forms it is seen that a significant interaction means that the difference in B_1 and B_2 when measured in A_1 is different from the difference in B_1 and B_2 when measured in A_2, or that the difference in A_1 and A_2 when measured in B_1 is different from the difference in A_1 and A_2 when measured in B_2.

On the other hand, a simple effects analysis never examines differences in differences. Instead, the contrasts:

$$\psi_{A(B_1)} = \mu_{11} - \mu_{21}$$

$$\psi_{A(B_2)} = \mu_{12} - \mu_{22}$$

or:

$$\psi_{B(A_1)} = \mu_{11} - \mu_{12}$$

$$\psi_{B(A_2)} = \mu_{21} - \mu_{22}$$

are examined separately for significance.

These same considerations extend to their multivariate analogs. Even in these cases, a researcher must decide what constitutes a meaningful research question, be it an interaction question or a simple effects question. No attempt was made to illustrate the latter type of question since it is comparable to a one-way MANOVA in each level of one of the independent variables and, since that model was clearly explicated in Chapter 8, there was no need to reproduce the method in this chapter.

For the most part, no new multivariate theory was required to illustrate the testing of multivariate mean effects hypotheses or corresponding interaction hypotheses. Again, a researcher could choose between a concentrated or a diffuse alternative and then proceed to use tests based on Roy's or Wilks's criterion. Rejected hypotheses are examined in terms of post hoc comparisons based on the Roy-Bose model described in Chapter 8. The only differences are that degrees of freedom values change but, other than that, the statistical procedures are identical.

However, new theory is required to analyze correctly the repeated measures designs so that a test of:

$$\text{H}_{0_B}\text{:} \quad \mu_{X_1} = \mu_{X_2} = \cdots = \mu_{X_P}$$

can be attained. To generate a valid test, we begin by creating $P - 1$ differences in X. A convenient transformation is to select one of the repeated measures as a standard. A common choice is to select the Pth measure. With this as a standard, $P - 1$ new variables are generated. Specifically, they are defined as:

$$\begin{aligned}
Y_1 &= X_1 - X_P \\
Y_2 &= X_2 - X_P \\
&\vdots \\
Y_{P-1} &= X_{P-1} - X_P
\end{aligned}$$

With these new variables, H_{0_B} can be restated as:

$$H_{0_B}: \quad \mu_{Y_1} = \mu_{Y_2} = \ldots = \mu_{Y_{P-1}} = 0$$

and can be tested with the one-sample Hotelling T^2 statistic as:

$$F = \frac{v_2}{v_1}\left(\frac{T^2}{N-1}\right)$$

where:

$$\begin{aligned}
v_1 &= P - 1 \\
v_2 &= N - P + 1 \\
T^2 &= N\,\bar{\mathbf{Y}}'\hat{\Sigma}^{1}_{YY}\,\bar{\mathbf{Y}} \\
\bar{Y}' &= (\bar{Y}_1, \bar{Y}_2, \ldots, \bar{Y}_{P-1}) \\
\hat{\Sigma}_{YY} &= \text{variance-covariance matrix of the } Y \text{ values} \\
N &= \text{number of subjects}
\end{aligned}$$

In practice, T^2 is rarely computed, since the associated characteristic equation has only one root. Once this root is found, we can use the fact that Wilks's Λ is simply related to λ as:

$$\Lambda_B = \frac{1}{1+\lambda}$$

so that:

$$F = \frac{v_2}{v_1}\left(\frac{1-\Lambda_B}{\Lambda_B}\right)$$

can be employed directly.

Surprisingly, the same procedure is used to test the repeated measures hypothesis in the K-group (split-plot) model. The only difference is that the eigen value is determined from the pooled within variance-covariance matrix, which is computed as:

$$\mathbf{MS_W} = \frac{1}{N-K}\left[(N_1-1)\hat{\Sigma}_1 + (N_2-1)\hat{\Sigma}_2 + \cdots + (N_K-1)\hat{\Sigma}_K\right]$$

where $\hat{\boldsymbol{\Sigma}}_k$ is the variance-covariance matrix for Y in the kth sample. In addition, F is defined as:

$$F = \frac{v_2}{v_1}\left(\frac{T^2}{N - K}\right)$$

where:

$v_1 = P - 1$

$v_2 = N - P - K + 2$

Similar to the one-sample case:

$$\Lambda_B = \frac{1}{1 + \lambda}$$

so that:

$$F = \frac{v_2}{v_1}\left(\frac{1 - \Lambda_B}{\Lambda_B}\right)$$

can be employed directly.

For both the one- and K-sample models, contrasts can be defined directly in terms of the original variables as:

$$\hat{\psi} = a_1\bar{X}_{.1.} + a_2\bar{X}_{.2.} + \cdots + a_P\bar{X}_{.P.}$$

where:

$a_1 + a_2 + \cdots + a_P = 0$

with:

$$SE^2_{\hat{\psi}} = \frac{1}{N}\mathbf{A}'\,\mathbf{MS_W}\,\mathbf{A}$$

$$= \frac{1}{N}\left(\sum_{p=1}^{P} a_p^2 MS_{W_p} + 2\sum_{p=1}^{P}\sum_{p'=1}^{P} a_p a_{p'} MS_{W_{pp'}}\right) \qquad p < p'$$

and where:

$N = N_1 + N_2 + \cdots + N_K$

In addition:

$$\mathbf{S}_B = \sqrt{\frac{v_1}{v_2}(N - K)\,F_{v_1,v_2:1-\alpha}}$$

In the one-sample case, $N = N_1$ and $N - K = N - 1$.

Testing the main effects for groups is exceedingly simple in that this test reduces to a univariate F test of the form:

$$F = \frac{MS_B}{MS_W}$$

where $v_1 = \mathrm{K} - 1$ and $v_2 = N - K$. To generate the measures for this test, we simply sum the observed values across the repeated measures for each subject. Thus the analysis is performed on the:

$$X_{k.i} = X_{k1i} + X_{k2i} + \cdots + X_{kPi}$$

Post hoc procedures use the MS_W of the F test and:

$$\mathbf{S}_A = \sqrt{v_1 F_{v1,v2:1-\alpha}}$$

Finally, the test of the $A \times B$ interaction is also very simple in that it reduces to a one-way MANOVA on the difference scores across the K groups of subjects. That this is indeed a test of the interaction is easy to demonstrate. As an illustration, suppose $P = 4$ and $K = 2$. In this case, $H_{0_{AB}}$ can be written as:

$$\psi_1 = \mu_{Y_{11}} - \mu_{Y_{21}} = 0$$

$$\psi_2 = \mu_{Y_{12}} - \mu_{Y_{22}} = 0$$

$$\psi_3 = \mu_{Y_{13}} - \mu_{Y_{23}} = 0$$

In terms of the original X variables, this is identical to:

$$\psi_1 = (\mu_{X_{11}} - \mu_{X_{14}}) - (\mu_{X_{21}} - \mu_{X_{24}})$$

$$\psi_2 = (\mu_{X_{12}} - \mu_{X_{14}}) - (\mu_{X_{22}} - \mu_{X_{24}})$$

$$\psi_3 = (\mu_{X_{13}} - \mu_{X_{14}}) - (\mu_{X_{23}} - \mu_{X_{24}})$$

which are seen to be simple tetrad differences or difference of differences.

Similar to the repeated measures hypothesis, post hoc comparisons can be made directly in terms of the X variables, since all interaction contrasts reduce to main effect contrasts on the Y variables. In this case, contrasts as described in Section 8-6 will need to be investigated. In the most general case, we might wish to examine contrasts across the K sample means, $\bar{C}, \bar{C}_2, \ldots, \bar{C}_K$, where:

$$\bar{C}_k = a_1\bar{X}_{k1.} + a_2\bar{X}_{k2.} + \cdots + a_P\bar{X}_{kP.}$$

Contrasts in the $\bar{C}_k$ values are defined as:

$$\hat{\psi} = b_1\bar{C}_1 + b_2\bar{C}_2 + \cdots + b_K\bar{C}_K$$

where:

$$b_1 + b_2 + \cdots + b_K = 0$$

Such contrasts can be tested for significance with:

$$SE^2_{\hat{\psi}} = MS_{W_C} \sum_{k=1}^{K} \frac{b_k^2}{N_k}$$

where:

$$MS_{W_C} = \mathbf{A}'\,\mathbf{MS_W}\,\mathbf{A}$$

$$= \sum_{p=1}^{P} a_p^2 MS_{W_p} + 2 \sum_{p=1}^{P} \sum_{p'=1}^{P} a_p a_{p'} MP_{pp'(W)} \qquad p < p'$$

where MS_{W_p} and $MP_{pp'(W)}$ values are selected from the pooled within-group variance-covariance matrix. Critical values may be determined from the Roy-Bose model described in Chapter 8.

9-8. Exercises

Each of the exercises in this chapter utilizes the 'sleep' data reported in Appendix Table A-3.

9-1. Classify the subjects of the 'sleep' study according to two factors: hours of sleep permitted (0, 3, 6, and 9) and IQ (High = 110 and above; Low = less than 110). With a single dependent variable defined as the subject's score on the 60-item test (that is $V + R + A$):

a. Perform a two-factor ANOVA according to the interaction model, using $\alpha = .05$ for each test.

b. Conduct Scheffé post hoc comparisons for any significant sources of variance.

c. Redo the preceding analysis, but this time examining the amount of sleep factor in terms of the trend coefficients given in Table B-10. Test the linear and quadratic components using $\alpha = .025$ for each. Do the same for each of these components in interaction with IQ.

d. Perform a two-factor ANOVA according to the simple effects model in which sleep treatments are compared within IQ levels. Use $\alpha = .05$ for each simple effects test.

e. Conduct Scheffé post hoc comparisons for any significant simple effects.

f. Redo the preceding analysis, but this time examining the amount of sleep factor in terms of the trend components of Table B-10. Test the linear and quadratic components within each IQ level, using $\alpha = .025$ for each.

9-2. Using the same two factors as in Exercise 9-1, conduct a two-factor interaction model MANOVA with three dependent variables defined by subjects' vocabulary, reasoning, and arithmetic scores.

a. Test each source of variance according to Roy's criterion ($\alpha = .05$) followed by simultaneous confidence intervals where appropriate.

b. Assess each source of variance according to Rao's test of Wilks's Λ ($\alpha = .05$).

9-3. Perform a one-factor multivariate analysis of covariance, with the treatment factor given by amount of sleep, the covariate given by IQ, and the dependent variables given by vocabulary, reasoning, and arithmetic scores.

a. Use Roy's criterion based on $\alpha = .05$.

b. Use Rao's approximate F test based on $\alpha = .05$.

9-4. Treating the 16 subjects as a single sample, conduct a multivariate repeated measures analysis to determine whether there are mean differences associated with the three variables, vocabulary, reasoning, and arithmetic ($\alpha = .05$). If there are differences, perform the associated post hoc comparisons.

9-5. Redo the analysis of Exercise 9-4 according to a 'split-plot' design in which the between-subjects factor is amount of sleep.

a. Test the repeated measures effect using $\alpha = .05$, followed by post hoc comparisons if necessary.

b. Test for an amount of sleep by repeated measures interaction according to Roy's criterion ($\alpha = .05$) followed by post hoc comparisons if necessary. Reexamine the interaction hypothesis in terms of Rao's test of Wilks' Λ ($\alpha = .05$).

c. Create three differences, $V - R$, $V - A$, and $R - A$, for each subject. Using the amount of sleep factor, conduct a one-way univariate ANOVA on each of these differences ($\alpha = .01$ for each), followed by Scheffé post hoc comparisons where necessary. Compare the results of this analysis with those in the preceding part.

CHAPTER TEN

MULTIVARIATE ANALYSIS OF CONTINGENCY TABLES

10-1. Multidimensional contingency tables

Researchers in the social sciences have a long history of using the traditional Karl Pearson Chi-square tests of homogeneity and independence for analyzing two-dimensional tables of frequency data. These tests are based on the statistic:

$$X^2 = \sum_{i=1}^{I} \sum_{j=1}^{J} \frac{(O_{ij} - E_{ij})^2}{E_{ij}}$$

where:

O_{ij} = the observed frequency in the ith row and jth column of an $I \times J$ table of frequencies

E_{ij} = the corresponding expected or estimated expected frequencies

However, problems arise for tables that involve three or more dimensions. A number of methods have been proposed for multidimensional tables, some of which have been reviewed by Marascuilo and McSweeney (1977). In their review, they selected for presentation a number of nonparametric and distribution-free procedures that are easy to perform using only a hand calculator. However, other more effective methods exist that they did not consider. Some of these methods are based on the techniques presented in earlier chapters. In this chapter, we present some of these methods. As will be seen, these methods require the use of an electronic computer. In some cases, standard multivariate computer programs can be used directly, simply by making modifications in the data input. In other cases, commercial computer programs are available for purchase so that it is not necessary to write special programs. In our presentation, we will continue to denote levels of the independent variable by X, but will replace the dependent variable Y by P. We will let Y refer to frequencies of occurrence of a specified event, so that over N trials, $\hat{P} = Y/N$ serves as an estimator of the population probability or proportion.

10-2. Trend analysis for binomial proportions in an $I \times 2$ contingency table

Consider the data of Table 10-1 which are taken from Marascuilo and McSweeney (1977), and which represent the number of learning trials provided, X, and corresponding success in learning a list of 15 nonsense syllables to criterion, Y, by independent groups of subjects who were randomly assigned to one of six experimental conditions. Subjects in Group 1 were given 5 trials to learn the list of 15 nonsense syllables. Subjects in Group 2 were given 10 trials. Subjects in the

TABLE 10-1. Summary statistics for learning 15 nonsense syllables by six independent groups of subjects

Group	X_i	N_i	Y_i	$\hat{P}_i$	$SE^2_{\hat{P}_i}$
1	5	30	2	0.06667	0.002074
2	10	30	10	0.33333	0.007407
3	15	29	11	0.37931	0.008118
4	20	30	23	0.76667	0.005963
5	25	30	22	0.73333	0.006519
6	30	28	22	0.78571	0.006013

remaining groups were given 15, 20, 25, or 30 trials. Summary statistics are reported in Table 10-1 for Group $i = 1, 2, \ldots, 6$. Because of the quantitative nature of the independent variable, we may expect to find a relationship between X, the number of trials, and P, the probability of success in learning the list. As a first approximation for an $I \times 2$ contingency table, a linear relation represented by:

$$P = \beta_0 + \beta_1 X$$

should suffice. This can be examined by testing:

$$\text{H}_0: \quad \beta_1 = 0$$

against:

$$\text{H}_1: \quad \beta_1 \neq 0$$

Since, in this case, it is reasonable to expect a positive value for β_1, we can justify the testing of H_0 against a directional alternative:

$$\text{H}_1: \quad \beta_1 > 0$$

Unfortunately we cannot use the methods of Section 3-5 on these data because the homoscedasticity and independence-of-observation assumptions are both violated. Since the criterion variables are binomial, their variances, P_iQ_i/N_i, change as the P_i change.

As illustrated by Marascuilo and McSweeney, for samples yielding expected cell frequencies greater than 5, we can perform a test for equally spaced independent variables by defining a contrast $\hat{\psi}$ in terms of the linear trend coefficients of Table B-10. The resulting statistic:

$$\text{X}^2 = \frac{\hat{\psi}^2_{\text{linear}}}{SE^2_{\hat{\psi}_{\text{linear}}}}$$

can be referred to the Chi-square distribution with $v = 1$. For a one-tailed test, X^2 is replaced by $Z = \sqrt{\text{X}^2}$ and is referred to the standard normal distribution. For this example, with $\alpha = .05$, a one-tailed hypothesis is rejected if $Z > Z_{.95} = 1.645$ or if $\text{X}^2 > 1.645^2 = 2.71$.

Since, in this example, the levels of the independent variable are equally spaced, we may use the linear trend coefficients of Table B-10. With $I = 6$, the linear trend contrast is defined by:

$$\psi_{\text{linear}} = -5P_1 - 3P_2 - 1P_3 + 1P_4 + 3P_5 + 5P_6.$$

It can be easily shown that if $\beta_1 = 0$, then $\psi_{\text{linear}} = 0$. In addition,

$$\psi_{\text{linear}} = 0 \quad \text{if} \quad P_1 = P_2 = \cdots = P_6 = P_0.$$

For the data of Table 10-1,

$$\begin{aligned}\hat{\psi}_{\text{linear}} &= -5\hat{P}_1 - 3\hat{P}_2 - 1\hat{P}_3 + 1\hat{P}_4 + 3\hat{P}_5 + 5\hat{P}_6 \\ &= -5(.06667) - 3(.33333) - \cdots + 5(.78571) = 5.1826.\end{aligned}$$

The assumed common P_0 is estimated as:

$$\hat{P}_0 = \frac{Y_1 + Y_2 + \cdots + Y_6}{N_1 + N_2 + \cdots + N_6} = \frac{2 + 10 + \cdots + 22}{30 + 30 + \cdots + 28} = \frac{90}{177}$$

Under H_0, the variance of $\hat{\psi}_{\text{linear}}$ is estimated as:

$$SE^2_{\hat{\psi}_{\text{linear}}} = (-5)^2 \frac{\hat{P}_0\hat{Q}_0}{N_1} + (-3)^2 \frac{\hat{P}_0\hat{Q}_0}{N_2} + \cdots + (5)^2 \frac{\hat{P}_0\hat{Q}_0}{N_6}$$

$$= \left(\frac{90}{177}\right)\left(\frac{87}{177}\right)\left[\frac{(-5)^2}{30} + \frac{(-3)^2}{30} + \cdots + \frac{(5)^2}{28}\right] = .5983$$

so that:

$$X^2 = \frac{\hat{\psi}^2_{\text{linear}}}{SE^2_{\hat{\psi}_{\text{linear}}}} = \frac{5.1826^2}{.5983} = 44.89$$

Thus, the alternative that $\beta_1 > 0$ is supported. (It should be mentioned that under some conditions the variance of $\hat{\psi}_{\text{linear}}$ could have been estimated using the individual $\hat{P}_i\hat{Q}_i$ rather than the common $\hat{P}_0\hat{Q}_0$, but this will not be pursued here.)

Selection of linear trend coefficients from Table B-10 requires that the levels of the independent variable be equally spaced. This condition is satisfied for the present example, where $X_1 = 5$, $X_2 = 10, \ldots, X_6 = 30$ are separated by a constant five units. If we were interested in the linear trend, but the independent variable levels are not equally spaced, a simple adaptation of the present procedure is available. In particular, we need only devise coefficients that preserve the pattern represented by the levels of the independent variable and, at the same time, sum to zero. This is easily accomplished by applying the following strategy:

1. Obtain the mean of the values associated with the independent variable.
2. Use as coefficients the signed deviation of each level of the independent variable from that mean.

For example, suppose that first, fifth, eighth, and tenth graders were compared on some task and the researcher were interested in the linear component of the grade effect. Here, $X_1 = 1$, $X_2 = 5$, $X_3 = 8$, and $X_4 = 10$. Following the two-step strategy, we find that the mean of these values is $(1 + 5 + 8 + 10)/4 = 6$, so that the coefficients for a linear trend become $a_1 = 1 - 6 = -5$, $a_2 = 5 - 6 = -1$, $a_3 = 8 - 6 = 2$, and $a_4 = 10 - 6 = 4$. Such a procedure can be legitimately applied even when the sample sizes at the various levels of X are unequal. We now provide directions for obtaining the coefficients for a linear trend when the X values are not equally spaced.

Procedure for determining the coefficients for a linear trend.

Step 1. Let the values of the independent variable be denoted by $X_1, X_2, \ldots, X_I$. Find the unweighted mean value of the X_i. Let this mean be denoted by:

$$\bar{X} = \frac{1}{I}\sum_{i=1}^{I} X_i$$

Step 2. Define the linear trend coefficients by:

$$a_1 = X_1 - \bar{X},\ a_2 = X_2 - \bar{X}, \ldots, a_I = X_I - \bar{X}$$

Sometimes, however, we are interested in more than just the linear trend. With equally spaced intervals and equal sample sizes, the higher order trend coefficients of Table B-10 are appropriate. If either of these conditions does not hold and if we want the trend components to be mutually orthogonal, the orthogonal polynomial solutions of Gaito (1965) – see Kirk (1982) – may be employed.

More recently, Wood (1978) has provided a different method for dealing with the question of linear and higher order trends in proportions based on a dichotomous dependent variable. This method does not assume that the levels of the independent variable are equally spaced, nor that the sample sizes are equal. The method is based on the principle of weighted least squares, as has been applied throughout this book in other contexts and as was first described in Section 1–9.

One of the hypothesis-testing assumptions implicit in the least squares model, as presented in Section 2-3, is that the dependent measure has constant variance across all levels of the independent variable. For binomial variables, such as success-failure, live-dead, yes-no, pass-fail, and go-stop, this assumption is violated, since:

$$\mathrm{Var}(\hat{P}_i) = \frac{P_iQ_i}{N_i}$$

is clearly a function of both P_i and N_i. To overcome this variation in the variances of the dependent measures, Wood proposes the use of the weighted least squares model originally described by Neyman (1949). In particular, instead of minimizing:

$$U = \sum_{i=1}^{I} (\hat{P}_i - \beta_0 - \beta_1 X_i)^2$$

we minimize:

$$U_0 = \sum_{i=1}^{I} W_i (\hat{P}_i - \beta_0 - \beta_1 X_i)^2$$

The problem now reduces to choosing the correct weights W_i.

To generate the solution, consider each level of the independent variable X_i and:

$$Z_i = \frac{\hat{P}_i - E(\hat{P}_i)}{\sqrt{\mathrm{Var}(\hat{P}_i)}} = \frac{\hat{P}_i - P_i}{\sqrt{\dfrac{P_iQ_i}{N_i}}} = \frac{\hat{P}_i - (\beta_0 + \beta_1 X_i)}{\sqrt{\dfrac{P_iQ_i}{N_i}}}$$

$$= \sqrt{\frac{N_i}{P_iQ_i}}(\hat{P}_i - \beta_0 - \beta_1 X_i)$$

Under large-sample theory, each Z_i has a normal distribution with a mean of zero and a standard deviation of 1. Thus:

$$\mathrm{X}^2 = \sum_{i=1}^{I} Z_i^2 = \sum_{i=1}^{I} \frac{N_i}{P_iQ_i}(\hat{P}_i - \beta_0 - \beta_1 X_i)^2$$

possesses a Chi-square distribution with $v = I$ degrees of freedom, but what is of greater interest is that we now see that the appropriate weights are defined by N_i/P_iQ_i, the reciprocals of the $\mathrm{Var}(\hat{P}_i)$. In addition, we see that minimizing U_0 is the same as minimizing X^2. The estimates obtained from this minimizing operation are called *minimum Chi-square estimates* and possess the desirable property of having sampling distributions that are normal with means and variances that can be estimated. The unfortunate part is that the estimates are difficult to obtain. While the solution could be programmed for a computer, a simpler procedure exists and is the one we will describe.

Many years ago, before the computer era, Neyman (1949) proposed a general model for frequency data that is quite easy to execute. He suggested that the W_i be replaced by their sample estimators, $\hat{W}_i = N_i/\hat{P}_i\hat{Q}_i$, and that:

$$U_0' = \sum_{i=1}^{I} \frac{N_i}{\hat{P}_i\hat{Q}_i}(\hat{P}_i - \beta_0 - \beta_1 X_i)^2$$

be minimized. When this modification is introduced, the weighted least squares problem becomes trivial, and the resulting *modified minimum Chi-square estimates*, as they were called by Neyman, can be used for testing the hypothesis of interest. Under this model, the normal equations are given by:

$$\left(\sum_{i=1}^{I} \hat{W}_i\hat{P}_i\right) = \left(\sum_{i=1}^{I} \hat{W}_i\right)\hat{\beta}_0 + \left(\sum_{i=1}^{I} \hat{W}_iX_i\right)\hat{\beta}_1$$

and

$$\left(\sum_{i=1}^{I} \hat{W}_i\hat{P}_iX_i\right) = \left(\sum_{i=1}^{I} \hat{W}_iX_i\right)\hat{\beta}_0 + \left(\sum_{i=1}^{I} \hat{W}_iX_i^2\right)\hat{\beta}_1$$

These equations may be solved using Cramer's rule as discussed in Section 1-9. In this case, the values of $\hat{\beta}_0$ and $\hat{\beta}_1$ are given by:

$$\hat{\beta}_1 = \frac{\left(\sum_{i=1}^{I} \hat{W}_i\right)\left(\sum_{i=1}^{I} \hat{W}_i\hat{P}_iX_i\right) - \left(\sum_{i=1}^{I} \hat{W}_iX_i\right)\left(\sum_{i=1}^{I} \hat{W}_i\hat{P}_i\right)}{\left(\sum_{i=1}^{I} \hat{W}_i\right)\left(\sum_{i=1}^{I} \hat{W}_iX_i^2\right) - \left(\sum_{i=1}^{I} \hat{W}_iX_i\right)^2}$$

and

$$\hat{\beta}_0 = \frac{\sum_{i=1}^{I} \hat{W}_i\hat{P}_i}{\sum_{i=1}^{I} \hat{W}_i} - \hat{\beta}_1\frac{\sum_{i=1}^{I} \hat{W}_iX_i}{\sum_{i=1}^{I} \hat{W}_i}$$

Up to this point, we have been somewhat restrictive in our presentation in that the model has centered on a linear trend only. A little thought should help us realize that the model can be extended to quadratic, cubic, quartic, and higher order polynomials. Estimates are readily determined by substituting $\hat{W}_i$ values in the corresponding normal equations. Since solution of these equations becomes quite complex, we recommend using a computer to obtain the appropriate estimates. Even here, complications arise and, before we illustrate the method, we need to backtrack and discuss how the decision-testing model operates, since it differs slightly from the one presented in earlier chapters.

With the advent of the computer, researchers have been treating the problems of estimation and hypothesis testing through a technique that is usually referred to as *model building* or model fitting. In model building, we construct an analysis that parallels that of stepwise regression, as presented in Section 3-13. Technically speaking, stepwise regression, as presented, represents a model-building approach to regression analysis. If we review the model briefly, we see how it can be extended to the solution of the problem at hand. As we recall, stepwise regression begins at Step 1 with the selection of a variable, such as X_1, that is most highly correlated with Y. Y is then regressed on X_1 to obtain $\hat{R}^2_{Y \cdot X_1}$. If the residual variance is statistically significant, a second variable, such as X_2, is selected. A regression analysis using both X_1 and X_2 is then performed and $\hat{R}^2_{Y \cdot X_1 X_2}$ is determined. To decide whether or not X_2 is to be retained in the system, $\hat{R}^2_{Y \cdot X_1 X_2}$ is not examined directly, but rather $r^2_{Y(X_2 \cdot X_1)} = \hat{R}^2_{Y \cdot X_1 X_2} - \hat{R}^2_{Y \cdot X_1}$ is tested for statistical significance. If the residual variance is larger than can be explained by chance, a similar test is made of X_3, X_4, and so on. The process terminates when a nonsignificant residual is achieved. The reason for this termination is that the observed data are successively fitted to more elaborate models. Once the fit is so good that the deviation from the last tested model is minimal, the rest of the additional variance accounted for by a more elaborate model will not be statistically significant. At that point, we adopt the last-tested model as an adequate description for the data. Essentially this provides a fair statement of model building as it is practiced by researchers. For frequency data, Chi-square statistics are substituted for F ratios and differences in squared correlations are replaced by differences in Chi-square values.

In classical regression analysis, as discussed in Chapter 3, sequential hypothesis testing is not necessary because the models assume the existence of estimable errors with common variance. With frequency data, such an analog does not exist. On the other hand, residual sums of squares are automatically generated as we go from a simpler model to one that is more complex. Because the process terminates when the residual ceases to be significant, we cannot in practice know in advance at what point this will happen, and so stepwise procedures are required.

Before providing procedural directions, let us note that in the most general case we begin, not with a simple linear regression model, but with a polynomial regression model given by:

$$P_i = \beta_0 + \beta_1 X_i + \beta_2 X_i^2 + \cdots + \beta_{I-1} X_i^{I-1}$$

In this model, each $\beta_i (0 \leq i \leq I - 1)$ is examined in a stepwise fashion. In practice, we will find that one or more of the β_i will be statistically zero, because certain hypotheses will not be rejected. When this happens, we still proceed in a forward direction, using zero values for those parameter estimates. Because this could complicate the directions on how to analyze the data, we have decided to present the procedural section as though this does not happen. In practice, this should cause no problem since the analysis is certain to be performed by a computer in which parameter estimates can be set equal to zero as the process unfolds. Thus, although we provide directions assuming that each β_i is statistically significant, we should note that the procedure is operational even with one or more zero values in the polynomial equation.

The hypothesis-testing model for binomial trend analysis is as follows.

Procedure for performing a trend analysis on binomial probabilities for an $I \times 2$ contingency table.

Step 1. To determine the total X^2 that can be partitioned into $I - 1$ trend components, compute:

$$U'_{0(\beta_0)} = \sum_{i=1}^{I} \hat{W}_i(\hat{P}_i - \hat{\beta}_0)^2$$

where:

$$\hat{\beta}_0 = \frac{\sum_{i=1}^{I} \hat{W}_i P_i}{\sum_{i=1}^{I} \hat{W}_i}$$

$$\hat{P}_i = Y_i/N_i$$

$$\hat{Q}_i = 1 - \hat{P}_i$$

$$\hat{W}_i = N_i/\hat{P}_i\hat{Q}_i$$

and

Y_i = number of binomial successes for X_i

Step 2. To test for a linear component:

H_0: $\beta_1 = 0$ vs. H_1: $\beta_1 \neq 0$

compute a new $\hat{\beta}_0$, as well as $\hat{\beta}_1$, using either the weighted normal equations or a computer program.

Step 3. Determine the value of the component Chi-square statistic:

$$X^2_{(\beta_1)} = U'_{0(\beta_0)} - U'_{0(\beta_0, \beta_1)}$$

where:

$$U'_{0(\beta_0, \beta_1)} = \sum_{i=1}^{I} \hat{W}_i (\hat{P}_i - \hat{\beta}_0 - \hat{\beta}_1 X_i)^2$$

represents the residual Chi-square based on a polynomial equation with a linear component built into it.

Step 4. If:

$$X^2_{(\beta_1)} < \chi^2_{1:1-\alpha}$$

do not include the linear component β_1 in the model. If:

$$X^2_{(\beta_1)} > \chi^2_{1:1-\alpha}$$

include β_1 in the model.

Step 5. Test the significance of $U'_{0(\beta_0, \beta_1)}$ to determine whether the process should be terminated. If:

$$U'_{0(\beta_0, \beta_1)} < \chi^2_{I-2:1-\alpha}$$

terminate the process. If:

$$U'_{0(\beta_0, \beta_1)} > \chi^2_{I-2:1-\alpha}$$

proceed to Step 6.

Step 6. To test for a quadratic component:

H_0: $\beta_2 = 0$ vs. H_1: $\beta_2 \neq 0$

compute new $\hat{\beta}_0$ and $\hat{\beta}_1$ terms, as well as a $\hat{\beta}_2$, using either the weighted normal equations or a computer program.

Step 7. Determine the value of the component Chi-square statistic:

$$X^2_{(\beta_2)} = U'_{0(\beta_0,\beta_1)} - U'_{0(\beta_0,\beta_1,\beta_2)}$$

where:

$$U'_{0(\beta_0,\beta_1,\beta_2)} = \sum_{i=1}^{I} \hat{W}_i(\hat{P}_i - \hat{\beta}_0 - \hat{\beta}_1 X_i - \hat{\beta}_2 X_i^2)$$

represents the residual Chi-square for a polynomial equation with a quadratic component built into it.

Step 8. If:

$$X^2_{(\beta_2)} < \chi^2_{1:1-\alpha}$$

do not include the quadratic component β_2 in the model. If:

$$X^2_{(\beta_2)} > \chi^2_{1:1-\alpha}$$

include β_2 in the model.

Step 9. Test the significance of $U'_{0(\beta_0,\beta_1,\beta_2)}$ to determine whether the process should be terminated. If:

$$U'_{0(\beta_0,\beta_1,\beta_2)} < \chi^2_{I-3:1-\alpha}$$

terminate the process. If:

$$U'_{0(\beta_0,\beta_1,\beta_2)} > \chi^2_{I-3:1-\alpha}$$

proceed to Step 10.

Step 10. Repeat the preceding sequence until the U'_0 statistic tested last is not significant.

Note that $U'_{0(\beta_0)}$ measures how well the model $P_i = \beta_0$ fits the data, whereas $U'_{0(\beta_0,\beta_1)}$ measures how well the model $P_i = \beta_0 + \beta_1 X$ fits the data. This means that $X^2_{\beta_1} = U'_{0(\beta_0)} - U'_{0(\beta_0,\beta_1)}$ measures the amount of the total explained variance that can be attributed to the inclusion of a linear component in the model, since $U'_{0(\beta_0)}$ is based simply on β_0. Since $U'_{0(\beta_0)}$ is based on one estimate from the data, $v_{(\beta_0)} = I - 1$. On the other hand, $U'_{0(\beta_0,\beta_1)}$ requires the estimation of two population parameters. For that reason, $v_{(\beta_0,\beta_1)} = I - 2$. Under H_0, both measures possess Chi-square distributions with parameters $I - 1$ and $I - 2$, respectively. Finally, $X^2_{\beta_1}$ has $(I - 1) - (I - 2) = 1$ degrees of freedom. If the residual $U'_{0(\beta_0,\beta_1)}$ is statistically large, we can fit a quadratic equation to the data and see how well it fits. In fact, all higher level polynomials can be fitted to the data until a perfect fit is found. This will happen when all $\beta_0, \beta_1, \ldots, \beta_{I-1}$ terms are included in the model. In practice, we stop the process when a given residual U'_0 statistic is not significant, indicating an adequate fit between data and model.

In many psychological studies, increases in the independent variable may not show a linear relationship with the probabilities of success. In some cases, transforming data to a logarithmic or square root scale will achieve the desired linear relationship. Many sociological investigations are based on a single sample which is then classified according to the two dimensions of the resulting contingency table. This means that both margins represent random variables and, as a consequence, binomial probability theory is violated. If a researcher is willing to perform the analysis contingent upon the marginal frequencies obtained, the proposed method is justified. For further discussion of this topic, see Wood (1978).

Finally, standard regression programs such as *BMD*, *SPSS*, and *Multivariance* can be used to analyze, directly, data similar to those of Table 10-1. The only adjustment required is that the independent and dependent variables must be introduced, not as Y and X, but as $\sqrt{\hat{W}_i}\,\hat{P}_i$ and $\sqrt{\hat{W}_i}\,X_i$. With these weighted values, standard stepwise regression procedures are invoked, but the corresponding F-ratios are ignored. Rather, the component Chi-square tests:

$$X^2_{(\beta_i)} = U'_{0(\beta_0,\beta_1,\ldots,\beta_{i-1})} - U'_{0(\beta_0,\beta_1,\ldots,\beta_i)}$$

are performed with one degree of freedom, whereas the residual Chi-square tests, U_0', are based on $I - 1 - i$ degrees of freedom. For completeness, we illustrate the model in terms of computations which are summarized in Tables 10-2 and 10-3 and which are taken from a computer program written by Rob Slaughter of the Department of Education, University of California at Berkeley.

We begin by computing $\hat{\beta}_0$ that is needed for the computation of $U'_{0(\beta_0)}$. Here:

$$\hat{\beta}_0 = \frac{\sum_{i=1}^{6} \hat{W}_i\hat{P}_i}{\sum_{i=1}^{6} \hat{W}_i} = \frac{495.60317}{1227.73361} = .40367$$

Making use of the computational algorithm:

TABLE 10-2. Weighted least squares computations for the data of Table 10-1

Group	$\hat{W}_i$	$\hat{W}_i\hat{P}_i$	$\hat{W}_i\hat{P}_iX_i$	$\hat{W}_iX_i$	$\hat{W}_iX_i^2$
1	482.14286	32.14286	160.71429	2410.71429	12053.57143
2	135.00000	45.00000	450.00000	1350.00000	13500.00000
3	123.17677	46.72222	700.83333	1847.65152	27714.77273
4	167.70186	128.57143	2571.42857	3354.03727	67080.74534
5	153.40909	112.50000	2812.50000	3835.22727	95880.68182
6	166.30303	130.66667	3920.00000	4989.09091	149672.72727
Total	1227.73361	495.60317	10615.47619	17786.72125	365902.49859

TABLE 10-3. Goodness of fit of $P_i = \beta_0 + \beta_1X_i$.

Group	$\hat{P}_i$	$\hat{\beta}_0 + \hat{\beta}_1X_i$	$\hat{P}_i - \hat{\beta}_0 - \hat{\beta}_1X_i$	$\hat{W}_i$	$\hat{W}_i(\hat{P}_i - \hat{\beta}_0 - \hat{\beta}_1X_i)^2$
1	0.0667	0.1025	− 0.0358	482.14286	0.6179
2	0.3333	0.2612	0.0721	135.00000	0.7018
3	0.3793	0.4199	− 0.0406	123.17677	0.2030
4	0.7667	0.5786	0.1881	167.70186	5.9336
5	0.7333	0.7373	− 0.0040	153.40909	0.0025
6	0.7857	0.8960	− 0.1103	166.30303	2.0232
Total				1227.73361	9.4820

$$U'_{0(\beta_0)} = \sum_{i=1}^{6} \hat{W}_i(\hat{P}_i - \hat{\beta}_0)^2 = \sum_{i=1}^{6} \hat{W}_i\hat{P}_i^2 - \hat{\beta}_0^2 \sum_{i=1}^{6} \hat{W}_i$$

$$= (482.14286)(.06667)^2 + \cdots + (166.30303)(.78571)^2 - (.40367)^2(1227.73361)$$

$$= 118.54$$

To test for a linear component, we compute:

$$\hat{\beta}_1 = \frac{(1227.73361)(10615.47619) - (17786.72125)(495.60317)}{(1227.73361)(365902.49859) - (17786.72125)^2}$$

$$= \frac{4217821}{132863340} = .03174$$

and:

$$\hat{\beta}_0 = \frac{495.60317}{1227.73361} - (.03174)\frac{17786.72125}{1227.73367} = -.05624$$

Thus:

$$\hat{P} = -.05624 + .03174X$$

represents the best-fitting line. When $X = 5$:

$$\hat{P} = -.05624 + .03174(5) = .10245$$

Remaining estimated predicted values are reported in Table 10-3, along with the computations for the residual $U'_{0(\beta_0,\beta_1)}$. In this case:

$$U'_{0(\beta_0,\beta_1)} = 9.48$$

so that the linear component Chi-square is given by:

$$X^2_{\beta_1} = U'_{0(\beta_0)} - U'_{0(\beta_0,\beta_1)} = 118.54 - 9.48 = 109.06$$

With a positive β_1, the directional test decided on earlier is significant at $\alpha = .05$, since $Z = \sqrt{X^2_{\beta_1}} = \sqrt{109.06} = 10.44$ exceeds the critical Z value of $Z_{.95} = 1.645$. We now know that the relationship between X and P has a linear component. As an aside, we note that $X^2_{\beta_1} = 109.05$ is much larger than the previously performed test based on the linear contrast, where $X^2 = 44.89$. The larger Chi-square in this model can be attributed to the use of the individual standard errors of the binomial proportions as weights in the normal equations. In addition, we see that the residual Chi-square statistic, $U'_{0(\beta_0,\beta_1)} = 9.48$ is not significantly large, since $\chi^2_{4:.95} = 9.49$. As a result, we conclude that a linear fit to the data is a reasonable model to adopt. The analysis is summarized in Table 10-4.

One of the problems associated with a model-building approach is that the risk of

TABLE 10-4. Summary Chi-square table for the data of Table 10-1

Source of variance	*Degrees of freedom*	*Chi-square*
Total	5	118.54
Linearity	1	109.05
Residual	4	9.48

a type I error remains unknown because of the conditional nature of the statements that must be made as the analysis proceeds. That is, the risk of a type I error for the test of deviation from linearity, as well as that for all subsequent tests remain unknown, since they are performed conditional upon decisions made at previous stages.

10-3. Comparison of linear trends in K contingency tables of size $I \times 2$

The example of Section 10-2 shows how we can analyze data in which the dependent variable is dichotomous and the independent variable is quantitative. Although it represents a frequently encountered design in behavioral research, another common situation is to have the $I \times 2$ data matrix repeated over a number of K different experimental conditions. For example, the data of Table 10-1 may actually refer to the control condition of a learning study. Another set of I experimental groups of independent subjects may be told to learn the list and at the same time be given a strategy to learn the list by linking adjacent nonsense syllables. For this complete design, we could assess the effects that the strategy has on learning. Such a design would give rise to data similar to that reported in Table 10-5. Here the statistical research question has progressed from an analysis about a single line to a hypothesis that focuses on whether or not the $K = 2$ lines are identical, parallel, or at angles to one another. If the lines are not parallel, we would conclude that an interaction exists between experimental and control conditions and the number of trials given to learn the list of 15 nonsense syllables. If the lines are parallel but not identical, the effects of the strategy are constant across all trials, so that there exists only a main effect for conditions. If the lines should prove to be identical, the effects of the strategy would be of little or no consequence.

Although the research questions can be formulated as tests of parallelism and equal intercepts, as in an analysis of covariance, that model cannot be justified since the variances of the various dichotomous variables are not equal. As might be expected, however, direct use of the model presented in Section 10-2 can be made. As before, we begin by determining the total X^2 that is partitionable. Once this has been computed, we proceed in a stepwise fashion to test the following hierarchy of hypotheses:

1. Across all K groups, there is a linear relationship between X and P, given by $\beta_{1(T)}$, so that:

$$P_k = \beta_{0(T)} + \beta_{1(T)}X$$

TOTAL 10-5. Summary statistics for learning 15 nonsense syllables by six independent groups of subjects given a strategy

Group	X_i	N_i	Y_i	$\hat{P}_i$	$SE^2_{\hat{P}_i}$
7	5	29	3	0.10345	0.003198
8	10	30	12	0.40000	0.008000
9	15	30	15	0.50000	0.008333
10	20	26	18	0.69231	0.008193
11	25	29	24	0.82759	0.004920
12	30	30	22	0.73333	0.006519

2. All K regression lines have the same slope, $\beta_{1(W)}$, so that:

$$P_k = \beta_{0(k)} + \beta_{1(W)}X$$

3. All K regression lines have the same intercept, $\beta_{0(W)}$. Assuming parallelism in the immediately preceding model, this model is one of identity:

$$P_k = \beta_{0(W)} + \beta_{1(W)}X$$

whereas assuming nonparallelism, this model is one of different regression lines:

$$P_k = \beta_{0(k)} + \beta_{1(k)}X$$

4. Each of the preceding models may be augmented to include higher order polynomials.

As indicated, the model-building approach proceeds from a model of an across-groups linear relationship, to K parallel lines, to K lines with possible different slopes or intercepts. As may be seen, this hierarchy of increasing complexity of models can be modified to include quadratic, cubic, and higher order polynomials, if desired. If the residual, after the testing of different slopes and different intercepts is still large, testing for quadratic components in the relationship is certainly in order. If this were necessary, the use of standard stepwise regression programs is required since the computations become exceedingly complex. However, this would be of minor significance if *BMD*, *SPSS*, or *Multivariance* were employed since each of these programs can solve the problem in a stepwise manner. In any case, the linear portion of the analysis would proceed as follows.

Procedure for testing hypotheses about slopes and intercepts in K independent $I \times 2$ contingency tables where the dependent variable is binomial.

Step 1. To determine the total X^2 that is partitionable into $IK - 1$ trend components, compute:

$$U'_{0(\beta_{0(T)})} = \sum_{k=1}^{K} \sum_{i=1}^{I} \hat{W}_{ik} (\hat{P}_{ik} - \hat{\beta}_{0(T)})^2$$

where:

$$\hat{\beta}_{0(T)} = \frac{\sum_{k=1}^{K} \sum_{i=1}^{I} \hat{W}_{ik}\hat{P}_{ik}}{\sum_{k=1}^{K} \sum_{i=1}^{I} \hat{W}_{ik}}$$

$$\hat{W}_{ik} = \frac{N_{ik}}{\hat{P}_{ik}\hat{Q}_{ik}}$$

$$\hat{P}_{ik} = \frac{Y_{ik}}{N_{ik}}$$

$$\hat{Q}_{ik} = 1 - \hat{P}_{ik}$$

Y_{ik} = number of successes in the ith level of condition k

Step 2. To test for an across-groups linear relationship

H_0: $\beta_{1(T)} = 0$

vs.

H_1: $\beta_{1(T)} \neq 0$

compute a new $\hat{\beta}_{0(T)}$, as well as $\hat{\beta}_{1(T)}$, using either the following formulas or a computer program.

$$\hat{\beta}_{1(T)} = \frac{\left(\sum_{k=1}^{K}\sum_{i=1}^{I} \hat{W}_{ik}\right)\left(\sum_{k=1}^{K}\sum_{i=1}^{I} \hat{W}_{ik}\hat{P}_{ik}X_{ik}\right) - \left(\sum_{k=1}^{K}\sum_{i=1}^{I} \hat{W}_{ik}X_{ik}\right)\left(\sum_{k=1}^{K}\sum_{i=1}^{I} \hat{W}_{ik}\hat{P}_{ik}\right)}{\left(\sum_{k=1}^{K}\sum_{i=1}^{I} \hat{W}_{ik}\right)\left(\sum_{k=1}^{K}\sum_{i=1}^{I} \hat{W}_{ik}X_{ik}^2\right) - \left(\sum_{k=1}^{K}\sum_{i=1}^{I} \hat{W}_{ik}X_{ik}\right)^2}$$

and:

$$\hat{\beta}_{0(T)} = \frac{\sum_{k=1}^{K}\sum_{i=1}^{I} \hat{W}_{ik}\hat{P}_{ik}}{\sum_{k=1}^{K}\sum_{i=1}^{I} \hat{W}_{ik}} - \hat{\beta}_{1(T)}\frac{\sum_{k=1}^{K}\sum_{i=1}^{I} \hat{W}_{ik}X_{ik}}{\sum_{k=1}^{K}\sum_{i=1}^{I} \hat{W}_{ik}}$$

Step 3. Determine the value of the component Chi-square statistic:

$$X^2_{\beta_{1(T)}} = U'_{0(\beta_{0(T)})} - U'_{0(\beta_{0(T)},\beta_{1(T)})}$$

where:

$$U'_{0(\beta_{0(T)},\beta_{1(T)})} = \sum_{k=1}^{K}\sum_{i=1}^{I} \hat{W}_{ik}(\hat{P}_{ik} - \beta_{0(T)} - \beta_{1(T)}X_{ik})^2$$

represents the residual Chi-square associated with the across-groups regression line.

Step 4. If $X^2_{\beta_{1(T)}} < \chi^2_{1:1-\alpha}$, conclude that there is no across-groups linear relationship between X and P. If $X^2_{\beta_{1(T)}} > \chi^2_{1:1-\alpha}$, conclude that there is an across-groups linear relationship between X and P.

Step 5. Test the significance of $U'_{0(\beta_{0(T)},\beta_{1(T)})}$ to determine whether the process should be terminated. If $U'_{0(\beta_{0(T)},\beta_{1(T)})} < \chi^2_{IK-2:1-\alpha}$, terminate the process. If $U'_{0(\beta_{0(T)},\beta_{1(T)})} > \chi^2_{IK-2:1-\alpha}$, continue the process by proceeding to Step 6.

Step 6. To test for parallelism of the K regression lines:

H_0: $\beta_{1(1)} = \beta_{1(2)} = \cdots = \beta_{1(K)} = \beta_{1(W)}$

vs.

H_1: H_0 is false

compute $\hat{\beta}_{1(W)}$ and $\hat{\beta}^*_{0(k)}$ using either the following formulas or a computer program:

$$\hat{\beta}_{1(W)} = \frac{\sum_{k=1}^{K}\left[\left(\sum_{i=1}^{I} \hat{W}_{ik}\hat{P}_{ik}X_{ik}\right) - \frac{\left(\sum_{i=1}^{I} \hat{W}_{ik}X_{ik}\right)\left(\sum_{i=1}^{I} \hat{W}_{ik}\hat{P}_{ik}\right)}{\sum_{i=1}^{I} \hat{W}_{ik}}\right]}{\left[\sum_{k=1}^{K}\left(\sum_{i=1}^{I} \hat{W}_{ik}X_{ik}^2\right) - \frac{\left(\sum_{i=1}^{I} \hat{W}_{ik}X_{ik}\right)^2}{\sum_{i=1}^{I} \hat{W}_{ik}}\right]}$$

and

$$\hat{\beta}^*_{0(k)} = \left(\frac{\sum_{i=1}^{I} \hat{W}_{ik}\hat{P}_{ik}}{\sum_{i=1}^{I} \hat{W}_{ik}}\right) - \hat{\beta}_{1(W)}\left(\frac{\sum_{i=1}^{I} \hat{W}_{ik}X_{ik}}{\sum_{i=1}^{I} \hat{W}_{ik}}\right)$$

Step 7. Determine the value of the component Chi-square statistic:
$X^2_{\beta_{1(W)}} = U'_{0(\beta_{0(T)},\beta_{1(T)})} - U'_{0(\beta^*_{0(k)},\beta_{1(W)})}$

where:

$$U'_{0(\beta^*_{0(k)},\beta_{1(W)})} = \sum_{k=1}^{K}\sum_{i=1}^{I} \hat{W}_{ik}(\hat{P}_{ik} - \hat{\beta}^*_{0(k)} - \hat{\beta}_{1(W)}X_{ik})^2$$

represents the residual Chi-square associated with the pooled within-group regression line.

Step 8. If $X^2_{\beta_{1(W)}} < \chi^2_{K-1:1-\alpha}$, conclude that the K regression lines are parallel. If $X^2_{\beta_{1(W)}} > \chi^2_{K-1:1-\alpha}$, conclude that nonparallelism exists.

Step 9. Test the significance of $U'_{0(\beta^*_{0(k)},\beta_{1(W)})}$ to determine whether the process should be terminated. If $U'_{0(\beta^*_{0(k)},\beta_{1(W)})} < \chi^2_{IK-K-1:1-\alpha}$, terminate the process. If $U'_{0(\beta^*_{0(k)},\beta_{1(W)})} > \chi^2_{IK-K-1:1-\alpha}$, proceed to Step 10.

Step 10. To test for equality of the K intercepts:

H_0: $\beta_{0(1)} = \beta_{0(2)} = \cdots = \beta_{0(K)} = \beta_{0(W)}$

vs.

H_1: H_0 is false

compute $\hat{\beta}_{1(k)}$ and $\hat{\beta}_{0(k)}$, using either the following formulas or a computer program:

$$\hat{\beta}_{1(k)} = \frac{\left(\sum_{i=1}^{I} \hat{W}_{ik}\right)\left(\sum_{i=1}^{I} \hat{W}_{ik}\hat{P}_{ik}X_{ik}\right) - \left(\sum_{i=1}^{I} \hat{W}_{ik}X_{ik}\right)\left(\sum_{i=1}^{I} \hat{W}_{ik}\hat{P}_{ik}\right)}{\left(\sum_{i=1}^{I} \hat{W}_{ik}\right)\left(\sum_{i=1}^{I} \hat{W}_{ik}X^2_{ik}\right) - \left(\sum_{i=1}^{I} \hat{W}_{ik}X_{ik}\right)^2} \quad \text{and}$$

$$\hat{\beta}_{0(k)} = \frac{\sum_{i=1}^{I} \hat{W}_{ik}\hat{P}_{ik}}{\sum_{i=1}^{I} \hat{W}_{ik}} - \hat{\beta}_{1(k)}\frac{\sum_{i=1}^{I} \hat{W}_{ik}X_{ik}}{\sum_{i=1}^{I} \hat{W}_{ik}}$$

Step 11. Determine the value of the component Chi-square statistic:

$X^2_{\beta_{1(k)}} = U'_{0(\beta^*_{0(k)},\beta_{1(W)})} - U'_{0(\beta_{0(k)},\beta_{1(k)})}$

where:

$$U'_{0(\beta_{0(k)},\beta_{1(k)})} = \sum_{k=1}^{K}\sum_{i=1}^{I} \hat{W}_{ik}(\hat{P}_{ik} - \hat{\beta}_{0(k)} - \hat{\beta}_{1(k)}X_{ik})^2$$

represents the residual Chi-square associated with K different regression lines.

Step 12. If $X^2_{\beta_{1(k)}} < \chi^2_{K-1:1-\alpha}$, conclude that the K intercepts are equal. Further, if the parallelism hypothesis was not rejected in Step 8, conclude that the K regression lines are identical. If $X^2_{\beta_{1(k)}} > \chi^2_{K-1:1-\alpha}$, conclude that there are differences among the K intercepts.

Step 13. Test the significance of $U'_{0(\beta_{0(k)},\beta_{1(k)})}$ to determine whether the process should be terminated. If $U'_{0(\beta_{0(k)},\beta_{1(k)})} < \chi^2_{IK-2K:1-\alpha}$, terminate the process. If $U'_{0(\beta_{0(k)},\beta_{1(k)})} > \chi^2_{IK-2K:1-\alpha}$, proceed to the analysis of higher order components.

For the data of Tables 10-1 and 10-5, we begin by computing $\hat{\beta}_{0(T)}$ that is needed for the computation of $U'_{0(\beta_{0(T)})}$. We make use of the data summarized in Table 10-2 for the Control Group, $k = 1$, and Table 10-6 for the Experimental Group, $k = 2$. For the test of this model:

$$\hat{\beta}_{0(T)} = \frac{495.60317 + 507.54615}{1227.73361 + 1036.38580} = \frac{1003.14932}{2264.11940} = .44306$$

As shown in Table 10-7:

$$U'_{0(\beta_{0(T)})} = 207.69$$

Because one parameter has been estimated from the data, $\nu = IK - 1 = 12 = 1 = 11$. We now test the across-groups linear relationship for significance. For this test we compute a new $\hat{\beta}_{0(T)}$ based on $\hat{\beta}_{1(T)}$, as follows:

$$\hat{\beta}_{1(T)} = \frac{(1227.73361 + 1036.38580)(10615.47619 + 10831.73077) - (17786.72125 + 16737.82294)(495.60317 + 507.54615)}{(1227.73361 + 1036.38580)(365902.49859 + 361233.43289) - (17786.72125 + 16737.82294)^2}$$

$$= .03065$$

and:

$$\hat{\beta}_{0(T)} = \frac{(495.60317 + 507.54615)}{(1227.73361 + 1036.38580)} - (.03065)\frac{(17786.72125 + 16737.82294)}{(1227.73361 + 1036.38580)}$$

$$= -.02430$$

so that the best-fitting across-groups regression line is:

$$\hat{P} = -.02430 + .03065X$$

The best-fitting probabilities are reported in Table 10-7. As shown there:

$$U'_{0(\beta_{0(T)},\beta_{1(T)})} = 19.19$$

so that the component Chi-square statistic for measuring the across-groups linear relationship between X and P is given by:

$$X^2_{\beta_{1(T)}} = U'_{0(\beta_{0(T)})} - U'_{0(\beta_{0(T)},\beta_{1(T)})}$$
$$= 207.69 - 19.19 = 188.50$$

Since $U'_{0(\beta_{0(T)},\beta_{1(T)})}$ is based on two parameters estimated from the data,

TABLE 10-6. Weighted least square computations for the data of Table 10-5

Group	$\hat{W}_{i2}$	$\hat{W}_{i2}\hat{P}_{i2}$	$\hat{W}_{i2}\hat{P}_{i2}X_{i2}$	$\hat{W}_{i2}X_{i2}$	$\hat{W}_{i2}X^2_{i2}$
7	312.67949	32.34615	161.73077	1563.39744	7816.98718
8	125.00000	50.00000	500.00000	1250.00000	12500.00000
9	120.00000	60.00000	900.00000	1800.00000	27000.00000
10	122.05556	84.50000	1690.00000	2441.11111	48822.22222
11	203.24167	168.20000	4205.00000	5081.04167	127026.04167
12	153.40909	112.50000	3375.00000	4602.27273	138068.18182
Total	1036.38580	507.54615	10831.73077	16737.82294	361233.43289

TABLE 10-7. Fit of the hierarchical models to the data of Tables 10-1 and 10-5

		Total		Across-groups regression		Slopes		Intercepts	
Group	No. of words	Fit	$\hat{W}_{ik}(\hat{P}_{ik} - \hat{\beta}_{0(T)})^2$	Fit	$\hat{W}_{ik}(\hat{P}_{ik} - \hat{\beta}_{0(T)} - \hat{\beta}_{1(T)}X_{ik})^2$	Fit	$\hat{W}_{ik}(\hat{P}_{ik} - \hat{\beta}^*_{0(k)} - \hat{\beta}_{1(W)}X_{ik})^2$	Fit	$\hat{W}_{ik}(\hat{P}_{ik} - \hat{\beta}_{0(k)} - \hat{\beta}_{1(k)}X_{ik})^2$
Control	5	0.44306	68.31	0.12895	1.87	0.11449	1.10	0.10251	0.62
	10	0.44306	1.63	0.28220	0.35	0.26689	0.60	0.26126	0.70
	15	0.44306	0.50	0.43545	0.39	0.41929	0.20	0.42001	0.20
	20	0.44306	17.56	0.58870	5.31	0.57169	6.37	0.57876	5.93
	25	0.44306	12.93	0.74195	0.01	0.72409	0.01	0.73751	0.00
	30	0.44306	19.53	0.89520	1.99	0.87649	1.37	0.89626	2.03
Experimental	5	0.44306	36.06	0.12895	0.20	0.14987	0.67	0.16658	1.25
	10	0.44306	0.23	0.28220	1.73	0.30227	1.19	0.31148	0.98
	15	0.44306	0.39	0.43545	0.50	0.45467	0.25	0.45638	0.23
	20	0.44306	7.58	0.58870	1.31	0.60707	0.89	0.60128	1.01
	25	0.44306	30.05	0.74195	1.49	0.75947	0.94	0.74618	1.35
	30	0.44306	12.93	0.89520	4.02	0.91187	4.89	0.89108	3.82
Residual									
Chi-square			207.69		19.19		18.49		18.12
Deg. of freedom			11		10		9		8
Component									
Chi-square					188.50		0.70		0.38
Deg. of freedom					1		1		1

$\nu_{(\beta_{0(T)},\beta_{1(T)})} = IK - 2 = 12 - 2 = 10$, so that $X^2_{\beta_{1(T)}}$ is based on $\nu = \nu_{\beta_{0(T)}} - \nu_{(\beta_{0(T)},\beta_{1(T)})} = 11 - 10 = 1$. Because $X^2_{\beta_{1(T)}} = 188.50$ is larger than $\chi^2_{1:.95} = 3.84$, the hypothesis of no relationship between X and P is rejected. As mentioned in Section 2-7, this particular test confounds the relationship of interest with the between-group mean differences or, in this case, probabilities of success. As a result, interpretation of this test is problematical.

Because $U'_{0(\beta_{0(T)},\beta_{1(T)})} = 19.19$ is larger than $\chi^2_{10:.95} = 18.31$, we now proceed to test for parallelism of the regression lines. Based on the information of Tables 10-2 and 10-6:

$$\hat{\beta}_{1(W)} = \frac{\left[\left(10615.47619 - \dfrac{17786.72125(495.60317)}{1227.73361}\right) + \left(10831.73077 - \dfrac{16737.82294(507.54615)}{1036.38580}\right)\right]}{\left[\left(365902.49859 - \dfrac{17786.72125^2}{1227.73361}\right) + \left(361233.43289 - \dfrac{16737.82294^2}{1036.38580}\right)\right]}$$

$$= \frac{3435.45329 + 2634.76629}{108218.3802 + 90914.4871} = \frac{6070.21958}{199132.8673}$$

$$= .03048$$

For this model:

$$\hat{\beta}_{0(1)} = \frac{495.60317}{1227.73361} - (.03048)\frac{17786.72125}{1227.73361} = -.03795 \quad \text{and}$$

$$\hat{\beta}_{0(2)} = \frac{507.54615}{1036.38580} - (.03048)\frac{16737.82294}{1036.38580} = -.00258$$

so that:

$\hat{P}_1 = -.03795 + .03048X$

and:

$\hat{P}_2 = -.00258 + .03048X$

The best-fitting probabilities are reported in Table 10-7. As shown there:

$U'_{0(\beta^*_{0(k)},\beta_{1(W)})} = 18.49$

so that the component Chi-square statistic for assessing the parallelism hypothesis is given by:

$$\begin{aligned} X^2_{\beta_{1(W)}} &= U'_{0(\beta_{0(T)},\beta_{1(T)})} - U'_{0(\beta^*_{0(k)},\beta_{1(W)})} \\ &= 19.19 - 18.49 = .70 \end{aligned}$$

Since $U'_{0(\beta^*_{0(k)},\beta_{1(W)})}$ is based on three parameters estimated from the data, $v_{(\beta^*_{0(k)},\beta_{1(W)})} = IK - 3 = 9$, so that $X^2_{\beta_{1(W)}}$ is based on $v = v_{(\beta_{0(T)},\beta_{1(T)})} - v_{(\beta^*_{0(k)},\beta_{1(W)})} = 10 - 9 = 1$. Because $X^2_{\beta_{1(W)}} = .70$ is less than $\chi^2_{1:.95} = 3.84$, we cannot reject the parallelism hypothesis. Thus the two regression lines are concluded to be parallel, which implies there is no condition by linear trials interaction.

However, because $U'_{0(\beta^*_{0(k)},\beta_{1(W)})} = 18.49$ is larger than $\chi^2_{9:.95} = 16.92$, we proceed to test for the equality of the intercepts. In this case, this is consistent with testing for the identity of the two lines, since they have already been identified as parallel. At this point we deviate from the decisions made by the component tests and focus on the minimization procedure used to reduce the residual Chi-square statistic. Thus, even though we have to conclude that the two lines are parallel, if we were to use $\hat{\beta}_{1(W)} = .03048$, we would not obtain the minimum Chi-square value. For this reason, we estimate $\beta_{1(1)}$ and $\beta_{1(2)}$ and use them to estimate $\beta_{0(1)}$ and $\beta_{0(2)}$. The resulting estimates produce a reduction in the residual Chi-square. To test the hypothesis of equal intercepts, compute:

$$\hat{\beta}_{1(1)} = \frac{1227.73361(10615.47619) - 17786.72125(495.60317)}{1227.73361(365902.49859) - 17786.72125^2} = .03175$$

$$\hat{\beta}_{0(1)} = \frac{495.60317}{1227.73361} - (.03175)\frac{17786.72125}{1227.73361} = -.05624$$

$$\hat{\beta}_{1(2)} = \frac{1036.38580(10831.73077) - 16737.82294(507.54615)}{1036.38580(361233.43289) - 16737.82294^2} = .02898$$

and:

$$\hat{\beta}_{0(2)} = \frac{507.54615}{1036.38580} - (.02898)\frac{16737.82294}{1036.38580} = .02168$$

so that:

$\hat{P}_1 = -.05624 + .03175X$

and:

$\hat{P}_2 = .02168 + .02898X$

The best-fitting probabilities are reported in Table 10-7. As indicated:

$$U'_{0(\beta_{0(k)},\beta_{1(k)})} = 18.11$$

so that the component Chi-square statistic for assessing the equal intercepts hypothesis is given by:

$$X^2_{\beta_0(W)} = U'_{0(\beta^*_{0(k)},\beta_{1(W)})} - U'_{0(\beta_{0(k)},\beta_{1(k)})}$$
$$= 18.49 - 18.11 = .38$$

which does not lead to rejection of the equal intercepts hypothesis. However, the residual U'_0 is still significant, since $\chi^2_{8:.95} = 15.51$. The entire analysis is summarized in Tables 10-8 and 10-9.

Because the residual is significant, we know that a linear relationship is not sufficient to describe the data. The next model to be tested would be one that assumes parallel quadratic components for the two curves, followed by one assuming different quadratic components. Higher order trend components would be examined next.

This model can be extended in many different ways. We have just indicated that we can add higher order trend components to the relationship. Other quantitative independent variables can be incorporated into the regression model. In addition to number of trials, for example, we might build age categories into the model. Thus we might repeat the entire learning study using groups of 5-, 10-, 15-, and 20-year-old subjects. In such an analysis, trial trends, age trends, and their interaction could be examined using procedures similar to those just described.

10-4. Log-linear analysis of a two-dimensional contingency table

The contingency tables of Sections 10-2 and 10-3 involved a quantitative independent variable that could be analyzed by familiar regression methods. However, most contingency tables involve qualitative or ordered qualitative

TABLE 10-8. Summary Chi-square data for fitting two regression lines to the data of Tables 10-1 and 10-5

Step	*Component*	U'_0	X^2	d/f
1	Total	207.69	207.69	11
2	Across-groups linear regression	19.19	188.50	1
3	Parallel lines	18.49	0.70	1
4	Equal intercepts	18.11	0.38	1
5	Deviation from linearity	18.11	18.11	8

TABLE 10-9. Degrees of freedom for fitting K regression lines to $I \times 2$ contingency tables

Step	*Component*	d/f
1	Total	$IK - 1$
2	Across-groups linear regression	1
3	Parallel lines	$K - 1$
4	Equal intecepts	$K - 1$
5	Deviation from linearity	$IK - 2K$

variables, rather than truly quantitative ones. Qualitative variables consist of nominal categories with no numerical relationships among the categories, whereas the categories of an ordered qualitative variable form a monotonically increasing or decreasing scale, but with unknown distances between categories. With such variables, standard regression analyses cannot be performed. For qualitative variables, the traditional analysis is based on Karl Pearson's Chi-square statistic, with the more recent Light-Margolin (1971) categorical analysis of variance proposed as a competitor.

As an example of a contingency table based on two ordered qualitative variables, consider the frequency data of Table 10-10. These data are taken from a school desegregation evaluation study described by Marascuilo and Levin (1967). In this study, junior high school students were categorized according to race, Black or White, the number of new friends from the other race made during the previous school year (Many, Some, or None) and the perceived amount of social mixing of students of different races (Often, Sometimes, or Hardly Ever). The data in Table 10-10 are for the White students only.

Among the many research questions that could be asked from these data, the most obvious ones, stated as hypotheses to be tested, are:

1. There is a uniform distribution in the number of new Black friends made by the White students, or $P(A_i) = 1/3$, for $i = 1, 2, 3$.
2. There is a uniform distribution in the amount of social mixing perceived by the White students, or $P(B_j) = 1/3$, for $j = 1, 2, 3$.
3. The number of new Black friends made by the White students is independent of the amount of social mixing of the different races as perceived by the White students, or $P(A_i \text{ and } B_j) = P(A_i)P(B_j)$, for all i and j.

Most researchers would have no problem testing these three hypotheses. The first two can be tested by the goodness-of-fit Chi-square statistic whereas the third can be tested via the Chi-square independence statistic or the Light-Margolin C statistic. Since both variables of this example are ordered qualitative variables, the Goodman-Kruskal γ statistic (Hays, 1973) would also be appropriate here, as would Kendall's tau, corrected for ties (Marascuilo and McSweeney, 1977). However, if the study were expanded to include a third factor, such as race of the respondent, many researchers would not know what to do. Although researchers are aware of methods for partitioning Chi-square that have been programmed for computer analysis, we do not recommend their use. For example, the procedure described by Lancaster (1951) has been designed for this model, but since it gives rise to an interaction hypothesis that almost defies description, its utility is questionable.

TABLE 10-10. Perceived amount of social mixing and number of new Black friends made by White students during the first year of a school desegregation program

Perceived amount of social mixing	*Number of new Black friends*			
	B_1: Many	B_2: Some	B_3: None	Total
A_1: Often	230	246	9	485
A_2: Sometimes	130	478	47	655
A_3: Hardly Ever	15	83	54	152
Total	375	807	110	1292

We now develop the procedures based on multivariate theory, following the approach of Everitt (1977).

10-5. Omnibus tests for two-dimensional tables: The interaction model

In this section, we present an alternative two-factor analysis procedure that we extend in Section 10-6 to cover multidimensional contingency tables, that is, contingency tables with more than two factors. As will be seen, the procedure has many of the characteristics of the analysis of variance and multiple regression. As in Chapter 9, we will maintain the distinction between the interaction and simple effects ANOVA models when discussing the new procedure. Before we make the presentation, however, let us consider the more traditional interaction model analysis based on the Pearson Chi-square statistic.

If we let:

Y_{ij} = observed frequency in the ijth cell

$Y_{i.}$ = observed frequency in the ith row

$Y_{.j}$ = observed frequency in the jth column

$\hat{Y}_{ij} = N(Y_{i.}/N)\,(Y_{.j}/N)$ = estimated expected frequency in the ijth cell under the assumption of independence of the two factors

$\hat{Y}_{i.} = N(1/I)$ = expected frequency in each row under the assumption of row homogeneity

$\hat{Y}_{.j} = N(1/J)$ = expected frequency in each column under the assumption of column homogeneity

then we can test the following three hypotheses:

H_{0_A}: All $P_{i.} = 1/I$. There is no row main effect.

H_{0_B}: All $P_{.j} = 1/J$. There is no column main effect.

$H_{0_{AB}}$: All $P_{ij} = P_{i.}P_{.j}$. There is no two-factor interaction.

by, respectively, referring:

$$X_A^2 = \sum_{i=1}^{I} \frac{(Y_{i.} - \hat{Y}_{i.})^2}{\hat{Y}_{i.}}$$

$$X_B^2 = \sum_{j=1}^{J} \frac{(Y_{.j} - \hat{Y}_{.j})^2}{\hat{Y}_{.j}}$$

$$X_{AB}^2 = \sum_{i=1}^{I} \sum_{j=1}^{J} \frac{(Y_{ij} - \hat{Y}_{ij})^2}{\hat{Y}_{ij}}$$

to Chi-square distributions with $\nu_A = I - 1$, $\nu_B = J - 1$, and $\nu_{AB} = (I - 1)(J - 1)$.

For the data of Table 10-10, the estimated expected frequencies for the three hypotheses are given by:

$$\hat{Y}_{i.} = \hat{Y}_{.j} = 1292(1/3) = 430.67 \quad \text{and}$$

$$\hat{Y}_{11} = 1292(485/1292)\,(375/1292) = 140.77, \ldots,$$

$$\hat{Y}_{33} = 1292(152/1292)\,(110/1292) = 12.94$$

The remaining estimated expected frequencies are reported in Table 10-11. With these values:

$$X_A^2 = \frac{(485 - 430.67)^2}{430.67} + \frac{(655 - 430.67)^2}{430.67} + \frac{(152 - 430.67)^2}{430.67}$$
$$= 304.02$$

$$X_B^2 = \frac{(375 - 430.67)^2}{430.67} + \frac{(807 - 430.67)^2}{430.67} + \frac{(110 - 430.67)^2}{430.67}$$
$$= 574.81$$

and:

$$X_{AB}^2 = \frac{(230 - 140.77)^2}{140.77} + \frac{(246 - 302.94)^2}{302.94} + \cdots + \frac{(54 - 12.94)^2}{12.94}$$
$$= 275.48$$

Note, in addition to these three Chi-square statistics, a total Chi-square statistic X_T^2 could be computed to reflect between-cell differences in proportion. If we let $\hat{Y}_{..} = N(1/IJ)$ represent the estimated expected cell frequency under the assumption of cell homogeneity, then:

$$\hat{Y}_{..} = 1292(1/9) = 143.56$$

so that:

$$X_T^2 = \sum_{i=1}^{I} \sum_{j=1}^{J} \frac{(Y_{ij} - \hat{Y}_{..})^2}{\hat{Y}_{..}}$$

$$= \frac{(230 - 143.56)^2}{143.56} + \frac{(246 - 143.56)^2}{143.56} + \cdots + \frac{(54 - 143.56)^2}{143.56} = 1293.12$$

If this model were completely analogous to the analysis of variance, it would follow that:

$$X_A^2 + X_B^2 + X_{AB}^2 = X_T^2$$

TABLE 10-11. Estimated expected frequencies for the data of Table 10-10 under the hypotheses of row homogeneity, column homogeneity, and independence

Perceived amount of social mixing	*Number of new Black friends*			
	B_1	B_2	B_3	*Row homogeneity*
A_1	140.77[c]	302.94[c]	41.29[c]	430.67[a]
A_2	190.11[c]	409.12[c]	55.77[c]	430.67[a]
A_3	44.12[c]	94.94[c]	12.94[c]	430.67[a]
Column homogeneity	430.67[b]	430.67[b]	430.67[b]	

[a] Row homogeneity
[b] Column homogeneity
[c] Independence

For this example:

$$X_A^2 + X_B^2 + X_{AB}^2 = 304.02 + 574.81 + 275.58 = 1154.31 \neq X_T^2$$

Clearly, the Pearson Chi-square statistic does not possess the property of additivity. For this statistic, the correspondence with analysis of variance sums of squares falls short. As a result, let us consider a model that provides us with a direct correspondence, that is, the log-linear model. Although a number of procedures have been advanced for performing a log-linear analysis, we will adhere to the procedures described by Bishop, Fienberg, and Holland (1975) and by Goodman (1971). Since our presentation includes only the bare essentials, it is recommended that researchers refer to the Bishop et al. and Goodman presentations for an in-depth justification of what is illustrated here. Furthermore, these sources provide directions for investigating other and more complicated statistical hypotheses.

The log-linear model is based on the assumption that the frequency of being a member of the *ij*th cell, defined by the intersection of the *i*th row and the *j*th column, has the latent structure:

$$Y_{ij} = e^{\mu + \alpha_{i.} + \alpha_{.j} + \gamma_{ij}}$$

where:

e = the base for the natural logarithms

μ = a standardizing constant

and:

$$\sum_{i=1}^{I} \alpha_{i.} = \sum_{j=1}^{J} \alpha_{.j} = \sum_{i=1}^{I} \gamma_{ij} = \sum_{j=1}^{J} \gamma_{ij} = 0$$

If we take logarithms to the base e, the model can be written as:

$$L_{ij} = \log_e Y_{ij} = \mu + \alpha_{i.} + \alpha_{.j} + \gamma_{ij}$$

which parallels the familiar ANOVA model. In this form, the three hypotheses of interest can be written as:

$$H_{0_A}: \quad \alpha_{1.} = \alpha_{2.} = \cdots = \alpha_{I.} = 0$$

$$H_{0_B}: \quad \alpha_{.1} = \alpha_{.2} = \cdots = \alpha_{.J} = 0$$

$$H_{0_{AB}}: \quad \gamma_{11} = \gamma_{12} = \cdots = \gamma_{IJ} = 0$$

These three hypotheses can be tested in terms of the log-linear statistic which is defined in a general form, without subscripts, as follows.

Definition of the general log-linear test statistic, G^2

Consider the set of observed frequencies Y and their estimated expected frequencies $\hat{Y}$ computed under the hypothesis H_0. If the hypothesis is true, the statistic:

$$G^2 = 2 \sum Y \log_e (Y/\hat{Y})$$

has a distribution that is approximately Chi-square with degrees of freedom equal to the number of independent parameters in the models that are set equal to zero.

For the total G^2 statistic, G_T^2, all parameters except μ are set equal to zero so that the number of degrees of freedom for G_T^2 is given by $\nu_T = IJ - 1$. For the test of homogeneity of the row effects, the $\alpha_{.j}$ and the γ_{ij} are set equal to zero. As a consequence, $\nu_A = (IJ - 1) - (J - 1) - (I - 1)(J - 1) = I - 1$. In like manner, the degrees of freedom for the column effects are given by $\nu_B = J - 1$ and for the interaction by $\nu_{AB} = (I - 1)(J - 1)$.

For the data of Table 10-10:

$$G_T^2 = 2[230 \log_e (230/143.56) + 246 \log_e (246/143.56) + \cdots + 54 \log_e (54/143.56)] = 1186.80$$

$$G_A^2 = 2[485 \log_e (485/430.67) + 655 \log_e (655/430.67) + 152 \log_e (152/430.67)] = 347.91$$

$$G_B^2 = 2[375 \log_e (375/430.67) + 807 \log_e (807/430.67) + 110 \log_e (110/430.67)] = 609.48$$

$$G_{AB}^2 = 2[230 \log_e (230/140.77) + 246 \log_e (246/302.94) + \cdots + 54 \log_e (54/12.94)] = 229.45$$

If H_{0_A}, H_{0_B}, and $H_{0_{AB}}$, are true, then G_T^2, G_A^2, G_B^2, and G_{AB}^2 are each approximately Chi-square distributed with $\nu_T = IJ - 1 = 3(3) - 1 = 8$, $\nu_A = I - 1 = 3 - 1 = 2$, $\nu_B = J - 1 = 3 - 1 = 2$, and $\nu_{AB} = (I - 1)(J - 1) = 2(2) = 4$. In this case, $\chi^2_{2:.95} = 5.99$ and $\chi^2_{4:.95} = 9.49$. As shown in Table 10-12, for this particular example, statistical decisions made for the familiar Pearson tests are consistent with those made for the log-linear model. In this case, both main effects and interaction are significant with $\alpha = .05$, using both approaches. The major difference is that:

$$G_A^2 + G_B^2 + G_{AB}^2 = G_T^2$$

whereas the Chi-square statistics do not possess this additivity.

We now provide directions for performing a log-linear analysis of an $I \times J$ contingency table.

TABLE 10-12. Chi-square and log-linear analyses of data from Table 10-10: The interaction model

Source of variance	*df*	X^2	G^2
Total	8	1293.12	1186.80
A	2	304.02	347.91
B	2	574.81	609.48
$A \times B$	4	275.48	229.45

Notes: $X_A^2 + X_B^2 + X_{AB}^2 \neq \chi_T^2$
$G_A^2 + G_B^2 + G_{AB}^2 = G_T^2$

Procedure for performing a log-linear analysis of an $I \times J$ contingency table: The interaction model.

Step 1. Compute the total G^2:

$$G_T^2 = 2 \sum_{i=1}^{I} \sum_{j=1}^{J} Y_{ij} \log_e (Y_{ij}/\hat{Y}_{ij})$$

where:

Y_{ij} = observed frequency in the ijth cell

$\hat{Y}_{ij} = N(1/IJ)$ = estimated expected frequency of the ijth cell

Step 2. Test the hypothesis of row homogeneity with:

$$G_A^2 = 2 \sum_{i=1}^{I} Y_{i.} \log_e (Y_{i.}/\hat{Y}_{i.})$$

where:

$Y_{i.}$ = observed frequency in the ith row

$\hat{Y}_{i.} = N(1/I)$ = estimated expected frequency in the ith row

Reject H_{0_A}: All $\alpha_{i.} = 0$ if $G_A^2 > \chi^2_{I-1:1-\alpha}$.

Step 3. Test the hypothesis of column homogeneity with:

$$G_B^2 = 2 \sum_{j=1}^{J} Y_{.j} \log_e (Y_{.j}/\hat{Y}_{.j})$$

where:

$Y_{.j}$ = observed frequency in the jth column

$\hat{Y}_{.j} = N(1/J)$ = estimated expected frequency in the jth column

Reject H_{0_B}: All $\alpha_{.j} = 0$ if $G_B^2 > \chi^2_{J-1:1-\alpha}$.

Step 4. Test the hypothesis of two-factor independence with:

$$G_{AB}^2 = 2 \sum_{i=1}^{I} \sum_{j=1}^{J} Y_{ij} \log_e (Y_{ij}/\hat{Y}_{ij})$$

where:

Y_{ij} = observed frequency in the ijth cell and

$\hat{Y}_{ij} = N(Y_{i.}/N)(Y_{.j}/N)$ = estimated expected frequency in the ijth cell

Reject $H_{0_{AB}}$: All $\gamma_{ij} = 0$ if $G_{AB}^2 > \chi^2_{(I-1)(J-1):1-\alpha}$.

Contrasts in two-dimensional tables: The interaction model. Other than the fact that $G_A^2 + G_B^2 + G_{AB}^2 = G_T^2$, we may wonder why the log-linear model has gained such widespread popularity among statisticians. One reason, as noted earlier, is that straightforward generalizations to higher order contingency tables are possible. But another major reason for adopting the model is that it leads to contrasts that parallel contrasts among parameters in the analysis of variance model. For example, rejection of the hypothesis, H_{0_A}: All $\alpha_{i.} = 0$, is equivalent to stating that not all ψ_A are equal to zero. As a result, simultaneous confidence intervals, based on a Chi-square analog to Scheffé's procedure, may be constructed to investigate as many contrasts of interest involving the A factor. Before we consider the contrast procedure, however, we must first present the estimation theory associated with the log-linear model. The complete log-linear model for an $I \times J$ contingency table, written as a multiple regression model, is given by:

$$L = \mu + (\alpha_{1.}X_{1.} + \alpha_{2.}X_{2.} + \cdots + \alpha_{I.}X_{I.}) + (\alpha_{.1}X_{.1} + \alpha_{.2}X_{.2} + \cdots + \alpha_{.J}X_{.J}) + (\gamma_{11}X_{11} + \gamma_{12}X_{12} + \cdots + \gamma_{IJ}X_{IJ})$$

where the $X_{i.}$, $X_{.j}$ and X_{ij} are dummy-coded values that may be zero or one.

In analogy with a two-way ANOVA represented as a dummy-coded multiple-regression problem, μ is analogous to β_0, the α and γ terms are analogous to the $I + J + IJ$ main effect and interaction terms, and the X terms are zero-one indicator variables to represent the presence or absence of a term when defining the value of a given cell.

Recalling the previously given restrictions that parameters sum to zero, we see that each main effect has one restriction, and that the interaction has $I + J$ restrictions. With these $2 + I + J$ restrictions, parameters can be estimated via Cramer's rule, or by solving the normal equations of multiple regression theory. For the data of Table 10-10, the normal equations are as shown in Table 10-13. The first row of Table 10-13 corresponds to the equation $\hat{\mu} + \hat{\alpha}_{1.} + \hat{\alpha}_{.1} + \hat{\gamma}_{11} = 5.43808$, which represents cell 11. We will solve these equations and show how similar the results are to the familiar ANOVA model. We begin by summing across the entire set of equations to obtain the single equation:

$$\begin{aligned} 9\hat{\mu} + 3\sum_{i=1}^{3}\hat{\alpha}_{i.} + 3\sum_{j=1}^{J}\hat{\alpha}_{.j} + \sum_{i=1}^{I}\sum_{j=1}^{J}\hat{\gamma}_{ij} &= \sum_{i=1}^{I}\sum_{j=1}^{J}\log_e Y_{ij} \\ &= \sum_{i=1}^{I}\sum_{j=1}^{J} L_{ij} \\ &= 5.43808 + \cdots + 3.98898 \\ &= 39.14379 \end{aligned}$$

Since each of the summed parameter terms is equal to zero, this equation reduces to:

TABLE 10-13. The normal equations for the data of Table 10-10

Cell	μ	$\alpha_{1.}$	$\alpha_{2.}$	$\alpha_{3.}$	$\alpha_{.1}$	$\alpha_{.2}$	$\alpha_{.3}$	γ_{11}	γ_{12}	γ_{13}	γ_{21}	γ_{22}	γ_{23}	γ_{31}	γ_{32}	γ_{33}	L_{ij}
11	1	1	0	0	1	0	0	1	0	0	0	0	0	0	0	0	5.43808
12	1	1	0	0	0	1	0	0	1	0	0	0	0	0	0	0	5.50533
13	1	1	0	0	0	0	1	0	0	1	0	0	0	0	0	0	2.19722
21	1	0	1	0	1	0	0	0	0	0	1	0	0	0	0	0	4.86753
22	1	0	1	0	0	1	0	0	0	0	0	1	0	0	0	0	6.16961
23	1	0	1	0	0	0	1	0	0	0	0	0	1	0	0	0	3.85015
31	1	0	0	1	1	0	0	0	0	0	0	0	0	1	0	0	2.70805
32	1	0	0	1	0	1	0	0	0	0	0	0	0	0	1	0	4.41884
33	1	0	0	1	0	0	1	0	0	0	0	0	0	0	0	1	3.98898

Note: Cell entries are 0 and 1 coded X terms to represent the inclusion of a given parameter in the normal equation.

$$9\hat{\mu} = 39.14379$$

so that:

$$\hat{\mu} = 4.34931$$

If we now sum across the first three rows, we obtain the equation:

$$3\hat{\mu} + 3\hat{\alpha}_{1.} = 5.43808 + 5.50533 + 2.19722 = 13.14063$$

so that:

$$\hat{\mu}_{1.} = \hat{\mu} + \hat{\alpha}_{1.} = \frac{1}{3}(13.14063) = 4.38021$$

and:

$$\hat{\alpha}_{1.} = \hat{\mu}_{1.} - \hat{\mu} = 4.38021 - 4.34931 = .03090$$

Values of $\hat{\alpha}_{2.}$ and $\hat{\alpha}_{3.}$ are found in a similar manner. These values are reported in Table 10-14. If we now sum across rows 1, 4, and 7 of the normal equations in Table 10-13, we obtain the equation:

$$3\hat{\mu} + 3\hat{\alpha}_{.1} = 5.43808 + 4.86753 + 2.70805 = 13.01366$$

so that:

$$\hat{\alpha}_{.1} = \hat{\mu}_{.1} - \hat{\mu} = \frac{1}{3}(13.01366) - 4.34931$$
$$= 4.33789 - 4.34931 = -.01142$$

Values of $\hat{\alpha}_{.2}$ and $\hat{\alpha}_{.3}$ are found in a similar manner. These values are reported in Table 10-14. From row one of Table 10-13, we see that:

$$\hat{\mu} + \hat{\alpha}_{1.} + \hat{\alpha}_{.1} + \hat{\gamma}_{11} = 5.43808$$

so that:

$$\hat{\gamma}_{11} = 5.43808 - 4.34931 - .03090 - (-.01142) = 1.06929$$

Remaining values are reported in Table 10-14. A little reflection shows that the solution to the normal equations is as follows.

TABLE 10-14. Estimated parameters for the row effects, column effects, and interaction effects associated with the data of Table 10-10

Perceived amount of social mixing	*Number of new Black friends*			
	B_1: *Many*	B_2: *Some*	B_3: *None*	*Row margin*
A_1: Often	1.06929[c]	0.10984[c]	− 1.17913[c]	0.03090[a]
A_2: Sometimes	− 0.08348[c]	0.19190[c]	− 0.10842[c]	0.61312[a]
A_3: Hardly Ever	− 0.98582[c]	− 0.30173[c]	1.28755[c]	− 0.64402[a]
Column margin	− 0.01142[b]	1.01528[b]	− 1.00386[b]	

[a] Row effects
[b] Column effects
[c] Interaction effects

The general solution to the normal equations for an $I \times J$ contingency table. Let Y_{ij} be the observed frequency in the ijth cell. Then:

$$\hat{\mu} = \frac{1}{IJ}\sum_{i=1}^{I}\sum_{j=1}^{J}\log_e Y_{ij} \qquad \hat{\mu}_{ij} = \log_e Y_{ij}$$

$$\hat{\mu}_{i.} = \frac{1}{J}\sum_{j=1}^{J}\log_e Y_{ij} \qquad \hat{\mu}_{.j} = \frac{1}{I}\sum_{i=1}^{I}\log_e Y_{ij}$$

so that:

$$\hat{\alpha}_{i.} = \hat{\mu}_{i.} - \hat{\mu} \qquad \hat{\alpha}_{.j} = \hat{\mu}_{.j} - \hat{\mu}$$

and:

$$\begin{aligned}\hat{\gamma}_{ij} &= \hat{\mu}_{ij} - \hat{\mu} - \hat{\alpha}_{i.} - \hat{\alpha}_{.j} \\ &= \hat{\mu}_{ij} - \hat{\mu} - (\hat{\mu}_{i.} - \hat{\mu}) - (\hat{\mu}_{.j} - \hat{\mu}) \\ &= \hat{\mu}_{ij} - \hat{\mu}_{i.} - \hat{\mu}_{.j} + \hat{\mu}\end{aligned}$$

Similar to the classical ANOVA model, parameter estimators of the log-linear model can be written as contrasts. Furthermore, for this model all contrasts can be written as a weighted sum in terms of the $\log_e Y_{ij}$ values. In the most general case:

$$\hat{\psi} = \sum_{i=1}^{I}\sum_{j=1}^{J} a_{ij}\log_e Y_{ij} = \sum_{i=1}^{I}\sum_{i=1}^{J} a_{ij}\,\hat{\mu}_{ij}$$

represents a linear contrast, provided:

$$\sum_{i=1}^{I}\sum_{j=1}^{J} a_{ij} = 0$$

One special property of these contrasts is that their standard errors are easy to compute, provided that the sample sizes are large. If at least 80% of the expected values across all IJ cells exceed five, a reliable value for the squared standard error of a contrast is given by:

$$SE_{\hat{\psi}}^2 = \sum_{i=1}^{I}\sum_{j=1}^{J}\frac{a_{ij}^2}{Y_{ij}}$$

We now give directions for testing contrasts for statistical significance based on a log-linear analysis of a two-dimensional contingency table.

Procedure for testing contrasts for statistical significance in a two-dimensional log-linear analysis: The interaction model.

Step 1. Define contrasts of interest as:

$$\hat{\psi} = \sum_{i=1}^{I}\sum_{j=1}^{J} a_{ij}\log_e Y_{ij} = \sum_{i=1}^{I}\sum_{j=1}^{J} a_{ij}\hat{\mu}_{ij}$$

where:

$$\sum_{i=1}^{I} \sum_{j=1}^{J} a_{ij} = 0$$

For row contrasts, the $\hat{\mu}_{ij}$ must be selected so that $\hat{\psi}_A$ reduces to one that includes only $\hat{\alpha}_{i.}$ terms; for a column contrast, $\hat{\psi}_B$ must reduce to one that involves only $\hat{\alpha}_{.j}$ terms; and for an interaction contrast, $\hat{\psi}_{AB}$ must reduce to one that involves $\hat{\gamma}_{ij}$ terms only.

Step 2. Estimate the standard errors for the contrasts as follows:

$$SE_{\hat{\psi}} = \sqrt{\sum_{i=1}^{I} \sum_{j=1}^{J} \frac{a_{ij}^2}{Y_{ij}}}$$

Step 3. Set up $100(1 - \alpha)$ percent confidence intervals as:

$$\psi = \hat{\psi} \pm \mathbf{S}^* \, SE_{\hat{\psi}}$$

where $\mathbf{S}^*$ is selected on an a priori or post hoc basis. For a post hoc analysis based on rows, use:

$$\mathbf{S}_A^* = \sqrt{\chi^2_{I-1:1-\alpha}}$$

For a post hoc analysis based on columns, use:

$$\mathbf{S}_B^* = \sqrt{\chi^2_{J-1:1-\alpha}}$$

For a post hoc analysis based on row by column interactions, use:

$$\mathbf{S}_{AB}^* = \sqrt{\chi^2_{(I-1)(J-1):1-\alpha}}$$

For a Dunn-Bonferroni planned analysis, count the number of contrasts of interest in a specific family of hypotheses and replace $\mathbf{S}^*$ by a critical value selected from Table B-4, with $\nu_2 = \infty$.

In the present example, both main effects and the interaction resulted in statistically significant G^2 statistics using $\alpha = .05$ per family, since all exceeded their respective tabled χ^2 values. As a result, one or more significant row contrasts, column contrasts, and interaction contrasts are guaranteed to differ from zero using the post hoc procedure just described. For the A main effect, let us compare the social mixing categories Often, A_1, and Hardly Ever, A_3. In this case, since the social mixing variable is ordered qualitative, such a comparison is synonymous with assessing the monotonic trend on that variable. Monotonicity can be examined in variables that are ordinal in nature, but where distances between levels of the variable are unknown. In this sense we ask whether there is a performance increase or decrease across the I levels of the variable. A test of monotonicity subsumes the possibility that a linear trend exists. However, linearity per se cannot be examined whenever distances between levels of an independent variable are unknown.

For monotonicity and $I = 3$, $a_1 = 1$, $a_2 = 0$, and $a_3 = -1$. Thus, to determine the significance of the contrast:

$$\begin{aligned}\hat{\psi}_A &= \hat{\mu}_{1.} - \hat{\mu}_{3.} \\ &= \frac{1}{3}(\hat{\mu}_{11} + \hat{\mu}_{12} + \hat{\mu}_{13}) - \frac{1}{3}(\hat{\mu}_{31} + \hat{\mu}_{32} + \hat{\mu}_{33})\end{aligned}$$

we use the values in Table 10-15 to find that:

TABLE 10-15. Estimated row values, $\hat{\mu}_{i.}$, column values, $\hat{\mu}_{.j}$, and cell values, $\hat{\mu}_{ij}$, for the data of Table 10-10

Perceived amount of social mixing	*Number of new Black friends*			
	B_1: *Many*	B_2: *Some*	B_3: *None*	*Row margin*
A_1: Often	5.43808	5.50533	2.19722	4.38021
A_2: Sometimes	4.86753	6.16961	3.85015	4.96243
A_3: Hardly Ever	2.70805	4.41884	3.98898	3.70529
Column margin	4.33789	5.36459	3.34545	4.34931

$$\hat{\psi}_A = \frac{1}{3}(5.43808 + 5.50533 + 2.19722) - \frac{1}{3}(2.70805 + 4.41884 + 3.98898)$$
$$= 4.38021 - 3.70529$$
$$= .67492$$

It is worth noting that we could determine $\hat{\psi}_A$ directly from the margin of Table 10-15, since $\hat{\psi}_A = 4.38021 - 3.70529 = .67492$. However, we are advised not to do the computations in this manner because it may well lead to errors in computing the standard error of $\hat{\psi}_A$ which is found from the Y_{ij} values and not the $Y_{i.}$ values.

In addition, using the cell frequencies in Table 10-10, we find that:

$$SE^2_{\hat{\psi}_A} = \frac{(1/3)^2}{230} + \frac{(1/3)^2}{246} + \cdots + \frac{(-1/3)^2}{54} = .02408$$

With $\alpha = .05$, $\mathbf{S}^{*2}_A = \chi^2_{2:.95} = 5.99$, and:

$$\psi_A = \hat{\psi}_A \pm \mathbf{S}^*_A \, SE_{\hat{\psi}_A}$$
$$= .67492 \pm \sqrt{5.99(.02408)}$$
$$= .67 \pm .38$$

Therefore, we can conclude that $P_{1.}$ and $P_{3.}$ differ signicantly or that a monotonic trend exists among levels of the A factor. As many other A effect contrasts as are of interest could be examined using this method. For example, the contrast, $\hat{\psi}_A = \frac{1}{2}(\hat{\mu}_{1.} + \hat{\mu}_{3.}) - \hat{\mu}_{2.}$ would assess deviations from monotonicity which, in the case of three levels of a factor, is equivalent to what is referred to as the *bitonic* trend.

For the B effect, let us compare the new friends categories Many, B_1, and None, B_3, with the same statement regarding monotonicity applying here as in the case of A_1 vs. A_3. For this contrast:

$$\hat{\psi}_B = \hat{\mu}_{.1} - \hat{\mu}_{.3}$$
$$= \frac{1}{3}(\hat{\mu}_{11} + \hat{\mu}_{21} + \hat{\mu}_{31}) - \frac{1}{3}(\hat{\mu}_{13} + \hat{\mu}_{23} + \hat{\mu}_{33})$$
$$= \frac{1}{3}(5.43808 + 4.86753 + 2.70805) - \frac{1}{3}(2.19722 + 3.85015 + 3.98898)$$
$$= 4.33789 - 3.34545$$
$$= .99244$$

from Table 10-15. From the cell frequencies of Table 10-10, we find that:

$$SE^2_{\hat\psi_B} = \frac{(1/3)^2}{230} + \frac{(1/3)^2}{130} + \cdots + \frac{(-1/3)^2}{54} = .02551$$

With $\alpha = .05$, $\mathbf{S}^{*2}_B = \chi^2_{2:.95} = 5.99$, and:

$$\begin{aligned}\psi_B &= \hat\psi_B \pm \mathbf{S}^*_B\, SE_{\hat\psi_B}\\ &= .99244 \pm \sqrt{5.99(.02551)}\\ &= .99 \pm .39\end{aligned}$$

Thus we can conclude that $P_{.1}$ and $P_{.3}$ differ significantly or that a monotonic trend exists among levels of the B factor. As many other B effect contrasts as are of interest could be examined using this method.

To define an interaction contrast in terms of the two main effect contrasts just examined, $\hat\psi_A$ and $\hat\psi_B$, we use the procedure outlined in Table 10-16. In that table, the interaction contrast $\hat\psi_{AB}$ is defined by multiplying the cell coefficients for $\hat\psi_A$ and $\hat\psi_B$, respectively. The result is given in the third row of that table. For convenience, we multiply each coefficient by 9 to obtain:

$$\hat\psi_{AB} = \hat\mu_{11} - \hat\mu_{13} - \hat\mu_{31} + \hat\mu_{33} = (\hat\mu_{11} - \hat\mu_{13}) - (\hat\mu_{31} - \hat\mu_{33})$$

which is the simple difference in differences, or tetrad, contrast discussed in Section 9-1. Here:

$$\hat\psi_{AB} = (5.43808 - 2.19722) - (2.70805 - 3.98898) = 4.52179$$

with:

$$SE^2_{\hat\psi_{AB}} = \frac{+1^2}{230} + \frac{-1^2}{9} + \frac{-1^2}{15} + \frac{+1^2}{54} = .20064$$

With $\alpha = .05$ and $\mathbf{S}^{*2}_{AB} = \chi^2_{4:.95} = 9.49$:

$$\begin{aligned}\psi_{AB} &= \hat\psi_{A_1B_1} \pm \mathbf{S}^*_{AB} SE_{\hat\psi_{AB}}\\ &= 4.52179 \pm \sqrt{9.49(.20064)}\\ &= 4.52 \pm 1.38\end{aligned}$$

Therefore, this interaction contrast is significant, indicating that students who made many new Black friends exhibited a larger difference in favor of Often over Hardly Ever responses on the social-mixing question, in comparison to students who made no new Black friends. Alternatively, a monotonic-by-monotonic interaction involving the two factors exists. (Note that if the categories of both A and B were

TABLE 10-16. The contrast coefficients for the interaction $\psi_{AB} = \psi_A \times \psi_B$, where $\psi_A = \mu_{1.} - \mu_{3.}$ and $\psi_B = \mu_{.1} - \mu_{.3}$

	A_1			A_2			A_3		
	B_1	B_2	B_3	B_1	B_2	B_3	B_1	B_2	B_3
$\hat\psi_A$	1/3	1/3	1/3	0	0	0	− 1/3	− 1/3	− 1/3
$\hat\psi_B$	1/3	0	− 1/3	1/3	0	− 1/3	1/3	0	− 1/3
$\hat\psi_{AB}$	1/9	0	− 1/9	0	0	0	− 1/9	0	1/9

equally spaced, the $A \times B$ contrast just examined would be termed a linear-by-linear interaction.) As many other interaction comparisons as are of interest could be investigated using this method.

Although tetrad interaction contrasts may not always be easy to interpret when defined in terms of the $\hat{\mu}_{ij}$, at this point we introduce an alternative representation that may simplify interpretation. Let us examine the interaction contrast:

$$\begin{aligned}\hat{\psi} &= \hat{\mu}_{11} - \hat{\mu}_{13} - \hat{\mu}_{31} + \hat{\mu}_{33} \\ &= \log_e Y_{11} - \log_e Y_{13} - \log_e Y_{31} + \log_e Y_{33} \\ &= \log_e (Y_{11} Y_{33}/Y_{13} Y_{31})\end{aligned}$$

If we let:

$$g = Y_{11} Y_{33}/Y_{13} Y_{31}$$

we have a statistical measure that is called the *cross-products ratio* or the *odds ratio*. Under the hypothesis of independence, $P_{11} = P_{1.}P_{.1}$, $P_{33} = P_{3.}P_{.3}$, $P_{13} = P_{1.}P_{.3}$, and $P_{31} = P_{3.}P_{.1}$, so that $g = 1$ and $\hat{\psi} = 0$. Thus, the log-linear hypothesis $H_{0_{AB}}$: All $\gamma = 0$ is identical to the hypothesis $H_{0_{AB}}$: All $E(g) = 1$.

For our example:

$$r_1 = Y_{11}/Y_{31} = 230/15 = 15.333$$

$$r_2 = Y_{13}/Y_{33} = 9/54 = .167$$

where r_1 measures the odds of having often seen social mixing relative to having hardly ever seen social mixing, among those White students who made many new Black friends; whereas r_2 measures the same odds among White students who made no new Black friends. Note that when the hypothesis of independence holds, $r_1 = r_2$. Clearly, in this example, perceptions of social mixing are related to the number of new black friends made. For the four cells:

$$\frac{r_1}{r_2} = \frac{Y_{11}/Y_{31}}{Y_{13}/Y_{33}} = \frac{Y_{11} Y_{33}}{Y_{31} Y_{13}} = g$$

In this case:

$$g = \frac{230(54)}{15(9)} = 92$$

is significantly different from $E(g) = 1$. In particular, the odds of responding *often* relative to *hardly ever* on the social-mixing question is 92 times greater for White students who made many new Black friends than for those who made no new Black friends.

Measures of association for two-dimensional contingency tables: The interaction model. In addition to hypothesis testing and defining contrasts based on a log-linear analysis, other analogs to the familiar ANOVA model also exist. In the two-factor analysis of variance model, the sum of squares total is partitioned into sum of squares explained by A, B, and AB and a sum of squares unexplained, as follows:

$$SS_T = SS_A + SS_B + SS_{AB} + SS_U$$

From this partitioning, the proportion of the total sum of squares accounted for by A, B, and AB are computed as:

$$\hat{\eta}_A^2 = \frac{SS_A}{SS_T}, \qquad \hat{\eta}_B^2 = \frac{SS_B}{SS_T}, \qquad \text{and} \qquad \hat{\eta}_{AB}^2 = \frac{SS_{AB}}{SS_T}$$

For a two-dimensional contingency table based on the Karl Pearson X^2 statistic, Cramér (1946) has proposed that:

$$V = \frac{X^2}{NM}$$

where $M = \min(I - 1, J - 1)$, be used as a measure of the strength of association between the two variables. In this case, V is the ratio of the observed Chi-square statistic to the maximum Chi-square possible for an $I \times J$ contingency table based on N observations. Analogous measures can be proposed for each source of variance in a log-linear analysis, as follows:

$$V^* = \frac{\text{observed } G^2}{\text{maximum } G^2}$$

Since it can be shown that the maximum G_A^2, G_B^2, and G_{AB}^2 possible in an $I \times J$ contingency table are given, respectively, by:

$$\max G_A^2 = 2N \log_e I$$

$$\max G_B^2 = 2N \log_e J$$

$$\max G_{AB}^2 = 2N \log_e M^* \qquad \text{where } M^* = \min(I, J)$$

it follows that measures of association for the log-linear model can be defined as:

$$V_A^* = G_A^2/2N \log_e I$$

$$V_B^* = G_B^2/2N \log_e J$$

$$V_{AB}^* = G_{AB}^2/2N \log_e M^*$$

For the G^2 statistics of Table 10-12:

$$V_A^* = \frac{347.91}{2(1292) \log_e 3} = .1226 \simeq .12$$

$$V_B^* = \frac{609.48}{2(1292) \log_e 3} = .2147 \simeq .21 \quad \text{and}$$

$$V_{AB}^* = \frac{229.45}{2(1292) \log_e 3} = .0808 \simeq .08$$

Thus, for example, the observed G_{AB}^2 represents a value that is 8% as large as the maximum G_{AB}^2 that could have been obtained for these data based on $I = 3$, $J = 3$ and $N = 1292$. (Note that the Cramér statistic for the $A \times B$ interaction is given by

$$V = \frac{275.48}{1292(2)} = .1066 \simeq .11)$$

10-6. Omnibus tests for two-dimensional tables: The simple effects model

Just as the two-way factorial ANOVA design can be examined in terms of simple effects hypotheses, so can contingency tables that are analyzed according to the log-linear model. As an example, suppose that a researcher wished to examine social-mixing perceptions within each level of the variable, number of new friends made, where the responses are Many, Some, and None. For such a model, one assumes that:

$$L_{ij} = \log_e Y_{ij} = \mu + \alpha_{.j} + \alpha_{i(j)}$$

and then tests the hypotheses:

H_{0_B}: There are no column main effects, All $P_{.j} = 1/J$

$H_{0_{A(B)}}$: There are no row within column effects, $P_{i(j)} = 1/I$ for all j

Of course, H_{0_B} is tested in exactly the same way as was discussed for the interaction model. Concerning $H_{0_{A(B)}}$, for each level of B, let:

$$\hat{Y}_{i(j)} = \frac{1}{I} Y_{.j} = \text{expected frequency in the } i\text{th row of the } j\text{th cell under the assumption of row within column homogeneity}$$

For the present example:

$$\hat{Y}_{i(1)} = \frac{1}{3}(375) = 125.0000$$

$$\hat{Y}_{i(2)} = \frac{1}{3}(807) = 269.0000$$

$$\hat{Y}_{i(3)} = \frac{1}{3}(110) = 36.6667$$

so that:

$$G^2_{A(B1)} = 2[230 \log_e (230/125) + 130 \log_e (130/125) + 15 \log_e (15/125)]$$
$$= 227.08$$

$$G^2_{A(B2)} = 2[246 \log_e (246/269) + 478 \log_e (478/269) + 83 \log_e (83/269)]$$
$$= 310.43$$

$$G^2_{A(B3)} = 2[9 \log_e (9/36.6667) + 47 \log_e (47/36.6667) + 54 \log_e (54/36.6667)]$$
$$= 39.86$$

Note that:

$$G^2_{A(B)} = G^2_{A(B1)} + G^2_{A(B2)} + G^2_{A(B3)}$$
$$= 227.08 + 310.43 + 39.86$$
$$= 577.37$$

From our earlier calculations, we know that:

$$G^2_{A(B)} = G^2_A + G^2_{AB} = 347.92 + 229.45 = 577.37$$

providing another analogy to the classical ANOVA model. Similarly:

$$\begin{aligned} \nu_{A(B)} &= \nu_{A(B_1)} + \nu_{A(B_2)} + \nu_{A(B_3)} \\ &= (I-1) + (I-1) + (I-1) \\ &= J(I-1) = 3 = 6 \end{aligned}$$

$$\begin{aligned} \nu_A + \nu_{AB} &= (I-1) + (I-1)(J-1) \\ &= I - 1 + IJ - I - J + 1 \\ &= IJ - J \\ &= J(I-1) = 3(2) = 6 \end{aligned}$$

Also, consistent with the rationale adopted in Section 9-1, if in the interaction model, each source of variance were tested using $\alpha = .05$, then:

$$\alpha_A + \alpha_{AB} = .05 + .05 = .10$$

could be divided among the three simple effects hypotheses in order to preserve the experimentwise type I error probability. With .10 equally divided among the three hypotheses, we have that $\alpha_{A(B_j)} = .10/3 = .033$. With these alpha levels, the critical Chi-square value needed for each test is given by $\chi^2_{2:.967}$. In Table B-3, we find that $\chi^2_{2:.95} = 5.99$ and $\chi^2_{2:.975} = 7.38$. With simple linear interpolation, $\chi^2_{2:.967} = 7.07$. Since all three $G^2_{A(B_j)}$ statistics exceed 7.07, all three simple effects hypotheses can be rejected. In particular, within each level of number of new Black friends made, there are differences in social-mixing perceptions. Results are summarized in Table 10-17.

We now provide directions for performing a simple effects analysis, using the log-linear model. In these directions, assume that B effects and A within B effects are the ones of interest.

Procedure for performing a log-linear analysis of an $I \times J$ contingency table: The simple effects model.

Step 1. Compute G^2_T as in the interaction model.

Step 2. Test the hypothesis of column homogeneity as in the interaction model.

Step 3. Test the hypothesis of row homogeneity in column one, with:

$$G^2_{A(B1)} = 2 \sum_{i=1}^{I} Y_{i1} \log_e (Y_{i1}/\hat{Y}_{i1})$$

where:

Y_{i1} = observed frequency for the $(i1)$ cell and

$\hat{Y}_{i1} = \frac{1}{I} Y_{.j}$ = expected frequency for the $(i1)$ cell.

Reject H_0: $P_{i(1)} = \frac{1}{I}$ if $G^2_{A(B1)} > \chi^2_{I-1:1-\alpha}$.

Step 4. Repeat Step 3 for the remaining columns.

Contrasts in the two-dimensional contingency tables: The simple effects model. For simple effect contrasts, repeat the analysis described for the interaction model, but define contrasts within columns or rows depending on which way the simple effects are defined. If the effects are defined by columns and rows within columns,

TABLE 10-17. Log-linear analysis of the data of Table 10-10: The simple effects model

Source of Variance	d/f	G^2
Total	8	1186.80
B	2	609.48
A in B_1	2	227.08
A in B_2	2	310.43
A in B_3	2	39.86

the simple effect contrasts are defined as:

$$\hat{\psi}_{A(B_j)} = \sum_{i=1}^{I} a_{ij} \log_e Y_{ij} = \sum_{i=1}^{I} a_{ij}\hat{\mu}_{ij}$$

where:

$$\sum_{i=1}^{I} a_{ij} = 0 \qquad \text{and} \qquad SE_{\hat{\psi}} = \sqrt{\sum_{i=1}^{I} \frac{a_{ij}^2}{Y_{ij}}}$$

For post hoc comparisons, critical values are defined by:

$$\mathbf{S}^*_{A(B_j)} = \sqrt{\chi^2_{I-1:1-\alpha}}$$

If type I error control is made across all J columns, alpha is set equal to $(1/J)\ \alpha$.

For our example for White students who made many Black friends, the pairwise contrast of *often* versus *hardly ever* is given by:

$$\hat{\psi}_{A(B_1)} = \log_e 230 - \log_e 15 = 5.43808 - 2.70805 = 2.73003$$

with:

$$SE^2_{\hat{\psi}_{A(B_1)}} = \frac{1^2}{230} + \frac{-1^2}{15} = .07101$$

In this case:

$$\mathbf{S}^*_{A(B_1)} = \sqrt{\chi^2_{2:.967}} = \sqrt{7.07}$$

so that:

$$\begin{aligned}\psi_{A(B_1)} &= \hat{\psi}_{A(B_1)} \pm \mathbf{S}^*_{A(B_1)}\, SE_{\hat{\psi}_{A(B_1)}} \\ &= 2.73003 \pm \sqrt{7.07(.07101)} \\ &= 2.73 \pm .71\end{aligned}$$

Therefore, we conclude that P_{11} and P_{31} are different or that a monotonic trend exists among levels of Factor A within B_1. Other contrasts can be examined in a similar fashion.

Measures of association for two-dimensional contingency tables: The simple effects model. For simple effects of rows within columns, we can define a measure of association by:

$$V^*_{A(B_j)} = G^2_{A(B_j)}/2N_j \log_e I$$

In like manner, for simple effects defined for columns within rows:

$$V^*_{B(Ai)} = G^2_{B(Ai)}/2N_i \log_e J$$

For the data of Table 10-17:

$$G^2_{A(B1)} = \frac{227.08}{2(375)(\log_e 3)} = .2756 \simeq .28$$

$$G^2_{A(B2)} = \frac{310.43}{2(807)(\log_e 3)} = .1751 \simeq .18$$

$$G^2_{A(B3)} = \frac{39.86}{2(110)(\log_e 3)} = .1649 \simeq .16$$

10-7. Log-linear models for higher-order contingency tables

Unlike tests of significance based on simple Chi-square partitionings, those based on G^2 partitionings extend in a straightforward fashion to contingency tables based on three or more dimensions. In much the same way that the two-way analysis of variance can be extended, log-linear models can be generated for the treatment of three- or four-factor interactions, univariate repeated measures, and split-plot designs, incomplete factorial designs, the analysis of covariance, and so on. Unfortunately, an in-depth treatment of these topics would require the expansion of this chapter into a complete book. Because of these limitations, we will examine only what is termed the *saturated three-factor design.* By *saturated* is meant that as many parameters are estimated as there are cells in the design. Thus the previous $3(3) = 9$ cell design was saturated because our log-linear analysis was based on estimates of μ, two $\alpha_{i.}$ *values, two* $\alpha_{.j}$ values, and four γ_{ij} values, or $1 + 2 + 2 + 4 = 9$ independent parameters. As we recall, the linear restrictions on the parameters means that, for any $I \times J$ contingency table, the number of independent parameters is given by:

$$1 + (I - 1) + (J - 1) + (I - 1)(J - 1) = IJ$$

Complicated designs can be analyzed using canned computer programs that are designed to cover unsaturated and more complex designs. Our goal here is to show how the analysis parallels that of the familiar ANOVA. With this in mind, consider the data of Table 10-18. These data, which include information for two races, Blacks

TABLE 10-18. Perceived amount of social mixing and number of new friends made from the other race by Black and White students during the first year of a school desegregation program[a]

	C_1			C_2		
	B_1	B_2	B_3	B_1	B_2	B_3
A_1	230	246	9	244	191	19
A_2	130	478	47	109	259	49
A_3	15	83	54	12	59	37

[a] See Table 10-10 for definitions of A and B. C_1 Corresponds to White and C_2 to Black.

and Whites, are taken from the study described in Section 10-4. The three-factor saturated model for these data is based on the latent structure:

$$L_{ijk} = \log_e Y_{ijk} = \mu + \alpha_{i..} + \alpha_{.j.} + \alpha_{..k} + \gamma_{ij.} + \gamma_{i.k} + \gamma_{.jk} + \gamma_{ijk}$$

where:

$$\sum_{i=1}^{I} \alpha_{i..} = \sum_{j=1}^{J} \alpha_{.j.} = \sum_{k=1}^{K} \alpha_{..k} = \sum_{i=1}^{I} \gamma_{ij.} = \sum_{j=1}^{J} \gamma_{ij.}$$
$$= \sum_{i=1}^{I} \gamma_{i.k} = \sum_{k=1}^{K} \gamma_{i.k} = \sum_{j=1}^{J} \gamma_{.jk} = \sum_{k=1}^{K} \gamma_{.jk}$$
$$= \sum_{i=1}^{I} \gamma_{ijk} = \sum_{j=1}^{J} \gamma_{ijk} = \sum_{k=1}^{K} \gamma_{ijk} = 0$$

and:

$$\mu = \text{a standardizing constant}$$

The α's represent main effect parameters, the double-subscripted γ's represent two-factor interaction parameters, and the triple subscripted γ's represent three-factor interaction parameters. The hypotheses to be tested, along with the degrees of freedom associated with each test, are given by:

H_{0_A}: All $\alpha_{i..} = 0$ $\quad \nu_A = I - 1$

H_{0_B}: All $\alpha_{.j.} = 0$ $\quad \nu_B = J - 1$

H_{0_C}: All $\alpha_{..k} = 0$ $\quad \nu_C = K - 1$

$H_{0_{AB}}$: All $\gamma_{ij.} = 0$ $\quad \nu_{AB} = (I - 1)(J - 1)$

$H_{0_{AC}}$: All $\gamma_{i.k} = 0$ $\quad \nu_{AC} = (I - 1)(K - 1)$

$H_{0_{BC}}$: All $\gamma_{.jk} = 0$ $\quad \nu_{BC} = (J - 1)(K - 1)$

and:

$H_{0_{ABC}}$: All $\gamma_{ijk} = 0$ $\quad \nu_{ABC} = (I - 1)(J - 1)(K - 1)$

At this point we note that, although the saturated model was initially developed for situations in which a single sample of N individuals is cross-classified on the basis of two or more response variables, Goodman (1971) has argued that the model is also appropriate when there are one or more *population* variables combined with one or more *response* variables. According to this usage, population variables correspond to independent variables whose levels have sample sizes that are fixed prior to data collection, whereas response variables correspond to dependent variables whose levels have sample sizes that can be determined only after data collection. In the present example, all the students in one grade of a particular high school were administered a questionnaire. On the basis of their responses, students were cross-classified on the basis of race, number of new friends made, and perceived social mixing. Thus, here, the data will be analyzed in accordance with the originally conceived log-linear model, that is, a single sample with two or more response variables. Under such conditions, all main effects are potentially interesting and testable, in addition to the interactions of major interest. In practice, the proper distinction between fixed population variables and random response variables should be made and analyzed in accordance with models contained in available computer programs, such as *Everyman's Contingency Table Analyses (ECTA)*, *MULTIQUAL*, *Generalized Linear Model (GLIM)*, and *BMDP Biomedical Computer Programs, Series R*. Through these programs, we can test hypotheses of a response variable effect in a model containing one or more population variables. Finally, we should note that the hypothesis of complete independence can also be tested, if desired.

Before we provide analysis of the data of Table 10-18, we need to comment on the lack of orthogonality among the higher order interactions. The resulting tests are not independent. In the classical three-factor ANOVA design with unequal sample sizes, we encounter this problem of nonorthogonality by noting that the sum of squares of the components does not sum to the sum of squares total. In addition, the tests of hypothesis are interrelated and the problem of the appropriate mean squares for the tests is in question. This lack of independence exists for the tests of 2-, 3-, or higher-order interactions in multidimensional contingency tables. No clear solution exists for this problem, but the solution suggested by Brown (1976) is presented in the next section.

10-8. Omnibus tests for higher order contingency tables: The saturated interaction model

To analyze the data of Table 10-18, we use the general approach described in Section 10-5 for the interaction model. In doing this, however, we recognize that alternative techniques are available, including those in which individual model parameters are estimated and tested for significance, and those that rely on the stepwise, model-building approach discussed in Sections 10-2 and 10-3.

Extensions of the tests described in Section 10-5 to a three-dimensional or higher-order contingency table require a number of adjustments, even though the basic theory is not different. The source of the problem is tied to the problem of defining independence for three or more variables. For example, consider three events A, B, and C. These events are said to be independent if, and only if, the following four relationships are satisfied:

1. $P(A \text{ and } B \text{ and } C) = P(A)P(B)P(C)$
2. $P(A \text{ and } B) = P(A)P(B)$
3. $P(A \text{ and } C) = P(A)P(C)$
4. $P(B \text{ and } C) = P(B)P(C)$

This means that the tests of $A \times B$, $A \times C$, and $B \times C$ cannot be conducted *free* of the test of $A \times B \times C$. This problem creates a few modifications in the methods used for two-dimensional contingency tables.

The first modification requires that G^2_{ABC} be computed before the test of the two-variable contingency tables is performed. In Step 8, we will show that $G^2_{ABC} = 6.32$. This value will be used in the three two-factor tests of our example.

The second modification results from the fact that in this context, a two-factor interaction can be defined in two different ways. For example, consider the $A \times B$ test of $H_{0_{AB}}$: All $\gamma_{ij.} = 0$. This test is confounded by the possible existence of a three-factor interaction where some of the $\gamma_{ijk} \neq 0$. Brown (1976) has suggested a solution to this problem. His suggestion is to make both an *unconditional* and a *conditional* test of the hypothesis.

As will be seen, the estimates of Y_{ijk} for testing the $A \times B$ interaction can be obtained according to different procedures. These are:

1. Estimate the Y_{ijk} by fixing the totals in the expected table to agree in both their A marginal totals and their B marginal totals, and:
2. Estimate the Y_{ijk} by summing the observed frequencies across C, and then use the methods of Section 10-5 to test the hypothesis.

The first procedure provides a test of *partial association*, a conditional test, whereas the second procedure provides a test of *marginal association*, an unconditional test.

Brown recommends that both tests be performed. If both tests lead to rejection, then the hypothesis of no $A \times B$ interaction, $H_{0_{AB}}$, is rejected. If both tests are not significant, $H_{0_{AB}}$ is not rejected. Finally, if one of the tests rejects $H_{0_{AB}}$ and the other does not, decisions must be made on theoretical or practical considerations.

If we let G^2_{AB} refer to fixing the A and B margins for each level of C, the degrees of freedom for G^2_{AB} are given by:

$$\begin{aligned}\nu_{AB} &= \nu_{AB\cdot C_1} + \nu_{AB\cdot C_2} + \cdots + \nu_{AB\cdot C_K}\\ &= (I-1)(J-1) + (I-1)(J-1) + \cdots + (I-1)(J-1)\\ &= K(I-1)(J-1)\end{aligned}$$

The test statistic for the partial, or conditional, test of association,

$H_{0_{AB\cdot C}}$: All $(\gamma_{ij})_k = 0$ is given by:

$$G^2_{AB\cdot C} = G^2_{AB} - G^2_{ABC}$$

with degrees of freedom:

$$\begin{aligned}\nu_{AB\cdot C} &= \nu_{AB} - \nu_{ABC}\\ &= K(I-1)(J-1) - (K-1)(I-1)(J-1)\\ &= (I-1)(J-1)\end{aligned}$$

In contrast, for the marginal or unconditional test of $H_{0_{AB}}$: All $\gamma_{ij.} = 0$, we sum the Y_{ijk} across $k = 1, 2, \ldots, K$ to obtain:

$$Y_{ij.} = Y_{ij1} + Y_{ij2} + \cdots + Y_{ijK}$$

The method of Section 10-5 is now applied to these summed (marginal) frequencies. If we denote the corresponding test statistic, $G^2_{AB\cdot M}$, we make a decision about $H_{0_{AB\cdot M}}$ by referring $G^2_{AB\cdot M}$ to the Chi-square distribution with $\nu_{AB\cdot M} = (I-1)(J-1)$. Note that the degrees of freedom for both the conditional and unconditional test are the same.

We now return to our example. Because of the complexity of the computations, however, we do not provide directions. The analysis would normally be done on a computer and, thus, we simply describe the results for the data of Table 10-18. Because of the notational complexities, we perform the analysis step-by-step, keeping symbolism to a minimum. Throughout the analysis, we report results to two-place decimal accuracy.

Step 1. To check subsequent computations, we compute G^2_T, under the assumption of equality of proportions in the $IJK = 3(3)(2) = 18$ cells. For the data of Table 10-18, $N = 2271$ and $\hat{Y}_{ijk} = 2271(1/18) = 126.17$, so that:

$$G_T^2 = 2[230 \log_e (230/126.17) + \cdots + 37 \log_e (37/126.17)] = 1939.79$$

For completeness, we note that $\nu_T = IJK - 1 = 18 - 1 = 17$.

Step 2. We now test the hypothesis of homogeneity for Factor A:

$$\text{H}_{0_A}\text{:} \quad P_{i..} = 1/I$$

For the data of Table 10-18, $\hat{Y}_{i..} = 2271(1/3) = 757$. Using the marginal frequency values reported in Table 10-19, we find that:

$$G_A^2 = 2[939 \log_e (939/757) + 1072 \log_e (1072/757) + 260 \log_e (260/757)]$$
$$= 594.84$$

With $\alpha = .05$, we reject the hypothesis of homogeneity for Factor A because, with $\nu_A = (I - 1) = 3 - 1 = 2$, $G_A^2 = 594.84$ is greater than $\chi^2_{2:.95} = 5.99$.

Step 3. We now test the hypothesis of homogeneity for Factor B:

$$\text{H}_{0_B}\text{:} \quad P_{.j.} = 1/J$$

For the data of Table 10-18, $\hat{Y}_{.j.} = 2271(1/3) = 757$. Using the marginal frequencies reported in Table 10-19, we find that:

$$G_B^2 = 2[740 \log_e (740/757) + 1316 \log_e (1316/757) + 215 \log_e (215/757)]$$
$$= 880.60$$

With $\alpha = .05$ and $\nu_B = (J - 1) = (3 - 1) = 2$, we reject the hypothesis of homogeneity for Factor B because $G_B^2 = 880.60$ is greater than $\chi^2_{2:.95} = 5.99$.

Step 4. We now test the hypothesis of homogeneity for Factor C:

$$\text{H}_{0_C}\text{:} \quad P_{..k} = 1/K$$

For the data of Table 10-18, $\hat{Y}_{..k} = 2271(1/2) = 1135.5$. Using the marginal frequencies reported in Table 10-19, we find that:

$$G_C^2 = 2[1292 \log_e (1292/1135.5) + 979 \log_e (979/1135.5)] = 43.28$$

TABLE 10-19. Observed totals for the data of Table 10-18 With $N = 2271$

A Totals	A_1	A_2	A_3						
	939	1072	260						
B Totals	B_1	B_2	B_3						
	740	1316	215						
C Totals		C_1	C_2						
		1292	979						
$A \times B$ Totals	A_1B_1	A_1B_2	A_1B_3	A_2B_1	A_2B_2	A_2B_3	A_3B_1	A_3B_2	A_3B_3
	474	437	28	239	737	96	27	142	91
$A \times C$ Totals		A_1C_1	A_1C_2	A_2C_1	A_2C_2	A_3C_1	A_3C_2		
		485	454	655	417	152	108		
$B \times C$ Totals		B_1C_1	B_1C_2	B_2C_1	B_2C_2	B_3C_1	B_3C_2		
		375	365	807	509	110	105		

With $\alpha = .05$ and $\nu_C = (K - 1) = (2 - 1) = 1$, we reject the hypothesis of homogeneity for Factor C because $G_C^2 = 43.28$ is greater than $\chi^2_{1:.95} = 3.84$.

Step 5. We now test the conditional hypothesis that Factors A and B do not interact:

$$\text{H}_{0_{AB \cdot C}}\text{: All } (\gamma_{ij})_k = 0, \qquad \text{or} \qquad P_{ijk} = P_{i..}P_{.j.}$$

To obtain the expected values for this test, we sum the frequencies across the C factor of Table 10-18 and obtain the familiar estimated expected frequencies for an $I \times J$ contingency table. Thus the estimated expected frequency for cell $A_1B_1C_1$ is computed from Table 10-19 as:

$$\hat{Y}^{(1)}_{111} = N(\hat{P}_{1..}\hat{P}_{.1.}) = N(Y_{1..}/N)(Y_{.1.}/N)$$
$$= 2271(939/2271)(740/2271) = 305.97$$

The remaining estimated expected frequencies are reported in Table 10-20 under the heading, first iteration; hence the designation, $\hat{Y}^{(1)}_{ijk}$. Unfortunately these estimates cannot be used to compute $G^2_{AB \cdot C}$ because the marginal totals do not equal the marginal totals of Table 10-18, as reported in Table 10-19. Thus we must adjust the estimated expected frequencies so that they will yield marginal totals that correspond to those of the observed frequency table. In general, in order to obtain an appropriate test of a particular interaction, we must adjust the table of expected frequencies so that the marginal totals correspond to those of the observed table *for every effect other than the one of interest.* At this point in the present example, we seek to reproduce all the totals reported in Table 10-19, except the $A \times B$ totals. To achieve this requires one or more adjustments of the expected frequencies obtained by the first iteration.

We illustrate the adjustment procedure for the $\hat{Y}^{(1)}_{111}$ entry. For the C_1 part of the complete table and for the A_1 level in C_1, we see from Table 10-19 that the total is equal to 485, whereas in Table 10-20 for the first iteration, summing across levels of B yields:

$$305.97 + 544.13 + 88.90 = 939$$

Clearly, 305.97 is too large an expected frequency for cell $A_1B_1C_1$. If we were to keep

TABLE 10-20. Estimated expected frequencies for testing the hypothesis that all $\gamma_{ij.} = 0$

First iteration ($Y^{(1)}_{ijk}$)					
305.97	544.13	88.90	305.97	544.13	88.90
349.31	621.20	101.49	349.31	621.20	101.49
84.72	150.66	24.61	84.72	150.66	24.61
Second iteration ($Y^{(2)}_{ijk}$)					
158.04	281.05	45.92	147.93	263.08	42.98
213.43	379.56	62.01	135.88	241.64	39.48
49.53	88.08	14.39	35.19	62.58	10.22
Third iteration ($Y^{(3)}_{ijk}$)					
140.77	302.94	41.29	169.26	236.04	48.69
190.11	409.12	55.76	155.47	216.81	44.73
44.12	94.94	12.94	40.26	56.15	11.58

the proportions in the two series the same, we should reduce $\hat{Y}^{(1)}_{111}$ to satisfy the equation:

$$\hat{Y}^{(2)}_{111}/\hat{Y}^{(1)}_{111} = 485/939$$

so that:

$$\hat{Y}^{(2)}_{111} = \hat{Y}^{(1)}_{111}\,(485/939) = 305.97(485/939) = 158.04$$

In like manner:

$$\hat{Y}^{(2)}_{112} = \hat{Y}^{(1)}_{112}\,(454/939) = 305.97(454/939) = 147.93$$

The remaining estimated expected frequencies are reported in Table 10-20 under the heading, second iteration. Here, even though the various A_iC_k totals can be shown to correspond to those in Table 10-19, the totals involving the B_j are still in error, and thus the adjustment procedure must be continued. For example, from Table 10-19 we see that the observed B_1C_1 total is equal to 375, whereas in the expected table for the second iteration, the B_1C_1 total is given by:

$$158.04 + 213.43 + 49.53 = 421.00$$

Maintaining equal proportions for the two sets of figures, we have that:

$$\hat{Y}^{(3)}_{111}/\hat{Y}^{(2)}_{111} = 375/421$$

so that:

$$\hat{Y}^{(3)}_{111} = \hat{Y}^{(2)}_{111}(375/421) = 158.04(375/421) = 140.77$$

In like manner:

$$\hat{Y}^{(3)}_{112} = \hat{Y}^{(2)}_{112}(365/319) = 147.93(365/319) = 169.26$$

Remaining values are shown in Table 10-20 under the heading, third iteration. At this point, our adjustment procedure has proven successful, for now it can be seen that all marginal totals, with the exception of $A \times B$, match those reported in Table 10-19. Consequently, we compute:

$$G^2_{AB} = 2[230 \log_e (230/140.77) + \cdots + 37 \log_e (37/11.58)]$$
$$= 377.69$$

At this point, we recall that the Y_{ijk} values are found conditional on the $Y_{i.k}$ and $Y_{.jk}$ marginal frequencies. The degrees of freedom associated with G^2_{AB} are found by noting that for $C = 1$, $\nu_{AB\cdot 1} = (I - 1)(J - 1) = (3 - 1)(3 - 1) = 4$ and for $C = 2$, $\nu_{AB\cdot 2} = (I - 1)(J - 1) = (3 - 1)(3 - 1) = 4$, so that $\nu_{AB} = \nu_{AB\cdot 1} + \nu_{AB\cdot 2} = 4 + 4 = 8$. For $C = K$, $\nu_{AB} = K(I - 1)(J - 1)$. In Step 8, we show that $G^2_{ABC} = 6.32$ with $\nu_{ABC} = (I - 1)(J - 1)(K - 1) = (3 - 1)(3 - 1)(2 - 1) = 4$. We use these values for the partial association test. With these figures:

$$G^2_{AB\cdot C} = G^2_{AB} - G^2_{ABC} = 377.69 - 6.32 = 371.37$$

and:

$$\nu_{AB\cdot C} = \nu_{AB} - \nu_{ABC} = (I - 1)(J - 1) = (3 - 1)(3 - 1) = 4$$

With $\alpha = .05$, we reject $\text{H}_{0_{AB \cdot C}}$, since 371.37 is considerably larger than $\chi^2_{4:.95} = 9.49$.

We reiterate that $G^2_{AB \cdot C}$ provides a test of no partial association, which can be stated as:

$$\text{H}_{0_{AB \cdot C}}\text{:}\quad \text{All } (\gamma_{ij})_k = 0$$

According to Brown's (1976) recommendation, we must also test the unconditional hypothesis:

$$\text{H}_{0_{AB \cdot M}}\text{:}\quad \text{All } \gamma_{ij.} = 0$$

We do this by finding the $Y_{ij.}$ frequencies and applying the methods of Section 10-5 to them. The expected values for this marginal test of association appears in Table 10-20 as the first iteration, $\hat{Y}^{(1)}_{ijk}$, values. The corresponding marginal frequencies $Y_{ij.}$, are reported in Table 10-19. With these values:

$$G^2_{AB \cdot M} = 2[474\log_e(474/305.97) + 437\log_e(437/544.13) + \cdots + \log_e(91/24.61)]$$
$$= 377.95$$

The degrees of freedom for this test are given by:

$$\nu_{AB \cdot M} = (I - 1)(J - 1) = (3 - 1)(3 - 1) = 4$$

With $\alpha = .05$, the marginal test of $\text{H}_{0_{AB}}$ is rejected. Because both tests lead to the same decision, we reject the hypothesis of no $A \times B$ interaction with confidence.

Step 6. We now test the hypothesis that Factors A and C do not interact, by way of the tests:

$$\text{H}_{0_{AC \cdot B}}\text{:}\quad \text{All } (\gamma_{ik})_j = 0, \text{ or } P_{ijk} = P_{i..}P_{..k}$$

$$\text{H}_{0_{AC \cdot M}}\text{:}\quad \text{All } \gamma_{i.k} = 0$$

We repeat the process of Step 5 to find the expected frequencies needed for these test statistics. We do not show the arithmetic for this set of iterations, but summarize the results in Table 10-21. To obtain the expected frequencies for the first iteration, we consider the set of 3 × 2 contingency tables defined by A and C for each level of B.

TABLE 10-21. Estimated expected frequencies for testing the hypothesis that all $\gamma_{i.k} = 0$

	B_1		B_2		B_3	
	C_1	C_2	C_1	C_2	C_1	C_2
Zero iteration (original data)						
A_1	230	244	246	191	9	19
A_2	130	109	478	259	47	49
A_3	15	12	83	59	54	37
First iteration						
	534.21	404.79	534.21	404.79	534.21	404.79
	609.87	462.13	609.87	462.13	609.87	462.13
	147.92	112.08	147.92	112.08	147.92	112.08
Third iteration						
	240.20	233.79	267.98	169.02	14.32	13.67
	121.11	117.89	451.94	285.06	49.12	46.88
	13.68	13.32	87.08	54.92	46.56	44.44

For this hypothesis:

$$\hat{Y}^{(1)}_{111} = 2271(939/2271)(1292/2271) = 534.21$$

$$\hat{Y}^{(2)}_{111} = 534.21(474/939) = 269.67$$

and:

$$\hat{Y}^{(3)}_{111} = 240.20$$

For the third iteration, for which all expected totals except $A \times C$ match those of Table 10-19, we have that:

$$G^2_{AC} = 2[230 \log_e (230/240.20) + \cdots + 37 \log_e (37/44.44)] = 18.29$$

The degrees of freedom for G^2_{AC} are given by:

$$\nu_{AC} = J(I-1)(K-1)$$

For the test of $\mathrm{H}_{0_{AC \cdot B}}$, we compute:

$$G^2_{AC \cdot B} = G^2_{AC} - G^2_{ABC} = 18.29 - 6.32 = 11.97$$

The degrees of freedom for this statistic are given by:

$$\nu_{AC \cdot B} = \nu_{AC} - \nu_{ABC} = (I-1)(K-1) = (3-1)(2-1) = 2$$

With $\alpha = .05$, we reject the hypothesis of no partial association, $\mathrm{H}_{0_{AC \cdot B}}$: All $(\gamma_{ik})_j = 0$, between A and C because $G^2_{AC \cdot B} = 11.97$ is greater than $\chi^2_{2:.95} = 5.99$.

For the marginal test of no association, $\mathrm{H}_{0_{AC \cdot M}}$: All $\gamma_{i.k} = 0$, we have:

$$G^2_{AC \cdot M} = 2[485 \log_e (485/534.21) + 454 \log_e (454/404.79) + \cdots + 108 \log_e (108/112.08)] = 18.74$$

In this case we also reject $\mathrm{H}_{0_{AC \cdot M}}$ and conclude that A and C interact. Thus, once again, the conditional and unconditional tests lead to the same conclusion.

Step 7. We now test the hypothesis that Factors B and C do not interact, in terms of the two tests of:

$\mathrm{H}_{0_{BC \cdot A}}$: All $(\gamma_{jk})_i = 0$, or $P_{ijk} = P_{.j.}P_{..k}$

$\mathrm{H}_{0_{BC \cdot M}}$: All $\gamma_{.jk} = 0$

We repeat the process of Step 5 to find the expected frequencies needed for these test statistics. We do not show the arithmetic, but summarize the results in Table 10-22, for the set of 3×2 contingency tables for B and C at each level of A. For this hypothesis:

$$G^2_{BC} = 2[230 \log_e (230/244.82) + \cdots + 37 \log_e (37/37.80)] = 24.78$$

The degrees of freedom for G^2_{BC} are given by:

$$\nu_{BC} = I(J-1)(K-1)$$

We now compute $G^2_{BC \cdot A}$ as:

$$G^2_{BC \cdot A} = G^2_{BC} - G^2_{ABC} = 24.78 - 6.32 = 18.46$$

TABLE 10-22. Estimated expected frequencies for testing the hypothesis that all $\gamma_{.jk} = 0$

	A_1			A_2			A_3		
	B_1	B_2	B_3	B_1	B_2	B_3	B_1	B_2	B_3
Zero iteration (original data)									
C_1	230	246	9	130	478	47	15	83	54
C_2	244	191	19	109	259	49	12	59	37
First iteration									
	421.00	748.69	122.32	421.00	748.69	122.32	421.00	748.69	122.32
	319.00	567.31	92.68	319.00	567.31	92.68	319.00	567.31	92.68
Third iteration									
	244.82	225.71	14.46	146.03	450.31	58.66	15.78	83.02	53.20
	229.18	211.29	13.54	92.97	286.69	37.34	11.22	58.98	37.80

The degrees of freedom for this statistic are given by:

$$\nu_{BC \cdot A} = \nu_{BC} - \nu_{ABC} = (J - 1)(K - 1) = (3 - 1)(2 - 1) = 2$$

With $\alpha = .05$, we reject the hypothesis of no partial association, $\mathrm{H}_{0_{BC \cdot A}}$: All $(\gamma_{jk})_i = 0$, between B and C because 18.46 is greater than $\chi^2_{2:.95} = 5.99$.

For the test of no marginal association:

$$G^2_{BC \cdot M} = 2[375 \log_e (375/421.00) + 807 \log_e (807/748.69) + \cdots + 105 \log_e (105/92.68)] = 25.05$$

We reject $\mathrm{H}_{0_{BC \cdot M}}$ and conclude that B and C interact. Thus, once again, we have reached consistent decisions.

Step 8. We now test the hypothesis that the three-factor interaction is zero:

$$H_{0_{ABC}}: \text{ All } \gamma_{ijk} = 0$$

If the three-factor interaction were not significant, then the $A \times B$ interactions for C_1 and C_2 would be identical. Thus, in the first iteration portion of Table 10-23, C_1 and C_2 have been combined, with the resulting cell frequencies obtained by averaging over the two levels of C. Thus, since it can be seen from Table 10-19 that the A_1B_1 total is 474:

$$\hat{Y}^{(1)}_{111} = \frac{1}{2}(474) = 237$$

The remaining first iteration estimates are shown in Table 10-23. We now apply the iteration process to these first iteration estimates. After 10 iterations, all expected frequency totals come within .01 of the corresponding observed totals. At that point:

$$G^2_{ABC} = 2[230 \log_e (230/226.69) + \cdots + 37 \log_e (37/43.83)] = 6.32$$

with
$$\nu_{ABC} = (I - 1)(J - 1)(K - 1) = (3 - 1)(3 - 1)(2 - 1) = 4$$

TABLE 10-23. **Estimated expected frequencies for testing the hypothesis that all $\gamma_{ijk} = 0$**

Zero iteration (original data)

	C_1			C_2		
	B_1	B_2	B_3	B_1	B_2	B_3
A_1	230	246	9	244	191	19
A_2	130	478	47	109	259	49
A_3	15	83	54	12	59	37

First iteration

	237	218.5	14	237	218.5	14
	119.5	368.5	48	119.5	368.5	48
	13.5	71	45.5	13.5	71	45.5

Tenth iteration

	226.69	245.85	12.46	247.31	191.15	15.55
	133.41	471.21	50.38	105.59	265.79	45.62
	14.90	89.94	47.17	12.10	52.06	43.83

With $\alpha = .05$, we do not reject the hypothesis that the three-factor interaction is zero, since $G^2_{ABC} = 6.32$ is less than $\chi^2_{4;.95} = 9.49$. The complete analysis is summarized in Table 10-24. It should be noted that the seven constituent G^2 statistics do not sum to G^2_T. This difference arises because of the hierarchical nature and nonorthogonality of the tests.

We now wish to comment about the nonorthogonality of the analysis. For this, note that:

$$G^2_A + G^2_B + G^2_C = 594.84 + 880.60 + 43.28 = 1518.72$$

$$G^2_{AB \cdot C} + G^2_{AC \cdot B} + G^2_{BC \cdot A} = 371.37 + 11.97 + 18.46 = 401.80$$

and:

$$G^2_{ABC} = 6.32$$

so that:

$$1518.72 + 401.80 + 6.32 = 1926.84$$

does not equal $G^2_T = 1939.79$. The nonorthogonality is related to the fact that $G^2_{AB \cdot C}$, $G^2_{AC \cdot B}$, and $G^2_{BC \cdot A}$ are confounded with G^2_{ABC}. A similar confounding exists in terms of $G^2_{AB \cdot M}$, $G^2_{AC \cdot M}$, and $G^2_{BC \cdot M}$.

In our example, we have illustrated the analysis of a three-dimensional set of frequencies in the form of a three-factor ANOVA with interactions. The specific model that we used is not necessary, since the entire analysis can be approached from a flexible model-building approach. This approach can be illustrated for the data of Table 10-18 and the summary statistics obtained from the computer program *BMDP3F* of the *BMDP Biomedical Computer Programs P-Series*, 1977, University of California Press. Statistics appear in Table 10-25. This table can be used to generate the results of Table 10-24 and other tests.

Because the *BMD* program takes computational advantage of the hierarchical properties of G^2-type statistics, one can analyze multidimensional contingency tables with ease and with considerable flexibility. Consider the hypothesis:

$$H_{0_B}: \quad \text{All } \alpha_{\cdot j \cdot} = 0$$

TABLE 10-24. Full log-linear model

Source of variance	d/f	G^2 (Conditional)	G^2 (Marginal)	Statistical decision
A	2	594.84	594.84	Significant
B	2	880.60	880.60	Significant
C	1	43.28	43.28	Significant
$A \times B$	4	371.37	377.95	Significant
$A \times C$	2	11.97	18.74	Significant
$B \times C$	2	18.46	25.05	Significant
$A \times B \times C$	4	6.32	6.32	Not significant
Total		1926.84*	1946.78*	

* Total does not equal $G_T^2 = 1939.79$

TABLE 10-25. All possible models for a three-factor study based on log-linear statistics

Model	Variables in the model	d/f	G^2
1	None	17	1939.91
2	A (Mixing)	15	1345.06
3	B (Friendship)	15	1059.31
4	C (Perceiver)	16	1896.63
5	A, B	13	464.47
6	A, C	14	1301.79
7	B, C	14	1016.03
8	A, B, C	12	421.19
9	A, B, AB	9	86.57
10	A, C, AC	12	990.99
11	B, C, BC	12	1283.28
12	A, B, C, AB	8	43.29
13	A, B, C, AC	10	396.15
14	A, B, C, BC	10	402.68
15	A, B, C, AB, AC	6	18.25
16	A,B, C, AB, BC	6	24.78
17	A, B, C, AC, BC	8	377.64
18	A, B, C, AB, AC, BC	4	6.32
19	A, B, C, AB, AC, BC, ABC	0	0.00

This hypothesis can be tested in a number of different ways. For this discussion, let us denote G_T^2 as G_0^2 to indicate that only the mean value, $P_{ijk} = (1/IJK)\,N$ is fitted to the data. With this notation:

$$G_B^2 = G_0^2 - G_{0,B}^2 = 1939.91 - 1059.31 = 880.60$$

with $\nu_B = \nu_0 - \nu_{0,B} = 17 - 15 = 2$.

Alternatively:

$$G_B^2 = G_A^2 - G_{A,B}^2 = 1345.06 - 474.47 = 880.60$$

$$G_B^2 = G_C^2 - G_{B,C}^2 = 1896.63 - 1016.03 = 880.60$$

$$G_B^2 = G_{A,C}^2 - G_{A,B,C}^2 = 1301.79 - 421.19 = 880.60$$

The log-linear statistic for the marginal test of the $A \times B$ interaction can be obtained in four ways as:

$$G_{AB}^2 = G_{A,B}^2 - G_{A,B,AB}^2 = 464.47 - 86.57 = 377.90$$

$$G_{AB}^2 = G_{A,B,C}^2 - G_{A,B,C,AB}^2 = 421.19 - 43.29 = 377.90$$

$$G^2_{AB} = G^2_{A,B,C,AC} - G^2_{A,B,C,AB,AC} = 402.68 - 24.78 = 377.90$$

$$G^2_{AB} = G^2_{A,B,C,BC} - G^2_{A,B,C,AB,BC} = 396.15 - 18.25 = 377.90$$

These values differ from the $A \times B$ interaction G^2_{AB} of Table 10-24, since the figures in Table 10-24 were computed by hand with only two-place accuracy. The *BMD* figures are determined with three-place accuracy. Finally, the conditional test of no $A \times B$ interaction can be obtained as:

$$G^2_{AB \cdot C} = G^2_{A,B,C,AB,AC,BC} - G^2_{A,B,C,AC,BC} = 337.64 - 6.32 = 371.32$$

Table 10-25 can be used for model building since the G^2 values correspond to goodness-of-fit statistics. The closer to zero, the better is the fit. In this sense, Model 19 yields the best fit, since for this model, $G^2 = 0$. However, it is a model with little utility, since all sources of variance must be included, so that $\nu = 0$. Model 18 is the next best-fitting model. Model 18 requires all three main effects and all three two-factor interactions to provide an adequate fit to the data. Model 15 serves as the next best description for the data. It is based on five significant sources of variance, *A*, *B*, *C*, *AB*, and *BC*. Even so, there is a significant residual G^2 of 86.57. Model 9 might also be considered as a competitor to Model 18, in that it is more parsimonious in requiring only three sources of variance, *A*, *B*, and *AB*.

Finally, we should note that the Brown recommendation to perform both the conditional and unconditional test has been questioned by Fienberg (1980) mainly because it can lead to inconsistent decisions. As he states, "Since the two test statistics used for a given effect do not bound all possible values of the conditional test statistic for that effect, Brown's screening approach is fallible, and it should be used with caution" (p. 81).

Contrasts in higher-order contingency tables: The saturated interaction model. Planned and post hoc contrasts based on main effects and two-factor interactions follow directly from the corresponding material discussed in Section 10-5. In particular, main effect contrasts are defined in the following terms:

$$\hat{\mu}_{i..} = \frac{1}{JK} \sum_{j=1}^{J} \sum_{k=1}^{K} \log_e Y_{ijk} \qquad (A \text{ main effect})$$

$$\hat{\mu}_{.j.} = \frac{1}{IK} \sum_{i=1}^{I} \sum_{k=1}^{K} \log_e Y_{ijk} \qquad (B \text{ main effect})$$

$$\hat{\mu}_{..k} = \frac{1}{IJ} \sum_{i=1}^{I} \sum_{j=1}^{J} \log_e Y_{ijk} \qquad (C \text{ main effect})$$

whereas two-factor interaction contrasts are defined in terms of the:

$$\hat{\mu}_{ij.} = \frac{1}{K} \sum_{k=1}^{K} \log_e Y_{ijk} \qquad (A \times B \text{ interaction})$$

$$\hat{\mu}_{i.k} = \frac{1}{J} \sum_{j=1}^{J} \log_e Y_{ijk} \qquad (A \times C \text{ interaction})$$

$$\hat{\mu}_{.jk} = \frac{1}{I} \sum_{i=1}^{I} \log_e Y_{ijk} \qquad (B \times C \text{ interaction})$$

as in Section 10-5.

Three-factor interaction contrasts are defined directly in terms of the $\hat{\mu}_{ijk} = \log_e Y_{ijk}$. In this case, however, differences in the difference-in-difference, or tetrad, contrast of Section 10-5 are legitimately subsumed by the three-way interaction. To illustrate, consider the $A \times B$ interaction contrast investigated previously; that is:

$$\hat{\psi}_{AB} = (\hat{\mu}_{11} - \hat{\mu}_{13}) - (\hat{\mu}_{31} - \hat{\mu}_{33})$$

but augmented to include differences associated with the two levels of Factor C. In particular, if we cross $\hat{\psi}_{AB}$ with $\hat{\psi}_C = \hat{\mu}_{..1} - \hat{\mu}_{..2}$, we obtain:

$$\begin{aligned}\hat{\psi}_{ABC} &= [(\hat{\mu}_{111} - \hat{\mu}_{131}) - (\hat{\mu}_{311} - \hat{\mu}_{331})] - [(\hat{\mu}_{112} - \hat{\mu}_{132}) - (\hat{\mu}_{312} - \hat{\mu}_{332})] \\ &= \log_e Y_{111} - \log_e Y_{131} - \cdots - \log_e Y_{332} \\ &= \log_e 230 - \log_e 9 - \cdots - \log_e 37 \\ &= .84305\end{aligned}$$

As before:

$$\begin{aligned}SE^2_{\hat{\psi}_{ABC}} &= \sum_{i=1}^{3} \sum_{j=1}^{3} \sum_{k=1}^{2} \frac{a^2_{ijk}}{Y_{ijk}} \\ &= (1/230 + 1/9 + \cdots + 1/37) \\ &= .36773\end{aligned}$$

With the critical value given by:

$$\mathbf{S}^*_{ABC} = \sqrt{\chi^2_{(I-1)(J-1)(K-1):1-\alpha}} = \sqrt{\chi^2_{4:.95}} = \sqrt{9.49}$$

we obtain:

$$\begin{aligned}\psi_{ABC} &= \hat{\psi}_{ABC} \pm \mathbf{S}^*_{ABC}\, SE_{\hat{\psi}_{ABC}} \\ &= .84305 \pm \sqrt{9.49(.36773)} \\ &= .84 \pm 1.87\end{aligned}$$

thereby indicating a nonsignificant difference. Naturally this is to be expected of all contrasts involving the $A_iB_jC_k$, inasmuch as the omnibus G^2_{ABC} test was also statistically nonsignificant. Finally, it should be apparent that the Dunn-Bonferroni procedure could replace the post hoc approach just discussed.

Measures of association for higher-order contingency tables: The saturated interaction model. Measures of association, based on the V^* statistic, parallel those discussed in Section 10-5 for two-factor contingency tables. Thus:

$$V^*_A = G^2_A/2N \log_e I$$

$$V^*_B = G^2_B/2N \log_e J$$

$$V^*_C = G^2_C/2N \log_e K$$

$$V^*_{AB} = G^2_{AB}/2N \log_e M^*$$

$$V^*_{AC} = G^2_{AC}/2N \log_e M^*$$

$$V^*_{BC} = G^2_{BC}/2N \log_e M^*$$

and:

$$V^*_{ABC} = G^2_{ABC}/2N \log_e M^*$$

where M^* = the number of levels of the constituent variable with the minimum number of levels. Thus, for V^*_{AB}, $M^* = \min(I, J)$; for V^*_{AC}, $M^* = \min(I, K)$; for V^*_{BC}, $M^* = \min(J, K)$; and for V^*_{ABC}, $M^* = \min(I, J, K)$. Results for the present example may be computed using the values in Table 10-24. Based on these values, the B main effect may be found to be the largest, with the obtained G^2_B representing about 18% of the maximum G^2_B for a table based on three columns and $N = 2271$ observations.

10-9. Canonical analysis of a two-dimensional contingency table

At first thought, it would seem that the application of quantitative methods to qualitative data would prove fruitless. Yet, as was indicated in Chapter 5, it is possible to apply the general canonical correlation model to investigating the association between the two qualitative variables of a two-dimensional contingency table. The procedure we use here follows the presentation of Kendall and Stuart (1967) and is based on the definition of $I + J$ indicator variables to represent the margins of a typical $I \times J$ contingency table.

In the discussion that follows, we will always assume that $I \leq J$. We illustrate the method using the data of Table 10-26, which are taken from an exercise found in Marascuilo and McSweeney (1977, p. 242). The data are based on a nationwide survey of the American public's attitude toward abortion. In particular, 500 men were asked the question:

> Does a woman have the right to decide whether an unwanted birth can be terminated during the first three months of pregnancy? *Yes* *No* *No opinion*

Responses were broken down according to religious preference, as shown in Table 10-26. We begin by defining I zero-one indicator variables to represent the row categories. Thus let the elements in the first row be coded as $X_{1.} = (1, 0, \ldots, 0)$, the elements in the second row be coded as $X_{2.} = (0, 1, \ldots, 0)$, and the elements in the last row be coded as $X_{I.} = (0, 0, \ldots, 1)$. In like manner, we define J zero-one indicator variables to represent the column categories, with $Y_{.1} = (1, 0, \ldots, 0)$, $Y_{.2} = (0, 1, \ldots, 0), \ldots, Y_{.J} = (0, 0, \ldots, 1)$. Note that for each factor, we define as many indicator variables as there are categories, unlike the dummy coding system discussed in Chapter 3, where one less variable than the number of categories of a factor is defined. With the present system, then, linear dependence exists in each set of coded variables. However, the nonsingularity in the resulting matrix will be taken care of in the characteristic equation generated from the data. In terms of the $I + J$ coded variables, we now consider the two canonical variates:

$$\hat{X}^{(1)} = a_1^{(1)}X_1 + a_2^{(1)}X_2 + \cdots + a_I^{(1)}X_I$$

$$\hat{Y}^{(1)} = b_1^{(1)}Y_1 + b_2^{(1)}Y_2 + \cdots + b_J^{(1)}Y_J$$

As with the canonical correlation problem of Chapter 5, we wish to select the $a_i^{(1)}$ and $b_j^{(1)}$ values so that the correlation between $\hat{X}^{(1)}$ and $\hat{Y}^{(1)}$ is maximized, subject to the restrictions that $\text{Var}(\hat{X}^{(1)}) = 1$ and $\text{Var}(\hat{Y}^{(1)}) = 1$. With Lagrange multipliers, λ_1^* and λ_2^*, and with the $a_i^{(1)}$ and $b_j^{(1)}$ values chosen to make $\mu_{X^{(1)}} = 0$ and $\mu_{Y^{(1)}} = 0$, we consider the function:

TABLE 10-26. Two-dimensional contingency table representing 500 men's religious preferences and attitudes toward abortion

	Religion				
Response	*Catholic*	*Protestant*	*Jewish*	*Other*	*Total*
Yes	76	115	41	77	309
No	64	82	8	12	166
No opinion	11	6	2	6	25
	151	203	51	95	500

$$Q = \text{Cov}(\hat{X}^{(1)}, \hat{Y}^{(1)}) + \lambda_1^*[\text{Var}(\hat{X}^{(1)}) - 1] + \lambda_2^*[\text{Var}(\hat{Y}^{(1)}) - 1]$$
$$= \frac{1}{n}\sum_{i=1}^{I}\sum_{j=1}^{J} a_i^{(1)}b_j^{(1)}\hat{X}_i^{(1)}\hat{Y}_j^{(1)} + \frac{1}{n}\lambda_1^*\left(\sum_{i=1}^{I} a_i^{(1)2}\hat{X}_i^{(1)2} - 1\right)$$
$$+ \frac{1}{n}\lambda_2^*\left(\sum_{j=1}^{J} b_j^{(1)2}\hat{Y}_j^{(1)2} - 1\right)$$

Once $\hat{X}^{(1)}$ and $\hat{Y}^{(1)}$ are determined, we introduce $\hat{X}^{(2)}$ and $\hat{Y}^{(2)}$, $\hat{X}^{(3)}$ and $\hat{Y}^{(3)}$, . . . , and $\hat{X}^{(I-1)}$, $\hat{Y}^{(I-1)}$, as described in Section 5-3. Upon completion of the algebra, we obtain $(I - 1)$ eigen values which are generated from the resulting characteristic equation. For the general solution, let:

n_{ij} = the frequency in the ijth cell

$n_{i.}$ = the frequency in the ith row

$n_{.j}$ = the frequency in the jth column.

Q reduces to:

$$Q = \frac{1}{n}\sum_{i=1}^{I}\sum_{j=1}^{J} a_ib_jn_{ij} + \frac{1}{n}\lambda_1^*\left(\sum_{i=1}^{I} n_{i.}a_i^2 - 1\right) + \frac{1}{n}\lambda_2^*\left(\sum_{j=1}^{J} n_{.j}b_j^2 - 1\right)$$

Performing the differentiation on the a_i, b_j, λ_1^*, and λ_2^*, to determine the maximum value of Q, we are led to the determinantal equation:

$$\left|\begin{array}{cccc|cccc}
\lambda_{n1.}^* & 0 & \cdots & 0 & n_{11} & n_{12} & \cdots & n_{1J} \\
0 & \lambda_{n2.}^* & \cdots & 0 & n_{21} & n_{22} & \cdots & n_{2J} \\
\vdots & \vdots & & \vdots & \vdots & \vdots & & \vdots \\
0 & 0 & \cdots & \lambda_{nI.}^* & n_{I1} & n_{I2} & \cdots & n_{IJ} \\
\hline
n_{11} & n_{21} & \cdots & n_{I1} & \lambda_{n.1}^* & 0 & \cdots & 0 \\
n_{12} & n_{22} & \cdots & n_{I2} & 0 & \lambda_{n.2}^* & \cdots & 0 \\
\vdots & \vdots & & \vdots & \vdots & \vdots & & \vdots \\
n_{1J} & n_{2J} & \cdots & n_{IJ} & 0 & 0 & \cdots & \lambda_{n.J}^*
\end{array}\right| = \mathbf{0}$$

For $\hat{X}^{(1)}$ and $\hat{Y}^{(1)}$, the solution to this equation is given by:

$$\lambda_1 = \lambda_1^* = \lambda_2^* = \hat{R}^2_{\hat{X}(1)\hat{Y}(1)} = (S_{\hat{X}(1)\hat{Y}(1)})^2$$

with $\hat{R}_{\hat{X}(1)\hat{Y}(1)}$ being the correlation coefficient between $\hat{X}^{(1)}$ and $\hat{Y}^{(1)}$. Remaining eigen values are determined in a similar way. To obtain all eigen values, let:

$$E_{ij} = n_{ij}/\sqrt{n_{i.}n_{.j}}$$

and set up the matrix:

$$\mathbf{N} = \begin{bmatrix} E_{11} & E_{12} & \dots & E_{1J} \\ E_{21} & E_{22} & \dots & E_{2J} \\ \cdot & \cdot & \cdot & \cdot \\ \cdot & \cdot & \cdot & \cdot \\ \cdot & \cdot & \cdot & \cdot \\ E_{I1} & E_{I2} & \dots & E_{IJ} \end{bmatrix}$$

In this form, we are led to the characteristic equation:

$$| \mathbf{NN}' - \lambda\mathbf{I} | = 0$$

which will have as solutions:

$$\lambda_0, \lambda_1, \dots, \lambda_{I-1}$$

Thus, as was shown in Chapter 5, there are as many solutions as the minimum of predictor and criterion variables; here, $\min(I, J) = I$. Because of the linear dependence in each set of indicator variables, $\lambda_0 = 1$ is always a solution. The remaining solutions give rise to eigen vectors that are the values of the a_i and b_j. According to Kendall and Stuart, interest will focus only on the canonical variates associated with λ_1, since the remaining eigen values are functions of it. For this reason, we will investigate only the largest eigen value and its corresponding canonical variates.

The vector equation:

$$\mathbf{NN}'\mathbf{A}^* = \lambda_1\mathbf{A}^*$$

does not give a direct solution of the a_i values since the transformation to the E_{ij} has introduced a change of scale. To obtain the correct values, we normalize the $\mathbf{A}_i^*$ and define:

$$a_i^* = a_i^* \Bigg/ \sqrt{\sum_{i=1}^{I} a_i^{*2}}$$

In terms of these normalized weights:

$$a_i = a_i^*\sqrt{n/n_{i.}}$$

and:

$$b_j = \frac{1}{n_{.j}\sqrt{\lambda_1}} \sum_{i=1}^{I} n_{ij}a_{i.}$$

We now illustrate the method for the data of Table 10-26, which has been set up so that $I \leq J$. For this example, $I = 3$ and $J = 4$. This means that the matrix **NN**′ will be of size 3 by 3, so that the characteristic equation will have three roots, one of which is equal to 1. If we worked for the four-category variable, the resulting **NN**′ matrix would be of size 4 by 4, and two of the roots would be equal to 1. The arithmetic would be more involved, and for this reason, we should always define X and Y so that $I \leq J$. This further implies that the number of eigen values not equal to unity is given by:

$$M = \min(I - 1, J - 1) = I - 1$$

A little reflection suggests that M is identical to the divisor required to transform the Pearson Chi-square independence statistic into Cramér's coefficient of association. As we recall, Cramér's V is defined as:

$$V = X^2/NM$$

For the data of Table 10-26, $X^2 = 40.17462$, so that:

$$V = 40.17462/500(2) = .04018$$

Thus, even though $X^2 = 40.17$ is larger than $\chi^2_{4:.95} = 9.49$, the degree of association is quite small, being equal to $V = .04$.

We now perform a canonical analysis using the same data. The needed **N** and the **NN**′ matrices are presented in Tables 10-27 and 10-28. The resulting characteristic equation is given by:

$$\lambda^3 - 1.08035\lambda^2 + .08091\lambda - .00056 = 0$$

As stated, this equation has the unusual property that one of its roots is equal to 1. This means that the characteristic equation has only two roots that are of interest or are meaningful. Since $\lambda = 1$ is a root of the equation, we can factor it out. This gives rise to the quadratic equation:

$$\lambda^2 - .08035\lambda + .00056 = 0$$

TABLE 10-27. The N matrix associated with Table 10-26

	B_1	B_2	B_3	B_4
A_1	0.35184	0.45917	0.32660	0.44942
A_2	0.40424	0.44670	0.08695	0.09556
A_3	0.17903	0.08422	0.05601	0.12312

TABLE 10-28. The NN′ matrix associated with Table 10-26

	A_1	A_2	A_3
A_1	0.64327	0.41868	0.17529
A_2	0.41868	0.37964	0.12663
A_3	0.17529	0.12663	0.05744

whose roots are given by the quadratic formulas as:

$$\lambda = \frac{.08035 \pm \sqrt{(-.08035)^2 - 4(.00056)}}{2} = \frac{.08035 \pm .06493}{2}$$

so that:

$$\lambda_1 = .07264 \qquad \text{and} \qquad \lambda_2 = .00771$$

Before we find the eigen vector corresponding to λ_1, let us compute the average of the $I - 1$ meaningful eigen values. In this case:

$$\bar{\lambda} = \frac{\lambda_1 + \lambda_2}{2} = \frac{.07264 + .00771}{2} = .04018$$

which is seen to equal Cramér's V. This represents a general result, in that Cramér's V is simply equal to the average values of the M eigen values that are different from 1. Put a different way, and as Serlin (1982) has shown, $\bar{\lambda} = V$ is also equivalent to the average of the s successive Roy criteria of Chapter 5, which in turn represents the Pillai-Bartlett trace criterion divided by s. Thus, in general:

$$V = \frac{\lambda_1 + \lambda_2 + \cdots + \lambda_M}{M}$$

Since the trace of a matrix is equal to the sum of its eigen values, we can alternatively define V as:

$$V = \frac{\text{trace of } \mathbf{NN}' - (J - I)}{M}$$

For our example:

$$V = \frac{(.64327 + .37964 + .05744) - (4 - 3)}{2} = .04018$$

Once the eigen values have been determined, we would like to know which ones represent statistically significant relationships between the canonical variates. If n is relatively large, we can test the hypothesis that the largest meaningful eigen value, λ_1, differs significantly from zero, using Roy's criterion, as described in Section 5-4. Adopting present terminology, $P = I - 1$ and $Q = J - 1$, and we have that:

$$s = \min(I - 1, J - 1) = \min(2, 3) = 2$$

$$m = \tfrac{1}{2}[\,|(I - 1) - (J - 1)| - 1] = \tfrac{1}{2}[\,|2 - 3| - 1] = 0$$

and:

$$n = \tfrac{1}{2}[N - (I - 1) - (J - 1) - 2] = \tfrac{1}{2}(500 - 2 - 3 - 2) = 246.5$$

With $\alpha = .05$, we see from Table B-7 that the critical value of λ is given by $\lambda_{1:.95} \simeq .02$. Since $\lambda_1 = .07$, we reject the hypothesis, H_0: $\lambda_1 = 0$, and conclude that the relationship between $\hat{X}^{(1)}$ and $\hat{Y}^{(1)}$ is significantly different from zero.

To test that the average eigen value $\bar{\lambda}$ differs significantly from zero is equivalent to testing that Cramér's V differs from zero, which in turn is equivalent to testing the significance of the Pearson Chi-square. In terms of $\bar{\lambda}$:

$$X^2 = NM\,\bar{\lambda}$$

The hypothesis of no association would be rejected if

$X^2 > \chi^2_{(I-1)(J-1):1-\alpha}$. For our example:

$$X^2 = 500(2)(.04018) = 40.18$$

With $\alpha = .05$, $\chi^2_{6:.95} = 12.59$. Since $X^2 = 40.18$, we reject the hypothesis of no association and conclude that religious preference is related to attitude toward abortion.

We now return to our example, and find the eigen vector associated with λ_1. In this case:

$$\mathbf{N}\,\mathbf{N}'\,\mathbf{A}^* = \lambda_1\,\mathbf{A}^*$$

is defined by:

$$\begin{bmatrix} .64327 & .41868 & .17529 \\ .41868 & .37964 & .12663 \\ .17529 & .12663 & .05744 \end{bmatrix} \begin{bmatrix} a_i^* \\ a_2^* \\ a_3^* \end{bmatrix} = .07264 \begin{bmatrix} a_1^* \\ a_2^* \\ a_3^* \end{bmatrix}$$

which reduces to the set of three homogeneous equations:

$$.57063a_1^* + .41868a_2^* + .17529a_3^* = 0$$

$$.41868a_1^* + .30700a_2^* + .12663a_3^* = 0$$

and:

$$.17529a_1^* + .12663a_2^* - .01520a_3^* = 0$$

Since there is an infinite set of solutions to this set of equations, we can obtain one solution by finding a_2^* and a_3^* in terms of a_1^*. For equations 2 and 3, we have:

$$a_2^* = \frac{\begin{vmatrix} -.41868a_1^* & .12663 \\ -.17529a_1^* & -.01520 \end{vmatrix}}{\begin{vmatrix} .30700 & .12663 \\ .12663 & -.01520 \end{vmatrix}} = \frac{.02856a_1^*}{-.02070} = -1.37971a_1^*$$

and:

$$a_3^* = \frac{\begin{vmatrix} .30700 & -.41868a_1^* \\ .12663 & -.17529a_1^* \end{vmatrix}}{\begin{vmatrix} .30700 & .12663 \\ .12663 & -.01520 \end{vmatrix}} = \frac{-.00080a_1}{-.02070} = .03865a_1^*$$

so that a_1^*, a_2^*, and a_3^* are given by:

$$a_1^* = \frac{a_1^*}{\sqrt{a_1^{*2} + (-1.37971)^2 a_1^{*2} + (.03865)^2 a_1^{*2}}} = .58670$$

$$a_2^* = \frac{-1.37971a_1^*}{\sqrt{a_1^{*2} + (-1.37971)^2 a_1^{*2} + (.03865)^2 a_1^{*2}}} = -.80948$$

and:

$$a_3^* = \frac{.03865a_1^*}{\sqrt{a_1^{*2} + (-1.37971)^2 a_1^{*2} + (.03865)^2 a_1^{*2}}} = .02268$$

With $a_i = a_i^* \sqrt{n/n_{i.}}$, we have that:

$$a_1 = .58670\sqrt{500/309} = .74631$$

$$a_2 = -.80948\sqrt{500/166} = -1.40487$$

and:

$$a_3 = .02268\sqrt{500/25} = .10143$$

With $b_j = \dfrac{1}{n_{.j}\sqrt{\lambda_1}} \sum_{i=1}^{3} n_{ij}a_i$ we have that:

$$b_1 = \frac{1}{151\sqrt{.07264}}[76(.74631) + 64(-1.40487) + 11(.10143)] = -.78817$$

$$b_2 = \frac{1}{203\sqrt{.07264}}[115(.74631) + 82(-1.40487) + 6(.10143)] = -.52575$$

$$b_3 = \frac{1}{51\sqrt{.07264}}[41(.74631) + 8(-1.40487) + 2(.10143)] = 1.42321$$

and:

$$b_4 = \frac{1}{95\sqrt{.07264}}[77(.74631) + 12(-1.40487) + 6(.10143)] = 1.60974$$

As a check on our computations, we now verify that $\hat{R} = \sqrt{.07264} = .2695 = \lambda_1$. For this check:

$$\sum_{i=1}^{I} X_i = 309(.74631) + 166(-1.40487) + 25(.10143) = -.06288$$

$$\sum_{i=1}^{I} X_i^2 = 309(.74631)^2 + 166(-1.40487)^2 + 25(.10143)^2 = 499.99109$$

$$\sum_{j=1}^{J} Y_j = 151(-.78817) + \cdots + 95(1.60974) = -.23191$$

$$\sum_{j=1}^{J} Y_j^2 = 151(-.78817)^2 + \cdots + 95(1.60974)^2 = 499.38665$$

$$\sum_{i=1}^{I} \sum_{j=1}^{J} X_i X_j = 76(.74631)(-.78817) + \cdots + 6(.10143)(1.60974) = 134.59367$$

$$\hat{R} = \frac{500(134.59367) - (-.06288)(-.23191)}{\sqrt{500(499.99109) - (-.06288)^2}\sqrt{500(499.38685) - (-.23191)^2}}$$
$$= .2694$$

If there had been no rounding errors, we would have seen that

$$\sum_{i=1}^{I} X_i = \sum_{j=1}^{J} Y_j = 0$$

$$\sum_{i=1}^{I} X_i^2 = \sum_{j=1}^{J} Y_j^2 = 500$$

and:

$$\sum_{i=1}^{I}\sum_{j=1}^{J} X_i Y_j = S_{XY}$$

Let us now consider the meaning of what we have done. Normally we would consider religion to be an independent variable and response to the question as the dependent variable. Let us make this switch in X and Y for this discussion and let us reduce the coefficients of the canonical variates to two-place decimal accuracy. Thus:

$$\hat{X} = -.79X_1 - .53X_2 + 1.42X_3 + 1.61X_4 \quad \text{and}$$

$$\hat{Y} = .75Y_1 - 1.40Y_2 + .10Y_3$$

Consider males who respond *Yes* to the question on abortion. Such males would be coded as $Y_{1.} = (1, 0, 0)$ and their value on the Y variate would be given by:

$$\hat{Y} = .75(1) - 1.40(0) + .10(0) = .75$$

Clearly the coefficients serve as scale values for each category. Most likely, in the absence of a canonical analysis, many researchers would code the categories as:

Yes	*No opinion*	*No*
+ 1	0	− 1

This would give an equal spacing between the categories and place the *No opinion* response in a neutral position. The canonical analysis has produced a different scaling of these responses:

Yes	*No opinion*	*No*
+ .75	+ .10	− 1.40

suggesting that a *No* response is a much stronger statement of opinion about abortion than a *Yes* response is. In point of fact, we see that a *No* response is scored almost twice as much as a *Yes* response. At the same time, we see that a *No opinion* response is more like a *Yes* response than it is like a *No* response. In other words, in the context of the present data, *No opinion* does not represent a neutral position.

Generally we think of religion as an unordered qualitative variable, but when examined in the context of certain social or political issues, subjective orderings are often predictable. For the present abortion question, the subjective orderings seem to be consonant with common beliefs about the precepts of different religions. Catholics are thought to be against abortion, whereas other groups are more supportive. In this example, the scaling of the religions is given by:

Catholic	*Protestant*	*Jewish*	*Other*
− .79	− .53	1.42	1.62

Whatever is being measured by the labels, *Catholic*, *Protestant*, *Jewish*, and *Other* in the context of the question on abortion, it is clear that the Christian followers, Catholics and Protestants, are quite different in that characteristic from the non-Christians, assuming that those labeling themselves as Other are primarily non-Christian. Further, the Jewish and other groups are more positive in their position than the Catholics and Protestants are negative in theirs. From these observations, it seems reasonable to conclude that the scale defined by X in this context corresponds somewhat to a liberal-conservative scaling of these four religious categories, with respect to the question of abortion.

Other methods are available for the scaling of unordered categories. This method is just one of them. It has the advantage of simplicity of theory, as well as the generation of interpretable results. As such, it should be of interest to researchers in the social sciences.

We now provide directions for performing a canonical analysis on a two-dimensional contingency table.

Procedure for performing a canonical analysis of a two-dimensional contingency table.

Step 1. Define the two marginal variables of the contingency table so that the X variate is associated with the smaller of I and J, that is, so $I \leq J$.

Step 2. Define the **N** matrix with elements:

$$E_{ij} = n_{ij}/\sqrt{n_{i.}n_{.j}}$$

where:

n_{ij} = frequency in the ijth cell

$n_{i.}$ = frequency in the ith row

$n_{.j}$ = frequency in the jth column

Step 3. Find the eigen values of:

$$|\mathbf{N}\,\mathbf{N}' - \lambda\,\mathbf{I}| = 0$$

and retain the largest value that is not equal to 1. Denote this largest meaningful eigen value as λ_1. This largest eigen value is the squared correlation coefficient between:

$$\hat{X}^{(1)} = a_1^{(1)}X_1 + a_2^{(1)}X_2 + \cdots + a_I^{(1)}X_I$$

$$\hat{Y}^{(1)} = b_1^{(1)}Y_1 + b_2^{(1)}Y_2 + \cdots + b_J^{(1)}Y_J$$

Step 4. Find the eigen vector $\mathbf{A}^*$ as a solution of the homogeneous set of equations:

$$\mathbf{N}\,\mathbf{N}'\,\mathbf{A}^* = \lambda_1\,\mathbf{A}^*$$

Let the solution be found in terms of a_1^* and denote the complete solution by:

$$a_1^*, a_2^*, \ldots, a_I^*$$

Normalize this solution and determine:

$$a_i^* = \frac{d_i^*}{\sqrt{\sum_{i=1}^{I} d_i^{*2}}}$$

Step 5. From the a_i^*, compute:

$$a_i = a_i^* \sqrt{n/n_{i.}}$$

$$b_j = \frac{1}{n_{.j}\sqrt{\lambda_1}} \sum_{i=1}^{I} n_{ij}a_i$$

10-10. Simplified statistics for contingency table analysis

We close by noting that no extended simplified statistics section is included in this final chapter. This is because the methods presented here represent more sophisticated and, more than likely, more complex competitors to those typically employed by applied researchers. In other words, the simplified statistics here would simply be the traditional Chi-square analyses and simple Likert scaling of items for which the present procedures were offered as improvements. There clearly exist a number of other statistical procedures for analyzing contingency table data, and books such as Marascuilo and McSweeney (1977), Kendall and Stuart (1967), and Bishop et al. (1975) should be consulted for a number of possibilities. Also see the first three exercises that follow the chapter summary.

10-11. Summary

This chapter dealt with the multivariate analysis of qualitative data that can be presented in contingency tables. Although social science researchers have relied on Chi-square analyses over the years, the methods introduced here represent more versatile, and frequently more powerful, alternatives for testing specific hypotheses about proportions.

The first test discussed was a test for trend in an $I \times 2$ contingency table, and follows the presentation of Wood (1978). The test is based on an adaptation of the two-variable linear regression model and uses what are called modified minimum Chi-square estimates. It also relies on what we have called a model-building approach, which represents a departure from the standard approach to significance testing. The model-building approach was discussed in analogy with stepwise multiple regression where differences in the goodness of successive *models* are examined. In the present context, differences in successive Chi-square statistics are computed to yield a *component* Chi-square. On the basis of statistical tests of these components, as well as of the *residual* Chi-square, we decide whether the trend in the binomial probabilities can best be described by a linear component, by a linear plus higher order trend components, or by no systematic trend components at all.

In the next section, this model was extended to include more than a single $I \times 2$ contingency table. In particular, the question of interest was whether the trends observed in the K different tables (populations) are the same. Specific details were given for assessing the parallelism or the identity of the regression lines (that is, slopes, or slopes plus intercepts) in K populations, where the dependent variable is binomial rather than continuous.

We then present the focal statistical procedure of this chapter, log-linear analysis. The procedure represents an important advance over standard methods of analyzing contingency table data. Unlike the preceding trend procedure, which depends on known quantitative levels of the independent variable, with log-linear analysis no such quantitative metric is needed. Moreover, log-linear analysis can be easily extended in parallel with the analysis of variance model to encompass contingency tables with more than two dimensions. The log-linear procedures described follow those of Bishop et al. (1975) and of Goodman (1971), using a statistic G^2. In particular,

$$G^2 = 2 \sum Y \log_e (Y/\hat{Y})$$

where:

Y = the observed cell frequencies in a contingency table

$\hat{Y}$ = the corresponding expected cell frequencies

G^2 is referred to the Chi-square distribution, with degrees of freedom equal to the number of independent parameters in the appropriate model that are set equal to zero. Both omnibus tests and individual contrasts were discussed according to the log-linear approach. The approach was presented to test hypotheses subsumed by each of the two ANOVA models described in Chapter 9, namely, the interaction model and the simple effects model. Following the statistical tests, measures of association were introduced that parallel Cramér's V statistic in standard Chi-square analyses.

We then show how a two-dimensional contingency table can be analyzed according to the canonical correlation model introduced in Chapter 5. The presentation follows that of Kendall and Stuart (1967). A relationship between the average eigen value of the solution, Cramér's V, and the Pillai-Bartlett multivariate test criterion is indicated. The canonical correlation approach produces weights that are useful in scaling the levels of the two qualitative variables under consideration.

No simplified statistics were included in this final chapter inasmuch as standard Chi-square analyses were seen as the simplified approach to what was presented here.

10-12. Exercises

10-1. Some educators believe that some tests used to measure academic achievement are biased against certain minority groups. One way to test for bias associated with specific items is to perform a *latent trait analysis* on the minority group of interest, and then to compare the results with those based on a majority group. In latent trait analysis, we examine the *operating* *characteristic curves* of the two groups, that is, the relationship produced by regressing the probability of a correct response to a particular item Y on total test scores X. In practice, this leads to a set of equations that must be solved by iteration. The methods of Sections 10-2 and 10-4 serve as a simplified procedure that can be substituted for the more complex procedure. The simplification is described as follows.

Scores on a test with 15 items have been grouped into four intervals. The frequencies of success and failure for 200 Black students on Item 1 are given by the following figures:

Total score interval	0–5	6–11	12–13	14–15	Total
Midpoint	2.5	8.5	12.5	14.5	
No. of successes	18	25	26	29	98
No. of failures	56	28	13	5	102
Total	74	53	39	34	200

Use the method of Section 10-2 to see whether a linear trend is sufficient to describe these data. That is, is the linear compoment significant, with no significant deviations from linearity? Use $\alpha = .05$ for each test.

10-2. Frequencies for a sample of White students are as follows:

Total score interval	0–5	6–11	12–13	14–15	Total
Midpoint	2.5	8.5	12.5	14.5	
No. of successes	30	81	95	275	481
No. of failures	60	34	10	15	119
Total	90	115	105	290	600

An item can be said to be unbiased if the regression line for the minority group is identical to the regression line for the majority group. Incorporating the data of Exercise 10-1, use the method of Section 10-3 to see whether the item is biased. Use $\alpha = .05$.

10-3. The model of Section 10-3 can also be used for simultaneously comparing more than two regression lines. Suppose that frequencies for a group of Chicano students were as follows:

Total score interval	0–5	6–11	12–13	14–15	Total
Midpoint	2.5	8.5	12.5	14.5	
No. of successes	10	15	13	8	46
No. of failures	28	17	7	2	54
Total	38	32	20	10	100

a. Use the method of Section 10-3 to see whether the item is biased, $\alpha = .05$. That is, determine whether the three regression lines are identical.

b. Would it be wiser statistically to compare the three ethnic groups in a single test, or to compare each minority group to Whites via two pairwise comparisons, using the Dunn-Bonferroni procedure? Why?

c. Should the Dunn-Bonferroni comparisons of Exercise 10-3b be directional. Why or why not?

10-4. Analyze the data of Exercise 10-1 using the log-linear model of Section 10-5; $\alpha = .05$.

10-5. Analyze the three contingency tables of Exercises 10-1, 10-2, and 10-3 by applying the log-linear model to a $3 \times 4 \times 2$ contingency table. Test each source of variance using $\alpha = .05$.

10-6. Perform a planned Dunn-Bonferroni analysis of all simple three-factor interaction contrasts of Exercise 10-5. The number of such 8-cell contrasts is given by: $C = \binom{3}{2}\binom{4}{2}\binom{2}{2} = 18$. For this analysis, use a familywise alpha of .05, equally divided among the 18 comparisons.

10-7. Determine the seven V^* values associated with the analysis of Exercise 10-5. Which sources of variance seem to be most highly associated with the dependent variable, success/failure?

10-8. Analyze the data of Table 10-10 as a canonical correlation problem, as described in Section 10-6. Use $\alpha = .05$ to test the hypothesis that there is no relationship between number of new friends made and amount of perceived social mixing.

10-9. The study of Table 10-26 was repeated using a sample of 640 females. Results are as shown.

	Catholic	*Protestant*	*Jewish*	*Other*	*Total*
Yes	61	117	63	71	312
No	146	126	3	14	289
No opinion	9	12	8	10	39
Total	216	255	74	95	640

a. Perform a canonical analysis on these data. Use $\alpha = .05$ to test the hypothesis that there is no relationship between religious preference and attitude toward abortion.

b. Make a descriptive comparison of the results in Exercises 10-9a and those associated with the males in Table 10-26.

10-10.

a. Perform a separate log-linear analysis of the data in Exercise 10-9 and Table 10-26, using $\alpha = .05$ for each. Make a descriptive comparison of the results associated with each analysis.

b. Analyze the data of Exercise 10-9 and Table 10-26 in a single log-linear analysis as applied to a $2 \times 4 \times 3$ contingency table. Use $\alpha = .05$ for each source of variance tested.

c. In terms of V^* statistics, which sources of variance seem to be most highly associated with subjects' attitudes?

APPENDIX

TABLES

TABLE A-1. Hypothetical Data for 216 Students Enrolled in a Beginning Sociology Class. Data include: Code Number (CN); Social Class (SC); Sex (Sex); High School Grade Point Average (GPA); College Board Score (CB); Took High School Sociology (HSS); College Major (M); Pretest Score (PT); Midterm One Score (M1); Midterm Two Score (M2); Final Score (F); Score on Course Evaluation Item (E); and Subsequent Career Field (C). (See Chapter 1, p. 7, for interpretation of coded values. A – indicates that information is missing for the student on that variable.)

CN	*SC*	*Sex*	*GPA*	*CB*	*HSS*	*M*	*PT*	*M1*	*M2*	*F*	*E*	*C*
001	1	1	3.98	650	1	5	29	78	96	156	1	1
002	1	0	3.47	390	0	4	20	57	63	140	1	1
003	2	1	3.55	410	0	1	17	43	61	129	3	2
004	2	1	2.70	390	0	2	20	50	47	60	1	1
005	2	0	3.17	450	1	4	16	39	48	62	5	2
006	3	1	3.69	500	1	3	18	78	64	140	2	1
007	3	0	3.52	590	0	3	10	53	67	106	3	1
008	1	0	3.97	710	1	2	30	82	69	160	3	1
009	2	1	4.00	650	1	5	30	68	72	129	3	2
010	2	1	3.50	510	0	4	22	47	79	119	1	1
011	2	1	2.98	520	1	–	6	38	60	78	3	2
012	2	0	3.38	400	0	5	21	52	79	95	2	1
013	3	1	3.59	700	0	2	14	47	75	150	2	–
014	3	1	2.91	430	0	1	13	24	40	–	1	2
015	1	1	3.90	800	1	1	26	88	93	140	3	1
016	1	0	3.38	580	0	5	14	56	58	91	3	2
017	2	1	3.59	480	1	2	7	49	81	128	1	1
018	2	1	3.10	600	0	–	16	47	60	79	–	1
019	2	0	3.41	620	0	2	23	57	61	103	3	1
020	3	1	3.49	610	0	2	28	57	59	99	1	1
021	3	1	2.86	470	0	5	21	51	30	49	1	1
022	1	1	3.69	710	0	3	30	62	90	116	4	1
023	3	1	3.48	600	0	2	19	45	58	84	1	2
024	2	1	2.65	470	–	4	18	27	51	76	4	1
025	1	0	3.20	560	0	1	15	40	51	79	3	2
026	2	1	3.44	690	0	2	30	49	63	103	4	1
027	2	0	3.28	450	1	1	15	41	50	94	1	2
028	3	0	3.91	630	1	1	16	68	73	163	2	1
029	1	1	3.41	550	1	5	28	50	90	92	1	2
030	3	1	3.64	610	1	5	20	50	61	120	1	1
031	2	1	3.20	470	1	2	6	50	60	91	1	1
032	1	0	3.17	610	0	4	14	42	61	92	3	1
033	2	0	3.75	430	1	5	30	63	79	145	1	1
034	2	1	3.49	520	0	4	22	30	66	91	1	2
035	3	1	3.70	530	0	2	21	40	58	70	1	2
036	3	1	3.75	820	0	1	30	73	77	126	1	2
037	1	1	3.70	510	1	5	24	53	–	–	1	2
038	2	1	3.01	410	0	–	4	40	39	79	1	2
039	1	0	–	450	0	3	–	44	49	73	3	2
040	2	1	3.57	560	0	4	10	42	79	107	2	2
041	2	0	3.70	560	1	4	16	48	63	115	1	2
042	3	1	3.70	460	1	1	16	45	23	73	1	2
043	1	1	3.90	470	1	5	27	70	100	132	2	2
044	3	1	3.65	510	1	3	2	70	80	120	2	2
045	2	1	3.20	420	1	2	17	45	58	78	1	2
046	1	0	3.30	490	0	2	19	36	50	86	3	2
047	2	0	2.99	390	–	5	12	40	57	68	2	1
048	2	1	3.59	550	1	2	16	48	82	91	1	2
049	3	0	2.91	410	0	1	28	41	37	77	5	1
050	3	1	3.76	700	1	1	28	69	83	156	1	1

TABLE A-1. (Continued)

CN	*SC*	*Sex*	*GPA*	*CB*	*HSS*	*M*	*PT*	*M1*	*M2*	*F*	*E*	*C*
051	1	0	3.80	640	1	5	27	72	64	130	4	1
052	2	0	3.81	460	1	1	30	48	67	110	1	2
053	2	1	3.60	390	1	1	14	55	66	89	4	2
054	2	1	3.45	470	1	2	8	38	–	–	2	1
055	2	0	3.60	590	1	3	28	59	74	116	1	1
056	3	0	3.40	430	1	1	10	43	47	77	1	1
057	1	0	3.50	410	0	2	10	50	50	99	3	2
058	3	1	3.70	620	0	2	16	61	97	147	1	1
059	2	1	3.59	610	1	2	8	50	63	119	1	1
060	2	0	3.76	570	1	5	24	60	82	129	2	1
061	2	1	3.23	610	1	1	18	51	62	95	3	1
062	2	–	–	500	–	–	12	22	41	91	3	1
063	3	–	–	480	0	–	–	40	37	55	–	2
064	2	1	3.70	690	1	1	19	65	96	110	3	2
065	3	1	3.30	500	0	2	10	51	40	70	3	1
066	1	0	3.51	580	1	1	28	64	77	143	2	1
067	2	0	3.96	550	1	5	27	65	87	121	1	2
068	2	1	3.23	510	1	1	17	37	38	79	3	2
069	2	–	3.10	460	0	4	18	23	50	34	2	2
070	3	–	3.10	500	1	1	15	21	40	49	1	1
071	1	0	3.22	390	0	2	27	49	47	98	–	1
072	1	1	–	410	0	4	24	52	71	107	5	2
073	3	1	3.37	440	1	1	13	35	37	70	2	2
074	2	1	3.25	460	1	2	4	50	53	65	2	1
075	2	1	3.11	510	0	2	13	47	71	85	1	1
076	2	–	3.50	470	1	5	15	35	40	125	1	1
077	3	0	3.50	600	0	3	15	44	58	97	1	2
078	1	0	3.60	580	0	5	30	55	70	145	1	2
079	1	–	3.16	410	0	4	14	18	60	39	3	2
080	2	1	3.43	210	1	5	26	35	57	64	5	2
081	3	1	3.39	410	0	1	–	52	45	90	1	1
082	2	0	3.76	580	0	2	20	50	61	121	2	2
083	2	0	3.39	610	0	1	16	59	58	100	1	1
084	3	0	3.60	510	0	3	1	16	60	50	–	2
085	1	0	3.19	560	0	2	25	39	63	110	–	1
086	1	0	3.79	490	1	5	24	59	68	84	1	1
087	3	1	3.50	510	0	1	30	56	73	115	2	2
088	2	1	3.47	580	0	3	15	27	73	116	1	1
089	2	0	3.76	510	1	1	25	68	66	138	2	1
090	2	0	3.59	500	0	1	17	45	61	110	1	2
091	3	0	3.71	600	0	1	3	38	58	63	1	1
092	2	1	3.60	470	1	3	–	61	79	122	3	1
093	3	1	3.39	420	0	5	12	40	40	88	1	2
094	1	0	3.79	470	1	3	26	61	51	129	5	2
095	2	1	3.09	410	1	5	5	41	46	67	3	2
096	2	1	3.27	470	1	1	9	40	39	94	1	2
097	2	–	3.60	470	1	–	12	43	41	91	1	2
098	3	1	3.20	550	1	1	8	47	62	88	1	1
099	2	1	3.60	480	0	2	17	51	70	99	2	2
100	1	0	3.90	790	1	1	29	73	63	126	3	2
101	3	1	3.40	460	1	–	8	49	43	88	1	1
102	2	1	3.30	410	1	1	16	52	62	76	1	1
103	2	1	3.00	470	1	–	5	45	24	82	3	1
104	2	0	–	460	0	5	16	37	48	73	3	1
105	3	0	2.71	430	1	2	16	22	–	–	–	2
106	2	1	3.69	800	1	2	28	54	100	132	2	1

TABLE A-1. (Continued)

CN	SC	Sex	GPA	CB	HSS	M	PT	M1	M2	F	E	C
107	3	1	3.49	540	0	2	16	50	69	101	2	1
108	1	1	3.24	610	0	3	13	45	83	87	2	1
109	2	0	3.90	710	1	3	15	74	74	145	1	1
110	2	1	3.45	420	0	2	13	43	52	84	3	2
111	2	0	2.71	500	0	–	–	13	–	–	2	2
112	3	–	3.47	470	0	5	28	57	56	101	–	1
113	2	1	3.70	500	1	4	28	70	71	111	1	1
114	2	1	2.70	600	0	1	21	22	39	70	1	2
115	1	1	3.49	410	–	2	29	55	77	130	1	1
116	3	1	3.45	560	1	2	22	58	58	101	4	1
117	2	1	3.46	490	0	2	9	31	70	89	2	2
118	2	0	3.39	470	0	2	13	39	48	99	1	2
119	3	0	3.40	470	0	2	2	43	56	95	2	2
120	2	1	3.69	610	0	5	30	54	72	146	1	2
121	1	1	2.97	410	1	4	8	39	71	98	2	1
122	2	1	2.70	410	0	1	9	28	40	51	2	1
123	2	1	3.40	480	0	4	–	50	69	101	2	1
124	3	1	3.58	680	1	3	17	60	66	150	1	1
125	2	0	3.59	550	0	1	15	51	70	108	2	1
126	3	0	3.46	590	0	5	17	57	55	79	5	2
127	1	0	3.46	490	0	4	19	47	63	116	2	2
128	2	0	3.90	610	1	3	30	67	85	119	–	1
129	1	1	2.90	390	–	3	25	55	60	42	3	2
130	3	1	3.57	400	1	4	19	55	59	73	1	2
131	2	1	3.50	620	1	5	15	43	65	132	4	1
132	2	0	3.28	510	0	1	14	44	65	88	1	1
133	3	0	3.29	460	0	5	–	47	43	109	3	1
134	1	–	2.91	400	1	1	4	27	40	98	1	1
135	1	1	3.70	660	1	3	26	67	100	135	2	1
136	2	1	2.91	620	–	–	12	49	41	90	1	1
137	2	0	3.39	710	0	1	18	40	49	111	1	2
138	2	1	3.51	400	1	5	21	40	58	94	5	2
139	3	1	3.47	510	0	3	16	44	61	73	1	2
140	3	1	2.71	590	1	3	8	66	23	73	1	2
141	2	1	3.10	510	0	1	9	50	55	39	2	2
142	1	1	3.06	470	1	4	10	40	65	94	2	2
143	1	–	2.76	580	0	3	10	30	14	–	1	2
144	2	1	3.30	490	1	1	20	18	40	96	2	2
145	2	0	3.08	490	–	5	16	25	–	–	1	2
146	3	1	3.47	430	1	1	15	40	53	94	1	1
147	3	0	3.19	600	0	1	15	34	40	87	4	2
148	1	0	3.31	650	1	2	14	54	33	103	3	1
149	1	1	3.69	720	0	3	3	49	57	118	3	2
150	2	1	2.70	410	0	2	13	19	–	–	2	2
151	2	0	3.36	390	0	1	16	49	72	98	1	1
152	2	1	3.57	600	1	2	9	52	72	111	2	1
153	3	1	3.69	640	1	5	27	56	90	146	2	2
154	3	0	3.40	410	0	1	16	41	55	63	1	2
155	1	0	3.40	550	–	5	16	61	55	115	3	1
156	2	0	3.90	720	1	3	8	56	72	115	2	1
157	1	1	3.88	490	0	1	14	59	71	139	3	2
158	2	0	3.37	390	0	1	30	47	57	84	2	2
159	2	1	3.58	480	0	1	18	59	77	116	1	1
160	3	1	3.56	600	1	1	21	58	58	114	1	1
161	3	1	3.16	410	1	2	13	45	51	83	2	1

TABLE A-1. (Continued)

CN	*SC*	*Sex*	*GPA*	*CB*	*HSS*	*M*	*PT*	*M1*	*M2*	*F*	*E*	*C*
162	2	1	3.06	390	0	1	10	50	47	65	5	1
163	2	1	4.00	820	1	3	18	63	87	148	4	1
164	2	1	3.57	570	1	3	20	50	68	115	2	2
165	2	0	3.41	610	1	1	10	50	52	94	2	2
166	1	1	3.77	630	1	–	8	71	100	166	3	1
167	3	1	3.49	530	0	2	17	44	90	104	2	2
168	3	0	3.90	710	1	2	27	51	90	125	5	2
169	2	1	3.10	500	0	3	12	54	68	82	2	1
170	2	1	3.56	560	0	5	30	49	57	85	2	1
171	2	1	4.00	790	1	4	29	80	94	111	2	1
172	1	1	3.20	470	1	4	10	46	66	70	2	2
173	2	0	3.10	500	–	1	13	26	41	59	–	2
174	3	1	3.40	490	0	4	17	47	45	110	1	2
175	3	0	3.41	550	0	2	13	50	67	94	–	1
176	2	0	3.98	670	1	5	26	59	90	141	5	2
177	2	1	3.99	720	1	3	27	59	74	126	1	2
178	2	1	3.33	500	0	1	15	25	63	79	2	1
179	2	0	3.09	400	0	–	–	46	58	93	1	1
180	1	1	3.16	620	1	5	27	50	76	115	2	1
181	3	1	3.40	410	0	4	15	50	49	83	1	1
182	3	0	3.61	510	0	1	28	49	71	106	2	2
183	2	1	3.80	610	1	1	16	59	90	141	2	1
184	2	1	3.10	560	0	4	30	50	50	59	2	2
185	2	0	3.16	510	0	1	21	47	68	62	4	1
186	2	1	3.17	510	0	5	13	33	66	89	–	2
187	3	1	3.65	500	1	5	27	56	75	107	1	2
188	1	1	3.28	610	1	1	13	48	84	99	2	2
189	3	0	3.71	760	1	1	27	60	83	130	4	1
190	1	0	3.00	600	1	3	7	45	59	63	4	1
191	2	0	3.20	390	0	2	12	50	63	76	2	1
192	2	1	3.01	390	0	5	1	42	49	85	5	1
193	1	1	3.70	500	1	2	30	68	81	114	5	1
194	3	1	3.65	700	1	4	29	75	77	136	1	1
195	2	1	3.42	430	1	1	17	43	49	96	1	1
196	3	1	3.09	540	0	1	17	31	54	39	1	2
197	2	0	3.28	560	0	2	2	37	39	79	2	2
198	1	–	3.40	510	0	5	28	31	51	70	3	2
199	1	1	3.70	610	0	3	25	64	87	149	4	2
200	2	1	3.03	470	0	2	3	46	44	78	3	2
201	2	1	3.41	440	1	1	18	39	47	60	1	2
202	3	1	3.63	670	1	1	13	61	80	91	3	2
203	3	1	3.15	460	0	1	10	38	49	67	3	2
204	2	0	3.20	420	0	2	18	31	43	65	1	2
205	1	1	3.37	610	1	5	–	59	85	99	2	1
206	1	0	2.90	410	0	2	5	51	50	100	2	1
207	2	1	2.69	400	0	3	10	19	36	53	3	2
208	3	1	3.40	390	0	4	23	43	51	39	1	2
209	2	1	3.41	600	0	2	10	47	51	95	1	1
210	3	1	3.08	410	0	2	18	38	60	58	3	1
211	1	0	2.95	490	0	2	18	20	–	–	1	2
212	2	0	3.19	600	0	2	27	60	57	72	3	1
213	2	0	3.98	800	1	5	20	77	96	155	1	1
214	2	1	3.40	510	0	–	12	36	40	59	1	2
215	3	1	3.61	510	0	1	15	66	73	130	5	1
216	3	1	3.10	510	0	1	6	46	43	70	1	1

TABLE A-2. Summary Data for the Ghatala et al. (1975) Experiment (See Exercise 2-12 for a description.)

		Task			
		1 (FJ)		2 (MJ)	3 (DL)
Condition					
Vocalization-Control ($N = 30$)	Mean	10.4667		14.8000	7.0333
	SD	3.5982		6.1330	3.2535
	$r_{12} = -.0456$		$r_{13} = .3963$		$r_{23} = .1576$
Vocalization-Strategy ($N = 30$)	Mean	10.5000		15.9333	3.5333
	SD	3.1156		7.4460	2.6488
	$r_{12} = -.1486$		$r_{13} = .0418$		$r_{23} = .6400$
Imagery-Control ($N = 30$)	Mean	10.3000		21.1667	7.7333
	SD	2.9261		8.6745	3.1506
	$r_{12} = -.0020$		$r_{13} = .4017$		$r_{23} = .1531$
Imagery-Strategy ($N = 30$)	Mean	10.5000		20.7667	5.0000
	SD	3.5209		10.2644	2.9361
	$r_{12} = .1045$		$r_{13} = -.0767$		$r_{23} = .6384$

TABLE A-3. "Sleep" Data Set (See Exercise 2-15 for a description.)

Subject No.	*Sleep (hrs.)*	*IQ*	*Vocabulary*	*Reasoning*	*Arithmetic*
1	3	115	17	6	7
2	6	130	16	18	16
3	0	108	8	4	5
4	9	109	12	9	10
5	6	107	12	8	9
6	9	91	9	8	11
7	3	123	18	8	5
8	0	129	17	13	16
9	6	111	13	15	15
10	3	101	7	1	2
11	0	90	8	6	5
12	9	122	18	18	18
13	3	98	8	2	0
14	0	115	15	14	13
15	6	95	11	5	7
16	9	114	12	13	14

TABLE A-4. "Medical" Data Set (See Exercise 5-7 for a description.)

X_1	X_2	X_3	X_4	X_5	X_6	X_7	X_8	X_9	X_{10}	X_{11}	X_{12}	X_{13}
2	001	2	66	60	54	79	87	84	80	85	82	1
2	005	1	42	40	38	83	75	82	82	85	84	4
2	007	3	59	33	47	83	86	76	82	80	84	4
2	008	4	40	55	60	77	76	71	71	75	75	4
2	009	2	36	48	55	79	75	69	75	75	77	4
2	010	4	49	37	49	87	81	87	91	83	88	5
2	011	4	51	41	70	86	82	84	87	83	89	4
2	012	2	50	54	44	82	84	78	84	77	75	4
2	013	2	17	59	70	83	75	73	79	72	85	1
2	015	2	51	43	48	82	89	78	78	75	84	5
2	016	1	35	59	51	88	84	86	89	88	93	1
2	017	1	59	54	43	83	82	79	81	79	79	1
2	020	4	31	54	64	80	78	75	77	84	82	4
2	023	1	39	60	65	87	82	77	89	79	89	2
2	024	3	51	49	33	78	81	81	78	78	78	5
2	025	1	57	43	49	83	86	78	84	90	86	1
2	026	3	32	54	45	84	77	77	82	79	87	4
2	027	3	48	39	38	92	84	88	94	89	94	1
2	029	2	31	44	54	84	87	75	79	83	76	4
2	032	3	46	58	40	76	77	77	79	73	79	1
2	034	2	42	39	54	75	83	78	83	76	78	4
2	035	1	49	61	65	84	79	83	85	86	89	1
2	036	4	33	59	50	76	73	73	78	79	77	4
2	040	1	49	42	72	84	80	85	77	84	87	1
2	042	2	64	40	38	79	78	79	79	81	81	1
2	043	1	71	42	53	85	83	84	83	81	87	5
2	044	1	27	62	64	82	78	77	75	77	81	4
2	045	1	56	39	52	82	83	84	79	81	85	3
2	046	3	47	49	44	78	75	75	75	75	76	1
2	047	3	52	43	48	80	85	81	75	78	84	5
2	052	1	57	38	59	82	84	86	82	83	81	1
2	053	2	56	48	48	81	57	82	78	86	82	1
2	055	2	50	30	44	77	76	75	78	73	78	3
2	056	1	73	41	33	80	87	80	84	87	76	4
2	057	2	54	38	60	80	78	73	82	78	80	4
2	059	1	48	37	54	81	81	80	85	82	81	2
2	060	4	41	52	36	84	86	87	82	81	89	1
2	061	1	26	57	52	84	76	75	80	77	78	3
2	063	2	38	46	41	77	75	75	73	81	81	3
2	064	1	58	49	44	76	83	75	68	79	77	4
2	066	2	51	55	37	72	76	76	70	72	73	5
2	069	1	49	47	52	83	81	78	86	82	84	1
2	071	3	54	39	52	89	79	82	86	75	88	1
2	072	4	68	51	50	71	82	77	75	78	73	1
2	073	3	47	30	63	80	88	77	80	81	80	4
2	074	1	44	49	61	72	82	75	77	76	76	1
2	077	4	64	52	60	83	87	89	90	79	86	4
2	080	3	54	54	47	79	70	78	81	75	85	2
2	082	3	66	40	37	83	76	76	86	79	79	1
2	083	1	41	43	39	79	83	69	75	69	80	5
3	002	3	66	56	32	75	79	75	76	71	71	1
3	003	2	52	45	46	75	81	69	73	79	75	1
3	005	2	54	46	48	82	76	85	85	75	83	1
3	006	3	36	55	59	81	79	80	88	78	79	1
3	008	2	83	44	52	73	86	76	75	79	71	1
3	009	2	54	57	47	80	80	78	78	75	78	5
3	010	4	43	40	67	91	77	82	91	82	83	1
3	011	2	51	38	58	86	82	82	91	92	83	1
3	013	1	73	47	54	85	85	84	87	86	82	1

TABLE A-4. (Continued)

X_1	X_2	X_3	X_4	X_5	X_6	X_7	X_8	X_9	X_{10}	X_{11}	X_{12}	X_{13}
3	018	3	57	42	62	81	80	81	87	83	82	2
3	019	1	51	33	50	82	82	78	85	85	82	3
3	021	1	65	44	39	83	83	79	84	77	84	1
3	022	2	39	46	46	81	77	83	84	78	76	1
3	023	2	59	41	48	77	75	82	76	81	76	4
3	024	4	58	51	44	77	83	79	81	87	78	1
3	025	3	74	40	50	79	87	84	82	82	78	5
3	029	4	33	49	55	76	72	78	73	75	75	1
3	030	4	52	52	51	73	72	77	77	81	72	5
3	033	1	46	51	36	75	78	80	80	83	79	2
3	034	1	49	43	62	75	73	81	78	76	81	5
3	035	3	47	40	32	81	76	83	88	77	86	1
3	037	2	45	31	54	75	70	77	75	70	78	1
3	040	2	67	44	56	76	82	82	85	89	81	1
3	041	1	59	45	45	87	72	88	84	85	85	1
3	042	1	55	40	57	80	76	81	82	73	83	3
3	043	2	39	68	52	72	66	71	77	70	75	4
3	046	2	54	46	47	78	78	76	75	79	76	2
3	048	1	60	32	50	87	81	79	89	90	83	2
3	049	2	64	52	50	86	81	81	83	86	83	1
3	050	1	84	48	33	89	92	85	88	89	87	1
3	052	4	68	35	46	91	96	88	88	84	86	2
3	056	3	46	61	62	82	77	89	87	81	91	1
3	057	4	56	55	49	81	86	83	86	77	79	4
3	058	1	52	38	58	78	75	80	73	78	76	1
3	060	1	39	50	50	77	83	78	73	77	83	4
3	062	2	58	41	54	84	81	84	87	86	87	1
3	063	1	36	69	47	76	75	75	77	75	77	4
3	064	2	57	58	48	82	78	82	86	80	80	5
3	065	4	43	50	50	86	81	85	84	80	76	1
3	066	1	41	57	54	73	75	71	70	75	71	1
3	068	1	66	50	34	78	81	86	85	84	82	2
3	069	4	60	49	66	85	78	80	80	79	81	1
3	070	2	57	52	35	75	73	81	82	82	79	3
3	071	2	38	49	42	76	76	75	71	76	71	1
3	072	2	52	56	70	80	78	77	87	79	79	1
3	073	2	39	54	60	75	78	78	75	81	81	1
3	074	1	47	47	64	77	77	76	75	77	72	1
3	077	1	71	41	45	75	79	81	76	86	78	2
3	078	4	45	44	44	85	86	76	83	78	82	5
3	080	2	39	44	53	76	72	78	75	77	77	4
3	081	2	64	37	39	81	85	81	80	82	81	1
3	083	3	56	40	36	84	90	79	87	87	85	2
4	001	1	41	62	54	85	83	83	80	77	89	5
4	003	2	38	66	32	88	84	83	84	84	79	4
4	004	4	70	32	60	92	88	86	95	86	90	2
4	005	2	57	56	56	81	78	86	77	82	80	5
4	008	2	52	42	39	88	75	71	79	84	75	1
4	009	1	38	72	59	85	71	82	81	81	84	1
4	010	2	58	72	60	92	75	79	87	78	85	4
4	013	1	83	49	51	80	82	75	77	73	80	5
4	014	3	52	65	56	78	75	71	76	73	75	1
4	015	2	45	63	57	83	73	76	78	76	85	4
4	016	1	38	46	52	82	76	75	80	82	76	5
4	017	2	41	52	45	80	76	80	76	75	77	1
4	018	1	75	69	51	77	77	80	76	82	81	5
4	019	4	63	55	32	80	77	80	81	84	80	5
4	020	3	43	61	60	84	84	84	80	84	86	5
4	021	2	42	61	53	79	81	85	81	84	85	1

TABLE A-4 (Continued)

X_1	X_2	X_3	X_4	X_5	X_6	X_7	X_8	X_9	X_{10}	X_{11}	X_{12}	X_{13}
4	024	3	42	73	37	80	80	79	76	80	81	5
4	026	1	44	61	41	83	83	75	83	86	87	3
4	027	1	53	44	46	79	76	75	75	77	77	4
4	029	2	40	65	45	88	83	81	81	82	85	1
4	031	1	56	46	40	89	78	78	87	87	84	1
4	032	3	57	52	41	88	75	81	81	81	78	1
4	033	1	66	53	34	84	80	84	87	81	87	1
4	034	2	35	53	42	84	75	79	80	81	84	5
4	035	1	76	46	40	83	82	78	80	81	82	4
4	036	1	67	54	38	75	84	78	77	80	78	1
4	038	1	46	47	48	82	80	80	80	86	81	5
4	039	1	80	54	49	78	85	83	85	89	81	1
4	040	2	45	46	43	84	82	84	8	77	83	1
4	042	2	70	71	36	78	79	69	78	81	81	4
4	044	2	36	64	41	78	78	75	76	78	77	1
4	046	4	40	41	42	82	77	79	72	77	85	5
4	047	2	41	42	54	83	79	80	84	75	68	5
4	048	1	65	73	70	70	79	73	73	78	64	1
4	049	2	82	53	29	94	79	88	91	81	90	3
4	051	1	68	57	58	76	88	75	77	79	71	3
4	053	4	64	69	46	87	84	82	90	81	84	5
4	055	3	54	54	36	72	88	80	81	79	84	1
4	057	2	43	56	32	83	80	80	83	83	84	1
4	059	1	44	68	47	81	84	81	73	81	82	1
4	060	2	28	68	59	77	69	69	65	75	72	1
4	061	4	75	49	49	83	83	83	82	72	80	3
4	062	1	61	56	45	75	73	76	80	70	79	4
4	063	3	55	51	52	80	75	73	82	81	80	5
4	064	2	56	56	50	77	75	77	68	81	76	3
4	065	1	50	58	52	85	84	83	84	83	85	4
4	066	2	45	60	69	84	78	76	81	85	81	2
4	067	1	46	69	46	84	81	80	72	82	81	1
4	068	1	53	65	38	82	75	76	72	76	76	5
4	069	1	75	56	43	83	81	80	85	81	80	4
4	070	2	66	55	43	85	78	75	83	80	81	3
4	071	1	81	49	58	84	81	90	83	85	84	4
4	072	2	41	59	61	79	85	82	87	85	79	1
4	075	1	62	52	42	80	70	75	80	77	76	2
4	076	2	62	53	40	75	83	70	70	79	73	1
4	077	1	40	69	64	75	70	71	75	75	80	1
4	078	2	58	63	58	83	76	79	83	85	82	5
4	079	2	55	69	32	83	76	79	83	85	82	3
4	080	1	60	70	52	75	75	75	72	75	76	5
4	081	1	50	65	66	85	73	79	82	71	75	1
4	082	1	67	60	62	83	54	87	76	85	68	3

TABLE B-1. Percentage points of the F distribution

$\alpha = .05$

Degrees of Freedom	ν_1								
ν_2	1	2	3	4	5	6	7	8	9
1	161.4	199.5	215.7	224.6	230.2	234.0	236.8	238.9	240.5
2	18.51	19.00	19.16	19.25	19.30	19.33	19.35	19.37	19.38
3	10.13	9.55	9.28	9.12	9.01	8.94	8.89	8.85	8.81
4	7.71	6.94	6.59	6.39	6.26	6.16	6.09	6.04	6.00
5	6.61	5.79	5.41	5.19	5.05	4.95	4.88	4.82	4.77
6	5.99	5.14	4.76	4.53	4.39	4.28	4.21	4.15	4.10
7	5.59	4.74	4.35	4.12	3.97	3.87	3.79	3.73	3.68
8	5.32	4.46	4.07	3.84	3.69	3.58	3.50	3.44	3.39
9	5.12	4.26	3.86	3.63	3.48	3.37	3.29	3.23	3.18
10	4.96	4.10	3.71	3.48	3.33	3.22	3.14	3.07	3.02
11	4.84	3.98	3.59	3.36	3.20	3.09	3.01	2.95	2.90
12	4.75	3.89	3.49	3.26	3.11	3.00	2.91	2.85	2.80
13	4.67	3.81	3.41	3.18	3.03	2.92	2.83	2.77	2.71
14	4.60	3.74	3.34	3.11	2.96	2.85	2.76	2.70	2.65
15	4.54	3.68	3.29	3.06	2.90	2.79	2.71	2.64	2.59
16	4.49	3.63	3.24	3.01	2.85	2.74	2.66	2.59	2.54
17	4.45	3.59	3.20	2.96	2.81	2.70	2.61	2.55	2.49
18	4.41	3.55	3.16	2.93	2.77	2.66	2.58	2.51	2.46
19	4.38	3.52	3.13	2.90	2.74	2.63	2.54	2.48	2.42
20	4.35	3.49	3.10	2.87	2.71	2.60	2.51	2.45	2.39
21	4.32	3.47	3.07	2.84	2.68	2.57	2.49	2.42	2.37
22	4.30	3.44	3.05	2.82	2.66	2.55	2.46	2.40	2.34
23	4.28	3.42	3.03	2.80	2.64	2.53	2.44	2.37	2.32
24	4.26	3.40	3.01	2.78	2.62	2.51	2.42	2.36	2.30
25	4.24	3.39	2.99	2.76	2.60	2.49	2.40	2.34	2.28
26	4.23	3.37	2.98	2.74	2.59	2.47	2.39	2.32	2.27
27	4.21	3.35	2.96	2.73	2.57	2.46	2.37	2.31	2.25
28	4.20	3.34	2.95	2.71	2.56	2.45	2.36	2.29	2.24
29	4.18	3.33	2.93	2.70	2.55	2.43	2.35	2.28	2.22
30	4.17	3.32	2.92	2.69	2.53	2.42	2.33	2.27	2.21
40	4.08	3.23	2.84	2.61	2.45	2.34	2.25	2.18	2.12
60	4.00	3.15	2.76	2.53	2.37	2.25	2.17	2.10	2.04
120	3.92	3.07	2.68	2.45	2.29	2.17	2.09	2.02	1.96
∞	3.84	3.00	2.60	2.37	2.21	2.10	2.01	1.94	1.88

TABLE B-1. (Continued)

ν_1									Degrees of Freedom	
10	12	15	20	24	30	40	60	120	∞	ν_2
241.9	243.9	245.9	248.0	249.1	250.1	251.1	252.2	253.3	254.3	1
19.40	19.41	19.43	19.45	19.45	19.46	19.47	19.48	19.49	19.50	2
8.79	8.74	8.70	8.66	8.64	8.62	8.59	8.57	8.55	8.53	3
5.96	5.91	5.86	5.80	5.77	5.75	5.72	5.69	5.66	5.63	4
4.74	4.68	4.62	4.56	4.53	4.50	4.46	4.43	4.40	4.36	5
4.06	4.00	3.94	3.87	3.84	3.81	3.77	3.74	3.70	3.67	6
3.64	3.57	3.51	3.44	3.41	3.38	3.34	3.30	3.27	3.23	7
3.35	3.28	3.22	3.15	3.12	3.08	3.04	3.01	2.97	2.93	8
3.14	3.07	3.01	2.94	2.90	2.86	2.83	2.79	2.75	2.71	9
2.98	2.91	2.85	2.77	2.74	2.70	2.66	2.62	2.58	2.54	10
2.85	2.79	2.72	2.65	2.61	2.57	2.53	2.49	2.45	2.40	11
2.75	2.69	2.62	2.54	2.51	2.47	2.43	2.38	2.34	2.30	12
2.67	2.60	2.53	2.46	2.42	2.38	2.34	2.30	2.25	2.21	13
2.60	2.53	2.46	2.39	2.35	2.31	2.27	2.22	2.18	2.13	14
2.54	2.48	2.40	2.33	2.29	2.25	2.20	2.16	2.11	2.07	15
2.49	2.42	2.35	2.28	2.24	2.19	2.15	2.11	2.06	2.01	16
2.45	2.38	2.31	2.23	2.19	2.15	2.10	2.06	2.01	1.96	17
2.41	2.34	2.27	2.19	2.15	2.11	2.06	2.02	1.97	1.92	18
2.38	2.31	2.23	2.16	2.11	2.07	2.03	1.98	1.93	1.88	19
2.35	2.28	2.20	2.12	2.08	2.04	1.99	1.95	1.90	1.84	20
2.32	2.25	2.18	2.10	2.05	2.01	1.96	1.92	1.87	1.81	21
2.30	2.23	2.15	2.07	2.03	1.98	1.94	1.89	1.84	1.78	22
2.27	2.20	2.13	2.05	2.01	1.96	1.91	1.86	1.81	1.76	23
2.25	2.18	2.11	2.03	1.98	1.94	1.89	1.84	1.79	1.73	24
2.24	2.16	2.09	2.01	1.96	1.92	1.87	1.82	1.77	1.71	25
2.22	2.15	2.07	1.99	1.95	1.90	1.85	1.80	1.75	1.69	26
2.20	2.13	2.06	1.97	1.93	1.88	1.84	1.79	1.73	1.67	27
2.19	2.12	2.04	1.96	1.91	1.87	1.82	1.77	1.71	1.65	28
2.18	2.10	2.03	1.94	1.90	1.85	1.81	1.75	1.70	1.64	29
2.16	2.09	2.01	1.93	1.89	1.84	1.79	1.74	1.68	1.62	30
2.08	2.00	1.92	1.84	1.79	1.74	1.69	1.64	1.58	1.51	40
1.99	1.92	1.84	1.75	1.70	1.65	1.59	1.53	1.47	1.39	60
1.91	1.83	1.75	1.66	1.61	1.55	1.50	1.43	1.35	1.25	120
1.83	1.75	1.67	1.57	1.52	1.46	1.39	1.32	1.22	1.00	∞

TABLE B-1. (Continued)

$\alpha = .01$

Degrees of Freedom	ν_1								
ν_2	1	2	3	4	5	6	7	8	9
1	4052	4999.5	5403	5625	5764	5859	5928	5982	6022
2	98.50	99.00	99.17	99.25	99.30	99.33	99.36	99.37	99.39
3	34.12	30.82	29.46	28.71	28.24	27.91	27.67	27.49	27.35
4	21.20	18.00	16.69	15.98	15.52	15.21	14.98	14.80	14.66
5	16.26	13.27	12.06	11.39	10.97	10.67	10.46	10.29	10.16
6	13.75	10.92	9.78	9.15	8.75	8.47	8.26	8.10	7.98
7	12.25	9.55	8.45	7.85	7.46	7.19	6.99	6.84	6.72
8	11.26	8.65	7.59	7.01	6.63	6.37	6.18	6.03	5.91
9	10.56	8.02	6.99	6.42	6.06	5.80	5.61	5.47	5.35
10	10.04	7.56	6.55	5.99	5.64	5.39	5.20	5.06	4.94
11	9.65	7.21	6.22	5.67	5.32	5.07	4.89	4.74	4.63
12	9.33	6.93	5.95	5.41	5.06	4.82	4.64	4.50	4.39
13	9.07	6.70	5.74	5.21	4.86	4.62	4.44	4.30	4.19
14	8.86	6.51	5.56	5.04	4.69	4.46	4.28	4.14	4.03
15	8.68	6.36	5.42	4.89	4.56	4.32	4.14	4.00	3.89
16	8.53	6.23	5.29	4.77	4.44	4.20	4.03	3.89	3.78
17	8.40	6.11	5.18	4.67	4.34	4.10	3.93	3.79	3.68
18	8.29	6.01	5.09	4.58	4.25	4.01	3.84	3.71	3.60
19	8.18	5.93	5.01	4.50	4.17	3.94	3.77	3.63	3.52
20	8.10	5.85	4.94	4.43	4.10	3.87	3.70	3.56	3.46
21	8.02	5.78	4.87	4.37	4.04	3.81	3.64	3.51	3.40
22	7.95	5.72	4.82	4.31	3.99	3.76	3.59	3.45	3.35
23	7.88	5.66	4.76	4.26	3.94	3.71	3.54	3.41	3.30
24	7.82	5.61	4.72	4.22	3.90	3.67	3.50	3.36	3.26
25	7.77	5.57	4.68	4.18	3.85	3.63	3.46	3.32	3.22
26	7.72	5.53	4.64	4.14	3.82	3.59	3.42	3.29	3.18
27	7.68	5.49	4.60	4.11	3.78	3.56	3.39	3.26	3.15
28	7.64	5.45	4.57	4.07	3.75	3.53	3.36	3.23	3.12
29	7.60	5.42	4.54	4.04	3.73	3.50	3.33	3.20	3.09
30	7.56	5.39	4.51	4.02	3.70	3.47	3.30	3.17	3.07
40	7.31	5.18	4.31	3.83	3.51	3.29	3.12	2.99	2.89
60	7.08	4.98	4.13	3.65	3.34	3.12	2.95	2.82	2.72
120	6.85	4.79	3.95	3.48	3.17	2.96	2.79	2.66	2.56
∞	6.63	4.61	3.78	3.32	3.02	2.80	2.64	2.51	2.41

TABLE B-1. (Continued)

ν_1 → Degrees of Freedom										
10	12	15	20	24	30	40	60	120	∞	ν_2
6056	6106	6157	6209	6235	6261	6287	6313	6339	6366	1
99.40	99.42	99.43	99.45	99.46	99.47	99.47	99.48	99.49	99.50	2
27.23	27.05	26.87	26.69	26.60	26.50	26.41	26.32	26.22	26.13	3
14.55	14.37	14.20	14.02	13.93	13.84	13.75	13.65	13.56	13.46	4
10.05	9.89	9.72	9.55	9.47	9.38	9.29	9.20	9.11	9.02	5
7.87	7.72	7.56	7.40	7.31	7.23	7.14	7.06	6.97	6.88	6
6.62	6.47	6.31	6.16	6.07	5.99	5.91	5.82	5.74	5.65	7
5.81	5.67	5.52	5.36	5.28	5.20	5.12	5.03	4.95	4.86	8
5.26	5.11	4.96	4.81	4.73	4.65	4.57	4.48	4.40	4.31	9
4.85	4.71	4.56	4.41	4.33	4.25	4.17	4.08	4.00	3.91	10
4.54	4.40	4.25	4.10	4.02	3.94	3.86	3.78	3.69	3.60	11
4.30	4.16	4.01	3.86	3.78	3.70	3.62	3.54	3.45	3.36	12
4.10	3.96	3.82	3.66	3.59	3.51	3.43	3.34	3.25	3.17	13
3.94	3.80	3.66	3.51	3.43	3.35	3.27	3.18	3.09	3.00	14
3.80	3.67	3.52	3.37	3.29	3.21	3.13	3.05	2.96	2.87	15
3.69	3.55	3.41	3.26	3.18	3.10	3.02	2.93	2.84	2.75	16
3.59	3.46	3.31	3.16	3.08	3.00	2.92	2.83	2.75	2.65	17
3.51	3.37	3.23	3.08	3.00	2.92	2.84	2.75	2.66	2.57	18
3.43	3.30	3.15	3.00	2.92	2.84	2.76	2.67	2.58	2.49	19
3.37	3.23	3.09	2.94	2.86	2.78	2.69	2.61	2.52	2.42	20
3.31	3.17	3.03	2.88	2.80	2.72	2.64	2.55	2.46	2.36	21
3.26	3.12	2.98	2.83	2.75	2.67	2.58	2.50	2.40	2.31	22
3.21	3.07	2.93	2.78	2.70	2.62	2.54	2.45	2.35	2.26	23
3.17	3.03	2.89	2.74	2.66	2.58	2.49	2.40	2.31	2.21	24
3.13	2.99	2.85	2.70	2.62	2.54	2.45	2.36	2.27	2.17	25
3.09	2.96	2.81	2.66	2.58	2.50	2.42	2.33	2.23	2.13	26
3.06	2.93	2.78	2.63	2.55	2.47	2.38	2.29	2.20	2.10	27
3.03	2.90	2.75	2.60	2.52	2.44	2.35	2.26	2.17	2.06	28
3.00	2.87	2.73	2.57	2.49	2.41	2.33	2.23	2.14	2.03	29
2.98	2.84	2.70	2.55	2.47	2.39	2.30	2.21	2.11	2.01	30
2.80	2.66	2.52	2.37	2.29	2.20	2.11	2.02	1.92	1.80	40
2.63	2.50	2.35	2.20	2.12	2.03	1.94	1.84	1.73	1.60	60
2.47	2.34	2.19	2.03	1.95	1.86	1.76	1.66	1.53	1.38	120
2.32	2.18	2.04	1.88	1.79	1.70	1.59	1.47	1.32	1.00	∞

From "Tables of Percentage Points of the Inverted Beta (F) Distribution," *Biometrika,* Vol. 33 (1943), pp. 73–88, by Maxine Merrington and Catherine M. Thompson. Reproduced by permission of Professor E. S. Pearson.

TABLE B-2. Percentage points of Student's t distribution

d/f	α .25 2α .50	.20 .40	.15 .30	.10 .20	.05 .10	.025 .05	.01 .02	.005 .01	.0005 .001
1	1.000	1.376	1.963	3.078	6.314	12.706	31.821	63.657	636.619
2	.816	1.061	1.386	1.886	2.920	4.303	6.965	9.925	31.598
3	.765	.978	1.250	1.638	2.353	3.182	4.541	5.841	12.924
4	.741	.941	1.190	1.533	2.132	2.776	3.747	4.604	8.610
5	.727	.920	1.156	1.476	2.015	2.571	3.365	4.032	6.869
6	.718	.906	1.134	1.440	1.943	2.447	3.143	3.707	5.959
7	.711	.896	1.119	1.415	1.895	2.365	2.998	3.499	5.408
8	.706	.889	1.108	1.397	1.860	2.306	2.896	3.355	5.041
9	.703	.883	1.100	1.383	1.833	2.262	2.821	3.250	4.781
10	.700	.879	1.093	1.372	1.812	2.228	2.764	3.169	4.587
11	.697	.876	1.088	1.363	1.796	2.201	2.718	3.106	4.437
12	.695	.873	1.083	1.356	1.782	2.179	2.681	3.055	4.318
13	.694	.870	1.079	1.350	1.771	2.160	2.650	3.012	4.221
14	.692	.868	1.076	1.345	1.761	2.145	2.624	2.977	4.140
15	.691	.866	1.074	1.341	1.753	2.131	2.602	2.947	4.073
16	.690	.865	1.071	1.337	1.746	2.120	2.583	2.921	4.015
17	.689	.863	1.069	1.333	1.740	2.110	2.567	2.898	3.965
18	.688	.862	1.067	1.330	1.734	2.101	2.552	2.878	3.922
19	.688	.861	1.066	1.328	1.729	2.093	2.539	2.861	3.883
20	.687	.860	1.064	1.325	1.725	2.086	2.528	2.845	3.850
21	.686	.859	1.063	1.323	1.721	2.080	2.518	2.831	3.819
22	.686	.858	1.061	1.321	1.717	2.074	2.508	2.819	3.792
23	.685	.858	1.060	1.319	1.714	2.069	2.500	2.807	3.767
24	.685	.857	1.059	1.318	1.711	2.064	2.492	2.797	3.745
25	.684	.856	1.058	1.316	1.708	2.060	2.485	2.787	3.725
26	.684	.856	1.058	1.315	1.706	2.056	2.479	2.779	3.707
27	.684	.855	1.057	1.314	1.703	2.052	2.473	2.771	3.690
28	.683	.855	1.056	1.313	1.701	2.048	2.467	2.763	3.674
29	.683	.854	1.055	1.311	1.699	2.045	2.462	2.756	3.659
30	.683	.854	1.055	1.310	1.697	2.042	2.457	2.750	3.646
40	.681	.851	1.050	1.303	1.684	2.021	2.423	2.704	3.551
60	.679	.848	1.046	1.296	1.671	2.000	2.390	2.660	3.460
120	.677	.845	1.041	1.289	1.658	1.980	2.358	2.617	3.373
∞	.674	.842	1.036	1.282	1.645	1.960	2.326	2.576	3.291

From Table iii of Fisher and Yates, *Statistical Tables for Biological, Agricultural and Medical Research,* published by Longman Group Ltd., London (previously published by Oliver & Boyd, Edinburgh). Reprinted by permission of the authors and publishers.

TABLE B-3. Percentiles of the χ^2 distribution

df	$P_{0.5}$	P_{01}	$P_{02.5}$	P_{05}	P_{10}	P_{90}	P_{95}	$P_{97.5}$	P_{99}	$P_{99.5}$
1	0.000039	0.00016	0.00098	0.0039	0.0158	2.71	3.84	5.02	6.63	7.88
2	0.0100	0.0201	0.0506	0.1026	0.2107	4.61	5.99	7.38	9.21	10.60
3	0.0717	0.115	0.216	0.352	0.584	6.25	7.81	9.35	11.34	12.84
4	0.207	0.297	0.484	0.711	1.064	7.78	9.49	11.14	13.28	14.86
5	0.412	0.554	0.831	1.15	1.61	9.24	11.07	12.83	15.09	16.75
6	0.676	0.872	1.24	1.64	2.20	10.64	12.59	14.45	16.81	18.55
7	0.989	1.24	1.69	2.17	2.83	12.02	14.07	16.01	18.48	20.28
8	1.34	1.65	2.18	2.73	3.49	13.36	15.51	17.53	20.09	21.96
9	1.73	2.09	2.70	3.33	4.17	14.68	16.92	19.02	21.67	23.59
10	2.16	2.56	3.25	3.94	4.87	15.99	18.31	20.48	23.21	25.19
11	2.60	3.05	3.82	4.57	5.58	17.28	19.68	21.92	24.73	26.76
12	3.07	3.57	4.40	5.23	6.30	18.55	21.03	23.34	26.22	28.30
13	3.57	4.11	5.01	5.89	7.04	19.81	22.36	24.74	27.69	29.82
14	4.07	4.66	5.63	6.57	7.79	21.06	23.68	26.12	29.14	31.32
15	4.60	5.23	6.26	7.26	8.55	22.31	25.00	27.49	30.58	32.80
16	5.14	5.81	6.91	7.96	9.31	23.54	26.30	28.85	32.00	34.27
18	6.26	7.01	8.23	9.39	10.86	25.99	28.87	31.53	34.81	37.16
20	7.43	8.26	9.59	10.85	12.44	28.41	31.41	34.17	37.57	40.00
24	9.89	10.86	12.40	13.85	15.66	33.20	36.42	39.36	42.98	45.56
30	13.79	14.95	16.79	18.49	20.60	40.26	43.77	46.98	50.89	53.67
40	20.71	22.16	24.43	26.51	29.05	51.81	55.76	59.34	63.69	66.77
60	35.53	37.48	40.48	43.19	46.46	74.40	79.08	83.30	88.38	91.95
120	83.85	86.92	91.58	95.70	100.62	140.23	146.57	152.21	158.95	163.64

For large values of degrees of freedom the approximate formula

$$\chi^2_a = \nu\left(1 - \frac{2}{9\nu} + z_a\sqrt{\frac{2}{9\nu}}\right)^3$$

where z_a is the normal deviate and ν is the number of degrees of freedom, may be used. For example $\chi^2_{.99} = 60[1 - .00370 + (2.326 \times .06086)]^3 = 60(1.1379)^3 = 88.4$ for the 99th percentile for 60 degrees of freedom. From *Introduction to Statistical Analysis,* 3rd ed., by W. J. Dixon and F. J. Massey, Jr.

TABLE B-4. Critical values of the Bonferroni t

($\alpha = .05$, familywise)

	Degrees of freedom																		
$a_i/\Sigma a_i$	10	12	14	16	18	20	22	24	26	28	30	35	40	45	50	60	80	100	250	500
1/32	3.87	3.68	3.56	3.48	3.41	3.36	3.32	3.28	3.26	3.23	3.21	3.17	3.14	3.12	3.11	3.08	3.05	3.03	2.98	2.97
3/32	3.21	3.09	3.01	2.95	2.91	2.87	2.85	2.82	2.81	2.79	2.78	2.75	2.73	2.72	2.70	2.68	2.66	2.65	2.62	2.61
5/32	2.91	2.81	2.75	2.70	2.67	2.64	2.62	2.60	2.59	2.57	2.56	2.54	2.52	2.51	2.50	2.49	2.47	2.46	2.43	2.43
7/32	2.71	2.63	2.58	2.54	2.51	2.49	2.47	2.45	2.44	2.43	2.42	2.40	2.39	2.38	2.37	2.35	2.34	2.33	2.31	2.30
9/32	2.56	2.50	2.45	2.41	2.39	2.37	2.35	2.34	2.32	2.32	2.31	2.29	2.28	2.27	2.26	2.25	2.24	2.23	2.21	2.20
11/32	2.45	2.39	2.34	2.31	2.29	2.27	2.26	2.24	2.23	2.22	2.22	2.20	2.19	2.18	2.18	2.16	2.15	2.14	2.13	2.12
13/32	2.35	2.29	2.26	2.23	2.21	2.19	2.18	2.16	2.16	2.15	2.14	2.13	2.12	2.11	2.10	2.09	2.08	2.07	2.06	2.05
15/32	2.27	2.22	2.18	2.15	2.13	2.12	2.11	2.10	2.09	2.08	2.07	2.06	2.05	2.04	2.04	2.03	2.02	2.01	2.00	1.99
1/30	3.83	3.65	3.53	3.44	3.38	3.33	3.29	3.26	3.23	3.21	3.19	3.15	3.12	3.10	3.08	3.06	3.03	3.01	2.96	2.95
7/30	2.67	2.60	2.54	2.51	2.48	2.46	2.44	2.42	2.41	2.40	2.39	2.37	2.36	2.35	2.34	2.33	2.31	2.30	2.28	2.28
11/30	2.41	2.35	2.31	2.28	2.26	2.24	2.22	2.21	2.20	2.19	2.19	2.17	2.16	2.15	2.15	2.14	2.12	2.12	2.10	2.10
13/30	2.31	2.26	2.22	2.19	2.17	2.16	2.14	2.13	2.12	2.12	2.11	2.10	2.09	2.08	2.07	2.06	2.05	2.05	2.03	2.03
1/28	3.78	3.61	3.50	3.41	3.35	3.30	3.26	3.23	3.20	3.18	3.16	3.12	3.10	3.08	3.06	3.03	3.00	2.98	2.94	2.93
3/28	3.13	3.02	2.94	2.89	2.85	2.81	2.79	2.77	2.75	2.73	2.72	2.70	2.68	2.66	2.65	2.63	2.61	2.60	2.57	2.56
5/28	2.83	2.74	2.68	2.64	2.61	2.58	2.56	2.54	2.53	2.52	2.51	2.49	2.47	2.46	2.45	2.44	2.42	2.41	2.38	2.38
9/28	2.49	2.42	2.38	2.35	2.32	2.30	2.29	2.28	2.26	2.26	2.25	2.23	2.22	2.21	2.20	2.19	2.18	2.17	2.16	2.15
11/28	2.37	2.31	2.27	2.24	2.22	2.20	2.19	2.18	2.17	2.16	2.16	2.14	2.13	2.12	2.12	2.11	2.10	2.09	2.07	2.07
13/28	2.27	2.22	2.18	2.16	2.14	2.12	2.11	2.10	2.09	2.08	2.08	2.06	2.06	2.05	2.04	2.03	2.02	2.02	2.00	2.00
1/26	3.74	3.57	3.46	3.38	3.32	3.27	3.23	3.20	3.17	3.15	3.13	3.10	3.07	3.05	3.03	3.01	2.98	2.96	2.92	2.90
3/26	3.08	2.98	2.90	2.85	2.81	2.78	2.76	2.74	2.72	2.70	2.69	2.67	2.65	2.63	2.62	2.61	2.59	2.57	2.54	2.54
5/26	2.79	2.70	2.64	2.60	2.57	2.55	2.53	2.51	2.50	2.48	2.47	2.45	2.44	2.43	2.42	2.41	2.39	2.38	2.36	2.35
7/26	2.59	2.52	2.47	2.44	2.41	2.39	2.37	2.36	2.34	2.34	2.33	2.31	2.30	2.29	2.28	2.27	2.25	2.25	2.23	2.22
9/26	2.44	2.38	2.34	2.31	2.29	2.27	2.25	2.24	2.23	2.22	2.21	2.20	2.19	2.18	2.17	2.16	2.15	2.14	2.12	2.12
11/26	2.33	2.27	2.23	2.21	2.19	2.17	2.16	2.14	2.14	2.13	2.12	2.11	2.10	2.09	2.08	2.08	2.06	2.06	2.04	2.04
1/24	3.69	3.53	3.42	3.34	3.28	3.23	3.20	3.17	3.14	3.12	3.10	3.07	3.04	3.02	3.00	2.98	2.95	2.93	2.89	2.88
5/24	2.74	2.66	2.60	2.56	2.53	2.51	2.49	2.47	2.46	2.45	2.44	2.42	2.41	2.40	2.39	2.37	2.36	2.35	2.33	2.32
7/24	2.54	2.48	2.43	2.40	2.37	2.35	2.33	2.32	2.31	2.30	2.29	2.28	2.26	2.25	2.25	2.24	2.22	2.21	2.19	2.19
11/24	2.28	2.23	2.19	2.16	2.14	2.13	2.12	2.11	2.10	2.09	2.08	2.07	2.06	2.05	2.05	2.04	2.03	2.02	2.01	2.00
1/22	3.64	3.48	3.37	3.30	3.24	3.20	3.16	3.13	3.11	3.08	3.07	3.03	3.01	2.99	2.97	2.95	2.92	2.90	2.86	2.85
3/22	2.99	2.89	2.82	2.77	2.73	2.70	2.68	2.66	2.65	2.63	2.62	2.60	2.58	2.57	2.56	2.54	2.52	2.51	2.48	2.48

5/22	2.69	2.61	2.56	2.52	2.49	2.47	2.45	2.43	2.42	2.41	2.40	2.38	2.37	2.36	2.35	2.34	2.32	2.31	2.30	2.28
7/22	2.49	2.43	2.38	2.35	2.33	2.31	2.29	2.28	2.27	2.26	2.25	2.24	2.22	2.22	2.21	2.20	2.18	2.18	2.16	2.15
9/22	2.35	2.30	2.25	2.22	2.20	2.19	2.17	2.16	2.15	2.14	2.14	2.12	2.11	2.10	2.10	2.09	2.08	2.07	2.06	2.05
1/20	3.58	3.43	3.33	3.25	3.20	3.15	3.12	3.09	3.07	3.05	3.03	3.00	2.97	2.95	2.94	2.92	2.89	2.87	2.83	2.82
3/20	2.93	2.84	2.77	2.72	2.69	2.66	2.64	2.62	2.60	2.59	2.58	2.56	2.54	2.53	2.52	2.50	2.49	2.48	2.45	2.44
7/20	2.44	2.38	2.33	2.30	2.28	2.26	2.25	2.24	2.22	2.22	2.21	2.19	2.18	2.17	2.17	2.16	2.14	2.14	2.12	2.11
9/20	2.29	2.24	2.20	2.18	2.15	2.14	2.13	2.12	2.11	2.10	2.09	2.08	2.07	2.06	2.06	2.05	2.04	2.03	2.02	2.01
1/18	3.52	3.37	3.27	3.20	3.15	3.11	3.07	3.05	3.02	3.00	2.99	2.96	2.93	2.91	2.90	2.88	2.85	2.83	2.80	2.78
5/18	2.57	2.50	2.46	2.42	2.39	2.37	2.36	2.34	2.33	2.32	2.31	2.30	2.28	2.27	2.27	2.26	2.24	2.23	2.21	2.21
7/18	2.38	2.32	2.28	2.25	2.23	2.21	2.20	2.18	2.18	2.17	2.16	2.15	2.14	2.13	2.12	2.11	2.10	2.09	2.08	2.07
1/16	3.45	3.31	3.21	3.15	3.10	3.06	3.02	3.00	2.98	2.96	2.94	2.91	2.89	2.87	2.86	2.83	2.81	2.79	2.76	2.75
3/16	2.80	2.72	2.66	2.62	2.58	2.56	2.54	2.52	2.51	2.50	2.48	2.46	2.45	2.44	2.43	2.42	2.40	2.39	2.37	2.36
5/16	2.50	2.44	2.39	2.36	2.34	2.32	2.30	2.29	2.28	2.27	2.26	2.24	2.23	2.22	2.22	2.21	2.19	2.18	2.17	2.16
7/16	2.31	2.25	2.22	2.19	2.17	2.15	2.14	2.13	2.12	2.11	2.10	2.09	2.08	2.08	2.07	2.06	2.05	2.04	2.03	2.02
9/16	2.16	2.11	2.08	2.06	2.04	2.03	2.02	2.01	2.00	1.99	1.99	1.98	1.97	1.96	1.95	1.95	1.94	1.93	1.92	1.91
11/16	2.04	2.00	1.97	1.95	1.94	1.92	1.91	1.91	1.90	1.89	1.89	1.88	1.87	1.86	1.86	1.85	1.84	1.84	1.83	1.82
13/16	1.94	1.90	1.88	1.86	1.85	1.84	1.83	1.82	1.81	1.81	1.80	1.80	1.79	1.78	1.78	1.77	1.77	1.76	1.75	1.75
15/16	1.85	1.82	1.80	1.78	1.77	1.76	1.75	1.74	1.74	1.74	1.73	1.72	1.72	1.71	1.71	1.70	1.70	1.69	1.68	1.68
1/15	3.41	3.27	3.18	3.12	3.06	3.03	3.00	2.97	2.95	2.93	2.92	2.88	2.86	2.84	2.83	2.81	2.79	2.77	2.74	2.72
2/15	3.00	2.90	2.83	2.78	2.74	2.72	2.69	2.67	2.66	2.64	2.63	2.61	2.59	2.58	2.57	2.55	2.53	2.52	2.49	2.48
4/15	2.60	2.52	2.48	2.44	2.41	2.39	2.38	2.36	2.35	2.34	2.33	2.31	2.30	2.29	2.28	2.27	2.26	2.25	2.23	2.22
7/15	2.27	2.22	2.18	2.16	2.14	2.12	2.11	2.10	2.09	2.08	2.08	2.06	2.05	2.05	2.04	2.03	2.02	2.01	2.00	1.99
8/15	2.19	2.14	2.11	2.09	2.07	2.05	2.04	2.03	2.02	2.02	2.01	2.00	1.99	1.98	1.98	1.97	1.96	1.96	1.94	1.94
11/15	2.00	1.96	1.94	1.92	1.90	1.89	1.88	1.87	1.87	1.86	1.86	1.85	1.84	1.83	1.83	1.82	1.82	1.81	1.80	1.80
13/15	1.90	1.87	1.84	1.82	1.81	1.80	1.79	1.79	1.78	1.78	1.77	1.76	1.76	1.75	1.75	1.74	1.74	1.73	1.72	1.72
14/15	1.86	1.82	1.80	1.78	1.77	1.76	1.75	1.75	1.74	1.74	1.73	1.72	1.72	1.71	1.71	1.70	1.70	1.69	1.68	1.68
1/14	3.37	3.24	3.15	3.08	3.03	3.00	2.96	2.94	2.92	2.90	2.89	2.86	2.84	2.82	2.80	2.78	2.76	2.75	2.71	2.70
3/14	2.72	2.64	2.59	2.55	2.52	2.50	2.48	2.46	2.45	2.44	2.43	2.41	2.40	2.38	2.38	2.36	2.35	2.34	2.32	2.31
5/14	2.43	2.36	2.32	2.29	2.27	2.25	2.24	2.22	2.22	2.21	2.20	2.18	2.17	2.16	2.16	2.15	2.14	2.13	2.11	2.11
9/14	2.08	2.04	2.01	1.99	1.97	1.96	1.95	1.94	1.93	1.93	1.92	1.91	1.90	1.90	1.89	1.88	1.88	1.87	1.86	1.85
11/14	1.96	1.92	1.90	1.88	1.86	1.85	1.84	1.84	1.83	1.83	1.82	1.81	1.80	1.80	1.80	1.79	1.78	1.78	1.77	1.76
13/14	1.86	1.83	1.80	1.79	1.78	1.76	1.76	1.75	1.74	1.74	1.74	1.73	1.72	1.72	1.71	1.71	1.70	1.70	1.69	1.68
1/13	3.32	3.20	3.11	3.05	3.00	2.96	2.93	2.91	2.89	2.87	2.86	2.83	2.81	2.79	2.78	2.76	2.73	2.72	2.69	2.68
2/13	2.92	2.82	2.76	2.71	2.68	2.65	2.63	2.61	2.59	2.58	2.57	2.55	2.53	2.52	2.51	2.50	2.48	2.47	2.44	2.43
3/13	2.68	2.60	2.55	2.51	2.48	2.46	2.44	2.43	2.42	2.40	2.40	2.38	2.36	2.35	2.34	2.33	2.32	2.31	2.29	2.28

TABLE B-4. (Continued)

$a_i/\Sigma a_i$	10	12	14	16	18	20	22	24	Degrees of freedom 26	28	30	35	40	45	50	60	80	100	250	500
4/13	2.51	2.45	2.40	2.37	2.34	2.32	2.31	2.30	2.28	2.28	2.27	2.25	2.24	2.23	2.22	2.21	2.20	2.19	2.17	2.17
5/13	2.38	2.32	2.28	2.26	2.23	2.22	2.20	2.19	2.18	2.17	2.16	2.15	2.14	2.13	2.13	2.12	2.10	2.10	2.08	2.08
6/13	2.28	2.22	2.19	2.16	2.14	2.13	2.11	2.10	2.09	2.09	2.08	2.07	2.06	2.05	2.04	2.04	2.02	2.02	2.00	2.00
7/13	2.18	2.14	2.10	2.08	2.06	2.05	2.04	2.03	2.02	2.01	2.01	2.00	1.99	1.98	1.98	1.97	1.96	1.95	1.94	1.93
8/13	2.10	2.06	2.03	2.01	1.99	1.98	1.97	1.96	1.95	1.95	1.94	1.93	1.92	1.92	1.91	1.90	1.90	1.89	1.88	1.87
9/13	2.04	2.00	1.97	1.95	1.93	1.92	1.91	1.90	1.90	1.89	1.88	1.87	1.87	1.86	1.86	1.85	1.84	1.84	1.82	1.82
10/13	1.97	1.94	1.91	1.89	1.88	1.86	1.86	1.85	1.84	1.84	1.83	1.82	1.82	1.81	1.81	1.80	1.79	1.79	1.78	1.77
11/13	1.91	1.88	1.86	1.84	1.82	1.82	1.81	1.80	1.79	1.79	1.78	1.78	1.77	1.76	1.76	1.75	1.75	1.74	1.73	1.73
12/13	1.86	1.83	1.81	1.79	1.78	1.77	1.76	1.75	1.75	1.74	1.74	1.73	1.72	1.72	1.72	1.71	1.70	1.70	1.69	1.69
1/12	3.28	3.15	3.07	3.01	2.96	2.93	2.90	2.88	2.86	2.84	2.82	2.80	2.78	2.76	2.75	2.73	2.70	2.69	2.66	2.65
5/12	2.34	2.28	2.24	2.21	2.19	2.18	2.16	2.15	2.14	2.14	2.13	2.12	2.10	2.10	2.09	2.08	2.07	2.06	2.05	2.04
7/12	2.14	2.09	2.06	2.04	2.02	2.01	2.00	1.99	1.98	1.97	1.97	1.96	1.95	1.94	1.94	1.93	1.92	1.92	1.90	1.90
11/12	1.87	1.83	1.81	1.79	1.78	1.77	1.76	1.76	1.75	1.75	1.74	1.73	1.73	1.72	1.72	1.71	1.71	1.70	1.69	1.69
1/11	3.22	3.11	3.02	2.97	2.92	2.89	2.86	2.84	2.82	2.80	2.79	2.76	2.74	2.73	2.71	2.70	2.67	2.66	2.63	2.62
2/11	2.82	2.73	2.67	2.63	2.60	2.57	2.55	2.54	2.52	2.51	2.50	2.48	2.46	2.45	2.44	2.43	2.41	2.40	2.38	2.37
3/11	2.58	2.51	2.46	2.43	2.40	2.38	2.36	2.35	2.34	2.33	2.32	2.30	2.29	2.28	2.27	2.26	2.25	2.24	2.22	2.21
4/11	2.42	2.36	2.31	2.28	2.26	2.24	2.23	2.22	2.21	2.20	2.19	2.18	2.17	2.16	2.15	2.14	2.13	2.12	2.10	2.10
5/11	2.28	2.23	2.20	2.17	2.15	2.13	2.12	2.11	2.10	2.09	2.09	2.07	2.06	2.06	2.05	2.04	2.03	2.03	2.01	2.00
6/11	2.18	2.13	2.10	2.07	2.06	2.04	2.03	2.02	2.01	2.01	2.00	1.99	1.98	1.97	1.97	1.96	1.95	1.94	1.93	1.93
7/11	2.08	2.04	2.01	1.99	1.98	1.96	1.95	1.94	1.94	1.93	1.93	1.92	1.91	1.90	1.90	1.89	1.88	1.88	1.86	1.86
8/11	2.00	1.97	1.94	1.92	1.91	1.89	1.88	1.88	1.87	1.86	1.86	1.85	1.84	1.84	1.83	1.83	1.82	1.81	1.80	1.80
9/11	1.94	1.90	1.88	1.86	1.84	1.83	1.82	1.82	1.81	1.80	1.80	1.79	1.78	1.78	1.78	1.77	1.76	1.76	1.75	1.74
10/11	1.87	1.84	1.82	1.80	1.79	1.78	1.77	1.76	1.76	1.75	1.75	1.74	1.73	1.73	1.72	1.72	1.71	1.71	1.70	1.69
1/10	3.17	3.06	2.98	2.92	2.88	2.84	2.82	2.80	2.78	2.76	2.75	2.72	2.70	2.69	2.68	2.66	2.64	2.63	2.60	2.59
3/10	2.53	2.46	2.42	2.38	2.36	2.34	2.32	2.31	2.30	2.29	2.28	2.26	2.25	2.24	2.23	2.22	2.21	2.20	2.18	2.18
7/10	2.03	1.99	1.96	1.94	1.93	1.91	1.90	1.90	1.89	1.88	1.88	1.87	1.86	1.86	1.85	1.84	1.84	1.83	1.82	1.82
9/10	1.88	1.84	1.82	1.80	1.79	1.78	1.77	1.77	1.76	1.76	1.75	1.74	1.74	1.73	1.73	1.72	1.72	1.71	1.70	1.70
1/9	3.11	3.00	2.92	2.87	2.83	2.80	2.77	2.75	2.73	2.72	2.71	2.68	2.66	2.65	2.64	2.62	2.60	2.59	2.56	2.55
2/9	2.70	2.62	2.57	2.53	2.50	2.48	2.46	2.44	2.43	2.42	2.41	2.39	2.38	2.37	2.36	2.35	2.33	2.32	2.30	2.29
4/9	2.30	2.24	2.21	2.18	2.16	2.14	2.13	2.12	2.11	2.10	2.10	2.08	2.08	2.07	2.06	2.05	2.04	2.04	2.02	2.02

5/9	2.17	2.12	2.09	2.06	2.05	2.03	2.02	2.01	2.00	2.00	1.99	1.98	1.97	1.96	1.96	1.95	1.94	1.94	1.92	1.92
7/9	1.96	1.93	1.90	1.88	1.87	1.86	1.85	1.84	1.84	1.83	1.83	1.82	1.81	1.80	1.80	1.79	1.79	1.78	1.77	1.77
8/9	1.88	1.85	1.83	1.81	1.80	1.79	1.78	1.77	1.77	1.76	1.76	1.75	1.74	1.74	1.74	1.73	1.72	1.72	1.71	1.70
1/8	3.04	2.93	2.86	2.81	2.78	2.74	2.72	2.70	2.68	2.67	2.66	2.63	2.62	2.60	2.59	2.58	2.56	2.54	2.52	2.51
3/8	2.40	2.34	2.30	2.27	2.25	2.23	2.21	2.20	2.19	2.18	2.18	2.16	2.15	2.14	2.14	2.13	2.12	2.11	2.09	2.09
5/8	2.10	2.05	2.02	2.00	1.99	1.97	1.96	1.95	1.95	1.94	1.94	1.92	1.92	1.91	1.90	1.90	1.89	1.88	1.87	1.87
7/8	1.89	1.86	1.84	1.82	1.81	1.80	1.79	1.78	1.78	1.77	1.77	1.76	1.75	1.75	1.74	1.74	1.73	1.73	1.72	1.71
1/7	2.96	2.86	2.80	2.75	2.71	2.68	2.66	2.64	2.63	2.61	2.60	2.58	2.56	2.55	2.54	2.52	2.50	2.49	2.47	2.46
2/7	2.56	2.49	2.44	2.41	2.38	2.36	2.34	2.33	2.32	2.31	2.30	2.28	2.27	2.26	2.26	2.24	2.23	2.22	2.20	2.20
3/7	2.32	2.26	2.23	2.20	2.18	2.16	2.15	2.14	2.13	2.12	2.12	2.10	2.09	2.08	2.08	2.07	2.06	2.05	2.04	2.03
4/7	2.15	2.10	2.07	2.05	2.03	2.02	2.01	2.00	1.99	1.98	1.98	1.97	1.96	1.95	1.95	1.94	1.93	1.92	1.91	1.91
5/7	2.02	1.98	1.95	1.93	1.92	1.90	1.89	1.89	1.88	1.87	1.87	1.86	1.85	1.85	1.84	1.84	1.83	1.82	1.81	1.81
6/7	1.91	1.87	1.85	1.83	1.82	1.81	1.80	1.79	1.79	1.78	1.78	1.77	1.76	1.76	1.75	1.75	1.74	1.74	1.72	1.72
1/6	2.87	2.78	2.72	2.67	2.64	2.61	2.59	2.57	2.56	2.55	2.54	2.52	2.50	2.49	2.48	2.46	2.44	2.44	2.41	2.40
5/6	1.92	1.89	1.86	1.85	1.83	1.82	1.81	1.81	1.80	1.80	1.79	1.78	1.78	1.77	1.77	1.76	1.75	1.75	1.74	1.74
1/5	2.76	2.68	2.62	2.58	2.55	2.53	2.51	2.49	2.48	2.47	2.46	2.44	2.42	2.41	2.40	2.39	2.37	2.36	2.34	2.33
2/5	2.36	2.30	2.26	2.24	2.21	2.20	2.18	2.17	2.16	2.15	2.15	2.13	2.12	2.12	2.11	2.10	2.09	2.08	2.06	2.06
3/5	2.12	2.08	2.05	2.02	2.01	1.99	1.98	1.97	1.97	1.96	1.96	1.94	1.94	1.93	1.92	1.92	1.91	1.90	1.89	1.88
4/5	1.95	1.91	1.89	1.87	1.86	1.84	1.84	1.83	1.82	1.82	1.81	1.80	1.80	1.79	1.79	1.78	1.77	1.77	1.76	1.75
1/4	2.63	2.56	2.51	2.47	2.44	2.42	2.40	2.39	2.38	2.37	2.36	2.34	2.33	2.32	2.31	2.30	2.28	2.28	2.26	2.25
3/4	1.99	1.95	1.92	1.90	1.89	1.88	1.87	1.86	1.86	1.85	1.84	1.84	1.83	1.82	1.82	1.81	1.80	1.80	1.79	1.78
1/3	2.47	2.40	2.36	2.33	2.30	2.28	2.27	2.26	2.25	2.24	2.23	2.22	2.20	2.20	2.19	2.18	2.16	2.16	2.14	2.13
2/3	2.06	2.02	1.99	1.97	1.95	1.94	1.93	1.92	1.91	1.91	1.90	1.89	1.88	1.88	1.88	1.87	1.86	1.85	1.84	1.84
1/2	2.23	2.18	2.14	2.12	2.10	2.09	2.07	2.07	2.06	2.05	2.04	2.03	2.02	2.01	2.01	2.00	1.99	1.98	1.97	1.96
1/1	1.81	1.78	1.76	1.75	1.73	1.72	1.72	1.71	1.71	1.70	1.70	1.69	1.68	1.68	1.68	1.67	1.66	1.66	1.65	1.65
(α = .01, familywise)																				
1/32	4.90	4.59	4.38	4.24	4.13	4.05	3.98	3.93	3.89	3.85	3.82	3.76	3.71	3.68	3.65	3.61	3.56	3.53	3.46	3.44
3/32	4.18	3.96	3.82	3.72	3.64	3.58	3.53	3.49	3.46	3.43	3.41	3.36	3.33	3.30	3.26	3.25	3.22	3.19	3.14	3.13
5/32	3.87	3.68	3.56	3.48	3.41	3.36	3.32	3.28	3.26	3.23	3.21	3.17	3.14	3.12	3.11	3.08	3.05	3.03	2.98	2.97
7/32	3.66	3.50	3.39	3.32	3.26	3.21	3.18	3.15	3.12	3.10	3.08	3.05	3.02	3.00	2.98	2.96	2.93	2.92	2.88	2.86
9/32	3.51	3.36	3.27	3.20	3.14	3.10	3.07	3.04	3.02	3.00	2.98	2.95	2.93	2.91	2.89	2.87	2.85	2.83	2.79	2.78
11/32	3.39	3.26	3.17	3.10	3.05	3.01	2.98	2.96	2.94	2.92	2.90	2.87	2.85	2.83	2.82	2.80	2.78	2.76	2.72	2.71
13/32	3.29	3.17	3.08	3.02	2.97	2.94	2.91	2.89	2.87	2.85	2.84	2.81	2.79	2.77	2.76	2.74	2.72	2.70	2.67	2.66
15/32	3.21	3.09	3.01	2.95	2.91	2.87	2.85	2.82	2.81	2.79	2.78	2.75	2.73	2.72	2.70	2.68	2.66	2.65	2.62	2.61

TABLE B-4. (Continued)

$a_i/\Sigma a_i$	10	12	14	16	18	20	22	24	Degrees of freedom 26	28	30	35	40	45	50	60	80	100	250	500
1/30	4.86	4.55	4.35	4.21	4.10	4.02	3.96	3.91	3.86	3.83	3.80	3.74	3.69	3.66	3.63	3.59	3.54	3.51	3.45	3.42
7/30	3.62	3.47	3.36	3.28	3.23	3.18	3.15	3.12	3.10	3.08	3.06	3.02	3.00	2.98	2.96	2.94	2.91	2.89	2.86	2.84
11/30	3.35	3.22	3.13	3.07	3.02	2.98	2.95	2.93	2.91	2.89	2.88	2.85	2.82	2.81	2.80	2.78	2.75	2.74	2.70	2.69
13/30	3.25	3.13	3.05	2.99	2.94	2.91	2.88	2.86	2.84	2.82	2.81	2.78	2.76	2.74	2.73	2.71	2.69	2.68	2.65	2.64
1/28	4.81	4.51	4.31	4.18	4.07	3.99	3.93	3.88	3.84	3.80	3.77	3.71	3.67	3.63	3.61	3.57	3.52	3.49	3.43	3.41
3/28	4.10	3.89	3.75	3.65	3.58	3.52	3.48	3.44	3.41	3.38	3.36	3.32	3.28	3.26	3.24	3.21	3.17	3.15	3.10	3.09
5/28	3.78	3.61	3.50	3.41	3.35	3.30	3.26	3.23	3.20	3.18	3.16	3.12	3.10	3.08	3.06	3.03	3.00	2.98	2.94	2.93
9/28	3.43	3.29	3.20	3.13	3.08	3.04	3.01	2.98	2.96	2.94	2.93	2.90	2.88	2.86	2.84	2.82	2.80	2.78	2.75	2.74
11/28	3.31	3.18	3.10	3.04	2.99	2.95	2.92	2.90	2.88	2.86	2.85	2.82	2.80	2.78	2.77	2.75	2.73	2.71	2.68	2.67
13/28	3.21	3.09	3.01	2.96	2.91	2.88	2.85	2.83	2.81	2.79	2.78	2.75	2.73	2.72	2.71	2.69	2.67	2.65	2.62	2.61
1/26	4.76	4.47	4.28	4.14	4.04	3.96	3.90	3.85	3.81	3.77	3.74	3.68	3.64	3.61	3.56	3.54	3.50	3.47	3.41	3.38
3/26	4.05	3.85	3.72	3.62	3.55	3.49	3.44	3.41	3.38	3.35	3.33	3.29	3.26	3.23	3.21	3.18	3.15	3.13	3.08	3.06
5/26	3.74	3.57	3.46	3.38	3.32	3.27	3.23	3.20	3.17	3.15	3.13	3.10	3.07	3.05	3.03	3.01	2.98	2.96	2.92	2.90
7/26	3.54	3.39	3.29	3.22	3.16	3.12	3.09	3.06	3.04	3.02	3.00	2.97	2.94	2.92	2.91	2.89	2.86	2.84	2.81	2.80
9/26	3.39	3.25	3.16	3.10	3.05	3.01	2.98	2.95	2.93	2.92	2.90	2.87	2.85	2.83	2.82	2.80	2.77	2.76	2.72	2.71
11/26	3.27	3.14	3.06	3.00	2.96	2.92	2.89	2.87	2.85	2.83	2.82	2.79	2.77	2.75	2.74	2.72	2.70	2.69	2.65	2.64
1/24	4.71	4.42	4.23	4.10	4.00	3.93	3.87	3.82	3.78	3.74	3.71	3.66	3.61	3.58	3.56	3.52	3.47	3.45	3.38	3.36
5/24	3.69	3.53	3.42	3.34	3.28	3.23	3.20	3.17	3.14	3.12	3.10	3.07	3.04	3.02	3.00	2.98	2.95	2.93	2.89	2.88
7/24	3.49	3.34	3.25	3.18	3.13	3.09	3.05	3.03	3.00	2.98	2.97	2.94	2.91	2.90	2.88	2.86	2.83	2.82	2.78	2.77
11/24	3.22	3.10	3.02	2.96	2.92	2.88	2.86	2.83	2.82	2.80	2.79	2.76	2.74	2.72	2.71	2.69	2.67	2.66	2.63	2.62
1/22	4.65	4.37	4.19	4.06	3.96	3.89	3.83	3.78	3.74	3.71	3.68	3.62	3.58	3.55	3.53	3.49	3.45	3.42	3.36	3.34
3/22	3.95	3.76	3.63	3.54	3.47	3.42	3.38	3.34	3.31	3.29	3.27	3.22	3.20	3.17	3.15	3.13	3.09	3.07	3.03	3.01
5/22	3.64	3.48	3.37	3.30	3.24	3.20	3.16	3.13	3.11	3.08	3.07	3.03	3.01	2.99	2.97	2.95	2.92	2.90	2.86	2.85
7/22	3.44	3.30	3.20	3.14	3.09	3.05	3.02	2.99	2.97	2.95	2.93	2.90	2.88	2.86	2.85	2.83	2.80	2.79	2.75	2.74
9/22	3.29	3.16	3.08	3.02	2.97	2.94	2.91	2.88	2.86	2.85	2.83	2.80	2.78	2.77	2.75	2.74	2.71	2.70	2.67	2.66
1/20	4.59	4.32	4.14	4.02	3.92	3.85	3.79	3.74	3.71	3.67	3.65	3.59	3.55	3.52	3.50	3.46	3.42	3.39	3.33	3.31
3/20	3.89	3.71	3.58	3.49	3.43	3.38	3.34	3.30	3.27	3.25	3.23	3.19	3.16	3.14	3.12	3.09	3.06	3.04	3.00	2.98
7/20	3.38	3.25	3.16	3.09	3.04	3.00	2.97	2.95	2.93	2.91	2.90	2.86	2.84	2.83	2.81	2.79	2.77	2.75	2.72	2.71
9/20	3.23	3.11	3.03	2.97	2.93	2.89	2.86	2.84	2.82	2.81	2.79	2.77	2.75	2.73	2.72	2.70	2.68	2.66	2.63	2.62

1/18	4.52	4.26	4.09	3.96	3.87	3.80	3.75	3.70	3.67	3.63	3.61	3.55	3.51	3.48	3.46	3.43	3.38	3.36	3.30	3.28
5/18	3.52	3.37	3.27	3.20	3.15	3.11	3.07	3.05	3.02	3.00	2.99	2.96	2.93	2.91	2.90	2.88	2.85	2.83	2.80	2.78
7/18	3.32	3.19	3.10	3.04	3.00	2.95	2.93	2.90	2.88	2.87	2.85	2.82	2.80	2.79	2.77	2.75	2.73	2.72	2.68	2.67
1/16	4.44	4.19	4.03	3.91	3.82	3.75	3.70	3.66	3.62	3.59	3.56	3.51	3.47	3.44	3.42	3.39	3.35	3.32	3.26	3.25
3/16	3.76	3.58	3.47	3.39	3.33	3.28	3.24	3.21	3.18	3.16	3.14	3.11	3.08	3.06	3.04	3.02	2.99	2.97	2.93	2.91
5/16	3.45	3.31	3.21	3.15	3.10	3.06	3.02	3.00	2.98	2.96	2.94	2.91	2.89	2.87	2.86	2.83	2.81	2.79	2.76	2.75
7/16	3.25	3.13	3.04	2.98	2.94	2.90	2.88	2.85	2.84	2.82	2.80	2.78	2.76	2.74	2.73	2.71	2.69	2.67	2.64	2.63
9/16	3.10	2.99	2.92	2.86	2.82	2.79	2.77	2.75	2.73	2.71	2.70	2.68	2.66	2.64	2.63	2.62	2.60	2.58	2.55	2.54
11/16	2.98	2.88	2.82	2.77	2.73	2.70	2.68	2.66	2.64	2.63	2.62	2.59	2.58	2.56	2.55	2.54	2.52	2.51	2.48	2.47
13/16	2.88	2.79	2.73	2.68	2.65	2.62	2.60	2.58	2.57	2.56	2.55	2.52	2.51	2.50	2.49	2.47	2.46	2.44	2.42	2.41
15/16	2.80	2.72	2.66	2.62	2.58	2.56	2.54	2.52	2.51	2.50	2.48	2.46	2.45	2.44	2.43	2.42	2.40	2.39	2.37	2.36
1/15	4.40	4.16	3.99	3.88	3.79	3.73	3.67	3.63	3.59	3.56	3.54	3.49	3.45	3.42	3.40	3.37	3.33	3.30	3.24	3.23
2/15	3.96	3.77	3.64	3.55	3.48	3.43	3.38	3.35	3.32	3.30	3.28	3.23	3.20	3.18	3.16	3.13	3.10	3.08	3.03	3.02
4/15	3.54	3.39	3.29	3.22	3.17	3.12	3.09	3.06	3.04	3.02	3.00	2.97	2.95	2.93	2.91	2.89	2.86	2.85	2.81	2.80
7/15	3.21	3.09	3.01	2.95	2.91	2.88	2.85	2.83	2.81	2.79	2.78	2.75	2.73	2.72	2.70	2.69	2.66	2.65	2.62	2.61
8/15	3.13	3.02	2.94	2.89	2.85	2.82	2.79	2.77	2.75	2.74	2.72	2.70	2.68	2.66	2.65	2.64	2.62	2.60	2.57	2.56
11/15	2.94	2.85	2.78	2.74	2.70	2.67	2.65	2.63	2.62	2.60	2.59	2.57	2.55	2.54	2.53	2.51	2.50	2.48	2.46	2.45
13/15	2.85	2.76	2.70	2.65	2.62	2.59	2.57	2.56	2.54	2.53	2.52	2.50	2.48	2.47	2.46	2.45	2.43	2.42	2.40	2.39
14/15	2.80	2.72	2.66	2.62	2.58	2.56	2.54	2.52	2.51	2.50	2.49	2.47	2.45	2.44	2.43	2.42	2.40	2.39	2.37	2.36
1/14	4.36	4.12	3.96	3.85	3.76	3.70	3.64	3.60	3.57	3.54	3.51	3.46	3.43	3.40	3.38	3.34	3.30	3.28	3.22	3.21
3/14	3.67	3.51	3.40	3.32	3.27	3.22	3.18	3.16	3.13	3.11	3.09	3.06	3.03	3.01	2.99	2.97	2.94	2.92	2.88	2.87
5/14	3.37	3.24	3.15	3.08	3.03	3.00	2.96	2.94	2.92	2.90	2.89	2.86	2.84	2.82	2.80	2.78	2.76	2.75	2.71	2.70
9/14	3.02	2.92	2.85	2.80	2.76	2.73	2.71	2.69	2.67	2.66	2.65	2.62	2.60	2.59	2.58	2.56	2.54	2.53	2.51	2.50
11/14	2.90	2.81	2.75	2.70	2.67	2.64	2.62	2.60	2.58	2.57	2.56	2.54	2.52	2.51	2.50	2.49	2.47	2.46	2.43	2.42
13/14	2.81	2.72	2.66	2.62	2.59	2.56	2.54	2.52	2.51	2.50	2.49	2.47	2.45	2.44	2.43	2.42	2.40	2.39	2.37	2.36
1/13	4.31	4.08	3.92	3.81	3.73	3.66	3.61	3.57	3.54	3.51	3.48	3.44	3.40	3.37	3.35	3.32	3.28	3.26	3.20	3.18
2/13	3.88	3.69	3.57	3.48	3.42	3.36	3.32	3.29	3.26	3.24	3.22	3.18	3.15	3.13	3.11	3.08	3.05	3.03	2.99	2.98
3/13	3.63	3.47	3.37	3.29	3.23	3.19	3.15	3.12	3.10	3.08	3.06	3.03	3.00	2.98	2.97	2.94	2.92	2.90	2.86	2.85
4/13	3.46	3.32	3.22	3.15	3.10	3.06	3.03	3.00	2.98	2.96	2.95	2.92	2.89	2.88	2.86	2.84	2.81	2.80	2.76	2.75
5/13	3.32	3.20	3.11	3.05	3.00	2.96	2.93	2.91	2.89	2.87	2.86	2.83	2.81	2.79	2.78	2.76	2.73	2.72	2.69	2.68
6/13	3.22	3.10	3.02	2.96	2.92	2.88	2.85	2.83	2.81	2.80	2.78	2.76	2.74	2.72	2.71	2.69	2.67	2.66	2.62	2.61
7/13	3.13	3.02	2.94	2.88	2.84	2.81	2.79	2.76	2.75	2.73	2.72	2.69	2.68	2.66	2.65	2.63	2.61	2.60	2.57	2.56
8/13	3.05	2.94	2.87	2.82	2.78	2.75	2.73	2.71	2.69	2.68	2.66	2.64	2.62	2.61	2.60	2.58	2.56	2.55	2.52	2.51
9/13	2.98	2.88	2.81	2.76	2.73	2.70	2.68	2.66	2.64	2.63	2.61	2.59	2.57	2.56	2.55	2.54	2.52	2.50	2.48	2.47
10/13	2.92	2.82	2.76	2.71	2.68	2.65	2.63	2.61	2.59	2.58	2.57	2.55	2.53	2.52	2.51	2.50	2.48	2.47	2.44	2.43

TABLE B-4. (Continued)

	Degrees of freedom																		
$a_i/\Sigma a_i$	10	12	14	16	18	20	22	24	26	28	30	35	40	45	50	60	80	100	250	500
11/13	2.86	2.77	2.71	2.67	2.63	2.61	2.58	2.57	2.55	2.54	2.53	2.51	2.49	2.48	2.47	2.46	2.44	2.43	2.40	2.40
12/13	2.81	2.72	2.67	2.62	2.59	2.56	2.54	2.53	2.51	2.50	2.49	2.47	2.46	2.44	2.44	2.42	2.40	2.40	2.37	2.36
1/12	4.26	4.03	3.88	3.77	3.69	3.63	3.58	3.54	3.51	3.48	3.45	3.41	3.37	3.34	3.32	3.29	3.25	3.23	3.18	3.16
5/12	3.28	3.15	3.07	3.01	2.96	2.93	2.90	2.88	2.86	2.84	2.82	2.80	2.78	2.76	2.75	2.73	2.70	2.69	2.66	2.65
7/12	3.08	2.97	2.90	2.85	2.81	2.78	2.75	2.73	2.71	2.70	2.69	2.66	2.64	2.63	2.62	2.60	2.58	2.57	2.54	2.53
11/12	2.81	2.73	2.67	2.63	2.59	2.57	2.55	2.53	2.52	2.50	2.50	2.48	2.46	2.45	2.44	2.42	2.41	2.40	2.37	2.37
1/11	4.20	3.98	3.84	3.73	3.65	3.59	3.54	3.50	3.47	3.44	3.42	3.38	3.34	3.32	3.29	3.26	3.23	3.20	3.15	3.14
2/11	3.77	3.60	3.49	3.40	3.34	3.29	3.25	3.22	3.20	3.17	3.16	3.12	3.09	3.07	3.05	3.03	3.00	2.98	2.94	2.92
3/11	3.53	3.38	3.28	3.21	3.16	3.12	3.08	3.05	3.03	3.01	3.00	2.96	2.94	2.92	2.90	2.88	2.86	2.84	2.80	2.79
4/11	3.36	3.23	3.14	3.07	3.02	2.99	2.96	2.93	2.91	2.90	2.88	2.85	2.83	2.81	2.80	2.78	2.76	2.74	2.71	2.70
5/11	3.22	3.11	3.02	2.97	2.92	2.89	2.86	2.84	2.82	2.80	2.79	2.76	2.74	2.73	2.71	2.70	2.67	2.66	2.63	2.62
6/11	3.12	3.01	2.93	2.88	2.84	2.81	2.78	2.76	2.74	2.73	2.71	2.69	2.67	2.66	2.64	2.63	2.61	2.59	2.56	2.56
7/11	3.03	2.92	2.86	2.80	2.77	2.74	2.71	2.69	2.68	2.66	2.65	2.63	2.61	2.60	2.58	2.57	2.55	2.54	2.51	2.50
8/11	2.95	2.85	2.79	2.74	2.70	2.68	2.65	2.63	2.62	2.60	2.59	2.57	2.56	2.54	2.53	2.52	2.50	2.49	2.46	2.45
9/11	2.88	2.79	2.73	2.68	2.65	2.62	2.60	2.58	2.57	2.55	2.54	2.52	2.51	2.49	2.48	2.47	2.45	2.44	2.42	2.41
10/11	2.82	2.73	2.67	2.63	2.60	2.57	2.55	2.54	2.52	2.51	2.50	2.48	2.46	2.45	2.44	2.43	2.41	2.40	2.38	2.37
1/10	4.14	3.93	3.79	3.69	3.61	3.55	3.50	3.49	3.44	3.41	3.38	3.34	3.31	3.28	3.26	3.23	3.20	3.17	3.12	3.11
3/10	3.47	3.33	3.23	3.16	3.11	3.07	3.04	3.01	2.99	2.97	2.96	2.93	2.90	2.88	2.87	2.85	2.82	2.81	2.77	2.76
7/10	2.97	2.87	2.81	2.76	2.72	2.69	2.67	2.65	2.64	2.62	2.61	2.59	2.57	2.56	2.55	2.53	2.51	2.50	2.48	2.47
9/10	2.82	2.74	2.68	2.64	2.60	2.58	2.56	2.54	2.52	2.51	2.50	2.48	2.47	2.46	2.45	2.43	2.42	2.40	2.38	2.37
1/9	4.08	3.87	3.73	3.64	3.56	3.51	3.46	3.42	3.39	3.37	3.34	3.30	3.27	3.24	3.22	3.20	3.16	3.14	3.09	3.08
2/9	3.65	3.49	3.38	3.31	3.25	3.20	3.17	3.14	3.12	3.09	3.08	3.04	3.02	3.00	2.98	2.96	2.93	2.91	2.87	2.86
4/9	3.24	3.12	3.04	2.98	2.93	2.90	2.87	2.85	2.83	2.81	2.80	2.77	2.75	2.74	2.72	2.70	2.68	2.67	2.64	2.63
5/9	3.11	3.00	2.92	2.87	2.83	2.80	2.77	2.75	2.73	2.72	2.71	2.68	2.66	2.65	2.64	2.62	2.60	2.59	2.56	2.55
7/9	2.91	2.87	2.75	2.71	2.67	2.64	2.62	2.60	2.59	2.58	2.56	2.54	2.53	2.52	2.50	2.49	2.47	2.46	2.44	2.43
8/9	2.83	2.74	2.68	2.64	2.61	2.58	2.56	2.54	2.53	2.52	2.51	2.49	2.47	2.46	2.45	2.44	2.42	2.41	2.39	2.38
1/8	4.00	3.81	3.68	3.58	3.51	3.46	3.41	3.38	3.35	3.32	3.30	3.26	3.23	3.20	3.18	3.16	3.12	3.10	3.05	3.04
3/8	3.34	3.21	3.12	3.06	3.01	2.97	2.94	2.92	2.90	2.88	2.87	2.84	2.82	2.80	2.79	2.77	2.74	2.73	2.70	2.68
5/8	3.04	2.93	2.86	2.81	2.78	2.74	2.72	2.70	2.68	2.67	2.66	2.63	2.62	2.60	2.59	2.58	2.56	2.54	2.52	2.51
7/8	2.84	2.75	2.69	2.65	2.62	2.59	2.57	2.55	2.54	2.52	2.52	2.49	2.48	2.47	2.46	2.44	2.43	2.42	2.39	2.38

1/7	3.92	3.72	3.61	3.52	3.45	3.40	3.36	3.32	3.29	3.27	3.25	3.21	3.18	3.16	3.14	3.11	3.08	3.06	3.01	3.00
2/7	3.50	3.36	3.26	3.19	3.14	3.10	3.06	3.04	3.01	2.99	2.98	2.94	2.92	2.90	2.89	2.87	2.84	2.82	2.79	2.78
3/7	3.26	3.14	3.06	3.00	2.95	2.92	2.89	2.86	2.84	2.83	2.81	2.78	2.76	2.75	2.74	2.72	2.70	2.68	2.65	2.64
4/7	3.09	2.98	2.91	2.86	2.82	2.78	2.76	2.74	2.72	2.71	2.70	2.67	2.65	2.64	2.63	2.61	2.59	2.58	2.55	2.54
5/7	2.96	2.86	2.80	2.75	2.71	2.68	2.66	2.64	2.63	2.61	2.60	2.58	2.56	2.55	2.54	2.52	2.50	2.49	2.47	2.46
6/7	2.85	2.76	2.70	2.66	2.63	2.60	2.58	2.56	2.55	2.53	2.52	2.50	2.49	2.48	2.47	2.45	2.43	2.42	2.40	2.39
1/6	3.83	3.65	3.53	3.44	3.38	3.33	3.29	3.26	3.23	3.21	3.19	3.15	3.12	3.10	3.08	3.06	3.03	3.01	2.96	2.95
5/6	2.87	2.78	2.72	2.67	2.64	2.61	2.59	2.57	2.56	2.55	2.54	2.52	2.50	2.49	2.48	2.46	2.44	2.44	2.41	2.40
1/5	3.72	3.55	3.44	3.36	3.30	3.25	3.21	3.18	3.16	3.14	3.12	3.08	3.06	3.03	3.02	2.99	2.96	2.95	2.90	2.89
2/5	3.30	3.18	3.09	3.03	2.98	2.94	2.92	2.89	2.87	2.86	2.84	2.81	2.79	2.78	2.76	2.74	2.72	2.71	2.67	2.66
3/5	3.06	2.96	2.88	2.83	2.79	2.76	2.74	2.72	2.70	2.69	2.67	2.65	2.63	2.62	2.61	2.59	2.57	2.56	2.53	2.52
4/5	2.89	2.80	2.74	2.69	2.66	2.63	2.61	2.59	2.58	2.56	2.55	2.53	2.52	2.50	2.49	2.48	2.46	2.45	2.42	2.42
1/4	3.58	3.43	3.33	3.25	3.20	3.15	3.12	3.09	3.07	3.05	3.03	3.00	2.97	2.95	2.94	2.92	2.89	2.87	2.83	2.82
3/4	2.93	2.84	2.77	2.72	2.69	2.66	2.64	2.62	2.60	2.59	2.58	2.56	2.54	2.53	2.52	2.50	2.49	2.48	2.45	2.44
1/3	3.41	3.27	3.18	3.12	3.06	3.03	3.00	2.97	2.95	2.93	2.92	2.88	2.86	2.84	2.83	2.81	2.79	2.77	2.74	2.72
2/3	3.00	2.90	2.83	2.78	2.74	2.72	2.69	2.67	2.66	2.64	2.63	2.61	2.59	2.58	2.57	2.55	2.53	2.52	2.49	2.48
1/2	3.17	3.04	2.98	2.92	2.88	2.84	2.82	2.80	2.80	2.76	2.76	2.72	2.70	2.69	2.68	2.66	2.64	2.63	2.60	2.59
1/1	2.76	2.68	2.62	2.58	2.55	2.53	2.51	2.49	2.48	2.47	2.46	2.44	2.42	2.41	2.40	2.39	2.37	2.36	2.34	2.33

From Dayton, C.M., & Schafer, W.D. Extended tables of t and Chi-square for Bonferroni tests with unequal error allocation. *Journal of the American Statistical Association*, 1973, **68**, 78–83. Reprinted by permission.

TABLE B-5. Random normal deviates, $\mu = 0$ and $\sigma = 1$

01	02	03	04	05	06	07	08	09	10
0.464	0.137	2.455	−0.323	−0.068	0.296	−0.288	1.298	0.241	−0.957
0.060	−2.526	−0.531	−0.194	0.543	−1.558	0.187	−1.190	0.022	0.525
1.486	−0.354	−0.634	0.697	0.926	1.375	0.785	−0.963	−0.853	−1.865
1.022	−0.472	1.279	3.521	0.571	−1.851	0.194	1.192	−0.501	−0.273
1.394	−0.555	0.046	0.321	2.945	1.974	−0.258	0.412	0.439	−0.035
0.906	−0.513	−0.525	0.595	0.881	−0.934	1.579	0.161	−1.885	0.371
1.179	−1.055	0.007	0.769	0.971	0.712	1.090	−0.631	−0.255	−0.702
−1.501	−0.488	−0.162	−0.136	1.033	0.203	0.448	0.748	−0.423	−0.432
−0.690	0.756	−1.618	−0.345	−0.511	−2.051	−0.457	−0.218	0.857	−0.465
1.372	0.225	0.378	0.761	0.181	−0.736	0.960	−1.530	−0.260	0.120
−0.482	1.678	−0.057	−1.229	−0.486	0.856	−0.491	−1.983	−2.830	−0.238
−1.376	−0.150	1.356	−0.561	−0.256	−0.212	0.219	0.779	0.953	−0.869
−1.010	0.598	−0.918	1.598	0.065	0.415	−0.169	0.313	−0.973	−1.016
−0.005	−0.899	0.012	−0.725	1.147	−0.121	1.096	0.481	−1.691	0.417
1.393	−1.163	−0.911	1.231	−0.199	−0.246	1.239	−2.574	−0.558	0.056
−1.787	−0.261	1.237	1.046	−0.508	−1.630	−0.146	−0.392	−0.627	0.561
−0.105	−0.357	−1.384	0.360	−0.992	−0.116	−1.698	−2.832	−1.108	−2.357
−1.339	1.827	−0.959	0.424	0.969	−1.141	−1.041	0.362	−1.726	1.956
1.041	0.535	0.731	1.377	0.983	−1.330	1.620	−1.040	0.524	−0.281
0.279	−2.056	0.717	−0.873	−1.096	−1.396	1.047	0.089	−0.573	0.932
−1.805	−2.008	−1.633	0.542	0.250	−0.166	0.032	0.079	0.471	−1.029
−1.186	1.180	1.114	0.882	1.265	−0.202	0.151	−0.376	−0.310	0.479
0.658	−1.141	1.151	−1.210	−0.927	0.425	0.290	−0.902	0.610	2.709
−0.439	0.358	−1.939	0.891	−0.227	0.602	0.873	−0.437	−0.220	−0.057
−1.399	−0.230	0.385	−0.649	−0.577	0.237	−0.289	0.513	0.738	−0.300
0.199	0.208	−1.083	−0.219	−0.291	1.221	1.119	0.004	−2.015	−0.594
0.159	0.272	−0.313	0.084	−2.828	−0.439	−0.792	−1.275	−0.623	−1.047
2.273	0.606	0.606	−0.747	0.247	1.291	0.063	−1.793	−0.699	−1.347
0.041	−0.307	0.121	0.790	−0.584	0.541	0.484	−0.986	0.481	0.996
−1.132	−2.098	0.921	0.145	0.446	−1.661	1.045	−1.363	−0.586	−1.023
0.768	0.079	−1.473	0.034	−2.127	0.665	0.084	−0.880	−0.579	0.551
0.375	−1.658	−0.851	0.234	−0.656	0.340	−0.086	−0.158	−0.120	0.418
−0.513	−0.344	0.210	−0.736	1.041	0.008	0.427	−0.831	0.191	0.074
0.292	−0.521	1.266	−1.206	−0.899	0.110	−0.528	−0.813	0.071	0.524
1.026	2.990	−0.574	−0.491	−1.114	1.297	−1.433	−1.345	−3.001	0.479
−1.334	1.278	−0.568	−0.109	−0.515	−0.566	2.923	0.500	0.359	0.326
−0.287	−0.144	−0.254	0.574	−0.451	−1.181	−1.190	−0.318	−0.094	1.114
0.161	−0.886	−0.921	−0.509	1.410	−0.518	0.192	−0.432	1.501	1.068
−1.346	0.193	−1.202	0.394	−1.045	0.843	0.942	1.045	0.031	0.772
1.250	−0.199	−0.288	1.810	1.378	0.584	1.216	0.733	0.402	0.226
0.630	−0.537	0.782	0.060	0.499	−0.431	1.705	1.164	0.884	−0.298
0.375	−1.941	0.247	−0.491	0.665	−0.135	−0.145	−0.498	0.457	1.064
−1.420	0.489	−1.711	−1.186	0.754	−0.732	−0.066	1.006	−0.798	0.162
−0.151	−0.243	−0.430	−0.762	0.298	1.049	1.810	2.885	−0.768	−0.129
−0.309	0.531	0.416	−1.541	1.456	2.040	−0.124	0.196	0.023	−1.204
0.424	−0.444	0.593	0.993	−0.106	0.116	0.484	−1.272	1.066	1.097
0.593	0.658	−1.127	−1.407	−1.579	−1.616	1.458	1.262	0.736	−0.916
0.862	−0.885	−0.142	−0.504	0.532	1.381	0.022	−0.281	−0.342	1.222
0.235	−0.628	−0.023	−0.463	−0.899	−0.394	−0.538	1.707	−0.188	−1.153
−0.853	0.402	0.777	0.833	0.410	−0.349	−1.094	0.580	1.395	1.298

TABLE B-5. (Continued)

11	12	13	14	15	16	17	18	19	20
−1.329	−0.238	−0.838	−0.988	−0.445	0.964	−0.266	−0.322	−1.726	2.252
1.284	−0.229	1.058	0.090	0.050	0.523	0.016	0.277	1.639	0.554
0.619	0.628	0.005	0.973	−0.058	0.150	−0.635	−0.917	0.313	−1.203
0.699	−0.269	0.722	−0.994	−0.807	−1.203	1.163	1.244	1.306	−1.210
0.101	0.202	−0.150	0.731	0.420	0.116	−0.496	−0.037	−2.466	0.794
−1.381	0.301	0.522	0.233	0.791	−1.017	−0.182	0.926	−1.096	1.001
−0.574	1.366	−1.843	0.746	0.890	0.824	−1.249	−0.806	−0.240	0.217
0.096	0.210	1.091	0.990	0.900	−0.837	−1.097	−1.238	0.030	−0.311
1.389	−0.236	0.094	3.282	0.295	−0.416	0.313	0.720	0.007	0.354
1.249	0.706	1.453	0.366	−2.654	−1.400	0.212	0.307	−1.145	0.639
0.756	−0.397	−1.772	−0.257	1.120	1.188	−0.527	0.709	0.479	0.317
−0.860	0.412	−0.327	0.178	0.524	−0.672	−0.831	0.758	0.131	0.771
−0.778	−0.979	0.236	−1.033	1.497	−0.661	0.906	1.169	−1.582	1.303
0.037	0.062	0.426	1.220	0.471	0.784	−0.719	0.465	1.559	−1.326
2.619	−0.440	0.477	1.063	0.320	1.406	−0.701	−0.128	0.518	−0.676
−0.420	−0.287	−0.050	−0.481	1.521	−1.367	0.609	0.292	0.048	0.592
1.048	0.220	1.121	−1.789	−1.211	−0.871	−0.740	0.513	−0.558	−0.395
1.000	−0.638	1.261	0.510	−0.150	0.034	0.054	−0.055	0.639	−0.825
0.170	−1.131	−0.985	0.102	−0.939	−1.457	1.766	1.087	−1.275	2.362
0.389	−0.435	0.171	0.891	1.158	1.041	1.048	−0.324	−0.404	1.060
−0.305	0.838	−2.019	−0.540	0.905	1.195	−1.190	0.106	0.571	0.298
−0.321	−0.039	1.799	−1.032	−2.225	−0.148	0.758	−0.862	0.158	−0.726
1.900	1.572	−0.244	−1.721	1.130	0.495	−0.484	0.014	−0.778	−1.483
−0.778	−0.288	−0.224	−1.324	−0.072	0.890	−0.410	0.752	0.376	−0.224
0.617	−1.718	−0.183	−0.100	1.719	0.696	−1.339	−0.614	1.071	−0.386
−1.430	−0.953	0.770	−0.007	−1.872	1.075	−0.913	−1.168	1.775	0.238
0.267	−0.048	0.972	0.734	−1.408	−1.955	−0.848	2.002	0.232	−1.273
0.978	−0.520	−0.368	1.690	−1.479	0.985	1.475	−0.098	−1.633	2.399
−1.235	−1.168	0.325	1.421	2.652	−0.486	−1.253	0.270	−1.103	0.118
−0.258	0.638	2.309	0.741	−0.161	−0.679	0.336	1.973	0.370	−2.277
0.243	0.629	−1.516	−0.157	0.693	1.710	0.800	−0.265	1.218	0.655
−0.292	−1.455	−1.451	1.492	−0.713	0.821	−0.031	−0.780	1.330	0.977
−0.505	0.389	0.544	−0.042	1.615	−1.440	−0.989	−0.580	0.156	0.052
0.397	−0.287	1.712	0.289	−0.904	0.259	−0.600	−1.635	−0.009	−0.799
−0.605	−0.470	0.007	0.721	−1.117	0.635	0.592	−1.362	−1.441	0.672
1.360	0.182	−1.476	−0.599	−0.875	0.292	−0.700	0.058	−0.340	−0.639
0.480	−0.699	1.615	−0.225	1.014	−1.370	−1.097	0.294	0.309	−1.389
−0.027	−0.487	−1.000	−0.015	0.119	−1.990	−0.687	−1.964	−0.366	1.759
−1.482	−0.815	−0.121	1.884	−0.185	0.601	0.793	0.430	−1.181	0.426
−1.256	−0.567	−0.994	1.011	−1.071	−0.623	−0.420	−0.309	1.362	0.863
−1.132	2.039	1.934	−0.222	0.386	1.100	0.284	1.597	−1.718	−0.560
−0.780	−0.239	−0.497	−0.434	−0.284	−0.241	−0.333	1.348	−0.478	−0.169
−0.859	−0.215	0.241	1.471	0.389	−0.952	0.245	0.781	1.093	−0.240
0.447	1.479	0.067	0.426	−0.370	−0.675	−0.972	0.225	0.815	0.389
0.269	0.735	−0.066	−0.271	−1.439	1.036	−0.306	−1.439	−0.122	−0.336
0.097	−1.883	−0.218	0.202	−0.357	0.019	1.631	1.400	0.223	−0.793
−0.686	1.596	−0.286	0.722	0.655	−0.275	1.245	−1.504	0.066	−1.280
0.957	0.057	−1.153	0.701	−0.280	1.747	−0.745	1.338	−1.421	0.386
−0.976	−1.789	−0.696	−1.799	−0.354	0.071	2.355	0.135	−0.598	1.883
0.274	0.226	−0.909	−0.572	0.181	1.115	0.406	0.453	−1.218	−0.115

From tables of the RAND Corporation, by permission

TABLE B-6. Graphs of the percentiles of the Roy criterion for $s = 2$ to $s = 5$

a. $s = 2; \alpha = .05$

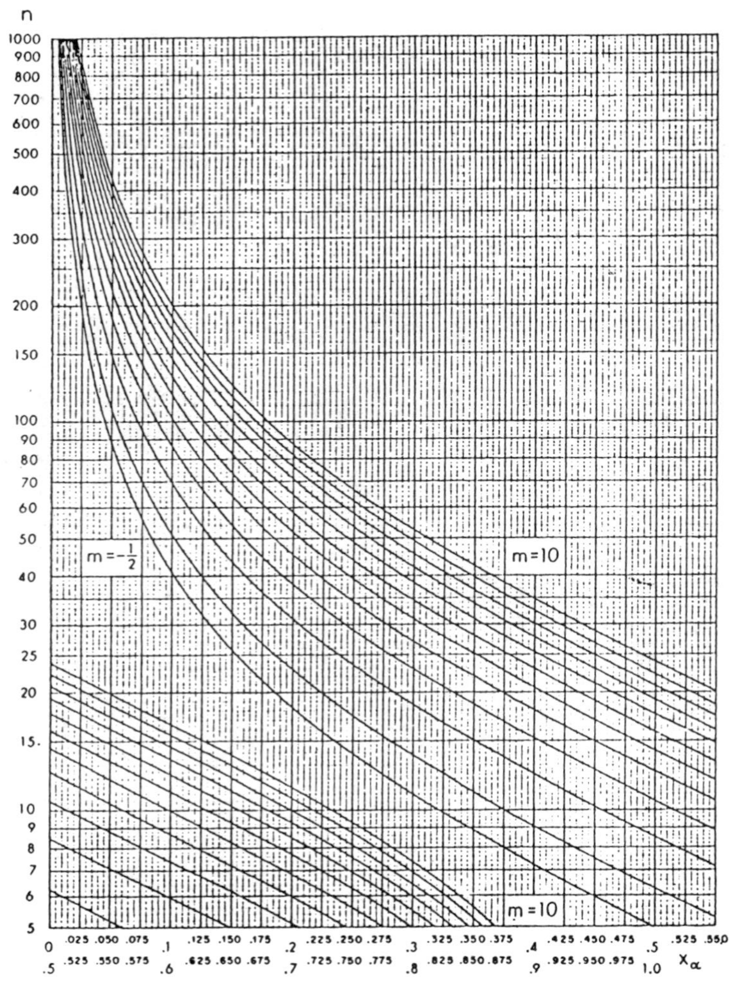

b. $s = 2; \alpha = .01$

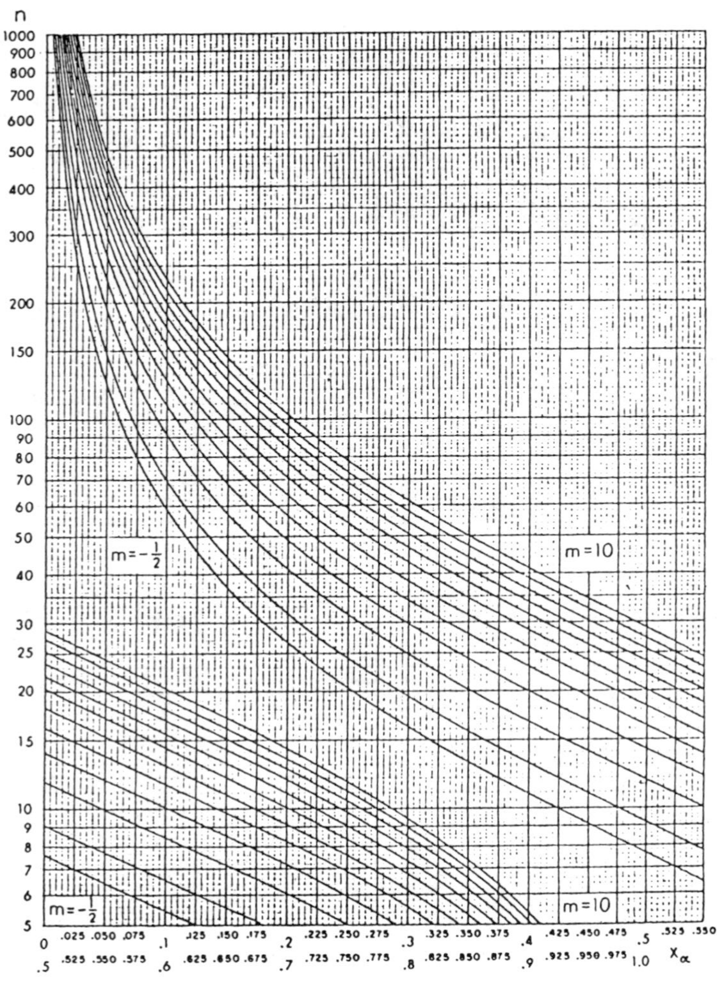

TABLE B-6. (Continued)

c. $s = 3; \alpha = .05$

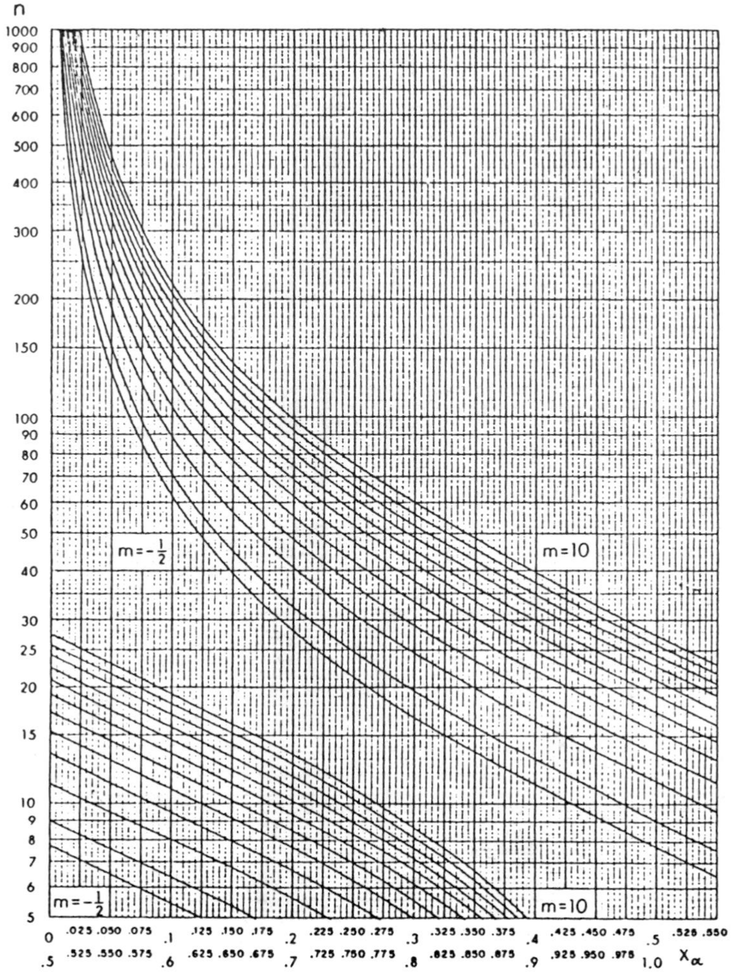

d. $s = 3; \alpha = .01$

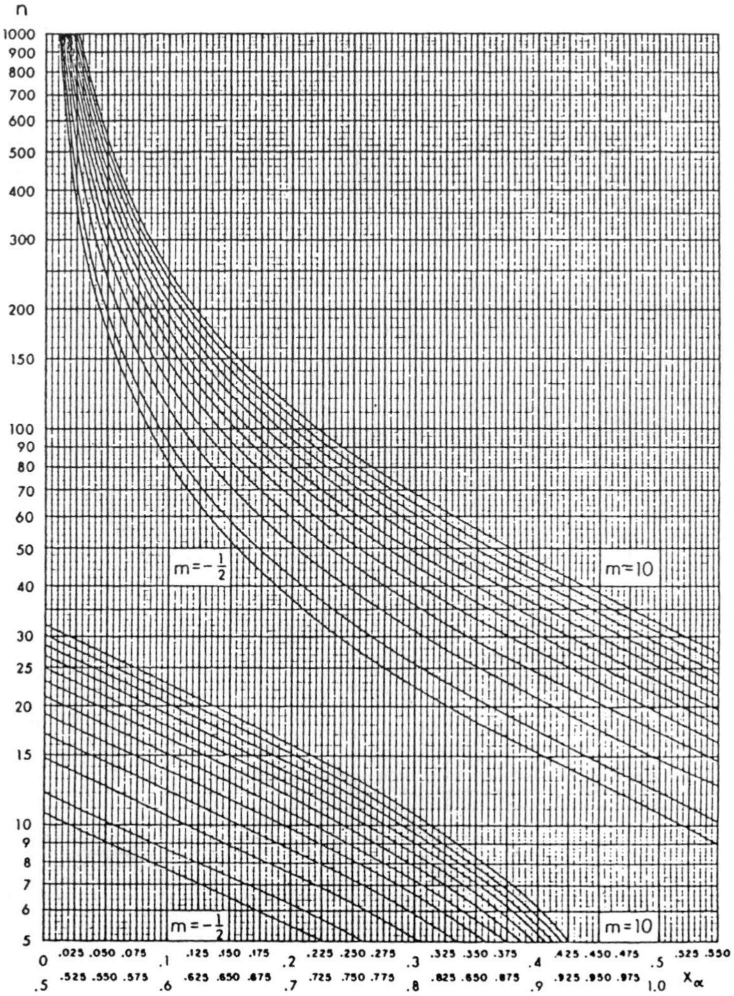

TABLE B-6. (Continued)

e. $s = 4; \alpha = .05$

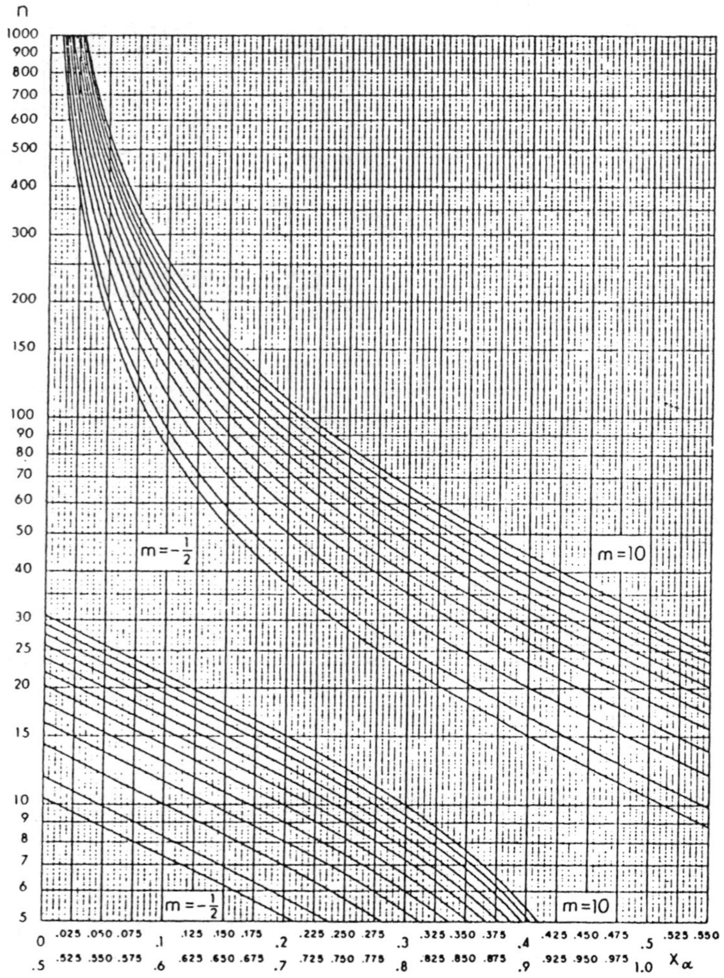

f. $s = 4; \alpha = .01$

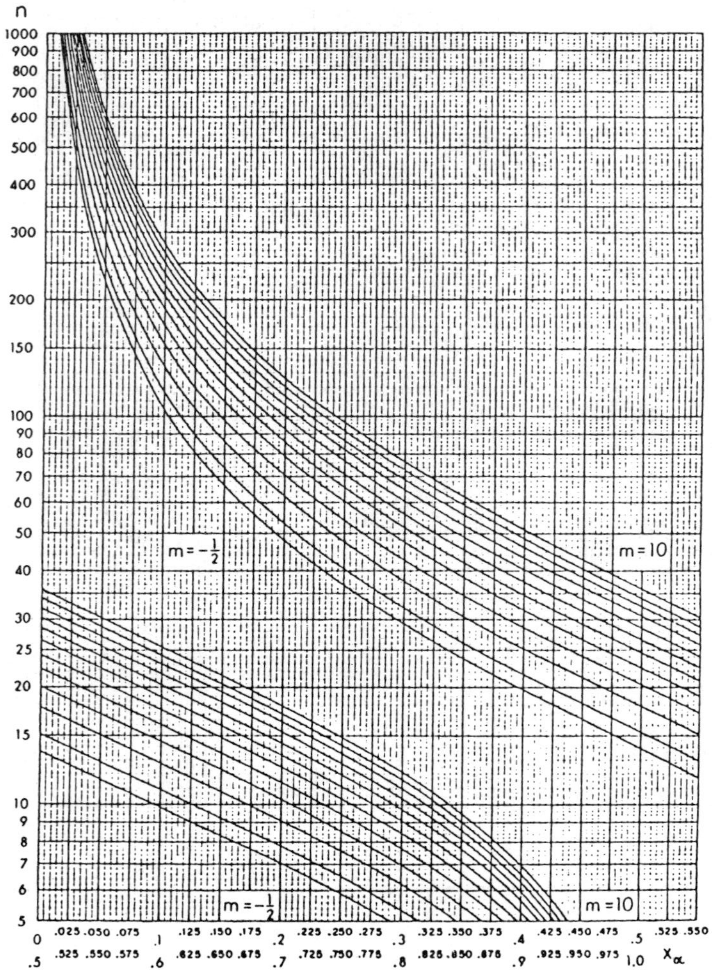

TABLE B-6. (Continued)

g. $s = 5; \alpha = .05$

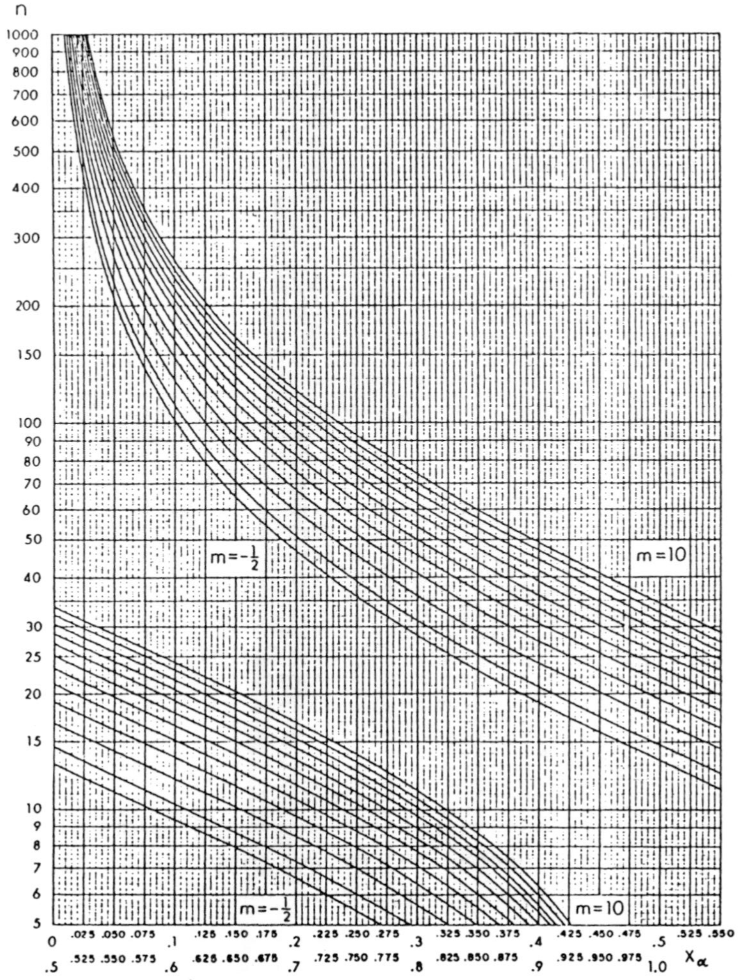

h. $s = 5; \alpha = .01$

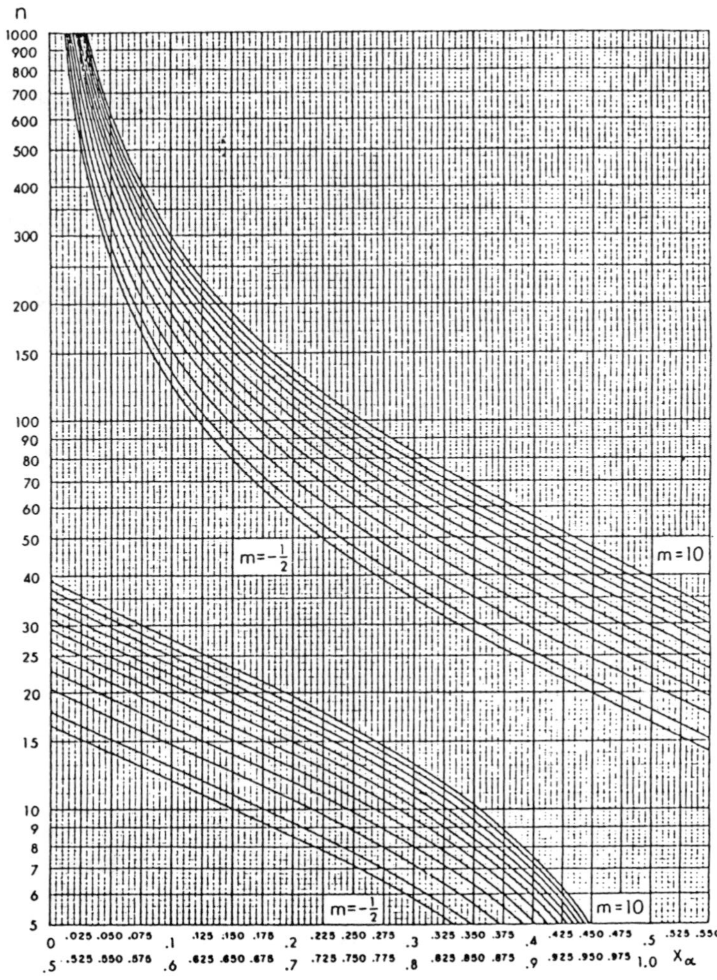

From "Charts of some upper percentage points of the distribution of the largest characteristic root," by D. L. Heck, *Annals of Mathematical Statistics,* 1960, Vol. 31, pp. 625–642. Reprinted by permission.

TABLE B-7. Percentiles of the Roy criterion for $s = 6$ to $s = 20$

$n \backslash m$	0	1	2	3	4	5	7	10	15
a. Upper 5% points of the largest root for $s = 6$									
5	0.8246	0.8499	0.8685	0.8830	0.8945				
10	0.6552	0.6917	0.7206	0.7442	0.7639				
15	0.5371	0.5758	0.6077	0.6346	0.6577				
20	0.4535	0.4912	0.5231	0.5505	0.5746				
25	0.3918	0.4276	0.4583	0.4852	0.5091				
30	0.3447	0.3782	0.4074	0.4332	0.4564				
40	0.2775	0.3069	0.3329	0.3563	0.3776				
60	0.1995	0.2225	0.2433	0.2624	0.2801				
80	0.1556	0.1745	0.1916	0.2075	0.2224				
100	0.1275	0.1434	0.1580	0.1716	0.1843				
130	0.10036	0.11319	0.12504	0.13615	0.14666				
160	0.08272	0.09348	0.10388	0.11284	0.12175				
200	0.06702	0.07586	0.08409	0.09186	0.09926				
300	0.04545	0.05156	0.05728	0.06281	0.06790				
500	0.02765	0.03143	0.03498	0.03835	0.04160				
1000	0.01397	0.01590	0.01772	0.01946	0.02113				
b. Upper 1% points of the largest root for $s = 6$									
5	0.8745	0.8929	0.9065	0.9169	0.9255				
10	0.7173	0.7482	0.7724	0.7922	0.8086				
15	0.5986	0.6334	0.6619	0.6858	0.7063				
20	0.5111	0.5462	0.5757	0.6010	0.6231				
25	0.4450	0.4790	0.5081	0.5335	0.5559				
30	0.3936	0.4261	0.4542	0.4789	0.5011				
40	0.3194	0.3484	0.3739	0.3969	0.4177				
60	0.2315	0.2548	0.2757	0.2948	0.3125				
80	0.1814	0.2006	0.2181	0.2342	0.2493				
100	0.1491	0.1654	0.1803	0.1942	0.2072				
130	0.11762	0.13091	0.14314	0.15457	0.16536				
160	0.09713	0.10830	0.11901	0.12834	0.13754				
200	0.07880	0.08803	0.09659	0.10466	0.11232				
300	0.05355	0.05996	0.06594	0.07160	0.07701				
500	0.03270	0.03661	0.04034	0.04388	0.04727				
1000	0.01651	0.01855	0.02046	0.02229	0.02405				

From "On the distribution of the largest of six roots of a matrix in multivariate analysis," by K. C. Pillai and C. G. Bantegui, *Biometrika,* 1959, Vol. 46, p. 239. Reprinted by permission.

TABLE B-7 (Continued)

$n \backslash m$	0	1	2	3	4	5	7	10	15
c. Upper 5% points of the largest root for $s = 7$									
5	0.85229	0.87214	0.88715	0.89893	0.90846	0.91632	0.9288	0.9445	
10	0.69490	0.72561	0.75028	0.77064	0.78778	0.80243	0.8264	0.8540	
15	0.57912	0.61295	0.64111	0.66505	0.68575	0.70387	0.7342	0.7695	
20	0.49436	0.52818	0.55698	0.58197	0.60396	0.62353	0.6570	0.6970	
25	0.43049	0.46310	0.49132	0.51617	0.53832	0.55827	0.5929	0.6352	
30	0.38090	0.41189	0.43903	0.46319	0.48495	0.50472	0.5395	0.5825	
40	0.30923	0.33684	0.36144	0.38367	0.40398	0.42267	0.4561	0.4987	
60	0.22433	0.24644	0.26650	0.28496	0.30209	0.31811	0.3474	0.3858	
80	0.17590	0.19414	0.21088	0.22642	0.24098	0.25471	0.2801	0.3141	
100	0.14463	0.16011	0.17441	0.18776	0.20036	0.21230	0.2345	0.2647	
130	0.11417	0.12676	0.13845	0.14945	0.15987	0.16981	0.1885	0.2141	
160	0.094297	0.104892	0.114774	0.124101	0.132975	0.14147	0.15750	0.17965	
200	0.076532	0.085273	0.093455	0.101205	0.108603	0.11570	0.12917	0.14792	
300	0.052023	0.058098	0.063813	0.069251	0.074465	0.079493	0.08909	0.10258	
500	0.031710	0.035480	0.039040	0.042442	0.045714	0.048883	0.05496	0.06357	
1000	0.016046	0.017979	0.019811	0.021566	0.023261	0.024905	0.02807	0.03259	
d. Upper 1% points of the largest root for $s = 7$									
5	0.89470	0.90908	0.91991	0.92839	0.93522	0.9408	0.9498	0.9614	
10	0.75082	0.77656	0.79714	0.81405	0.82824	0.8403	0.8600	0.8818	
15	0.63628	0.66646	0.69144	0.71260	0.73083	0.7467	0.7732	0.8038	
20	0.54905	0.58029	0.60677	0.62966	0.64973	0.6675	0.6978	0.7336	
25	0.48171	0.51253	0.53909	0.56238	0.58308	0.6016	0.6338	0.6727	
30	0.42859	0.45835	0.48430	0.50732	0.52798	0.5467	0.5795	0.6198	
40	0.35059	0.37767	0.40170	0.42335	0.44306	0.4612	0.4934	0.5342	
60	0.25649	0.27866	0.29872	0.31712	0.33415	0.3500	0.3789	0.4168	
80	0.20204	0.22055	0.23748	0.25317	0.26783	0.2816	0.3071	0.3409	
100	0.16660	0.18243	0.19700	0.21058	0.22336	0.2354	0.2579	0.2882	
130	0.13187	0.14483	0.15684	0.16810	0.17875	0.1889	0.2079	0.2338	
160	0.109113	0.120064	0.130255	0.139852	0.148966	0.15767	0.17406	0.19664	
200	0.088695	0.097764	0.106235	0.114242	0.121870	0.12918	0.14300	0.16220	
300	0.060419	0.066754	0.072702	0.078351	0.083759	0.08896	0.09888	0.11277	
500	0.036892	0.040839	0.044561	0.048111	0.051521	0.05482	0.06113	0.07005	
1000	0.018692	0.020724	0.022645	0.024483	0.026254	0.02798	0.03127	0.03597	

TABLE B-7. (Continued)

n \ m	0	1	2	3	4	5	7	10	15
e. Upper 5% points of the largest root for $s = 8$									
5	0.87386	0.88974	0.90198	0.91173	0.91968	0.92630	0.93670	0.94773	0.95948
10	0.72804	0.75412	0.77534	0.79300	0.80798	0.82085	0.84191	0.86546	0.89206
15	0.61550	0.64525	0.67024	0.69164	0.71022	0.72656	0.75402	0.78589	0.82359
20	0.53065	0.56108	0.58718	0.60997	0.63010	0.64806	0.67886	0.71565	0.76068
25	0.46544	0.49524	0.52122	0.54420	0.56475	0.58331	0.61561	0.65503	0.70464
30	0.41408	0.44274	0.46800	0.49059	0.51099	0.52957	0.56228	0.60290	0.65518
40	0.33876	0.36473	0.38799	0.40909	0.42841	0.44623	0.47816	0.51881	0.57296
60	0.24794	0.26912	0.28844	0.30627	0.32286	0.33838	0.36679	0.40411	0.45600
80	0.19537	0.21303	0.22931	0.24447	0.25871	0.27215	0.29703	0.33034	0.37787
100	0.16115	0.17623	0.19022	0.20334	0.21572	0.22748	0.24942	0.27915	0.32232
130	0.12759	0.13993	0.15145	0.16231	0.17263	0.18247	0.20099	0.22638	0.26392
160	0.10559	0.11602	0.12579	0.13504	0.14386	0.15230	0.16827	0.19034	0.22335
200	0.085849	0.094482	0.10260	0.11032	0.11769	0.12478	0.13824	0.15698	0.18531
300	0.058496	0.064526	0.070225	0.075663	0.080887	0.085929	0.095564	0.109119	0.12993
500	0.035726	0.039482	0.043047	0.046463	0.049755	0.052946	0.059074	0.067768	0.08119*
1000	0.018105	0.020038	0.021878	0.023645	0.025355	0.027016	0.030219	0.03480*	0.04201*
f. Upper 1% points of the largest root for $s = 8$									
5	0.91031	0.92176	0.93055	0.93754	0.94323	0.94796	0.95537	0.96320	0.97152
10	0.77855	0.80027	0.81787	0.83248	0.84482	0.85541	0.87267	0.89189	0.91349
15	0.66867	0.69502	0.71708	0.73589	0.75218	0.76647	0.79039	0.81803	0.85053
20	0.58250	0.61043	0.63429	0.65505	0.67334	0.68961	0.71741	0.75045	0.79066
25	0.51467	0.54266	0.56696	0.58839	0.60751	0.62472	0.65456	0.69080	0.73614
30	0.46038	0.48773	0.51176	0.53317	0.55245	0.56997	0.60071	0.63869	0.68727
40	0.37948	0.40480	0.42741	0.44786	0.46653	0.48371	0.51438	0.55327	0.60475
60	0.28011	0.30123	0.32046	0.33814	0.35456	0.36990	0.39787	0.43447	0.48507
80	0.22175	0.23958	0.25597	0.27120	0.28547	0.29892	0.32375	0.35686	0.40386
100	0.18344	0.19878	0.21298	0.22626	0.23878	0.25064	0.27271	0.30251	0.34559
130	0.14565	0.15829	0.17007	0.18115	0.19165	0.20166	0.22043	0.24609	0.28386
160	0.12076	0.13149	0.14152	0.15100	0.16002	0.16865	0.18492	0.20734	0.24074
200	0.098336	0.10725	0.11562	0.12356	0.13114	0.13841	0.15219	0.17132	0.20013
300	0.067151	0.073412	0.079320	0.084948	0.090347	0.095551	0.105476	0.119400	0.14070
500	0.041086	0.045003	0.048715	0.052266	0.055685	0.058994	0.065337	0.074316	0.08822*
1000	0.020850	0.022872	0.024794	0.026638	0.028420	0.030148	0.033477	0.03824*	0.04573*

g. Upper 5% points on the largest root for $s = 9$

5	0.89098	0.90390	0.91402	0.92217	0.92889	0.93453	0.94348	0.95305	0.96347
10	0.75598	0.77833	0.79670	0.81213	0.82529	0.83666	0.85538	0.87647	0.90052
15	0.64727	0.67357	0.69584	0.71503	0.73178	0.74656	0.77150	0.80063	0.83527
20	0.56307	0.59053	0.61426	0.63508	0.65353	0.67006	0.69848	0.73257	0.77449
25	0.49716	0.52447	0.54841	0.56969	0.58878	0.60606	0.63622	0.67314	0.71978
30	0.44455	0.47111	0.49465	0.51577	0.53491	0.55237	0.58319	0.62156	0.67108
40	0.36633	0.39077	0.41278	0.43280	0.45118	0.46816	0.49864	0.53752	0.58940
60	0.27040	0.29069	0.30929	0.32650	0.34254	0.35757	0.38512	0.42136	0.47178
80	0.21408	0.23118	0.24699	0.26177	0.27567	0.28880	0.31315	0.34578	0.39237
100	0.17713	0.19182	0.20550	0.21836	0.23052	0.24208	0.26368	0.29297	0.33552
130	0.14066	0.15275	0.16408	0.17480	0.18499	0.19472	0.21305	0.23822	0.27542
160	0.11663	0.12689	0.13654	0.14570	0.15444	0.16283	0.17869	0.20065	0.23349
200	0.094986	0.10351	0.11156	0.11922	0.12656	0.13362	0.14704	0.16575	0.19404
300	0.064875	0.070856	0.076532	0.081961	0.087184	0.092232	0.10189	0.11548	0.13636
500	0.039699	0.043440	0.047005	0.050427	0.053733	0.056939	0.063104	0.071859	0.08542*
1000	0.020149	0.022080	0.023925	0.025702	0.027423	0.029097	0.032330	0.036952	0.04416*

h. Upper 1% points of the largest root for $s = 9$

5	0.92264	0.93192	0.93917	0.94499	0.94979	0.95381	0.96017	0.96696	0.97430
10	0.80179	0.82030	0.83548	0.84818	0.85899	0.86832	0.88362	0.90079	0.92029
15	0.69676	0.71994	0.73951	0.75631	0.77093	0.78381	0.80548	0.83067	0.86048
20	0.61221	0.63727	0.65886	0.67774	0.69444	0.70936	0.73493	0.76547	0.80282
25	0.54440	0.56992	0.59221	0.61197	0.62965	0.64561	0.67339	0.70724	0.74977
30	0.48940	0.51462	0.53691	0.55685	0.57486	0.59126	0.62013	0.65591	0.70182
40	0.40632	0.43003	0.45131	0.47064	0.48833	0.50464	0.53383	0.57092	0.62013
60	0.30247	0.32262	0.34104	0.35804	0.37386	0.38866	0.41570	0.45114	0.50020
80	0.24060	0.25778	0.27365	0.28844	0.30232	0.31542	0.33965	0.37199	0.41796
100	0.19966	0.21454	0.22837	0.24134	0.25359	0.26521	0.28688	0.31617	0.35853
130	0.15901	0.17134	0.18288	0.19377	0.20411	0.21398	0.23252	0.25789	0.29524
160	0.13209	0.14260	0.15248	0.16183	0.17075	0.17929	0.19541	0.21766	0.25082
200	0.10775	0.11652	0.12479	0.13265	0.14017	0.14739	0.16110	0.18015	0.20885
300	0.073760	0.079948	0.085812	0.091413	0.096795	0.10199	0.11191	0.12584	0.14716
500	0.045220	0.049108	0.052807	0.056355	0.059777	0.063093	0.069460	0.078480	0.09243*
1000	0.022983	0.024997	0.026918	0.028767	0.030555	0.032293	0.035644	0.040426	0.04788*

TABLE B-7. (Continued)

n \ m	0	1	2	3	4	5	7	10	15
i. Upper 5% points of the largest root for $s = 10$									
5	0.90483	0.91547	0.92393	0.93083	0.93656	0.94141	0.94916	0.95759	0.96720
10	0.77978	0.79907	0.81509	0.82864	0.84026	0.85037	0.86708	0.88605	0.90789
15	0.67519	0.69855	0.71848	0.73575	0.75090	0.76431	0.78704	0.81372	0.84561
20	0.59217	0.61704	0.63867	0.65772	0.67468	0.68990	0.71619	0.74784	0.78695
25	0.52606	0.55114	0.57325	0.59297	0.61073	0.62684	0.65503	0.68966	0.73355
30	0.47623	0.49728	0.51923	0.53901	0.55697	0.57339	0.60245	0.63872	0.68566
40	0.39214	0.41517	0.43599	0.45499	0.47248	0.48865	0.51774	0.55494	0.60465
60	0.29180	0.31125	0.32914	0.34574	0.36124	0.37580	0.40248	0.43765	0.48664
80	0.23209	0.24864	0.26400	0.27839	0.29194	0.30477	0.32857	0.36050	0.40613
100	0.19260	0.20690	0.22028	0.23287	0.24480	0.25616	0.27739	0.30622	0.34812
130	0.15339	0.16524	0.17638	0.18693	0.19699	0.20660	0.22473	0.24963	0.28647
160	0.12743	0.13752	0.14704	0.15610	0.16476	0.17307	0.18882	0.21063	0.24327
200	0.10396	0.11237	0.12034	0.12794	0.13523	0.14226	0.15562	0.17427	0.2025*
300	0.071167	0.077098	0.082744	0.088157	0.093372	0.098418	0.10808	0.12169	0.1426*
500	0.043634	0.047358	0.050918	0.054344	0.057657	0.060875	0.067067	0.07585*	0.08948*
1000	0.022179	0.024107	0.025955	0.027739	0.029470	0.031155	0.03441*	0.03905*	0.04632*
j. Upper 1% points of the largest root for $s = 10$									
5	0.93258	0.94020	0.94624	0.95116	0.95524	0.95869	0.96419	0.97016	0.97680
10	0.82149	0.83740	0.85058	0.86170	0.87122	0.87948	0.89311	0.90854	0.92620
15	0.72134	0.74183	0.75927	0.77433	0.78751	0.79916	0.81886	0.84189	0.86931
20	0.63873	0.66133	0.68093	0.69814	0.71344	0.72714	0.75072	0.77900	0.81378
25	0.57137	0.59468	0.61519	0.63344	0.64982	0.66465	0.69054	0.72222	0.76217
30	0.51602	0.53932	0.56002	0.57862	0.59547	0.61085	0.63798	0.67172	0.71517
40	0.43131	0.45356	0.47362	0.49189	0.50867	0.52416	0.55195	0.58733	0.63440
60	0.32368	0.34292	0.36058	0.37692	0.39216	0.40644	0.43257	0.46688	0.51445
80	0.25867	0.27524	0.29059	0.30495	0.31844	0.33120	0.35482	0.38640	0.43132
100	0.21530	0.22974	0.24321	0.25588	0.26786	0.27924	0.30049	0.32925	0.37088
130	0.17197	0.18401	0.19532	0.20602	0.21619	0.22592	0.24420	0.26925	0.30617
160	0.14313	0.15344	0.16315	0.17238	0.18119	0.18963	0.20560	0.22765	0.26054
200	0.11696	0.12559	0.13375	0.14153	0.14898	0.15615	0.16977	0.18871	0.2173*
300	0.080258	0.086375	0.092191	0.09776	0.10312	0.10830	0.11820	0.13213	0.1534*
500	0.049301	0.053160	0.056844	0.060386	0.063808	0.067128	0.073509	0.08258*	0.09661*
1000	0.025096	0.027100	0.029020	0.030871	0.032666	0.034411	0.03778*	0.04260*	0.05013*

From "Largest characteristic root of a matrix in multivariate analysis," by K. C. Pillai, *Biometrika,* 1965, Vol. 52, pp. 412–414. Reprinted by permission.

TABLE B-7. (Continued)

n \ m	0	1	2	3	4	5	7	10	15
k. Upper 5% points of the largest root for $s = 14$									
5	0.9403	0.9457	0.9503	0.9541	0.9574	0.9602	0.9649	0.9701	0.9761
10	0.8470	0.8584	0.8681	0.8766	0.8840	0.8906	0.9017	0.9146	0.9299
15	0.7590	0.7742	0.7875	0.7992	0.8096	0.8189	0.8350	0.8543	0.8779
20	0.6834	0.7006	0.7159	0.7296	0.7419	0.7531	0.7726	0.7966	0.8267
25	0.6196	0.6378	0.6542	0.6689	0.6824	0.6947	0.7165	0.7436	0.7784
30	0.5657	0.5843	0.6011	0.6165	0.6305	0.6435	0.6666	0.6958	0.7340
40	0.4807	0.4990	0.5158	0.5313	0.5457	0.5590	0.5832	0.6144	0.6565
60	0.3683	0.3848	0.4001	0.4145	0.4279	0.4407	0.4641	0.4952	0.5387
80	0.2980	0.3125	0.3261	0.3390	0.3512	0.3628	0.3844	0.4136	0.4554
100	0.2500	0.2629	0.2751	0.2866	0.2976	0.3081	0.3278	0.3546	0.3938
130	0.2013	0.2122	0.2226	0.2325	0.2419	0.2510	0.2682	0.2919	0.3271
160	0.1685	0.1779	0.1869	0.1955	0.2038	0.2117	0.2269	0.2479	0.2795
200	0.1383	0.1463	0.1539	0.1612	0.1683	0.1751	0.1881	0.2064	0.2340
300	0.09556	0.1013	0.1068	0.1121	0.1172	0.1222	0.1318	0.1454	0.1662
500	0.05904	0.06269	0.06621	0.06962	0.07293	0.07616	0.08240	0.09130	0.1052
1000	0.03019	0.03210	0.03395	0.03575	0.03750	0.03921	0.04253	0.04730	0.05482
l. Upper 1% points of the largest root for $s = 14$									
5	0.95784	0.96171	0.96493	0.96764	0.96996	0.97197	0.97527	0.97897	0.98317
10	0.87660	0.88590	0.89386	0.90075	0.90678	0.91210	0.92107	0.93152	0.94385
15	0.79444	0.80757	0.81903	0.82914	0.83812	0.84617	0.86001	0.87655	0.89674
20	0.72109	0.73655	0.75023	0.76245	0.77346	0.78342	0.80082	0.82205	0.84866
25	0.65775	0.67449	0.68948	0.70300	0.71529	0.72651	0.74634	0.77095	0.80248
30	0.60342	0.62078	0.63645	0.65071	0.66376	0.67577	0.69718	0.72412	0.75929
40	0.51631	0.53380	0.54979	0.56452	0.57815	0.59082	0.61373	0.64320	0.68278
60	0.39883	0.41495	0.42993	0.44392	0.45705	0.46941	0.49218	0.52229	0.56430
80	0.32422	0.33862	0.35212	0.36484	0.37687	0.38830	0.40957	0.43817	0.47908
100	0.27291	0.28576	0.29788	0.30937	0.32030	0.33073	0.35028	0.37689	0.41558
130	0.22042	0.23140	0.24181	0.25173	0.26122	0.27033	0.28753	0.31121	0.34623
160	0.18481	0.19435	0.20343	0.21212	0.22045	0.22848	0.24372	0.26486	0.29651
200	0.15203	0.16012	0.16786	0.17528	0.18243	0.18933	0.20250	0.22090	0.24874
300	0.10529	0.11114	0.11675	0.12217	0.12741	0.13249	0.14224	0.15602	0.17718
500	0.065179	0.068928	0.072541	0.076040	0.079437	0.082746	0.089131	0.098227	0.11239
1000	0.033379	0.035350	0.037256	0.039107	0.040910	0.042671	0.046084	0.050981	0.058685

TABLE B-7. (Continued)

n \ m	0	1	2	3	4	5	7	10	15
m. Upper 5% points for the largest root for $s = 16$									
5	0.9510	0.9551	0.9586	0.9615	0.9641	0.9663	0.9701	0.9743	0.9793
10	0.8695	0.8786	0.8864	0.8933	0.8993	0.9047	0.9139	0.9248	0.9378
15	0.7892	0.8017	0.8127	0.8225	0.8313	0.8392	0.8529	0.8695	0.8901
20	0.7178	0.7324	0.7454	0.7571	0.7677	0.7774	0.7945	0.8154	0.8421
25	0.6561	0.6719	0.6861	0.6990	0.7108	0.7216	0.7409	0.7650	0.7963
30	0.6031	0.6194	0.6342	0.6478	0.6603	0.6719	0.6926	0.7189	0.7536
40	0.5177	0.5342	0.5493	0.5633	0.5764	0.5886	0.6107	0.6393	0.6781
60	0.4018	0.4170	0.4312	0.4446	0.4572	0.4691	0.4910	0.5202	0.5613
80	0.3276	0.3413	0.3541	0.3663	0.3778	0.3889	0.4094	0.4372	0.4771
100	0.2763	0.2886	0.3001	0.3111	0.3217	0.3317	0.3506	0.3765	0.4143
130	0.2237	0.2341	0.2441	0.2537	0.2628	0.2716	0.2883	0.3113	0.3456
160	0.1878	0.1969	0.2056	0.2140	0.2221	0.2298	0.2446	0.2652	0.2962
200	0.1547	0.1625	0.1699	0.1771	0.1840	0.1907	0.2035	0.2214	0.2487
300	0.1074	0.1130	0.1184	0.1236	0.1287	0.1337	0.1432	0.1566	0.1774
500	0.06656	0.07017	0.07366	0.07705	0.08035	0.08357	0.08981	0.09872	0.1127
1000	0.03413	0 03603	0.03788	0.03968	0.04143	0.04315	0.04649	0.05129	0.05887
n. Upper 1% points of the largest root for $s = 16$									
5	0.96542	0.96833	0.97078	0.97288	0.97469	0.97628	0.97892	0.98193	0.98540
10	0.89495	0.90231	0.90868	0.91425	0.91916	0.92353	0.93097	0.93973	0.95022
15	0.82050	0.83127	0.84075	0.84918	0.85672	0.86352	0.87530	0.88951	0.90705
20	0.75190	0.76491	0.77652	0.78696	0.79641	0.80501	0.82011	0.83869	0.86220
25	0.69124	0.70562	0.71858	0.73034	0.74108	0.75094	0.76842	0.79028	0.81850
30	0.63825	0.65340	0.66716	0.67975	0.69132	0.70200	0.72113	0.74534	0.77716
40	0.55156	0.56719	0.58155	0.59484	0.60718	0.61868	0.63956	0.66653	0.70294
60	0.43151	0.44634	0.46017	0.47314	0.48534	0.49686	0.51813	0.54634	0.58585
80	0.35351	0.36698	0.37966	0.39164	0.40301	0.41382	0.43398	0.46118	0.50018
100	0.29912	0.31128	0.32278	0.33372	0.34415	0.35412	0.37285	0.39840	0.43564
130	0.24286	0.25335	0.26335	0.27289	0.28204	0.29084	0.30749	0.33045	0.36449
160	0.20433	0.21352	0.22230	0.23071	0.23881	0.24662	0.26147	0.28212	0.31308
200	0.16862	0.17647	0.18399	0.19123	0.19822	0.20498	0.21789	0.23597	0.26338
300	0.11730	0.12302	0.12854	0.13387	0.13903	0.14405	0.15371	0.16736	0.18838
500	0.072890	0.076586	0.080162	0.083631	0.087008	0.090300	0.096667	0.10575	0.11992
1000	0.037439	0.039394	0.041291	0.043138	0.044941	0.046704	0.050127	0.055047	0.062803

o. Upper 5% points of the largest root for $s = 18$

5	0.9590	0.9622	0.9649	0.9673	0.9693	0.9711	0.9741	0.9777	0.9819
10	0.8874	0.8947	0.9011	0.9067	0.9118	0.9163	0.9240	0.9332	0.9444
15	0.8140	0.8244	0.8336	0.8419	0.8494	0.8561	0.8679	0.8824	0.9004
20	0.7469	0.7593	0.7705	0.7806	0.7898	0.7982	0.8132	0.8317	0.8554
25	0.6876	0.7013	0.7137	0.7250	0.7354	0.7450	0.7622	0.7837	0.8119
30	0.6358	0.6502	0.6633	0.6754	0.6866	0.6969	0.7156	0.7394	0.7709
40	0.5509	0.5657	0.5794	0.5921	0.6040	0.6151	0.6354	0.6617	0.6976
60	0.4326	0.4467	0.4599	0.4724	0.4841	0.4952	0.5158	0.5433	0.5820
80	0.3553	0.3682	0.3803	0.3918	0.4028	0.4132	0.4328	0.4592	0.4974
100	0.3012	0.3128	0.3239	0.3344	0.3444	0.3541	0.3723	0.3972	0.4336
130	0.2450	0.2551	0.2647	0.2739	0.2827	0.2912	0.3074	0.3298	0.3631
160	0.2064	0.2152	0.2237	0.2318	0.2397	0.2472	0.2617	0.2818	0.3121
200	0.1706	0.1781	0.1854	0.1924	0.1991	0.2057	0.2183	0.2359	0.2628
300	0.1189	0.1244	0.1297	0.1349	0.1399	0.1448	0.1542	0.1675	0.1882
500	0.07397	0.07753	0.08100	0.08437	0.08765	0.09086	0.09708	0.1060	0.1199
1000	0.03804	0.03993	0.04177	0.04357	0.04533	0.04705	0.05040	0.05522	0.06285

p. Upper 1% points of the largest root for $s = 18$

5	0.97112	0.97336	0.97528	0.97693	0.97838	0.97965	0.98180	0.98428	0.98723
10	0.90947	0.91539	0.92057	0.92513	0.92919	0.93283	0.93906	0.94649	0.95550
15	0.84185	0.85079	0.85873	0.86584	0.87223	0.87803	0.88814	0.90045	0.91580
20	0.77780	0.78886	0.79880	0.80778	0.81596	0.82344	0.83663	0.85299	0.87387
25	0.71996	0.73240	0.74369	0.75399	0.76343	0.77212	0.78762	0.80712	0.83249
30	0.66859	0.68189	0.69405	0.70521	0.71551	0.72505	0.74221	0.76405	0.79293
40	0.58298	0.59701	0.60996	0.62198	0.63318	0.64366	0.66272	0.68745	0.72103
60	0.46148	0.47515	0.48796	0.49999	0.51135	0.52209	0.54196	0.56842	0.60560
80	0.38083	0.39345	0.40537	0.41666	0.42740	0.43763	0.45675	0.48261	0.51979
100	0.32383	0.33534	0.34628	0.35669	0.36664	0.37617	0.39411	0.41863	0.45446
130	0.26424	0.27429	0.28388	0.29306	0.30188	0.31038	0.32647	0.34873	0.38179
160	0.22307	0.23193	0.24041	0.24857	0.25643	0.26401	0.27847	0.29862	0.32887
200	0.18465	0.19226	0.19959	0.20664	0.21347	0.22008	0.23273	0.25047	0.27741
300	0.12901	0.13462	0.14003	0.14527	0.15036	0.15531	0.16485	0.17837	0.19921
500	0.080467	0.084114	0.087650	0.091089	0.094440	0.097713	0.10405	0.11311	0.12727
1000	0.041452	0.043392	0.045280	0.047121	0.048921	0.050684	0.054112	0.059048	0.066841

TABLE B-7. (Continued)

n \ m	0	1	2	3	4	5	7	10	15
q. Upper 5% points of the largest root for $s = 20$									
5	0.9653	0.9677	0.9699	0.9718	0.9735	0.9749	0.9774	0.9804	0.9840
10	0.9018	0.9078	0.9131	0.9178	0.9220	0.9258	0.9323	0.9402	0.9499
15	0.8346	0.8434	0.8512	0.8583	0.8647	0.8705	0.8807	0.8933	0.9092
20	0.7716	0.7823	0.7920	0.8008	0.8088	0.8162	0.8294	0.8458	0.8670
25	0.7149	0.7269	0.7378	0.7478	0.7570	0.7655	0.7808	0.8002	0.8256
30	0.6646	0.6773	0.6890	0.6998	0.7098	0.7192	0.7360	0.7575	0.7863
40	0.5806	0.5940	0.6065	0.6181	0.6289	0.6391	0.6577	0.6819	0.7151
60	0.4611	0.4742	0.4864	0.4980	0.5090	0.5194	0.5387	0.5646	0.6011
80	0.3814	0.3934	0.4049	0.4158	0.4261	0.4360	0.4546	0.4799	0.5163
100	0.3248	0.3358	0.3464	0.3564	0.3660	0.3753	0.3927	0.4166	0.4517
130	0.2655	0.2751	0.2844	0.2933	0.3018	0.3100	0.3257	0.3474	0.3798
160	0.2244	0.2329	0.2411	0.2490	0.2566	0.2640	0.2781	0.2977	0.3274
200	0.1859	0.1933	0.2004	0.2072	0.2138	0.2202	0.2326	0.2499	0.2763
300	0.1301	0.1355	0.1408	0.1459	0.1509	0.1557	0.1650	0.1782	0.1987
500	0.08127	0.08480	0.08823	0.09158	0.09484	0.09804	0.1042	0.1131	0.1271
1000	0.04192	0.04380	0.04563	0.04742	0.04918	0.05090	0.05426	0.05910	0.06678
r. Upper 1% points for the largest root for $s = 20$									
5	0.97552	0.97728	0.97880	0.98013	0.98130	0.98234	0.98411	0.98618	0.98870
10	0.92115	0.92599	0.93026	0.93405	0.93744	0.94050	0.94578	0.95214	0.95995
15	0.85957	0.86708	0.87379	0.87984	0.88531	0.89030	0.89904	0.90977	0.92329
20	0.79980	0.80928	0.81785	0.82565	0.83277	0.83931	0.85090	0.86538	0.88402
25	0.74479	0.75564	0.76553	0.77459	0.78293	0.79064	0.80444	0.82191	0.84480
30	0.69519	0.70694	0.71773	0.72768	0.73689	0.74544	0.76089	0.78065	0.80695
40	0.61113	0.62377	0.63549	0.64640	0.65660	0.66616	0.68361	0.70635	0.73736
60	0.48906	0.50169	0.51356	0.52475	0.53533	0.54536	0.56396	0.58878	0.62380
80	0.40637	0.41821	0.42943	0.44008	0.45023	0.45991	0.47805	0.50264	0.53810
100	0.34717	0.35809	0.36848	0.37840	0.38790	0.39701	0.41418	0.43771	0.47217
130	0.28465	0.29428	0.30349	0.31233	0.32083	0.32902	0.34459	0.36614	0.39822
160	0.24109	0.24963	0.25783	0.26573	0.27336	0.28073	0.29480	0.31443	0.34398
200	0.20016	0.20755	0.21468	0.22156	0.22822	0.23468	0.24706	0.26446	0.29092
300	0.14045	0.14594	0.15125	0.15640	0.16142	0.16630	0.17571	0.18908	0.20972
500	0.087921	0.091519	0.095016	0.098422	0.10175	0.10500	0.11130	0.12033	0.13446
1000	0.045423	0.047349	0.049227	0.051061	0.052857	0.054618	0.058048	0.062993	0.070818

* Value extrapolated.

From "Upper percentage points of the largest root of a matrix in multivariate analysis," by K. C. Pillai, *Biometrika,* 1967, Vol. 54, pp. 190–193. Reprinted by permission.

TABLE B-8. Table of common logarithms

N	0	1	2	3	4	5	6	7	8	9
10	0000	0043	0086	0128	0170	0212	0253	0294	0334	0374
11	0414	0453	0492	0531	0569	0607	0645	0682	0719	0755
12	0792	0828	0864	0899	0934	0969	1004	1038	1072	1106
13	1139	1173	1206	1239	1271	1303	1335	1367	1399	1430
14	1461	1492	1523	1553	1584	1614	1644	1673	1703	1732
15	1761	1790	1818	1847	1875	1903	1931	1959	1987	2014
16	2041	2068	2095	2122	2148	2175	2201	2227	2253	2279
17	2304	2330	2355	2380	2405	2430	2455	2480	2504	2529
18	2553	2577	2601	2625	2648	2672	2695	2718	2742	2765
19	2788	2810	2833	2856	2878	2900	2923	2945	2967	2989
20	3010	3032	3054	3075	3096	3118	3139	3160	3181	3201
21	3222	3243	3263	3284	3304	3324	3345	3365	3385	3404
22	3424	3444	3464	3483	3502	3522	3541	3560	3579	3598
23	3617	3636	3655	3674	3692	3711	3729	3747	3766	3784
24	3802	3820	3838	3856	3874	3892	3909	3927	3945	3962
25	3979	3997	4014	4031	4048	4065	4082	4099	4116	4133
26	4150	4166	4183	4200	4216	4232	4249	4265	4281	4298
27	4314	4330	4346	4362	4378	4393	4409	4425	4440	4456
28	4472	4487	4502	4518	4533	4548	4564	4579	4594	4609
29	4624	4639	4654	4669	4683	4698	4713	4728	4742	4757
30	4771	4786	4800	4814	4829	4843	4857	4871	4886	4900
31	4914	4928	4942	4955	4969	4983	4997	5011	5024	5038
32	5051	5065	5079	5092	5105	5119	5132	5145	5159	5172
33	5185	5198	5211	5224	5237	5250	5263	5276	5289	5302
34	5315	5328	5340	5353	5366	5378	5391	5403	5416	5428
35	5441	5453	5465	5478	5490	5502	5514	5527	5539	5551
36	5563	5575	5587	5599	5611	5623	5635	5647	5658	5670
37	5682	5694	5705	5717	5729	5740	5752	5763	5775	5786
38	5798	5809	5821	5832	5843	5855	5866	5877	5888	5899
39	5911	5922	5933	5944	5955	5966	5977	5988	5999	6010
40	6021	6031	6042	6053	6064	6075	6085	6096	6107	6117
41	6128	6138	6149	6160	6170	6180	6191	6201	6212	6222
42	6232	6243	6253	6263	6274	6284	6294	6304	6314	6325
43	6335	6345	6355	6365	6375	6385	6395	6405	6415	6425
44	6435	6444	6454	6464	6474	6484	6493	6503	6513	6522
45	6532	6542	6551	6561	6571	6580	6590	6599	6609	6618
46	6628	6637	6646	6656	6665	6675	6684	6693	6702	6712
47	6721	6730	6739	6749	6758	6767	6776	6785	6794	6803
48	6812	6821	6830	6839	6848	6857	6866	6875	6884	6893
49	6902	6911	6920	6928	6937	6946	6955	6964	6972	6981
50	6990	6998	7007	7016	7024	7033	7042	7050	7059	7067
51	7076	7084	7093	7101	7110	7118	7126	7135	7143	7152
52	7160	7168	7177	7185	7193	7202	7210	7218	7226	7235
53	7243	7251	7259	7267	7275	7284	7292	7300	7308	7316
54	7324	7332	7340	7348	7356	7364	7372	7380	7388	7396
55	7404	7412	7419	7427	7435	7443	7451	7459	7466	7474
56	7482	7490	7497	7505	7513	7520	7528	7536	7543	7551
57	7559	7566	7574	7582	7589	7597	7604	7612	7619	7627

TABLE B-8. (Continued)

N	0	1	2	3	4	5	6	7	8	9
58	7634	7642	7649	7657	7664	7672	7679	7686	7694	7701
59	7709	7716	7723	7731	7738	7745	7752	7760	7767	7774
60	7782	7789	7796	7803	7810	7818	7825	7832	7839	7846
61	7853	7860	7868	7875	7882	7889	7896	7903	7910	7917
62	7924	7931	7938	7945	7952	7959	7966	7973	7980	7987
63	7993	8000	8007	8014	8021	8028	8035	8041	8048	8055
64	8062	8069	8075	8082	8089	8096	8102	8109	8116	8122
65	8129	8136	8142	8149	8156	8162	8169	8176	8182	8189
66	8195	8202	8209	8215	8222	8228	8235	8241	8248	8254
67	8261	8267	8274	8280	8287	8293	8299	8306	8312	8319
68	8325	8331	8338	8344	8351	8357	8363	8370	8376	8382
69	8388	8395	8401	8407	8414	8420	8426	8432	8439	8445
70	8451	8457	8463	8470	8476	8482	8488	8494	8500	8506
71	8513	8519	8525	8531	8537	8543	8549	8555	8561	8567
72	8573	8579	8585	8591	8597	8603	8609	8615	8621	8627
73	8633	8639	8645	8651	8657	8663	8669	8675	8681	8686
74	8692	8698	8704	8710	8716	8722	8727	8733	8739	8745
75	8751	8756	8762	8768	8774	8779	8785	8791	8797	8802
76	8808	8814	8820	8825	8831	8837	8842	8848	8854	8859
77	8865	8871	8876	8882	8887	8893	8899	8904	8910	8915
78	8921	8927	8932	8938	8943	8949	8954	8960	8965	8971
79	8976	8982	8987	8993	8998	9004	9009	9015	9020	9025
80	9031	9036	9042	9047	9053	9058	9063	9069	9074	9079
81	9085	9090	9096	9101	9106	9112	9117	9122	9128	9133
82	9138	9143	9149	9154	9159	9165	9170	9175	9180	9186
83	9191	9196	9201	9206	9212	9217	9222	9227	9232	9238
84	9243	9248	9253	9258	9263	9269	9274	9279	9284	9289
85	9294	9299	9304	9309	9315	9320	9325	9330	9335	9340
86	9345	9350	9355	9360	9365	9370	9375	9380	9385	9390
87	9395	9400	9405	9410	9415	9420	9425	9430	9435	9440
88	9445	9450	9455	9460	9465	9469	9474	9479	9484	9489
89	9494	9499	9504	9509	9513	9518	9523	9528	9533	9538
90	9542	9547	9552	9557	9562	9566	9571	9576	9581	9586
91	9590	9595	9600	9605	9609	9614	9619	9624	9628	9633
92	9638	9643	9647	9652	9657	9661	9666	9671	9675	9680
93	9685	9689	9694	9699	9703	9708	9713	9717	9722	9727
94	9731	9736	9741	9745	9750	9754	9759	9763	9768	9773
95	9777	9782	9786	9791	9795	9800	9805	9809	9814	9818
96	9823	9827	9832	9836	9841	9845	9850	9854	9859	9863
97	9868	9872	9877	9881	9886	9890	9894	9899	9903	9908
98	9912	9917	9921	9926	9930	9934	9939	9943	9948	9952
99	9956	9961	9965	9969	9974	9978	9983	9987	9991	9996

TABLE B-9. Ordinates of the normal curve

	Second decimal place in Z									
Z	0.00	0.01	0.02	0.03	0.04	0.05	0.06	0.07	0.08	0.09
0.0	0.3989	0.3989	0.3989	0.3988	0.3986	0.3984	0.3982	0.3980	0.3977	0.3973
0.1	0.3970	0.3965	0.3961	0.3956	0.3951	0.3945	0.3939	0.3932	0.3925	0.3918
0.2	0.3910	0.3902	0.3894	0.3885	0.3876	0.3867	0.3857	0.3847	0.3836	0.3825
0.3	0.3814	0.3802	0.3790	0.3778	0.3765	0.3752	0.3739	0.3725	0.3712	0.3697
0.4	0.3683	0.3668	0.3653	0.3637	0.3621	0.3605	0.3589	0.3572	0.3555	0.3538
0.5	0.3521	0.3503	0.3485	0.3467	0.3448	0.3429	0.3410	0.3391	0.3372	0.3352
0.6	0.3332	0.3312	0.3292	0.3271	0.3251	0.3230	0.3209	0.3187	0.3166	0.3144
0.7	0.3123	0.3101	0.3079	0.3056	0.3034	0.3011	0.2989	0.2966	0.2943	0.2920
0.8	0.2897	0.2874	0.2850	0.2827	0.2803	0.2780	0.2756	0.2732	0.2709	0.2685
0.9	0.2661	0.2637	0.2613	0.2589	0.2565	0.2541	0.2516	0.2492	0.2468	0.2444
1.0	0.2420	0.2396	0.2371	0.2347	0.2323	0.2299	0.2275	0.2251	0.2227	0.2203
1.1	0.2179	0.2155	0.2131	0.2107	0.2083	0.2059	0.2036	0.2012	0.1989	0.1965
1.2	0.1942	0.1919	0.1895	0.1872	0.1849	0.1826	0.1804	0.1781	0.1758	0.1736
1.3	0.1714	0.1691	0.1669	0.1647	0.1626	0.1604	0.1582	0.1561	0.1539	0.1518
1.4	0.1497	0.1476	0.1456	0.1435	0.1415	0.1394	0.1374	0.1354	0.1334	0.1315
1.5	0.1295	0.1276	0.1257	0.1238	0.1219	0.1200	0.1182	0.1163	0.1145	0.1127
1.6	0.1109	0.1092	0.1074	0.1057	0.1040	0.1023	0.1006	0.0989	0.0973	0.0957
1.7	0.0940	0.0925	0.0909	0.0893	0.0878	0.0863	0.0848	0.0833	0.0818	0.0804
1.8	0.0790	0.0775	0.0761	0.0748	0.0734	0.0721	0.0707	0.0694	0.0681	0.0669
1.9	0.0656	0.0644	0.0632	0.0620	0.0608	0.0596	0.0584	0.0573	0.0562	0.0551
2.0	0.0540	0.0529	0.0519	0.0508	0.0498	0.0488	0.0478	0.0468	0.0459	0.0449
2.1	0.0440	0.0431	0.0422	0.0413	0.0404	0.0396	0.0387	0.0379	0.0371	0.0363
2.2	0.0355	0.0347	0.0339	0.0332	0.0325	0.0317	0.0310	0.0303	0.0297	0.0290
2.3	0.0283	0.0277	0.0270	0.0264	0.0258	0.0252	0.0246	0.0241	0.0235	0.0229
2.4	0.0224	0.0219	0.0213	0.0208	0.0203	0.0198	0.0194	0.0189	0.0184	0.0180
2.5	0.0175	0.0171	0.0167	0.0163	0.0158	0.0154	0.0151	0.0147	0.0143	0.0139
2.6	0.0136	0.0132	0.0129	0.0126	0.0122	0.0119	0.0116	0.0113	0.0110	0.0107
2.7	0.0104	0.0101	0.0099	0.0096	0.0093	0.0091	0.0088	0.0086	0.0084	0.0081
2.8	0.0079	0.0077	0.0075	0.0073	0.0071	0.0069	0.0067	0.0065	0.0063	0.0061
2.9	0.0060	0.0058	0.0056	0.0055	0.0053	0.0051	0.0050	0.0048	0.0047	0.0046

	First decimal place in Z									
Z	0.0	0.1	0.2	0.3	0.4	0.5	0.6	0.7	0.8	0.9
3	0.0044	0.0033	0.0024	0.0017	0.0012	0.0009	0.0006	0.0004	0.0003	0.0002
4	0.0001	0.0001	0.0001	0.0000	0.0000	0.0000	0.0000	0.0000	0.0000	0.0000

Reprinted by permission from *Statistical Methods*, 7th Edition by G. W. Snedecor and W. G. Cochran. Copyright © 1980 by the Iowa State University Press.

TABLE B-10. Coefficients of orthogonal polynomials (linear, quadratic, and cubic)

	$n = 3$		$n = 4$			$n = 5$			$n = 6$			$n = 7$		
	$f_1(x_i)$	$f_2(x_i)$	$f_1(x_i)$	$f_2(x_i)$	$f_3(x_i)$	$f_1(x_i)$	$f_2(x_i)$	$f_3(x_i)$	$f_1(x_i)$	$f_2(x_i)$	$f_3(x_i)$	$f_1(x_i)$	$f_2(x_i)$	$f_3(x_i)$
	-1	1	-3	1	-1	-2	2	-1	-5	5	-5	-3	5	-1
	0	-2	-1	-1	3	-1	-1	2	-3	-1	7	-2	0	1
	1	1	1	-1	-3	0	-2	0	-1	-4	4	-1	-3	1
			3	1	1	1	-1	-2	1	-4	-4	0	-4	0
						2	2	1	3	-1	-7	1	-3	-1
									5	5	5	2	0	-1
												3	5	1
c_j	2	6	20	4	20	10	14	10	70	84	180	28	84	6

	$n=3$	$n=4$	$n=5$	$n=6$	$n=7$
$f_1(x)$	$x - 2$	$2x - 5$	$x - 3$	$2x - 7$	$x - 4$
$f_2(x)$	$3x^2 - 12x + 10$	$x^2 - 5x + 5$	$x^2 - 6x + 7$	$\frac{1}{2}(3x^2 - 21x + 28)$	$x^2 - 8x + 12$
$f_3(x)$	$\cdots$	$\frac{1}{3}(10x^3 - 75x^2 + 167x - 105)$	$\frac{1}{6}(5x^3 - 45x^2 + 118x - 84)$	$\frac{1}{6}(10x^3 - 105x^2 + 317x - 252)$	$\frac{1}{6}(x^3 - 12x^2 + 41x - 36)$

	$n = 8$			$n = 9$			$n = 10$			$n = 11$			$n = 12$		
	$f_1(x_i)$	$f_2(x_i)$	$f_3(x_i)$	$f_1(x_i)$	$f_2(x_i)$	$f_3(x_i)$	$f_1(x_i)$	$f_2(x_i)$	$f_3(x_i)$	$f_1(x_i)$	$f_2(x_i)$	$f_3(x_i)$	$f_1(x_i)$	$f_2(x_i)$	$f_3(x_i)$
	-7	7	-7	-4	28	-14	-9	6	-42	-5	15	-30	-11	55	-33
	-5	1	5	-3	7	7	-7	2	14	-4	6	6	-9	25	3
	-3	-3	7	-2	-8	13	-5	-1	35	-3	-1	22	-7	1	21
	-1	-5	3	-1	-17	9	-3	-3	31	-2	-6	23	-5	-17	25
	1	-5	-3	0	-20	0	-1	-4	12	-1	-9	14	-3	-29	19
	3	-3	-7	1	-17	-9	1	-4	-12	0	-10	0	-1	-35	7
	5	1	-5	2	-8	-13	3	-3	-31	1	-9	-14	1	-35	-7
	7	7	7	3	7	-7	5	-1	-35	2	-6	-23	3	-29	-19
				4	28	14	7	2	-14	3	-1	-22	5	-17	-25
							9	6	42	4	6	-6	7	1	-21
										5	15	30	9	25	-3
													11	55	33
c_j	168	168	264	60	2772	990	330	132	8580	110	858	4290	572	12012	5148

	$n=8$	$n=9$	$n=10$	$n=11$	$n=12$
$f_1(x)$	$2x - 9$	$x - 5$	$2x - 11$	$x - 6$	$2x - 13$
$f_2(x)$	$x^2 - 9x + 15$	$3x^2 - 30x + 55$	$\frac{1}{2}(x^2 - 11x + 22)$	$x^2 - 12x + 26$	$3x^2 - 39x + 91$
$f_3(x)$	$\frac{1}{3}(2x^3 - 27x^2 + 103x - 99)$	$\frac{1}{6}(5x^3 - 75x^2 + 316x - 330)$	$\frac{1}{6}(10x^3 - 165x^2 + 761x - 858)$	$\frac{1}{6}(5x^3 - 90x^2 + 451x - 546)$	$\frac{1}{3}(2x^3 - 39x^2 + 211x - 273)$

Donald B. Owen, HANDBOOK OF STATISTICAL TABLES, ©1962. U.S. Department of Energy. pp: 516. Published by Addison-Wesley Publishing Company, Inc., Reading, MA. Reprinted with permission of the publisher.

TABLE B-11. Selected percentiles of the standard normal distribution, $\mu = 0$, $\sigma = 1$

Cumulative Probability	*Value of Z*	*Value of X*	*Cumulative Probability*	*Value of Z*	*Value of X*
.000005	−4.42	$\mu - 4.42\,\sigma$	.51	.03	$\mu + 0.03\,\sigma$
.00001	−4.26	$\mu - 4.26\,\sigma$	.52	.05	$\mu + 0.05\,\sigma$
.00005	−3.89	$\mu - 3.89\,\sigma$	.53	.08	$\mu + 0.08\,\sigma$
.0001	−3.72	$\mu - 3.72\,\sigma$	.54	.10	$\mu + 0.10\,\sigma$
.0005	−3.29	$\mu - 3.29\,\sigma$	.55	.13	$\mu + 0.13\,\sigma$
.001	−3.09	$\mu - 3.09\,\sigma$	.56	.15	$\mu + 0.15\,\sigma$
.005	−2.58	$\mu - 2.58\,\sigma$	.57	.18	$\mu + 0.18\,\sigma$
.01	−2.33	$\mu - 2.33\,\sigma$	.58	.20	$\mu + 0.20\,\sigma$
.02	−2.05	$\mu - 2.05\,\sigma$	.59	.23	$\mu + 0.23\,\sigma$
.025	−1.96	$\mu - 1.96\,\sigma$	.60	.25	$\mu + 0.25\,\sigma$
.03	−1.88	$\mu - 1.88\,\sigma$	.61	.28	$\mu + 0.28\,\sigma$
.04	−1.75	$\mu - 1.75\,\sigma$	.62	.31	$\mu + 0.31\,\sigma$
.05	−1.645	$\mu - 1.645\,\sigma$	.63	.33	$\mu + 0.33\,\sigma$
.06	−1.56	$\mu - 1.56\,\sigma$	.64	.36	$\mu + 0.36\,\sigma$
.07	−1.48	$\mu - 1.48\,\sigma$	.65	.39	$\mu + 0.39\,\sigma$
.08	−1.40	$\mu - 1.40\,\sigma$	.66	.41	$\mu + 0.41\,\sigma$
.09	−1.34	$\mu - 1.34\,\sigma$	.67	.44	$\mu + 0.44\,\sigma$
.10	−1.28	$\mu - 1.28\,\sigma$	.68	.47	$\mu + 0.47\,\sigma$
.11	−1.23	$\mu - 1.23\,\sigma$	.69	.50	$\mu + 0.50\,\sigma$
.12	−1.18	$\mu - 1.18\,\sigma$	.70	.52	$\mu + 0.52\,\sigma$
.13	−1.13	$\mu - 1.13\,\sigma$	.71	.55	$\mu + 0.55\,\sigma$
.14	−1.08	$\mu - 1.08\,\sigma$	.72	.58	$\mu + 0.58\,\sigma$
.15	−1.04	$\mu - 1.04\,\sigma$	.73	.61	$\mu + 0.61\,\sigma$
.16	−0.99	$\mu - 0.99\,\sigma$	.74	.64	$\mu + 0.64\,\sigma$
.17	−0.95	$\mu - 0.95\,\sigma$	.75	.67	$\mu + 0.67\,\sigma$
.18	−0.92	$\mu - 0.92\,\sigma$	.76	.71	$\mu + 0.71\,\sigma$
.19	−0.88	$\mu - 0.88\,\sigma$	.77	.74	$\mu + 0.74\,\sigma$
.20	−0.84	$\mu - 0.84\,\sigma$	.78	.77	$\mu + 0.77\,\sigma$
.21	−0.81	$\mu - 0.81\,\sigma$	.79	.81	$\mu + 0.81\,\sigma$
.22	−0.77	$\mu - 0.77\,\sigma$	.80	.84	$\mu + 0.84\,\sigma$
.23	−0.74	$\mu - 0.74\,\sigma$	.81	.88	$\mu + 0.88\,\sigma$
.24	−0.71	$\mu - 0.71\,\sigma$	.82	.92	$\mu + 0.92\,\sigma$
.25	−0.67	$\mu - 0.67\,\sigma$	.83	.95	$\mu + 0.95\,\sigma$
.26	−0.64	$\mu - 0.64\,\sigma$	.84	.99	$\mu + 0.99\,\sigma$
.27	−0.61	$\mu - 0.61\,\sigma$	.85	1.04	$\mu + 1.04\,\sigma$
.28	−0.58	$\mu - 0.58\,\sigma$	.86	1.08	$\mu + 1.08\,\sigma$
.29	−0.55	$\mu - 0.55\,\sigma$	.87	1.13	$\mu + 1.13\,\sigma$
.30	−0.52	$\mu - 0.52\,\sigma$	.88	1.18	$\mu + 1.18\,\sigma$
.31	−0.50	$\mu - 0.50\,\sigma$	.89	1.23	$\mu + 1.23\,\sigma$
.32	−0.47	$\mu - 0.47\,\sigma$	.90	1.28	$\mu + 1.28\,\sigma$
.33	−0.44	$\mu - 0.44\,\sigma$	.91	1.34	$\mu + 1.34\,\sigma$
.34	−0.41	$\mu - 0.41\,\sigma$	.92	1.40	$\mu + 1.40\,\sigma$
.35	−0.39	$\mu - 0.39\,\sigma$	.93	1.48	$\mu + 1.48\,\sigma$
.36	−0.36	$\mu - 0.36\,\sigma$	.94	1.56	$\mu + 1.56\,\sigma$
.37	−0.33	$\mu - 0.33\,\sigma$	.95	1.645	$\mu + 1.645\,\sigma$
.38	−0.31	$\mu - 0.31\,\sigma$	.96	1.75	$\mu + 1.75\,\sigma$
.39	−0.28	$\mu - 0.28\,\sigma$	.97	1.88	$\mu + 1.88\,\sigma$
.40	−0.25	$\mu - 0.25\,\sigma$	.975	1.96	$\mu + 1.96\,\sigma$
.41	−0.23	$\mu - 0.23\,\sigma$	.98	2.05	$\mu + 2.05\,\sigma$
.42	−0.20	$\mu - 0.20\,\sigma$	.99	2.33	$\mu + 2.33\,\sigma$
.43	−0.18	$\mu - 0.18\,\sigma$	.995	2.58	$\mu + 2.58\,\sigma$
.44	−0.15	$\mu - 0.15\,\sigma$	.999	3.09	$\mu + 3.09\,\sigma$
.45	−0.13	$\mu - 0.13\,\sigma$	.9995	3.29	$\mu + 3.29\,\sigma$
.46	−0.10	$\mu - 0.10\,\sigma$	.9999	3.72	$\mu + 3.72\,\sigma$
.47	−0.08	$\mu - 0.08\,\sigma$	.99995	3.89	$\mu + 3.89\,\sigma$
.48	−0.05	$\mu - 0.05\,\sigma$	.99999	4.26	$\mu + 4.26\,\sigma$
.49	−0.03	$\mu - 0.03\,\sigma$	.999995	4.42	$\mu + 4.42\,\sigma$
.50	−0.00	$\mu - 0.00\,\sigma$			

REFERENCES

Atkinson, R. C. Mnemotechnics in second-language learning. *American Psychologist*, 1975, *30*, 821–828.

Bartlett, M. S. Further aspects of the theory of multiple regression. *Proceedings of the Cambridge Philosophical Society*, 1938, *34*, 33–40.

Bartlett, M. S. Tests of significance in factor analysis. *British Journal of Psychology (Statistics Section)*, 1950, *3*, 77–85.

Bartlett, M. S. A further note on tests of significance in factor analysis. *British Journal of Psychology (Statistics Section)*, 1951, *4*, 1–2.

Birnbaum, A., and Maxwell, A. E. Classification based on Bayes's formula. *Applied Statistics*, 1960, *9*, 152–169.

Bishop, Y. M. M., Fienberg, S. E., and Holland, P. W. *Discrete multivariate analysis: Theory and practice*. Cambridge, Mass.: MIT Press, 1975.

Box, G. E. P. Problems in the analysis of growth and linear curves. *Biometrika*, 1950, *6*, 362–389.

Brown, M. B. Screening effects in multidimensional contingency tables. *Applied Statistics*, 1976, *25*, 37–46.

Carlson, J. E., and Timm, N. H. Analysis of nonorthogonal fixed-effects designs. *Psychological Bulletin*, 1974, *81*, 563–570.

Cattell, R. B. *Handbook of multivariate experimental psychology*. Chicago: Rand McNally, 1966.

Chou, R.-J., and Muirhead, R. J. On some distribution problems in Manova and discriminant analysis. *Journal of Multivariate Analysis*, 1979, *9*, 410–419.

Cohen, J. A coefficient of agreement for nominal scales. *Educational and Psychological Measurement*, 1960, *20*, 37–46.

Cohen, J. Partialed products *are* interactions; partialed powers *are* curve components. *Psychological Bulletin*, 1978, *85*, 858–866.

Cohen, J., and Cohen, P. *Applied multiple regression/correlation analysis for the behavioral sciences*. Hillsdale, N.J.: Erlbaum, 1975.

Cramer, E. M., and Appelbaum, M. I. The validity of polynomial regression in the random regression model. *Review of Educational Research*, 1978, *48*, 511–515.

Cramér, H. *Mathematical methods of statistics*. Princeton, N.J.: Princeton University Press, 1946.

Cronbach, L. J., and Snow, R. E. *Aptitudes and instructional methods: A handbook for research on interactions*. New York: Irvington, 1977.

Darlington, R. B., Weinberg, S. L., and Walberg, H. J. Canonical variate analysis and related techniques. *Review of Educational Research*, 1973, *43*, 433–454.

Davidson, M. I. Univariate versus multivariate tests in repeated-measures experiments. *Psychological Bulletin*, 1972, *77*, 446–452.

Dayton, C. M., and Schafer, W. D. Extended tables of *t* and Chi Square for Bonferroni tests with unequal error allocation. *Journal of the American Statistical Association*, 1973, *68*, 78–83.

Dixon, W. J., and Brown, M. B. (Eds.), *Biomedical computer programs (P-series)*. Berkeley: University of California Press, 1979.

Dixon, W. J., and Massey, F. J., Jr. *Introduction to statistical analysis* (3rd ed.). New York: McGraw-Hill, 1969.

Dorans, N., and Drasgow, F. Alternative weighting schemes for linear prediction. *Organizational Behavior and Human Performance*, 1978, *21*, 316–345.

Draper, N., and Smith, H. *Applied regression analysis* (2nd ed.). New York: Wiley, 1981.

Dretzke, B. J., Levin, J. R., and Serlin, R. C. Testing for regression homogeneity under variance heterogeneity. *Psychological Bulletin*, 1982, *91*, 376–383.

Dunn, O. J. Multiple comparisons among means. *Journal of the American Statistical Association*, 1961, *56*, 52–64.

Elashoff, J. D. Analysis of covariance: A delicate instrument. *American Educational Research Journal*, 1969, *6*, 383–401.

Everitt, B. C. *The analysis of contingency tables*. London: Chapman and Hall, 1977.

Feldt, L. S. A comparison of the precision of three experimental designs employing a concomitant variable. *Psychometrika*, 1958, *23*, 335–353.

Fienberg, Stephen E. *The analysis of cross-classified categorical data* (2nd ed.). Cambridge, Mass.: MIT Press, 1980.

Finn, J. D. *Multivariance: Univariate and multivariate analysis of variance, covariance, and regression* (Version 5). Ann Arbor: National Educational Resources, Inc., 1972.

Finn, J. D. *A general model for multivariate analysis*. New York: Holt & Co., 1974.

Fisher, R. A. The use of multiple measurements in taxonomic problems. *Annals of Eugenics*, 1936, *7*, 179–188.

Gaito, J. Unequal intervals and unequal *n* in trend analyses. *Psychological Bulletin*, 1965, *63*, 125–127.

Ghatala, E. S., Levin, J. R., and Subkoviak, M. J. Rehearsal strategy effects in children's discrimination learning: Confronting the crucible. *Journal of Verbal Learning and Verbal Behavior*, 1975, *14*, 398–407.

Girshick, M. A. On the sampling theory of the roots of determinantal equations. *Annals of Mathematical Statistics*, 1939, *10*, 203–224.

Glass, G. V., Peckham, P. D. and Sanders, J. R. Consequences of failure to meet assumptions underlying the fixed effects analyses of variance and covariance. *Review of Educational Research*, 1972, *42*, 237–288.

Glass, G. V., and Stanley, J. C. *Statistical methods in education and psychology*. Englewood Cliffs, N.J.: Prentice-Hall, 1970.

Goodman, L. A. The analysis of multidimensional contingency tables: Stepwise procedures and direct estimation methods for building models for multiple classifications. *Technometrics*, 1971, *13*, 33–61.

Gordon, R. A. Issues in multiple regression. *American Journal of Sociology*, 1968, *73*, 592–616.

Guilford, J. P. *Psychometric methods* (2nd ed.). New York: McGraw-Hill, 1954.

Hanushek, E. A., and Jackson, J. E. *Statistical methods for social scientists*. New York: Academic Press, 1977.

Harman, H. H. *Modern factor analysis* (2nd ed.). Chicago: University of Chicago Press, 1967.

Hays, W. L. *Statistics for the social sciences* (2nd ed.). New York: Holt & Co., 1973.

Heck, D. L. Charts of some upper percentage points of the distribution of the largest characteristic root. *Annals of Mathematical Statistics*, 1960, *31*, 625–642.

Hotelling, H. The generalization of Student's ratio. *Annals of Mathematical Statistics*, 1931, *2*, 360–378.

Hubert, L., and Baker, F. B. Data analysis by single-link and complete-link hierarchical clustering. *Journal of Educational Statistics*, 1976, *1*, 87–111.

Huberty, C. J., and Holmes, S. E. *Two-group comparisons and univariate classification*. Paper presented at the annual meeting of the American Educational Research Association, Toronto, March 1978.

Huynh, H., and Feldt, L. S. Conditions under which mean square ratios in repeated measurements designs have exact *F*-distributions. *Journal of the American Statistical Association*, 1970, *65*, 1582–1585.

Jennrich, R. I. An asymptotic χ^2 test for the equality of two correlation matrices. *Journal of the American Statistical Association*, 1970, *65*, 904–912.

Kaiser, H. F. The varimax criterion for analytic rotation in factor analysis. *Psychometrika*, 1958, *23*, 187–200.

Kaiser, H. F. The application of electronic computers to factor analysis. *Educational and Psychological Measurement*, 1960, *20*, 141–151.

Kendall, M. G. *A course in multivariate analysis*. New York: Hafner, 1961.

Kendall, M. G., and Stuart, A. *The advanced theory of statistics*. New York: Hafner, 1967.

Kerlinger, F. N., and Pedhazur, E. J. *Multiple regression in behavioral research*. New York: Holt & Co., 1973.

Kirk, R. E. *Experimental design* (2nd ed.). Belmont, Calif.: Brooks/Cole, 1982.

Knapp, T. Canonical correlation analysis: A general parametric significance-testing system. *Psychological Bulletin*, 1978, *85*, 410–416.

Lancaster, H. O. Complex contingency tables treated by partition of χ^2. *Journal of the Royal Statistical Society, Series B*, 1951, *13*, 242–249.

Laughlin, J. E. Comment on 'Estimating coefficients in linear models: It don't make no nevermind.' *Psychological Bulletin*, 1978, *85*, 247–253.

Levy, P. Substantive significance of significant differences between two groups. *Psychological Bulletin*, 1967, *67*, 37–40.

Li, C. C. *Introduction to experimental statistics*. New York: McGraw-Hill, 1964.

Light, R. J., and Margolin, B. H. An analysis of variance for categorical data. *Journal of the American Statistical Association*, 1971, *66*, 534–544.

Mandeville, G. K. *A power comparison of some multivariate procedures and their approximate testing analogues in repeated measures designs*. Paper presented at the annual meeting of the American Educational Research Association, San Francisco, April 1979.

Marascuilo, L. A. *Statistical methods for behavioral science research*. New York: McGraw-Hill, 1971.

Marascuilo, L. A., and Levin, J. R. Group differences in the perception of a social situation. *Urban Education*, 1967, *3*, 85–98.

Marascuilo, L. A., and Levin, J. R. Appropriate post hoc comparisons for interaction and nested hypotheses in analysis of variance designs: The elimination of Type IV errors. *American Educational Research Journal*, 1970, *7*, 397–421.

Marascuilo, L. A., and Levin, J. R. A note on the simultaneous investigation of interaction and nested hypotheses in two-factor analysis of variance designs. *American Educational Research Journal*, 1976, *13*, 61–65.

Marascuilo, L. A., and McSweeney, M. *Nonparametric and distribution-free methods for the social sciences*. Monterey, Calif.: Brooks/Cole, 1977.

Morris, J. D., and Guertin, W. H. *A comparison of regression prediction with data-level variables versus factor scores*. Paper presented at the annual meeting of the American Educational Research Association, New York, April 1977.

Morrison, D. F. *Multivariate statistical methods* (2nd ed.). New York: McGraw-Hill, 1976.

Mulaik, S. A. *The foundations of factor analysis*. New York: McGraw-Hill, 1972.

Neyman, J. Contribution to the theory of the χ^2 test. *Proceedings of the Berkeley Symposium on Mathematical Statistics and Probability*, Berkeley, Calif.: University of California Press, 1949.

Nie, N. H., Hull, C. H., Jenkins, J. G., Steinbrenner, K. S., and Bent, D. H. *Statistical package for the social sciences* (2nd ed). New York: McGraw-Hill, 1975.

Olson, C. L. Comparative robustness of six tests in multivariate analysis of variance. *Journal of the American Statistical Association*, 1974, *69*, 894–908.

Olson, C. L. On choosing a test statistic in multivariate analysis of variance. *Psychological Bulletin*, 1976, *83*, 579–586.

Overall, J. E., and Spiegel, D. K. Concerning least squares analysis of experimental data. *Psychological Bulletin*, 1969, *72*, 311–322.

Petrinovich, L. F., and Hardyck, C. D. Error rates for multiple comparison methods: Some evidence concerning the frequency of erroneous conclusions. *Psychological Bulletin*, 1969, *71*, 43–54.

Pillai, K. C. S. *Statistical tables for tests of multivariate hypotheses.* Manila: Statistical Center, University of the Philippines, 1960.

Pressley, M., Levin, J. R., Hall, J. W., Miller, G. E., and Berry, J. K. The keyword method and foreign word acquisition. *Journal of Experimental Psychology: Human Learning and Memory*, 1980, *6*, 163–173.

Pruzek, R. M., and Frederick, B. C. Weighting predictors in linear models: Alternatives to least squares and limitations of equal weights. *Psychological Bulletin*, 1978, *85*, 254–266.

Rao, B. R. An asymptotic expansion of the distribution of Wilk's criterion. *Bulletin of the International Statistics Institute*, 1951, *33*, 177–180.

Readence, J. E., and Baldwin, R. S. Effects of impulsivity-reflectivity and type of phonics in instruction on reading achievement. *National Reading Conference Yearbook*, 1978(a), *27*, 36–40.

Readence, J. E., and Baldwin, R. S. The relationship of cognitive style and phonics instruction. *Journal of Educational Research*, 1978(b), *72*, 44–52.

Robinson, W. S. Ecological correlations and the behavior of individuals. *American Sociological Review*, 1950, *15*, 351–357.

Romaniuk, J. G., Levin, J. R., and Hubert, L. J. Hypothesis-testing procedures in repeated-measures designs: On the road map not taken. *Child Development*, 1977, *48*, 1757–1760.

Roy, S. N. *Some aspects of multivariate analysis.* New York: Wiley, 1957.

Roy, S. N., and Bose, R. C. Simultaneous confidence interval estimation. *Annals of Mathematical Statistics*, 1953, *24*, 513–536.

Schatzoff, M. Exact distributions of Wilks's likelihood-ratio criterion. *Biometrika*, 1966, *53*, 347–358.

Schatzoff, M. Sensitivity comparisons among tests of the general linear hypothesis. *Journal of the American Statistical Association*, 1966, *61*, 415–435.

Scheffé, H. A method for judging all contrasts in the analysis of variance. *Biometrika*, 1953, *40*, 87–104.

Schluck, G. J. *A comparison of three confidence interval procedures for the multivariate general linear model.* Paper presented at the annual meeting of the American Educational Research Association, New York, February 1971.

Serlin, R. C. *Orthogonal polynomials for trend analysis with continuous independent variables.* Unpublished manuscript, University of Wisconsin, Madison, 1978.

Serlin, R. C. A multivariate measure of association based on the Pillai-Bartlett procedure. *Psychological Bulletin*, 1982, *91*, 413–417.

Serlin, R. C., and Levin, J. R. *R^2 explained.* Occasional Paper No. 20, Laboratory of Experimental Design, University of Wisconsin, Madison, 1978.

Serlin, R. C., and Levin, J. R. Identifying regions of significance in aptitude-by-treatment-interaction research. *American Educational Research Journal*, 1980, *17*, 389–399.

Sloane, L. If the IRS calls you . . . *Parade*, August 14, 1977, p. 12.

Stumpf, S. A. A note on handling missing data. *Journal of Management*, 1978, *4*, 65–73.

Sweet, R. A. *Distribution of canonical correlations and Gaussian rank canonical correlations for small samples from various distributions with various correlation matrices.* Unpublished doctoral dissertation, University of California, Berkeley, 1973.

Thurstone, L. L. *Multiple factor analysis.* Chicago: University of Chicago Press, 1947.

Timm, N. H. The estimation of variance-covariance and correlation matrices from incomplete data. *Psychometrika*, 1970, *35*, 417–438.

Timm, N. H. *Multivariate analysis with applications in education and psychology.* Monterey, Calif.: Brooks/Cole, 1975.

Tsutakawa, R. K., and Hewett, J. E. Comparison of two regression lines over a finite interval. *Biometrics*, 1978, *34*, 391–398.

Tukey, J. W. *The problem of multiple comparisons.* Unpublished manuscript, Princeton University, 1953.

Wainer, H. Estimating coefficients in linear models: It don't make no nevermind. *Psychological Bulletin*, 1976, *41*, 213–217.

Wainer, H. On the sensitivity of regression and regressors. *Psychological Bulletin*, 1978, *85*, 267–273.

Wall, F. J. *The generalized variance ratio of the U-statistic*. Albuquerque: The Dikewood Corporation, 1968.

Weinberg, S. L., and Darlington, R. B. Canonical analysis when number of variables is large relative to sample size. *Journal of Educational Statistics*, 1976, *1*, 313–332.

Whitla, D. K. (Ed.). *Handbook of measurement and assessment in behavioral sciences*. Reading, Mass.: Addison-Wesley, 1968.

Wood, C. L. Comparison of linear trends in binomial proportions. *Biometrics*, 1978, *34*, 496–504.

Wright, S. The method of path coefficients. *Annals of Mathematical Statistics*, 1934, *5*, 161–215.

SELECTED ANSWERS TO CHAPTER EXERCISES

2-11.

a. (i) No; $Z_1 = 3.10$; $Z_{0.975} = 1.96$
(ii) Yes; $Z_2 = -.34$; $Z_{0.025} = -1.96$

b. For H_{0_1}, the Dunn-Bonferroni procedure would be used in conjunction with Formula 1 to examine all pairwise difference. With an α of .0083 for each comparison, the critical value is given by $Z_{0.996} = 2.65$.

For H_{0_2}, three pairwise comparisons would be examined using the Dunn-Bonferroni method and a critical value of $Z_{0.9917} = 2.40$. The comparison, $p_{13} - p_{35}$, would employ Formula 1. The other two comparisons would employ Formula 2.

2-12.

	V–C	V–S	I–C	I–S
For $\rho_{13} = 0$, $t_{28:0.95} = 1.70$	$t = 2.28$*	$t = .22$	$t = 2.31$*	$t = -.41$
For $\rho_{23} = 0$, $t_{28:0.95} = 1.70$	$t = .84$	$t = 4.40$*	$t = .82$	$t = 4.39$*
For $\rho_{13} = \rho_{23}$, $z_{0.95} = 1.65$	$z = .98$	$z = -2.65$*	$z = 1.04$	$z = -3.61$*

* Significant

2-13.

a.

	V–C	V–S	I–C	I–S
$B_{1(k)}$	.0836	.2277	.0556	.1826
$MS_{\text{Res}(k)}$	10.69	4.29	10.04	5.29

The values for the two control groups are similar; and the values for the two strategy groups are similar.

b. (i) $F = 1.62$(NS); $F_{3,112:0.95} = 2.68$
(ii) $U_0 = 4.94$(NS); $\chi^2_{3:0.95} = 7.81$
(iii) $F^* = 1.61$(NS); $F_{3,60:0.95} = 2.76$

c. $-.05 < \psi < .31$ NS

2-14.

$F = 13.36$*, since $F_{3,115:0.95} = 2.68$.

Simultaneous multiple comparisons reveal that the V–C and I–C conditions each differs from the V–S and I–S conditions.

2-15.

a. $t = .46$(NS); $t_{8:0.975} = 2.31$
b. $t = .72$(NS); $t_{11:0.975} = 2.20$

2-16.

a. $r_{XY(W)} = .84$; $t = 5.13$*, since $t_{11:0.95} = 1.80$

b. $r_{XY(T)} = .69$; $t = 3.53$*, since $t_{14:0.95} = 1.76$

c. $r_{XY(W)}$ turned out to be slightly higher than $r_{XY(T)}$ for these data. See discussion in Section 3-2.

3.1. a., b., c. (Complete the data table)

	(**a.** $X_3 = X_1X_2$)	(**b.** $X_4 = X_1^2$)	(**c.** $X_5 = X_2^2$)
Student	X_3	X_4	X_5
1	1494	6889	324
2	1260	7056	225
3	1800	8100	400
4	1520	9025	256
5	1728	9216	324
6	2231	9409	529
7	1400	10000	196
8	1545	10609	225
9	1030	10609	100
10	990	12100	81
11	1725	13225	225
12	2806	14884	529
13	3429	16129	729
14	3354	16641	676
15	4448	19321	1024

3-11. Stepwise regression (all possible orders using X_1, X_2, X_3)

		$\hat{R}^2$	$\hat{R}^2$ change	Standardized beta
a. X_1, X_2, X_3	X_1	.574	.574	0.181
	X_2	.655	.081	− 0.386
	X_3	.661	.005	1.005
b. X_1, X_3, X_2	X_1	.574	.574	0.181
	X_3	.659	.085	1.005
	X_2	.661	.001	− 0.386
c. X_2, X_1, X_3	X_2	.466	.466	− 0.386
	X_1	.655	.189	0.181
	X_3	.661	.005	1.005
d. X_2, X_3, X_1	X_2	.466	.466	− 0.386
	X_3	.659	.194	1.005
	X_1	.661	.001	0.181
e. X_3, X_1, X_2	X_3	.612	.612	1.005
	X_1	.659	.047	0.181
	X_2	.661	.001	− 0.386
f. X_3, X_2, X_1	X_3	.612	.612	1.005
	X_2	.659	.047	− 0.386
	X_1	.661	.001	0.181

g. The best single predictor of Y is X_3 ($r_{YX_3} = .78$). After that, X_1 and X_2 are of almost equal utility ($r_{YX_1 \cdot X_3} = .347$, $r_{YX_2 \cdot X_3} = -.348$). It is interesting that although $r_{X_2X_3} = .95$, $r_{YX_2} \neq r_{YX_3}$; in fact, $r_{YX_2} = .68$ and $r_{YX_3} = .78$. It is also interesting that although the zero-order correlations of X_1 and X_2 with Y are unequal ($r_{YX_1} = .76$ and $r_{YX_2} = .68$), their partial correlations with Y after X_3 is removed are nearly equal (though opposite in sign).

h. (1) Means and SDs for computations:

	$\bar{X}$	S
Y	61.33	14.55
X_1	106.20	16.98
X_2	18.73	6.43
X_3	2050.67	1010.10
X_4	11547.53	3740.72
X_5	389.53	262.27

(2) Z-scores

Student	Z_Y	Z_{X_1}	Z_{X_2}	Z_{X_3}	Z_{X_4}	Z_{X_5}
1	−0.64	−1.37	−0.11	−0.55	−1.25	−0.25
2	−0.78	−1.31	−0.58	−0.78	−1.20	−0.63
3	−0.98	−0.95	0.20	−0.25	−0.92	0.04
4	−0.57	−0.66	−0.43	−0.53	−0.67	−0.51
5	−0.44	−0.60	−0.11	−0.32	−0.62	−0.25
6	−0.37	−0.54	0.66	0.18	−0.57	0.53
7	−0.85	−0.37	−0.74	−0.64	−0.41	−0.74
8	0.73	−0.19	−0.58	−0.50	−0.25	−0.63
9	0.46	−0.19	−1.36	−1.01	−0.25	−1.10
10	−1.53	0.22	−1.51	−1.05	0.15	−1.18
11	−0.44	0.52	−0.58	−0.32	0.45	−0.63
12	1.28	0.93	0.66	0.75	0.89	0.53
13	1.21	1.22	1.29	1.36	1.22	1.29
14	1.49	1.34	1.13	1.29	1.36	1.09
15	1.42	1.93	2.06	2.37	2.08	2.42

3-12. Stepwise regression using X_1, X_2, X_4

Source Step one-linear	d/f	SS	MS	F	$\hat{R}^2$	Increment in $\hat{R}^2$
Regression on X_1 and X_2	2	1943.30	971.65	11.41	.66	.66
Residual	12	1022.03	85.17			
Total	14	2965.33				
Step two-quadratic						
Regression	3	1948.88				
X_1 and X_2	2	1943.30				
X_4	1	5.58	5.58	0.06	.66	.00
Residual	11	1016.45	92.40			
Total	14	2965.33				

4-1.
$$\begin{bmatrix} 5 & -1 & 7 & -5 \\ 3 & 11 & 4 & 0 \\ 4 & 8 & 11 & 12 \end{bmatrix}$$

4-2. No, the number of columns in A_1 does not equal the number of rows in A_2.

4-3. $\begin{bmatrix} 7 & 7 \\ 20 & 7 \\ 29 & 8 \end{bmatrix}$

4-4. No. A 4×2 matrix cannot be postmultiplied by a 3×4 matrix.

4-7. There is no inverse since $|\Delta_{y'}| = 0$

4-8. $\Delta_5^{-1} = \begin{bmatrix} \frac{6}{56} & -\frac{2}{56} \\ \frac{-2}{56} & \frac{10}{56} \end{bmatrix}$

5-7.

V	λ	$\hat{R}$	Λ	χ^2	ν
1	.2364	.4862	.7302	49.53	18
2	.0347	.1864	.9562	7.06	10
3	.0094	.0971	.9906	1.49	4

5-8.

(1) Roy's criterion:

H_0: $\lambda_1 = 0$

H_1: $\lambda_1 \neq 0$

$\lambda_1 = .23638$

$s = \min(P,Q) = 3$

$m = \frac{1}{2}(|P - Q| - 1) = 2$

$n = \frac{1}{2}(N - P - Q - 2)$
$= \frac{1}{2}(163 - 3 - 6 - 2) = 76$

$\alpha = .05$

The critical value for $s = 3$, $m = 2$, $n = 76$, $\alpha = .05$ is approximately .148. Therefore, H_0 is rejected.

(2) Rao's test of Wilks's Λ:

H_0: $\lambda_1 = \lambda_2 = \lambda_3 = 0$

H_1: H_0 is false

$\alpha = .05$

$\Lambda = (1 - \lambda_1)(1 - \lambda_2)(1 - \lambda_3)$
$= (1 - .23638)(1 - .03473)(1 - .00943)$
$= .7301$

$$F = \left[\frac{ab - \frac{1}{2}PQ + 1}{PQ}\right]\left[\frac{1 - \Lambda^{1/b}}{\Lambda^{1/b}}\right]$$

$$a = (N - 1) - \tfrac{1}{2}(P + Q + 1)$$
$$= 162 - \tfrac{1}{2}(10) = 157$$

$$b = \sqrt{\frac{P^2Q^2 - 4}{P^2 + Q^2 - 5}} = \sqrt{\frac{9(36) - 4}{9 + 36 - 5}} = \sqrt{\frac{320}{40}}$$
$$= 2.8284$$

$$F = \left[\frac{157(2.8284) - \tfrac{1}{2}(3.6) + 1}{3.6}\right]\left[\frac{1 - .7301^{1/2.8284}}{.7301^{1/2.8284}}\right] = 2.8489$$

$$v_1 = PQ = 18$$

$$v_2 = ab - \tfrac{1}{2}PQ + 1 = 436.0631$$
$$F_{18,436:0.95} \simeq 1.63$$

Therefore, H_0 is rejected.

(3) Bartlett's Sequential Procedure

H_{0_1}: $\lambda_1 = \lambda_2 = \lambda_3 = 0$

H_{1_1}: H_{0_1} is false

$\Lambda_1 = \Lambda = .7301$

$$\alpha_1 = \frac{2(1)}{3(4)}(.05) = .0083$$

$$X_1^2 = -[(N - 1) - \tfrac{1}{2}(P + Q + 1)] \ln(\Lambda_1)$$
$$= -[162 - 5] \ln(.7301)$$
$$= 49.39$$

The critical value is $\chi^2_{PQ:1-.0083} = \chi^2_{18:0.9917} = 37.16$

Reject H_0

H_{0_2}: $\lambda_2 = \lambda_3 = 0$

H_{1_2}: H_{0_2} is false

$$\alpha_2 = \frac{2(2)}{3(4)}(.05) = .0167$$

$\Lambda_2 = (1 - \lambda_2)(1 - \lambda_3) = .9562$

$X_2^2 = -157 \ln(\Lambda_2) = 7.03$

The critical value is $\chi^2_{(P-1)(Q-1):\,1-.0167} = \chi^2_{10:0.9833}$
The table shows that $20.48 < \chi^2_{10:0.9833} < 23.21$.

Therefore, H_{0_2} is not rejected, and the analysis is discontinued. Only the first canonical variate would be retained according to this criterion.

5-9.

Pattern Matrix

	v_1	v_2	v_3
X_4	−.8826	.5011	−.2339
X_5	.3691	.7073	−.6285
X_6	−.0782	.6900	.7571
X_7	.1562	−.1616	.3000
X_8	−.5520	−.6886	−.2605
X_9	−.6645	.4877	.1893
X_{10}	−.3011	.3907	.6513
X_{11}	−.2676	.1012	−.5938
X_{12}	.5668	−.7237	.3525

It is very difficult to interpret this analysis using the pattern matrix. Among the variables of the first set, only MAT score receives a large weight on the first canonical variate. In the second set, knowledge of psychiatry and obstetrics are weighted heavily in the same direction as MAT score, while knowledge of surgery is weighted in the opposite direction. Ordinarily, no attempt is made to interpret canonical variates which are not retained. However, a glance at the weights for canonical variates 2 and 3 reveals similar uninterpretable patterns.

5-10.

Structure Matrix

	v_1	v_2	v_3
X_4	.93	.22	−.30
X_5	−.52	.66	−.55
X_6	−.14	.62	.78
Y_7	.18	−.33	.60
Y_8	.66	−.71	−.07
Y_9	.65	.02	.41
Y_{10}	.46	.09	.72
Y_{11}	.57	−.09	−.08
Y_{12}	.10	−.58	.59

In this example, the structure matrix also fails to yield easily interpretable results. Among the variables of the first set, MAT score has a high positive correlation (.93) with the first canonical variate; need for order has a fairly high negative correlation (−.52). Among the variables of the second set, knowledge of psychiatry, obstetrics, and public health all have correlations of over .50 on the first canonical variate.

5-11.

a. Specialty $F = 1.57$

b. Social class $F = 1.21$

c. Year of medical school $F = 2.29$

The null hypothesis H_0: All $\psi = 0$ cannot be rejected for any of these analyses.

6-10. The following matrices were produced when the 164 medical students' data was subjected to a principal components analysis

Knowledge Area	Second year* 1st component	Third year* 1st component	Fourth year 1st component	Fourth year 2nd component
Medicine	.86	.87	.83	.05
Psychiatry	.36	.63	− .05	.92
Ob-Gyn	.82	.79	.63	.38
Pediatrics	.85	.88	.60	− .09
Public health	.71	.72	.57	.31
Surgery	.86	.84	.57	.57

* Rotation was bypassed as only one component was extracted

6-11.

Social class	N	Mean	Variance
1 (high)	18	.27	0.85
2	13	− .54	0.41
3	11	.10	1.09
4 (low)	8	.13	1.89
Total sample	50	0	1.0

Source	d/f	SS	MS	F	$\hat{\eta}^2$
Between	3	5.415	1.805	1.905(NS)	.11
Within	46	43.585	0.947		
Total	49	49.000			

There appears to be no significant difference between the four social classes on the principal component for second-year students.

8-6.

a. Effect—Soc. class

Multivariate tests of significance ($s = 3$, $m = 2\frac{1}{2}$, $n = 74\frac{1}{2}$)

Test name	Value	Approx. F	Hypoth. d/f	Error d/f	Sig. of F	Crit. value
Pillai	.22108	1.35246	27.00	459.00	.113	$F \simeq 1.49$ N.S.
Hotelling	.24133	1.33772	27.00	449.00	.122	$F \simeq 1.49$ N.S.
Wilks	.79384	1.34557	27.00	441.64	.118	$F \simeq 1.49$ N.S.
Roy	.10810					$\theta \simeq 0.145$ N.S.

Eigenvalues and canonical correlations

Root No.	Eigenvalue	Pct.	Cum. Pct.	Canon. Cor.
1	.12120	50.22112	50.22112	.32878
2	.07424	30.76300	80.98412	.26289
3	.04589	19.01588	100.00000	.20947

Dimension reduction analysis

Roots	Wilks's lambda	F	Hypoth. d/f	Error d/f	Sig. of F
1 to 3	.79384	1.34557	27.00	441.64	.118
2 to 3	.89005	1.13568	16.00	303.00	.321
3 to 3	.95612	.99648	7.00	152.00	.436

Standardized discriminant function coefficients

Function No.

Variable	1	2	3
MAT	.21418	−.48546	.73574
Order	.25241	−.22941	.23569
Nurturance	.08949	−.76837	−.10827
Medicine	.12796	−.15136	−.69585
Psychiatry	−.43846	−.26899	−.21389
Ob-Gyn	−.44732	−.30967	−.42906
Pediatrics	−.57776	.09289	.07208
Public health	.73095	−.21620	.04099
Surgery	−.24895	.23097	1.10072

Canonical discriminant functions evaluated at group means (group centroids)

Group	Function 1	Function 2	Function 3
1	−0.13590	0.23081	0.18689
2	−0.29365	−0.21015	−0.15995
3	0.55503	−0.39502	0.21485
4	0.51880	0.32589	−0.34545

b. Effect—Special

Multivariate tests of significance ($s = 4$, $m = 2$, $n = 74$)

Test name	Value	Approx. F	Hypoth d/f	Error d/f	Sig. of F	Crit. value
Pillai	.19327	.86311	36.00	612.00	.699	$F \simeq 1.42$ N.S.
Hotelling	.20649	.85177	36.00	594.00	.716	$F \simeq 1.42$ N.S.
Wilks	.81896	.85736	36.00	563.86	.708	$F \simeq 1.42$ N.S.
Roy	.08704					$\theta \simeq 0.160$ N.S.

Eigenvalues and canonical correlations

Root No.	Eigenvalue	Pct.	Cum. Pct.	Canon. Cor.
1	.09533	46.16796	46.16796	.29502
2	.06037	29.23430	75.40226	.23860
3	.03643	17.64116	93.04342	.18748
4	.01436	6.95658	100.00000	.11900

Dimension reduction analysis

Roots	Wilks lambda	F	Hypoth. d/f	Error d/f	Sig. of F
1 to 4	.81896	.85736	36.00	563.86	.708
2 to 4	.89704	.69528	24.00	440.22	.858
3 to 4	.95119	.54655	14.00	302.00	.904
4 to 4	.98584	.36271	6.00	151.50	.902

Standardized discriminant function coefficients

Function No.

Variable	1	2	3	4
MAT	−.26370	.46073	−.42139	−.23461
Order	.57842	.06309	.14457	−.06140
Nurturance	−.09958	−.50700	.22133	.24682
Medicine	.05270	.27218	−.31301	.24655
Psychiatry	.29762	−.67244	.15690	−.63452
Ob-Gyn	.36460	.49201	.92749	−.38287
Pediatrics	−.28699	−.21044	−.34490	−.12389
Public health	−.68581	−.07964	.53633	.44758
Surgery	−.19387	−.22671	−.35745	−.35957

Canonical discriminant functions evaluated at group means (group centroids)

Group	Function 1	Function 2	Function 3	Function 4
1	− 0.02168	− 0.00274	0.20088	− 0.04536
2	0.88946	0.13870	− 0.05035	0.15299
3	0.17467	− 0.59405	− 0.25905	− 0.14949
4	− 0.12264	0.32724	− 0.22595	− 0.08349
5	− 0.31619	− 0.12119	− 0.07385	0.20254

c. Effect—year

Multivariate tests of significance ($s = 2, m = 3, n = 75$)

Test name	Value	Approx. F	Hypoth. d/f	Error d/f	Sig. of F	Crit. value
Pillai	.53665	6.23430	18.00	306.00	0.0	$F \simeq 1.61$ Sign.
Hotelling	.85667	7.18652	18.00	302.00	0.0	$F \simeq 1.61$ Sign.
Wilks	.51226	6.70810	18.00	304.00	0.0	$F \simeq 1.61$ Sign.
Roy	.42029					$\theta \simeq 0.110$ Sign.

Eigenvalues and canonical correlations

Root No.	Eigenvalue	Pct.	Cum. Pct.	Canon. Cor.
1	.72499	84.62843	84.62843	.64829
2	.13168	15.37157	100.00000	.34112

Dimension reduction analysis

Roots	Wilks's lambda	F	Hypoth. d/f	Error d/f	Sig. of F
1 to 2	.51226	6.70810	18.00	304.00	0.0
2 to 2	.88364	2.51022	8.00	152.50	.014

Standardized discriminant function coefficients

Function No.

Variable	1	2
MAT	− .52785	− .24684
Order	− .93196	.01990
Nurturance	.14247	.07628
Medicine	− .77477	.26345
Psychiatry	.11877	.24728
Ob-Gyn	.22821	− .78332
Pediatrics	.43253	− .27124
Public health	− .14052	− .17284
Surgery	.20776	.92184

Canonical discriminant functions evaluated at group means (group centroids)

Group	Function 1	Function 2
2	− 0.68695	0.45433
3	− 0.61846	− 0.45436
4	1.09029	0.01493

8-7. There were no significant mean differences among the four social classes or five specialties, i.e., all four equal 0. The three pairwise comparisons of the mean standardized first discriminant scores for year of medical school are as follows:

$$\psi = \hat{\psi} \pm \mathbf{S}\, SE_{\hat{\psi}}$$

$$\mathbf{S} = \sqrt{\left[\frac{\theta^{\alpha}_{(s,m,n)}}{1 - \theta^{\alpha}_{(s,m,n)}}\right](N - K)} = \sqrt{\left[\frac{\theta^{.05}_{(2,3,75)}}{1 - \theta^{.05}_{(2,3,75)}}\right](N - K)}$$

$$= \sqrt{\left[\frac{0.125}{1 - 0.125}\right](163 - 3)} = \sqrt{22.875} = 4.78$$

$$\psi_1 \text{ (Year 2 } vs. \text{ Year 3)} = (\bar{L}_2 - \bar{L}_3) \pm \mathbf{S}\sqrt{\frac{1}{N_2} + \frac{1}{N_3}}$$

$$= [(-0.68695) - (-0.61846)] \pm 4.78\sqrt{\frac{1}{50} + \frac{1}{52}}$$

$$= -0.06849 \pm 0.95 \quad \textit{Not significant}$$

$$\psi_2 \text{ (Year 2 } vs. \text{ Year 4)} = -1.77724 \pm .91 \quad \textit{Significant}$$

$$\psi_3 \text{ (Year 3 } vs. \text{ Year 4)} = -1.70875 \pm .90 \quad \textit{Significant}$$

8-8.

Source	d/f	Sum of squares	Mean square	F ratio	Prob.	Crit. value
Between groups	3	19.2703	6.4234	6.423	0.0004	$F \simeq 2.60$ (Sig.)
Within groups	159	158.9993	1.0000			
Total	162	178.2696				

The two omnibus tests come to different conclusions. After careful consideration, however, the reasons for the differences are apparent. For the one-way MANOVA in Exercise 8-6a the null hypothesis is H_0: For the four social classes, all linear contrasts in all possible linear combinations of the nine variables are equal to zero, versus the alternative hypothesis, H_1: At least one contrast does not equal zero. Thus the MANOVA omnibus hypothesis tests all possible one-variable contrasts, all possible two-variable contrasts, and so on, as well as all possible contrasts in the discriminant functions. For the univariate ANOVA in this exercise, however, the null hypothesis is much more restricted, that is, H_0: All linear contrasts in the first discriminant function are equal to zero. In essence, the MANOVA spreads the risk of a Type I error over a much 'larger' universe of infinite contrasts than does the univariate ANOVA on the first discriminant function. This difference is particularly apparent when the multiple comparison post hoc critical values for the two omnibus procedures are compared:

$$\text{MANOVA: Roy-Bose } \mathbf{S} = \sqrt{\left[\frac{.145}{(1 - .145)}\right]159} = 5.19$$

$$\text{ANOVA: Scheffé } \mathbf{S} = \sqrt{3(2.60)} = 2.79$$

8-9.

a. Social class

Classification results

Actual group	No. of cases	Predicted group membership 1	2	3	4
Group 1 higher	61	22	17	11	11
		36.1%	27.9%	18.0%	18.0%
Group 2	56	15	18	13	10
		26.8%	32.1%	23.2%	17.9%
Group 3	24	1	4	13	6
		4.2%	16.7%	54.2%	25.0%
Group 4 lower	22	3	6	3	10
		13.6%	27.3%	13.6%	45.5%

Percent of 'grouped' cases correctly classified: 38.65%

b. Medical specialty

Classification results

Actual group	No. of cases	Predicted group membership 1	2	3	4	5
Group 1	71	15	16	11	12	17
primary care		21.1%	22.5%	15.5%	16.9%	23.9%
Group 2	14	1	7	4	2	0
sub-specialty		7.1%	50.0%	28.6%	14.3%	0.0%
Group 3	15	1	2	6	4	2
surgery		6.7%	13.3%	40.0%	26.7%	13.3%
Group 4	33	3	6	6	11	7
miscellaneous		9.1%	18.2%	18.2%	33.3%	21.2%
Group 5	30	6	5	4	4	11
none, undecl., unknown		20.0%	16.7%	13.3%	13.3%	36.7%

Percent of 'grouped' cases correctly classified: 30.67%

c. Year of medical school

Classification results

Actual group	No. of cases	Predicted group membership 2	3	4
Group 2	50	33	13	4
second year		66.0%	26.0%	8.0%
Group 3	52	15	29	8
third year		28.8%	55.8%	15.4%
Group 4	61	6	9	46
fourth year		9.8%	14.8%	75.4%

Percent of 'grouped' cases correctly classified: 66.26%

Classification by year of medical school produces the lowest proportion of misclassified subjects.

9-1.

a. ANOVA Table

Source	*d/f*	*SS*	*MS*	*F*
IQ	1	1764.00	1764.00	83.01*
Sleep	3	766.25	255.41	12.02**
S × IQ	3	41.50	13.83	< 1
Error	8	170.00	21.25	

*$F_{1,8:0.95} = 5.32$
**$F_{3,8:0.95} = 4.07$

b. Conditions 3 and 6, and 3 and 9 differ significantly

c. Main effect linear: $F = 12.88$*, since $F_{1,8:0.975} = 7.57$
Main effect quadratic: $F = 7.35$(NS)
Interaction linear: $F = 1.72$(NS)
Interaction quadratic: $F < 1$(NS)

d. ANOVA Table

Source	d/f	SS	MS	F
IQ	1	1764.00	1764.00	83.01*
Sleep in High IQ	3	353.375	117.79	5.54**
Sleep in Low IQ	3	454.375	151.45	7.12**
Error	8	170.00	21.25	

* $F_{1,8:0.95} = 5.32$
** $F_{3,8:0.95} = 4.07$

e. Sleep in High IQ: No pairwise comparisons are significant.
Sleep in Low IQ: Conditions 3 and 9 differ significantly.

f. High IQ linear: $F = 2.60$(NS), since $F_{1,8:0.975} = 7.57$
High IQ quadratic: $F = 4.29$(NS)
Low IQ linear: $F = 12.00$*
Low IQ quadratic: $F = 3.11$(NS)

9-2.
a. Sleep main effect: $\theta = .9715$ (Sig.), since $\theta_c \simeq .7$
Variable by variable comparisons: Conditions 9 and 6 exceed Condition 3 on the reasoning subtest; all conditions exceed Condition 3 on the arithmetic subtest. Trend comparisons and comparisons based on the first discriminant function could also be examined.

IQ main effect: $\theta = .9357$, $F = 29.10$ (Sig.), since $F_{3,6:0.95} = 4.76$.
High IQ greater than Low IQ on all three subtests.

Sleep $\times$ IQ interaction: $\theta = .8839$ (Sig.), since $\theta_c \simeq .7$
No significant variable-by-variable tetrad differences.

b. Sleep main effect:

$\Lambda = .0257$, $F = 5.74$ (Sig.), since $F_{9,14:0.95} = 2.65$

c. IQ main effect:

$\Lambda = .0643$, $F = 29.10$ (Sig.), since $F_{3,6:0.95} = 4.76$

d. Sleep $\times$ IQ interaction:

$\Lambda = .0750$, $F = 3.11$ (Sig.), since $F_{9,14:0.95} = 2.65$

9-3.
a. $\theta = .8002$ (Sig.), since $\theta_c = .65$
b. $\Lambda = .1858$, $F = 2.44$ (Sig.), since $F_{9,22:0.95} = 2.34$

9-4. $F = 5.78$ (Sig.), since $F_{2,14:0.95} = 3.74$.

The vocabulary subtest mean is significantly higher than the reasoning subtest mean.

9-5.

a. $F = 12.61$ (Sig.), since $F_{2,11:0.95} = 3.98$.

The vocabulary subtest mean is higher than either the reasoning subtest mean or the arithmetic subtest mean.

b. $\theta = .7470$ (Sig.), since $\theta_c = .675$
$\Lambda = .2464$, $F = 3.72$ (Sig.), since $F_{6,22:0.95} = 2.55$

c. V–R: $F = 6.34$ (Sig.), since $F_{3,12:0.99} = 5.95$

(No significant pairwise or trend post hoc comparisons)

V–A: $F = 11.77$ (Sig.); Condition 3 is higher than Conditions 6 and 9

R–A: $F = .88$ (NS)

10-1.

Source	*d/f*	X^2
Homogeneity	3	65.08
Linearity	1	63.64
Deviation from Linearity	2	1.45

H_0: $\beta_1 = 0$

H_1: $\beta_1 > 0$

$Z = \sqrt{X^2_{\beta_1}} = \sqrt{63.64} = 7.98$ therefore reject H_0 since $Z > Z_{.95} = 1.645$.

Conclusion: A significant linear component exists without a significant deviation from linearity.

10-2.

Step	Test	U_0	*d/f*	X^2	*d/f*
1.	Homogeneity ($P_{ijk} = \alpha_0$)	364.92	7	364.92	7
2.	One regression line ($\beta_0 = 0$)	23.00	6	341.93	1
3.	Parallel lines ($\alpha_1 = \alpha_2$)	5.84	5	17.16	1
4.	Nonparallel lines ($\beta_1 = \beta_2$)	5.84	4	0.00	1
5.	Deviation from linearity	5.84	3	5.84	4

Since $17.16 > \chi^2_{1:.95}$, the hypothesis of equal intercepts is rejected—the item is differentially difficult. However, since $5.84 < \chi^2_{5:.95}$, the goodness of fit test is rejected at Step 3. Assume, then, that the best-fitting model contains two parallel lines with different intercepts.

10-3.

a. This test should not be done. Instead, one would compare each group to the majority group. See **10-6** below.

b. It would be much wiser, statistically, to compare each minority group to the White group via pairwise comparisons using the Dunn-Bonferroni procedure because of greater power and interpretability. If one opted for the omnibus procedure, rejection of H_0 would not indicate where the bias was occurring. In the planned method, rejection of planned H_0's would be readily interpretable.

c. The comparisons should be directional, since increased power would result. Also, if one suspects bias, it should be possible to predict the direction of the bias.

10-4.

Source	d/f	G^2	Probability	Decision (at $\alpha = .05$)
Score interval	3	18.59	.0003	Reject
Outcome	1	0.08	.7774	NS
S × O	3	43.72	.0000	Reject
Total (Homogeneity)	7	62.40	.0000	

10-5.

Source	d/f	G^2	Probability	Decision (at $\alpha = .05$)
Score interval	3	69.48	0	Reject
Outcome	1	139.77	0	Reject
Ethnic group	2	449.87	0	Reject
S × O	3	211.31/279.03*	0	Reject
S × E	6	56.15/123.88*	0	Reject
O × E	2	27.30/95.03*	0	Reject
S × O × E	6	5.84	.4417	NS
Total (Homogeneity)	23	1095.17	.0000	

* Partial association/Marginal association (see Section **10-8**, Step 8)

10-6.

Contrast	$\hat{\psi}$	$SE^2_{\hat{\psi}}$	$S^*SE_{\hat{\psi}}$
1. $[(\mu_{111}-\mu_{211}) - (\mu_{121}-\mu_{221})] - [(\mu_{112}-\mu_{212}) - (\mu_{122}-\mu_{222})]$	0.53958	0.24088	2.19492
2. $[(\mu_{111}-\mu_{211}) - (\mu_{121}-\mu_{221})] - [(\mu_{113}-\mu_{213}) - (\mu_{123}-\mu_{223})]$	−0.11719	0.41033	2.86472
3. $[(\mu_{112}-\mu_{212}) - (\mu_{122}-\mu_{222})] - [(\mu_{113}-\mu_{213}) - (\mu_{123}-\mu_{223})]$	−0.65678	0.35296	2.65692
4. $[(\mu_{111}-\mu_{311}) - (\mu_{121}-\mu_{321})] - [(\mu_{112}-\mu_{321}) - (\mu_{122}-\mu_{322})]$	1.11631	0.34932	2.64319
5. $[(\mu_{111}-\mu_{311}) - (\mu_{121}-\mu_{321})] - [(\mu_{113}-\mu_{313}) - (\mu_{123}-\mu_{323})]$	−0.17947	0.54429	3.29937
6. $[(\mu_{112}-\mu_{312}) - (\mu_{122}-\mu_{322})] - [(\mu_{113}-\mu_{313}) - (\mu_{123}-\mu_{323})]$	−1.29578	0.51602	3.21254
7. $[(\mu_{111}-\mu_{411}) - (\mu_{121}-\mu_{421})] - [(\mu_{112}-\mu_{412}) - (\mu_{122}-\mu_{422})]$	0.70903	0.42820	2.92643
8. $[(\mu_{111}-\mu_{411}) - (\mu_{121}-\mu_{421})] - [(\mu_{113}-\mu_{413}) - (\mu_{123}-\mu_{423})]$	−0.47692	1.06861	4.62301
9. $[(\mu_{112}-\mu_{412}) - (\mu_{122}-\mu_{422})] - [(\mu_{113}-\mu_{413}) - (\mu_{123}-\mu_{423})]$	−1.18595	0.88102	4.19766
10. $[(\mu_{211}-\mu_{311}) - (\mu_{221}-\mu_{321})] - [(\mu_{212}-\mu_{312}) - (\mu_{222}-\mu_{322})]$	0.57673	0.34338	2.62062
11. $[(\mu_{211}-\mu_{311}) - (\mu_{221}-\mu_{321})] - [(\mu_{213}-\mu_{313}) - (\mu_{223}-\mu_{323})]$	−0.06227	0.53637	3.27527
12. $[(\mu_{212}-\mu_{312}) - (\mu_{222}-\mu_{322})] - [(\mu_{213}-\mu_{313}) - (\mu_{223}-\mu_{323})]$	−0.63900	0.49755	3.15453
13. $[(\mu_{211}-\mu_{411}) - (\mu_{221}-\mu_{421})] - [(\mu_{212}-\mu_{412}) - (\mu_{222}-\mu_{422})]$	0.16944	0.42226	2.90605
14. $[(\mu_{211}-\mu_{411}) - (\mu_{221}-\mu_{421})] - [(\mu_{213}-\mu_{413}) - (\mu_{223}-\mu_{423})]$	−0.35973	1.06069	4.60584
15. $[(\mu_{212}-\mu_{412}) - (\mu_{222}-\mu_{422})] - [(\mu_{213}-\mu_{413}) - (\mu_{223}-\mu_{423})]$	−0.52917	0.86255	4.15343
16. $[(\mu_{311}-\mu_{411}) - (\mu_{321}-\mu_{421})] - [(\mu_{312}-\mu_{412}) - (\mu_{322}-\mu_{422})]$	−0.40729	0.53070	3.25790
17. $[(\mu_{311}-\mu_{411}) - (\mu_{321}-\mu_{421})] - [(\mu_{313}-\mu_{413}) - (\mu_{323}-\mu_{423})]$	−0.29746	1.19465	4.88804
18. $[(\mu_{312}-\mu_{412}) - (\mu_{322}-\mu_{422})] - [(\mu_{313}-\mu_{413}) - (\mu_{323}-\mu_{423})]$	0.10983	1.02561	4.52904

No significant contrasts. This would be expected since the omnibus $G^2_{S \cdot E}$ test was not significant.

10-7.

Source	V^*
Score interval	0.02784[a]
Outcome	0.11203[a]
Ethnic group	0.22749[a]
S × O	0.22364
S × E	0.06264
O × E	0.07617
S × O × E	0.00468

[a] These V^* values are not interpretable in this study. The Score-interval × Outcome interaction (0.22364) seems to be the largest source of association, with the Ethnic × Outcome interaction (0.07617) having secondary importance.

10-8.

$$\mathbf{N} = \begin{bmatrix} 0.5393136 & 0.3932126 & 0.0389651 \\ 0.2623053 & 0.6574617 & 0.1750979 \\ 0.0628281 & 0.2369843 & 0.4176146 \end{bmatrix}$$

$$\mathbf{NN}' = \begin{bmatrix} 0.4469936 & & \\ 0.4068098 & 0.5317192 & \\ 0.1433417 & 0.2454117 & 0.2345109 \end{bmatrix}$$

Eigenvalue of NN':

$\lambda_0 = 1.00000$
$\lambda_1 = 0.16714$
$\lambda_2 = 0.04608$

Normalized eigenvector for largest non-unity eigenvalue (λ_1):

$[0.59476 \; - 0.12959 \; - 0.79339]$

If X = No. of new black friends

and Y = Perceived amount of social mixing,

then: $\hat{X} = (1.03560)X_1 - (0.22485)X_2 - (3.26535)X_3$

$\hat{Y} = (0.97074)Y_1 - (0.18200)Y_2 - (2.72276)Y_3$

Cramer's $V = \bar{\lambda} = .10661$

$$X^2 = NM\bar{\lambda} = 1292\,(2)\,(.10661) = 275.48$$

With $\alpha = .05$, $\chi^2_{4:.95} = 9.49$, therefore reject hypothesis of no association. The number of new Black friends one has is associated with the amount of social mixing that one perceives.

10-9.

$$\mathbf{N} = \begin{bmatrix} 0.2349772 & 0.4147997 & 0.4147173 & 0.4124006 \\ 0.5843554 & 0.4641427 & 0.0205143 & 0.0844923 \\ 0.0980581 & 0.1203314 & 0.1489162 & 0.1642880 \end{bmatrix}$$

$$\mathbf{NN'} = \begin{bmatrix} 0.5692548 & & \\ 0.3731867 & 0.5644595 & \\ 0.2024506 & 0.1300877 & 0.07326162 \end{bmatrix}$$

Eigenvalues:
$\lambda_0 = 1.00000$
$\lambda_1 = 0.20588$
$\lambda_2 = 0.00110$

Normalized eigenvector for λ_1:

[0.62967 − 0.74052 0.23485]

If $\hat{X}$ = Religious preference

and $\hat{Y}$ = Attitude toward abortion

then $\hat{X} = (-0.99295)X_1 + (-0.18945)X_2 + (1.82031)X_3 + (1.34823)X_4$

$\hat{Y} = (0.90183)\,Y_1 + (-1.10199)\,Y_2 + (0.95137)\,Y_3$

Cramer's $V = .10349$

$X^2 = 132.47 \rightarrow$ Reject hypothesis of no association since $\chi^2_{6:.95} = 12.59$

The results of the Males and Females are very similar, with one exception—the females' "No Opinion" attitude appears to have a larger scale value than the males'. The two variables seem to be about equally associated for males and females since $V_{\text{males}} = 0.10661$ and $V_{\text{females}} = 0.10349$ are so similar.

10-10.

a. The results from the two analyses are very similar. The interaction term accounts for more variance for the females, however.

	Source	d/f	G^2	Probability	V^*
Females:	Religion	3	154.18	0	0.0869
	Attitude	2	280.13	0	0.1992
	R × A	6	151.85	0	0.1080
Males:	Religion	3	110.35	0	0.0796
	Attitude	2	285.33	0	0.2597
	R × A	6	44.16	0	0.0402

b.

Source	d/f	G^2	Probability	V^*
Religion	3	260.02	0	0.0823
Attitude	2	545.93	0	0.2180
Sex	1	17.24	0	0.0109
R × A	6	177.67/178.81†	0	0.0714
R × S	3	3.37/4.51†	.338/.2115	0.0029
A × S	2	18.40/19.53†	.0001	0.0124
R × A × S	6	18.34	.0054	0.0116

† Partial association/Marginal association

c. None of the sources of variance indicates a high level of association with subjects' attitudes. The highest seems to be religion.

INDEX